unraveled

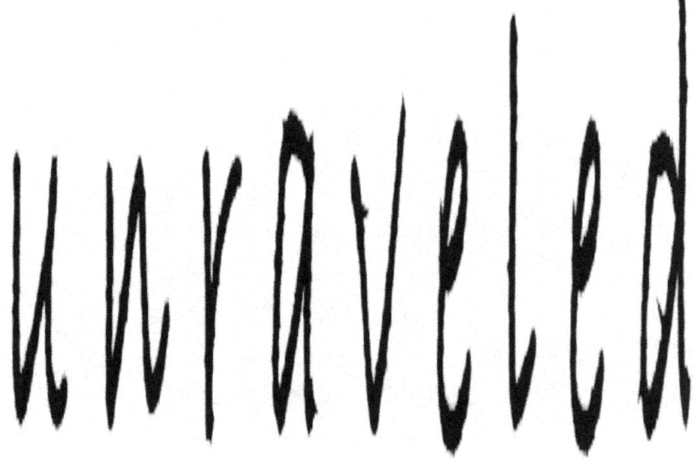

James Randall Chumbley

Lighted Tree Press

Alabama Snow (2009)

Before the Last Dance (2006)

In the Arms of Adam: a diary of men (1997)

Lighted Tree Press
 Library of Congress Class Number: 1-14475299991

Unraveled / James Randall Chumbley
Printed in the United States of America.
First edition 2025.
ISBN 979-8-218-43581-3

For more information, send correspondence to:
lightedtreepress@gmail.com

For Dugan and Bradley

You both will always live between each of my heartbeats—always loved and never forgotten.

table of contents

In the underlay—under the deepest layer of human existence, ever since I can remember, I've felt entrapped. And in relation to the world, a larger part of me has always known that I've never belonged; and have never wanted to stay.

If certain circumstances of my young life had been different, feasibly I would have felt otherwise. Yet here I still remain despite several exit attempts. Why, I'm uncertain although peradventure—out of some sense of obligation. Not for myself—but others.

unraveled

preface

An important component of this writing deals with my virtual death and being returned to life due to the interference of five friends who played a role in blocking my exit from this earth. That interference resulted in the dispatch of my body to an operating table the night of July 4, 2009.

Much of what transpired was recounted to me by them, and to a great degree by my sister, Sandra, who had been notified by phone to meet them at Davy Hospital. All were, unfortunately, witnesses to the aftermath of what that act inflicted upon them.

What literary license I've taken was in transcribing the depiction from asking my sister what she and those friends talked about, the individual thoughts shared, their moods, and that of their surroundings during those precarious five-plus hours as they waited in Davy's ER while I was in surgery, to be as accurate as possible in the drawing of a picture. As well, the amassing days before and those following, while I grappled back to consciousness.

Imparting has been a piercing exercise in personal trauma and perseverance as it has required the tolerance of a life-changing event, culminating in a near-death by point-of-fact actual-death experience. Hopefully, you will begin to visualize the passion and trepidation of what I'm about to share. In no way is it my intent to glorify or romanticize suicide, proffer murder as a solution, offer any advice, or suggest any course of medical treatment.

The purpose of this telling is to share the begetting occurrences surrounding the dejected desperation experienced in seeking death and to possibly why—mostly, the long-reaching shadows of past events of an abhorrent childhood of which, countless children tragically are trapped within as well; and those into my young adulthood where I once again found myself captured in caustic and life-threatening circumstances, and in order to escape, I had to act to free myself as I had as a child—if only physically.

Although I've shared some of those real-life childhood nightmares in previous books, I've not to the full extent experienced as I've never shared others in either direction or beyond—until now, and as before only widened those events but not given in full measure. These warping and excruciating events are of the magnitude that we have been gravely changed and may never fully mentally overcome. The aftermath of those events often follows us—creeping behind.

Life is full of maybes, what ifs, chance, truth, lies, omissions, in-betweens, heroes and villains. Concerning the latter and what those villains inflict on us—depending on the intensity and to what degree and length, where we find ourselves severely endangered, a choice—no matter how regrettable but necessary or so we have judged, sometimes has to be made if we feel it's imperative to do so. A choice—one of two that we find ourselves caught between, that can be as excruciating as those inflictions.

One of two, which we believe there is no other alternative and therefore must be chosen—one over the other. And once one has been selected, and if successfully executed, we must trust it was life-saving—because there is no undoing. And as a result, we are left to carry that choice and action alone from day to day and year to year. A burdensome secret, which can never see the light of day but can haunt in the darkest of nights. And if it were to see the light, we attempt to separate ourselves from it with lies and omissions.

Addressing omissions, George Orwell stated: "Omission is the greatest form of a lie." Although referring to the events ignored in the writing of history, I believe the same can apply to many of our individual lives—unquestionably mine. The things we're not willing to admit fully, but perhaps in part, or not at all, for grievous reasons.

Nonetheless, I believe we often skew the details for degrees of protection, in fear of possible prosecution, and from self-incrimination, the avoidance of embarrassment and judgment, and even self-esteem issues. I am guilty of both: making a choice and the omission of it. They, too, have impacted my life in the worst possible way, and another factor that led me to choose death over life once they caught up with me. I'll address those further in this telling.

There is a massive space between the white and the black—the light and the darkness. Sometimes, we get caught somewhere in the middle—the in-between. I obviously know truths of arduous choices I've made in my life and admit to being guilty of some omissions and skewing certain life-and-death events for several of the reasons I've listed. I've done the same in my first and third books, but the truth, in one form or another, has always been written between the lines.

In keeping, I've purposefully endeavored to confuse the reader in parts of "Unraveled." Thus, leaving you to wonder—however, I'm sure many will see through the wanton uncertainties. But I must present some in such a manner as I have on the pages to follow—attempting to free myself from that self-incrimination and for that protection of which I've mentioned. While I may be guilty of certain choices, I'll let you decide what you believe and what you choose not to allow credence. At this junction of my life, I couldn't care less either way. It is the pieces of my scattered soul I'm trying to collect and not yours—my peace, I seek. Perhaps, even some degree of rescue.

While in junior high school, I began chronicling a young boy's life in journals. From the first words written, those journals became his only friends as their pages filled from one to the next. The very pages he bled tears upon with the strokes of countless pens scribbled dry. Friends, he could lean on. They were the eyes and ears—even the heartbeats that fully know, in detail, the truths of those horrors of what really took place.

In the beginning days of that accounting, I never imagined what I entrusted in those journals would echo throughout the chasing years. Nor did I know that my very survival would divide me into three distinctive people tethered to one heart and one soul. Three people, each carrying the weight of their own secrets and truths, while protecting each other. But mostly, to disguise one of the three who was a monster molded by father by his fracturing acts. It wasn't a choice of my making—to become three people, but out of innate necessity.

As a result of that childhood: the stripping of innocence stolen by savage events of madness and that necessity to split into three different people, I do not believe I've ever known any part of the person I could have become—when I left the safety and comfort of my mother's womb. Instead, I was left a lost and faceless child searching for moments of a sense of freedom, oftentimes sitting on a wooden swing. Its ropes fraying—swing-by-swing in a playground of isolation.

A lopsided roundabout whining as blasts of wind pushed it. Around and around in a circle, much like the retuning events of abuse and violence—the debasement, and even rape. Swinging while quietly singing my own lullaby: "I'm going to be okay. Nothing will hurt me. I'm going to be okay." And much like the fraying of the swing's ropes, I've unknowingly been unraveling since.

I've never fully been able to shatter that mold—as others have their own. In many ways, I remained on that swing.

I'm certain, despite my editor's best efforts, there are mistakes that managed to slip beyond the view of each focused edit and proofing cycle of laborious rewrites, my dyslexia, and pure exhaustion over nine years. This book has exceeded the boundaries of what we originally envisioned. Above all, please know that I did my best, given my fluctuating state of mind.

Nevertheless, the time has arrived—overdue as it is to let it go so, I can hopefully step forward in the few years I have left—regardless of what end will take me. But I'll admit this enterprise has pushed me to the edge many times—the edge that separates life and death. Plus, good or bad, I need an accomplishment. I need to have finished something after not having done so since before 2009.

The names of people, some institutions, and locations have been changed for the obvious.

prologue

Many kids wish for superpowers much like the comic book characters they worship. The ones whose mothers replicate costumes while hunched over sewing machines or purchasing them at Walmart for All Hallows' Eve. Some of the kids want to be White Knights—protectors who use their powers for good to save the vulnerable and the innocent. However, others prefer to be villains—many, creatures of the night from folklore: behemoths, witches, ghosts, goblins, and the like to rain down havoc and even death. And whichever, they wait for sunset to rush the houses in their neighborhoods to fill their bags with a bounty of candy—the more the better.

I, too, wanted superpowers. In a boy's mind, they were a necessity to end my father—the biggest and scariest villain of them all. To end his reign of abuse and violence. That power, the ability to destroy him. To wipe my father from the face of the earth—erase every trace of him, along with every bad person who would inflict harm on good people. I'm just wondering, once you finish reading this telling, if you will see me as a White Knight or one of those evil villains?

It all took place some sixty years ago in the whilom of decay; during the dogged years of my childhood in what was once the small cow-town of Warner Robins, where I grew up, located in Middle Georgia. And within its boundary, abundant peach orchards ruled. Their fruit's sweet-sticky fragrance bathed the ferocious and aggressive humidity of the long-suffocating and burning summers.

Ripe for the picking, I would snatch one from the lower branches within arm's reach. At the first bite into the peach's yellow-orange and fuzzy outer layer, plentiful streams of juice drizzled down my chin as I ate around its oval teeth-cracking pit—while watching hoarsely-cawing large black crows circle overhead in the glaring sunlight.

It was there, in those peach orchards where I hid from the chaos and hell of the abhorrent things no child should be burdened with or witness, much less be the recipient.

Unrestrained memories of those young years rush backward like fast-flowing water. They often awaken me sweaty and abnormally shaky as an empty heart races—snarled in loneliness. A sense of paralyzing fear and foreboding apprehension lingers. As much as I've attempted to leave it all in the past, I'm fettered—the long steel chain, too lengthy as it is unbreakable. And once again, I'm that boy. That boy, living in the gripping, looming dreariness inside a red and white house on Shirley Drive. A house that became a ghost, collectively joined by others. Its odor—musty. Its dampness—swamping.

The images remain clear as if that house is calling me back. The living room, with old furniture on top of thick-piled dark green carpet. The large brick fireplace. Once white, yellowish worn lace curtains hung on rods over two windows. The paneled knotted wood. The adjoining dining room the same. A large picture window overlooking the backyard—generous with tall and thin pines. The shed at the back of the property with tools and a cot where inescapable events took place—remains indelible. The only beautiful thing was the mighty magnolia with its large almond-shaped waxy green leaves and massive paper-white flowers it gifted.

The kitchen sink filled with dirty dishes; the faucet dripping like slow rain. The adjoining breakfast room overlooking the backyard. Its jalousie windows—some cracked, others chipped. The walls of both, a dirty-yellow layered by nicotine, a result of years of my parents' chain-smoking. The air, choked by the pervasive wafting of parched and stale cigarette smoke.

On the left side of the hallway, across from my parents' bedroom, was a half bathroom with a toilet and sink. Next to it, was a full bathroom. The fake white tile board around the tub was edged with mold. Both had crappy, unpredictable plumbing. All part of a house that was never filled with laughter and joy but pulsated with yelling and fighting, fueled by my father's drunken explosions and the fallout of his abuse and violence. All—my normal, although for years I knew there was nothing right under the roof of that house. A roof that only kept the rain off my head. A roof that was only a roof.

At times, it seems as though I existed in that house on Shirley Drive a million years ago, and in another lifetime—others, just minutes before. But time doesn't always distance the collection of years in one's mind. But to this day, knowing all I know and all I've done and accomplished in my life since, I'm still not free or completely sure how he—that boy, managed to survive or even found the courage to do the things necessary to do so.

As much as I wish I could disown those visions and memories—vanquish the ghosts' haunting screams that bleed my eardrums, I know I never will in entirety. They are a part of me as everything that happened within the walls of that house.

Therefore, a greater part of me will inhabit those early years. Mentally knotted and rooted, from the embryonic seedlings of those peach trees planted in southern soil—their roots growing thicker, longer, and deeper over the amassing of years as they continue to dig. Much of every aspect of my being was in those seeds as other elements were presented in childhood by the behavioral and emotional traits of troubled parents—consumed with the events of their own horrific, self-involved drama and its resulting pain and suffering. A multitude in the mix of the DNA in those seeds as well, and the environment of early life events: a collision of threatening uncertainties merging while scorching an indelible, traumatizing imprint. All formulating the person I remain at my core.

Early on, the plan was undefined but had one goal: getting through high school, then get the hell out of Warner Robins and head to California. And by doing so, escape my father and his reign of terror—escape before he could kill me. A legitimate fear I may not live to see my eighteenth birthday. But it was not only my life that was in danger—my mother's and siblings were equally.

So, if I were going to move out West, my father had to die. I had to commit parricide.

one

the sword

I owed my father nothing. Not even the utterance of a last word. Not a last look into his cold and inert eyes. Not even forgiveness. My father deserved nothing but the swing of the sword.

His punishments of choice serve as caustic weapons: abusive degrading words drowning in anger and delivered raucously; pinning to the ground leaving me immobilized under smothering restrain, as his bloodshot eyes cut into mine and as his liquored breath choked; slapping me around; twisted, violent advances and depraved torments of ineffable acts of humiliation performed in that grimy, dirt-floor shed; whippings with the buckle of his belt while butchering my flesh lash-by-lash until the sphincter muscles of my anus failed, the stemming odor sickening as it increasingly overwhelmed the surrounding oxygen. My father wanted to hear me cry out in pain until those cries morphed into screams.

I have no doubt that abuse partly executed, believing he'd seeded a sissy played a primal role in what transpired as some form of retaliation. To my father's dismay, Sandra and I would play with her Barbie Dolls. I often rolled her hair to create elaborate hairdos. I'm sure my girl's play and zero interest in the manly sports, along with him overhearing my grandmother as others, at times, tell Mother: "Randy's too pretty to be a boy." How it all must have shamed him. Deflated the image of himself as a man's man as it layered rage on his face. The knowledge, intolerable that his masculine seed had produced such a boy.

"Boys don't do those kinds of sissy things," he would yell between those lashes and during those acts of perversions.

Perhaps, my father believed he was teaching me some lessons even as warped and sick his modus.

Once I turned fifteen, the depravity ceased but his verbal humiliations continued. No doubt, the shift, due to my physical maturity. I'd grown bigger and angrier enough to fight back. We became nothing more than two humans swimming past each other in a toxic miasma, masquerading as father and son. But we did have one thing in common: our repugnance for each other.

Around the age of sixteen, my mind was forsaken to run amuck on how to kill my father and get away with it—get away with murdering him, fully aware he could never be trusted or shed his skin. I'd given him enough chances to not return on each occasion he left the house, whether for work or off drinking and philandering with his buddies—leaving a prolonged trail of the smell of Aqua Velva aftershave long after he'd exited the house. "Good fucking riddance!" I thought, each time. But my father kept returning with his loitering tyranny. Both reappearing to where they were not welcomed.

I knew if my father continued to return, it was up to me to ensure—the day would come, when his exit was permanent. An instinctive consciousness of thought; the conceptualization of unthinkable diabolical and merciless plots soon after took on a life of their own.

But it wasn't just for my benefit, despite any degree of abuse I endured at my father's will—his death was more so to give my mother another chance at life. That realization was clear; but first, she needed protection. As a child, yet big or strong enough, I had to fight back, if only to put myself between my parents—even jump on my father's back, fully knowing I would fail but willing to afford Mother the time needed to get away while sacrificing myself—knowing I would take the beatings instead. And it was about Sandra. At some point, feeling she was at risk as well from the theft of her innocence and any possible depravity.

When adults, Sandra reminded me that when he was intoxicated, I'd ride my bicycle before old enough to drive a car, to bring school clothes for the next day so she could spend the night with girlfriends and therefore, out of harm's way. Even though our father did beat Stephen at times; he was big for his age and eventually became a strong adversary. But despite the violence between them, Stephen was favored—a school athlete. If our father and his oldest son shared any commonality: they were ashamed of me. And because of that, Stephen and I were never close. Eventually, he internally isolated himself from the chaos and kept his distance. Stephen became very much like an occasional visitor—sanitizing himself of the systemic toxicity of a sham domicile. He may as well have been some random kid living down the street. So, I was left alone to be a guardian when he should have been as well.

For some years to follow, I could not always succeed at diverting my father's battering of Mother—especially, while I was in school. And along with the abuse was his indifference; both sucking her lifeblood like a vampire and with it her spirit, strength, and dreams until she was just an empty vessel.

He was the cause of Mother's mental derailments—exasperating and maturating them while leading her to the bottle. And in it, drowning herself in the alcohol they contained in a futile attempt to forget and to self-medicate when the legions of shock treatments and the mountainous pills didn't unlock the shackles—liberate my mother from her psychological pain and emotional torment. But to his pleasure, when wanted, my father expected Mother to do her wifely duties—including spreading her legs while he fucked other women.

He never deserved the love my mother once gave him or her gentle nature—certainly, not the pleasures he took and enjoyed due to her unmistakable physical beauty. I wonder if he'd treated those other women he fucked as cruelly as he did my mother and moved on to the next—like popping and guzzling cans from six-packs of Falstaff beer. Downing one—and moving onto the next as my mother sank deeper into the pits of darkness and despair. All—sufficient calculus to ensure the day came that my father would never draw another breath—without mercy. It was because of his treatment of my mother; I wanted to be one of those superheroes as a kid—to again ensure her safety from him. And In the process: protect all of us, so we would no longer be his victims. And to make that happen, my father would have to be sliced in half with laser eyes—mine. That need, to be a protector, remained with me into adulthood; to cut down anyone who would hurt a good person.

The fact he often slept on the cot in the shed was an opportunity as was his habit of drinking himself near unconsciousness. The use of a large garden tool was one of those added possibilities—actual scenarios that I knew, one must be played out to the end.

I know it all sounds so fucked-up—it was, maybe even psycho but you have yet to know the entirety of it. Some adults severely seized by abuse as children in dangerously volatile environments, understand the culmination of violence directed at the abuser. Eventually, the trauma reaches an apogee where they strike back. In my mind, it was self-defense.

The more time consumed with thinking about the satisfaction it would offer, the more ideas cemented in my brain. Planning it. How to pull it off without being caught. The best place to do the deed. Assessing the optimum opportunity. The story I would concoct for the police.

I've never publicly written about it. Too terrified to reveal that side of myself—the capability of murder, stripped of remorse or regret. Instead, I kept it hidden on those pages between the covers of my journals. Where many would dismiss such as illusionary insanity—I calculated it as garden-variety insurance for our safety more akin to inoculation against a life-threatening disease than a crime. A gruesome, yet quintessential labor of love. Granted—contemplating the murder of his father may have been all too much for a teenage boy. But my father was an existential villain. As long as he was still alive, he would remain roosted as an ominous threat to our safety.

Immersed in the lurking shadows of night, I stood over my father as he lay in a drunken stupor on the cot in the shed. My hand tightly gripped the garden shovel—my sword, as I began to draft the plans to become the architect of his death.

Months into my seventeenth year, after all the planning—I was ready to swing the sword.

the genesis

It's within the fragmented, provisional hours—each one tender and dubious when the sky is draped by night; the fleeting quietude as its companion solitude, is when the truths of my life sit closest beside me.

Although it had all been executed some three decades before he was born, a random email from a stranger received on Monday, January 2, 2007, at 1:41 a.m., reaching out after having read an excerpt from my first book, "In the Arms of Adam: a diary of men," published in 1997, concerning staying faithful to one's authenticity—would eventually stir much of it back to the surface. The email was received some forty-five days after my mother's death that would lead to my undoing two years into the future. And open an old wound seeping of the misery, pain, heartache, and the hopelessness. The guilt. And worst of all—the blinding darkness after I believed I'd made some sort of armistice years before with the past.

If the email had been received a few months later, I would have already moved out of Atlanta to finally fulfill a dream sparked by a teenage boy of getting the hell out of Georgia and the South to live in Los Angeles, California in a house in the Hollywood Hills.

That email was from Christopher, thirty years my junior. Several months later, I mistakenly believed I knew him to be honest, mature beyond his years, and of a good heart. Well aware, I was in the middle of relocating to the West Coast—while professing pressing love, Christopher begged I wait three more years until he finished law school. Then, we would go to California together. Although I resisted offering a long toilet paper list of cons, eventually, that email migrated into a fool's relationship. Me, being the fool.

Perhaps, I saw Christopher as a last chance to feel loved in degrees. Even when I'd agreed to stay three more years and regardless of what I'd written in "Alabama Snow," I never anticipated the relationship would be forever. I knew it would end one day. Perhaps, within some five years—if that. I was not naive to think Christopher would stay until I was an old man and he have to wipe my ass. I knew my life would not end with him standing over my deathbed crying. I just didn't expect he would end it so quickly and ruthlessly.

So let me jump ahead and rip off the bandage from my flesh as if it were adhered by Super Glue. It's too painful to read those words in any form—to know I'd once written them, much less read them aloud and in public no less. And that people read them in "Alabama Snow." That, at one time, I believed they carried any truth. Because I did, I feel like a fool even today and cringe out of humiliation.

If only it were possible to extract those five words as if they were cancerous: "the love of my life." That statement couldn't be any further from reality concerning Christopher. But why should I be surprised? My mine was not anywhere within the vicinity of reality for the longest time. And the worst part: that pathetic declaration is impertinent to the memory of Bradley. Christopher was nothing—he is nothing. Perhaps, I am as well. But in all actuality, Christopher was a cancer in my life and not just those mistaken words spoken and written. As a notation: if you decide to continue reading, "Unraveled," you will learn of this person I refer to as Bradley.

On a January morning, he walked into my home-office—discharging slashing, vile, and harsh words. I was caught off guard in the worst of ways.

"It's over. We're over" The news, announced with a windstorm of arrogance.

"I can't handle law school and a relationship," he declared. "Besides, you're too old," he castrated. "It'll never work," he gelid, glaring with impassive eyes.

Bewildered, I remained seated. Shock surely covered my face as he heartlessly delivered his message. I remember thinking at the time, "How did I get too old in two years? It worked for two years."

"I was planning on leaving you sooner… just waiting for you to finish that stupid book, but I can't any longer." Christopher was referring to "Alabama Snow," which at the time, I was three-quarters into writing it. The story, about a mother's and son's relationship. "And I'm not responsible for the pain you're feeling because I'm leaving," each word Christopher spoke fired like bullets.

Within minutes, he turned around and walked out of the room. I remained seated. I heard the front door quickly opened then slam. The selfsame door, for two years, he'd so eagerly entered. I got up from behind the desk. Stunned, walked to the full-view glass door. Watched Christopher's back grow smaller with each step he took to his car. And then, drive away in the cold early morning's mist of winter.

His exit at that pivotal, engrossing point of the book triggered the return of an array of emotions captured within my relationship with my mother and surrounding childhood that I would come to experience—reaching further into the years to follow.

The pain of those eruptive years and her death returned, tangled with gouging loss that seemed unbearable—all serving as the blade of mass confusion and my execution. Then, unknowingly at the time of Christopher's exit, there would come to be his unforgivable actions that took place five months later when I was forced to face him in court.

I found myself on the edge. A fucked-up mess journeying to a homecoming back in time and to three bottles of prescription drugs,

Benadryl, a razor blade, and a bathtub full of water. It wasn't until some seven turbulent years later, I came to realize it had nothing to do with Christopher but what he symbolized. Among other issues: fear of abandonment. And with that, how a man named Bradley and his own exit—the deadliest loss in my life, forty-eight years before, made me feel forsaken in the undertow of drowning despondency. How I felt the universe had abandoned me—had abandoned us: Bradley and me.

the good son

In the sedateness of the early morning hours, as night hangs in the placid air and sunrise delays outside my window, I think about her—my mother. I miss her. My soul misses her. My heart, too. My mind is a pool of still clear spring water. In its reflection: I see the light that once sparkled in her pecan-colored eyes looking back at me, I see her smile as she slightly tilts her head and her lips curl upward, and I see her unmistakable beauty. Then, the water ripples as if a single pebble breaks the surface: I see tears rolling down her cheeks, bruises on her flesh, and a stream of blood running out the corner of her swollen lips. Another pebble drops. The water ripples once more: I see a beast standing behind her—and my mother's eyes scream fear.

In those fragile hours, I heard her spirited-laughter riding the wind—what joy the sound before it was silenced when my father's violence erupted like a once dormant volcano. Then,—her laughter, was rarely heard through the ash.

The wind suddenly stirs, and I hear her cries in my sleep. Her rages. And at times—the sounds of her insanity even if no one else can. Why? Because they're all mine as well—what I've witnessed. What I heeded. And when I awakened, my eyes teared and heart bled puddles.

Amid the chaos and the aftermath, in different ways, she protected me as I did her in others. Mother wanted me to be smart and savvy—certainly, not remain a small-town boy as she was once a dirt-road poor kid growing up on a small cotton farm. I wish I could have protected my mother more when my best didn't seem good enough. And, again, while at school, I could not stand guard and thus left her at risk.

Without hesitation, I would have given my life so my mother could have freely lived hers to the fullest--gladly given her every ounce of happiness I'd experienced once my life transformed from an ugly duckling into a beautiful swan and traded it in equal measure for that of her sadness. I owed my mother that—and more. I owe the woman who gave me life. Gave me her love. Her beauty. Her compassion. Her kindness. I'm her son—her beautiful boy, as she always called me even into my later years.

Now that she's left this earth, I find some sense of peace that my mother knew I was the child who stayed. The child who didn't run even though he wanted to, and desperately so. The child who helped her to bed when she had too much to drink and laid beside her while holding her hand until she fell to sleep. The child who never strayed too far from her bosom regardless of wherever he may have been in the world at any given time. The important thing: he always returned. The child who kept her between each of his heartbeats. Today, she goes on living there. My heart beats for hers now. The heart of the child who never forgot his mother while she was alive and never will as long as his heart goes on beating.

But as much as I loved my mother—and always will, she could infuriate me and cause me great pain when she drank and when her mental afflictions took over her being. But, again, I never fully blamed her. I blamed him—my father. I blamed his mayhem for destroying her—every part of her. Thankfully, my father got what he deserved in the end: a bloody death.

After two years of physical calamities, including lung and heart disease—incubated from years of chain-smoking and drinking, my mother sadly inched into a coma. I remember how her eyes fixedly looked at me while connected to a ventilator to insure her more breaths of life; I knew my mother was afraid as her stares attempted to speak to me. The day she slipped into a coma—her life was perishing. Once we released her, Mother languished for four days; I believed it was what was left of her soul that was still trying to hold onto life despite how each breath her lungs had drawn for years where tormented.

Her doctors were certain she would never open her eyes again—destine to remain a vegetable hooked up to tubes and wires connected to repetitive beeping medical telemetry.

From the ICU bed where Mother's last days of consciousness

where spent with the breathing tube down her throat connected to a ventilator to insure her more breaths of life, the memory of how fear and desperation wailed from her eyes that fixedly looked at me as she attempted to speak through them seeking comfort and reassurance as her life was perishing clung; her favorite music softly played from a CD player in hopes of doing just that: to offer some degree of that comfort.

Durning those few precious days that followed, all I could do was tell my mother how much I loved her and reassure her that she would be okay.

"Well get through this together as we have so many other tribulations of life that had kicked down the door."

Still her fear never left.

"The doctor is going to take out the tube when you get better… and then you can return home again. Trust me."

But no matter how many times I told her, all I could see in her beautiful eyes was life inching away. Even I tried to convince myself that the words I spoke were true, the reality remained constant as it surrounded me—surrounded us both.

Once we cut off everything that would sustain life to release Mother, she languished for four days. I believed it was that which was left of her soul, still trying to hold onto life despite how each breath her lungs had drawn for years where tormented.

Once her eyes closed for the last time—just minutes before the drop of midnight, my mother's world stopped spinning. Sandra, Joann, and I were at her bedside. As I wrote in "Alabama Snow," in some devout way, as I held the hand of the woman who gave me my first breath of life by bring me into this would: it was an honor to be by her bedside to lay witness to my mother taking in her last breath before giving it back to the world upon her exit.

And with that last exhale—all the mental and physical pain along with the bad and the ugly left with it. I was relieved to know her protracted mortal suffering had come to an end. My dear mother found her long-awaited peace. Her death certificate states, she passed on the other side of midnight—technically, the next day because it took the doctor some twenty minutes to arrive at the ICU room to pronounce her death.

Well aware our mother would not outlast that fourth night, instead of holding vigilance with us, our older brother was home in bed. After Sandra called him, Stephen showed up at the hospital—only staying five or so minutes before leaving. It would be the second time he'd left me alone with a dead parent. The first, was of what was left of our father.

I didn't grieve her death but rather the life she deserved but never obtain—the one I wanted for her before and after my father's demise. Of course, I would have wished for a different denouement for my mother. One free of any fear and pain associated with life and that of death, regardless of their source. Concerning the latter, many of our endings are rarely in our control in the way we would prefer to leave this earth. And in most cases, even how long we stay. It was a truth that I would have to learn the hard way—some three years later. If there is a god, surely, my mother is cradled in his arms.

Today, the sun warms the grass covering my mother's grave. Spring and summer rains give life to that grass—as it does the tree that shades her headstone. Cool billowing breezes dance the fallen-colored leaves of fall over her resting place. The winter cold never touches her; the ground covering her grave is like a blanket. Now, her damaged soul rests. All that pain and heartache is no longer her burden. Now, I carry it for her. Someone must remember my mother. That, someone—is me.

With my mother's passing, came my freedom as well. The latitude to disclaim any existence of Georgia. Or at least, I thought as I began making plans for my departure after I put Mother to rest. That is, until I derailed myself.

far side of perfect

Some eight months after the receipt of that email—I was in California with someone I foolishly believed loved me and I, him. I was with Christopher. We'd flown into Laguna Beach mid-evening from Atlanta. I'd spared no expense, including first-class tickets and prearranged the rental of a black, four-door jeep at John Wayne Airport. I wanted him to have the total California experience. I'd lost count of the times I'd been since my early twenties, but this was Christopher's first trip to the West Coast. I wanted to share it with him—the state

I'd made the commitment to delay moving until he finished law school. The agreement to stay in Atlanta for three more years added to thirty-two—by far, was not an easy decision to make.

The draperies of the wall of windows were pulled open, allowing in spectacular views while Christopher and I lay naked aloft in the Laguna Hills. Plentiful lights from the houses below dotted the hillside—reaching out into the enigmas of night as a full moon hovered in a black-blue sky. The large sphere's silvery-white light glistened as it pranced over the Pacific, easing a path into the bedroom of the vacation home—a splendid contemporary in the sky owned by my friend, William.

The bed was clad in white sheets—cool and silky to the skin. The moment seemed near-perfect from a distance but blemished. Flawed. Even wrong. It felt as though my stomach had dropped—liked I'd eaten something that hadn't agreed with my constitution, rendering me somewhat bilious. But I hadn't—nothing disagreeable physically. As with every trip to California, it was impossible not to intermittently think of Bradley. But he was not the reason for my discomfort either.

Days before, I began experiencing refashioned thoughts. Despite Christopher's declarations, the relationship began to feel forced. But I kept dismissing those feelings. Dismissed the vacillating intuitions until they were sucked from reality. I knew whatever the root, it was emotionally seeded. Possibly, due to the rising belief Christopher was the best I could obtain at that junction of my life or was going to get. All I knew for certain: any excitement felt was due to my return to the state of California. Christopher was a second—or even a third-place prize. Or at best, what I settled for to feel loved again.

My eyes squinted open as they met the sunrise painting the room. The smell of sex lingered from the night before. My chest hair was matted from where I'd scooped Christopher's cum from his flat belly and rubbed it over me as if skin lotion. Its taste, still present on my lips after having licked the remainder from his flesh.

Twisted bedsheets partly covered his lower body—exposing the top portion of a round, bubble butt and a teasing hint of its crack. Tousled, dirty-blonde hair covered the back of Christopher's head. Small reddish-brown freckles sparingly spotted paper-white smooth skin. I affectionately slid my hand around Christopher's warm body, expanding its fingers once they reached his stomach. I leaned in. Brushed my lips over the nape of his neck before my bare chest met his back. A yawning inhaled breath of mirth followed a convincing moan of pleasure by Christopher as I pulled him close.

"You, awake?"

"Yes," he sleepily uttered, turning his head to look at me with dozy eyes.

Chapped lips from a night of impetuous hunger smiled.

"Can we just stay in bed all day?" he implored.

"Anything you want."

"Anything?"

"Yes, anything."

Our lips touched. My instinct was to devour Christopher again as I'd done before we'd fallen asleep. He lustfully opened his mouth—an invitation. The kiss became wetter and deeper. I slowly pulled the sheet from his lower body until he was fully exposed.

"Climb on top of me," he whimpered.

Christopher rolled onto his back; alluringly, spread his large athletic legs apart while cloyingly sliding his feet back until his knees pointed upward—exposing a pink anus. Christopher grabbed his ball sack. Once again, he smiled. My hands reached out, rubbing his smooth belly before greedily digging my fingers into his flesh as if he were prey.

I aggressively took hold around the back of his waist. Quickly, pulled him toward me before moving on top. Youthful precum leaked from his rigid penis; the muscles of my abdomen glided over his body. Uniformed. Slowly. Wittingly. By design, as if orchestrated by Three Dog Night's, "Eli's Coming," steadily escalated until its sweaty finish—until both our bellies were slippery with jism.

In seconds, he released a warm load of ejaculate in long-measured peristaltic paroxysms—amazingly fecund after a night of multiple sustained orgasms. A prolonged sigh followed. I lifted my body off his. Set back. Our eyes made contact as I scooped up his cum from our bellies in the palm of my hand—the smell of sex, once again, tangled in the air around us.

"You're not going to get off that easily."

"I hope not."

I eagerly rubbed the cum cupped in my hand on his anus. He whimpered again. I moved two fingers to my lips. Sucked cum from one before bringing the other to Christopher's lips; and circled them as if my finger were a paint brush before lying back down on top of his body. Again, we kissed while tasting the inebriating cum. Christopher and I were seemingly wrapped in voluminous bands of euphoria dangling over the cliffs of ecstasy.

Our mouths locked. I repositioned. Eased my dick into his ass—slowly, at first. Instinctively, my hands grabbed his round muscled ass-cheeks. Christopher's legs cuffed my waist. Then, mercilessly, I took him like the waves crashing on the beach below. Anger replaced my impassionate forceful jabs. Jabbing, until I came inside his warm ass with numerous jolts of my body. I remained on top of Christopher long enough to kiss him again, before rolling onto my back.

"I… I love you, Randy," Christopher spoke—near-breathless.

Those words would prove to be lies. Perhaps, even a lie when I told him the same. A lie, from the day he'd convinced me to stay as he wept crocodile tears. It was all another opportunist's deception—or even my own. Although, admittedly, I should have known better; perhaps I was too caught up in a middle-aged man's foolish attempt to reclaim his lost youth.

two

seven 'til midnight

In this determining moment, I'm screaming. You just cannot hear me—you never could. Perhaps—it's for the best…

Sandra received the call in the late afternoon of July 4, 2009. She was living in a small apartment in Fort Valley, Georgia—eighteen miles west of Warner Robins. The call interrupted an episode of the television series, Law and Order occupying her attention. Sis loved detective and crime stories; her interest was generated early-on during her long stint in the U.S. Army's Jag Corps.

Sandra instinctively reached for the phone before questioning if the unfamiliar number highlighted on the screen, was another annoying unsolicited sales call. Instead of letting it go to voicemail, which was her habit for unknown callers, something in her gut told her to hit the receive button. A man clearing his throat, was on the other end.

"Hello."

A silent pause followed. A throat cleared.

"Are you Randy's sister, Sandra?"

"Yes."

"I'm Marty, a friend of your brother's. I'm sorry, but I have some upsetting news," he inhaled deeply and purposefully.

"What's wrong?" she asked, her emotions on high alert.

"Are you sitting down?"

"Just tell me, please. Has something happened to him?"

Another pause.

"He tried to commit suicide. We're at Davy Memorial Hospital… Randy's in surgery now."

"Oh my God. He what?"

"Try to take some deep breaths… "

Marty waited.

"Is, is he okay… will he be, okay?" her voice leached.

"I don't know any details yet, but you should come. I'm here at Davy hospital with some of your brother's friends."

He went on to explain: the nurse at the front desk would not tell them much of anything because they were not related to me.

"I'm… I'm on my way," her words stuttered. "Wait, where's the hospital?"

"Off I-75 on the left. You can't miss it," he directed. "How long will it take you?"

"Maybe an hour and a half," she answered. "What… what did he do?"

"Just get here. Okay. We'll be here waiting on you."

The cell phone dropped from her hand to the floor. Sheer terror mounted within, overtaking Sandra's body as it trembled like a single leaf trying to hold on to a tree branch in a windstorm. She was trying to hold on like that leaf.

Her mind dredged up thoughts from the past of our father's labeled suicide. They rattled Sandra.

Frantically, she threw some random clothes into an overnight bag before rushing out the door. Within seconds, her white BMW hatchback sped out of the parking lot.

Our relationship as brother and sister had been somewhat rocky since our mother's passing; but we did stay in touch and saw each other on a few occasions. She'd moved a number of times after Mother's affairs were settled.

I'd moved her to San Antonio Texas. Later, Sandra relocated to Columbus, Georgia to be close to Mother's grave. Then, surprisingly to Fayette, Alabama before moving back to Middle Georgia.

My sister had known I'd been depressed; but not to the degree of its growing severity. I'd only shared with her that I was experiencing an involved and stressful breakup; but had kept the deals marginal.

Sometime later, she expressed I no longer sounded like the brother who had once been her champion. But Sandra never thought that depression would lead to such news. Or, to the coursing precariousness and heartache she was driving toward the night of Marty's phone call. Sandra had also shared, she had wondered about the odds of being able to tell her big brother she loved him—at least, one more time if the worst was at hand.

The ER was chaotically crammed with Atlanta's afflicted—especially so, on a holiday weekend. Sandra's heart pounded with despair as she entered a buzz of engulfing conversations. All sorts of people were standing or sitting, waiting to be seen while others for news. Sandra's head moved from side to side looking until she caught sight of four well-groomed, ostensibly upscale white guys huddled apart from the other waiting people—glaring standouts in the milieu of Davy's otherwise disheveled clientele of inner diversity. Sandra made a beeline for them.

"Excuse me. Is one of you… Marty?" Sandra barely gasped, winded from her veritable footrace.

"I am," answered a tall, blonde, and exceptionally handsome man in his mid-to-late thirties.

Her breath of relief was as exaggerated as it was obvious.

"Is he okay? Is my brother okay?"

Worry and measured caution hung on her words.

"We still don't know anything... not a word as of yet," Marty allowed, while shaking his head.

After a quick introduction of Russ, Hal, and Mitch by Marty, Sandra nervously commented, "If Randy saw me like this, he would die. I just rushed out of the house without showering or changing… or anything."

Sandra paused for a long moment, suddenly regretting her choice of words—too late to swallow them but wishing she could.

"I… I can't believe I said that. I mean… die that is," she softly confessed.

Sandra palmed her forehead in direful disbelief.

Subdued nervous laughter ensued by the guys.

"Well, we know what you meant. It's okay. It's just good you're here now," Mitch chimed in. "Your brother would likely get a chuckle… too," he added.

They each gave Sandra a warm hug of support—instantly taking a shine to her and Sandra's thick, quite authentic Southern accent.

No one really knew what to say or how to console her.

Marty suggested she let someone know of her arrival. Together, they proceeded to the admissions desk where two women were all-consumed, performing inscrutable hospital tasks: one typing on a computer, the other intently rifling through what appeared to be a medical file. A doctor approached the desk and interrupted the typing woman in a protracted discussion.

"Ma'am, ma'am," Sandra addressed while peering directly into the other woman's face, attempting to make eye contact.

She sat the folder down on the desk.

"Yes. How can I help you?"

"I'm Randy's… I mean, James Randall Chumbley's sister. Can you give me an update on his status? I understand he's in surgery."

"I'll let someone know you're here. Just try to sit tight."

The woman offered a smile of sympathy. She then stood up. Patted Sandra's nervously shaking hand before taking her leave.

Marty and Sandra looked at each other before walking back to where the others were sitting. Russ stood up to see if there was any news offered. Sandra shook her head, no.

"This… this is Christopher's doing," Mitch blurted.

"What do you mean?" Sandra asked.

"Your brother never told you about him?"

"No. But he did mention he was dating someone."

Mitch lowered his head.

"Does he even know?" Russ asked.

"I didn't call him," Marty informed.

"Well, I'm sure he had something to do with it."

The boys looked at each other.

"I know this is scary," Marty directed his statement to Sandra. "Let's just focus on your brother. Don't worry about Christopher… don't give him a second thought," he spoke with conviction.

Sandra covered her face with both hands.

"He did put Randy through hell," Hal surprisingly interjected.

"You know… the court thing. It tore your brother up. I went by his house the day after. Randy was pale… white as a sheet. He looked like his soul had been shredded."

"Court case?" Sandra asked.

"You didn't know?" Russ questioned.

"No... Randy never mentioned it. What was it all about?"

"Well, that psycho party boy slapped a restraining order on him. Randy had to go to court."

"He what? When did this happen?"

"Just last month," Hal interjected.

"Don't worry about it, Sandra. I'll fill you in later. Let's not waste any more energy on Christopher," Marty insisted.

"Oh, I'm sure Christopher will find out soon enough… but

likely won't give a damn. He showed his true colors… at least to a few of us," Mitch offered. "Atlanta may be a big city but it's just a country town when it comes to gossiping queens. Your brother is known and liked by lots of folks who really care about him. You need to know that… Sandra," Mitch jumped in.

"Your brother is a good person, maybe too good for his own sake," Marty expressed with assurance.

"You're familiar with the term queen, yes?" he asked.

"Oh, yes. Randy has filled me in on all the gay slang."

They all chuckled a bit. It helped to fracture the severity surrounding them.

"Well, Christopher's an opportunist. I'm surprised Randy never saw it. But... I guess he just sees the good in people, not that there is any good in that one," Russ spoke up. "William and I had our concerns when they came to visit us in Florida last year… that Christopher was using Randy," he added.

"Never knew what your brother saw in him. We go way back. Almost every gay man in this town wanted to get with Randy back then... and there are a good number now." Mitch stated. "Now, his life has come to this tragic moment," he added.

Marty gave everyone a stern look of authority; one translating to move on from the topic of Christopher as he'd moments before insisted. The conversation lulled for want of immediacy, consuming long moments. Sandra's new-found friends fell silent. A few minutes passed.

"I need a smoke," Sandra abruptly announced. "It's my nasty habit."

"We all have at least one. Right?" Marty agreed.

"I ought to stop," Sandra announced. "Randy would like that… if I'd stop, that is. He's such a health nut."

Hal shrugged his shoulders. He gave a look of innocence concerning nasty habits as if he had none.

"Not me. I'm perfect," he said to the group, attempting to add more humor to the dreadful night of waiting.

"Do I need to remind you of that time… " Marty started to say before he was interrupted.

"No, you don't," Hal insisted.

Another low chuckle from the group followed.

"I'll join you," Russ told Sandra.

By then, what minuscule pieces of light was waning. Squeezed out of the sky as a midsummer night draped the city.

Sandra and Russ headed for the sliding doors. They parted to allow a young lady pushing an elderly, white-haired woman in a wheelchair.

A feeling of déjà vu washed over Sandra as she watched the woman in the wheelchair pass—too much of a reminder of the last year of our mother's life, when there were many repeated trips to the hospital. Particularly, that late night toward the end when Sandra called 911 after Mother rolled off the bed onto the floor—painfully calling out for help. Within a month, Mother was dead.

Once Sandra and Russ were outside, by contrast to the air conditioning in the hospital, the Atlanta night's sultry humidity hit them in the face like a steamy blanket.

While outside, Sandra pressed Russ for more details of what actually happened earlier in my Midtown home. He was reluctant to give any additional information than she was given upon her arrival at the hospital—believing, by keeping Sandra in the dark was best under the circumstances to spare her the gory details. Russ only reiterated about the pills and that I was found in my bathtub.

Two hours had passed since Sandra's arrival, and three and a half since my body was rolled into surgery. My sister and Russ returned from their smoke to rejoin the others back in the waiting area at approximately 10:30, noted on the standard-issued institutional clock hanging on the wall across the room.

Everyone tried to resettle into the less-than-comfortable chairs. The waiting continued for any news as their agitation and worry fluctuated from hope to dread. One by one, the entourage stood and paced the floor; occasionally, looking back in the direction of the clock—more out of habit than anything else. For them, its hands seemed to move in slow motion.

The hours continued to lengthen. The uneasiness languished. Their eyes and voices fatigued. Sandra and her new friends' verbal interactions lessened to infrequent intervals of sentences and expressions crisscrossing among them to that of hushed support—merely vulnerable facades on their faces. Underneath those slight smiles and momentary looks, their concerns seeped through their eyes. With the expanding hours, so did the burden each one carried—those burdens, regrettably of my doing.

Those burdens weighed heavier and heavier on their minds of just how surreal and hostile that night was: my lifeless body, the pills, the razor, the blood—all of it. But for my sister—unknowing of the razor and bloody scene of my bathroom, still what I did pulled her back in time to another ugly place neither one of us would ever completely escape—certainly me.

The group's exchanges eventually settled into coasting mode, then into near silence. Sandra and my friends surrendered their voices to the waffling of other peoples' concerns and emotions, waiting as well, in Davy's ER: occasional coughs, moans and groans, while a few raised verbal expressions of frustration. All ongoing, circling around them, in the duration of their gathering. But for the most part, had gone unnoticed earlier by their concentrated assiduousness.

Understandably, they had become too drained and worried to find the energy to speak anymore. I can only imagine how the night must have seemed to erode until the abrasive realities began to crumble. Sandra and my friends were stuck somewhere between the gray and the pitch of night—and at its mercy. It crawled at its own pace, regardless of the circumstances and what prayers may have been spoken under their breaths.

the rebirth

Sandra's and my friends' restlessness built; the waiting had passed insufferably. The sustained torture as the strain of concern remained on their faces—especially Sandra's. Persistent anxiety weighed as if a mountain were crushing the night. Randomly, they soon began to relinquish their chairs to pace, and then eventually took another seat. The outlying intermittent bangs, whizzing, and thunderous thuds of fireworks set off at the State Capitol building and the nearby campus of Georgia State University became annoying, as did the firecrackers exploding on the downtown streets.

They continued to check the clock on the wall as its hands creeped toward midnight. Almost five hours of waiting had elapsed. Interminable doctors, nurses, and endless functionaries entered and exited the ER's waiting area. Sandra, as the boys, were hoping one of them was about to bring good news.

Within another thirty minutes or so, as Sandra was about to ask Russ if he wanted another smoke outside, she noticed a pretty, tall, and lean female dressed in blue surgical scrubs appearing to walk straight for her. My sister stood as did her bodyguards of her heart, much like the wall of a bastion and consolation.

Their breaths were seized. Eyes widened with the speculation of pending news. Sandra tried to read the woman's face the closer she approached for any signs of hope—that the good news she'd prayed for with every tick of the clock and breath her lungs inhaled would be delivered. The women came to a stop just feet from them.

"I understand… you're Mr. Chumbley's sister."

The prolonged silence shattered; a rush of fear-fueled adrenaline pounding in Sandra's heart. Her mouth opened but only a garble in mid-breath escaped. The massiveness of the moment was dwarfing; the surroundings grew larger as she—smaller. Sandra attempted to clear her throat of the lodged uncertainty.

"Yes… yes. Please tell me he's okay."

Tears once again coated her eyes.

"I'm, Dr. Bernard."

In an expression of kindness, the doctor reached for Sandra's hand—gently embraced it with hers.

The doctor articulated that they would have to wait and see.

"Your brother did a great deal of damage to his body. He really must have wanted to end his life."

Sandra instinctively lowered her head. Raised her free hand to cover her face. She wept. Not just because of the circumstances of the immediate, but also for those of the years past—all leading to the moment at hand. A collision of tears and years, and unwanted life-choking events. The wall of support moved in even closer as Marty placed his hand on Sandra's shoulder. All eyes were on Dr. Bernard, except Sandra's—still covered with her hand until she managed to look up at the doctor.

"What did my brother do?"

Dr. Bernard explained to Sandra that they finally got my heart beating on its own again. That, it was touch and go. The cut on my left arm was severe. I'd cut through muscle and tendons. Also, understanding that my arm was very vascular, the cut had severed several veins.

She paused before continuing as dispassionately as possible. Sandra was certain Dr. Bernard's eyes teared with each added detail as she broadened to address the ingestion of the pills. Adding, it was fortunate the EMTs had brought in the empty pill containers.

"He hadn't eaten in a while. We're giving Mr. Chumbley nutrients through an IV… just as a precaution, he's on a respirator for now."

Sandra's body leaned back into Marty.

"Do you want more details?" Dr. Bernard asked. "I understand this is very troubling."

"No… no. I… I mean yes. Please continue. I have to know."

"Okay then. Try to stay positive," the doctor consoled.

Sandra waited as Dr. Bernard paused for another moment.

"Randy will get through this… he will," Russ encouraged.

The doctor soon proceeded to express possible concern for any brain impairment. Addressing, I'd lost a considerable amount of blood by the time I was found. Telling Sandra and the boys it was too soon to know if there was any degree of oxygen deprivation due to the amount of time my body remained in the tub. But to know she was hopeful and for Sandra to be as well.

Sandra shared that the doctor's voice came in and out as she watched her lips move as well as her hand gestures. Nausea took over. The ER started to spin.

"Why don't you sit down," Dr. Bernard suggested. "I don't need another patient to take care of."

Mitch helped Sandra into a seat.

"Again… I know this is extremely upsetting. Your brother has some good friends."

Dr. Bernard looked at Russ and Hal, then back at Sandra. She explained that if it wasn't for their persuasive angst pleading for them to do something—she would have gone with the opinion of her medical colleague, who believed I was too far gone. But because of them, she dismissed it and instead, decided to try.

"Yes. Yes, he does. I'm grateful for them and you," Sandra said as she looked around at the guys.

"They'll be moving him to recovery soon, but…"

Sandra interrupted her before the doctor could finish.

"Just please tell me he's not going to die."

"Again, let's be hopeful."

As I understand it, Bernard imparted that the outcome was possibly in my favor because I was physically strong and in excellent shape. That, I obviously knew the inside of a gym; and other than my physical prowess, one big aspect of survival was a question of will.

"Can I see him?

"As soon as he's settled in ICU."

"Thank you."

"If there aren't any further complications… well, let's just say he'll be one lucky man."

Everyone scanned over each other. Then, back at the doctor.

"Let's hope your brother sees it that way as well."

gasping for air

Voices swam. Distant. Vague. Whispered. Mixed and mingled. A sensation of wetness. Submerged. Cold. Eyelids, swollen. Glued-shut. Sticky. Mass darkness. Dense. Swallowed up in complete nothingness. Struggling. Arms, restrained. Legs, the same. Jerks.

"I think he's waking up," the nebulous words crept, but quickly scampered backward—as if back into a long, narrow corridor until briskly gone. Silence returned. Hushed. Back to—nothingness.

Time floated. Limitless. Futile. Wasted. Cold—then melts quickly like snow into water. Warmth hastened, rising into heat. Fire. Nauseating panic clutched. Something in my chest pounds. My heart? Yes, my heart. It beats at a rapid pace. Even faster. Tepid, dank, sweat collects. More, I feebly struggle as if fighting an unknown opponent. Vulnerable. Defenseless. Concentrated peril. Fear. My lungs labor for air. I want to run—escape escalating terror. The fire. I remain trapped. Death surrounds. Sleep. Perhaps, in a coffin in the ground. That's what I remember—unaware of who or where I was.

More time waits. Stagnant. I languish before the recurrence of the voices. Gradually, they statically rise like the volume of an old radio. Their intensity amplifies, stabbing at my eardrums—long, prickly needles. I attempt to reach the palms of my hands to cover my ears, but they still won't move. More voices. Captors. Then, again, they cease—almost as soon as they came. The stabbing sensation stops.

My head starts to throb, explosively as if my brain hammers

against the inside of my skull—as if, coming out from under a drunken hangover. Flickers of light begin to go on and off. Black-and-white. Black-and-white. Black-and-white. The feel of wetness returns. So very wet, as if I'm being soaked by heavy rain.

Tattered and discolored images drift into view. They come in spurts like short-circuiting electric wires sparking in my mind's eye: a woman sitting next to a child on a porch swing; a winding dirt road; a man and woman, their faces angry; yelling; a child's chaotic pencil sketch filling a page, scribbled; a shirtless boy on his knees, and a man sitting on a cot in front of him; a finger pulling a trigger; a splattered wall and a bucket on carpet; flashes of men dancing; a hand holding a bloody knife; a young man in a suit; two naked men kissing in an embrace; a hand reaching out in desolate longing. The images whiten until they fade into nothing only to return jumbled with others less distinguishable. They come and go like the light.

The wetness—grows heavier. Water rises higher around me. An oversized picture window appears in my brain with an early evening sky on the other side of cloudy, spotted glass. I look further out the window. Tall trees full of green. Oddly, only the leaves have color. A waning, frail rays of sunlight moderately retreats through branches of bountiful foliage. The trees began to fall one by one to the ground. Noiselessly. Then,—calm comes over me.

Light continues to dim. The color red streaks through the water like little rushing rivers. My body becomes immersed in the red. The voices return, again—coming back as quickly as they had left like a tug-of-war. Needles prick more rapidly than before like that of a sewing machine puncturing fabric. Like millions of needles—like a seamstress pressing the contraption's pedal all the way to the floor.

A sense of consciousness levels then falls and rises again. I feel the pressure of strange hands on my body. I'm afraid. Can't open my eyes as if their lids are sealed. I wonder what is happening. What's happening to me?

A distinct voice registers in a fraction of my brain—a part that barely separates consciousness from the raging fevered swamp in my head.

"Randy, Randy, you're okay, you're okay. Stop struggling."

The words repeat. I fight harder to free myself but again to no avail. The tug-of-war of the voices and lapsing consciousness continue until everything just stops again—sucked back into silence. I drift deeper into the blackness where I seem to have come from. A place where I feel safe.

"Randy, can you hear me?" whispers through the abyss.

I recognize the name.

"I'm Randy. Yes, that's my name."

I think it's my mother's voice but not sure. The scent of her CHANEL N°5 whiffs like a benignant gust of air as it did while on the floor with Dugan in my arms when I first tried in early January of 2009. Maybe she's coming to take me home. Random images flash back again in my brain. A lifetime of them—imagines of her.

One after the other. Quickly. Again. Some blurry. Others, clear. A familiar panic resurfaces. My body begins shaking uncontrollably like a seizure.

"Randy… it's me, Sandra."

The tug-of-war continues, pulling at my arms and legs. Perhaps, a struggle between Heaven and Hell. The fog around me grows thicker again until I'm back in its clammy core.

I remained adrift without consciousness of time, space, or reality. Later, I was told I wandered in and out for two days. Two days of body jerks, incomprehensible babbling, and gasps for air. At times, mumbling for my mother. Others, for Dugan and names unfamiliar to Sandra. Many times, for Bradley as my sister told me. Any memories I recall—however faintly during that period consist of interrupted sounds, voices, words, more distorted blurred pictures of faces, and events in the visage of dreams and nightmares. All seemingly came in and out of focus like a bad television signal. The screen—snowy, hazy, and pixelating wildly.

two nights and three days

Eyes squint open. Fuzzy figures circle. An airy fog surrounds…

At some provisional state of semi-lucidness while in recovery, although my mind was still somewhat fogged and loopy—restricted in some measure, it slowly began to resurface, cracking the shield that hindered consciousness.

I recall moving my head to assess where I am. Sandra's talking to someone. Then, the reality hits me. Everything floods my mind like a dam has burst open. I find myself back in the world I tried so desperately and laboriously to leave. The one I'd believed I'd exited. I didn't want to believe it—believe I was alive.

The first thought screamed in my head: "Fuck! Fuck! Fuck!" This had better be Hell because it damn sure doesn't look like Heaven." But in truth, I didn't want either. I didn't want Hell or Heaven. I wanted nothing.

A deluge of tears flooded my eyes. My whole body hurt, but the pain could not compare to what I was feeling in my heart. All the emotional amputation returned. That, ugly splintering convulsive torment had been resurrected as my body had, along with the very sorrow that had utterly paralyzed me for so many months—maybe even a lifetime. Many thoughts rolled in my head—some intelligible but many massacred. While others were unable to completely formulate.

It's impossible to even begin to explain the overload of confusion in my head or the fear that beat in my chest—much less, the anguish and desperation of it all. Of how it throbbed—the reality that I was still alive. But I was. Tied down to a hospital bed. A guard standing in the corner—rigid, like a life-sized cardboard cutout.

I thought of my mother as I struggled. Panic quickly took over. Suddenly, I could not breathe. I felt as though I was drowning. My lungs naturally searched in gulps for pockets of air. Purposefully. Laborious. Fraught. But air—was the last thing I wanted. Then, I remember turning to see Sandra sitting by the bed. She's holding my hand while telling me that I'm okay.

"You're okay, Randy. You… you're okay."

My brain starts to roll again. Then, abruptly stops. An image of a woman walks toward the edge of the hospital bed. At the time, I didn't know who she was. Or the role she'd played that returned me to the living.

The blanks were later filled in by Sandra concerning Dr. Bernard's visit of which I can barely grasp—if at all. She told me the kindness the doctor offered didn't measure well with my anger after the narration of her onerous five-some hours at the operating table—that she'd given up just minutes before midnight to call my death. But due to some unexpected indication on the monitor, prompted her to continue.

Upon that accounting—Sandra made it known that I began screaming at the doctor. Lunging for her but held back by the restraints. Riotously shouting questions as if my persona changed into a monstrous madman.

"Who works on a suicide case for five hours? Wasn't it clear I wanted to die? You've no idea of what you've done—what you've done to my soul."

Even Bernard's fuzzy efforts to comfort me by sharing that she'd too once found herself on that crumbling edge of life. That, if it wasn't for that personal experience, combined with the persuasive angst of my friends begging her to do something, is why she ignored the professional opinion of her medical colleague. And therefore, I was rolled into an operating room. Furthermore, Bernard told me that she was okay, and I would eventually be—as if her abilities as a doctor, included having the power to see into my heart or foresee my future.

And as Sandra recounted: Dr. Bernard insisted that nothing she and her team had done was what saved me. But rather some internal will to live that still existed within me. That, it was not my time to die as if she had a direct phone line to God.

Apparently, I attempted to lunge at Bernard a second time in retaliation, only to be held back again by the restraints. From that recall, my last words were, "Get the fuck out of my face!" Sandra then told me that I was administered a sedative.

Before Hal had kicked in my front door, I'd made peace with life. I'd welcomed death to free myself from the nihility of darkness—over which my world had plummeted; and I'd found myself entangled. For that, I resented the doctor who brought me back to life.

I get that Dr. Bernard thought she was doing her sworn job—her Hippocratic Oath of the Ages; but alive or not, she and I both knew a line had been crossed. She'd reached too far to pull me back from death—when in fact, after Bernard's and her staff's laborious efforts, they had saved nothing. It's not a matter of my being ungrateful for her momentary, clinical, umpire call to resuscitate me but more of having my wishes to die on my own terms disrespected. A subtlety altogether unobserved in such circumstances.

I'd already crossed the threshold of death's door, where I wanted to remain. Not dragged back across it—certainly, not by such extreme measures. All resulting in a tug-of-war between the sentinels of life and death. I did carry some animosity toward my friends who intervened, but I acknowledged the difficult and impossible choices with which they were confronted—in the milieu of their own complicated lives.

If all had gone as planned uninterrupted—my ashes entrusted to Allen, as per my will, would have already been on a plane to California. He and Sandra, along with a faithful Dugan would have spread them off Mulholland Drive in the Hollywood Hills, at a curve in the road looking out over Los Angeles. I was determined to get back to the Hollywood Hills where I'd fallen in love with Bradley—one way or another. If not in life, then in death. When Dugan's time came, I'd requested Allen and Sandra to fly back to Los Angeles to spread Dugan's ashes in the same spot. I'd opened a separate bank account with fifteen-thousand-dollars exclusively to cover the cost of four, round-trip plane tickets, hotel, and other expenses.

Once my mind returned to clearer thought, all I could think about was how to kill the never-ending sense of loss, abandonment, betrayal, and the accompanying panic that had returned with a vengeance along with my life. All of it swelling over the years. I was mourning my rebirth after being ripped from Death's arms by Dr. Bernard. And by doing so, Dr. Frankenstein, in a sense, had kept the Grim Reaper at bay while desecrating the grave that had been waiting for my body.

purgatory

Thoughts vacillate indiscriminately. I'm caught within a sense of threatening danger. I want to be anywhere but where I am. I want to flee. But I can't. I'm still feeling somewhat drugged—immersed. Loopy. Unsure. Confused. Disoriented. Still groggy from the drugs I'd been administered once on and after the operating table. The complex combination of drugs merged in my body. I felt the painkillers were expiring. My left arm started to burn. I felt as if I'd barely walked away from a horrific car crash and was the only survivor. But that never was my intent: to survive. Even still, I knew I was dead inside. Weakness had taken over my body. Spent. I felt spent, emptied out. Limp as a child's rag doll. My mind and spirit are possessed by the feeling of helplessness, but helplessness had been running through my veins the months before.

I sense it's late in the night. Hovering voices talk behind me. Their presence, certain. My mind struggled to process the words. Then, I realize I'm sitting in a wheelchair inside of an elevator. I feel exposed in the flimsy gown—violated. I wonder where my clothes are. Incomplete thoughts gather but break apart and crumble before they can broaden. Before I can grasp them intelligently.

Netted in my peripheral vision, a pointed finger reaches past me. I'm too afraid to look anywhere but forward. The finger presses a round button in a row of round buttons with numbers. The half dollar size circle lights up. The doors close. I'm trapped. It's too late to run—that is, if I were capable. The elevator makes a mechanical sound, then jerks. The sensation of traveling upward follows.

The metal box comes to a jolting stop. The doors open. I find myself surrounded by the intangible stillness. The deafening quiet. The dimness. Combined, they validate my belief it's the midpoint of night.

I'm wheeled down a long corridor. More like a tunnel. Spaced, random, noises dampened. Or so I thought. Perhaps, more so in a fuddled mind. The wheelchair stopped in front of a desk. I vaguely remembered papers presented to me and instructed to sign. The wheelchair started rolling again. Rolled into a bare room. A harsh light goes on as I'm pushed to a bed. An orderly. Yes, I sensed it had to be an orderly who assisted me onto a bed. He soon departed as if never there. The light goes off. The door closed. Immediately, the room—grimy-gray. I recall feeling like a terrified little boy afraid of the dark and left alone to fend for himself. Afraid to move an inch. Afraid to look around the room to see what might be lurking. So, I lay in bed like a dead body—my mind, scrambled.

In the unsettling hours of what persisted in that inexplicit night—a woman's frail, crippling voice ruptured the emotionless silent cold and sterile isolation. I remained unstirred while listening to the faint tolling of her words ghosting up and down the wide corridors, desperate, fatal cries. "Help me. Someone… please help," leached from somewhere—seemingly far away. She repeatedly called out eerie breaths of despair.

I'd instantly thought of my mother—perhaps, it was her cries haunting me. Knowing a truth, I'd never dare divulge to her. Now that her spirit was in death's kingdom, surely, she knew that truth and either was indignant with me for what I'd done and for burying her body in the same grave as my father's—even though the coffin in which her body rested was on top. By me entombing her there, my mother was perhaps still suffering from his torment and abuse she'd endured in life and would for eternity as he'd done the many years of their volatile wreck of a marriage.

The only reason I did, preferring not to have my mother's body anywhere near his, was because Sandra told me Mother once said, "Just put me there." As I questioned a number of times, maybe I was not the good son I'd once believed—and this was payback.

That was my first night on the 13th floor of Davy Hospital's mental ward. I woke in unfamiliar surroundings and in a strange bed as daylight pushed the daunting night from the room. A glaring reality met my sleepy eyes as they opened. My body: stiff and sore. My left arm still burned. I stared at the ceiling; my mind raced with discombobulated thoughts in search of explanations. Even those thoughts hurt as my brain attempted to process everything past and present. In the middle of it all, I hoped I was only caught in a nightmare. One from which I would eventually awaken.

Not until later that morning, I realized I'd been delivered as if a package rather than a human being by an employee of the United Parcel Service—processed from one location to another: from the bathtub of my master bathroom in my home, to an ambulance, to an ER, to an operating table, to recovery, and then to a mental ward. I'd arrived at the next holding station and may as well have had a tracking number tattooed on my arm.

A nondescript woman enters the room unannounced. She eyes me disappointingly, before taking a few steps toward the bed.

"You need to get up and come with me," she blatantly orders, like I'm her bitch.

No good morning or how are you feeling. Nothing of any remote politeness is offered. I looked in her direction but said nothing.

"Can you hear me?" she asked.

I continued to look at her.

"Mr. Chumbley…"

"Yes… yes, I can."

"Then, follow me."

"Why?"

"To check your vitals… and take some blood. Now get up," she scolded.

Grudgingly, I get out of bed rubbing my eyes. I follow the woman like a newborn animal imprinting on the first moving creature it sees—out the room and down the hallway. An array of people walked around: most evidently, patients; the majority, unkempt in appearance; poverty-stricken faces; a few in hospital gowns, and others in street clothing—long passed a good washing; employees and staff caring things or holding folders; other people indistinguishable. The environment is all too familiar from a decade or so ago. I start feeling scared again. The sensation of entrapment consumes me as does rawness. I feel extremely out of place, convinced a mistake has been made. My brain switches on high alert: "Danger Will Robinson, Danger!"

Once the nurse finishes her poking and prodding, she directs me to the common area. I sit. Just sit. Frozen—I sit. Watching. Waiting. Wondering. After irresolute minutes, I notice a man with bad posture standing several yards away; he glances in my direction while talking to what appears to be a staffer. I spy them. More minutes stumble by. The staffer looks at me while pointing as if giving directions to the closest Pizza Hut. The man nods before heading in my direction. The closer he gets—I realize that he was in fact, a woman. It was an honest mistake or more like, mistaken identity. In my defense, she did in fact look like a man in her amplified and exaggerated choice of attire suitable for a Mr. Rogers' Halloween costume: a baggy light-colored button-down shirt with what appeared to be a mustard stain; khaki pants; brown belt; ugly, slightly worn brown men's shoes to match.

I remained seated—watching her every stride until she briskly stopped in front of me before arrogantly introducing herself as if I was supposed to be impressed—dispassionately, as the nurse had been earlier, she announced, without a hint of human empathy. Not that I was looking for any.

"I'm Dr. Barbara Albridge… head psychiatrist here at Davy," she declared, cold and hard as the concrete floor underneath the tile. Her introduction spoken in a manner that I expected a drumroll at any moment.

Long moments ensured as her hard-bitten eyes stared accusingly; Albridge's arms were locked across her flat chest. I remember asking when I could leave—hoping it would be soon. One night in that wretched place was enough. Even in my state of mind, I realized it was a hellhole.

Dr. Albridge's stare hadn't shied as she oh-so-clinically responded, "You need to sit here and realize what a very bad thing you did." Talking down to me like one might a misbehaved kid put in detention. Like a kid, who'd toilet-papered the school cafeteria. Her words fell outrageously. Her voice, flat-toned and void of compassion. Her face, expressionless. The fact I surely looked scared and disoriented—more like terrified, was lost on her.

That was it. Albridge pivoted and walked away—walked fucking away without another word.

"Realize what a very bad thing I did. Very bad. I did. Bad? Very. To whom?" my mind riffled.

I wanted to stand up and scream at her, "Who the fuck are you to judge me… you cunt bitch?" But I didn't.

Directly, I took a strong dislike to this quack—this Dr. Albridge who had just made an enemy with a target on her back. I was certain, a lesbian but no matter—her possible persuasion was not the issue. But ostensibly, a hardened one with seemingly an ideological axe-to-grind from what I could ascertain from her curtness. Hurled such, as if we'd known each other many years before, and I'd wronged her in some terrible fashion. As if I'd once bitch-slap her. I summoned up, from fathomless depths—instantaneous, visceral, antipathy for her from that moment onward. I hated that bitch. Dr. Albridge had already made her anecdotal assumptions about me: male, white, privileged, and another sob story. I was nothing more to her than a statistic, formulated in her mind from years of medical journal studies and countless patients before me.

Clearly, I possessed more compassion in the tip of my little finger than she had in her whole body—or seemingly so. If she was a doctor, then I was Pope Francis.

"God help them… her patients," I thought.

I'd convinced myself I was in purgatory waiting for the elevator to the bottom. Surely, the next stop—the next and last delivery station. Everything around me screamed: it was only going to get worse. Dr.

Albridge looked like something from Hell—perhaps the Devil's Gatekeeper. For all I knew—the keeper of souls waiting to be sent to Hell.

"She might be out to fuck me, but not in the way I would prefer," I remembered thinking.

Not long after Albridge's introduction, a plump woman approached with a clipboard securely positioned under her arm.

"Are you Mr. Chumbley?" she cuts to the chase.

"Yes."

"Do you have health insurance?"

"Blue Cross Blue Shield."

"Do you have your card?"

I shook my head, no.

"Can someone bring it?"

"I'll ask my sister."

The woman with the clipboard scampers away.

"Is everyone so curt in this fucking place?" I thought.

Shortly after Ms. Clipboard, a honey-colored skinned, perhaps late-twenties, clean-cut-stick-of-a-man, short with wide eyes, tight hair, and cinnamon breath introduced himself as my social worker, Abdul. Again, no one had yet to directly ask me: how was I'm feeling or doing for that matter. I would have appreciated either.

He immediately gave a sales pitch on the efficiency and prestige of the mental facility—going as far as exclaiming famous people like actors and athletes had been patients at Davy on this very ward as if it rivaled, The Betty Ford Center. All I had to do was look around to know that was bullshit. Any person of prominence might have been held there briefly, but their caregivers, handlers, assistants, private doctors, or attorneys would have had them transferred out in a matter of hours.

I realized I was still being processed as the day dragged. By mid-afternoon, the nurse brought some pills in a little white paper cup.

"Take these," she ordered.

She doesn't inform why—just to take them.

By the late afternoon, Sandra came with Russ and Marty. They told me I looked good, but I knew I looked like shit-warmed-over as I felt the same.

"Have you eaten much today?" Sandra asked.

"I don't have much of an appetite. But if I did, after seeing what they served for breakfast... that was been enough to squash it."

"You do look pale. You should eat something."

"Clearly not from here. Please tell me I didn't eat any hospital food while I was in recovery?"

"Really, just Jello... you were out of it most of the time. I can run to the grocery to get you something, that is... if they'll let me."

"Well, either way, when we leave... I'll pick up something and bring it back," Sandra insisted.

"Maybe just a few protein bars."

Sandra told me that Allen, another good friend and an attorney, called to let her know he would be driving over from Birmingham the next day to visit. I asked about Dugan. I remember being so worried about my boy most of the day. I'm informed that Hal's good friend, Liz is looking after him at her home.

"No. I want Dugan at the house. I don't want him in some unfamiliar place with a stranger. Like... like I am, Sandra. You can look after him. You're staying at the house, anyway," I adamantly insisted.

"You know I would... but I'm going to be here as much as they'll allow. That way, Dugan will have somebody with him most of the time."

"But... Sandra... "

"Randy... you and I know Dugan has never met a stranger. Think of him as being on vacation," she reasoned.

"Then... I want to talk to Hal about his friend. I've got to know they will take good care of him."

"He's coming with us tomorrow."

Hal told us to give you his love," Marty comforted. "I know his friend... Liz. She loves animals."

"Hey... hey, listen. Liz fell in love with Dugan the second she laid eyes on him," Russ chimed in.

At that point, I completely broke down thinking about Dugan. I was certain, he was surely wondering where I was.

"Sis... will you take the picture of Dugan and me from the frame in my bedroom?" I asked. "Will... will you bring it tomorrow?" I then covered my face with my hands, feeling pathetic.

"Of course. Really, Randy... Dugan is perfectly fine," she tried to console even more.

this isn't the – w - atlanta midtown

The grace of night ended a directionless garbled day of vexations to a close on Davy's mental ward of the broken—some forgotten. A day without a single person associated with the hospital offering a kind and supportive word of encouragement to a man who'd arrived lifeless in the ER some seventy-two hours before. I was on a countdown. One day down, but how many more to go? How many would it take to satisfy Dr. Bitch, "I'd realized what a very bad thing I did?"

I found an uneasy refuge but refuge all the same in my assigned room away from the rest of the inmates—facing the wall and curled up in the bed like a child. And as had the day, I lingered with the night lying embedded in those vulnerable hours. In time, once again, the woman's cries heard the night before began to ghost the corridors. As before, they were remote but piercing. At first, they mirrored those of a dying animal's, drifting out into those remote and murky hours of what seemed to be a void of nonexistence. The hollowness of her voice remained pitiful, chilling, weeping cries and hauntingly sung—ringing through the blackness as well; interrupting the tranquil sleep of innocence—if sleep could be found.

A thin pillow wrapped over my ears—held securely with both hands in a nugatory effort to deafen the intransigent callousness of her muffled howling. Even still, they remained unsilenced and inescapable in some alternate veracity without foundation.

The meagerly thin mattress of the twin, metal-framed bed was unyielding as if laid out on concrete. The cheapest possible polyester sheets, and an itchy lightweight cotton-blend blanket—both enough to rash flesh, poorly stayed tucked. Certainly, a far cry from the 1200 thread count Egyptian cotton sheets I'd taken for granted that dressed my bed at home.

To make this flea infested motel equally physically unpleasant, the bed was positioned a few feet from the wall and bolted to the floor. The bolting—preventing me from pushing my body up against the wall as I wanted, rather needed, to penetrate the sheetrock in order to hide as much as to become invisible.

I wore the same T-shirt and shorts as I had during the day. The same socks, too. My athletic shoes were at the side of the bed. All in an effort of readiness if indeed an opportunity arose, I could somehow make an escape unnoticed. A second bed was positioned on the far side of the room I shared with a stranger. Across from the foot of each bed was a brown bookcase where the patients stored what little belongings were allowed. I'd been informed by Abdul earlier in the day during his sales pitch: the attendants checked them regularly to ensure there was nothing sharp with which to harm ourselves or drugs. They may as well have strip searched us every day.

With the morning, I found myself in the same reality as I sat in the dingy common area—glowering at the thick, iron gate. A six-foot-six guard—the Gatekeeper, dwarfed a desk where he sat on the other side. Just beyond him, a metal detector was visible. I would surmise the detector was for the benefit of the hospital as a precautionary measure if a visitor brought a concealed weapon onto the ward. Plausibly, to break someone out or prevent a disgruntled ex-patient from going postal on the doctors, nurses, and staff—perhaps dissatisfied with the services rendered.

I continued to plot and scheme for an escape as I memorized the layout—all the while, envying the staff, doctors, nurses, and visitors freely coming and going as they flashed pass cards over a small square box a few feet from the gate. I coveted one of those cards. I would have killed for one. Vigilantly, I continued to watch the gate, like a hawk looking for its next rat to catch.

I toyed with the notion of hiding in some doorway off a corridor with a blind spot. Waiting for a doctor or nurse—anyone, wearing a white lab coat or scrubs, to knock them out cold before dragging their body out of sight. From there: I would steal their pass card, strip them of any professional attire; dress in them, and make my getaway. Then, I would mosey out as if I worked at the hospital. But I was as bolted to the ward as much as those beds.

A small, obsolete television was mounted high on the grubby wall. Its screen, staticky as it broadcasted a four-decade-old episode of Gilligan's Island. That alone, was depressing enough—too reminiscent of a piece of my childhood: a boy sitting on the sofa in the living room watching the same show—the exact episode, no less: the Professor fixing a radio in hopes of being rescued; that was, until an inept Gilligan dropped a load of firewood on it. And just like those stranded castaways on that fake remote island television show set, I needed rescue from Davy's 13th floor. But the ward was not artificially constructed. After five minutes or so, I returned to my VIP hotel room.

The mental ward was a wretched habitat to the degree of toxicity. It offered no visual pleasantries or emotional comfort, much less stability—rather, an insipid colorless environment. I was reluctant to touch anything. The furniture in the common area was circa 1980s: two long ratty straight-line sofas covered in faded-blue cracked vinyl; two side chairs on wobbly legs with well-worn armrests, surely tattered from countless patients. Some of the damage likely caused by the digging and scratching of the vinyl by patients' fingernails in a repetitive, nervous manner like crazy people are perceived to do in horror movies; magazines, ragged and outdated, stacked on a beaten and nicked up side table with the scratched initials, BFK—stood out like a monogram. Perhaps, done by a former patient as a silent statement, "I was here."

Underfoot, the floor was covered in institutional vinyl-composite square tiles—yellowed and chipped over time and from foot traffic that no amount of mopping and buffing could render like-new. In the rear of the sitting area was a conference table and chairs. I would soon come to learn, the hub of the common area where patients were authoritatively ordered to assemble several times a day for meals and workshops. If any were to refuse, they were considered antisocial by the staff. As if like watchdogs, some collecting copious notes to provide the doctors and certainly, the head dragon—Dr. Albridge.

Through my continued education, I quickly came to know those workshops primarily dealt with drug abuse and the importance of taking medications after being released. Fascinatingly, the subjects of depression or suicide were never broached. Not being a druggie—these so-called workshops were a useless waste of my time. They may as well have passed out coloring books and crayons.

"Be sure to take your medications… so you won't end up back here," the staff, nurses, and doctors monotonously intone as if it were the ward's mantra—belabored day-in-and-day-out, like a prerecorded announcement looping on the intercom system to brainwash. "If only I could click my heels like Dorothy from the Wizard of Oz; and click, click, click-the-fuck out of the ward," I thought. Due to my unanticipated resurrection, I was branded hopelessly sick and locked up with others who were viewed as unfit to walk among the masses—in a place where the air was thick with the smell of apathy and any perception of reality was illusory.

It may have seemed like a high-end hotel to the impoverished patients; the attendants, the concierges. From the accommodations I was accustomed to: this was not the W Atlanta – Midtown. Rather, more like Hotel Hell—tripled refried.

coming full circle

At any given time—I was one of some twelve people. Twelve stories—twelve hardships to be told. Twelve reasons that brought us to this hellish place. That is, unless more were hiding under beds like mice or sequestered in another section of the ward.

I would not be left aghast to know that the latter were locked away—left unbathed, their clothes dirty and tattered, and made to sleep on the floor in soundproof rooms made of concrete walls. Hidden and out-of-sight while restrained, medieval-style, in rusty wrought iron neck and wrist shackles—fed scraps of food thrown at them once a day as they fought for those scraps with cat-size rats. Those scraps, much like the ones my grandmother threw on the ground for my mother's black dog that lived under the sun-bleached, wooden shack-of-a-house in which she grew up.

Those in view walked up and down the corridors as if in an episode of "The Walking Dead." All appearing as if lost and severely defeated souls. This was the only place for them, perhaps, other than some correctional facility, when their questionable actions and behaviors crossed the line dividing what society could and could not abide.

Sluggishly, they shuffled past each other—but seldom made eye contact. I surmised, if we dared to do so, it would be like peering at an oddity—some freak show of psychological rarities who didn't fit the norm. No one hurried along. There was nowhere to go. Each patient, quarantined in their own feces of their dysfunction and within the walls of Davy—lab rats in a glass aquarium. If not peering out the windows of sleeping quarters at what could be seen of the Atlanta skyline, then huddled in corners—in languid-like states having found a safe zone. Perhaps, some like me were pondering their existence, too.

They were not my contemporaries—they were strangers and nothing more. And none of which I might remotely identify socially. I assertively attempted to convince myself: none of them were a reflection of me; that I had nothing in common with any of them. But in the coming days, I would arrive at the comprehension: I was as mentally imperfect and damaged as those strangers who surrounded me. All of us—haphazardly assembled without any rhyme and reason. All seen as numbers and not human beings.

As they were, I was involuntarily carried through the portal of the dreaded 13th floor of Davy. I was—without argument, one of them hermetically sealed—confined and removed from the rest of the world. I'd lost my freedom as they had. The real question: did I ever have any—freedom, that is? The factors I didn't share with them: white, privileged, educated, and economically solid.

It would be close to impossible to portray how I felt during my mandatory stay. Certainly, unable to collect the words to convey such a hellish experience I'd found myself in. In shock might be a good start, followed by pure fear and overwhelming panic, again, I was still alive. My head continued to hurt as did my left arm where I'd laid it open.

The isolation was indescribable as one day circled around to the next and the next; there was not anything to do on the ward but wait. Just wait. And more waiting. But for what: pull sanity out of the air. Thus, there was not anything to distract from the obvious detestable environment and the cold shoulders of the majority of the staff. Instead, I was left to face segments of my life whether I wanted to or not—coerced to face the enter-mingling of fifty-four years.

My brain swam in unwanted and superfluous emotions that dredged up like vomit from the pit of my stomach, forcing me to relive certain unpleasant moments that had faded with each passing year into remote, hidden corners of my psyche. Then, there were the horrors that had never faded or would for that matter but lived in suspension—that is until now.

One minute, my mind raced with blurred thoughts like a speeding car. The next, they slowed to a crawl—inched along at a snail's pace before accelerating again even faster. Then, suddenly, those thoughts came to a screeching halt—all colliding like a twenty-car pile-up on I-75. My life had become that accident.

They say all roads lead somewhere. Despite the dividing years, the many miles of my winding road led from my birthplace of Fayette, Alabama, to Columbus, Georgia, to Manheim, Germany, back to Columbus, to that house on Shirley Drive in Warner Robins, Georgia, to Macon, Georgia, to Atlanta, Georgia, to Los Angeles, California, to Miami, Florida, to New York, to cities in France, Italy, and Spain. But my mind never completely left the events that took place in Columbus, especially those in that shit-town of Warner Robins where they escalated until they climaxed. And in early July 2009, that road landed me in the mental ward of Davy Memorial Hospital.

As you know, after moving to Atlanta, I kept being pulled back to Warner Robins and that house to the degree of losing count of the trips back and forth on I-75. Each drive returning to look after my mother to the best of my abilities was, indeed, like being jetted back in time. Back to that house where I stood within the boundaries where madness lived and cried and bled—and where I thought that madness had finally died.

Each time, hoping. Hoping, Mother would get better mentally. Hoping, she would triumph over alcoholism. Hoping, she would never feel unloved. Never feel alone as if the world had abandoned her—among other things (the same is true concerning me, concerning feeling unloved and alone even when I thought otherwise). Wishing I possessed the superpowers to make it all so. Such hypocrisy that I once thought I was dissimilar to my mother concerning her mental instabilities.

As I frequently thought of her while I was locked up in the ward, I also did of the many cards and notes I'd written her over the years. Cards and notes telling Mother: she needed to try harder and that she could become unstuck and find her way out of the mental illnesses that entangled her and out of the bottle. Each card ending in: always know you're loved and cherished. But I was wrong. I realized I was wrong to tell her she, needed and could—whether in those cards and notes or face-to-face, as I'd learned firsthand and would continue to do so. Even more enormously in the future.

It's true what they say: You have to walk in someone else's shoes to know. But even still, we never fully do—certainly, not in its magnitude. And although I saw the tremendous sadness and pain in Mother's eyes for years on end—heard it in the quiver of her voice and saw it rolling down her cheeks, I was not her regardless of how close we were. Regardless, how we were much alike. Regardless, of the pain I felt for my mother. Regardless, of how many times I held her in my arms. How many times she cried on my shoulders. Put her to bed. Watched her sleep. After all I'd witnessed and despite my love for my mother, it was impossible for me, again, to know over all those years until she died.

Now, I was labeled as she had been. I just hope by my writing to her—by those written words and even speaking them, telling Mother she needed and could—that, again, she would be okay if she just tried harder didn't make her feel more alone—more removed from the world than she must have already felt. Like the way I did when people told me comparatively, as well-meaning as their words may have been and as well-meaning as mine to her were. Now that I was locked up as my mother had been several times. We were misunderstood. Even harshly judged as weak among others. And, in many ways—unseen.

Yes, I knew more than before. Borne it much deeper. Even, felt much closer to her regarding the desperation that had stolen her breath as it did a huge part of her life because of what she was forced to endure from all sides of life. As my mother's, I came to feel the loneliness—soaked by the years as if it fell from the sky like black rain; even with Sandra and the friends who stayed surrounding me—it poured.

As a child, I only thought I was witnessing Mother's debilitating despair caused by the mental illnesses from a close proximity—but I was too young to know; it was my own as well. At Davy, I came to understand more of how she must have felt firsthand. I was living some of the same confined torment—added on top of a pile of it that had encased her like a second layer of skin. As well, my mother's desperation for freedom had become mine.

As on the pages of "In the Arms of Adam: a diary of men" and "Alabama Snow," I was no longer the little sweet boy standing on the pavement in the parking lot of a hospital in Columbus, Georgia, looking up at my mother's silhouette. Her standing, too, but behind chain-link fencing high up on a terrace. Mother's frail body and troubled mind, limply pressed against it. Her fingers white-knuckling the diamond-shaped links—grabbing hold as if for dear life while other patients slowly marauded in the background like sedated caged animals. Mother seemed so physically distant—out of reach of my short extended arms.

She looked small—like one of my sister's dolls while dressed in a long, pale-colored gown as she called out, "I love you." But her faint, weak words were carried off on the wind before they could fully reach my ears. Even at that young age, I knew my father was responsible for her imprisonment. That, his abuse had led her there as to other hepatizations. But he blamed my mother and not himself.

My father could not understand why his wife was not always happy making a roast or fried oysters for dinner. Why, she was resistant to lie in their bed with her legs spread. Why she spent days at a time in bed and when she was not, wore her night clothes and a robe from morning to night.

There were more hospitalizations. More times locked up inside similar walls like Davy's 13th floor as my mother's mental illness continued to spread overtime like a cancer: severe, more paralyzing, lengthy episodes of melancholy; anxiety; later the rage brought on by her bipolar condition; the confusion and paranoia to follow, seeded by the onset of schizophrenia; the resulting PTSD fueled by years of my father's all-inclusive abuse. They walked—hand-in-hand like old fraternity sisters. One often without one or more of the others. All to the point her mental afflictions had amalgamated into one, and the alcohol—the binding agent. All of it chewed at her life.

While caught in the isolation of Davy, I was often swamped by many recollections of my mother as if reading her memoir—that is, until mine collided with hers and they became entangled as one—colliding with such force, even breathing proved to be arduous.

Through a polished picture window, I see a boy watching as his mother is being taken from a house on a stretcher, fighting two paramedics trying to control her. His father stands on the back steps. His arms are crossed over his chest—his face unmarked by pity or compassion.

She is strapped down by wide and thick wrist restraints with longer ones across her violently writhing body. The boy witnesses with his siblings as the stretcher rolls down over the cracked and uneven, bumpy driveway. He feels helpless and sad. The boy's heart is filled with hatred for his father as his mother's eyes dart back and forth while her screams of, "why, why, why" go unacknowledged. At that moment, his mother's confused distress becomes his.

I clearly remembered how my mother suddenly stopped her struggling—as if the world had stopped spinning. Pensively, my mother looked at me. Our eyes locked as the paramedics were about to slide her into the back of the ambulance. At that moment, I instinctively knew how deep her pain ran—every fear and sorrow and the blood of her emotions—in entirety, all told by her eyes as if we were telepathically connected. That day of confession has never left me: the day my mother was taken away but not before she shared her darkness with me by some form of transference—as our eyes met and locked, only broken when the paramedics closed the door of the ambulance, and she disappeared but not what she had transferred.

As a man, that little boy found himself sitting next to her in the visiting room of Milledgeville's Georgia State Mental Hospital—where she was confined by a court order. My mother crumbled one too many times, and to the degree she was a danger to herself more than ever as she continued to live in that house alone. Even though I remained devoted to her; I would not live in Warner Robins again. I knew she wanted me to do so, but I was not going to live within those scorching flames of Hell.

By then, I'd seen other parts of the world as I had some experiences of beauty and what I believed was happiness. Regardless, not even God could make me ever return there to live. And because my mother remained steadfast in her refusal to sell and move to Los Angeles or hadn't remarried in the some-ten-year span of time since I'd moved to Atlanta, again, that devotion forced me to continue to return—where, each time, I stood alongside her surrounded by the flames.

After stays in mental wards of hospitals spread out over the preceding years, and regardless of various stretches of time where Mother seemed well and in control, the disease had grown too big for both of us—too immense, for her regardless of the ever-changing combinations of medications or me to manage her. I was not equipped to help my mother the deeper it dug its claws into her.

I realized there was no amount of love or attempted emotional support I could give that I already had. They too—succumbed to the flames of the disease. I was unable to repress their riotous darkness. Those years of love and devotion were not enough to save my beloved mother from the ugliness in the small world she suffered within. And I could not save her from the ghost of my father—her husband, who had betrayed her and worse. Each link in the chain it rattled represented an injury of great proportion inflicted on her and what each had stolen from her very being. Regardless of how painful it was, committing my mother seemed the only solution at the time for her physical safety and any hope for stability in her future.

Three years of her life was locked away, added to the prison sentence that jailed her for years as if my mother had committed a crime. But her confinement was due to being born into a family whose DNA carried the sickness; but more so, for marrying the wrong man—a lethal one, whose actions lit the match that ignited it. He was the criminal and not my mother, and the reason she was in Milledgeville. I felt as though I'd ultimately failed her and grievously so, even though I gave my soul in banknotes to the Devil in a split second. And if indeed there was more to my father's exit from this earth, it really didn't matter—he'd still won in death.

On each visit, I could barely manage to walk through the front doors of the massive Greek Revival edifice. I found it excruciating to sit beside my mother and directly look into her eyes as her sadness and emotional pain circled while the madness lurked. All the while, wondering if she hated me; and if that were the case, too sedated to scream and raise her hands to slap at me. Perhaps, the history of the hospital added to my grave discomfort as did knowing my mother went from that house on Shirley Drive and my father's ghost, to a state hospital full of moth-eaten ones.

Conceived in 1837, the hospital's main structure governs a pecan grove on its campus with much smaller buildings. Five years later, its doors opened to house the lunatics, the perceived idiots, the epileptics, and others not wanted to be seen by society—hidden away in a veritable dumping ground as many were abandoned by families to rot within its walls. First abrasively christened: The Georgia Lunatic Asylum—once known as one of the world's largest mental hospitals. It housed some 12,000-plus patients in the 1960s—its walls hiding the stifling pain and anguish of thousands of men, women, and children over the many years of its operation.

Those walls not only hid the agony and sorrow of the mentally ill, they concealed: grave abuse and neglect; lobotomies intended to alter behaviors of patients afflicted with unmanageable depression, psychosis, and schizophrenia; torturous experiments and other treatments equally harrowing; the rapes of patients by other patients and by attendants, even by doctors; women having a difficult time going through menopause, their confusion and odd actions deemed the work of the Devil; the deformed, unwanted and scoffed by society; elderly people falsely deemed mentally incompetent, locked up by greedy family members for control of estates and inheritances.

Untold numbers lived the better part of their lives within those walls. Not even in death, were some set free—their dead bodies removed from the confinement of its walls to wooden coffins buried on the grounds. Even today, from sunup to sundown, the shifting shadows of the institution looms, washing over unmarked graves as similar institutions around the world. Surely, many of their souls still in torment as their ghosts walk the vacated halls. Today, the living walk over that dirt unaware of the bones and bones lying beneath.

In 2010, the hospital closed out of disquiet concerns about how the patients were treated over its years of operation. Irrefragable—what few numbers of the surviving patients left, remain haunted by their confinement and ill-to-barbaric treatment.

Every second as we sat, the heartache I saw in my mother's eyes gnawed at me. My moral support continued to be perpetual. But I knew all I could hope for were that my words—I love you, to be comprehended while dispelling any doubts by her that I might one day stop being there for her. That, my love would remain constant and unwavering—no matter how frustrated or angry she'd made me at times. Some, resulting in raising my voice to the point of yelling at her. And the two times I regrettably, to my own self-disgust, slapped my mother.

The first time, while I was in college. That day, she had been drinking on and off from morning until night. I was studying at the desk in my bedroom—my back to the doorway. The hour had grown tired. Mother kept disturbing me as she swore and yelled. My attempts to ignore my mother pushed her anger forward. Several times, I got up to take her back to her bedroom, but Mother would not settle down.

Each interruption was worse than the one before. Her remarks were cruel and hurtful—my mother's demeanor highly aggressive, quite unlike her when she was sober. They were directed toward me and my father as if he was in the room—as if I were shapeshifting between the two of us.

"You're a fag… just like your father. I wish you were never born. I hate you, Wilson."

Mother eventually seemed to have finally settled down. The beer cans stopped popping. Her voice went adrift somewhere deep into her mind; and for the moment, her internal chaos appeared as if it had traveled someplace else outside the confines of the four walls of the house. But I knew better. Other than in her mind where my father had created and nurtured it, that's where it lived as well. Still, for the moment, the house returned to an ambiguous quiet as the hour grew late. All that could be heard, where the creeks and cracks of an old house where his ghost remained lurking and hovering—and the occasional clamors outside of any other night.

Weary and dismayed—but mostly always for her, I went back to my studies. I didn't even hear my mother walk back into my room. I was caught by immediate surprise as I felt her hand rip a clump of hair from the back of my head. Reflexively and within seconds, I got up and turned around—slapping my mother even before I knew I had. How I loathed myself at the realization of what I'd done. It was of no comfort; she was too intoxicated to remember the next day.

A few years later, I'd drove to Warner Robins to spend the Christmas holiday with her. Some days before, Mother told me she wasn't well enough to come to Atlanta as we'd planned. I made her promise not to drink so we could have a nice Christmas together; but I knew I couldn't depend on promises. Upon walking into the house, the next morning with presents in hand, I found Mother dunk and hysterical. Unable to reason with her and calm Mother down and that she had broken that promise as I feared she might, I angrily poured out all the liquor I could find in the cabinets after already having done so with the bottle on the kitchen table; fulling knowing it would intensify her state of mind as she yelled and tried to take them away from me.

As a result, I stupidly slapped her thinking it would help to bring her around. The shock of the slap did somewhat work; but all the same, I'd loathed myself as I had the time some years before. We both cried as we hugged each other. But I'll never forget or forgive myself. As I remember to this very day, the heartache and shame continues to shackle me. After the second time as I had the first—I told myself that I would rather die a billion times than to ever slap her again, no matter how wrathful she made me. I saw my father in myself both times.

I could not repeatedly keep going back to that house, not knowing in what condition I would find her or it. But increasingly, she became more discombobulated, slipping further away from reality. And the more she did, my mother began to fight me as if I were the enemy. Or could I keep cleaning it, overwhelmed by the mess during the worst periods of my mother's emotional distress.

The times I tried to hire a housekeeper, Mother would argue she didn't want a stranger in the house. That too, was a sign of her mushrooming paranoia. In time, the kitchen became roach infested. No matter how many times I fogged it, they eventually returned.

For my mother, it was three years of looking through more chain-link fencing out into the world. A world that should have always belonged to her. Early on, as I stated previously, mistakenly, I believed she could change if she tried harder—if I tried harder to save my mother. Many years later, in the confines of the wretched hospital of Davy as the months before—I came to know: why she could not completely change; could not keep her stable periods in a holding pattern and stay there; why she kept returning to the bottle after periods of staying sober; why she could not remain authentically happy; why she could not leave the past in the past.

And I came to understand, why my mother never fully found herself again after my father was removed from our lives. But years before, I'd foolishly believed she could. As well, I understood why she remained, for years to follow, in the dark of winter—intimately knowing too many cold and bleak days more than ones with sunshine. Perhaps, deep down, I'd known all along but refused to see it—refused to accept the measurement of her illness until it became mine.

At Davy, I was in my mother's shoes—where she had been. Sitting in a psychiatric ward feeling alone with a dispirited heart barely beating in my chest. A heart plunged with pain riding on a sharp-bladed knife. And surely as she must have felt, I was an outcast locked up with strangers—crazy people whom a large part of society looked down upon, made fun of, ran in the other direction of, and even feared. Then, there were those who found amusement as if viewing an animal at the zoo behind a cage or in the circus under the Big Top. No doubt, some in the audience, waiting as they hoped the lions, tigers, or bears would devour their trainer to add to their entertainment. I certainly wanted to devour Dr. Albridge for mine.

Surely, as my mother must have while confined at Georgia State Mental Hospital—I wanted and did scream at Davy. In my mind, I saw my mother's tormented eyes staring back at me as they had each time I'd sat with her over those three years. Often, feeling they were shooting bullets at me for locking her up. At Davy, I got an embittered crash-course taste of what she endured a hundredfold. And as my mother did time and time again, I existed in a stagnant world. Motionless. Controlled. Measured. Regulated. Airless. No windows to open to let out the stench of quarantined insanity.

There had been a time when I was one of those who were freely able to walk in and out of such a psychiatric ward. As ludicrously foreign as Davy may have seemed, it was also abstractly familiar and too reminiscent of the asylum where my mother was housed. On each of my visits, she begged me to get her out. At Davy, I came to understand how she must have felt firsthand. I was living some of the same torment—added on top of a pile of it that had encased her like a second layer of skin. Her desperation for freedom had become mine. All leaving me to again wonder: had I really been a good son? My mother's and mine—our inextricable lives, had brought me full circle. I was the one on the inside looking out. The caged circus animal—on display.

an imposed penance

Nights passed. Days crawled. Both dawdling in suspension. Time seemed perpetual—no beginning or end. Just dark melting into light and light into dark. Like the first night, I watched, listened, and waited. I quickly forgot what day of the week it was, much less the hour. In some ways, I didn't want to know—fearing, in knowing, time would drag even more.

The only delineation of time was when the stainless containers of food raddled onto the ward while patients gathered around the conference table. The sound's effect on them was much like Pavlov's studies training dogs to salivate by exposing them to repeated bell ringing; and then feeding them until the dogs began salivating at each ring.

The advancement of another unmarked night announced the demise of one more ambiguous day. It unforgivingly pierced the heart of the sky—slowly releasing the day's light like that of the air from a pin hole in a balloon. After fully gone—and the darker it became, the hidden shadows exposed themselves along with the unyielding bane of the mysterious woman's cries. Still, they went unheeded.

Her cries accompanied the heavy footsteps of the night attendants making their rounds—each step bouncing off the walls as if someone were beating a drum. Their probing heads prowled into the patient's doorways, unleashing the explosive harsh light from the hallways—shockingly invading the grainy-black.

I was snared in a total miasma of bewilderment, a man without a clue. My mind fried—still disoriented as it filled with childhood terrors and more. I seemed unable to distinguish if my beliefs—my thoughts, were based on actualities or illusions the more my mind populated. My biggest phobia of snakes ascended as if from the Devil's storehouse—snakes eating their way through my brain, rapidly leaving it inert. I felt the slithering in the confines of my skull until they took ownership.

I began to believe the crying woman was a ghost in my head since no one ever seemed to come to her aid—to placate her suffering. As the days and nights, there was no division between what was real and what was nonexistent. Like a tornado whipping truths and lies—both real and imagined to the point of delusion. I found myself questioning if my mind had surrendered to a world of perpetual obscurities with no escape.

Were the mysterious woman's cries those my mother's—again, angry for forcing her into those hospitals over my adult years as she had been when I was a child. Again, including the Georgia State Mental Hospital in Milledgeville for three of them. After all, I'd once believed she was angry and held resentment toward me. But I was angry, too—angry because I had to deal with all the crazy as I was heartbroken at the same time for both of us. But, again, angrier at my father—again, the root of all the misery and her confinements. Within the realm of possibilities, those wraithlike nightly cries may have been both of our merged connectivity.

The ultimate realism: I'd lost control of a considerable part of my life. I was broken but unaware. Shattered in those early years where I saw things and experienced others as I'd executed some, all feeding on purity—unhinged actions I took before and after leaving Warner Robins. Those I'd kept hidden—as I had most events for a time from the light.

I was in prison of damnation, ostensibly impenetrable to any form of forgiveness. But that is not surprising because I have never fully forgiven myself. Like a criminal, this was my incarceration—for offenses unknown to my keepers, and not a razor blade and pills. But each action eventually took a sliver of flesh until little, if anything, was left—left of me. What penance imposed, must I pay?

how was your day

Each night as if the patients were cattle grazing in a field, we were called back to the barn. All corralled in the common room for story time followed by a bedtime snack like children in a daycare would receive. A hefty, dark-skinned, night-shift attendant with a thick annoying-to-decipher accent, from the Dominican Republic, I think—served as the officiator. He reeked of tobacco and had an alarming smoker's cough. It was questionable if anyone in the group could even point out the location of the Dominican Republic on a map.

In order to be get our snack, like it was a gift basket from See's Candies, the cattle first had to listen to what Mr. Dominican Republic referred to as, A Life Lesson. I sat wondering exactly what staggering poppycock he might have to offer the heavily and deliberately medicated—as if his strong regional pronunciation, more akin to an ancient dialect, was even able to be comprehended regarding psychiatric involuntary hospitalization? My four years of French was of no assistance in translation. "I shouldn't have taken French," I thought.

He'd read some spiritual rigmarole from a nameless book as if it were the Bible—like some self-appointed, almighty authority or freelance guru on life. His minimum wage credentials stamp certified, were surely obtained online from a quick study course. Once he finished reading, then came Mr. Dominican Republic's insufferable, sententious harangues expounding on what he'd just read. As far as the patients were concerned, he may as well have been addressing the corpses in the morgue in the hospital's basement.

Most sat limply in chairs staring off into empty space—if not near comatose. Others just wanted their snack. I wanted neither: the life lesson or the snack—rather preferring to stick a pair of my rolled-up dirty socks in his mouth. Once he finished, a question followed—the same one every night, "How was your day?" When my turn came around to answer, I shrug my shoulders and cock my head to the side as if I were mute or even a simpleton. And if I were to answer, it would be the same response regardless of whichever day had passed, "It excruciatingly sucked, and then some!"

But I wasn't the only one not to answer; those few remained unresponsive or perhaps unmoved by the life lesson or what little, again, could be understood of it. I even doubted if Mr. Dominican Republic could.

As I continued to sit among the others, I felt dirty from the grimy surroundings—the poor hygiene of some patients not helping. All spoiling my Atlanta staycation. It was all pure shit running out of Dominican Republic's moving lips. A concerning bad case of diarrhea of the mouth.

After the Life Lesson thankfully ended, the cattle were herded to stand in line at the nurse's station. The medications were handed out in little white cups containing our prescribed magic pills, followed by the coveted promised snack. I'd ceased taking my pills on the second night. Instead, I concealed them under my tongue while pretending to swallow. Forgoing the gift basket, I then beelined-it to the bathroom to spit the pills into the toilet and flush them into the sewage.

I was sane enough to know, those pills were not going to make a difference. They were some of the same stuff I'd been taking before ending up in the hospital. It goes without saying: the pills obviously didn't have a positive impact on my state of mind or the desire to live.

Like every night before and those to follow, the intercom system blasted from the night nurse's mouth as she reiterated—in her tart tone: "Be good and take all your medicine so you can go home and not have to come back." Translation: be good little children. Growing more agitated from hearing that maxim, I factually wanted to staple everyone's mouth shut who spoke it. But then again, every aspect of Davy's 13th floor caused great agitation.

I so wanted to punch the night nurse in the face due to her shitty attitude in the way she addressed the patients, as I did Mr. Dominican Republic for his clear enjoyment of listening to his own voice and his useless Life Lessons. And a few others employed at Davy. Admittedly, I was a candidate for Anger Management. Even still, I know myself enough that the anger and hatred that lives within is here to stay—regardless of any management classes or none.

By all accounts, as I was told, I'd a history of that—punching, since being hospitalized. Sandra, to my genuine shame, informed me that I'd cold-cocked a nurse while still in recovery. An act of which I have no memory. While still coming back to full consciousness, feeling swamped in a bayou of panic, I begged an attending nurse to untie the restraints. When she gave in to my pleas, I regrettably did the deed when the nurse tried to block my ill-fated attempt to escape. Only to be quickly apprehended by the guard and put back into restraints. According to my sister, it was quite the scene: I bolted for the door in a wide-eyed frantic, my flimsy hospital gown half off with the urinary catheter in tow.

To add more insult to injury, late one night after believing I was done with another seemingly incessant day and the Life Lesson, the Dominican put in a personal appearance—invading my seclusion or what there was of it as my roomie snored across the way. I was awake lying on my back trying to find some peace in the gray-blackness of the confining space. All the while, attempting, as challenging as it were, to keep the crap in my head from bleeding out my ears.

Suddenly and without warning—the door rapidly opened spilling the hallway light into the room. The sharp click of the light switch followed, instantly chased by the harsh overhead fluorescents flickering on like micro-explosions. The act, instinctively, gave cause to cover my squinting eyes with both hands. The intensity of the brightness startled me; I sat up in bed like a dead man coming back to life after a massive jolt of Frankenstein's electricity.

"You got to sign the night nurse's evaluation form," he insisted, unapologetically in broken English while thrusting a clipboard securing a piece of paper and a pen at me.

"What?" I asked, confused and drained.

"Check the boxes and sign your name."

I grabbed the clipboard. Looked over the form. Then up at him.

"You're fucking nuts!" I blurted.

He didn't answer while maintaining his stance.

"You want me to sign an evaluation form of the night nurse's performance!"

"Yes."

"You want a crazy person to give his opinion of how the nurse is doing her job!" I reiterated.

"Yes."

"Do you know what time it is!" I presented, more of a statement than a question.

"Yes."

"Sign it your fucking self and... and turn off the goddamn light on your way out," I scoffed, chucking the clipboard back in his direction.

The brute hesitated. He looked at me and then at the clipboard that had bounced off him to the floor. Mr. Dominican Republic-Life-Lesson's eyes grew as large as a pair painted in one of Margaret Keane's big-eyed children's portraits. While his size was intimidating—especially from my supine position, I held my ground. I was not signing any more damn forms—for him or anyone else except for a fucking release from the hospital on Nightmare Street.

"How ridiculous," I thought as I laid back down and pulled the covers over my head.

"But you have to sign it!" he demanded in an institutional authoritative tone.

I pulled the covers away from my face, holding them at my neck. I stared at him trying not to blink. The harsh light made my eyes burn.

"Like fucking hell, I do!"

He grunted like a troll who lives under a bridge in a creepy fairy tale. Mr. Dominican Republic-Life-Lesson reminded me of a troll.

I rolled over on my stomach and waited for him to leave. I could sense the troll standing frozen, perhaps feeling disrespected. I could not care less. His heavy breathing, audible. A few minutes must have passed before I heard his lumbering footsteps scuffle away from the bed. Within seconds, I felt a draft as he must have quickly opened the door pulling in the added air. He grunted. The lights flickered off. The room went back to gray and then darker as the door completely closed—shuttering the hallway light.

"It was a small victory won," I thought, purchasing some pleasure from it. After the Life Lessons that followed, Mr. Dominican Republic skipped over me when asking each person in the group, "How was your Day?"

does the caged bird remember, it could once fly

Even though I've experienced a sense of great freedom during periods of my adult life, I still felt the drift of confinement in one way or another: whether trapped within certain events of the past; certainly, within my mother's many life calamities; at times, engulfed in fear of the future or even the next moment to follow; mostly, within my own actions done in hopes of ensuring real liberation. Concerning the latter: never thinking, much less believing, certain extreme efforts served to add more fortified steel bars to my own personal cage. The only times I did feel completely free, without restraints were those spent tightly wrapped within Bradley's strong and loving arms.

Many caged birds never take flight as they were meant to. Never allowed to fulfill their undeniable birthright—the freedom to master the skies. Instead, they are enslaved once hatched or stolen from their habitat. Their wings clipped. Condemned to exist in confinement—their liberties denied for the selfish amusement and pleasure of humans. But I wonder if they have an innate sense, they were meant to take flight.

Alternatively, what if those humans were confined within bars like the very birds they imprisoned? That seems fitting as it does more than fair. Maybe then, they would come to grasp firsthand what a cruel and arrogant act it is—impeding those birds to soar. I would suggest, such people get a dog or a cat. But, whatever you do, do not tie that dog to its doghouse or a tree in the yard. Do not be that kind of human trash! And those who do, should be tied to those dog houses and trees instead.

Locked up at Davy, I felt like one of those grounded birds—which no doubt, Dr. Albridge found some amusement as a result. My cage was made of walls with locked exits from the outside as the iron gate—the gateway to freedom from the 13th floor. I'd been enslaved in a box left to remember those periods of what it was like to be free. What it felt like to think I'd been happy—to soar much like a bird as I had after relocating to Atlanta, and before January of 2009. Up until then, I hadn't fully comprehended my wings had been clipped in childhood.

While at Davy, I'd often thought of Pebbles, my sister's pet yellow canary she had as a child—the memory oddly surfaced, occupying my mind after having long-forgotten about the bird. Pebbles was such a small part of our childhood, or so I thought. Never having noted the parallels to our reality as children. I don't even know why Sandra had the damn bird in the first place. But I would theorize, Pebbles was a subconscious attempt to add childhood normalcy depicted on television shows like The Brady Bunch—although, I'm not sure if there was a bird on the program. Regardless, even though it was, again, Sandra's, I'm the one who changed the paper at the bottom of the cage—as I made sure Pebbles had seeds and a filled water container.

One Halloween, anticipating going trick-or-treating, Mother made costumes for my siblings and me. After arriving home from school, I found Pebbles dead on her back with her little legs curled. I'd always stressed to see Pebbles caged up. On so many occasions, I'd wanted to set her free, but my mother said the bird's wings had been clipped and she could not survive outside her cage. I remember feeling remorseful that afternoon and throughout that night—I was never able to let Pebbles fly free as I knew she'd been born to do. Instead, her short life was confined behind bars.

The months before finding myself within Davy, I was no longer able to believe many of the things I'd told myself when the moment warranted—as I'd done countless times under my breath: it's going to be okay; no one's going to hurt me; my life belongs to me and not the past; I can run fast enough; I'll survive this; it will pass. Those silent pep talks stopped carrying any weight—thus, of no use anymore as once believed. Even hope seemed unreachable, wrapped in all the internal confusion and mayhem.

I tried to refocus on my present dilemma during periods of lucidness: the predicament of my forced concentration. I held steadfast, calculating a way to fly the coop or rather the cuckoo's nest as it were. My mind continued plotting how to steal a pass card—my thoughts growing more devious while giving much attention to the obvious obstacle of making it past the mammoth guard unnoticed—he, being distracted or not. After several days of waiting and watching the gate; he grew more familiar with my face. And again, I continued to stand out from the motley group like a cauliflower in a basket of coconuts—no pun intended. Nuts, that is. A muscular man, and a white one at that, is hard to miss in such an environment.

Admittedly, the keeper of the key to the Gate to Freedom was exceptionally sexy. The expression: a tall drink of water was certainly appropriate in his description. In all actuality, a tasty, tall, XXL, solid, muscled, dark chocolate bar would even be more fitting. In moments of successful attempts to forget everything and anything—rerouting thoughts of my current situation, I found some pause fantasizing about him while I watched from the common area as he sat at the desk on the other side—wanting this hotter than hot guard. Wanting his exquisite nocturne black pearl skin on top of that of my titanium white. The contrast, beautiful as it was alluring. And wanting him to spring me, and then we would run off together under a waxing crescent moon-lit night.

Each morning, sunrise broke up the gaunt oppressive-grayness of my assigned room as it pushed its light through the thick-glassed large picture window at the far end. Uncertain of the day ahead—certainly, of my life, I would stand in front of it. I knew I was witnessing a new day to be celebrated; but I saw no reason to do so. Actually, I mourned its return as a sick feeling of dread filled my gut.

Ten-stories below, I watched cars and people bustling around free of a cage while I remained immobile; not only in my being but in a mental ward. As a result, anger swelled within as it grew each day I was caged—it greeted as did the sunrise as I returned to stand at that window wishing I could open it and fly. The onslaught of suicidal ideations continued unabated—running wildly in my head. Being locked up made them fester.

Not a night passed that I was able to fully engage sleep, adding to the mounting neurosis. Once I did manage to but only for short intervals from utter emotional exhaustion, and despite the woman's cries and the orchestration of unidentifiable creepy noises, I'd waken afraid and plagued with anxiety.

In those long and arduous hours—those seemingly endless nights where sleep was elusive, desperation continued to follow like a low-hanging stench with each passing night. Preoccupation with escape elongated wider—either on my own two legs or lifeless on a gurney.

Late within the teetering hours, I crept from the bed to the bathroom down the hall. Cagily, I pushed open the door—my nostrils met by a lingering smell of urine and human excrement.

Despite the offensive odors, I dropped to my knees in front of the toilet as if kneeling at a church's altar—like I was before God ready to face my last moments of life. I lifted the lid to expose its porcelain rim. A solemn coarseness of the eeriness of the moment enfolded me. The periphery of the bathroom—airless as I focused on the edge of that porcelain rim like lining up a shot through the scope of a rifle. With forethought, I attempted to determine how hard I could slam my forehead onto it and at the right spot: the kill spot. And debating, if I could muster up enough force with one quick blow to the head. The only fear: would it be possible to whack it hard enough to finish the job I'd started in the bathtub some days before. I didn't want to fail again. The blow had to be severe and quick—brutal, like a bullet to the head.

I didn't want to only self-inflict damage to end up unconscious for a period of time or brain injured: the very reason I took the pills before stepping into the bath water and then cut open my arm was to ensure death. I feared the pills alone would possibly sentence me to a coma-like state, where I would be brain-impaired but still retain some memory of life. It would be torturous—to have any recall, no matter how vaporous. Not even a shadow.

In the nothingness of night—at the blackest moment before dawn and still wedged at the midpoint between life and death, I returned to that bathroom. Finding myself again and again on my knees trying to gather more courage to bash my head into the rim of the toilet. Gather the confidence that I would be successful—to free myself from the cage.

fade to black

Little had changed. Time still seemed reluctant to advance forward. Hours seemed like days. Days like months. It hung. Motionless. Torpid. Stagnant. One day, no different or unique from the one before or the one following. I began to believe in effect, I was sick. Feasibly, I was. In resistance, I repeatedly narrated in my mind that I was not: "Randy, you're not sick. They simply do not understand you. How could they possibly? You're not sick. Your heart is not beating in their chests. So, how would they know?"

Hal informed that he'd received numerous calls from various people, including the owner of the Midtown bookstore regarding an upcoming scheduled reading of my third book, and the owners of two local galleries who represented my artworks. Clearly, the news had begun to spread like a bad rash. However, I didn't expect the three other owners of those that were out-of-state would hear about my mental dilemmas. It did cross my mind: if I were more prominent throughout the country as an artist and a writer, my art would have increased in value as books sales would have likely boosted.

Of course, if I'd been successful at dying—the element of suicide certainly would have peaked more interest; and I would have been view as the troubled artist and writer who was constantly in a mental state overrun with angst. Well, actually, I was mental, but that state of mind had nothing to do with my work.

Hal also was receiving calls from my friends and acquaintances—some coming out of the woodwork from years past. All inquisitive about what had happen—having heard bits and pieces. Likely, some calling more so for the sensationalism than concerns for my well-being.

Like most inner city communities, it has its own network of how information flows. The more sordid and seedier—the quicker it travels from ear to ear through the tunnel of the rumor mill. And the more exchanges, the more the facts become distorted and even exaggerated.

Attempted suicide, to such a degree, by a known local individual—the knowledge of it, is not easily cauterized. That, added to what Christopher and his friends were spreading around town, not only about me being in a mental ward but also concerning the event of June 9, 2009, at the Superior Court of Fulton County—had quickly seethed into a wildfire. Hal and the boys as well as Sandra resisted sharing what they had been hearing around town, but I kept pressing them to do so until they did—feeding me in limited amounts.

Sandra had shared; it had gotten to the point she'd stopped answering my cell—oddly having survived the tub better than I. It was found in one of the pockets of the shorts I wore that day when I was pulled out of the tub. As a result, I'd asked Hal to convey to those calling about my condition: Randy appreciates your concerns as he does your friendship. But please understand this was a very confusing and troubling time. And because of the situation, it would be best for him not to have visitors.

Sandra did bring me the cards and notes that had been mailed to the house from the few friends who had remained loyal. I was warmed by them and asked Sandra to answer each one to show my appreciation.

There was only so much more I could put on Sandra and my loyal friends. I knew their visits were hard on them—returning to the den of morbid discontent. I didn't my want them to see me in such a fucked-up state—both of mind and physical appearance.

The visitor list remained eight people: Sandra, Hal, Mitch, Marty, Russ and his partner William, Allen, and Oliver. Allen and William were more like brothers to me, while Oliver, in his early seventies, was a father figure. I'd met him and his partner in the early 1980s. William divided his time, flying to Miami to work a few shifts at the hospital and then back to Atlanta. Allen's Birmingham legal practice was consuming but he called Sandra daily. I'd become friends with Marty through Hal and Mitch shortly after Christopher's exit.

Eight names. Eight people who loved me. Eight people I needed to tell me I was not crazy. Instead, I saw what I perceived to be seeping pity regardless of their forced counterfeit faces. Counterfeit, in that they attempted to fake smiles and conversations. I heard their patronizing in conversations—saying anything they thought I needed to hear but not believing it themselves. Certainly, the worry on Sandra's was evidence regardless of how hard she tried to hide it.

On occasions, it was detectable when I noticed they found difficulty looking me directly in the eyes at rigid, burdensome moments as theirs wandered to avoid mine. Rather, they searched each other's for allied succor and transitory words. I saw all of it without them speaking a word. There was no camouflaging the meaning of certain body movements.

As they continued to visit, the more revealing the expressions on their faces became. Markedly, increasingly showing what they were trying to hide: their uncertainty of my future; concern, I was broken beyond repair; how what I'd done had changed them—that grave, near-death suicide attempt that warped what they and many others in my community once believed about me before July 9, 2009, as strong and independent. And for many, it would give credence to Christopher's lies concerning an incident that took place back in May—give credence, that I was indeed a nut case.

After each visit ended—especially, as Sandra looked back before walking through the gate, the isolation returned as my heart broke for her; and I was left consumed by guilt. Still, I didn't know how to stay alive—not even for her. If it were not for the smothering monotony of the 13th floor, I would have asked them not to visit. But if I had, Sandra would keep coming—regardless.

Even though I'd hit rock bottom—I needed to lessen much of the mayhem. As I'd done on and off for years, when necessary, once again, I attempted to put on a good face. But regardless of how good-of-a-face, I knew there was a strong possibility some would not be so easily fooled. Still, I hoped much of my frenzied distress would remain hidden—and they could not see all of what was on the other side of the mask. I didn't want them to be privy to the truest of thoughts and feelings—as they remained pellucid. But I knew there was very little Sandra could not sense.

We were all playing a game of hide and seek. I didn't want them to see my desperation. I could not tell them: I wished I'd never been brought back to life—how the emotional pain was eating a hole through my soul. And obviously, my confinement at Davy, made me feel trapped as I had by life. Most of all: I didn't want them to see how that darkness was still pulling me down in rapid consumption. I didn't want them to witness me completely—fade to black.

breath-to-breath

It was as if it were any other day; but it wasn't. On that July Fourth morning, in a matter-of-fact manner, I drove the Rover to the Walgreens next to the Publix's grocery store on Piedmont Avenue in South Midtown. There—I purchased four boxes of Benadryl before driving over to Home Depot to acquire the container of razor blades. I thought the antihistamine would aid the sleeping and anxiety pills in slowing my breathing until my heart stopped beating—the razor blade was meant as a fail-safe to ensure death.

At the time of my decision to end my life—the second time, I clearly knew what I was planning to the degree of being regimented and calculating. It was not a knee-jerk reflex as the first attempt in early January of 2009, seven months before where I'd failed. As I'd shared in "Alabama Snow:" when I awakened one random morning, I was ravaged with an indescribable, overpowering, deep sadness feeling as much physical as it did emotional—as if I were having major surgery without anesthesia. It was sudden, involuntary, and automatic rather than contemplated. I felt as if I needed to die as painlessly and quickly as possible. I remember wishing I owned a handgun; and if so, within seconds—I could blow my brains out to end the refractory agony. To stop it—completely.

I've already admitted, and likely will again, that I was a fucking-fucking mess. It was days, perhaps a week at most since Christopher walked out. I understand now, all of the boohooing over him was no more than the representation of the many losses in my life and had very little to do with Christopher. But he was the most recent loss—regardless of how minuscule in measure to the others. I should have seen his exit as a win-win—certainly, for my bank accounts.

But what I hadn't shared concerning my state of mind that morning: I'd awaken from a terrorizing dream. One which repeatedly haunted me like indignant howling wolves throughout the night. I was a young man standing in the middle of Beckman Road in the Hollywood Hills. My body, weighted down by heavy chains that ringed me—preventing any movement. The Griffith Park Observatory—fogged in the far distance. The late afternoon lazed in the western sky.

Without warning, a truck sped by within inches—catching the end of the chain. Within seconds, I was pulled over the steep hillside with the truck. As I'd awaken, thoughts of impending death took possession of my mind.

The second time, my mind was unclouded even though I was shrouded in an eclipse of caliginosity—again, my mind was clear about what I was planning. I believed my thoughts were lucid. I believed I was sane. I'd detached my heart from my brain as much as possible. I had convinced myself it was my body, and my life and only belonged to me—it was my choice.

I placed two large bowls of water, and a large open bag of Dugan's dog food I'd regularly purchased from the veterinarian's office—in the bathroom, along with his favorite toys and one of my sweatshirts. As well, his oversized dog bed so he'd have a comfortable place to lie instead of on the travertine tile floor. Earlier, I'd filled his Kong with peanut butter and dog treats. All of which, I thought would comfort and occupy him before I closed the bathroom doors and my life. I knew if my plan played out the way I'd hoped, Dugan would be in the bathroom for two days and one night at most before I was found. The thought of him being alone in the bathroom with my dead body in the tub hurt my heart for him—my Dugan. But I felt I was of no use anymore to him or anyone else.

Letting go of Dugan—leaving him was excruciatingly heart-wrenching; the pain of it was piercing that I would not see Dugan again. I would never again laugh as he made me do while I watched him run around in whipping circles nipping to catch his tail. I would never lie in bed again with him snuggled up next to me while watching television at night—never be comforted by the sound of his breathing in the bed next to me. I wished I felt Dugan was enough for me to go on living, but the emotional pain was too overpowering as I was overwhelmed by it. He was all I treasured in life, but I still had to say goodbye to my sweet, loving creature.

After ingesting the pills, I'd place the container of razor blades on the windowsill of the large picture window over the jacuzzi tub; that looked out over the backyard. Before I stepped into the tub as it slowly filled with water, I laid on the travertine floor with Dugan to love on him. The pills did put me into a relaxed state. I do not remember how long; I just remember holding Dugan as close to me as possible, trying not to cry to keep from upsetting him—but crying all the same as my tears soaked into his white fur. Dugan repeatedly licked them from my face. I do recall being comforted by him in the bathroom with me. Even to this day, memories circle in my head—a few clear while others remain distant and weak. Perhaps, the latter is for the best.

I was not crying because I believed I was about to end my life, but, again, for the reason that I was leaving Dugan behind and the accompanying guilt. Time lapsed, although I do not markedly remember how long.

Not until I stood over the large bathtub watching it nearly overflow with water, did the world around me suddenly befall. I knew I had a choice to step into the tub or not. I recall focusing on the package of razor blades. Without question, I indubitably knew why I'd placed them there and what I intended to do.

When I made that choice to step into the tub and as I eased my body down into the steamy water, I don't remember feeling afraid as I had incessantly for many months before. A similar fear as I'd felt most of my childhood.

Dugan sat by the tub looking up at me. I rested my chin on its edge as I reached out my hand to pet him on his head. Dugan then raised up on his hind legs in order to put his front paws on the edge of the tub. I remember then hugging him once again—as I do, kissing Dugan many more times.

In my Last Will and Testament, I left my wishes that Sandra take him and keep my boy safe—knowing she would and likely viewing; by taking Dugan, he was somehow bringing us back together as brother and sister. I had no doubts she would love him and see that Dugan was well taken care of. I'd seen to the latter—setting aside funds for Dugan.

I grabbed his Kong, stuffed with doggie treats and peanut butter, from where I'd earlier set it on the ledge behind the tub. At the sight of it, Dugan perked up—his tail wagged like a revving engine. Then, it was time. I knew it. I felt it. I tossed the Kong toward the doggy bed. As expected, he went for it without delay and lay down as he eagerly licked at its opening. I do remember smiling as I watched him. Then, I looked away.

I pulled a single razor from the container and placed it on the edge of the tub. Then, I looked over at Dugan again. Watched him.

"Be a good boy, Dugan. Your Daddy loves you. Don't forget me, my sweet boy," I called out, even though I knew he couldn't hear me.

I wiped the tears from my eyes while fighting their return. The razor blade came back into sight. I reached for it while I told myself, "Do it deep and fast without hesitating." I hoped it would not hurt as I pressed the tip of the razor on the flesh of my arm without breaking the skin. I turned my head to look out the window. I recall taking a breath. In one mechanical, quick, and long motion—the sharp point punctured my skin and perfunctory slashed deeply crossing the large, antecubital fossa protruding veins of my muscular arm. It didn't hurt as I'd hoped. I do not remember even feeling the razor's passage. As I turned back, my blood was already gushing out—quickly swirling the water red. I watched as the razor dropped to the bottom of the tub. "It's done… I'm done," I thought.

I recall feeling relief and a sense of calm as I rested my head on the back edge of the tub. The low, incessant fear that had always existed under my skin—sharpened over time, likely since a boy, was gone. And with it, the heavy weight lifted off my chest. I felt light. My heart stopped hurting. My head stopped thinking of anything sad—I do not remember feeling sad my life was ending or that there was no reversing what I'd done. I was fully aware that within minutes, I would take my last shallow breath as my body emptied of blood—leaving my heart with no more to pump.

The chirping birds outside flew away. Voices of the partiers in my neighbor's backyard celebrating the Fourth of July holiday drifted further away until their laughter ceased. The popping and crackling of fireworks extinguished. Everything hushed. What was left of the soft late afternoon light of the sun's rays filtering down through the canopy of the lofty trees shading the backyard diminished to gray as I turned my head away from the window to look at Dugan on his dog bed still licking and chewing his Kong. I remember smiling. Yes, I clearly remember smiling at him. The gray deepened—growing blacker.

Complete blackness quickly followed. I felt life leaving my body. Then, there was nothing—not even the blackness.

381 seventh street

The morning of July 4, 2009, at fifty-four years of age, I told myself: nothing pertaining to my life would matter in another fifty years—even less. Eventually, my deeds and actions—good or bad or somewhere in-between and any resulting consequences would be swallowed in the abyss of time and space.

I never wanted it to be a fuss—my suicide, much less raise a commotion for the neighborhood if all had gone as planned. Rather, preferring to have dissipated into thin air or melted as if I were made of ice. And indeed, if my plan had unfolded in the way of my design, only the police would have found my dead body.

Some employees of the Fulton County Medical Examiner's Office would have been summoned to take over where I'd left off. They would put my body in a black body bag and load it in the back of a van and drive away. That would be the end of it. Unfortunately, that's not how it played out.

I can envision—what a circus it must have become the closer the sirens approached Seventh Street until they crescendo in front of the house on that Day of Judgement.

First, a solitary police car racing up the street as Hal waits on the front porch. He and the officer run into the house. Shortly thereafter, a fire truck tailed an ambulance—both arriving within veritable minutes of each other before coming to a screeching, abrupt stop in front of my home while all three blocked the street.

The mechanical upsurge of all the sirens in unison—ear-piercing, deafening, and shattering. All annoyingly sending birds flying out of the trees while dogs barked and howled throughout the neighborhood; and pulling neighbors—all friends I'd known for years, out of their homes as they gathered in front yards and on the sidewalks to see what all the hullabaloo was about interrupting the holiday; and the usually sleepy street.

How jaws must have dropped while many covered their ears to keep eardrums from hurting until the sirens stopped. But leaving the orchestration of blue and red—perhaps yellow emergency lights to continue flashing and circling. The array of colors, washing over the faces of the on-lookers. Pulsating. Whipping. Hypnotic. Repetitive. Persisting through the air in the late afternoon's milieu of the tree-lined street—brushing through the branches and altering the appearance of the sun to the west. The decrescendo giving way to the sounds of conjoined voices of the first responders, the desultory static emergency radio frequencies, and that of the neighbors' expressive chatter—fusing in the hot Atlanta air.

As I understand it: my neighbor, Jacob, had been strolling up the street with his two little fussy dogs—likely holding while sipping a well-aged glass of wine as was his custom habit at that time of the day—as if on cue, at the time when the police car raced by. He saw it coming to a sudden stop in front of my home, instinctively causing him to pick up his pace. There, he saw the glass of the full-view front door had been kicked in and the scattered fragments on the porch. By then, a few of the neighbors of our tight-knit group—always looking out for each other, quickly began to join him—including, Gavin who lived two blocks over on Mentelle Drive. They both would later play a role—in this tragic, real-life scenario. A role, I never wanted them or anyone to play in the face of my best-laid plans.

I envisioned that the expressions on their faces morphed even more so—perhaps, some covering their mouths with a hand and the unconscious reflex-like gasps as the EMTs, rolled the gurney out of the house as they feverishly attempted to resuscitate my water-soaked lifeless body—a veritable corpse on delivery into the back of the ambulance.

I imagined their eyes watching the ambulance, as well as the fire truck and police car speed away back in the direction they came—listening once again to the return of their high-pitched sirens while watching the nonstop light show until the emergency vehicles turned at the intersection of Charles Avenue and out of sight; but continuing to hear the urgency of the sirens until they eventually were lost some miles away, leaving the neighborhood to slip back into its quiet norm.

In my mind, I see my neighbors slowly dispersing—some voyeuristically lingering back to get a glimpse of my violated premises, thinly disguised as concern or wanting to help. Others, peeling off into groups of two or three to editorialize on the grisly spectacle they had just witnessed—the neighborhood gossip on an endless feedback loop replaying for days thereafter. I've wondered, after my neighbors knew the truth of that event, how their opinions of me may have been skewed?

Christopher had confided that as a child; comic books had been an escape from the real world—offering brief reprieves from the taxing confusion and the incontrovertible smothering truth that he was gay. As many children, he lived for the next addition to follow the story lines of his comic book heroes—nosing his face between the pages while lost in a suspended world of make-believe. Or was it? Make-believe, that is in his and those other children's susceptible minds. And how—if at all, would those chosen heroes, whether villain or protector, play out in their futures.

I did enjoy some of the time we spent together in that house; if I were to state otherwise, I'd be lying: the lazy Sundays; those long soaks in the tub together; the walks with Dugan in Piedmont Park and around the neighborhood; lying in bed watching movies; making Christopher breakfast; so many dinners together; lying on the large lounge in the den with a young Dugan between us; Christopher's law books spread out on the dining room table as he studied, and Dugan always at his feet.

However, those times were little in comparison to the reality. Admittedly, with Christerpher, most of the time was forced. I was trying to make us something I didn't even want and didn't feel right about much of the time; similar to how I felt before I took him to Laguna the first time. I knew deep down inside that I should have moved on to California. But I didn't fully realize the truth of why I let him convince me to stay—not until some years later. Actually, I did know but much of it was buried deep inside of me. Then, darkness fell upon my quaint home on that lovely street.

Foolishly, I never saw the menacing looming dark clouds that rode on Christopher's coattails of the comic book cape he wore that would aid in bringing disaster to Seventh Street. Moreso, partly opening the door when he closed it. As depicted in those comic books—he indeed was the villain.

Today, and thankfully so, those memories have dwindled until they are nothing—as if they never were reality; and as fake as those characters drawn with pen and ink.

the undoing

"The brave may not live forever but the cautious do not live at all…"
Richard Branson

Markedly—a brief phone call impeded the plan to die. They say timing is everything. In my case, it was against me. A short chain of freak events and that timing were the undoing of my plan. But it was the fiasco of the night before—that set everything in motion.

It seems strange to me that I don't remember my cell phone ringing or pulling it from the pocket of my shorts. Nor do I, talking to William or even slipping the phone back into the pocket. But as I've shared earlier in this telling, I do remember Dugan being with me. I remember those last minutes with him as I do stepping into the tub and lowering my body into the bath water. Remember, feeling comforted by the wet-warmth—then looking out the large picture window above the tub into the backyard. I remember the razor blade and the blood. I can only surmise, William called at some point after I had taken the pills and before getting into the water.

William and his partner, Russ, were flying back from William's second home in Laguna on route to Miami—requiring a short layover at Hartsfield-Jackson Atlanta International on that July Fourth. During that short timeframe, William called to check in—surely concerned about the alarming events of the night before conveyed to him by Marty. Apparently, I'd gone on a drug-induced rampage at Jason's Deli on Tenth Street, just before closing—causing quite the scene as I was later told while in the hospital. I have no recollection of the events that transpired at the deli.

Later, William related my words were slurred and unintelligible over the phone, making it clear to him I was in distress. As I have no recollection of the original conversation, I have none of being transported to an ER in an ambulance the night before. An ER doctor, himself, William was concerned due to those events at the deli that I'd over-medicated and was in danger of overdosing. But the thought of his friend intentionally taking his own life seemed improbable to him.

To be safe and out of that concern for my well-being, and a gut feeling, William asked Russ to rent a car to drive to my house to see what was up so he could make the connecting flight in order to work his shift that evening at the Miami hospital. Russ called Hal to ask him to meet at my residence, explaining the concern.

Hal arrived first—just under an hour after receiving Russ' call, who in transit got caught in bumper-to-bumper traffic on I-75. Hal saw both my cars in the driveway as he parked behind them. He walked over the 12 inch by 12 inch square concrete pavers set in pea gravel and contained by bricks that connected from the driveway to the main walkway from the street up to the brick steps of the porch. Once at the front door, while peering through its full-view thick glass, he aggressively knocked; but to no response.

Hal returned to the driveway, opened the purposefully rusted large iron gates. Each one, an 8-foot square made from 4-inch steel tubing with two bars crossing at each corner forming an X with a circle in the middle—under an arbor spanning the width of the driveway covered in abundant white jasmine. He then walked along the side of the house toward the security gates of the fence leading into the backyard. Hal heard the partiers in the backyard of my neighbor's house but didn't think I was with them due to the concerns Russ had shared with him. Hal's gut, too, stirred worry that something was wrong.

He forced open the gates and proceeded to walk over the pea gravel turn-around leading to the two-car garage I'd converted into an art studio, but I was not in there working. Hal then walked back across the yard to the large patio. He peered through the back door. It too, a solid sheet of glass exposing the den. Knocked there, as he did at the front door. Followed by another and another. Each one louder than the one before. Still, no response. As he did at the front, Hal began yelling out my name to come to the door… "Randy… Randy." Still nothing. The house seemed empty of life. Dead-quiet—no movement that he could see. Not even any sign of Dugan.

Growing increasingly concerned, he walked the few feet to the large picture window of the master bathroom. Hal looked through it to see what I didn't want anyone to witness except the police. In fact, that was part of my plan that I'd set in motion weeks before.

I can only imagine what thoughts rushed Hal's mind. What horror and disbelief. Hal called 911 as he ran back to the front porch; where he kicked in the glass door as he waited for the police and the ambulance to arrive. The responding police officer did arrive within minutes after Hal discovered my body. He and Hal rushed back to the bathroom where they used one of the laces from a pair of my athletic shoes to tie off my arm. Russ showed up some minutes later after the ambulance and fire truck.

Dugan was pacing in circles. They'd startled him. He stopped. Backed up against the tub while barking and growling—and Dugan rarely barked. His white coat was stained with watery blood. Clearly, at some point, he'd climbed in and out of the tub after I slipped into unconsciousness—which explains the deep scratch marks on my torso made from his hind claws digging into my skin as he scrambled to get out of the tub for whatever reason; then tracked blood on the floor. Splattering it everywhere as he instinctively shook it off his body in great soaking torrents on the travertine tile, the large window, the shower, and surrounding walls.

It slashes my heart to know Dugan was in distress, and of the confusion and fear he must have felt. I should have known better; but I was not in any condition of knowing anything. But he likely climbed into the bathtub as he often did when I took a bubble bath. I always laughed watching how Dugan would bite at the bubbles.

You must remember: Dugan was everything to me as he still is. Tears are rolling from my eyes as I type at this very moment—so many years later since that day. And I still do, every time that memory returns; I see him in my mind's eye, imagining what confusion must have circled Dugan.

I was also told, due to his distress, Russ locked him in the garage-studio; and left my boy alone throughout that night. Once I walked back into the studio, some weeks later, I discovered Dugan had knocked over easels, chewed on canvases, dragged them over the floor as he had done other destructive things. But I didn't fault him for doing so.

kappa kappa loco

"We are all born mad. Some remain so… "
Samuel Becker

I'd become a ward of the State of Georgia with a complimentary induction into a coed Greek fraternity—rather a parody of one:

Kappa Kappa Loco. All the while, attempting to keep a comfortable distance from the other brothers and sisters—to avoid group bonding activities including: any additional hazing practices similar to the ones already paddled courtesy of the Headmasters of Davy to the degree of mental and bodily endangerment. Certainly, House Mother Albridge, drilling more holes into the paddle for added injury to my ass. I'd been a bad boy—a really, really bad one per Albridge's psychiatric analysis without her asking a single question.

The taking of one's life carries many stigmas in societies throughout the world. In many cases, suicide is viewed as iniquitous and for the offenders there is little or no benevolence. To a larger degree, these stigmas are long-rooted in religious ideologies: a mark of shame—a stain.

Those who succeeded were seen as selfish and cowardly to leave family and friends behind to suffer with little or no regard given to the suffering of the departed. In my case: I was engulfed by unyielding emotional distress, but I knew my action would leave Sandra with a heavy heart beating in her chest, while asking herself: why hadn't she seem the signs—and even feel some measure of guilt as some of my friends would. I live with many of those stains—and my own guilt.

During the Middle Ages, many respected people of great prominence: philosophers, such as Socrates, Plato, and Aristotle; other teachers; doctors; religious leaders; governments all had similar views on suicide. They believed the human body to be of moral magnitude—a temple, and the devastation of it was a horrendous act of the highest degree of damnation. Therefore, deserving of harsh penalties.

People were viewed as the property of the State and before that, of the Gods; a person who committed suicide was robbing it of their municipal and monetary contributions. Their families were banished socially and their names slandered; any property and financial means were taken, leaving them destitute. The survivors were severely punished and imprisoned while those who didn't, were decapitated and their bodies buried in unmarked graves.

At Davy, I did my best to stay within an invisible boundary line circling my body. But nowhere in that hospital would prove to be enough of a comfortable distance. I was acutely aware there was nothing comfortable about the 13th floor. A few of my brothers and sisters didn't understand the concept of personal space. Most of them frightened me.

If I'd had a choice, it would not have been my preferred social club of Greek life to pledge. But it was the only Greek house on the row that allowed the strange and freakish—the lost and the broken. We all had a commonality that brought us to this very coed fraternity. Our initiation: our individual mental instabilities, with seemingly no discernible way out.

Despite the concept of bonding—segregation was alive and well in our little frat. For the most part, the Blacks hung with the Blacks as did the Hispanics—well, that is, if one could refer to "hanging" as a metaphor for sluggishly walking in circles

A county frat house—Davy's mental ward was a revolving door, much like a school of detention. Its students, from the streets: drug addicts and alcoholics, some with violent predispositions to the degree of having criminal behaviors and, of course, those mental afflictions. The real animal house of fraternity row—rebuffed by the more traditional and prestigious snobby Greek houses.

New pledges were rushed every few days or so. For some, it was not their first hazing at Kappa Kappa Loco while for others, it would not be their last. Some of their returns were based on which of them survived another stent of freedom in the sordid bowels of Atlanta where they existed. I was pledged because Kappa Kappa Loco was the closest trauma fraternity to my comfortable Midtown home.

A few brothers and sisters were mute as if their lips were sewn; they stood almost invisible on the sidelines. Perhaps, too traumatized by certain hazing life events. But there were a few exceptions: the rowdy ones as if at a nonstop, beer-funneling, drunken frat party. Once they were liquored-up to the point of alcohol poisoning, their anger was released. That anger ricocheted off the walls of the fraternity house and continued until the point of exhaustion or were ordered back to their rooms by the big brothers or big sisters. Usually, scolded by House Mother Albridge. Admittedly, I was angry as well and had my own outbursts.

With the prolonged fear of continued containment, I felt I would forever be a member of the frat wearing a sweatshirt with, Kappa Kappa Loco across the chest. Thus, freedom seemed impossible unless I was able to convince the powers that be at Davy—particularly, Albridge to viewed me as reformed into a model member of society void of suicidal ideations. In the rare event, I was set free of any obligations to fraternity life, which would require Hell freezing over. And if that were to happen, I had no intentions of ever attending any future alumni reunions.

i'll have take out

Unpalatable. The hospital food was inedible by my standards. Diarrhea in-the-making on a tray: powdered eggs; fatty bacon; over-processed chicken—that is, if it had even been part of a real chicken; mystery meat; white bread; over-cooked vegetables that disintegrated into nothing at the touch of a plastic fork. Of course, for obvious concerns, real utensils weren't allowed. In my case, likely for the safety of the staff and more so, for Dr. Albridge's.

I'm not sure why I cared; I guess, because I was used to eating healthy food out of years of habit—perhaps, I'd rather be a decent-looking corpse out of vanity than one grossly out of shape.

The only nourishment I had for two and a half days were the protein bars Sandra had smuggled in as if contraband. And if caught, would result in a five-to-ten-year prison sentence of hard labor. By day three, my sister insisted my food be brought in from the outside.

Abdul got into an uproar, instructing me to eat what I was given as if I were a kid who was told he couldn't leave the table until his plate was licked squeaky-clean. He accused me of thinking I deserved better treatment than the other patients because I was white.

"Just because you're white, doesn't mean you can have special treatment."

"You may as well hook me up to a feeding tube," I screamed at Abdul. "Are you really that stupid? Look at my body… you skinny-ass prick. Do you think I got this by eating processed foods?" I added.

The munchkin stood there with his mouth agape as I kept cutting him off every time he attempted to slither a word.

As Abdul, Dr. Al-bitch didn't want to allow my food to be brought in. Conveying, it would set an unwanted precedent of special treatment. Sandra immediately threatened to contact FOX 5 News that

I was on a hunger strike due to the hospital food making me sick because I was on a special diet; and by Davy refusing to allow her to personally see to my nutritional needs at her own expense, they were putting my health in danger. Understanding the possible public ramifications, Albridge begrudgingly relented.

The only stipulation was that the food be brought in discreetly as if Top Secret and having to do with national security but without being accompanied by Secret Service personnel. I would have to eat the meals in a small conference room unseen by the other patients. It was obvious, Abdul didn't take the defeat well.

For the remainder of my time in the ward, Sandra brought in meals from Jason's Deli, Flying Biscuit Café, Whole Foods Market, and MetroFresh. She continued to keep me supplied in protein bars, health drinks, and Diet Sprite. To this day, I can no longer drink the latter, finding the soda too unpleasantly reminiscent of my time at Davy. by Davy refusing to allow her to personally see to my nutritional needs at her own expense, they were putting my health in danger. Understanding the possible public ramifications, Albridge begrudgingly relented.

The only stipulation was that the food be brought in discreetly as if Top Secret and having to do with National Security. I would have to eat the meals in a small conference room unseen by the other patients. It was obvious, Abdul didn't take the defeat well.

For the remainder of my time in the ward, Sandra brought in meals from Jason's Deli, Flying Biscuit Café, Whole Foods Market, and MetroFresh. She continued to keep me supplied in protein bars, health drinks, and Diet Sprite.

three

unlikely roommates

Weighty and broad, wild-eyed Lily, perhaps with fifty rough and tumultuous years behind her, was undoubtedly jockeyed long and hard by life. I dubbed her as the president of Kappa Kappa Loco. Gallingly loud—with great exaggeration, Lily often threw her head back in glass-shattering laughter, displaying brownish-gray teeth, chipped and generously spaced in her mouth. Her ebony skin, blotchy and flaky deserved a good rubdown with some NIVEA body lotion. Surely, out there in movie land, there's a starring role for Lily as a character in a movie about incarcerated women in prison. After all, we were all incarcerated.

At times, her voice breached the flatlined dreariness of the common area with her caterwaul prattling. Lily imposed herself—with no apologies. Uninvited, she poked her nose into everyone's business. She often chattered non-stop as she asked senseless and repetitive questions while proffering unsolicited advice as if a staff therapist. In the process, cyclically picking at her thinning, mid-1960s, afro with a wide-toothed comb.

By her curbed vocabulary, broken grammar, and anomalous punctuation, Lily was surely deprived of an adequate education. It was a reasonable assessment: likely the product of the enraged, gang-ridden streets of the worst neighborhoods of Southwest Atlanta; a casualty of a street culture of predatory socialization; a parentless adolescent; possible apprentice to a repeat-offender adult criminal code of illicit drugs and prostitution. To put it simply—a shitty and unfair start in life.

"How'd a big, clean-cut white chile like you, git ya-self inna' dis goddamn mudda-fuckin' shit'ole?" Lily inquired, the second day after my arrival. From that day forward, Lily baptized me with the name: Man-Chile and other times, addressed me as Honey—with great inflection on, hun-EE. By her introductory question, I knew we were on the same page concerning Davy. However, as our interactions populated, there were instances I felt the need for a translator during some verbal interactions. Conversely, finding Lily somewhat bothersome I attempted to avoid her—much like maneuvering as not to step on a land mine. Over time, despite her pitfalls, I found something endearing about her.

Her large, yellowish-brown expressive eyes bulged and whizzed around in their sockets like balls in an arcade pinball machine as she talked. Conceivably, a defense tactic from years of living on the streets to assess her surroundings or possibly a medical-related condition.

With little imagination, I could visualize Lily's blinking snaggletooth visage as a homunculus animatron inside its mechanics—the steel ball banging, clinking, and ding-dinging in and out of her gaping orifices until the flippers sent it careening back for another go-around. Of such, Lily looked acutely disturbed—on the verge of internal panic. I could identify with the feeling.

At this point, I feel I must elucidate before I go any further: I know how my descriptions may come across as disrespectful and judgmental, but that is far from my intent. It's just how that little confined world was. Even while I was locked up with everyone, empathy was not lost on me for my fellow inmates.

Another Black woman, possibly mid-thirties—whose name I never knew, was definitely some kind of creature from the underworld, where voodoo and witchcraft are a way of life. With a broken arm and leg, she surprisingly dexterously maneuvered herself around in a wheelchair as if it were her own appendage. Her skin was shiny and faceted like a crystal goblet and dark like unsweetened chocolate. Her hair—rigidly long and thick, was twisted into cornrows. It resembled snakes moving in different directions. Her head mechanically moved from side to side like Medusa from Metro-Goldwyn-Mayer's, "Clash of the Titan." In fear of turning to stone, I did my best to avoid eye contact.

In light of the resemblance, I christened her: Medusa, Princess of the Dark. She spoke with a thick and mawkish—syrupy Cajun accent, displaying straight teeth with a noticeable space between the two front central incisors. Medusa's hospital gown was forever riding her thighs, exposing a hairy vagina gone wild. Although she was somewhat scary, there was a strange androgynous sexual appeal to her brassiere-less, well-shaped copiously rounded voluptuous melon breasts.

Even though, she may have been indeed alarming to some from the neck-up, her stripper-like body under the loose-fitting hospital gown would have made any exotic dancer proud. I imagine Medusa was pretty at one time in her life—long before whatever the hell inside her was unleashed and broke free.

One female staffer or another habitually ordered Medusa back to her room to put on a pair of panties. I could not blame the bitch, believing a person should take advantage of any attractive physical attributes that by chance had been given at birth or by plastic surgery.

Seemingly untamable like a wild beast, she constantly made sexual advances to male staff and patients alike. Medusa hovered about them like a persistent fly buzzing a summer picnic. If you ignored her, or she didn't get her way, the Voodoo Princess would do a one-eighty—Linda Blair impersonation from, "The Exorcist."

The rumor going around was that Medusa hailed from New Orleans. While in Atlanta—for what purpose unknown but I would guess likely performing tarot card readings at a Walmart location, she'd gotten into an unfortunate auto accident with a Metropolitan Atlanta Rapid Transit bus. During Medusa's subsequent hospitalization at Davy, she wigged-out on a nurse. And despite Medusa's injuries, had beaten the nurse to a pulp—so badly, the nurse had to be admitted for care. Soon after the incident, Medusa was dispatched straight to the 13th floor for psychiatric observation.

Her oddities and incalculable behavior didn't seem enough to keep two of the male attendants from finding amusement or perchance, bewitched by a casted voodoo hex. They especially seemed to take pleasure in getting a peep show now and then.

On more than one occasion, I distinctly overheard them make comments about wanting to tag her. And vividly remember witnessing one of them grab his meaty package as he dangled an impressive tongue while winking at our Cajun Queen in residence.

Formulating an educated guess: in conjunction with the length of his tongue in comparison to the bulge in his pants, his cock had to be at least a good twelve inches—surely envied by Dr. Albridge wishing she could stand while taking a piss.

After having survived another night, as every morning, a nurse took my blood pressure and blood as if the lab technicians would be able to find my suspected insanity under a microscope—as if the epic clusterfuck of my suicide attempt hadn't taken enough. Soon thereafter, before returning to my room—where I hid away most of the time, I found myself sitting in the common area thumbing through an outdated magazine—the cover story: Elvis Is Still Alive. As usual, Medusa anxiously rolled up and down the corridor—as if waiting for someone to come out of a bathroom so she could take a dump. Or, more likely, looking for her next victim.

Two patients were antagonistically quarreling over the phone—for most, their only connection to the outside world. Aggressively so, I expected a fist fight to begin at any moment. Others seemed to be retreating to the seclusion of their rooms since breakfast was over. I'd already had two protein bars and a Diet Sprite. Most of the staffers were behind their glass enclosure as if it were a barrier; a blockade to protect them from the wild animals in the surround—the patients, being the animals.

A pretty young Hispanic female had shown up sometime in the night. A new face in the group of nonconformists of good mental health—as if they could help it. Rose, apparently her name as Lily-the-informant eagerly announced, sat quietly at the end of one of the sofas. Her dark, almond eyes focused on the television; Rose appeared mesmerized by the people moving around and talking inside a box on the wall like it was a magic trick. One of her arms rested over an indisputably ample baby bump while the other occasionally pulled at her shoulder-length, abundant curly auburn hair.

Unable or unwilling to speak English, an interpreter attempted to translate for Dr. Ching who had also been assigned to me. A seriously cute Asian but as cute as he was, Dr. Ching had the personality of day-old burnt toast and a matter-of-fact attitude like Albridge. Their attempt to communicate with Rose proved fruitless as she—as she ignored them; her still in a trance-like state as Rose kept her eyes forward continuing to gaze unresponsively at the television. Eventually, the interpreter and the doctor shrugged and gave up. They walked a few steps away to have a conversation of their own. Dr. Cute wrote something in his black notepad before they parted ways.

Lily had taken a shine to the newbie. It was not uncommon to find her standing behind Rose; mothering her as she combed Rose's long locks—Lily using her hair pick. I guess the spreading of lice was not a concern on the ward. I do not recall being sprayed down with a pesticide, but again there is little I remember when first rolled onto the ward. If I had been coherent, I certainly would have fought tooth and nail from involuntary admission.

The pregnant woman returned daily to the same, well-worn sofa to stare at the television as if being paid by Nielsen ratings for her input. Without fail, a faithful Lily combed the young woman's hair as if reunited with a long-lost child separated at birth.

Rose had landed on the tarmac of our little group; rumor had it—Lily's of course, after apparently accosting her boyfriend with a knife. As the story goes: once the police arrived, Rose turned the knife on her bulging baby-belly, threatening to traumatically rip her unborn child from her womb. Thus, the crazy—13th floor was her sentence. Rose's boyfriend had done something horrible to her and deserving of a good slicing or so Lily alluded, surprisingly without the usual explicit details.

A middle-aged, skeleton of a woman with vapid eyes, seeped an odor of a musty closet that hadn't been opened in years. As per Lily, her name was Lucy. She could be seen during the early hours with a haggard look of petrified unhappiness that coated her face, walking up and down the long hallway as a low constant whimper escaped her thinning lips.

Soberly, Lucy paced in fluffy, dirty green slippers—as her feet slid along with some difficulty as if dragging a ball and chain. The ball and chain, perhaps the metaphor of her life. Lucy's oversized hospital gown and robe loosely hung off her body—as she continued as if having lost her way due to once taking a wrong turn on the long and ever twisting road of life.

Lucy looked as though she was about to crumble into pieces at the times, she stood like a statue several feet back from the steel gate leading to freedom—people coming and going around her as if Lucy was invisible.

I was familiar with the feeling of crumbling, but to do so might not have been so bad; especially, if a strong wind kicked up blowing our pieces—Lucy's and mine, through its bars. Perhaps, for Lucy, to a real kind of freedom she'd never known before. But likely, would sadly never have the chance.

In ways—although we'd never spoken a single word but only a disclosed glance in passing, I felt I related with Lucy during the duration of her time in the ward. Call it a shared a commonality—the kind that remains unspoken; but one shared all the same.

Things were looking up, well sort of, as much as they could with another new arrival: a good-looking man, surely mid-thirties, seemingly of Italian provenance, kept staring at me from the other sofa. I felt his eyes, as dark as a moonless night gaze at me. I resisted darting mine directly toward him—uncertain of his intentions. At first notice, I felt enamored as I had toward the robust sentinel on the other side of the gate.

The Italian continued his jetting stares each time I quickly glanced his way. It didn't take long for Lily to rush over and whisper his name in my ear. Why she didn't scream it out like a fire alarm, as would be expected, I do not know: Carlos. Or rather, hot and sexy Carlos would be more accurate.

His weight-trained muscular body was a good 5'10" tall: thick-necked, wide shoulders, ample biceps, vascular forearms, and all around well-proportioned. His chest highlighted a dingy, well-worn, white wife-beater; a stain crossed it looked as though Carlos wiped a soiled hand on it after eating a Big Mac bacon burger with Thousand Island dressing. Both arms—were full-sleeved with colorful gang-like tattoos. I assumed his chest, too from what peeked out above the top and bled through the thin cotton fabric.

On day two of Carlos' addition to our dozen or so cracked-egg group, I was sitting on the same distressed vinyl sofa waiting on Sandra's visit while ignoring the baseball game Rose was watching. I had no interest in the sport—finding it slow and yawningly boring; but admittedly, I liked the crotch and ass watching offered by the tight-fitting knickers of the uniforms. As I was considering returning to my room for a protein bar, bad-boy made his approach.

Carlos' gait was purposely cocky and self-assured—as I watched his lax-thuggish strides in my direction. He plopped down beside me—close enough our thighs unmistakably touched. Carlos smelled like pungent cologne—sharp like sweet and sour whiffs of a dying Dianthus flower. He exuded pure man-sex. Wild. Passionate. Sizzling. Sticky. Wet. Drenched-in-sweat, kind of sex. Could not stay out of trouble—that kind of sexy.

Carlos immediately looked over at Rose; he steadied his gaze on her for a long minute before transferring it to me. Close up and personal, I noticed that even though his hair was shaved close to his scalp—Carlos had a perfect hairline. A four-or-five-inch scar curved over his skull in the direction of his right ear. Each one, pierced with a one-and-a-half-carat diamond stud. I assumed—cubic zirconia, and surprised he was allowed to keep them while in detention unless they were semi-permanent. Though, I imagine Carlos would have put up a good fight to keep them.

"I've been noticing your tatts," he stated, referring to those on my arms, without a proper introduction like everyone in the neighborhood of the ward already knew him by reputation.

"They mean anything?" Carlos smiled, showing his white teeth, somewhat straight with a character-giving, small chip in one of his incisors.

"Thanks. Yes... yes, they do," I deepened my voice.

"Cool. Cool."

"I see you have a few tatts yourself," I, jested.

Carlos seemed to catch the understatement concerning having a few tatts by releasing a laugh in response. He pulled up his wife-beater, proudly exposing a tightly ripped six-pack. As I'd thought, he was covered with desultory haphazard jailhouse tatts without much bare skin to spare. At the time, I could not help but notice the bulge in his well-worn jeans, indicating he was packing.

"Yeah, I'm pretty well covered. Got my first when I was thirteen," he informed, as Carlos began pointing out the ones more crudely done—as if permanently etched into the dermis layer of his skin with a jail-made tattoo instrument while serving a stench in juvie.

"They look awesome," I flattered.

I declined to ask what any of them meant—if anything. There were just too many: crosses and hearts of various sizes; a rather large one of Jesus; skulls; dragons; the phrase, I WILL OVERCOME across his chest in a script font.

Not surprisingly, Carlos was the only verbal connection of sorts I'd made with any of the other patients. Obviously—over tattoos and weight training. His body radiated heat as our thighs still touched. I lost myself in imagining him naked within the throes of a midnight-dripping, sweaty tryst: a little or a lot of gangster jailhouse sex.

My imagination took increasing flight. At least, I could still fantasize—and now, I had distractions to help occupy my mind: Carlos and the Gatekeeper. I mean, what else was there to do? I was in prison after all. As I understand it, male straight inmates engage in penitentiary sex—in such circumstances, a hole is a hole. The mouth is a given. Especially for the pretty ones who needed big men to necessitate protection from gangbangs and beatings in the showers by making them their personal-property-bitches. And certainly, a plus for gay prisoners to get their fill.

"You like baseball?" he asked.

"Not really. But apparently Rose does."

"Is that her name?"

"That's what I hear."

"Looks like she got knocked up."

"It would appear so."

"You got kids?" I asked, more so to feel him out about his possible sexual orientation.

I admit, for a few inhales of air, talking with Carlos almost made me forget where I was. And why.

"Not any... I know of, but likely. I've lost count of the bitches I've fucked," he proudly answered.

At that response, my fantasy deflated like a flat tire—purposefully slashed by a gang rival.

He looked over at Rose again. As far as I could tell, her eyes hadn't veered away from the television. She still appeared to be in a trance; a permanent blank look as if painted on her face. There was an evident vacancy in her eyes, and I would surmise, in her heart as well. Something else I could also relate to.

"You work out?" Carlos asked.

"Do you have to ask? Yes... I do."

"I can tell, Bro."

"I see... you do as well. Looks like you've been bench pressing cars," I complimented.

"It keeps me sane," he offered.

I almost burst out in laughter but caught myself.

"Sane," I mused. "Then, what the fuck are you doing here?" I asked him in my head, humored by his statement. "Perhaps, not sane enough," my brain rambled.

"Maybe we can lift sometime," Carlos suggested.

"Sure," I responded, even though positive it was extremely doubtful, since we'd likely never cross paths again.

During our interaction, Carlos still hadn't offered his name. My brain persisted in its need for him to introduce himself in the proper manner even though Lily had told me. I wanted to know more of Carlos' story—the only one I wished to ascertain as I could have cared less about many of the others, Lily had verbally podcast. At the very least, Carlos and I could have been Facebook friends if I knew his last name—if he had a profile, that is. I was certain, I could bribe one of the attendants a few hundred bucks to look in his file.

I soon after abandoned the quest. "Probably better that way," I thought. But thanks to Lily, most everyone else probably already knew it, or some version of the News at 5 story and I was not in earshot when she had. It was most likely among the abundance of his tatts—what his real story was up to that point in time.

Hot Carlos remained in the ward for just a few days before he was gone. I surmised, his crime must have called for a much lesser incarceration than mine.

Ben stood alone as if an island in uncharted waters. A seemingly gentle, elderly Black gentleman severed from the world. A mystery—thin and tall as a stick with hunched over shoulders and grayed-nappy hair. His face was acutely wrinkled, surely marking the depth of the hills and valleys Ben had traveled in life—taking on the appearance of a shriveled avocado. He appeared as if he hadn't bathed or changed clothes—that is if had any other than those on his back, in a good month or more—and smelled as such.

He walked with a limp in incessant circles—sometimes standing in a corner while loudly speaking in rhymes; garbled words with no apparent meaning—none I could comprehend as if it was a dead language.

With caramel-colored skin, Alice's pixie haircut complemented her perfect bone structure. To the eye, in her mid-twenties, she had quite a resemblance to Halle Berry—as if they could have been sisters. By far, Alice was the least threatening-looking roommate—at the furthest end of the scale; appeared wholesome.

Of course, like every good reporter, Lily sniffed out what delivered

Alice to us: a single divorced mother of two young children. She'd attempted to overdose while her ex-husband had taken them for the weekend. Upon his return, he found Alice barely alive.

I imagined she was the young woman everyone admired and caught their eyes as she walked down the street. Just from looking at Alice, in a different environment, one would likely believe she had her life together or as much as anyone could. And as long as Alice kept whatever turmoil lived inside her, then most would think she was content. But like the rest of us at Davy, what they couldn't see was the storm that must have brewed inside of her.

Each of us locked in Davy's 13th floor (as every human in the world) begins life as a book of blank pages. As we age from moment-to-moment and year-to-year with the transit of time—those pages fill; and become chapters that tell the collective events of our individual journeys. On the pages of my unlikely roommates' and those of mine, mark the factors—those of our life events which led us to madness if not within inches of it.

Why Alice wanted to die—even to the moment she ingested those pills, is written in one or more of the chapters in her book of life: the sadness and desperation, and even the method of her expiration although she was found in time. And as to why, is written as well—why time was not on her side, Alice will never know. Why: because our books are never meant for us to read.

A few more souls—like outlines, came and went; and for the most part, unnoticed except by Lily.

Interestingly, I never came to know her real story, just the scenarios I imagined. She could have been wedged within purgatory—like the spinning wheels of a car stuck in a ditch with a full tank of gas. The driver, nowhere in sight as if snatched by aliens. Thirteen is known to be an unlucky number and we all had been unlucky in one way or another.

Perhaps, Lily's story was so beyond fucked-up that it was more self-humane for her to search out others with sadder narratives of hardships. Doing so was better than to face her own truth which plausibly could be why Lily remained so obstinate—to the point of exhaustion in seeking the one story that would top hers.

I believe in a better life, without the years of the wear of a hardened condemnation, Lily could have been a talk show host like

Oprah Winfrey or a news anchor—even an investigative reporter. She may have been the resident busybody, but I'm sure she had a good heart—as battered as it must have been.

On the other hand, and more concisely, it seemed more definable to rather believe Lily was a ghost who had been murdered by another patient years in the past; and was left to haunt the rooms and hallways of Davy's 13th floor—unable to find the exit to the next life and therefore left trapped for eternity. Perhaps, that would be more explicable why Lily was always around and for so long.

Feasibly, we were all ghosts—ghosts who perpetually lingered between yesterday and tomorrow. On the record, I believe in ghosts—I have faced many in my life.

I had no interaction with my first roomie. Just a blur. Faceless. Gone after my second day. At least what little I remember, again, still somewhat drugged up from the surgery and recovery. As far as number two, during the duration of his stay, all I saw was the back of his head sticking out of the bedsheet and cover. That was, until startled out of an edgy sleep one night to find his shadowy face haloed from what backlighting seeped from the large window offered by downtown Atlanta, looming inches from mine.

That night, I remember holding the breath forced into my lungs from a gasp of fear—unsure of his motives. First, I thought I was dreaming—hoping that was the case as I continued blinking the night out of my eyes. Then, suddenly, he reached out his hand toward me but quickly withdrew it to his side due to my intense scream, "WHAT THE FUCK!" I'd managed to propel from my mouth.

His body reacted with a jolt as if he'd been pushed with great force. He stumbled backward before rotating to return to his bed where he once again disappeared under the bed dressings. Needless to state, my eyes remain open—not even long enough to blink.

Late the following evening, I walked into the nebulous room having returned from the bathroom attempting another go at meeting an end with the porcelain rim of the toilet. As the times before, not finding the confidence that I could bash my head with the force I believed required. Any added slight hesitation could have been: I didn't want to die in that wretched environment of Davy—in a bathroom smelling of piss and shit.

In the dimness of the wraithlike light, I found the roomie standing in the center of the room naked and facing his assigned bed while urinating on the floor. I turned around. Walked out and up the hallway to inform one of the night attendants a mop and some disinfectants were needed. He was gone that night as if he never was—not having stayed long enough for even Lily to get the story.

The unnamed man, too, evaporated without much notice—but only after marking his territory. The next to take his place, was just another obscurity with a story I didn't care to know.

Ghost or not, as was the only consistency that possessed the ward—and the norm, Lily's inquisitive mind persistently roamed; and continued to freely inform anyone who would listen about the pain and heartaches—their tales of woe that lived under our skin and walked among us.

I sometimes think of Lily, wondering what happened to her and where she ended up in life—if she ever found that exit.

lunatics in lust

Under the circumstances, I thought Medusa deserved her 15 minutes of fame and hence her own little chapter. The phrase, made famous by Andy Warhol's statement that was printed in the program of his art exhibition of work at the Moderna Museet in Stockholm, Sweden in 1968: "In the future, everyone will be world-famous for 15 minutes."

After the rigmarole of one too many Life Lessons and look-alike, Nurse Ratched from "One Flew Over the Cuckoo's Nest" had finished passing out the pills—the inmates with their snack sought-out the seclusion of their rooms. As every night, I found it near-impossible to even close my eyes, much less sleep. So much so, I'd reached the point of full exhaustion—the kind where sleep becomes elusive.

In sock covered feet, I made my way down the lifeless and dismal hallway. Paranoia setting in—I fully expected Albridge to reach out from the walls to pull me through the sheetrock; thus, forever becoming trapped within the bowels of the building. The cheaply made blanket in-tow (and a shitty pillow) as if the thumb-sucking character, Linus van Pelt, in the "Peanuts" comic strip; the destination, a deserted common area. No, I was not sucking my thumb; but would not rule it out at some point in the near future as a form of much-needed comfort.

As I was about to stretch out on one of the sofas, I ensnared a glimpse of Medusa perched in her wheelchair outside her room. Medusa's gown was on backward and open, revealing her vajayjay; her breasts, spilled-out of the thin garment as she massaged and squeezed them as if milking a cow.

The two attendants I'd noticed a few days before showing unapologetic infatuation directed at her, who I'd nicked-named, Moe and Curly from the knee-slapping show, "The Three Stooges" (the Black version)—were mouth-watering Medusa.

As he did before, Curly rubbed his cock through his pants. I assumed Larry was on an extended suspension—missing his comrades eyeballing the Voodoo Princess like dogs would the bone of an eaten rib eye steak. I was tempted to look around for the cameras and the film crew—seemingly having walked into the filming of a bad porn movie in the making—perhaps titled: "Lunatics In Lust."

Curly momentarily looked in my direction; however, aware of my presence, it didn't seem to be of concern. He then returned his attention to Medusa and her sweet spot. I laid down on the sofa; an episode of "The Andy Griffith Show" was on the television. Sweet little Opie—was being gingerly scolded at the dining table for doing something unfitting of a boy whose father was the sheriff of Mayberry while a devoted grandmotherly, Aunt Bee pulled a pie out of the oven.

I heard Medusa's squirrely laughter over the low volume of the television show's corny dialogue. The Voodoo Princess was obviously teasing the two attendants. It was my impression—they seldom, got any.

Moe and Curly were at the bottom of the food chain when it came to good looks. Life had severely cheated them in the department of desirable physical enhancements—unless any were hanging between their legs.

As in the comedic show, Curly was bald and ashy-headed. Dumpy in stature; and looked as if he'd never missed a starchy, sugary, and salt-ladened meal. Curly's belly hung out and low over his belt, straining the buttons of his shirt close to the point of popping from holding his girth in place. On the other hand, Moe was tall and pencil-thin with taut braids on his head like freshly plowed rows in a farmer's field.

The Princess of the Dark lured them like a spider would a fly into its web. I thought about returning to my room but could not help sneaking a sporadic peek or two or three over the back of the sofa—like rubbernecking a bad car accident on the other side of a highway.

I found myself thinking: "Surely, there must be cameras in the common area." That is, until it dawned on me that perhaps the attendants-in-heat knew how to turn them off or redirect them or stay in their blind spots. As well, I wondered where the night nurse and the doctor on duty were. I humored myself—assuming, perhaps screwing in the broom closet; and would later join Medusa and her boy toys in a free-for-all orgy in scene three of the movie.

I soon thereafter returned to a reclining position while tossing out some fake snores to give the impression I'd fallen asleep while occasionally taking a quick look-see.

I caught an unsurprising glimpse of Moe pulling at Medusa's nipples as Curly rolled her into the tie-down room a few yards across the hall from the common area—the dreaded room the patients were threatened with if they got out of control. The Devil Princess laughed and giggled like a mischievous goblin, having succeeded in capturing her prey. The door closed.

I quietly sat up. Although cracked, the vinyl of the sofa squeaked but not loud enough to travel. My ears raptly listened for any sounds—finding the situation troubling as I did somewhat curious in the dryness of my surroundings. The latter more so than the 1960s television series about pies and small-town life in North Carolina.

It was not long before the sounds of grunts thickened through the door and into the hall as Medusa's wicked laughter persisted. I walked over and pressed my ear against the closed door.

Their voices intensified. Medusa's whimpers of pleasure extended; an attendant told the other to hold the cast of her broken leg higher. Sucking noises and moans were heard—thrusts as well as flesh hit flesh, and the accompanying and aggressive commands: "Yeah bitch, take it… damn take it." Clearly, one was going to town inside Medusa.

"You want more of this… you crazy fucking bitch?"

The Voodoo Princess evidently liked a bit of dirty talk as she laughed again—wickedly. One male's voice egged his comrade on, "Fuck her hole. Fuck yeah… juice her pussy.

More nasty prattle rambled on by the custodians: "Take your turn at the bitch? She's all lubed-up with cum for you."

"Hell yeah. I want my turn to fuck the whore."

At that realization, of what was really taking place, any curiosity turned into disgust—even for myself, since I'd been raped three times and also forced to performed deprave acts by my father on him.

The attendants' actions were obviously criminal by law as they were immoral and held severe consequences, regardless of being the instigator and Medusa's flaunting her exposed body and blatant advancements to employees and patients alike—she had been grossly violated.

Even if she had reported it—which was unlikely, or I did as a witness to the hospital, the rape would likely have never been reported to the authorities—understanding, Medusa was under Davy's care. And the hospital would not want to face any culpability, much less public outrage concerning Davy's inability to protect its patients. Plus, we might have seen delirious or just making up the situation. But although I should have: I had my own grave life-and-death concerns, and I didn't need to complicate my world any more than it had been. However, that didn't mean I was not horrified.

As if a three-toed sloth, I slowly made my way back down the long hallway to my room—home sweet home. The mysterious woman, who'd been crying out since my first night, awakened her pleas: "Someone, help me. Please help me."

The following morning, Medusa rolled my way; she didn't seem outwardly affected from the events of the night before. That aside, she was obsessed with collecting quarters from the patients. We all have our hobbies and clearly, she was no different in that respect. Although I went to measures of what I thought was a safe distance; I didn't always see Medusa coming as I had that next day and by then, it was too late. If I'd darted off, Medusa would have run me down in her wheelchair.

"Mister… Mister. You have a quarter?" she asked, in a harsh, scary-movie Caribbean voice.

"No. No. I keep telling you, I don't have a quarter," I reiterated.

"I'm going to kill you if you don't," she impishly growled.

I had made several reports to the staff about the threats, and a few from other patients. But they were not taken seriously. It was better to attempt to keep trying to avoid the Voodoo Princess and the others, as if they were carriers of the bubonic plague.

the melt down

There were other issues to deal with. While on the operating table, I'd obviously been catheterized. Shortly before leaving recovery, the catheter was removed. As I've shared, I do not remember much of anything once the light left the window over the bathtub until the morning I'd awaken on the 13th floor. What few spotted memories I had were bled thin—like a washed-out watercolor.

Unable to urinate, feeling as though my bladder would explode—accordingly, I was catheterized two more times before I could relieve myself. However, the pain continued to be almost unbearable—intense to the point of tears from the searing and burning that resulted from taking a garden-variety piss. I would have rather been repeatedly stabbed in the ass with a butcher knife by a serial killer.

Each time I needed to take a dump, I hunched over the toilet seat while biting down on a towel trying to refrain from screaming my head off—as if watching a marathon of all thirteen of the "Halloween" movies. I'd never liked horror flicks but seemingly was living one off the big screen.

It felt as though my guts were going to come out due to the extreme force I had to put on my bowels. As a result, I'd quickly developed an alarming bleeding motherfucker-of-a-hemorrhoid the size of an egg. I demanded to the day nurse: I needed to be released to see my private physician. But was sternly informed there were plenty of doctors at Davy to take care of it.

"Oh, fuck no!" I yelled, inadvertently spraying spit at her pigeon-eyed face.

The short white woman, shaped like a hot air balloon, looked at me with disagreeable haughtiness as she angrily wiped her face with the back of her hand. She glared with a butt-ugly attitude. Possibly she was nice early on in her career, full of compassion for her patients—dedicated to the profession of the healing arts.

Over time—both apparently had been long-abandoned to years of demanding patients, lengthy hours, late nights, swollen ankles, and annoying fuming corns that deformed her feet and pushed out the leather of her shoes with each excruciating step up and down the halls of each interminable, unrewarding shift. I guess—I too, added to her torment. But the only person's torment I was concerned about at the time—was MINE!

"Hell, no! No one here is going to touch my asshole!" I staunchly declared as I hurled a pair of bloody underwear in her direction that I'd been holding behind my back. Well, actually, that's not true in reference to my asshole: I would indeed let the huge guard on the other side of the gate.

She jumped back like an edgy rabbit, surprisingly agile for her age and the condition of her feet.

"Mr. Chumbley, you need to calm yourself."

"Calm myself in this shit hole!"

"Mr. Chumbley, please."

"Please what? Do you see all this blood? What, do you want me to bleed to death? Wait, I sort of did that already… that's why I'm here," I raged on, with my steel shiny spurs sharpened and out while everyone in earshot gathered around as if a cockfight was about to take place. I would not be surprised if they were placing bets on who would be the winner.

The bleeding to death was not a concern for me, but again, not at Davy. I may still have wanted to die, but not in the depressing and dismal confines of the hospital.

"Again, Mr. Chumbley… let me get a doctor to look at you," the nurse insisted.

"No, no, no! Didn't I already tell you, NO?!?!"

"Well then. There's nothing I can do for you."

"Listen!" I yelled, again. Then, added, "Let me tell you what you're going to do!"

I took a breath. Maybe two. The nurse looked as if she was moments from running for the hills.

"Get me a package of gauze, and some tubes of antibiotic ointment so I can pack my asshole," I demanded as if I were some CEO and she an underling.

The nurse's mouth opened to speak, but I didn't give her a chance.

"And… and do you think you could get me some damn pain pills?" I questioned.

At that point, I would have started smoking crack if I could have gotten my hands on some product. Perhaps, Moe and Curly might be a possible source of acquisition?

The nurse scoldingly pointed her finger—as if I could care. I wanted to reach out and break it in half.

"Mr. Chu…"

"Don't Mr. Chumbley me! And while you're at it… and for the umpteenth time, find out what's the deal with… no fucking hot water."

At that, I believed I was within seconds from bringing on a brain aneurysm.

"I'll, I'll talk to the doctor and get back with you," she replied, with increased irritation.

"Yeah. You do that!" I squawked, stomping away while leaving the underwear where it had landed.

Hours later—Nurse Haughty returned with the requested gauze and a handful of individual packets of ointment—TYLENOL, as well. But nowhere an ample quantity to prevent developing more complications. Still, without access to hot water—galled the situation; the limited supplies proved useless, preventing any ability to properly clean the hemorrhoid and surrounding area.

I shivered in the cramped shower as the freezing cold water spit out of the shower head—surely, indistinguishable from that of the melting ice of the iceberg that sank the Titanic. I felt like crying. If I had, surely the tears would have instantly frozen into crystals.

In reluctance, I took the soap and lathered it up in my hands before bending over and spreading my legs—exposing my ass to the spray. That alone, mercilessly stung as the inflamed throbbing hemorrhoid protested. Raw. Pulsating. Agonizing. Excruciating to the touch. I yowled—holy hell. Basically unsuccessful, I could not exit the shower fast enough.

While continuing to shiver and with teeth chattering, I first used one of the thin towels to dry off my body as my legs remained spread.

Then, took another to gently pat-dry my ass and the offending hemorrhoid. Each pat delivered more intensifying raw pain. The towels used to blot splotchy areas of fresh blood may as well have been made of sandpaper. Bloody-fucking, OUCH!

I proceeded to self-doctor using the contents of the packets of ointment as I squeezed the oily proportions on a finger before cautiously dabbing it on the hemorrhoid. Then, packed my anus with gauze as if I were a proctologist.

Finding the TYLENOL useless, I had Sandra call a friend who I knew could get their hands on some oxycodone. At the right price, she smuggled in a few pills but only enough to dull the racking discomfort.

I unremittingly complained to the staff, especially to Abdul only to get the same insipid non-reply: "We're working on it." Eventually—I realized, no one was working on it at all. Davy's half-century-old infrastructure was beyond failing on many levels and any semblance of maintenance had been long abandoned to apathy, lack of funds due to being insolvent and embezzlement, and total absence of immediacy. And, likely could not give a rat's ass about a bunch of crazies hidden away.

Even though in the capital of the New South—Atlanta Fucking Georgia USA—the Mecca, we may as well have been locked up at Guantanamo Bay. Its capital building's dome, gilded in native gold leaf mined from Lumpkin County—bedazzling skyscrapers illuminating the firmament. A global banking headquarters. Coveted major league sports franchises. Home of CNN, the global media news and information arbiter. Expensive, tax-gorged neighborhoods with manicured loans and shrubbery—but Davy, the healthcare institution of last resort for Atlanta's poor and its uninsured masses, could not fix the plumbing or possibly pay for the gas to heat the water. And again, I was not one of them in that respect—uninsured or poor!

In any other Western industrialized democracy—save the United States, such a social travesty would be worthy of international derision. Yet, in Republican political majorities, Davy is the inevitable—politically correct, God-ordained alternative to the retail, for-profit, over the counter, insured, moneyed, and privileged capitalist elite. They—the anecdotal, anonymous, and irresponsible didn't give a goddamn there just wasn't any hot water to be had to wash out my bleeding and pus-oozing infected ass. Someone needed to climb up on the capitol dome and scrape some gold off to make much-needed improvements or get me the fuck out! Preferably, the latter.

The last time I mentioned it—having realized I was wasting my breath, my social worker commented, "What, do you think this is some fancy hotel? Would you like turn-down service, too?"

"I want the hell out of this pit of hell!" I jaggedly responded.

Abdul turned around and huffed away like a prissy little bitch.

Yes, I wanted a five-star hotel and turn-down service—and a chocolate on my $150.00 pillow.

I endured within degrees but much like existing in a metal shoebox—the top soldered. Tiny holes, drilled to allow minimal air in which to breathe in halting breaths. Pocket-sized choices or none. No access to the roof from which to jump. No openable windows to do the same. No sharp objects. Not even a visible place to hang myself or anything to do the deed—except perhaps, the use of torn strips from bed sheets braided to make an inventive noose or socks obtained from skulking around in the middle of the night, stealing them from the other patients' rooms would accomplish the need to die. But hanging would likely be too painful: choking to death while desperately grabbing at the noose to attempt to pull it from my neck—legs and feet precipitously floundering and kicking.

The porcelain rim of the toilet continued to seem the only possible way out of life and Davy. By that point, I would have been satisfied by the latter and taken care of the rest later. The truth be told: if I'd come out of recovery in a safe and comfortable—reassuring environment, I might have been in a position to reconsider life. And, again, Albridge's attempt at tattooing shame on my flesh by so gruffly scolding: "I needed to sit there and realize what a really bad thing I'd done," was enough to live. To live long enough, to facilitate my desire to slit her throat before pushing the bitch out of a window to watch her guts spatter on the street below; at the entrance of the hospital.

play nice

The viscous murkiness of funk rose higher around me, growing thicker. Once again, my head had become a battlefield of indecision, mercilessly and repeatedly questioning my real state of mind. Was I truly crazy or sane—or in limbo between the two? I was losing ground of what I perceived as the last remaining thin fibers of lucidity. The back-and-forth—the mental ping-pong game, kept me confused. But what if the doctors and everyone else were right? What if I were just fooling myself and living in some false reality? Maybe I was delusional as my mother had become—on and off as she treacherously maneuvered through a larger part of her life.

The sketch of utterly losing it, filled the page to its edges with scribbles. Totally losing it to the point of possibly gnawing off a leg as if I was shackled to the gate—the gate of freedom, as if a rabid dog would constrained to a tree. I questioned if it was just a matter of time, even minutes, before the swelling raged nosedived toward another rampage as I had with the Troll, the nurse, and ongoing battles with Abdul—but more severe. Austere to the degree, I would end up restrained in a straitjacket. I had no doubts that Dr. Albridge's spies were updating her, and as those black marks tallied, possibly adding more days to my stint at Davy. And speaking of a straitjacket and the tie-down room, oh how I fantasized about getting Al-bitch in one of them and performing unspeakable acts of torture on her.

A handsome middle-aged Black woman, and professionally well-dressed, approached me.

"Excuse me, you're Mr. Chumbley… right?" she inquired, with welcoming eyes.

"Oh, God… what did I do now?" I asked.

The woman let out a slender laugh.

"Nothing really, that I know of… I'm Peggy. Can I have a moment of your time?"

"Like what else is there to do? They took away my manicure kit… so I can't do my nails."

"That's cute," Peggy replied to my comment.

I hadn't noticed her around the ward. At her introduction, Peggy explained she was a floor coordinator at Davy. Her position involved overseeing some of the day-to-day operations on the ward. Basically, dealing with staffing, equipment, and supplies. Peggy—like almost everyone else on the ward had, witnessed the outburst with the nurse as she had others.

At the time, a few of my fellow patients were mindlessly standing around. Two were sitting in the common area engrossed in an episode of "The Price Is Right" on the staticky television; the audience cheering on a contestant to pick the right door with the biggest prizes.

I was beginning to believe, the static from that television omitted a message from outer space. Ben paced while swatting his hands in the air as if mosquitoes were swarming around him for fresh blood. Another patient vigorously alternated from picking inside his nose and pressing a thumb on one of his nostrils attempting to dislodge a booger onto the floor. Aggressively and determinedly so—that it was thinkable, likely a boulder-sized of dried mucus possibly requiring the use of heavy excavation equipment. Once dislodged, it might be a world record—in fact, one for the Guinness Book.

"Let's walk over and take a seat at the end of the conference table."

My first impression of Peggy: she seemed quite the contrast from many of her co-workers and the overall surroundings of the 13th floor; and appeared as out of place as I felt.

I lagged behind to the unoccupied table. The hemorrhoid unceasingly made strides a challenge—necessitating remaining obligated to spread my legs as if freshly plowed and fisted in some leather daddy's basement's sex room. Additionally, blood chronically soaked into the gauze.

Peggy motioned to take a seat. I steadied myself with my hands on the table as if an elderly man with arthritic knees in order to gingerly sit—the act of sitting, much like doing so on a bed of carpenter nails.

"I don't usually have much contact with the patients, but I've been noticing you. You're a bit of a fighter… certainly, stirring things up around here. And I should tell you, that I took a look at your file. I'm sorry about what happened."

I tilted my head down. Locked my fingers.

"And… by the way, I don't care much for the food in the cafeteria downstairs either."

"So, you heard about that."

"Oh, yes. And good for you… "

"Like I said, I've been watching you, Mr. Chumbley."

"Please call me, Randy."

"Well, I'll try but it's a habit. I want the patients to feel respected."

"It seems like you're one of the very few."

Peggy placed her hand on mine. Leaned in closer. I looked up.

"I know this must be so hard," she confirmed. "We both know you don't belong. I'm not suggesting you don't need treatment, but there are much better places for you to get care," Peggy expounded.

She paused while offering an endearing look.

"Heck, this environment depresses me sometimes," she added, while slightly tilting her head back and chuckled.

I just listened.

"I can only imagine what it does to many of the patients… most have had a hard life. And I can see what it's doing to you, Randy."

She was right; the ward was poisonous—infecting.

"Peggy, my life is over. Being locked up here is just prolonging the inevitable."

"Don't repeat that. I didn't hear you. Understand? Hearing a patient say such, would require reporting them. And that's the last thing you need right now. Okay?"

I agreed.

"I don't want you to give up. Don't even think that. Give life more time. You have made it this far, and I'm convinced you can go the rest of the way. I believe life is telling you it's not your time to leave this earth."

"Yes, I've been told that before… Peggy."

"Now, about your hemorrhoid… regardless of what you told the nurse, why won't you allow one of the doctor's… to examine it?"

"I already feel violated enough. I have a doctor… a good one. Dr. Bozo Albridge needs to release me so I can see him."

Peggy felt my forehead.

"You do feel a bit warm. Did the nurse take your temperature this morning?"

"I don't remember."

"Well, if you start having a fever… let them know. Certainly, if it worsens. There's always the concern of possible blood poisoning."

"I will. But what's with the hot water?"

"Honestly, there's never enough on this floor. You're not the first to complain," Peggy confessed.

"Yep, I figured that out already. I'll keep cleaning the hemorrhoid the best I can. But if I could just get a hot shower… in fact, a bath would be better."

"I know."

"I'll get the nurse to give you some ibuprofen or something. Leave it to me."

I didn't mention to Peggy about the oxy Sandra had been delivering as if she were a drug-pusher; although she was concerned it might show up in my blood. I told my sister; I didn't care if it did. And doubted they even tested it. Just something they could stick my insurance for.

Despite the wreckage-beleaguered environment I'd found myself immersed, I sensed Peggy had quickly taken a liking to me as I had to her. Although but not likely, her interest may have been influenced due to Sandra—proudly informing, I was an artist and writer of some prominence while grossly aggrandizing as if I were a celebrity who swam regularly in Mariah Carey's pool on the weekends and attended White House State Dinners.

I'd finally felt I could indeed confide in someone associated with Davy without undesirable consequences. Yes, finally, someone genuine and separate from the hospital's institutionalized bull.

As the days before, especially after the issues with the hospital food and confrontations with the nurse and the ongoing ones with Abdul, my agitation mounted—more like caught fire. I was losing any last remaining control of my wits due to the ongoing confinement, the patients, the overall atmosphere, or lack thereof, and what I perceived as the arrogant attitude of most of the so-called professionals on the ward.

The conversation steered as we remained at the table—further addressing my outbursts. Peggy told me I would have to play nice in order to convince Albridge I was transformed enough to go home. Basically, that I say the required number of Hail Marys to satisfy her that I'd found Jesus. That I had sat there long enough to, "realize what a very bad thing I'd done." And make her think that I was once a lost sheep that had found my way back to the flock. In my thinking, more like—gaslighting the witch.

"I understand, Peggy… all of it makes perfect sense. Still, I know Albridge is going to continue to keep a tight hold… without laying her hands on me but rather letting her posse do the squeezing."

I wanted to tell Peggy how I longed to rip out Albridge's pussy. That is, if she still had one; and if she did, I was certain it was all dried-up and crusty like her demeanor; but to do so—to tell Peggy, would have been disrespectful on my part—but as far as I was concerned: it was open season on Dr. Albridge.

"She tends to be on the harsh side."

"You think? Talk about a bad bedside manner."

"And… you've made an enemy," Peggy interjected.

"Yes. Abdul's out to get me like a bad bout of diarrhea."

"You've got to reel it back with him," Peggy warned.

"That line has already snapped."

"Randy… snapped or not, play nice as if you and Abdul are best friends."

"Best friends? Never… unless Hell freezes over. And that's not a guarantee."

"Well, again, just pretend. It's in your best interest."

"That might require my lips stitched."

I planned on taking Peggy's generous advice to heart—attempt to play nice with Abdul on the playground at recess—even let him win at dodgeball, if that's what it took. And if necessary, go as far as letting him suck my dick behind the bleachers at the end of the school day; but by no means: would there be any reciprocation!

all dressed up with nowhere to go

Peggy didn't hold back on addressing my appearance…

"Randy… you need to shave… spruce yourself up. Show your handsome face," she insisted. "You're looking ragged. Have your sister bring some change of clothing."

"Well, don't hold back on the flattery," I said, in an attempt to lighten the mood. "Should I have her bring my Ralph Lauren tux?"

"Ha, ha."

"Just don't have the energy… besides, everyone locked up with me looks like crap, anyway. What difference is that going to make?"

"Dr. Ching… and certainly, Abdul wants to see you take pride in your appearance… they want to see the person they're convinced you once were," she, added.

"You mean, Dr. Albridge's spies. And I really don't believe Abdul wants me to… clean myself up, that is. I think he's trying to bend me to his will. I'm surprised he hasn't subjected me to waterboarding."

"Randy… come on now. It's true Ching and Abdul are keeping notes on you as are staff and nurses. Notes on your progress."

"I can understand that, Peggy. But I have no doubts, Abdul wants to make me look as incapable as possible because I won't put up with is crap… and I agree with you that my outbursts are digging my own grave."

"Again… just keep trying harder. Keep biting your tongue."

"If I do any more biting, I won't have one."

Peggy concurred concerning the topic of the other patients' appearance but insisted I was different. However, by then, I really didn't feel that way anymore as I had viewed myself when first thrown into the bowels of Davy—more and more, I was melting into my surroundings. Peggy used my sister and friends as an example as to how everyone—including some patients on the 13th floor saw me.

"Regardless of how worn down you feel… how defeated, your friends and sister… tell a different story."

Peggy was referring to Sandra's fashion style and how clean-cut my friends were.

"It's not like we're the Rockefellers or live on Tuxedo Road… in Buckhead."

"You know what I mean. And as far as anyone… Ching, Albridge, and Abdul are concerned—you may as well be."

"Relating to Abdul… I hate to say this, not wanting to come across as being elitist, but admittedly… in the beginning, I did throw that in his face out of spite," I confessed.

Peggy nodded her head.

I was aware by giving that impression, it had hammered another nail in my coffin, as far as Abdul was concerned. He did believe I was arrogant—although that was not true. But because of his belief, I was sure he wanted to cut me off at the knees.

Peggy let me keep talking.

"I've never thought I was better than anyone else… well, I mean that in general terms. But there are times, I believe I'm actually less. Even a homeless person's life is just as important as mine… and feeling that way has nothing to do with low self-esteem or wanting to die."

"More people than not wouldn't see things that way. You're a caring person… that's clear. But the fact remains, being white makes you stand out like a sore thumb around here."

"Yes, I'm White… at least the last time I checked. That shouldn't matter either. And I'm sure, there have been lots of white people locked up here as there will be…"

Peggy agreed. But as I knew, she confirmed they were poor or didn't have insurance. Quite contradicting Abdul's bullshit that celebrities had been guests on Davy's mental ward.

Peggy also directed: I need to be seen and stop spending most of the time hidden away in my room. That, by being seen along with looking presentable, I'd have even a better chance of getting out sooner than later.

"You mean… stay out of my five-star hotel suite and check out the local flair? Besides, Abdul would rather see me stay until the apocalypse. But I'm beginning to think something is fishy around here."

Peggy smiled.

"I've got to get to a meeting. I'll see you later. Remember what I said… clean yourself up and be seen."

I watched until she exited through the iron gate to freedom—wishing, Peggy could have put me in her pocket.

I knew Peggy was right. I hadn't shaved since several days before my body arrived at Davy. I'd been resorting to wearing the same clothes—even sleeping in them night after night. I was disheveled, clothes wrinkled, and I ranked. And I doubt, in my state of an unsettled mind, I would have not bothered to shower even if there had been hot water—and didn't have the hemorrhoid of hemorrhoids. And the fact remains, the ice-cold water impeded me from staying in long enough, again, to clean it as it kept me from washing my armpits and genitals.

I gave Sandra a list of items to bring from home: a nice pair of jeans and a few pair of shorts; some pocketed T-shirts and short sleeves—more underwear was a given; two pair of athletic shoes; socks; deodorant; face scrub and hair grooming products—I figured; I could stand it long enough to wash my face and hair in the sink; skin lotion; nail clippers. The latter would likely have to be turned in once I used them—as if I could do harm to myself with it. At best, perhaps, cut a cuticle too close.

An attendant gave me a razor to shave after he rummaged through a drawer. It was the cheap kind—although surprisingly unpackaged. The type that nicks one's face. I asked for a few packets of alcohol wipes, wondering if they were only rinsed off and given to other patients instead of properly discarded. After all, again, Davy was strapped for cash.

Hospital rules mandated a staff member be with a patient while shaving for obvious reasons, and to make sure the razor was taken back. Even if I'd considered slashing my wrists, the worst that razor could do was a paper cut.

The following Thursday afternoon, Peggy stopped me as she was leaving for a long weekend.

"You look great… handsome. I'm glad you took my advice."

"Well, I'm surprised they just don't put us in orange jumpsuits… and load us on a bus like a chain gang to dig ditches."

"Well… that's not going to happen."

"I'm certain… it would if Albridge had her way."

"Who knows… you just might get released in a few more days."

"I hope so. Did you hear something?"

"No… just a feeling."

"Well, I hope you're right. Abdul almost made me flip out a few hours after our conversation."

"What happened?"

"He bitched… I mean, complained again about me having too many visitors at once. Then, mumbled something under his breath… as he walked away."

Peggy reminded me not to rock the boat with him. That was not a problem, because I needed it to row back to shore after I drowned him in the middle of Lake Lanier.

"I'd tell you to have a good weekend… but I know better, Randy. Try to keep your chin up… just know I'm in your corner."

I began to tear-up.

"Now… now," Peggy caringly smiled.

"Well… I hope your weekend is good. At least, Sandra and a few of the guys will be coming around as usual… regardless of Abdul's crap."

"Good. You have a devoted and loving sister… and some nice friends. Just try to keep your focus on them. And of course, your Dugan waiting for you to come home. He's so adorable in the picture you showed me."

"Yes, I guess I'm lucky in some respects."

"I'd say in a lot of ways," Peggy added.

She winked before turning to walk toward the gate. I watched as Peggy stepped through the portal to freedom.

I was hopeful she was right. Right, I could blow this joint in a matter of days if not over the weekend. Until then, I was all dressed up for a summer picnic at the Swan House on West Paces Ferry Road, but unable to attend. Or for that matter—nowhere else.

the stare down

As the days and nights chronically splintered into the next with no signs of being released—rage sweltered within the expanding confinement…

Sandra arrived later than originally planned—at least two hours. A strained look of displeasure was evident on her face as she sat the grey insulated tote with my lunch and dinner down on the table. I presumed the annoyance was caused by traffic delays due to the sheets of rain that had been washing the city all morning with no signs of relenting.

"I thought I'd never get here… the traffic was a mess!" Sandra flustered.

"I saw that earlier out of the window of my room," I agreed as I stood up from a chair to give her a hug. "I was worried. Glad you got here okay… but I should have told you not to come."

Sandra kissed me on the cheek.

“Well, you know I wouldn’t let the rain deter me from coming to see my brother even if it took all day to get here and… I wasn’t going to let you starve.”

We sat down next to each other at a table in a small room that appeared to have once been an office. Now, it was my private dining room where I ate my meals out of the way from the other patients, since Sandra defeated Dr. Albridge concerning my diet.

The annoyance on her face narrowed as she smiled. A light laugh followed.

“What?”

“I just remembered the afternoon we got tons of snow while you were still in college.”

“Oh, yes… yes. I’d forgotten.”

My mind rolled back to that atypical snowy day—quirky for Southern skies. Mercer’s campus thickly blanketed with innocence as lace-like flakes whispered in hurried flurry and quickly clustered while covering everything white—moving or not. The resulting frosted air fogged the university in entirety like an Anthony Klitz painting. Ghostlike shadows of random groups of students and faculty alike, were transformed into children as they playfully ran and jumped around engaged in snowball combat as snowmen appeared here and there—echoing voices mitigated by the falling wonder. My shoes crunched leaving a trail of prints to the parking lot.

The car tires kept spinning as the heavily falling snow challenged the windshield wipers for visibility. Spinning such that I almost hit another before sliding off the road. Stranded and unsure, I eventually decided it best to ride out the storm overnight in the student lounge—maybe longer, until the roads were cleared.

At the time, Sandra was a senior at Warner Robins High. I’d called home to let Mother know. Some three hours later, Sandra showed up after battling the elements. The drive would have normally taken thirty minutes. My little sister came the rescue—just like now.

The laugher soon stopped. Annoyance widened her face as she shifted gears and got serious. She conveyed she wasn’t upset about the long delay, but something Marty and Hal had told her that morning.

"They were out last night and ran into you-know-who," Sandra words madly spit from her mouth like a hellcat's.

Marty and Hal had run into a drunken Christopher at Blake's On The Park. As she shared, he'd asked them, "How's the nutcase doing?" They had all planned on keeping the incident from me. But Sandra said she was just too pissed and thought that I should know.

I wasn't shocked by his knife-jabbing callousness—drunk or otherwise. Although the news did spike rage; I knew Christopher was going to continue to pump every possible ounce of blood into his lies—while bleeding my reputation dry.

The days and nights continued to expand. Both, accompanied by nightmares regardless of whether my eyes were open or closed. I was beginning to believe that Dr. Albridge was right: that I'd really done a very bad thing and as a result, I was indeed a bad person. That, I deserved to be locked up—maybe for good. That, I'd lost the right to decide for myself how I wanted to meet death or even how to live. Still, I continued to force myself to stay cleaned-up and dress every day as Peggy had earlier suggested.

By then, although totally disheartened, I kept it from Sandra and the guys. That shifted, when my sister spilled the beans that Dr. Ching and Abdul, undoubtedly at Albridge's orders, started privately pressing her and my friends for details—their intentions: to glean as much information as if bloodhounds searching for a dead body. Up to that point, all they knew was of the severity of my near-death suicide attempt and some miss information.

Pulling Sandra aside was one thing; but by questioning my friends, they'd crossed a line. Their tactics snapped me out of it—kept me from raising the white flag. Especially, when I found out that Hal had mentioned Christopher one too many times, including that we ended up in court. That had encourage Ching and his buddy, Abdul, to keep digging for that dead body.

I told Sandra to tell everyone to zip-it and not mention any more details about the court case. As I wrung out of Sandra, like wet socks, she expounded that the quacks kept sniffing around anyway. Allen came to my defense as my attorney and told Ching and Abdul they were in violation of HIPAA laws.

In a so-called heart-to-heart sit-down, Abdul brought it up. I looked at him with a stony face. I reminded that ass, that my attorney had already clarified: he, Ching, Albridge—as Davy, could face serious consequences. And concerning what they already think, it's miss information. Furthermore, no one will discuss the situation any further. Following, Abdul looked pissed because he'd been stopped in his tracks.

"You're clearly not as smart as you think…are we done now?"

"Well… there's something else I want to cover with you."

Abdul brought up my exceptional muscular build for a man in his mid-fifties and probed if I used steroids. I would imagine in his mind; anything was exceptional in comparison to Abdul's toothpick build. Accordingly, out of love and concern, nonetheless, I felt dismayed and betrayed to learn William, while in that meeting with the toothpick that in the aftermath of my dismantled suicide attempt—as if a lieutenant of a drug task force, had searched my home for all drugs.

In the process: numerous vials of testosterone, deca, and syringes, as well as other medications, including more sleeping pills, antidepressants, and anxiety pills—required him to rummage through my dresser and under the master bathroom's vanity. Subsequently, he'd bagged them as if damning evidence before transporting the motherload to Hal's house for safekeeping. The hardest to swallow was finding out William had told Abdul—who in turn told Dr. Ching, who told Dr. Albridge, that he believed I needed serious help. It was another heartbreaking perfidy even though I knew William had done it out of concern and love.

During the meeting, Abdul preached about the ill effects of using steroids—that they caused roid rage: uncontrollable outbursts of psychotic aggression, severe depression, paranoia, and mood swings. I was quickly aware the knowledge of the steroids were damning if I didn't get into damage control.

"There're other ways of having a good physique, even for a man of your age," he lectured.

Remembering Peggy's cautioning to play nice and censor my words, I seriously tried to hold my tongue. But the more I looked at Abdul's face and watched his lips flap—all control eventually disintegrated.

"A man of my age? That's rich coming from a stick figure," I goated.

"Mr. Chumbley, the doctors and I are concerned that the long-term somatopsychic effects of your illicit anabolic steroid abuse for weight training, may have substantially contributed to your suicidal ideations and obvious anger issues among other things."

"My anger issues?" I mocked.

"Yes, you clearly have a problem."

I looked away. Scratched my head without saying a word. Allowing a few moments to collect myself.

"Look… it's clear you don't like me. As you've alluded more than once, you think I'm some white privileged crybaby," I attacked. "And trust me, any anger issues I'm having at this very moment aren't from steroid use. It's sitting in front of me, and from being in this shithole."

"Of course not, Mr. Chumbley. I don't think such… and you don't have any reason to be angry at me."

"Oh, cut the bull… Abdul."

"Mr. Chumbley… "

"Well, you've got half of it right, I'm privileged," I cut him off. "I'm sure I make more in a week than you do in a month."

Abdul cleared his throat. He cowered a bit. My statement caught him off guard. And no matter how likely my statement may or may not have been accurate, I was purposefully being arrogant to piss him off.

"Look, let's get back on topic," Abdul tried to redirect.

"The topic is… I shouldn't be in this hospital. I want to be released!"

"Well, that's up to Dr. Albridge."

"Yeah… yeah."

"Now, Mr. Chumbley. Again, about the steroids."

"What the fuck about them?"

"Well for one, they're illegal. You could get into a whole lot of trouble. How long have you been taking them?"

"Not that it's any of your business, but for quite some time," I answered, in a matter-of-fact attitude while maintaining an unaltered gaze.

"Aren't you concerned about legal repercussions? Even jail?

I couldn't help but laugh in Abdul's face.

"I'm already in fucking jail!"

"We're here to help you, Mr. Chumbley. This is not a jail."

I exhaled long and hard.

"You know… it might help you to do a cycle or two to bulk up your skinny ass," I offered.

"Well. Well… don't you have anything better to say to properly address the matter?"

"You mean I could get into trouble?" I spooned-fed in exaggerated consternation.

"Yeah… big trouble. I could insist your friend bring in what he found."

"Oh, so William's the one who told you." I stated, faking a surprised look on my face, having already known.

"Yes. He's trying to look out for you… and he's a doctor."

"I'm aware he's a doctor, Genius. We've been friends for some twenty years," I smarted.

"Well, like I told you… you could get in trouble."

I let out another bit of laughter.

"Sounds like you're threatening me. What… you, you going to report me to the steroid police?"

"I'm just stating facts… not giving threats."

I laugh, again.

"If you're not throwing threats at me, then you're not black and I'm not white, Abdul."

"Is that a racist comment?"

"No. It's a black-and-white comment. Just like you're being about this matter."

"I assure you… there's nothing to laugh about. Just how long do you want to stay confined in this ward?"

"You know the answer."

"Yes, I do. That's why I don't understand why you think it's a laughing matter."

Edgy moments passed as we kept our eyes directed at each other like kids in a stare-down contest to see who was going to blink first—see who would first break his gaze. Abdul tapped his thumb on the folder in front of him. I'm assuming, chock-full of info on me. Tap. Tap. Tap. Like he was waiting for an answer. Like he was waiting for me to break.

"So, you actually haven't seen the alleged illegal vials of steroids, have you." I posed my words more as a statement than a question.

The stare-down continued. So did Abdul's irritating tapping.

"It just takes a phone call," Abdul said, smugly.

"Well. Make that call… right now."

Abdul leaned back in his chair and crossed his arms. He puffed out what little chest he had. I viewed it as a show of dominance, like a male dog dry-humping my leg. He clearly loved the heady aura of authority—craved it. Abdul wanted to feel superior and wanted me to think he was. His arrogance was in-my-face like the tits of a large-breasted woman in a wet T-shirt contest.

I cleared my throat. He looked down, once again breaking our gaze.

"I WIN!" I silently congratulated myself, with a sarcastic grin.

I had Abdul right where I wanted—like a Thanksgiving turkey, plump and juicy ready for the carving.

"Well… once you get the vials, you'll see they're pre-scrip-tion," I exaggeratedly enunciated each syllable for my gratification. "Obviously, William had failed to disclose that part," I added.

Abdul looked like he'd swallowed a cow.

"Prescribed by my doc-tor for low testosterone."

Abdul looked insulted, which was my intent. His face reddened. Surely out of embarrassment.

"I've been taking them for several years… and no, as much as I wouldn't want to disappoint you and your theory… they're not the reason I tried to off myself… "

"Mr. Chumbley… your friend, William, thinks you're taking more than what you're being prescribed. And…"

"I'm not finished yet… "

Abdul's face soured. Turned a light tinge of green.

"As I was saying, they don't… and never have affected me in the manner you're inferring. The only thing making me angry… again, is you and your piss-poor, so-called professional research," I scornfully mocked.

I stood up. Tauntingly smiled—before walking out of the room.

stashing the evidence

Hurriedly, I walked toward the community phone—hopping-mad William had inventoried and confiscated my drugs. But he hadn't discovered all of them; and I needed to make sure no one would. The irony: I'd been on his case for years about drinking and taking sleeping pills on top of the liquor because he couldn't sleep well—after working long shifts at the hospital. It was an ongoing habit since we'd first become friends.

William had been teetering on the edge of alcoholism and substance abuse for years. On several occasions, I'd tried to talk to him about it; but my concerns fell on deaf and dismissive ears. I guess since he was a doctor, William knew best. He'd basically fucked me with professional impunity—under cover of our friendship concerning my steroid use.

I found Lily positioned in front of the phone. Her meaty hips pushed out through the openings under the armrests of a chair. Her voice was loud and demanding—the phone's headset secured in place by the fat under her chin. It looked like it had been smashed into Lily's face and needed to be surgically removed. She was insisting on getting something from whoever was on the other end. The conversation loitered like a comedy of errors. I could hear a woman on the other end shouting at the top of her lungs.

Lily's demands intensified into a delusional rant as she waved her arms and hands—well extended with her bat wings flying. If they—the bat wings were hooked up to an energy converter, the motion would surely be enough to provide electricity for half of Atlanta.

I stood rigid a few feet from and to the left of Lily—just enough distance to stay out of range of her flailing arms, but close enough she could see me from the corner of her eye as it jetted toward me and then away. My temples pounded—angered William had sold me out.

Finally, Lily sharply turned her head in my direction, still riding her rant. Then, she stopped. Lily's tone switched gears—from bad-ass-biker-bitch to sweet-and-motherly.

"Honey, you need the phone?"

I nodded.

She returned her focus to the fanatical conversation on the phone.

"Gotta get off now! Shirley, I'll call you back later."

Lily slammed the receiver back in the cradle with alarming force.

"That bitch never does a goddamn thing I tell her!" Lily advertised, as she glimpsed back a smile as cloying as powdered sugar on jelly-filled donuts—her personality changing like the character in the 1957, 20th Century Fox movie, "Three Faces of Eve."

Lily struggled from the chair. Two more patients joined the line. My mind persisted to reel since Abdul basically had divulged, he and Ching had essentially been giving the third-degree to Sandra and my friends—an in-depth investigation compiling a dossier like I was on the FBI's Ten Most Wanted list. Although intentions may have been for my benefit and well-being, again I felt betrayed. They could make all the erroneous assumptions and speculations concerning my true state of mind, but they were not me—and concerning my so-called relationship with Christopher, I certainly don't remember it being a free-for-all. To be more specific: none of my friends shared our bed.

I picked up the handset still hot and sweaty from Lily's meaty hand and chubby neck. There appeared to be spit on the mouthpiece from her overly animated and heated conversation, causing saliva to spray in most directions. I wiped it with my T-shirt before punching in Sandra's number. She answered after a few rings.

"Hey… it's me."

"How are you doing?" she asked, out of habit.

"You know, just hunky-dory… having the time of my life and making all kinds of new friends." I answered, sarcastically.

"Oh, I bet," Sandra replied, letting out a bony laugh of gibed amusement.

"Marty's coming with me in a bit to bring your lunch from Eats. You, want anything special?"

"Surprise me."

"I'll give it some thought."

"Have you checked on Dugan today?"

"Of course… he's doing well."

"Can't wait to see him… if I ever get out of this low-rent joint."

I shared that I'd just had another sit-down with Abdul.

"He said everyone has been talking to him and Dr. Ching about me. Especially… William and Russ, expressing concern I needed to stay longer."

"Have you been talking, too?"

"No. No, Randy. They've both approached me, but I've said very little."

"Come on Sandra. Tell me the truth."

"The only thing I've said is, that I want you to be okay… to get better."

"Look. You must tell everyone… especially, William and Russ to stop talking to them. I'm serious."

"They're just trying to help you."

"But they're not. Did you know William went through my house and confiscated drugs?"

"Yes."

"Sandra… and you didn't tell me!"

"I didn't want to concern you."

I told my sister to tell them to please stop talking to Ching and Abdul. That, I'm never going to get out of this madhouse if they keep blabbing.

"I get it that they think they're trying to help… I do and I love them. But I don't want them to say another damn word!"

"Okay. Okay, I'll make it clear to them."

"Look… I'm not sure if I'll ever be okay again. But… the longer I'm locked up, the worse it's going to be for me. Do you understand?"

"I do, I do, Randy."

I could tell she was seconds from crying but managed to contain the release of tears.

"I really need you to make sure they stop. I need all of you to let Abdul and Dr. Ching think that I'm doing better."

"I understand."

"I need you to do two things for me."

"What."

Luckily, William hadn't found the red Tupperware container in the bottom drawer of my fridge, pushed back out of sight. It did contain substances aiding muscle growth that might be considered illegal—certainly, the unprescribed types of steroids from my dealer. As well as others I stacked along with the use of HGH and insulin, plus a drug used on horses.

I told Sandra to take it from the fridge when no one was at my house and put it in the small one in the art studio—and not to say a word. She agreed.

Obviously, Abdul and Ching were trying to dig deep. I'd the consciousness of mind to also ask Sandra to lock my writing website. I gave her the necessary info to do so. I couldn't leave it up for them to find it and read what could become a damning excerpt from "Alabama Snow." The book had been released in early May. I didn't want the powers that be at Davy to find out I'd also tried to end my life in early January. I knew that knowledge would throw more fuel on the flames of the hellfire. And give them the upper hand.

I had every right to be angry about the circumstances of my life at the time—regardless of what role I may have played in the grand scheme of things. I was transforming into a huge ball of hate. Growing. Burning hotter. Spreading throughout until it was all-consuming—until I felt the burning in my bones. I knew it had to be contained before I became a mound of ashes on the floor.

I slammed the phone down harder than I should have—hard enough, it cracked the earpiece. Now, I could add vandal to my list of crimes.

A hand jetted from behind to arrest the handset—another patient wanted to make a call to the outside world through the phone portal. I stepped back into the middle of the open area. The room began to spin. I was losing weight. I felt weak. The sleep-deprivation had caught up with me. In fact, it was running ahead.

the almighty dollar

That weekend dragged like an ant pulling an extra-large sack of Idaho potatoes. The air conditioning system—chronically inadequate for its heavy summer payload, had given up the ghost. The hermetically sealed ward remained oppressive. Stifling. Airless. Insufferable. I was on pins and needles waiting for Dr. Ching—who, by-the-way, had maybe spoken a dozen words to me, or Abdul to approach with the news: to pack my bags as if once-lovers were going their separate ways. Perhaps, more so for my outbursts of arduous defiance than anything else. But nothing. No word. Nada. Zilch. Not even a furtive glance in my direction. In fact, I hadn't seen Abdul all weekend—he must had it off.

The only relief: the threading visits of Sandra and the loyal five. As the usual, bearing edible food from the outside—although, ongoing worry had still hovered concerning them having to share the surrounding toxicity. But toxicity or not, I had come to rely on them more and more—even though, as I'd stated earlier: I rather they stay away to spare them. But the consistency of those visits were much like a life preserver to keep me from drowning—as my state of mind bobbed.

Sandra religiously brought more pictures of Dugan, text to her by

Liz. Seeing them and knowing he was well-looked-after had somewhat lifted my spirits. Each one delivered a combination of tears and happiness as they did heartbreak.

That weekend, William had flown in from Miami. Russ had returned home. It was better that way; even though I loved him and appreciated his loyalty as well, Russ tended to be a bit bossy and controlling as he was too opinionated. Sandra told me she'd overheard them having a colossal falling-out concerning me, before Russ stormed out of my house to the airport. But she didn't go into specifics of the drama.

Marty and Hal had been spending more time with Sandra—keeping her busy around the city. At Hal's insistence, she'd started staying at his residence a few blocks from mine—sleeping over in one of the guest rooms. I'm sure Sandra didn't want to be alone at night in my house. No doubt, having everything to do with what I'd done there. I was grateful Sandra was bonding with my friends as they'd taken a strong liking to her.

Early-on, I'd told her to take my AMEX card from my wallet to cover anything she needed, including to make sure Liz had enough of Dugan's special dog food purchased from the veterinarian's office. When William was in town, I knew he'd spend a small fortune on Sandra. A generous attempt to push away as much of the gloom surrounding the present set of circumstances: lunch and dinners out, and without a doubt—shopping sprees.

Upon Peggy's return on Monday, she stopped in her tracks at the sight of me. A puzzled look covered her face. Peggy quickly approached.

"Did you act out over the weekend?"

"No. I was a good little boy. Scout's honor."

"I'm somewhat perplexed. I'd expected you to be released by now. Certainly, understanding you have a big support group."

Peggy's brow wrinkled.

"I don't know. Guess they still think I'm a threat to myself."

She tilted her head as in thought. It was obvious her mind was processing. I waited for Peggy to say something else.

"Wait, I think there's something you can look into."

"What's that?"

"I don't know why I didn't think of it before… you do have the right to be transferred to another hospital. See that sign over there on the wall?" she pointed.

PATIENT RIGHTS: You have the right to be transferred to a hospital of your choosing.

"I know… Allen is my Power of Attorney. He's already set things in motion. But it seems the process is moving as slow as molasses from the bark of a tree."

"That's good he's aware," Peggy said.

"No disrespect meant to anyone, but I felt like white trash waiting to be recycled."

She then patted me on the shoulder before briskly walking toward the staff station.

I decided to check in with Allen again; I took a place in line for the phone behind three other patients. I wasn't surprised to see Lily chitchatting while in a chair all comfy-looking while hogging the phone. As usual, totally ignoring the five-minute time limit sign. So, I waited. Fucking waited—anxiously tapping my right foot.

"If only I could figure out a way for Sandra to smuggle in my phone," I thought.

Suddenly, someone unapologetically passed a load of offensively malodorous gas into the area as if a bomb had exploded. It almost knocked me off my feet—certain, it was Lily's flatulence. What gave her away was how she nippily looked back at the line. Just the thought of breathing in the methyl mercaptan, methane, and dimethyl sulfides were enough to send me running out of the area, but I didn't want to lose my place in line. Instead, I covered my mouth and nose with both hands, holding my breath. The nauseating smell—quite appropriate for the ambiance of the 13th floor.

I momentarily paused to scramble-up Allen's digits from memory. He'd been consistent in checking-in with Sandra between his visits from Birmingham.

"Hey… I know the answer but I'm going to ask anyway. How you holding up?"

"Pretty much the same… but another patient threatened me yesterday. Told me that he was going to kick my brains in."

"Do you want me to make another complaint?"

"No, it's pointless like the others. Actually, he'd be doing me a favor."

"Don't say that… Randy. I'm coming the day after next. Just

keep your distance."

I told Allen what Peggy had said about my right to be transferred to another hospital.

"Yeah… I know. It's one of the matters I've been trying to address with the administration, but… as usual, they keep avoiding my verbal demands of either releasing you altogether, and if not… allowing me to get the ball rolling on having you transferred to a private facility. There's something very fishy going on."

Allen had presented the hospital administration's and Dr. Al-bitch's office the Power of Attorney along with a letter of a number of demands—both seemed unconcerned.

"Somethings up."

"Why am I not surprised?"

"Yeah, they're avoiding me like the plague… but don't worry, this bulldog's going for their throats."

During the phone conversation, Allen told me that he'd checked into their public finances—that they were gushing money like a break in a dam.

"I'm pretty certain they're keeping you hostage for your health insurance money… and that's highly illegal."

Sometime before the July 4th event, I'd seen on the news: Davy was perpetually careening toward the edge of bankruptcy. Again, being a county facility, they had to take the impoverished. Meaning, the majority of their patients didn't have a pot to piss in or a window to throw it out of—much less health insurance. Accordingly, a patient with health insurance was a rare cash cow to be milked dry.

As I've shared, it's all a blur the night I was rolled out of the elevator on to the 13th floor, but, again, I do remember that a woman came to me to verify my health insurance.

Subsequently to talking with Allen, it soon became glaringly apparent: I could have lounged about in the common area dressed in my Brunello Cucinelli virgin wool and silk tuxedo wearing spit-shined Prada patent leather oxfords and smelling of Eau Sauvage Christian Dior cologne, laughing and throwing my head back like "Dynasty's" Alexis Carrington drinking Adam's Apple Martinis and still wouldn't get released from Davy without inciting World War III.

Allen did come as promised. This time, he was able to address his concerns with someone in administration. They told him they would look into his allegations and get back to him. Allen told me he felt they were stalling.

After he left to return to Birmingham, it didn't take Abdul long before he pulled me into a private meeting room and closed the door. He was becoming more like a pesky infestation of pubic lice. Once again, Abdul attempted to intimidate me—threatening, if I continued to cause problems, they would go to a judge and say I was still a danger to myself and others; and obtain a court order to keep me as long as they wanted.

In the process, he put some papers on the table. Papers I apparently signed once I was wheeled onto the ward, giving Davy the authority to do so. It was my signature or some drug-induced variation. I questioned Abdul of the legitimacy of the documents from someone in my state at the time. Cleary for damage control, he remained firm they were legal and binding documents. But he wasn't an attorney.

I was convinced my only importance was a source of revenue once the accounting department found out I had health insurance. It was clear where it hadn't been before. I may have been just another number beforehand. But at the discovery of insurance, that number became a lucky lottery draw. No one with a medical degree was formulating a treatment plan for my best interest. They were stalling while some bigwigs deep in the bowels of Davy—were ciphering how much cash flow my confinement would produce over the maximum hospitalization time. Scamming my insurance company, and by proxy its paying policyholders.

Conclusively, I didn't need to just sit there and "realize what a very bad thing I had done," as Dr. Albridge had first scolded. I needed to sit there as many days and nights they could get away with—to rack-up my bill.

Following Abdul's stunt, I called Allen. He was halfway back to Birmingham. I told him about Abdul pulling me into a conference room and showing me the papers that I'd signed but didn't remember doing so, therefore didn't mention them to Allen.

As I believed, he agreed whatever I signed was only worth the paper. He told me it was good information to have and to sit tight. That, he wasn't finished with Davy. Again, he told me that he would get me out—but this time in a matter of days. At the end of our phone conversation, Allen expressed me not to kill anyone before he was able to get me released.

In the meantime, it began to sink in that I had to outsmart them. I understood my situation perfectly by that point. Unless Allen could prove Davy's deceit sooner than later, or faced any more stalling on the hospital's part, Albridge still held the key to my freedom. I had to become the perfect patient: so grateful to be alive, so obliged to be saved. I had to be the miracle.

In order to play the game, I'd do whatever I had to—whatever they wanted to hear. Whatever it took to blanket the truth to make them think I was okay. Make the whole dirty bunch believe I'd come to Jesus while I held on to Allen's reassurance, I'd soon be checking out of Hotel Psycho Ward Hell. I was discovering—a part of me still had some fight left.

the interrogation

The remaining two days of my stay vacation, at approximately the same time every mid-afternoon, I was summoned to a meeting room. And each day, commanded to sit at the end of a conference table as if I were a dog." Not, "Good afternoon." Not, "Please take a seat, Mr. Chumbley." Not even a cursory inquiry as to my well-being. Not, "Did you fuck anyone while you were here?" Again, just, "sit" but no doggy treat was offered.

Queen Bee Albridge, sat at the head of the table across from me as if she was Jesus-fucking-Christ—but without the tattered robe or a crown of thorns. She flipped the pages in a green folder—never looking up at me or saying a single word. As well, Albridge still had the same stone-cold and butt-ugly face.

With my keen sense of smell, a stiff odor of a musty and moldy fragrance waft—as if her choice of eau de toilette was formulated by a cheap perfumer from the elements of licked armpits and feet.

Eight people surrounded Jesus like devoted apostles at the Last Supper. I assumed: a doctor or two, including Ching; social workers—plus my nemesis, Abdul; nurses; interns. Their lifeless dissecting glances occasionally eyed like I was some lab rat—some medical experiment. If I caught them—eye-to-eye, each one couldn't stay my stare. Instead, they quickly looked down or away. As Dr. Albridge, the cast of characters randomly wrote notations in their own folders or notebooks. For all I knew, they might as well have been jotting down their grocery list for dinner.

The walls of the windowless room were the same dingy white as the rest of the joint. I found myself contemplating a fresh coat of paint and some decent art would do the place a shitload of good as Dr. Albridge and her posse rearranged and shifted their asses in the chairs. I would compare the sessions to one of Rod Sterling's episodes of the "Twilight Zone" television series playing on loop with him narrating the action—a fly-on-the-wall, unseen by everyone except for me. I was transmogrified into another play-actor. Cast in the role of a patient in a mental ward who had a very serious problem of not wanting to stay alive.

Repetitively, as if on trial by a lead prosecutor, I was lectured by a petite mid-thirties pretty Black woman—who I didn't know her name or title. Perhaps, Mouthpiece would be fitting. Maybe she was the one in the bunch who had drawn the smallest straw in the game of drawing straws: "Well, Mr. Chumbley, you're in a high statistical rate of harming yourself again: given your age; the severity of your mother's mental illness; certainly, understanding the violence you experienced as a child; especially your father's suicide," she clinically allowed—surely, academically practiced and delivered rote without a scintilla of human empathy. Along with everything else, I'd let them maintain whatever they wanted to believe.

As she notched off pieces of my family history, I was astonished and confused how the prosecutor had become privy to much of my family's morbid history. Then, I soon assessed, in moments of weakness—surely brought on by the anxiety of Sandra's concerns as if a double agent and had been somewhat forthcoming with Dr. Ching.

The list of my family's saga was followed by questions that also fell on deaf ears as did the integration: Do you understand why you're here? Do you realize the brutality of what you did to yourself? What's going to keep you from attempting suicide or harming yourself again? What are you going to do if you feel like you want to in the future? Do you have a plan?

Every time, I answered their questions with varying versions of a scripted nature: yes, I tried to kill myself; yes, I understand I've been given another chance at life; I don't plan on blowing it; I want to live; I realize I have a good life; if ever tempted again, I'll call a friend or my doctor or go to the ER; I'm going to focus on my art and writing as I did before.

The unabridged experience of being locked up was dehumanizing enough—especially due to Albridge's overall callousness, and disregard that I was a human being, but only an outlined figure with a number on my back. Those inquisitions had emotionally stripped me of my clothing as I sat in front of her and those nut pickers while they psychologically raped me.

After each interrogation, I would dutifully parrot: "You've all been so helpful, and I appreciate your concerns. I'm privileged for another chance at life due to the treatment I've received at Davy."

I would lie, and lie, and then lie some more—as if a triple Oscar winner for the best leading male in a psychiatric ward. Even to the point, I'd possibly might temporarily believe it myself, if necessary, in order to walk through that gate to the other side. As well, as unappetizing as it wouldn't be, I'd lick Albridge's nasty ass squeaky-clean while trying to keep from vomiting.

I gave my performance with the martyrdom of "Gone With The Wind's, Scarlett O'Hara. "As God is my witness, they're not going to lick me. I'm going to live through this and when it's all over, I'll never be crazy again. No, or any of my folk. If I have to lie, steal, cheat, or kill. As God is my witness, I'll never be crazy again."

when the dreams and nightmares come

Dreams and nightmares plagued from slices of years passed—paralleling life events while contaminating what purity is left of a soul. All reminders brought forward by malignant spirits riding on galloping steeds—cloaked by moonless night skies as I lay vulnerable with the darkness.

They threaten the present and the future while looming as accusers and adjudicators as I wait to be sentenced for sins; I've spent a lifetime running from only to find myself standing before an executioner. On the occasions not rushed by them at night, those dreams and nightmares haunted the days in the confinement of Davy's 13th floor.

I dreamt of Bradley coming to save me—to break me out of Davy. Encased within the dream, he stands next to me at the gate to freedom; exactly how I remember him from some thirty-one years ago as if no time had passed. The gate opens. I turn to look up at Bradley. Seconds later, it slams shut. The dream shifts into a nightmare as he stands on the other side without me.

Bradley lies next to me in bed surrounded by the graying decay of the room. Fluorescent lights from the long corridor outside emit a low hum as Bradley holds me in his arms—as they once did in a distant life and a different place. I feel safe as I once did. His voice reassures in whispers as if having traveled light-years through time and space: "It's going to be okay. I'm here now."

In a trice, that dream as the other rolled into a nightmare. Bradley releases me; a bright light flashes. Suddenly he's standing by the bed as I look up at him—so big and strong. Bradley's hand holds mine. He smiles. Takes a step back. Then, another. Our hands begin to slip apart. I fight to hold on to Bradley's—fight to pull him back. Fight to get out of bed, but I can't. Our hands inevitably break apart.

I keep reaching. Calling his name to come back, but Bradley won't—won't come back. Another few steps, he's swallowed-up in the decaying of night.

I'm poised, stripped of clothing while suspended in the center of a semi-cylinder hole in the ground. Above, a brilliant blinding titanium-white light beckons. Below, blackness as dark as if discharged from a squeezed tube of mars black oil paint abandoned on my studio work table wrenches. The odorous earthiness of soil brims my lungs. The air, cold. A mist-like rain falls. Chilling wind encircles my body—fast then slow plunging me down than jetting me upward. Then, it stops as my body hovers in suspension once again. Quietude bleeds.

Climb, climb, climb innate survival called, although barely able to touch the sides—roughened of dirt and clay, and various sizes of embedded jagged rocks protruded. Long and thin, whisker-like exposed roots trailed like vines. Blood and dirt engorged nails of fingers and that of the toes of feet stung with raw fire as every limb extended to take hold of anything so as to ascend.

What progress made was eventually lost each time the wind stirred up—breaking my hold. The opening grew smaller as my body fell; and larger as I was able to ascend in inches.

As the whipping stilled, once again I attempted to climb—grabbing the protruding rocks and vines. Some of the vines were too tenuous and brittle to service my weight. They snapped, liberating clumps of dirt and rock careening down. I watched until they vanished—swallowed by the unseeable extinction beneath. Exhausted but determined, with each panting breath of the rank, grimy air, I struggled and struggled and struggled.

Following what seemed hours, I made it within feet of the opening. The steep roofline of a house came into view—clarifying the hole was in the backyard of the house on Seventh Street. Oddly, Christopher and Dugan were looking at me; a nimbus, silver light haloed their forms. I breathed relief. Dugan barked. His tail wagged.

I called out for help, but no response was returned. Christopher's eyes locked in a stare—his face without expression. He didn't move as if a stone figure. Desperation returned.

Vehemently, once again, I start clawing at the dirt and rocks—reaching for the vining roots. But the whipping air picked up until it became a massive vortex. My body plummets into vacantness. A gut-wrenching sensation of death followed as the hole at the top closed shutting light. I awakened or I thought I had—fingertips pulsating pain, raw, and bloodied.

On what forbearing nights—as brief as they were, I the selfsame dreams that morphed into nightmares. Each recurrence, shivered into the ice-cold vacantness of the room.

is freedom really freedom

"Freedom's just another word for nothin' left to lose… "

Me and Bobby McGee
Janis Joplin

Allen had kept his promise: championing my release after several civil attempts to address Davy, keeping me much longer than was generally deemed by health care professionals in the field of psychiatry. Typically, a person with no known prior history of self-harm (I'd made sure no one was aware of the first attempt in January) are held for a period of 24 to 72 hours for evaluation. And regardless of the severity of the attempt, didn't give them the legal right to do so beyond that timeframe.

To summarize: over the max of 72 hours, I hadn't shown any behaviors of other mental disorders; any outbursts were understandable due to the resulting hemorrhoid due to the surgery and the fact there was no hot water in order to clean myself properly, much less take a garden variety shower; any with Abdul were goated by him and were motivated by his racial prejudice; Davy's audacity of dismissing Allen's demand to have me transferred to a private facility and let them decide if any additional steps were necessary; the fact that I hadn't received any counseling; the added dismissal of threats made by other patients jeopardized my life; additionally, I had a substantial support group—including my sister, a doctor who was a close friend as well as the others. Furthermore, the absolute indication of evidence: any papers I'd signed upon entry to the ward were null and void because I was heavily sedated, and the hospital knew that fact but had me sign them anyway.

The fact that Allen was continuously ignored: he burst open the doors of Davy's administration office—bombarding them with a stack of legal pages of other infractions in addition to those listed above: malpractice, patient endangerment, kidnapping and unlawful confinement, ignoring HIPAA compliances, and deceptive medical practices for the purpose to commit fraud on an insurance company for their financial gain. Also, notifying, we would sue: not only the hospital but named Dr. Albridge, Dr. Ching, and Abdul as co-conspirators to force Davy for my immediate release.

As mentioned, the hospital was already under the microscope for the misappropriations of funds among other wrongdoings. They didn't need another major public embarrassment. My unlawful incarceration would certainly make the headlines, and Allen would see to that. Davy had no choice but to say, uncle.

I was desperate to return home like a weary traveler—but terrified at the same time. Fearful of what I might do—what I'd been planning while a guest on the 13th floor.

I knew I was a different person; and as impossible as it surely might be for many to understand—in some ways, even for myself, in the knowledge of knowing what I'd done, I was worse off walking out of Davy than when my body was rolled on a gurney into the ER that late afternoon of July Fourth; after the light had left my eyes, and all thought had bled from my brain.

Whatever diminutive parts of my essence that may have managed to cling to my being, had been purged—not by the suicide attempt but the trauma of Davy's mental ward where the accumulation of hours-on-end into days and bleeding into nights and more of the same until there seem there was no delineation—as the surroundings continued blurring while sliding deeper into the abyss of nonexistence—that surviving essence, had been squeezed like water wrung from a sponge.

Even though Allen obtained my release, my paranoia was on high alert—concerned something would run amuck and Albridge would somehow get the upper hand again regardless of Allen having pushed the administration into a tight corner.

The night before my release, Abdul informed me he'd have me signed-out by 11:00 the next morning. How quickly he changed his tune after Allen eventually got through to the powers that be at Davy.

Sleep had escaped the last night of my incarceration—I hinged to an edgy wakefulness. Inquietude soon pulled me from the bed toward the window. I don't even remember walking to it, but I found my body standing rigidly just inches from the reinforced glass in the piffling ash of night—surrounded in the complete stillness. In the background as I'd heard since night one, the crying woman still sirened; her voice continued to haunt the ward as it had me.

While standing at the window—spinning took control of my thoughts. I looked down to the realization, the context of my life up to that moment in time had led and left me emotionally naked standing on two twelve-inch by twelve-inch square tiles of over-waxed, yellowed commercial grade linoleum.

Regardless of what had taken place before that moment of clarification or what would follow, those two squares symbolized the border of my present world—how small it had become in a matter of two and a half years. I'd lost so much: my self-respect; hope had vanished; chunks of my sanity had been bitten away; worst of all, I'd lost the person I once was—to what degree would be determined in measured time.

It was a night overtaken by a myriad of waffling precariousness. I continued to stand in the sheer immobility of the window's impedance; viewing the sleeping city on the other side. My mind was bound by shadows of gray; my eyes leered at what seemed to be a void of destitution and what I strangely perceived to be freedom—while waiting for the night's lethargic evolution into daylight. Waited, for the light to infiltrate the skyscrapers composing Atlanta's cityscape. Until then, I numbly loitered in the silhouette of discomposure. Tears began to leak onto the grimy tile. I was unsure if they were tears of relief, or those of realities. Whichever, I remained—as my body innately swayed.

counting the seconds

"There is more to life than simply increasing its speed… "
Mahatma Gandhi

Earth had made its rotation around the sun pulling light back to the yawning East Coast of the continent—back to me and my anticipation. Its peeking, yellow-bronze glow hesitatingly hovered on the outside of the glass while examining the human on the inside. Then, cautiously amassing its time as it eased upward and inward illuminating the room and eventually the dark spot standing in the center.

The materialization of daybreak beamed uncertainties and apprehensions of what might or might not be. Yes, the world had come back around, but I remained immobile. Feeling, at any moment, my life or what little there seemed to be left would finish collapsing around me and I would find myself trapped in the last of the rubble. Notwithstanding, I was ready to leave Davy. Beyond that, I didn't know. I wasn't sure or could I give the day ahead any contemplation—much less, the hours, days, and weeks to follow. Or even know if I would manage to survive them. I would have to live minute to minute to find out.

I rotated and walked across the room to the bed. Sat on its edge. Waited. Waited while my legs uneasily shook. Two white plastic bags of my stuff were inches from my feet like those of a vagabond's. Sandra had taken the black leather Coach overnight bag back to the house—concerned it would possibly be absconded by either a patient or one of the staff. At 8:00, Abdul came looking for me.

I caught a brief look at him standing in the doorway from the corner of my eye.

"Well, this is your day," he stated, in the manner befitting his egotism.

At Allen's insistence, Abdul agreed to have my release documents ready by 10:00.

He still nauseated me. Nothing would change my disfavor. I knew there continued to be no genuineness behind his words, and his attitude concerning me hadn't changed either. The detestation between us was still as strong as ever. Abdul's somewhat improved demeanor was forced, just as the crow that Allen had crammed down his throat, and—its distaste slapped on his face. Allen had beaten him at his game of intimidation. I knew it would pain Abdul's pride to watch me walk through the iron gate to the other side—no longer under his control.

"Yes," I replied.

"There's one small thing… "

"Of course, there is."

"The Chief Psychologist at Stalter University… associated with us, wants to meet with you before you're released."

"Why?"

"Dr. Albridge talked to her about your case."

"Seriously? Did I happen to sign another form giving her permission to disclose my medical information to another doctor… not directly associated with my case when I did all the others under heavy sedation?"

"Well… we're all under the same umbrella here at Davy."

I let out a slender laugh—in rebuff.

"You mean the leaky one? Do I need to have my attorney add another breach of patient confidentiality to the long list of Davy's egregious infractions?"

Abdul didn't respond. I offered an eat-shit look.

"The thing is, she can't get here until one o'clock," he added.

"Why am I not surprised?" I scoffed.

Abdul retained his stance.

"I want to go home now!"

"I know Mr. Chumbley. It's just a few more hours."

"May as well be five more days!" I scoffed.

Abdul glowed that Dr. Griffin was an important bigwig, who specialized in suicide cases. And due to the severity of my situation, she thought it would benefit me to talk to her. I found my derailed release time to be somewhat fishy since Albridge hadn't taken any direct interest in me. And, again, not had spoken another word after she informed me on that first day, "You need to sit here and realize what a very bad thing you did."

"Yeah, yeah, yeah! With the severity of my situation," I mocked.

"We'd prefer you wait on her."

I mulled for some moments. Looked away, then back at him.

"Okay. Okay!" I vexingly caved, again, concerned something shady might be going on with Albridge and this Dr. Griffin. Certainly, since Allen had forced Davy's hand.

"Good. Your case must have really intrigued her. She's a very busy woman."

"Really?" I responded, unimpressed.

My nemesis proceeded to apprise he would let me know as soon as Dr. Griffin arrived. Abdul reached-out a large envelope he'd been holding since first entering the room. Told me it contained my discharge papers and prescriptions for medications. Further including, was a list of recommendations for psychiatrists and therapists for me to consider. As well, information about coping skills and such.

I reached to take it. Didn't bother to thank Abdul or show any appreciation. There was none deserved. I returned my gaze toward the window.

"Since you've agreed to wait, I'll call your sister to update her," Abdul offered.

"Sure."

"Okay, then… "

Before exiting, Abdul offered the hospitality of a late checkout if I wished to wait in the room; but if they needed it for a new patient, he'd let me know.

"Gee whiz, so nice of you."

I watched his scrawny ass walk away. Clearly, my little Mr. Social Worker relished his last measure of pleasure knowing I'd be trapped a while longer; the iron gate wouldn't be flying wide open as soon as I'd thought for my exit. No doubt, Abdul was savoring it; savoring it, as if he was sitting at a table in Gladys Knights Chicken and Waffles restaurant licking his lips while waiting on his order.

I wondered what this super psychologist really wanted. This supposedly powerhouse-of-a-woman—this healer, who was believed to have some insight into the dark kingdom of the suicidal mind. Some appointed high-functionary—who I'd never laid eyes on, wanted to talk to me delaying my release. I already didn't like her or cared to know what parting insights she might bestow.

The ends of every fingernail had been chewed while awaiting her arrival. Nothing had changed—more sitting and waiting in nervous agitation on the edge of the crappy bed. Antsy, I habitually walked into the common area to check the clock before returning to the bed's edge.

What seemed like days later, Abdul popped his bald shiny head into the room.

"What fucking time is it?" I gallingly asked while looking past him.

Abdul paused; he checked the time on his fake gold cheap, Timex wristwatch.

"12:45."

"Well, is she here?"

"Dr. Griffin called. She just finished a meeting on the first floor and is making her way up. Should be any minute now."

Without hesitancy, I exited the room with the two white garbage bags in tow. Dropped them in a corner near the staff station before I began pacing. Narrowed my eyes on the gate. The caustic smell of bleach hung in the air as a janitor purposefully swabbed the floor from side to side with a large filthy mop, mindlessly spreading the contamination stroke-by-stroke. The vapors strong enough, my eyes burned. I avoided the plastic, yellow caution signs bearing the stern multicultural warning: Wet Floor—Piso Mojado.

In annoyed anticipation over this stranger's arrival, my teeth returned to biting what little was left of my fingernails. My eyes were locked on the bars of the gate—as Pebbles must had been every day of her short life.

The taste of liberation salivated. A new patient stood off to the side. His wide eyes looked as if they were those of a dear caught in headlights—another sad story I didn't care to know. I'd leave it to Lily—surely hungering to gather every detail to be collected for his dossier. She retained her position as the ringmaster of the Big Top—running the whole circus show, continuing to dig for the chew on the newbies. Perchance, her purpose in life was giving much needed attention to disconsolate souls.

A woman lamented to someone on the other end of the common phone. Her back was hunched—her face hidden as if shamed. The loud distress in her voice had distracted the immediacy of my pacing. I instinctively felt empathy—for her plight, whatever it was. Thankfully, I hadn't seen Medusa in a day and a half. Sweet Rose was back in her spot on the sofa staring at the television—her favorite pastime on the ward. All their surrounding images began blurring—pushed into the background.

"Must be one slow elevator, or this woman is taking the stairs," I surmised.

Peggy spied me; she approached with a smile on her face—her eyes bright.

"I'm so glad you're leaving… finally."

Peggy opened her arms to offer a sincere hug. She had been caring and kind—never treated me like a clinical lunatic. I was grateful; the only light in this downhearted place.

"Thank you, Peggy. I really appreciate all your advice."

She winked before heading off in another direction. A commotion erupted between one of the patients and a staffer. I returned to my pacing while facing the gate again for any sign of Dr. Wasting My Time. It was 1:05 p.m. An automatic deep sigh followed.

dr. miss america

A nondescript woman walked through the gate like she owned the joint—nodding and superfluously waving in short hand gestures as if she was Miss America having left her crown and sash at home; she briefly spoke to a few staff members. One took a short stack of green folders from her hand. A large black padfolio remained in Miss America's grip as she beelined in my direction; and came to a halt in front of me as if I was a stop sign.

"I assume you're, Mr. Chumbley?"

"What gave me away?"

"I was told you're a handsome, muscular man," she purposefully flattered. "And… you look eager to get out of here," she added.

"You'd be correct on the latter."

"Well, I appreciate you waiting. Let's go back to the staff conference room so we can get acquainted. I'm Dr. Griffin… if you don't already know."

"Yes, I do."

I followed her animated shuffle, waddling from side to side as a woman with overly large hips would; but she was slight in build. Perhaps, obese once-upon-a-time and owing to her unambiguous gait. But had been rendered normal-sized for her height from dieting or maybe a radical stomach-stapling procedure.

Griffin stopped at the conference room's door. With a side-wave of the hand, I was gestured to enter first and take a seat. I eyed Griffin from my peripheral vision, further calculating her intentions. She took a seat on the other side of the short table. Griffin folded her arms over her flat chest as if about to scold—certain it wasn't about the birds and the bees.

"Dr. Albridge has filled me in on your case."

I sat there. Was I supposed to affirm? Nod? Genuflect? Light up a stick of incense to set the mood? Instead, I smiled.

"I guess you're wondering why I asked to meet with you?"

"Yes… it had crossed my mind."

"Well, as I said, Dr. Albridge and I have discussed your case…"

I cut her off before she could speak another word.

"Albridge has only imparted one sentiment to me the entire time I've been here."

"Really? What's that?"

"Her apparently seasoned conviction my primary therapeutic regimen was to sit on this ward, presumably until she said-so… or perhaps, Hell froze over and contemplate what a very bad thing I'd done to myself… without benefit of ten minutes of her time or any conversation to follow," I dramatized.

Miss America hesitated—in a very clinical and knowing way.

"I would say, consuming a very large quantity of pills… cutting open your arm and practically bleeding-out in your bathtub was pretty bad."

"Yes, all true. And pertaining to the severity… is why I was transported to Davy because it's a level one trauma center. But I don't wish to relive it at this moment… much less have it spoon-fed to me again. Plus, it's not as black-and-white to the point of cold-hearted as you seem to think."

"I'm the professional here concerning your situation, Mr. Chumbley," Griffin insisted.

"Don't flatter yourself."

My irritation spouted wings. She was spitting what happened in my face.

"My situation? Really? I would be the professional at this table concerning that."

"Why?"

"Because I'm dealing with it. Not you!" I bitched in rebuttal.

"I do understand, Mr. Chumbley."

"Highly doubtful."

"What do you mean?"

"I mean… let's move on."

Griffin cleared her throat. Opened her mouth to speak. I cut the doctor off before whatever mumbo jumbo she was about say couldn't pass her Juvéderm-filled lips.

"Can we get to the point?"

A surprised look crossed her face. It was clear Griffin didn't like to be challenged.

"Okay, then… I wanted to meet to see if you would be interested in me taking you on as a client… as your therapist."

My mind or what was left of it, processed for a few moments—maybe more.

"Oh really. I didn't realize you were an ambulance chaser."

Griffin threw a shitty look at me. Then, managed to dismiss my reference to her profession—although clearly momentarily having left her at a loss for words. My brash comment evoked silence. A few unspoken moments froze.

"As I was trying to convey, I must be blunt. I don't want to if you're contemplating harming yourself again in any way."

"That's some contradiction."

"What do you mean?"

If Dr. Griffin couldn't see the paradox of her statement, expounding on it seemed pointless. Being the good doctor, she was touted to be, I don't believe Griffin would have made such a statement concerning not enrolling me under her care if I were going to off-myself.

By her conditions, it was apparent the doctor preferred to keep the headcount of her success stories—the patients she saved higher than the ones she couldn't. Therefore, Dr. Griffin could keep up the appearance to the psychiatric professional community to be a savior of the suicidal.

She went on to excessively roll out her credentials like the red carpet at the Oscars. The more Griffin talked, the more I viewed her as a snake oil saleswoman.

"I know you're troubled," she kicked back. "Many very troubled people do attempt… and unfortunately succeed in killing themselves."

Miss America went on to school me on how extremely lucky I was. There was that damn word again: lucky. The very word I felt I wasn't.

Griffin wouldn't give it a rest. Reminding me as if I needed to be—I was minutes from death upon arrival at the hospital. That, I should be grateful I'd survived. As I watched Griffin's lips move, I was waiting for the cherubs with their harps to float down from the ceiling while singing some celestial song in their ethereal voices.

"So, you think I'm troubled?" I rephrased.

"How would you diagnose yourself, Mr. Chumbley?"

"Ah, the clinical second-person query," I smirked.

"Please go on."

I informed Dr. Griffin that hers was the first and only real in-depth question I'd been asked since arriving in this godforsaken ward.

"Ding, ding, ding. You deserved a gold star."

"Ahem… " she cleared her throat. "Why do you say that?"

Pushing forward, I conveyed to this proclaimed miracle-making doctor: she and I both knew Davy's psychiatric ward is a clearinghouse for the poor and homeless with psychiatric issues—many with drug and alcohol addictions. Bottom-line: people who don't have health insurance and thus can't afford Betty Ford or some other posh, tennis, swim-and-sunbathe facility.

Griffin opened her padfolio. Flipped over a page and jotted down a few words. I wouldn't be surprised if arrogant was one of them. She tapped her pen a few times on the table before putting it down.

"Mr. Chumbley, continue?"

"I'm neither homeless or poor and I have insurance… and because of my insurance, is the only reason Davy wouldn't release me sooner or to a private facility because of it… "

Dr. Griffin's mouth opened to speak.

"Wait… I'm not finished. This was never the place for me. I've no prior history of any mental illness, personally… although I've had to deal with lots of family issues in that department. Lots. Actually, a fuck-load."

"Well, what you're stating about Davy's intentions would be unethical. I think it's more of a mix up."

"Yeah… you would say that. But his place stinks of unethical."

I gave Griffin an eat shit look. I wanted to say something else, but figured I'd said enough and best to hold my tongue—that is, until the end. Besides, she'd just find a way to deflect it. I was coming around to understand the real reason I was even asked to wait on her in the first place. However, regardless of how irritating I found her, I was beginning to find Miss America somewhat entertaining and wondering what her act would be: singing off key, bad piano playing, or perhaps baton twirling.

"I understand your father killed himself."

"It's best if we just move past that."

Dr. Griffin looked puzzled.

"Don't you think… we should discuss it?" she asked with a concentrated gaze.

"Well, I assure you I'm quite aware of my family history."

"Back to your father's death."

"You must have a hearing problem."

Her mouth gaped.

I purposely yawned. Then, yawned again, hoping Griffin would get the message.

"Can we talk a little bit more about it?"

"Let me ask you a question," I insisted.

"What's that?"

I thought a second or two. Looked down and then back up.

"Anyone in your family with a history of mental illness?"

The doctor looked surprised by the inquiry.

"I don't think it's an appropriate question."

"Why not?"

"Well…" she paused.

"You get to know all about my personal stuff, but I can't be privy to anything about you except some list of credentials."

Dr. Griffin didn't answer.

"I'll just take that as a no… "

By then, a good forty minutes must have passed. It was becoming difficult to control myself; my emotion ran wildly in my head. I wanted to reach over the table to shake her—to see what would fall out of her cracks. To look Dr. Griffin directly in the eyes and tell her: she was full of it! Instead, I reminded myself I was hopefully minutes away from walking out of this pit of misery.

At least I had enough presence of mind—crazy as I was, to realize a last-minute verbal knock-down-drag-out confrontation would jeopardize my impending escape. And I would call it an escape since Albridge or Griffin didn't have the first clue what was really going through my sick head. Plus, they had no inkling of my real family history. Certainly, the ugly and bloody dynamics surrounding it. They were two bloodhounds, having lost their sense of smell.

I leaned back in the chair as if in a pose. Cradled my chin with the thumb and index finger of my right hand of my right arm. Crossed the other across my torso to rest its elbow while I turned my head away as if Griffin were a portrait painter and I, her subject.

"Am I losing you, Mr. Chumbley?"

I rotated my face back in her direction.

"You never caught me."

It was clear that Griffin was losing her cool. I could almost see steam rising around her; I'd gotten her panties in a wad.

"Mr. Chumbley… "

"Look. I'm ready to leave now," I asserted.

"I get the feeling there's something else you want to say," she jostled.

I conveyed to Griffin that her attempts to dissect questions should have been asked the first or second day I was delivered to the ward. And that the answers, if there were any, are way too big and too long to get into today. All of which I had already expressed in so many words. I told her to stop pushing. Again, to leave it for now. I went on, like a freight train about to derail the tracks.

"Okay, Mr. Chumbley. Okay. I can see you're getting agitated."

"No. Just anxious… anxious to see my dog, take a hot shower, get some food in my stomach, and go to the gym," I straightforwardly stated. "Oh, and I'm in a calamitous need of a mani-pedi. Don't you agree?" I added, as I looked at my fingernails with expressive exaggeration.

But all the same, I was serious. I did need one.

"That's an ugly scar on your arm, and far from being fully healed. Do you think it's wise for you to be in the gym today?"

"Oh… so now you're a personal trainer, too?"

"I can work around the arm. There're lots of other body parts I can train… you must understand, before I was locked up in a zoo, I trained almost seven days a week."

"I can see."

My temperature gauge was registering well into the yellow—close to overheating due to Griffin and this supposedly non mandatory meeting; I took a breath.

"Look, as you well know, I've been locked up in this joint like a criminal on death row… accumulating some-two weeks. And for that timeframe, forced to inhale the stale circulated miasma of this ward and the decaying, tainted breath of my cellmates."

Miss America glared; I imagined a neon question mark floating above her head. A half-cocked inquisitive look distorted her face. After a lapse of mental discomfort—mine, she spoke.

"Well… answer my question before we wrap up… do you want to live?"

"Listen, you and your questions are exhausting. Forget about pills and a razor blade; I'm dying with each second, I've been at Davy."

I was getting out of Davy without any more delays. One way or the other—even if it meant cutting a hole through her.

the gangbang

As I was about to stand up. Dr. Griffin revved back up with the third degree. Or was it the fourth? Clearly having tunnel vision—evident throughout her interrogation, Griffin may have known a lot but didn't know the meaning of the word, STOP.

She had passed the point of annoyance—rapidly grating as I once again listened to her ear-bleeding, self-magniloquence, and eleventh-hour ambitious questioning. I'd rather be waterboarded. Asking one probing catechism after another like I was in the middle of a deposition, and the opposing attorney attempting to trick me up.

I viewed Griffin like an ambulance chaser soliciting clients like some lawyers do looking to represent auto accident victims. Actually, Our meeting unceasingly rambled more about her than it was concerning my situation and well-being. I wondered if Griffin had obtained her medical license from a school of medicine or more like, an online one-day quick study? Our little meet-and-greet had outstayed its unwelcomed visit.

I speculated what was next? Possibly, a full strip-down and butt finger-probe. As before, her voice began to fade in and out as did her face. The time was burgeoning on two-something o'clock, and I'd not eaten anything out of what was left of my stash of protein bars. My blood sugar was dropping as my patience—and fast.

"Mr. Chumbley… did you understand me?"

I vaguely heard her.

"What? Sorry. What did you say?" I questioned, trying to return to the moment.

"Are you okay? You look a bit pale."

"Yes… yes, I'm fine."

"We were on the topic of your life… whether or not you wanted to live," she summarized. "I will add, I'm a bit concerned you might attempt to end your life again."

"I didn't say that… not wanting to live. I just want to be okay again," I responded.

"Why not happy?"

"Be… because being just okay is realistic. Being okay will keep me alive."

A long pause tailed. I purposely yawned again while eyeing the door.

"So, what do you say… do you want me to council you on a regular schedule?"

I cocked my head. Slightly shook it from side to side. Then, I spoke. Then, I told her that Abdul had given me a list of recommended therapists and psychiatrists. That, I was sure my primary doctor could do the same. That, like I'd already said: I just want to see my dog, take a hot shower, eat, and get to the gym.

"Is that a no than?"

I told Griffin to give me a few days to adjust. That, I might call her office to make an appointment—in the vein of hoping that might pacify her for the moment.

"Are we now finally done here?" I asked

"I appreciate your patience. Can you indulge me a few more minutes so I can make a call?" Griffin asked.

"Seriously," I thought. "What the fuck had I been doing but indulging her?"

"Dr. Albridge asked me to call when we were about done."

A long, low grumble of disdain left my lips. Griffin ignored my discontentment. She reached for her cell next to the padfolio. Griffin picked it up. Scrolled for a number. My instinct was to rip the cell out of her hand. She pushed the prompt before pressing the phone to her face. I waited.

"I'm here with Mr. Chumbley. He doesn't want to commit to an appointment," she tells, looking up at me.

By then, my eyes were about to roll back in their sockets, permanently—demon roll. If she couldn't see killer in my eyes, she wasn't a very good doctor. Griffin kept saying, "Yes. Yes. Yes, I see."

Her eyes edged away, then back. I knew exactly what was in play. Griffin was attempting to take on the role of alpha—the dominatrix, trying to apply the pressure of intimidation into making me squirm—break me down until I agreed to an appointment; but it felt more like Griffin was coaxing me into a leather sling. Then, she and her buddy, Albridge would buckle up and adjust the straps of their dildos to give me a good gangbang. Perhaps, Adbul was waiting in the wings to join in.

Griffin spoke a few more, "I see… I see."

I stood up out of the chair. Took the large envelope off the table that Abdul had given me earlier.

"I'll check in with you later," she told Albridge.

Griffin closed her portfolio. Placed her phone on top of it. Then, pushed away from the table.

"Okay, Mr. Chumbley. I guess we're done."

"Yes, we are… by-the-way, I don't appreciate the little intimidation tactic you and Albridge just tried to pull," I scorned.

Griffin didn't offer a comeback. We exchanged an awkward

glance—as if we'd been on a first date gone bad.

I left the conference room first. Griffin's uniformed footsteps followed.

Although I didn't address it to Miss America: as I stated earlier that I was beginning to understand why I was asked to have a last minute meeting with her—it had become clear, its intent was to make it appear Davy was concerned about my wellbeing and not their bottom-line. A stunt—and a weak one at that, to attempt to ward off any possible lawsuit Allen had threatened.

freedom comes with a price

"One man's definition of insanity is another's definition of freedom…"
Unknown

The sight of Sandra waiting in the common area was reassuring—confirming my release from prison was real. I'd gotten my walking-papers after having paid my debt to society for the crime of attempted murder. And surprisingly set free without a mandated assigned parole officer or surprisingly, required to wear a tracking device—one that would trigger if I slit my wrists and-or downed a bottle of pills.

I left the plastic bags containing my clothes behind on the ward. I figured some of the patients needed them more than I, and many likely had never worn anything unless it were from the Salvation Army or some second-hand store. There was a closet-full of expensive designer garments back at the house. So many, I felt bad after spending weeks with the poverty-stricken from the streets of Atlanta. Compared to them, I was a millionaire several times over. But that didn't mean I was much different from them in other ways.

Sandra had come to collect a package. One misaddressed. Bounced around from addressee-to-addressee—worst for the wear and stamped with the warning: INSPECT FOR CONCEALED DAMAGE. PLEASE NOTE THE CONDITION BEFORE SIGNING. IF NECESSARY, MAKE SURE TO FILE THE PROPER CLAIM REPORTS.

I'd asked Sandra to come alone without the entourage—it was better my discharge took place without a fuss as I'd originally planned my failed release by suicide.

At my approach, Sandra offered a hyperbolized smile. Convincing as it may have appeared to others, I was keenly aware that it hid many vexations of troubling uncertainties as it did worry. I knew Sandra was afraid of what the next few days to follow would entail as much as I was—even the moments. Terrified and weakened by thoughts of how I would respond to being released. Petrified, of what I would possibly do once I stepped off of Davy's 13th floor and back into the world like a newborn—thrusted out into life again. We both knew I was fragile, but unsure of just how brittle. All of it—all those fears and concerns, were reflected in Sandra's eyes.

She leapt out of the chair toward me and swathed me in her arms.

"Hey… you ready to blow this joint?"

Sandra took my hand as if I were a little boy. It instantly sparked a flash-image pulled from the past. One of Mother bent down. My little hand in hers. Mother's lips pressed to my cheek.

I cautiously walked beside my sister toward the gate. Within a few feet, I paused. Quickly looked back as if to be sure no one was behind me—following me to yank me back. I noticed Abdul standing outside of the staff station watching. The scowl on his face was contemptuous as if he'd downed a jumbo-sized drink of vinegar. I'm sure, he'd already placed his bet that I would be back.

It crossed my mind that I should approach him. Approach Abdul to thank him for being a total douche bag during my stay. Doing so would require me to remain another two minutes on the 13th floor. But another two minutes—were two minutes too long.

The towering guard buzzed opened the gate. Our eyes met as Sandra, and I stepped to the other side.

At the elevator, we glanced at each other while wordlessly awaiting its arrival. The sounds of its mechanics—the stops and starts from the floors below grew increasingly louder as it moved upward. A few people gathered around and behind us. Collectively we waited until an unsettling clang delivered the elevator to an abrupt stop—followed by a ding-ding announcing it had reached our floor. I captured a breath as the doors grind open.

Sandra and I stepped into the cab first—the rest shuffled in as fluorescent tubes above flickered. The doors labored to close—obviously, in need of a good greasing. Another clanged. A sharp jolt followed as the cab lunged downward while throwing the passengers off balance.

I remember thinking: I managed to survive not one but two suicide attempts, and the stay at Davy; and how darkly poetic it would be if this old, antiquated piece of square machinery snapped its cables—gravity sending it at rapid speed to the bottom and to all our deaths. I imagined the headline: Death by Elevator.

The six-by-six-foot compartment stopped on the floor below. While one or two people made their exit, more piled in. Each body adding mounting stress to the cables suspending the metal box. Two more floors down, we were packed-in like sardines in a tin—surely filled past the recommended capacity for safe transport as the elevator continued its descent to ground zero. Increasingly, it trapped the smells of humans: hints of perspiration, residue of cigarette smoke absorbed into clothing, subtleties of applied body fragrances among others indistinguishable—all blending.

Generated from anxiousness and feeling claustrophobic, I pulled Sandra closer to the front—annoying our fellow daredevils as we slithered while unintentionally elbowing a few. Understanding my necessity, Sandra patted my upper back.

"You're going to be okay," she whispered.

Two nurses squeezed in the back uproariously laughed as one purred the other a joke. With no reaction from the rest of the hell-riders, the humor was lost to everyone else.

The elevator continued to jerk floor-by-excruciating-floor. At each stop, people continued shoving their way out-and-in as it expelled and ingested its human payload. I stared at the floor numbers ticking down.

Surprisingly, and after much delay—the elevator reached the lobby. Sandra and I had survived the deathtrap. Before the doors completely slid open, we were practically trampled out by the impatience of those who rode in the rear—bulldozing and jostling their way out before splitting off in different directions. Others waiting for a lift upward, discourteously sliced through the slower passengers before they could exit.

"Follow me," Sandra hastened.

I tread closely behind through a tangle of scattering people as if a boy in fear of being left behind. A boy afraid of the world in front of him. Foreign. Threatening. Numbing. Still, the thought of freedom from Davy remained constant. And with that goal, a distant memory shoved its way to the forefront—another one taking me back many years to alternative midsummer day. The day I picked my mother up from the State Mental Hospital in Milledgeville.

After almost three years, Mother walked out of the double doors of the institution that had been her forced home—dressed in the light-pink square-shouldered summer dress, and wearing the white sandals I'd bought her at Saks a few days before.

I took her hand; it slightly shook as we walked side-by-side toward the car. Mother's voice remained still. Her face, unreadable but the melancholy in her eyes—evident.

Halfway to the parking lot, Mother stopped. Abruptly she turned around to look at the massive white building.

"I'm never coming back here. Never," she determinedly spoke, before we continued our pace.

At the car, I opened the passenger door. Mother got in. I reached over to buckle the seat belt while her eyes stared forward. As the car pulled away, I turned on the radio. An Anne Murry song she was familiar with was playing. In a whisper, Mother began to sing along: "And speaks to me of flowers that will bloom again in spring… "

Her whisper trailed until the song ended. Then, stopped as she looked over at me.

"No, I'm never coming back to this place," Mother repeated.

As that day in Milledgeville, my eyes began to tear up while Sandra and I continued toward the revolving door.

I took a few deep heated breaths as the late July char punched as we exited. The intensity of the sunlight was near-blinding—my surroundings, blurred by white spots. By impulse, a hand shot up to shield my eyes. I hadn't been outside since that Fourth of July day I'd driven to Home Depot to purchase the packet of razor blades and Walgreens, where I acquired the Benadryl.

The heat of the day followed us as we entered the dark airless parking garage; by contrast, my eyes were able to focus.

"I'm just a few rows over," Sandra informed while motioning.

The automatic car door locks clicked open. Once inside, I felt safe—safe as if I'd just escaped from a maximum-security prison; but in many aspects I had, and Sandra's BMW was the getaway car.

"You do remember… William's flying back to Atlanta in a few hours?"

"That's right. I forgot."

"He wants to be here for your big day."

"There's nothing big about it… it's not like I'm getting some big award for saving the world," I thought.

"William's such an amazing friend to you," she added.

I nodded in agreement as I looked over at her; Sandra winked.

"I guess I should tell you, Russ and he had another big argument over the phone last night. Hal and I heard him in the kitchen bitching William out."

"Well… no doubt another one about me. I feel bad I'm the cause."

"The topic of their arguments aren't your fault. I've learned that Russ can be a hot head as I saw that for myself, Randy."

"I know… I know he can be."

"Well, if you ask me, it's selfish and ridiculous Russ was causing all the friction because a good friend was being there for another one in crisis," Sandra interjected.

I knew she was right. Russ hadn't a thing to complain about—even concerning William having put their trip to Europe on hold. Especially, since he footed the bill in their household. At the time, Russ wasn't working. But why would he, having a millionaire as a boyfriend? Plus, Russ was the one who zeroed-in on William and his money, fully aware he was having issues with his partner at the time.

"He left first thing this morning for the airport."

"Shit, he did?"

"Yes. And I don't think he's coming back to Atlanta," Sandra added.

"It must have been one hell of an argument."

"Just don't worry yourself. They'll work it out."

As supportive as Russ had been to me, I was certain he still held a grudge toward me concerning the trip—even though I asked William not to cancel their plans; but he wouldn't listen.

"William wants to take all of us out to dinner tonight… somewhere nice."

"Why don't you-guys go? I just want to be home with Dugan."

"He's not there."

"What do you mean?" I scoffed.

"Liz isn't bringing him until tomorrow morning."

"Then, we'll go get him. I want to see Dugan right now!" I demanded, surely sounding like a recalcitrant, unreasonable child.

"Randy. Please, you'll see him soon enough."

welcome home

Consternation reeled. Apprehension mounted concerning what might have to be relived—possibly recounted from the Fourth of July upon re-entering my home. After all, I obviously never intended to walk back into those premises again.

Heart palpitations tracked evoking sweat under my arms at the thought of tangled memories that might progressively wrap me tighter once the car crossed Ponce De Leon Avenue; then to Charles Allen Drive before turning right onto Seventh Street. At that, it would only take less than a minute for the car to turn into the driveway of the house—transferring me back to harsh reality. Even seeing it again would be chilling.

I wasn't ready to face anything—not past or present much less a marshaled jury of neighbors and friends. Concerns pressed of how their thoughts about me may have shifted and perhaps passed pious judgement weighed heavily. Would they view me as the crazy neighbor down the street?

I would be leaving the hospital with an enhanced résumé: the acquired stigma of the local artist and writer who had so violently—though unintended publicly attempted suicide and miraculously resurrected and returned in situ for all to behold. I felt as if the word suicide was burned into my forehead like the proverbial Scarlet Letter.

Then, there was the visible, dreadful scar—although bandaged, on my left arm to broadcast undeniable evidence to the community. For me, it was an unsightly reminder—to add more insult to the emotional injury I had somehow failed; a complete and utter washout. And I even feared my reflection in the mirror.

I closed my eyes. Tilted my head back on the seat's headrest the second Sandra turned the car onto Seventh Street; and kept them closed as I felt the car turn into the driveway. Sandra switched off the ignition. Surely, my distress was obvious. Moments passed. A thickness filled the car until Sandra kindly spoke.

"Randy… I can't imagine how hard this is… but you have to. You have to walk in your house."

"Let's sit here for… for a few. I need to pull myself together."

Although I was desperate to get out of Davy, I really hadn't thought much further than my exit.

"Sure… of course. As long as you need."

I leaned forward until my forehead was on the car's dashboard. Nausea whirled. The urge to vomit, as the reluctance remained as did the trepidation.

"We'll do this together. Okay? I'll be with you every step of the way," Sandra tried to reassure as her hand rubbed my back.

She closely guided me to the steps leading up to the front porch. I stopped.

"Wait."

I stood as I looked through the full-view glass front door into the house. The right section of the living room as did the large arch into the dining room came into view. My eyes followed the long hallway leading to the master bedroom. At that, I wanted to run but didn't. My body shook.

"Remember… you're not doing this alone."

I turned to look at Sandra before my eyes returned to the view on the other side of the glass.

"I think it would be easier if Dugan were waiting—looking out the glass as he always does."

"I know… he'll be soon enough."

Sandra inserted the key. I heard the lock turn. The door slightly creaked as she pushed it open. Sandra stepped over the threshold first. I followed. Oxygen escaped from my lungs; my eyes blurred.

I took a seat on the sofa. As in the car, my stomach kept stirring such, I was close to sprinting for the guest bathroom to set free the ululation that had remained in my gut to let it out in the toilet. But

I didn't. To do so, would mean I had to pass by the master bedroom—knowing it was where it all happened.

Sandra hired a cleaning crew to ensure the house sparkled for my return. The landscaper tidied up the front and backyards: made sure the boxwood shrubs and various bushes were trimmed; the flowerbeds, with cast iron plants, hydrangeas, and tall lazy grasses had been refreshed with white flowers; the large pots with evergreens on either side of the walkway at the sidewalk—as the ones leading from the driveway; those on the porch on either side of the front door; those in front of my art studio were attended to as well with more white flowers added to the existing moss and weeping Oxford ivy; the English ivy covering the brick on the left front side of the house that framed the double windows of my home-office were perfectly clipped as well.

Tall Phalaenopsis orchids grew from tree bark and moss, filled a large round industrial-like metal container positioned on the coffee table in the living room and another in the den. Freshly cut stately white tulips filled a sleek glass vase on the Finnley sideboard in the dining room.

Planning to work out was unrealistic as I'd earlier thought otherwise. Hyper-anxious to leave Davy, regardless of my emotional disposition, I'd mistakenly believed I could effortlessly pick up where I'd left off before July Fourth—robotically return to the gym. Training was rote to my existence. Innate, as if inborn.

The gym was a safe environment. A habitat controlled by a preset regiment of lifting and pushing. The fact I'd not taken off more than two days in years from working out, my internal schedule and need to retreat to the gym after having been deprived for half a month or thereabouts, was needed as if in withdrawal mode from a much-needed drug. Or was I capable with the shock of being back at the house like a maladjusted kid placed in a new foster home.

Unable to see Dugan was disappointing. However, unlike Davy's freezing water pumped in from the Arctic Ocean, I acquired the service of a long, hot shower—steering clear of the master bathroom by using the hallway's. I'd asked Sandra beforehand to keep its doors closed. And while showering, I didn't miss the aromatherapy of shit and piss of Davy's bathroom. A bath would have been better to sooth the Guinness World Record of hemorrhoids—but the thought of a bathtub filled with water freaked me out.

Within an hour, William arrived from the airport. He animatedly burst through the front door as if channeling Liberace from the other side; but without the fur coat and bejeweled bling—bringing takeout bags of food from Panera Bread. William took both Sandra and me in his arms; he squeezed us pale. I was happy to see him again since his last visit—tempted to ask about the situation with Russ but decided best not to.

William and Sandra set up the kitchen island to eat lunch. Afterward, as if a doting mother, he ordered me to lie down for a while. As with the master bathroom, I wasn't ready to enter my bedroom—rather using the guest room. William gave me one of his tranquilizers. My rolling mind fought its objective until the pill took hold. I'd awaken as the sun was setting and drawn to the living room by voices.

Friends and neighbors, Jacob and Gavin were sitting as they talked with William and Sis in the den. I was happy to see them as well. Not a word was spoken or questioned asked about what had transpired before and during my incarceration at Davy. At first, it was challenging to look them straight in the eyes—having been earlier told they'd taken it upon themselves to clean the tub and master bath of the blood on the following day after I was transported to the hospital. Although I'd wished my sister had hired a professional forensic cleanup company. And she likely would have if they hadn't so quickly interceded.

All the same, I was grateful to them. As I'd shared earlier, I never planned on anyone seeing my body much less any residuals from my act of suicide—but only the police and professionals. And I especially didn't want Sandra to witness any of it—as I'd prevented her from seeing the carnage in the living room of the house on Shirley Drive, by cleaning it up myself when we were teenagers.

I managed to maneuver through a packed, Midtown One Kitchen—humming in patrons' conversations. A light blue long sleeve shirt hid the bandage around my left arm; Sandra, William, and the boys, purposefully encircled me while we followed the hostess. Some stares followed from familiar faces—even some of them friends. But they kept their acknowledgments to themselves. My shoulders were inward; nervous perspiration collected on my forehead. William's hand remained on the back of my neck as I took what I perceived as a walk of shame.

"Keep your head up," he whispered.

William had remembered it was one of my favorite restaurants. But it was all-too-soon. Too much. Too overwhelming. I played along—not wishing to spoil the dinner for the others, when I would have rather been at the house than on display in a crowded restaurant. I knew it was William's attempt to propel me back into the world as quickly as possible—certainly doing so without wasting much time.

Integrated with the bustle of wait staff and general operations associated with such a popular eating establishment, where the draw was more to be seen than necessarily the menu—we were seated in the back near the outdoor patio. Surprisingly, while hors d'oeuvres were being shared, two friends approached the table. I felt awkward but stood up to welcome their embraces. They offered hellos and small talk without investigative lingering.

Sandra settled into my bedroom; William took the long contemporary lounge in the den. Under the sheets and comforter, holding a pillow tightly—I laid with ghosts throughout that first night in the guest bedroom.

The next morning, a mixture of jubilant voices awakened me from a vulnerable sleep of the nightmarish dream of waking up in that stiflingly toxic room at Davy.

Sandra's distinctive pitch of Southern, sweet as powdered sugar topped above them. William's seasoned laughs, undeniably his as Hal's baritone voice added to the orchestration. A fourth—definitely female was unfamiliar to my ears although I was certain it was midwestern. "He was the perfect house guest… you sure I can't have Dugan stay with me a bit longer?" the woman asked.

"Oh, I don't think Randy would allow that," Sandra responded, followed by a short laugh. "I know he's excited to see his boy."

My heart jumped at the sound of his name. I knew it was Dugan's homecoming as well.

Dugan's paws scampered up the hallway. I heard Sandra direct him to the guest room. Within seconds, he jumped on the bed wagging his tail while licking my face clean.

"Oh, there's my handsome boy."

I met Liz and thanked her for caring for my boy. I hugged her tightly as Dugan remained by my side. We all sat at the dining room table drinking coffee and conversing while the sun's rays striped the inside of the house with translucent yellow and white.

"Randy… Dugan was really an angel. A real pleasure."

Her lips modeled a kind-hearted smile. I couldn't help but wonder if it was offered due to what Sandra and my friends may have shared about my mental state. But at the moment, it was of no matter. I smiled back as I reached out my hand to squeeze hers.

Amid the pleasant conversation, Liz commented on two small artworks that hung under the contemporary sconces.

Without speaking, I got up and took them off the wall. Walked back to Liz and placed them on the table in front of her.

"I want you to have them. A gift for keeping Dugan safe."

"Are you sure?" she asked as excitement lit her face.

By far, Dugan was the best part of coming home; maybe even a reason to try to stay alive.

William insisted I give Dr. Griffin a try. After all he'd gone through and had done for me, I couldn't very well tell him, no. William even insisted that he drive me to the first appointment at her office on the Statler campus as if he was instead delivering me to KinderCare.

After a few sessions, the only insights discovered hadn't a thing to do with me but her—finding Griffin irredeemably irksome as I had the first day we met at Davy. She wore her arrogance and self-importance like a gold and emerald-encrusted crown. I may have been deeply troubled, but Dr. Griffin would never know my pain or how deep it ran. Never know its ferociousness—no matter how much education accumulated in her brain. How many case studies she read. How many despondent, soul-searching patients she counseled with forlorn and tragic stories.

She wasn't going to be my savior or I another one of her guinea pigs—to feed her ego. Sitting across from Griffin while looking at her face and listening to her clinical and judging voice—like fingernails raking across a chalkboard as on that last day locked up like a prisoner, was too much of a reminder. Too much of a souvenir of her association with Davy and Dr. Albridge—grisly reminders of that medieval institution's toxic purgatory were shackled to that damp and clammy microcosm of hopelessness and human misery.

Despite how annoying I found her, and more so those reminders of Davy she pushed to the forefront, I managed to endure several months looking at her face and listening to her screechy voice spurring mumbo jumbo until I couldn't look at her any more.

When I informed Griffin, I was ending our sessions, she didn't take the rejection well as if we'd been lovers. No doubt, it blistered her ego. I set out on a quest in search of a much better fit—one that might settle my tortured soul, and thus—keep me alive.

After ending my affair with Griffin, I found the acquisition of a new psychiatrist and therapist from the list of mind-benders given to me upon my exit from Davy to be a challenge. It was much like single's dating. Certainly, a costly endeavor being stuck with the bill and a hefty one at that—called a consultation fee as I found out with my first date. With a 20% tip, the bills ranged between one-hundred-fifty to three hundred. Note: psychiatrists and therapists don't come as two-for-one specials. So, that's times two. Then, there are the costs of medications—hors d'oeuvres aren't cheap either. And there's no going Dutch. At the cost, it would be better to hire a high class hooker.

It was an unsteady start. There were hits and misses before starting talking about moving in together—more like a three-way polyamorous relationship. Unlike real dates, where it's ill-advised to spill one's guts—or what you're willing to puddle on the floor, psychiatrist and therapist want the inside skinny on the neighborhood as if you're Mrs. Kravitz from the 1964 -1974 television series, Bewitched.

Over the next few years, I'd gone through quite a lot. Some old enough to be my son or daughter while others, my grandfather or grandmother—and those in-between on the age spectrum.

One psychiatrist seemed nothing more than a glorified street drug-pusher—undercover of the pretense of conducting a licensed medical practice. A therapist nodded off halfway through my second session. I still had to pay for the full hour. Another one, although still suffering emotionally, my sessions with her were much like sitting in the audience on comedy open mic night.

One memorable wild-eyed stunt-double, reminiscent of Grandmama's character in the 1964 ABC television series, The Addams Family clutching a grimy plush-toy giraffe—a lime sucker stuck in her hair. Quite a contradiction in her Ann Taylor suit.

Much of the time, I felt like an idiot. A lost cause. A babbling child. All the while, eyeing my wristwatch as I exposed those guts of my psyche in limited measure. Many of the psychiatrists and therapists were smartly dressed—sitting in their exquisitely furnished offices. Some cross-legged. Most seemingly in studied empathy—real or faked. They took copious academic and diagnostic notes casted with every stripe of anecdotal clinical psychoses known to man: from stolid rocking gazes; to repetitively babbling nonsense. It got to the point; I felt like the town drunk stumbling from one bar to the next.

four

all the margaritas you can drink

I wish I'd never gone out that mid-Sunday afternoon on May 17, 2009—although I had every right to…

Zocalo Mexican kitchen & Cantina is a popular Midtown restaurant on Tenth Street. Every Sunday afternoon—good weather permitting as the sun eases closer to the western horizon, its parking lot is transformed into one big extended happy hour for gay men getting in the last bit of weekend fun before Monday's rush-hour traffic back to reality. They congregate doing what gays do best in such a candy-store setting: cruising for their next hit of pure protein—and I don't mean the kind you scoop out of a container of whey from Costco.

Known for its margaritas with house-made sangria and other signature cocktails plus an assortment of South-of-the-Border beers among others—be forewarned: a pitcher of their margaritas may very well lead to another and another, and one hellfire of a hangover greeting the next morning. There is always the possibility of waking next to a new naked friend and your bed smelling of well-procured sex. The degree of new friendship all-weighed on how quickly or slowly you wish what-was-your-name's gathers their garments and such from the floor and exits your residence.

Predominantly gay men but all are welcome in the mix of the LGBT+ community. Of course, drag queens are a must dressed from glamour to the unexpected—leopard prints optional, they parade around in story-high heels defying the laws of gravity with surprising dexterity even with several vodka shots downed while cajoling among adoring fans. With unapologetic confidence, they show off their hairdos: many, Peg Bundy-like, teased and sculptured to high-heaven—a bit reminiscent of those from the 1960s, enough to make housewives of that decade proud. Others, to the polished and smooth quaffs of Madonna and Gwen Stefani look-alikes.

Dotted around in the multitude are the token straights, fag hags, and those on the down-low hanging back, as are the wannabees testing the waters. All fascinated by the pejorative—yet irresistible homosexual lifestyle. The absence of attendants on the street checking IDs makes for a perfect environment in favor of those under-twenty-one—easy to get an adult to accommodate them with drinks until their eyes blur and see double. They provide—the archetype made by nature to lure our inherited desires of youth and beauty for reproduction; in other words, an endless supply of fresh meat for those who never lost the preferred taste of smooth flesh, young ass, and sweet dick. I guess it can be said, I eventually had made the transition from one of those pretty boys serving the needs of older men—to the reversal of roles. Perhaps, like them, finding it an avenue to reach back to my own dwindled youth.

Prior to that Sunday, the closest I'd gotten to Zocalo's gays-gone-wild was walking Dugan on our usual route through Piedmont Park to Twelfth Street. West, one block—a left down Juniper, passing Einstein's and Joe's with their patios filled with more revelers. Another left on Tenth Street passing Zocalo on the opposite side—before crossing Piedmont. Five more blocks back to Charles Allen Drive—and a right on Seventh Street ending at the house.

On that May afternoon, I decided to forgo the weekly Sunday walk to be one of those random gay men standing in the parking lot with a beer in one hand while gesturing with the other. Talking to friends and checking out the abundance of the cornucopia. It was high time to make a serious effort to get out in public again instead of limiting my exposure except to the gym, those walks with Dugan, the pharmacy, and grocery store.

At fifty-five I was still a good catch, or so I was told. But it was imperative to believe that and ostracize the reawakening of the destructive voice in my head preaching otherwise—as if it were a man of the cloth standing behind the pulpit. Before that dreadful Sunday, I'd already begun taking steps toward looking at the bigger picture. Bigger than the boundary of the property of my Midtown home. Bigger than Atlanta. Bigger than the South.

I felt it was safe to go. Safe because Christopher had called that morning—for money. No doubt, he'd spent the last penny from our joint checking account. Even though he was the one who walked out—I wasn't going to run to the bank and close it even if it was my money to begin with. It didn't feel right to do so. But I'd made it clear: once the balance hit zero—the Bank of Chumbley was permanently closed. As expected, Christopher tried to charm me—tried to lure my generosity back like a struggling fish on a line; but I'd stopped falling for that crap—at least when it came to money.

During that conversation, he shared that he had a ton of studying—most likely into the late hours of the night. Since that was the case, I was confident I could hit Zocalo without the displeasure of seeing his face. Otherwise, I wouldn't have chanced it.

I showered and shaved. Put on my best naturally-worn jeans that flattered my muscular thighs and ass as they also showed a bulge; at least enough to be noticed; and a fitted light blue T-shirt that did the same for my upper body and arms and made my gray-blue eyes stand out. It was important to highlight my best assets—necessary since I was single and gay and older.

From experience, two out of the top three plus-points for long-term viability for an older single gay man in the community to get some ass: money; a sizable dick; a decent, passable body. A handsome, head-turning face plays into the formula—but again, from experience, it's an add-on like a gift-with-purchase at Bergdorf Goodman's department store. I'm not quite sure where a good personality comes into play. However, someone who is pompous with a shitty one will work when it comes to a one-night-fuck.

I kissed Dugan before heading out for what I hoped would be some fun and socializing. Never would I have imagined that afternoon would become one of those: at the wrong place, at the wrong time, and more like a clusterfuck. Or would—walking into Zocalo would have ramifications like getting a flat tire on my way to my own funeral at H M Patterson & Son on Spring Street.

I'd decided to drive instead of footing it from the house. The black XJS maneuvered west up Seventh, slicing through Midtown toward the storied Peachtree Street. I parked on Juniper and walked north a few short blocks—turning right on Tenth. Zocalo was in sight from the intersection. To my surprise, there weren't many people in the parking lot as expected. "Perhaps, I'm early," I thought.

I passed a few guys as I made my way toward the ramp leading up into the open-air restaurant and bar. Once inside, Zocalo as the parking lot was close to empty as if they had a fire drill. To my shock, the first person I saw was the last one I'd expected to see or cared to—Christopher. At the sight of him, by all rights I should have turned around and walked back to my car but inexplicably didn't—because of what I saw as his calamity-in-the-making. "Jesus fucking Christ," my brain yelped.

I blinked to assimilate what I was witnessing: Christopher in proud wasted glory—unambiguously drunk, or high, or both and barely managing to prop himself upright. He was leaning against a column while surrounded by four horny guys—much to their and his pleasure, each intently occupied in various stages of groping Christopher's ass and junk through his jeans. By all accounts, a gangbang in the making. If it weren't for the column and the four guys furiously fondling him, Christopher would surely be passed out on the floor.

I was acquainted with the horny little bastards of Christopher's fan club. Particularly Bart, taking enjoyment with Christopher's bubbly ass—had full-blown AIDS. Thanks to the available drug cocktails, he looked fine except for a slight distended belly characteristic of the virus.

I'd heard Bart had intentionally infected others, not caring—including my friend, Trent. A short time back, I came home to find him in tears while sitting on the porch stairs. From the scenario Trent described, was precisely what was in play: Bart and his buddies circling in on a mark as they had Trent after slipping a roofie into Trent's drink; and took him home while in a semiconscious state and went to town inside Trent's ass.

Bart was one of those guys who felt the rest of the world should suffer along with him. Even though it's illegal to knowingly infect someone with HIV, it was near impossible to prove—especially, if it were a one-night-fuck out of many.

Witnessing Christopher in such a state reminded me of what he once shared after we became a couple: "If it weren't for you, Randy… I'd most likely have already been infected with HIV." His comment had stunned me, but I let it go without elaboration.

After ordering a beer and two big gulps, I purposefully approached the foreplay taking place. Immediately the guys, including Bart stepped back away from Christopher. At closer observation, what I believed was confirmed: he was not only drunk as the contents of the drink in his hand sloshed around in the glass—his dilated pupils were telling.

My concerns were several. Did Christopher freely take the drugs as were the rumors of him drugging made their way to my front door? And if that were the case, they had just been solidified that fateful Sunday at Zocalo—when I saw with my own eyes. At that thought, I felt a sense of responsibility thinking my money had possibly funded part of his habit. With that validation, I understood why he'd called that morning. Or had his drink been spiked as Trent's had as I'm sure many others with something? Either way, Christopher's life was at risk.

On the face of it, Christopher had become the person he'd once swore he never wanted to become: a platinum card-carrying member of the Mile High Fag Club—and I don't mean fucking in the confined space of a Delta flight toilet some 30,000 feet or more above sea level. But this Mile High Club's members were caught up in the toxic gay world of drugs and alcohol, and random anonymous sex. The future had arrived, and from what I was painfully seeing—Christoper was slipping fast. I knew I had to get him out of Zocalo and away from those vultures. I'd just rather prefer it wasn't me, but my caregiver role—kicked in anyway. Shit!

"Hey Christopher… thought you said… you'd be studying all night," I blurted.

This fan club stepped further back.

"Wha… what… the fu… fu… the fuck are you doing here?" Christopher slurred. "U… you following me?"

I repeated myself, "You told me you'd be studying all night." Then, added, "You're the last person I expected, or wanted to run into. And now that I have, you're obviously drunk… and on drugs."

"Wha… what… did you say!?!?" he angrily stammered, barely able to hold his head upright as his body continued to stumble to the degree, I fully expected him to fall to the floor at any moment.

I collectively looked at the guys before directing my gaze at Bart.

"What fucking vultures… you are," I allowed.

"Well, he's not your boyfriend anymore," Paul, one the foursome offered.

"Yeah. Thanks for clarifying that little factoid, Genius."

I took ownership of the few steps up to Bart and got into his face.

"I know. I fucking know," I stated.

"Know what?" Bart arrogantly questioned.

"Trent. I'm referring to Trent. Need I say more?"

Bart's eyes leered; the cocky expression on his face retreated. Bart didn't speak another word.

"If you think you and your buddies are going to infect Christopher… you're about to get a very rude awakening."

Paul opened his mouth. Then closed it as he looked over at their ringleader.

"I'll be right back. Keep your hands off him."

My stomach soured. Uneasiness ballooned. I wanted out of the situation. The sheer quirk of fate of running into him—in such a state of tripping out in la-la land was too disruptive to my sensibility.

I didn't know if it was a good thing or not concerning the state of affairs that I was at Zocalo. If it was good, then it was for his sake and definitely not mine. Regardless, an intervention was in order even though reason pulled me toward the door. My concern outweighed it. If I did leave, doing so could possibly have dire consequences on Christopher's tomorrows. I decided to look for Jax—the guy Christopher had cheated with and left me for.

I'd heard he was druggy, and popular in the gay scene. Short and muscular, with a face looking as if it had been pushed into a box of nails. We'd seen each other at the gym but never had any interchange. If Jax was in the establishment, it meant I could leave without any guilt. Hopeful of that prospect, I walked through the restaurant. One eye scanned for Jax while the other kept sight on Christopher and the predators. I soon ascertained; Nail Face wasn't there. Not even in the restroom.

I returned to the column supporting Christopher. The vultures still circled at a distance like he was their next meal—he was. They were just marinating him for the grill.

I knew the situation was too much for me to handle due to Christopher's obstinance. Or did I want to. I'd sensed misplaced anger in his alcohol-drug-induced voice. Under the circumstances, I thought it better to call someone.

I put the beer down on the closest table.

"I'm going to walk outside to make a phone call. Remember, I'll be keeping an eye on the four of you."

Since Zocalo was an open-air joint meant they would be in full view. No one uttered a syllable, except for Christopher.

"Who… who… the fu… fuck do you think you are?" he stuttered, in pops of flying saliva.

I attempted to reach Jay in hopes I could get him to pick up Christopher out of harm's way. The call to Jay went to voicemail. I left a message. "Who else can I call?" I thought. Nicky came to mind. I quickly scrolled to her number before remembering she was teaching a class at her studio.

I raised an eye. Christopher was still waddling-in-place like a dashboard bobblehead doll. The vultures had circled back in. My attention partly returned to the call list on the phone, brain-racking as to whom else to call as I scrolled the contacts. By the time I peered up again—Christopher, braced by his four amigos were in the parking lot bearing in the direction of Blake's.

I shook my head in disgust as I thought, "He's just not your problem anymore. Walk away. Walk back to the car and be done with the whole pathetic situation."

Although mentally worn and disappointed my outing had mangled into a disaster, I was somewhat relieved that I took my own advice. Christopher's fate was now out of my hands. "What will be, will be," I thought as I turned to head back to the car—but I didn't fast enough. I should have run like a 100m gold medal Olympian.

The screaming screech of tires, followed by the insistent blast of a car horn, stopped me in my tracks and spun me back around—only to see Christopher foundering in the middle of Tenth Street; apparently having broken away from his adoring fans. The offended car, inches from his drunken visage; the driver yelled, "You faggot!!!" Then, sped away.

the shit show

Having averted the flatting-by-car, Christopher continued to cross the street as if a year-old-baby learning to walk—minus the pacifier. My concern mounted at the realization his direction appeared to be the parking garage shared by Jason's Deli and Post Parkside Lofts just on the other side of Tenth. All the while endeavoring to multitask—shakily holding his cell to his ear.

"Seriously… surely he's not going to attempt to drive?" I suddenly questioned.

At that point, the situation was developing from worst to fuck-me-worst. Afraid for Christopher, I reflexively darted across Tenth. Quickly catching up a few feet behind him, I noticed Christopher's car four vehicles in.

"Hey… Christopher. What are you doing?" I called out from behind.

He chaotically lowered his cell while floundering around to face me. Christopher stumbled backward—then forward. As at Zocalo, he aggressively hissed and stuttered. In a sudden burst, he lunged in my direction, bulldozing me back with both hands—surprisingly hard for someone in his compromised condition. Christopher's show of violence stunned me. We'd never had an incident of such inimical physical contact. Intensified anger malformed his face—his eyes aflame. I became angered by such disrespect.

"Is this really happening, or did I wake up in the middle of a segment of the low-rent, trashy Jerry Springer Show?" I wondered. But it didn't stop there. He began swinging the phone in the air, taking dead-aim at my face. It hit my chin with some force. Christopher swung it again. In defense, I reached up to block it. It struck and broke in half against the palm of my hand before falling to the pavement and splintering into several pieces.

"Look what… you… you did to my fuc… fucking… phone!" the obstinate slurs continued.

He stumbled.

"How… how am I going to call any… anyone?"

I remember thinking how pathetic and pitiful he was. If I hadn't known Christopher intimately enough to care for him, he may as well have been some random tweaker I passed on the street. How I wished that had been true—just a faceless woeful soul.

I was pissed Christopher had pushed me and hit my face with his phone—angry about the whole situation. I was angry I'd found him in such a state. Angry at myself for even going out. Worse, I had no idea what to do aside from hoping Jay would return my call at any second.

Christopher continued to act-out like a spoiled little boy throwing a temper tantrum because his toys were taken away. Actually, more like an avatar of Chucky Lee Ray, the possessed serial killer doll from the animated "Chucky" horror movies—that Chucky.

Despite continued efforts to calm him, Christopher remained hostile. I well-knew booze and drugs can bring out the worst in a person; and they can't be reasoned with—many times showing their true self. And to my embarrassment, random people passed by while looking concerned—some walking their dogs, others gawking. Once again, I told myself to walk away. But how could I leave him in such a state, especially with his car in plain sight?

I decided to try Jay again. As I was about to select his number, relief rushed across the street—the off-duty police officer manning the door at Blake's.

"What's going on?"

"I'm glad to see you, officer."

I informed Christopher was my ex and briefly explained what had taken place. Chucky continued to sway—as he gaped at the officer with uncertainty.

"You can see the state he's in…" I belabored the obvious.

"Yeah. I see."

"I don't know… but I'm concerned he might attempt to drive. There's his car parked in the garage… right there," I pointed. Then, added, "He was headed in that direction when I tried to engage him."

A pause clutched the moment.

"Why don't you let me handle this," the officer directed.

"Yes. I think that's an excellent idea. Thank you… so much."

I was more than thankful the police officer had shown up. A huge sense of responsibility lifted. I could finally walk away without any regrets. Walk away knowing I'd done the right thing by Christopher as I would any friend. Walk away not having to worry if he was going to drive, assuming that was his intention—and possibly injuring or killing himself and God-only-knows who else. And after seeing him in such a state, I felt I could totally walk away and not look back. Still, it would be difficult to erase the image of Christopher—drunk and drugged-out. The image of him being so unashamedly man-fondled and groped in a bar from my mind as if I were tied to a chair and forced to watch a week of bad porn movies in some dark and damp, dingy basement.

Emotionally spent, I turned in the direction to deliver myself to the car—believing the drama was over as the late afternoon pushed toward dusk. But it wasn't over. Within steps away from the mayhem, another car screech to a loud stop. A voice yelled out, "Randy. Get a fucking life! People break up all the time."

I froze. Slowly looked over my shoulder to see Jax in his car stopped between where I was standing, and Christopher and the police officer.

"What the hell! Seriously?" I thought. And after all Christopher's shit having wasted and taxed my late afternoon. Then, this short little cockroach of a drug-pushing-street-punk, had the nerve to mouth-off at me. I wondered the root of it. I asked myself, "What could Christopher have possibly said about me to Jax to warrant such a snide remark?"

Instantly, my anger from before returned—if not in increased measure. It took hold of me. Filled with animosity toward this Jax-fuck—and still pissed Christopher had pushed me and then hit my face with his phone when I was only trying to make sure he was okay, I lost it. My anger mounted as I stood looking at the drug-pusher. Then, over at Christopher. Then, at the officer. I was an atomic bomb seconds from annihilating all of Midtown. Without forethought the words spit from my mouth like bullets from a gun—one after the other. Bang. Bang. Bang.

"Well, I guess you need to ask Christopher about the warts," I yelled out.

A second of time after that last word—wards, shot out of my mouth, I wished I could have quickly sucked them back before they sliced the tepid air in their direction—before they could be heard. I knew how wrong it was to reveal a confidence, regardless of my anger or how it had been provoked. I'd promised Christopher I would never tell a soul. But it was done. The words were spoken regardless of the promise I'd made.

Weeks prior to that Sunday, Christopher and I were having coffee at Starbucks at Piedmont and Tenth. He seemed tensely wired. His eyes edgy. The fingers of his right hand annoyingly slid his Latte's back and forth on the table. He focused on the movement of the cup as he shared, he was afraid to tell Jax he was infected. He wanted my advice if he should—if he should tell him?

"Jax's a stand-up guy," Randy. I'm afraid if I tell... he won't like me anymore."

"Don't you think it's the right thing to do… to tell him? Wouldn't you want to know?"

"Jax's older… and like the doctor said, almost everyone has the virus. So, he most likely does."

"You're right. I'm sure that's true. But…"

"No… no! I'm not going to tell him. Have you told anyone? Are you going to tell?" Christopher asked, his paranoia ricocheting off the walls of the coffee shop—as if he was about to draw and quarter me at any second to make sure.

"It's a private matter. It's not my place to tell anyone."

"You've got to promise!" he demanded.

"I promise. But… you might regret not telling him one day."

"What makes you think that…?"

"Being deceitful is not a good way to start a relationship, Christopher."

"Fuck, Randy… I'm not going to," he scowled, then stormed out of the coffee shop.

I'd considered myself better than that—but I guess I wasn't. I looked at Christopher one last time, then turned and walked away.

stalker

Two days following the Zocalo fiasco—the front door was slighted by an overly-assertive knocking. I'd returned home approximately twenty minutes before from a two-hour workout. A tall and dark uniformed deputy sheriff stoutly stood on the other side of the full-view glass. My assumption interpreting his presence: the deputy was going door-to-door in light of a neighborhood crime or some such pedestrian reason—plausible due to a sudden tide of onslaught robberies in our tranquil little part of Midtown until I opened the door.

The starched officer sternly presented court papers instigated by Christopher, accusing me of the serious crime of STALKING. A false allegation. The only wrongdoing on my behalf was not taking heed of my first instinct to walk away when I saw him, regardless of his impaired state and what I knew of Brent. Regardless of being faced with a moral dilemma. Just fucking, regardless. I was wrong in showing him the kindness of looking after his well-being. Although not a crime—that of breaking his confidence because I was unable to control my anger. Those court pages would be more accurate if the bold lettering at the top had stated: PAYBACK. Payback for speaking the word: warts.

While informed by the deputy sheriff of my alleged crime, he appeared as if he was judging me—as if I were guilty in his eyes. By his constrained calculated movements, the deputy may as well have been an android, as he extended the papers over on a clipboard. My mind clouded. My eyes blinked to focus. The ink on them fuzzed as I briefly scanned the first page and flipped to the second. Following, I unintentionally composed a messy version of my signature with the pen the deputy had pulled from his left chest pocket and handed to me. Then, took back the clip board and his pen—separated my copies with one quick gesture before officially handing them over.

His eyes diverted from my face but not before brusquely looking me up and down a final time. The deputy turned smartly and headed to the walkway. I inched the door closed but remained in place watching his image shrink into the white vehicle with the Fulton County Sheriff's logo emblazed across the side of the vehicle. Within mere minutes, it backed out of the driveway and sped out of sight.

Within decomposing minutes, I made it to the doorframe of the bedroom—leaned against it while looking at Dugan asleep on the bed. In mentally assessing my new dilemma concerning Christopher—he could check off another item on his list of character flaws: an Academy Award-Winning deceptive and shrewd liar along with lack of morality and gross deficiency of judgement. I looked at the restraining order again while processing the quagmire of the past Sunday. Any concern I had for his well-being and future as I showed that day had thinned until it dissipated. Until it was extinct. Now, this was war.

It was evident, Jax had played a role in Christoper obtaining the restraining order. Weeks before the whole shit show, Christopher had told me Jax didn't want him to see me anymore—even as friends. And concerning any possible friendship between us, I was quite aware it would be defined by Christopher's own self-absorbed terms—namely, for an open-ended-ticket to stay aboard the gravy train he'd been riding for two years. But that train had derailed.

The night of that Sunday, I sent Christopher an email—a final attempt to pull him from the quicksand he was already waist-high in, marked again from what I witnessed, before it became his grave.

In that email, as well, I apologized for breaking my promise regarding the warts—expressing how shitty I felt. I copied his older sister, Linda, who I'd never met in person but only had communicated via email—hoping she would come to Christopher's rescue. I further expressed, I was done and believed it best we no longer have any kind of contact.

The millisecond after I hit the send key, it screamingly dawned that Linda most likely didn't know about her brother being infected with HPV—meaning, once again, I'd broken my promise but unintentionally. Now, I had told two people and likely anyone who was in earshot when I yelled it out several yards from Christopher, Jax, and the police officer. But I must interject: I seriously doubt Christoper would have remembered anything that transpired that Sunday due to how far he'd traveled down the Yellow Brick Road.

It had to have been Jax who told him I'd unleashed the word, "warts." And I can only imagine what went down between them later; but certain the HPV was a topic of discussion. Then, when Christopher read the email, he likely became more infuriated. I guess I was the "Wicked Witch of the East," who brought the house down. And once Christopher crawled out from under it—his paranoia spiked, likely believing I was going to broadcast it all over the Southeast using the News at 5 as a conduit. It goes without saying: that email failed its intended purpose.

If it hadn't been for Dugan, it's unlikely there wouldn't have been any correspondence with his sister. When Christopher visited his parents, just north of Atlanta, he often took Dugan under the pretense of dog sitting. After all, how could he explain acquiring the money to purchase a purebred English Bull Terrier?

During one of those visits, Dugan outed us because Linda had noticed both our names and phone numbers engraved on his ID tag. She'd discovered my oversight and inquisitively Googled my name—leading Linda to my art and writing websites and various other information written online—including, I was gay.

A meltdown followed due to the double whammy: discovering her younger brother was gay and cavorting with an older man. But I'd been uncomfortable that information would be discovered at some point. During her meltdown, Linda told Christopher she was disgusted by the discovery. Told him, I was deviant and a pervert: a dirty old man taking advantage of her innocent brother's youth—dragging him down a path of homosexuality and a life of sin. I was sure she wouldn't waste any time running to her parents and older brother. And if that were the case, his mother would surely come gunning as I'd expect the rest of his family to run right behind her.

I'd always worried, if something were to happen to Christopher while we were on vacation, I would have to be the one to make that dreaded phone call. As well, troubled as to what some of my friends might be thinking—even though a few were in older-younger relationships. The things they would never say to my face but think. Those concerns were more than enough for me to break things off—which I'd been close to doing several times.

Thankfully, Linda didn't make a beeline to her family— didn't out our relationship and as a result, I lived to see another day. Not after her younger brother explained he had pursued me. Told her how I'd changed his life for the better—how I supported his dreams and helped Christopher understand, being gay was only one part of him. However, I imagined he'd left out the part I was just a moneyed target. To both our relief, Linda agreed to keep Christopher's secret.

With such glowing accolades, Linda asked Christopher if she could contact me. I agreed. In a long electronic message, she showed remorse for so quickly jumping to conclusions and offered appreciation for all I was doing for her brother—that she supported our relationship and couldn't wait to meet me. I responded, letting Linda know how important her brother had become in my life—how I would always shelter him and put Christopher first. But that was my habit. Precisely the very thing I was doing on May 17, 2009.

None the less, I almost had to laugh while holding those damning papers in my hands—if it weren't so ludicrous. Laugh at being so libelously labeled a stalker by Christopher, with malice and aforethought. His mental machinations capable only of a spiteful, scheming, and spurned ex—devoid of any self-awareness or by point-of-fact—his self-interest.

When I think of this piss-poor excuse of a human, and his bogus restraining order, I'm reminded of how my mother, siblings, and I needed one from my father. Another, against Mr. Jones—his acts of molestation that I wrote about in my first book. The neighbor down the street, whose lawn I cut and trimmed the large hedge in the backyard on a regular basis as a kid, while he watched from window to window of his house. Another against the nameless man who stalked me for a time in the screen of night—while I was taking postgraduate classes at Mercer. Then, again, for protection from a terrorizing guy named Chip and his acts invoked on me akin to a rabid animal—taunting its prey with intimidation and threats among others, shortly after I'd moved to Atlanta.

I doubt Christopher knew what it was like to constantly look over his shoulder, as I had done a number of times when I was much younger due to the examples addressed above. Looked over his shoulder, from being watched and followed. I doubt Christopher knew the legitimate—heart-pounding fear of walking to his car and from his car to his apartment, wondering if one of those stalkers was going to come from around a corner or out of the bushes. Know the encapsulating fear—while feverishly jamming his key into a lock in order to get out of harm's way before it was too late.

And as I also touched on in my first book, I doubt Christopher knows the fear I experienced. The bloodcurdling terror executed by an older rich powerful mafia-connected New Yorker ex, who dispatched two goons to either force me back or kill me in retaliation for ending our relationship.

No, likely Christopher didn't have the first clue, not up to the period—he had those papers served. I'm perplexed how Christopher could even have taken out the order without anything to back it up but lies and a cute face; or possibly having traded favors by offering his ass to obtain it with the help of one of his professors—or unknowingly sucked into the collusion.

I can visualize his little performance after all this time and the truths I've learned. I had no criminal record. Only a traffic ticket for turning left at an intersection, prohibiting to do so between the hours of four and six o'clock where I'd mistakenly overlooked the sign.

At the time, for all intents and purposes, I'd basically been a pillar of the community for twenty-eight years, and as you know involved in many charities. But Christopher could march his bubbly ass to the Superior Court building to falsely accuse me, in the condition of what I would imagine was a whopper of a hung-over state.

Bottom line: if anyone were the stalker—it was Christopher. I was his mark from the get-go. But just in case he ever truly knows: the National Domestic Violence Hotline is 1-800-799-7233.

Contempt for Christopher rumbled in my brain the more it grappled with having been served with no basis or foundation of facts—along with reeling thoughts of the events at Zocalo. As I'd designed the plans for my father's death—contemplations of murdering the ungrateful little lying bitch took hold. But even if I did, there was no way I could get away scot-free. The best I could hope for was he'd OD before I had to face the music in court—as off-key as it were, as if the piano player was tone-deaf.

bang, bang

I was five and he was six
We rode on horses made of sticks.
He wore black and I wore white.
He would always win the fight.
Bang bang, he shot me down.
Bang bang, I hit the ground.
Bang bang, the awful sound.
Bang bang, my baby shot me down.

Sonny Bono

A consumed hour must have passed. Restive, I decided to call Allen. We had already talked the morning after the shit-show—at which time, I regurgitated the events of that awful Sunday. Every taxing detail. He knew Christopher; we'd spent quality time with Allen at his vacation home on Pensacola Beach—as Allen had visited us in Atlanta.

He answered right away. I told him what Christopher had done: filed criminal charges accusing me of stalking and engaging him in a physical confrontation.

"He what?"

"Had me bitched-slapped with a restraining order."

"Randy, this is serious. What a piece of shit… and after all you've done for him."

"What should I do? How do I handle this situation?"

He told me to hold on for a second. Allen had to switch to another call. Minutes advanced.

"I'm back. Sorry. I'm working on a murder case and had to take the call."

"It's okay."

"Randy… are you okay?"

"Frankly, more unsettled."

"Try not to worry… we'll nip this in the bud. This restraining order is bogus. Read me exactly what the order states."

I read what Christopher had written.

"Jeez. What a fucking psycho," Allen offered.

"Yeah, I never thought he'd go so low."

"Look. I know you care about him. You have a good heart."

"You mean, cared," I interrupted.

"Your ex will just keep shitting on people who care about him for the rest of his life. That's who he clearly is. He'll eventually get what's coming to him."

"You're likely right."

"Oh… trust me, I know I am. But don't let this new development throw you off track concerning California."

"Nope. I've already a new plan in the works… I'm not going to make the colossal mistake I did concerning staying in Atlanta for someone… not even an extra day," I confirmed.

"Good! You've taken care of enough people in your life. It's high time to put yourself first."

"I guess I have."

"And to think Christopher wants to be an attorney. The last thing the law profession needs… another dishonest lawyer. The very fact he would initiate and then willfully and vindictively lie, if exposed, could jeopardize things for him," Allen authoritatively stated. Then, added, "At the rate he's going, I hope he flunks out."

I refrained from saying anything.

"Listen, Randy… now, I need you to do four things. They're important. You can't let Christopher get away with this appalling crap!"

"Okay."

"Now write this down. You got a pen and paper?"

"Yes."

One: Allen instructed to enlist five professional people, he included, to write a letter attesting to my general character and conduct toward Christopher who'd known us as a couple.

Two: He specifically asked if Christopher had ever lost his temper with me and if so, had subsequently sent a card, note, or email to apologize. Anything you might have saved?

Interestingly, Christopher had done just that on more than one occasion. And I saved everything.

Three: Allen went on for me to gather other cards and emails where Christopher had wonderful, romantic, and effusively nice things to say about our relationship. I had those, too. All our emails were in a file in my laptop.

Four: The most critical was to identify and find the off-duty police officer at Blake's, who had intervened and ask him to write a report.

I wrote everything down. Verbatim. At the conclusion of the phone conversation—my marching orders in hand, I googled the number for Blake's before calling to inquire the name of the off-duty officer, and when he was working again. I was informed, Officer Lambert would be there the next evening.

Feeling depleted—a reboot was crucial. Not having the mental energy to accomplish what I'd planned for the balance of the day; I took Dugan out into the backyard. Once he had his fill of sniffing around in the bushes and chasing his tail, he sat beside me on the back stairs. Together, we lingered in the stillness offered by the afternoon—oblivious of the sustained placidity of time.

Once back inside, I took a sleeping pill and fell into bed. It was all too much to deal with. A drug-induced sleep—was the only way to stop my brain from plummeting any deeper into the void.

The next evening, I walked from the house to the popular neighborhood bar. The officer was sitting on a stool just outside the front door. He looked at me as I cleared my throat.

"Hello, Officer… do you remember me?" I questioned.

He scrutinized me for a few moments.

"Yes. I do," he answered to my relief.

"Do you remember what happened this past late Sunday afternoon?"

"Oh, yes… quite the scene. Your friend was really messed-up. I see it all the time working here on my off-hours."

"I hate to be of any trouble, but could I impose on you to write a police report?"

"Why do you need it?"

"My ex had me served with a restraining order yesterday," I explained. "In it… he stated, I stalked him across the street and engaged him in a physical confrontation."

"Really. Has anything like this happened before between the two of you?"

"No. I've never seen him drunk or in such a state until last Sunday."

"Yeah, it was clear he was more than drunk. I'm guessing he was on something… "

"I'm just glad you showed up when you did. I didn't know what to do."

"Funny thing is… one of the drag queens brought the situation to my attention. That's when I saw him push you."

"I just wanted out of there."

"It was obvious you were trying to help him… what's your name again?"

"It's Randy… well, James Chumbley."

The officer told me if Christopher's buddy hadn't shown up when he did, he was about to call in a report and have Christopher picked-up for public intoxication and disorderly conduct. And if he had drugs on him, that would be possession as well. Officer Lambert also shared that Christopher continued to be verbally combative after I began to walk away. Then, he dangled his handcuffs at him. Plus, since the officer had witnessed Christopher push me, he could have arrested him for that alone and I could have filed charges. I realized that's what I should have done—been the one to file charges.

"It was just a mess. I never wanted to get involved," I explained.

"It appears… he's got some serious issues. I'd say it was your ex's lucky day in that regard… that you were there."

"Well… it certainly wasn't mine."

The officer shook his head in agreement.

"Give me a minute to get my briefcase out of the truck."

"I really appreciate it, Officer Lambert."

It was parked a few yards away. I watched as he opened the passenger side door. Then, pulled out a briefcase. Set it on the hood. Pulled out his metal posse box. Lambert retrieved a blank form.

"Okay… you're James Chumbley. Did I remember that right?"

"Yes, correct."

"And your ex?"

"Christopher Wallis."

I watched as the officer began writing. Shortly, my attention was sidetracked as the door to Blake's pushed outward. A surge of music exited along with two drag Queens. One, in a long brunette wig and glittery eyeshadow, held the door open for three guys venturing into the bar.

"Hello, Sugars," she greeted with exaggeration.

As the door closed, for the most part, the music was sucked back in the bar but could still be heard. At that, the queens' heels scuffed over the sidewalk as she headed toward the corner. My focus returned to the officer as I waited for him to finish. In the meantime, a guy I recognized from the gym smiled as he entered the establishment. Another burst of music escaped into the mid-May evening.

I turned to look across the street at the scene of the shit show. Instantly thought, "How could I've been so stupid… so fucking stupid to stay in Atlanta for this lying piece of shit?"

Officer Lambert's voice directed my attention back to him. He walked toward me while separating the copies. Handed over one. I briefly scanned his somewhat scribbled writing, but still legible.

"Here's my card."

I looked back up at the officer. Took it.

"If this Christopher guy goes through with the stalking order, you'll get a notification in the mail about a week before… with the date and time to show up. Then, call me."

The officer further expressed, when I present the report to the judge, to give his card along with it.

"I'm often at the courthouse. Be happy to speak on your behalf… if indeed I'm there and can break away… or they can call me."

"Thank you, again… Officer Lambert. I can't thank you enough. Seriously."

"Sure. No problem. If your ex has a brain cell left, maybe he'll come to his senses."

I headed back to the house. A few blocks from the bar, it dawned on me that I should have asked the name of the drag queen. I would have liked to thank her. Possibly, given her a big kiss on the lips.

Even with the police report in hand, I was still in a state of disbelief and weighed down like a boat anchor with a monstrous wave of betrayal.

The summer night simmered on medium—listless and patchy,

chirped and rustled in disquiet. I retraced the city blocks back to the house. The anger and repugnance remained unchanged. They walked alongside as if to keep me company.

If I could have rewind to the events of that Sunday night, in light of the restraining order: I wished the car rushing down Tenth Street had run over Christopher—indeed had flattened him like a pancake and syruped him in a mangled-bloody mess. Then, there would have been nothing for me to feel guilty about. Christopher would have gotten what he deserved.

take one and call me in the morning

I remained convinced in his state of paranoia—Christopher was doing damage control. Sending me a message with the sham of a restraining order. He was afraid I would blow the lid off—not only about the warts, but what transpired that plagued night to everyone I could possibly tell—even to Pope Benedict XVI as if I had a direct line to the Vatican in Rome and His Eminence and I played poker every All Saints' Day.

But Christopher hadn't anything to fear except his seriously bad judgment, and some of the people he hung with. In retrospect, I had a sense there was more to the situation. And as I stated earlier: from personal life experience, true feelings are often exposed when someone is under the control of alcohol and-or drugs or both. That injurious evening, Christopher opened the cage he'd aways concealed from me.

Shortly after we'd become a sham of a couple, he revealed he was on a medication I was familiar with. When Christopher told me, I was already aware—having discovered the prescription bottle he'd apparently unintentionally left out on the bathroom counter.

At the time of his disclosure addressing the medication, Christopher expressed he was going off it—because he was feeling better and happier. I asked if he'd consulted with his doctor but was told he didn't feel it necessary. I knew otherwise. Going cold turkey on certain meds could have dangerous effects, as I had dealt with at times when my mother stopped taking some of her meds. But, at the time of Christopher's forthcoming, I said nothing concerning the matter.

Within the span of a week, I'd noticed varying changes in his demeanor but still said nothing. That is, until Christopher returned to the house on what should have been a peaceful day. He'd slammed the front door harder than it deserved. Hard enough, it could have shattered the glass. So hard, annoyance flashed through my mind for the glass and the careless and unnecessary treatment by Christopher—for his thoughtless and inconsiderate treatment of my property.

Sensing Christopher's return—Dugan raced from somewhere in the house until he was jumping up on him for the ecstatic dog-pleasure of human affection; but was dismissively pushed away.

Christopher looked at me without so much as a hello. Instead, grumbled as he headed down the hallway.

"Hey… come back here. What's your deal?" I called out.

Moments following, Christopher appeared in the doorway of the office. An ireful grimace stamped his face.

"What the hell do you mean?" he verbally splintered.

"You slamming the door… and the way you just treated Dugan. What's eating you?"

"I don't feel like talking," Christopher gibed.

Stunted, I garnered my thoughts. I'd never witnessed him act out to such a degree of disrespect—at least, not directed at me in a questionable manner.

Both displeased and concerned, I went to look for Christopher. He was on the lounge in the den with Dugan. I hovered just inside the doorway.

"Okay… spill it."

"Nothing. Nothing's the matter," he spat.

"I seriously doubt that."

"No. I told you… "

"Was it your brother and mother making crass gay jokes again… when you were with them today? I get that it's hard on you because they don't know… "

Christopher remained disconnected as did the scowl on his face.

Unaccepting of his answer and rude abruptness, I once more

brought up about him having gone cold-turkey on the medication—expressing I was certain doing so was the reason for his agitation that was becoming more prominent in his behavior.

"I think it's important to make an appointment with your doctor."

"God… lay off it."

"I only want you to be okay and happy."

"It's not necessary! Stop badgering."

I held my breath for a few moments to collect my thoughts as I watched him before I spoke.

"You need to rein in your attitude. I know what I'm talking about."

A red faced Christopher, sternly looked over at me.

"It's none of your goddamn business!" he propelled.

Suddenly, Christopher shoved Dugan off his lap onto the floor. Surely hurt and puzzled, he looked over at me. Obviously baffled by the abrupt mistreatment—something which Dugan was totally unaccustomed to. I became livid.

"Now… I'm the one getting pissed. It's one thing to be gratuitously mad at me… even if for no reason except stupidity, but I won't allow you to ever treat Dugan like you just did again. I've warned you once already."

Christopher didn't speak a word as he sat up—looking as though he was going to walk over and punch me in the face. I remained in the doorway.

"Look, Randy. Don't play shrink with me. I don't need your psychobabble… just because you had a fucked-up childhood, doesn't make you an authority on me or my family!"

Once again, I took a few moments to gather my thoughts. The hostility of Christopher's comments had more than shocked. They stung.

"Look, I refuse to argue. Or yell. Or be disrespected by anyone… certainly, not by you."

An edgy silence followed.

"I'm going to the bedroom and lie down," he announced.

In a huff, Christopher stomped out. Dugan followed. I didn't move an inch. Remained in place. Perplexed. Soon thereafter, I walked to the bedroom door. Christopher laid on his back; Dugan was snuggled next to him—so forgivingly. I wasn't.

I stood for what seemed like pricking moments as Christopher's eyes glared at the ceiling. His jaw, locked like a vise while defiantly ignored my presence as if I were his existential archenemy.

I intentionally cleared my throat. Christopher still averted my presence.

"I think you should head back to your place. Hang with your roommates."

That was enough to get Christopher's attention. He moved his head in my direction.

"No. I just want to stay here."

"I'm too upset. It's better you go. We can talk later," I dictated.

Christopher moved quickly off the bed. Swiftly and with effort, he stood in front of me. Our eyes aligned. I remained firm—serious about him leaving. The vexation earlier masking his face had allayed. Christopher pushed his lips on mine as his hands took hold of my waist; but I didn't kiss him back. I knew if I did—if I returned the kiss, it wouldn't feel the same. Not taste the same. The kiss would have been forced—feigned on my part. Instead, I stepped back. I wasn't going to change my mind. Still, he persisted. Tried again to kiss me. Surely in hopes I would soften my stance on the matter. I took Christopher's hands from my waist. Took another step back.

"Okay… okay. Randy, I'm sorry. I'm an ass. I shouldn't have reacted like I did," he apologized.

I held back a response.

"I get you're looking out for me."

For a moment, my eyes diverted to Dugan on the bed watching us. Then, I looked back at Christopher.

"Again… go back to your place. A night apart will be good for both of us."

"But I love you. You mean everything to me," Christopher expressed as his eyes watered.

I reframed from looking at him until we faced each other at the front door.

"Ran…"

"We'll talk later. Okay," I spoke with some insistence.

Christopher leaned in to attempt to kiss me again as he had in the bedroom. I looked away. Opened the door. Then, caught his eyes as Christopher threw the backpack he'd been carrying by his side over his left shoulder. A few seconds passed before he stepped over the threshold onto the porch.

Obviously, I knew Christoper was much younger; but I had no intentions of raising a child.

marta bus

As much as I'd hoped Christopher would be honest and upstanding, he proved incapable of doing the right thing. Incapable of growing a conscience. As Officer Lambert had informed—I received a notice in the mail of the impending court date. Apparently, there would be no cooling-off period for Christopher to develop any remorse for the appalling position he'd placed me in with this malicious prosecution. Serving as another dose of proof in my experience, he was a born liar—and clarification of his sociopathy.

Sometimes an individual has to lie. I should know—not necessarily white lies, but big-fat-dark ones and for good reason. Many kids and even adults of the LGBT+ community understandably lie if they're not ready to come out of the closet—if ever. Those who aren't, for whatever reason, hide their sexuality—their other status from those in our society harboring disdain. Anyone who isn't heterosexual, except the Allies to the community become targets for disownment, loss of job opportunities, housing, practicing their religious faith, bullying, violence, and even death.

Christopher presented himself as a heterosexual. It was easy for him on the outside. He looked the part. And I understood why he was hiding under his skin that he was gay. But there were times he would bald-face lie when it wasn't necessary. During our relationship, I didn't realize he was doing the same to me. I didn't know he was born with the talent.

While finishing his senior year of college, snuggled naked next to me in bed, he would call his mother on Sunday nights—informing, he'd made it back the hour and a half drive to school when he wasn't leaving until the next morning.

Christopher seemed as though he collected extreme pleasure by doing so—by lying to his mother. Perhaps, his deception was a form of payback for her vitriolic views on homosexuals. As he'd shared, his religious zealot and a harridan-of-a-mother, believed fags were going to Hell. And the only things they were good for in the meantime, were decorating and doing hair.

"I made it back," he seamlessly bullshitted, holding his cell in one hand while simultaneously groping my balls in the other.

On more than one occasion, I asked why he didn't tell her he was staying overnight with friends in Midtown.

"She thinks Midtown is full of fags."

"I know your mother is staunch on her religious views… but surely she knows that's not true."

"No… she believes that. She gets up in arms every time there's Gay Pride footage on the news with guys pumping and grinding in underwear on floats. You'll never see me do that and it's not because of her or anyone else. It's just not me."

"Well… maybe you should educate her. Your sister eventually accepted you when she found out you're gay."

Christopher sneered.

"My older brother feels the same. He calls us the rainbow people. He and my sister would always tell gay jokes. I bet Linda still does when I'm not around. She has referred to us as vulgar freaks more than once."

I told Christopher, chances were that once he came out to his mother or if she found out by other means, as Linda had—she'd have to choose between her religious views and her son. And in that event, his mother likely would choose him.

Christopher always canned my views on the topic. Certainly, when I attempted to convince him, it was better to not tell the whole truth than to tell an outright lie. It would be better in the long run: give the details of what his family could accept and leave out the rest.

That logic applied to vacations as well. Still, Christopher would concoct outrageous stories—lies of where he was going and with whom, as well as how he was getting there. That's where I finally put my foot down. I insisted Christopher had to at least tell his parents where he was going and how he was getting there—whether by car or plane. Eventually, I realized the only thing I shared with his mother: we were both clueless marks of his pathological fraudulence. And because of that, I give a lot of consideration to walking away.

Allen had insisted on driving over from Birmingham to go to court with me for moral support; but I told him not to—he'd done enough to help me. That I would be fine.

"I'm not concerned about the outcome… I'm worried in general how this fraudulent action has put you in a dark place."

"Trust me, I'll be okay. Thanks to you, I know exactly what to do. Please don't worry. Again… I'll be fine," I insisted, more to persuade myself rather than Allen.

"If… if, you're sure."

"Yes, I am."

"I love you, Randy. You know that. What Christopher's doing is horrendous… he needs to be properly and officially reprimanded for his actions. I want to let that little bitch see me in court with you," Allen offered.

"I just need to get this shitty mess over with."

Even though I would have liked a friendly face in court, specifically Allen's—I didn't want to add more to his case load. And I did. I did need this shit over with so I could find a way to reboot and somehow move forward. Allen was right. I'd been a heaping mess since everything went down at Zocalo. And being served those court papers had put the up in fucked-up. As a result, some of the darkness had returned—I felt it growing around me.

"Hey… maybe Christopher will get hit by a bus before court," Allen jested.

But there was nothing funny about this situation Christopher had invented. And at that point, I'd welcome the news he'd been flatten by a MARTA bus.

Allen yielded to my wishes, but my friend, Terrie, wouldn't take no for an answer.

"There's no way in Hell I'm going to let you go by yourself. You're one of the kindest… generous and good-hearted people I know," she persisted.

"Terrie, you know I appreciate your support and love you for it… but I'm fine. I'll be fine."

"No way, Randy! I'm coming with you. Got it? When and what time? I'll pick you up."

Terrie had always been strong-willed; a hard nut to crack—a good and loving friend to have on my side. Plus, someone who didn't take crap from anyone. I knew there was no changing her mind. Terrie gave me no choice in the matter—she would have shown up at the courthouse regardless. The truth was, I didn't want any of my friends to witness the embarrassment of being labeled a stalker—even though it was fiction.

the reckoning

Try as we might to postpone them, days of reckoning inevitably arrive…
Brandon Mull

My mind is ravaged by a perilous dream. It traps me somewhere between the past and the present—leaving me on the hem separating the darkness of night and the light of day, as an evil being waits by the bed. It displays voracious, razor-sharp teeth hungering for revenge—ready to attack.

The clock's alarm pulls me back to the present. As habit, my head turns to the dresser where it's positioned. It's 5:00 a.m. The day ahead weighs heavily. In about four hours, I must be in court.

Dugan stirs. He looks at me as he inches closer until his head lies on my neck. I urgently need medications. The anxiety I'm feeling rises like hot air; but I wait to get them from the bathroom. I wait, in order to apprize the provisional comforts Dugan offers in the daunting pubescent hours of the morning. I tell myself that I can wait a little longer. Dugan will be my medication until then.

In another few hours, Terrie will be using her key to unlock the front door—arrive early to support me for whatever comes of the day.

Terrie reached for my hand as we walked through the tall open doors of The Lady of Justice's courtroom—into a cacophony of human voices abounding disorder in the large chamber. Nameless faces of those there to accuse or be accused of some legal stipulation of intransigence—by commission or omission of violence. All blurred in black-and-white as if I'd just walked into the filming of a bad episode of Judge Judy—not that there are any good ones.

Regardless of Allen's reassurance, dread circles. Heat builds within the confines of my flesh as if devoured by a seething fever. My palms sweat. I feel claustrophobic within the congestion. Terrie squeezes my hand to show immediate encouragement that it all will work out. It is real now; the day has arrived. The pages served by the deputy sheriff weeks before—have come to life; and I have found myself surrounded by everything foreign, distant, and peculiar.

Terrie spotted Christopher toward the back of the chamber; I glanced from the corner of an eye. His sister and brother-in-law—ensconced on either side. They wedged him like self-righteous bookends. I remember thinking how Christopher had hit rock-bottom, and how his bookends—his only allies were victims as I was of his lies and deceitfulness. I'd expected to see Jax—but he was nowhere in sight.

They watched us as they sat like cardboard cutouts. All—mortal enemies. We were in court at Christopher's invitation to battle for the truth of what transpired that Sunday at Zocalo Mexican Kitchen and Cantina. Even with Terrie beside me, I felt alone as if I were a character in a Lifetime Movie—where the audience wrongly believed the good guy was the bad, and the bad one was the good. But that couldn't have been any further from the truth of the matter—as Terrie and I wove in and out as we looked to find seats somewhere in the middle of the mayhem.

A loud voice called the courtroom to order by a nondescript bailiff dressed in a well pressed deputy uniform. The intermix of chattered conversations and scuffling quieted to a low hum and eventually fell into silence—except for a few coughs and clearing of throats.

All eyes were directed onto a female judge as she entered from a side door—intimidating in a black robe. Blonde. Hair pulled smartly up-and-back in a twist. Perhaps, mid-forties to early fifties. She stepped up behind a massive, bull-nosed bench offering a bird's-eye view of the chamber. The judge sat; her posture straight with a staid look on her face.

The bailiff called the courtroom to order a second time under penalty of expulsion—before he introduced the honorable judge. Terrie and I sat, occasionally looking at each other as one case followed another—listening to the sorrows of broken relationships, stalking orders, and cases of domestic violence. A good hour had passed before the bailiff acutely called out: "Wallis vs. Chumbley."

Our turn—Christopher's and mine had finally come to engage

in battle. Standing before the judge and our backs to the spectators. Two knights-in-armor. The White Knight against the Black. If I were nothing else that late afternoon at Zocalo, I was his White Knight and he knew it—that is, if he could clearly remember after he sobered up despite me wrongly bringing up the warts. As amiss as I've admitted, those lies and dragging me into court were depraved. Now, instead of metaphoric metal, my armor was made of doubts, reservations, and uncertainties. However, Christopher's protective covering—nothing but those lies.

At the calling of our names, everything for me careered into slow motion. I remained seated next to Terrie for a few moments more—long enough to see Christopher walking toward the front in the gray, Hugo Boss suit I'd bought him. I have to say, it was a fine-looking suit which I'm sure he purposefully wore for the occasion. His sister and brother-in-law were dutifully in tow. They took the table to the left as directed by the bailiff.

Linda glared. Christopher's untruths had surely contaminated what she'd once believed about me after he'd told his sister I was a good guy and was guiding him through obstacles of him being gay. No doubt, Linda was unaware of her brother's stellar abilities at deception—and as result, they had filled her mind with falsehoods regardless of what I wrote in the email I'd copied to her, again sent subsequent the events at Zocalo. Likely, Christopher insisted the contents: finding him in a dangerous compromised condition was a ruse—fiction. In consequence, shut off the good light he'd once shined so brightly on me. Now that it had been extinguished, I was returned to the status of what Linda initially thought: predator.

Terrie grabbed my arm as I was about to stand. She leaned in. Whispered in my ear, "You got this, Randy. You got this."

In some ways, I did; but it didn't feel right—none of it. All I'd gotten was hurt. I stood. Paused a moment before stepping in the aisle. Looked back at Terrie. She smiled and then motioned me on like a mom dropping off her child on the first day of kindergarten.

Edgy, I took the seat at the defendant's table adjacent to Christopher and his bookends at the plaintiff's. I strongly resisted the temptation to look full-on in his direction.

The judge appeared to scrutinize the prey before her. Moved her head—controlled and methodically like an owl perched on a ledge.

I instinctively wondered what she thought about me during her examination: her assumptions of an older man in casual-Friday business attire against the accusations of one much younger in a suit and tie. Instantly, I felt as if at a party underdressed. Wishing I'd at least worn a long-sleeve shirt to cover my tattooed-muscled forearms. Two hundred thirty-five or so pounds—pushing forty-five depending on the day of the week and my calorie intake. I questioned if I looked too big and therefore, too aggressive and menacing to the judge—even though I was a teddy bear on the inside. But the judge had no way of weighing that.

In my defense, it was summer; and I didn't feel the need to wear a suit in such heated weather. Emphatically, not one causing profuse sweating initiated by the set of circumstances or a dress tie to choke my neck that Christopher was already trying to. It was a nice shirt all the same: a white Michael Bastian light-gray twill grid check. In addition: Banana Republic gray fitted flat fronts; a rectangle silver buckle black leather belt in case I needed to hang myself; black lace-up Cole Haan shoes. Regardless of my attire, I felt stripped down to nothing but raw flesh. Still, hopefully, at the very least I looked respectable. But in hindsight and despite the temperature, a suit would have been in order as one would for a funeral. The dearly departed: trust and honesty.

The judge called Christopher first. I surreptitiously watched as he stood from the table and empty-handed approached the lectern centered directly in front of the bench. I guess Christopher believed he could charm the judge without any documents, and she would believe every hollow word uttered from his mouth. But of course, he had nothing. There was nothing for him to present except that Hugo Boss suit. Christopher couldn't possibly have—apart from those lies. The audience remained as if gagged.

"Mr. Wallis, you have requested a twelve-month Petition For Stalking Temporary Protection Order against a Mr. Chumbley."

To all intents and purposes, I wasn't human or animal or vegetable or mineral, but an, "a."

"Yes, Your Honor, I have," he answered, directly and self- assuredly.

"Explain why you feel this order should be granted by the court?"

Now, was Christopher's audition for a starring role in his future legal career—that is, if he was going to have one. He went on to tell the judge we had been partners for two years. That, I had taken the breakup badly. Christopher reiterating the lie he had concocted on the petition—word-for-fucking-word.

"Are you in any way fearful for your safety," the judge asked.

"Yes, Your Honor."

At that answer—loudly stated and as it rang in my ears, I finally saw Christopher as soulless.

Hugo Boss had played the audition short and sweet—right out of central casting. That statement alone, "Yes, Your Honor," was like a direct hit by a bullet.

"Is there anything you wish to add?"

"No, Your Honor. Thank you."

Christopher had just perjured himself: the intentional act of swearing a false declaration to tell the truth, spoken or in writing. The latter—he did the day he filed the petition.

I felt the impulse to turn around. To look at Terrie, but afraid to see the crowd behind me—the possible looks I might see on their faces. I'd already felt the hundreds of eyes on me. Terrified of being judged by people who had never seen me before, much less didn't know anything about me.

Regardless of my innocence, I was certain they had already made up their minds—had found me guilty as I'd felt when the deputy sheriff served me weeks before. I managed to keep my head forward. The courtroom remained silent—surely on pins and needles like I was. Christopher stoically walked back to his seat—again bookend by his sister on his left and his brother-in-law on the right—closest to me.

The judge studied me for what seemed like long, tangled moments. Perhaps, she believed I was guilty as well. That, she believed the Hugo Boss suit was telling the truth.

"Mr. Chumbley, please approach the bench."

The bailiff motioned me forward. I stiffly remained seated for a moment or two—and although not surprised, I felt so betrayed by Christopher's testimony as brief as it was. I reached for the folder on the desk. Carefully took unhurried steps to the lectern while I intuitively felt every eye—including Christopher's, his sister's, and brother-in-law's zeroing in on me. I felt completely exposed as if nude. As if everyone could look totally through my clothing.

"Mr. Chumbley, can you explain why Mr. Wallis has requested this restraining order?" the judge asked, with a weathering eye.

I returned eye contact. Kept what self-possession I had remaining in my body. Cleared my throat to dislodge a thick phlegm of revulsion after listening to Christopher's unambiguous perjury. Proceeded to apologize to the judge for taking up the court's valuable time with this situation.

I told her it's true Christopher and I were in a relationship for two years. That, it was true I took the breakup hard. That, I was blindsided by it. That it was true I loved the Christopher I once knew, but I didn't know who he was anymore. I told her and the courtroom of people that I would never harm him in any way. That, Christopher knew that fact to be true having spent two years together. Then, I related—by stark contrast and as succinctly as possible, the facts of that fateful Sunday evening. That, due to his condition, I find it impossible that he could even remember what had transpired.

"I see, Mr. Chumbley."

"Your Honor, everything Christopher wrote in the petition and told you minutes ago is false."

I cleared my throat, again.

In closed accordion form, I shared some of the events that went down. That, I never expected to see him because Christopher had called the morning of that Sunday. At which time, he'd shared he would be studying throughout the night—the only reason I ventured out. Further sharing: how surprised I was that the parking lot of the open-air restaurant was near empty of people at the time of my arrival which was uncommon—that it was usually packed. How I wished I'd walked away once I caught sight of Christopher inside the establishment, that was until I noticed he was extremely drunk and possibly on drugs. That, again, I indeed wanted to leave, but in good conscience I felt I couldn't.

"Why is that Mr. Chumbley?"

Your Honor, if I had I would blame myself if Christopher had ended up being sexually taken advantage of by the guys eagerly groping him. And, if not for the post he was leaning against and the four guys—Christopher would have surely been on the floor.

I left out my concern of a possible gangbang—as I did, that he was in law school. But I did tell the judge, contrary to what he wrote on the petition, Christopher wasn't having dinner; but as I found out later it was a fundraiser: all the margaritas you can drink for five dollars.

I paused. It felt as if the weight of the entire courthouse was on my shoulders. The mental sensation grew heavier with each inhale of breath, as I again continued to feel the eyes of every person in the crowded courtroom. Sweat collected in my armpits and began to roll down the sides of my body.

"Continue, Mr. Chumbley."

As it was to me, I was sure my nervousness was obvious to her and everyone else. My voice may have cracked a time or two.

"We did exchange some words, but Christopher's were slurred and boorish… his eyes were red, and pupils dilated," I explained.

I continued to tell the judge more of what had transpired. What a big mess it was, and I really didn't know what to do. I told her I attempted to look for his boyfriend, but he wasn't present. Then, that I went outside to call a mutual friend only to leave a voicemail to call me back to see if he could pick Christopher up. Going on to expand, while on the phone, Christopher was leaving Zocalo with the guys as they steadied him.

"At that point, I decided there was nothing I could do… so, I decided to head back to my car…"

A spontaneous deep breath followed before proceeding.

"Your Honor, I turned away but within minutes I heard a car break to a sudden stop followed by a horn blasting. I looked back to see Christopher attempting to cross the street alone, stumbling toward a parking garage… while the driver of the car yelled at him. That's what prompted me to further offer my aid in the matter."

The judge looked over at Christopher, then asked if I had anything else to say. I told her: "Yes… I have several letters concerning my conduct with Christopher from friends who knew us as a couple."

The judge motioned to the bailiff to retrieve them.

"Do you have copies for Mr. Wallis?"

"Yes… yes, I do Your Honor."

The bailiff fetched a copy for the judge as I passed another to the threesome sitting at the plaintiff's table without turning my head. The brother-in-law aggressively took them as I felt the pages quickly slip from my grip. I heard a brief flutter. Glanced over my shoulder.

The stooge brother-in-law had fumbled the copies as they pin-wheeled haphazardly onto the floor.

I anxiously awaited as the judge leafed through her copies, nodding authoritatively while scanning them. Then, she looked up at me.

"Okay, Mr. Chumbley. Anything else?"

I told her I had several copies of emails from Christopher expressing how I took care of him and always put him first. I continued to tell her I also had emails from Christopher apologizing for outbursts of losing his temper. At that time, the judge cocked her head in interest.

"Really?" she questioned.

"Yes, that's correct."

Once again, the judge motioned the bailiff to get them.

"In your experiences, Mr. Chumbley… do you think Mr. Wallis has an uneven temper?"

"Yes. At times," I answered, directly and truthfully.

The bailiff motioned to me for another set of copies—without the judge asking him and presented them to her. I again handed a copy to my opponent's table next to me and as the other times, without looking.

The judge looked them over as she had the others. The courtroom remained silent.

"Anything else?" the judge inquired.

"Yes."

I took another deep breath.

"And… what would that be?"

I paused again. This time out of vacillation.

"I have a police report from the Atlanta police officer who witnessed and intervened in the incident. The officer was working off-duty at Blake's… the bar across the street. Contrary to Christopher's statement, the police were never called."

As I pulled the report from the folder, a low collective hum rolled from the peanut gallery of the courtroom. I fleetingly looked back at Terrie. She smiled.

Once again, I blindly handed a copy to Christopher's sentry. I then handed the original to the bailiff. Within seconds, the judge held it in both hands as she dissected it—clearly appearing to digest every word.

The assemblage seemed to be holding their breaths—not even a cough as if in a movie theater in anticipation if the pretty blonde girl was about to have her head removed with an axe wielded by her ex-boyfriend turned serial killer before the hero could arrive. Before her head went rolling across the floor as blood splattered the inside of the screen.

The judge looked up; I slightly turned toward Christopher. He dropped his chin into his chest. I was positive, at that moment—hearing my words and finding out I had a police report, Christopher realized he'd been caught. His string of lies were wrapping around his throat, impeding the flow of oxygen from entering his lungs.

"Your Honor, if I may… I have the officer's card," I added as I held it in the air.

I proceeded to tell the judge that Officer Lambert instructed me to give it to her. That, he was also in the courthouse today and to call him if she wishes. That, if he can break away, he will come to testify on my behalf.

The bailiff retrieved it as if on cue. There was another pause.

"That won't be necessary, Mr. Chumbley."

She looked over at Christopher. The pompous expression he'd been wearing was stripped from his face. The judge looked down at the report again—once more studying it for stretched moments. The courtroom held their suspended animation. She looked back up in the direction of Christopher—her eyes zero in on him like a rifle's scope. Then, she searingly spoke.

"So, Mr. Wallis, why did you write on the petition the police were called? This police report in my hand states otherwise. Either you were too drunk to remember, or you lied. Which is it?"

He said nothing.

"Mr. Wallis, would you answer my question? Were the police called… as you wrote on the petition?"

Christopher cleared his throat, surely to dislodge the stuck crow. But again, he didn't answer her.

The judge waited. Another pause. Then, she spoke again.

"Well, perhaps you can answer this question. Tell me what we're doing here today?"

I looked over at him again. Christopher remained silent—his

head still down not even looking at her. His sister and brother-in-law dropped their supercilious visages—stunned like two deer caught in headlights. Then, the judge spoke sternly to Christopher. Her eyes widened with what I perceived as annoyance.

"It appears to me, Mr. Wallis, that Mr. Chumbley was doing what he has always done for you… look out for your well-being. And the officer is willing to speak on his behalf."

Still, Christopher said nothing.

"The police report speaks for itself. You were drunk and your car was in clear sight."

I took a deep breath; it appeared the tables had turned.

"I'm dismissing this case," she emphatically stated.

The judge pounded the gavel on the sound block while still looking at Christopher. The blow of it—and abruptness of the summary verdict startled me. If it were physically possible, my life force would have quite literally jumped out-of-my-flesh as its reverberation cut through the sudden reflex of oral discharge from the courtroom's audience.

The bailiff instructed us to wait in the hallway for the paperwork. Terrie met me partway as I made my way back to where we had been sitting. A huge smile beamed on her face as she reached out to offer a hug of congratulations.

"You're a rock star, Randy. You showed that ass," She whispered in my ear.

We made our way to the double doors leading out of the courtroom as the next case was called. A few people pushed their way through as we followed into chattering voices. Terrie and I took a seat on one of several benches in the wide and long hallway. We sat silently, only exchanging smiles while observing the people already waiting. Most huddled in small groups while others waited individually. Some hugged. There were a few long faces. Others smiled. Some laughter could be heard—an indication of a good outcome of their cases.

Terrie winked at me. She motioned with her head to look to the left. I caught sight of Christopher scowling in our direction. He then quickly turned away.

"Christopher doesn't look very happy," Terrie tittered.

"No… he doesn't."

"I guess there are a few missing teeth behind those pouting lips from the judge's verdict kicking him in the mouth," she tittered again.

"I would imagine so."

"Well, how do you feel?"

"I... I guess, pretty good. Just glad it's over."

"Do me a favor, Randy."

"What's that?"

"From now on... leave the charity cases for Goodwill."

Terrie and I maneuvered our way through a maze of corridors toward the exit. The thick humid Atlanta air greeted as did the heat. Now that it was over, I would have thought I'd be more than relieved that I'd been freed from lies—after all, it was a victory; but the heaviness of Christopher's betrayal still weighed. I just wanted to hide—to go home and hide from the world.

We walked toward the garage through the barrage of bustling people. Some jaywalking. Others, dodging cars in the street. I pulled my cell from the back pocket of my slacks and turned it on to call Allen.

"Hey... the judge dismissed the case."

"I knew any judge would. Now, we're going to sue."

"We are?"

"Like... yes! Christopher bold-faced lied! Not only on court papers but also to a sitting judge. He wrongly accused you. With the dismissal... and the police report and the officer's willingness to speak on your behalf, the cards are stacked in my favor."

Allen verbally spelled it out that, I had a good case to sue for disparagement. Further explaining: what Christopher had done, likely negatively affected my standing and reputation—personally and professionally. The latter, having adversely impacted my livelihood. Plus, there was the emotional distress I endured by the whole ordeal.

"But... but."

"No buts about it. He needs a good fucking-over. I'll get one of my associates in Atlanta to take the case."

Allen elaborated: Christopher failed to consider the consequences of being caught in a huge lie—if that were the case; but too arrogant to give it a second thought that it might backfire. And if I didn't have the police report, the judge very likely would have ruled otherwise. And regardless of the dismissal, some people would believe otherwise—believe I was a stalker.

"Can I think it over?"

"Sure. I just want you to be happy again. I want the old Randy back."

Terrie dropped me at the house. Straightaway, I took a clonazepam and a sleeping pill as a chaser. Emotionally exhausted, I'd faced enough truths for one day still yet to be processed: one of which, was the shocking truth that the Christopher I thought I knew was a sociopath void of human morality. He was no more than an empty vessel in that Hugo Boss suit.

My mind reeled. It was clearly a case of: "Sometimes, the person you'd take a bullet for ends up being the one behind the gun (Tupac)." But had I been spared? Had the bullet missed me? Was the worst of it over? I made a mental note to look up the term: pyrrhic victory.

FAMILY VIOLENCE

THE SUPERIOR COURT FOR THE COUNTY OF Fulton

STATE OF GEORGIA

FILED IN OFFICE
DEPUTY CLERK SUPERIOR COURT
FULTON COUNTY, GA

[redacted]]
]
Petitioner,] Civil Action File
v.]
] No. [redacted]
James Randall Chumbley]
]
Respondent.]

PETITION FOR STALKING TEMPORARY PROTECTIVE ORDER

The Petitioner, pursuant to O.C.G.A. § 16-5-94, hereby files this Petition for a Stalking Temporary Protective Order and in support shows the Court the following:

1. The Petitioner is a resident of Fulton County, Georgia and is over the age of 18 years of age or is an emancipated minor.

2. The Respondent is a resident of Atlanta Georgia, and may be served at 381 7th Street Fulton County, Georgia.

OR

2. Respondent is a resident of the State of ______________. Under O.C.G.A. §§ 19-13-2(b) and 16-5-94(6) jurisdiction and venue are proper with this Court because the stalking occurred in the State of Georgia in ____________ County and the Petitioner lives in ____________ County. Respondent is subject to the jurisdiction of this Court and may be served at __________________________.

3. On or about May 17, 2009, the Respondent has knowingly and willfully committed the following acts of stalking under O.C.G.A. §§ 16-5-90 et seq.: Showed up at a restaurant where the (P) was eating. He began to follow the (P) once he had left. About a block down the road the (R) pushed (P) against the wall to start a fight. The Police were called. and similar events may occur in the future. These acts had no legitimate purposes, happened at places other than the residence of the Respondent, were without the consent of the Petitioner, and placed Petitioner in reasonable fear for her/his own safety and/or the safety of her/his immediate family.

ATLANTA POLICE DEPARTMENT

CONTINUED STATEMENT OF Off. [redacted]

PAGE #

I was working an extra job at Slakers Bar at 227 Tenth St. when I was advised on a disturbance on the corner of Tenth and Myrtle St. [redacted] was drunk and attempting to get in his car and drive away.

His ex boyfriend James Chumbley was attempting to stop him from driving away.

While I was investigating James Chumbley stated they were breaking up.

[redacted] new boyfriend pulled up and [redacted] left with him.

At that time no one wanted to press charges.

I HAVE READ / HAVE HAD READ TO ME THE ABOVE STATEMENT AND IT IS TRUE TO THE BEST OF MY BELIEF AND KNOWLEDGE AND HAS BEEN GIVEN FREELY AND VOLUNTARILY BY ME.

SIGNATURE [redacted]

WITNESS:

WITNESS:

WITNESS:

TYPIST:

DATE: TIME:

VICTIM:

COMPLAINT#:

UCR CRIME#:

IN THE SUPERIOR COURT OF FULTON COUNTY
STATE OF GEORGIA

Petitioner,

vs.

Civil Action File No.

James Randell Chumbley,
Respondent.

DISMISSAL OF PETITION FOR A 12-MONTH PROTECTIVE ORDER

IT IS HEREBY ORDERED, ADJUDGED, and DECREED that the Petition for a Temporary Protective Order is dismissed:

[ ] on Petitioner's motion to dismiss in open court.

[ ] on Petitioner's failure to appear and proceed.

[X] on Petitioner's failure to prove the occurrence of stalking or domestic violence as set out in the Petition for Temporary Protective Order by a preponderance of the evidence.

[ ] due to lack of service on the Respondent within the 30 days' time limit of the Ex Parte Order.

[ ] OTHER:

This 9th day of June, 2009.

Magistrate/Pro Hac Vice, Sitting by Designation
in the Superior Court of Fulton County, Georgia

five

stuck in the middle

Delta flight 487 from Atlanta to LAX was ticketed for Thursday, June 18, 2009. Dugan and I were scheduled to depart at 10:33 a.m. for an arrival time of 7:55 Pacific Coast time. I'd decided to spend two weeks looking for a house in or around the Hollywood Hills. My birthday was four days away, and what a great gift to give myself.

Realtor, David Askew was recommended by a friend, Cliff—from my old modeling days who was picking me up at LAX. My first introduction to David was shortly after my mother's passing in late November of 2006, as I was making plans to move to California and before I'd met Christopher. I'd contacted David again, after I'd found a somewhat flirtatious chat between Christopher and a soccer guy on my computer—some nine months into our relationship in 2007.

That, and his periods of childish paroxysms—resulted in rethinking the agreement to stay longer in Atlanta. The fact that he was communicating with another guy online, had little to do with possibly amending my situation. Again, to be clear, it had more to do with those periodical temper tantrums. At the time, and to my regret, I foolishly gave in to Christopher's pleas to change my mind.

David had emailed several listings of interest. Once I'd returned to Atlanta, I expected to have a solid contract. No time would be wasted hiring movers to deliver my household belongings to what would be my new home out West. The cars would go by auto transport. One of the leasing companies I'd interviewed back in early 2007, would be in charge of renting out my Midtown home for a source of additional income. At least, that was the original plan before meeting Christopher.

I'd made reservations at The Charlie Hotel on Sweetzer in West Hollywood. It was once the residence of Charlie Chaplin—the silent film star who'd made his entrance into movies in the early 1910s. His home, with its vintage English-style cottages and gardens was later remodeled into a hotel. I'd made the arrangements in early May of 2009, before that fateful Sunday where I walked into a hellfire.

Cliff had insisted I stay with him and his partner at their home. But I needed to spend time alone with Dugan in the city I loved: to walk him along bustling Sunset, have lunches outside the little restaurants lining Santa Monica Boulevard with Dugan as he homed-in on my food, sit next to him on a hill in Griffith Park overlooking Downtown, run with Dugan on the beach while catching the surf between my toes, among other adventures.

However, first and foremost, there was one important weighty and exceedingly emotional thing I had to do—regardless of how heart-wrenching it would be even after a long absence: visit Bradley's grave. Perhaps, having Dugan by my side would offer some small degree of comfort. I had to tell Bradley I was coming home. Equally difficult, would be to drive by the house on Vasanta Way, where amazing moments were shared as a single entity and as a family.

Understanding the importance for me to stay at the hotel when David wasn't showing me houses, Cliff and he had insisted on hosting an informal dinner on the Sunday following my arrival for my birthday. Since I'd decisively committed to the move, they wanted to introduce some of their friends and invite the few I already knew.

Life seemed to have promise once again. I was cautiously optimistic concerning the rejuvenation of my plans—back on my chosen path to live out West. The only immediate uneasiness that growled and stirred the night before, was how I would feel stepping back out of the airport after many years—years that had been eaten and then digested.

The luggage was packed; I'd placed them near the front door the night before—along with my backpack filled with sundry things, including a Ziploc bag containing dog treats.

The alarm went off at 4:45 a.m. I was already half awake, having tossed and turned throughout an unexpected soul-rending night. Like a reflex, I hit the snooze prompt set for an extra 15 minutes.

"Just a few more minutes," I told myself. "Then I'll have plenty of time to get Dugan and I situated with our morning routines. Once finished, a car service will deliver us in a timely manner to the airport to board the Delta flight."

That 15 minutes became 15 more. 30 became 45. 45 rolled into an hour. "Just another 15," I kept telling myself as I repeatedly hit the snooze—followed by another. Then, another. And another. With each 15 minutes, emotional fatigue swelled as did the sudden onset of depression that had tossed and turned with me.

The promise and optimism I'd been feeling beforehand had slipped out of reach. I couldn't get out of bed in such a way like I'd been strapped to it—unable to break free, even if the house was on fire. Needless to say—that Delta flight departed without Dugan and me. I found myself stuck in the middle on the tightrope of life fighting not to lose balance.

the disclosure

Eventually, life becomes shadows. Breaths of expelled air—and in the end, we are left with empty lungs and a still heart…

That June day in court and those following, I'd arrived at one of my lowest points—after believing life had taken a turn for the better after it had met its nadir months before in early January of 2009, when I first attempted to end my life.

Gale-force nights shrieked into panicked mornings—the isolation of desperation sealed the bedroom. My mind spun. Scenarios rushed like passing trains—while I sought a ticket to a painless way in which to die.

In synopsis, from what was shared in "Alabama Snow," I'd awakened that early January morning; the sensation of death aggressively pounded like multiple drums—one over the other. Boom. Broom. Boom.

I pulled the Jag into the two-car garage used solely as an art studio. The plan—obvious: banking-on the carbon monoxide fumes from the dual exhaust to deliver a painless and peaceful death. While the world outside of that garage continued on with life, all I wanted was to end it.

Reviewing in-part of what I'd written, I do remember the waning of day—the waning of life as I do how the "long murky winter shadows stretched through the tall windows."

Any words treading of actions taken that morning in the depiction of loss were later learned, had in actuality—although believed at the time, weren't those of Christopher but of what was years afore; and that of which I'd felt abandoned by were from the past as well.

The over-ingestion of drugs and leaching of carbon monoxide had mixed a false reality—as the past collided with the present resulting in misaligned and obstructive thoughts of the present. And what tears shed that day were those that had already been—in another place and time.

As the carbon monoxide began to poison in unison with the pills—nausea and dizziness began to set-in; but within a short window from total collapse, surrounded by artworks thought never to be finished—even in that diminished state, I'd noticed a few of Dugan's toys lying about on the studio floor. The sudden sight of them triggered the realization, he was locked in his crate in the home office and would certainly become dehydrated and possibly starve to death—plausible: I wouldn't be found for days if not more; and the thought of him being alone—I somehow managed to will my way back to the house—stumbling and crawling.

I vaguely recall opening the crate before caught by the floor with Dugan in my arms. And as I wrote in "Alabama Snow," I retained a memory of the unmistakable scent of CHANEL N°5—the perfume my mother always wore. And whether imagined or not, I felt her hand touch my shoulder as I heard the tearful whisper of her voice, "My son is not going to kill himself today." I never told a soul until I wrote of it in that third book. Until then, Dugan had been the silent witness of what transpired that day.

one-way ticket

Days collapsed into weeks; clouds of mass proportion moved inward thundering as confused desolation hurled. The humidity suffocated the air as it thickened. Darkening clouds closed in. Rather than running from the storm—I ran toward it although my direction should have been the antithesis.

It didn't seem to matter—nothing did, which was quite the opposite of how I felt at the time I was days from that upcoming flight to Los Angeles and back to where I belonged. But unlike the storm, I was running away from what I'd always wanted to run back toward.

The terseness of my life soon became very apparent. It jarringly filled me like poison: its bitterness, its briefness, how fleeting it struck me at any given moment, and how abruptly temporary. The same was true concerning the hope once reclaimed. Within a matter of months, I'd seemed to grow so much older—equating seconds to years lived. My life didn't feel fuller, richer, or deeper. The same was true concerning the moments lived: not any more precious as they once had. I was slowly becoming the shadow—nothing more than a vapor of spent air as hope for the future had as well.

As perishable as they are: youth and the beauty of the flesh it sleeves, can only be forgiving for so long. I'd lost both and the ability to forgive—even unable to offer any measure of absolution to myself. At that abating period, my forgiving youth were years left behind. To comprehend in any degree, you would have to know the intimacies that have no real elucidation of words—those that live and die between each heartbeat. But it's impossible, because mine—as yours only beat in our individual chest and no other human's. Those intimacies of the mind and heart had become weightless as they were no longer harbored in my soul.

Once again, Death and its finality levered. As I'd once shared: in my latter years of college—I could see a future though uncharted but a future all the same; and felt a breeze of happiness as new as it was raw offering everything to live for despite the circumstances of the past. But once the breeze waned until gone, there were times I became caught within the faithless hours of night recklessly speeding my car along a deserted road—pushing harder on the gas pedal while counting the telephone poles and daring myself to crash into one of them as if another person had taken control of my mind and the wheel of the car.

The day of early January 2009 had circled back around. The notion of my demise surfaced; it ballooned in the days to follow. But unlike the uncontrollable knee-jerk despondency in January, when I felt as if I were being dragged into a Stygian-like cave, this one was different. As different as if I were planning a vacation to some far-off destination with a non-refundable, one-way ticket.

mexican food and gay men

I might as well have been a ghost—he walked right through me…

Daylight saving time offered a few extra hours to enjoy a Friday's summer evening before the streetlights began to flicker on like strikes of matchsticks—dispelling the onset of the graying of night in spotted areas along the streets of Atlanta.

Most Friday nights, a majority of the cities' cream of the crop gays—pun intended, would travel West the-some 2.4 miles on Peachtree Street from Midtown's own little Emerald City of the Land of OZ. Their destination: Uncle Julio's Mexican Restaurant located at 1860. The food billed and priced as moderately upscale.

It was as a weekly ritual, or more like an invasion of the popular and spacious Uncle Julio's Mexican Restaurant. Undoubtedly, it must have been the cheap bulk-bar-blended margaritas. Otherwise, I never understood how greasy Mexican food and homosexuals so effortlessly meshed. Plus, I would think that the refried beans would make for a gassy night. Regardless, the gay onslaught commandeering the usually mainstream straight eatery, forced some intolerant hets to flee to alternative venues.

Ever since the breakup with Christopher, I'd steered clear of the midtown happening places—apprehensive of running into him. It's not like I made it a habit to patronize them anyway. Certainly, not after the whole Zocalo, B-movie horror show and the mortification and added humiliation of being wrongfully accused a stalker—again, even though I was fully vindicated. And regardless of the judge throwing the shit at Christopher—I was the one wearing the stink around town due to the: Extra! Extra! Read All About It, on-going tabloid article authored by him regardless of the outcome. But as it's commonly known: tabloid mags are notorious for frequently using false and exaggerated info for the purpose of sensationalism. I imagine as Medusa at Davy; Christopher wanted his five minutes of fame.

Difficult to avoid the whistle of the gossip train—news was as I'd witnessed first-hand of his continued escapades of out drinking many nights—and more, high as a kite public sexual exhibition. Nothing really surprised me at that point, even though Christopher once vowed he never wanted to be a barfly or wear his homosexuality on his sleeve like a Boy Scout would a merit badge. By all accounts, Christopher had hit the ground running, wearing coordinating short-shorts and tight tank tops into Atlanta's gay universe—much like an untamed beast breaking loose at the legendary, Running of the Bulls at the festival of San Fermin, in Pamplona, Spain.

This particular Friday was July 3, 2009. Twenty-four days after coming to blows in the Superior Court of Fulton County. Marty had convinced me to go to dinner with him and some of his buddies to Uncle Julio's. More like twisted my arm when I would have rather stayed home watching a good movie with Dugan while enjoying what was left of the Reese's Peanut Butter Cups, Snicker Bars, and Ben and Jerry's Cherry Garcia—after my most recent late-night run to the twenty-four-hour CVS.

"You've got to get out of the house more… and not just to go to the gym," Marty scolded.

"Well, it's the only thing I'm interested in… "

"There's more to life than being a gym rat. Besides, you're big enough. What you need is to get some nice ass."

I rolled my eyes."

"Come on… Randy. I know Adrian will be there."

"Who?"

"That hot guy I've seen you flirting with."

"No… no. We're just new friends," I insisted.

"Well. It's obvious he likes you. He's just waiting for you to make the first move."

"Look. I will when I'm ready… but if I wanted a lecture, I'd go back to college."

"Randy. Please. Don't be such a goddamn pathetic homo! Just go to dinner with us."

"I don't want to take the chance of seeing Christopher there… I'd rather jump off a cliff. And… I don't feel like being in a crowd full of sex-crazed guys."

"I've never seen the little prick at Uncle Julio's. Not a single Friday night since I've been going there."

Then he added: don't let that scum define you because of what he tried to do. Don't give him the power. Think about what an amazing person you are; you've done so much for other people, and he'll never live up to the kind of person you are.

Marty badgered until I gave in. He'd managed to convince me he was right. The chances were in my favor Christopher wouldn't be there.

We sat at the bar waiting for our table, surrounded in the buzz of conversations and laughter. I was working on my third margarita. I usually stopped after one. I began feeling anxious; I wondered who in the crowd knew—knew about the restraining order and the court case. More importantly, if any of them knew I was innocent all along? I took one of the clonazepam I'd put in the zippered compartment of my wallet before leaving the house. Washed it down with the last swig in the glass. As the anxiety grew, I felt compelled to call a cab to return home. But before I could, the bartender placed another drink in front of me.

"This ones on the house," he said.

I raised the glass as a thank you and forced a convincing smile. He wouldn't have known it wasn't real—the smile, but the comped drink was appreciated all the same. I took a sip. Redirected my attention to Marty and his friends standing around me. Their voices fading in and out as I listened to them jabber on. I politely invented interest in the topic of conversation—mostly men and big dicks.

My ears started ringing from the noisy establishment. Perhaps, the alcohol, too. I reached for my wallet again. Took another pill. I'd already lost count of how many I'd taken since waking up that morning. Suddenly, I was startled by the vibrating and chasing LED lights of the wireless pager on the bar—like it had super-animated Mexican Jumping Beans inside. The indication our table was ready. I retrieved fifty bucks out of the wallet before zipping it shut. Caught the eye of the bartender before sliding the cash in his direction.

"Thanks. Keep the change."

The bartender smiled back. Nodded his head while offering a wink.

"Hey, Marty… Marty, our table's ready," I called out over the boisterous bar area.

I grabbed the pager. Stood. My gaze moved from Marty toward the large window; a line of cars waited at the valet station. A mismatch of guys exited while others entered the double doors of Uncle Julio's. Then, to my shocking surprise, with sporadic and jerky movements as if a bad break dancer, Christopher burst through the cortege—

repeatedly scratching his head as if infested with lice. His specter mentally seared my mind's eye in a virtual slow-motion screen-capture, like a smarmy Garbo trailer. A PTSD déjà vu moment.

"Jesus motherfucking Christ! Really! Fuck me!" I internally fumed.

I took the few paces toward Marty. Touched him on the shoulder. He was finishing a drink while still engaged in the colloquy. Marty slightly turned to look at me.

"We have time… just a few more minutes."

"Gotta leave… I'll cab-it home," I hastily spoke.

I sat the pager on the round table Marty was leaning on.

"Randy. I saw him, too," he acknowledged.

"You got to stand your ground."

I turned in the direction of the exit. Marty caught my arm in mid-step. Pulled me back.

"But… " he cut me off.

"No buts. You have as much a right to be here as he does."

"I know, but I think I'm going to be physically ill. The sight of him makes me want to vomit."

My knees went flaccid as discomfort filled my stomach like a pregnancy. The sight of Christopher was sickening.

Bitter and with urgency—I evacuated the bar area for the safety of the restroom as if Russia were bombarding the city. In haste, I bumped shoulders with him as if flesh hitting metal. Christopher's head turned. Our gaze crossed.

The dining area appeared to theatrically open wider and longer—emotional disorder pursued. A captive audience's beady eyes witnessed the dismay oozing out every pore of my body—like a surrealistic horror movie. I picked up the convulsive gesticulation of my pace. I was the protagonist helplessly trapped in a room without doors or windows. My eyes blurred as my human form heedlessly navigated the maze of occupied tables—furrowed in the direction of the restrooms at the far end of the restaurant.

Once inside, the restroom was surprisingly empty. I double-timed it to the furthest stall. Rushed the door open. Bent over seconds before vomit hurled from my mouth. Mechanically, my hand blindly reached for the toilet paper—spooling a long length from the dispenser. I wiped my lips and chin. Then, closed the lid before turning around to sit down. I bolted the door. At that—I felt safe as buried my face in my hands.

The outer door of the restroom suddenly opened—accompanied by cheerful voices echoing off the tile walls. I took in a deep breath. Kept quiet. I heard someone pee; a toilet flushed. More laughter followed with brief, giddy conversations. After all, it was Girls-Gone-Wild night-out at Uncle Julio's.

The door to the stall next to mine opened; compromising the armor that boxed me. The sound of a belt unbuckling followed. Then, a zipper. A pair of pants unmistakably dropped to the floor in a swoosh. Moments later, the rapid-fire of potent farts echoed—surely, the result of too many refried beans. Someone in the group chokingly laughed.

I moved my hands to cover my ears. Their voices quieted. Even still, the quipping dialogue was audible. A high-pitched voice clowned about hoping to get lucky later that night. Another lamented, he hadn't been laid in a month of Sundays. Another voice, "Girlfriend, guess you need to shake your money-maker." Another toilet flushed. I heard water running out the faucets, then the electric hand dryer blowing.

Finally, the outer door functioned opened and then closed—taking the animated chirpy voices back into the restaurant. My stall neighbor left soon afterward, rendering the restroom silent and momentarily still. At that moment, the world seemed to stop. I stood up haltingly, reaching out my hand. Slide the lock back open. My legs took me over to the sinks; the scuff of my shoes echoed off the tile. I stopped in front of the large frameless mirror. I looked at my reflection.

As I exited the restroom, I'd hoped Christopher would be nowhere to be seen once I walked back through the restaurant. But I doubted that would be the case even though anyone with an ounce of decency would have left the moment he saw me. But I wasn't dealing with such a person, rather, a narcissistic, cold-hearted, and calculating ass with zero accountability. Circumspectly, I made way back in the direction of the bar. The crowd of faces and bodies filling the restaurant melted together. Their voices, of varying pitches and tones mixed into one riotous cacophony, cascading into a roomful of patrons talking over one another.

I walked with one foot implanted before the other. The deeper I got into the restaurant; there appeared to be no sign of Christopher. I felt relief, hopeful he had indeed left. Midway, someone called out my name.

"Randy. Hey, we're over here."

My eyes caught Marty motioning. They had been seated while I'd taken refuge in the restroom. Reluctantly, I walked to the table. Stood over it, preferring to turn around and head for the door. Marty's hand reached up to grab my arm. He practically pulled me down into the seat.

"You're going to be okay," he whispered, leaning into me.

I took an edgy position in the chair. My mind rolled—cautiously hoping Christopher had left. But, within minutes, that wish would be short-lived. A familiar laugh met my ears over the amalgamation of the integration of voices. I turned in its direction.

Three tables over, I spotted Christopher with a few of his rowdy buds. Again, a better person would have left. Surely, Christopher knew I would be disturbed by his presence. He likely took pleasure in it—wanted to make me uncomfortable as payback for him being humiliated in court with the truth of what happened and tarnishing his golden-boy image. And, I was certain, Christopher would do all he could to keep the judge's verdict sealed inside the courtroom doors.

I returned my attention to Marty and his friends. But that would be short-lived as well, when I heard another familiar voice. I quickly looked back—an autonomic reflex. The situation surged like an electrical overload at the sight of one of my best friends, Jay, taking a seat next to Christopher.

"Could this night possibly get any worse?"

a knife in the back

"Fuck! That BASTARD!"

I felt the sensation of the steel blade of betrayal cut through me at the sight of one of my closest friends in Christopher's company; chumming like life-long friends since elementary school—laughing and carrying-on as if they didn't have a care in the world. Then, again, two and a half years before—I would have never fathomed Christopher to be a Judas.

Just five days before, I ran into Jay while walking Dugan in front of Jason's Deli. He called out as he ran across the street with his dog, Kipper in tow.

"You doing… okay?"

"I'm fine."

"You sure? I see something else all over your face."

"What? Did a pigeon shit on it without my knowing?" I coerced a joke.

"No, silly man. I see the sadness in your eyes," Jay addressed. "You can't hide anything from your buddy," he added.

"Okay, Mr. Sleuth. You got me."

"It's obvious you're still bothered… by that court shit. But the judge exonerated you. You showed that turd."

I cut Jay off.

"Don't care to rehash it."

"Okay. I get it."

As Dugan and Kipper obligatorily sniffed each other's butts—Jay asked about Los Angeles. I offered the same rote answer I'd given everyone else who had asked: I'm rescheduling.

"I owe you a belated birthday dinner," he insisted.

"It's nice of you… but not necessary, Jay."

"You're not getting off that easily. How about I invite Nicky and Terrie as well? Sound good?"

"It might be fun," I answered.

"Of course, it will. I'll call you tomorrow to set it up for later in the week."

I nodded.

During our conversation, I asked if he'd heard any rumors circling town. Hesitantly, Jay disclosed there were a few about me being a stalker. He reassured the truth would get out soon enough. But I knew it wouldn't unless I rented a billboard to plaster a giant-size copy of the police report and the court's dismissal. Jay never called as he'd promised. I never got the belated birthday dinner he'd promised.

I'd known Jay for several years before Christopher entered my life. We'd met at Club One in Savanna and instantly hit it off. A big, sociable Black man from Alabama: handsome; thick in stature; large, blinding white teeth. I'd once believed Jay had a heart of gold and truly loved me as a friend—which he'd conveyed many times.

Jay's employment often required him to travel to Atlanta. When he'd discovered his partner had been cheating—more of a serial cheater, Jay took it extremely hard. There were numerous phone calls where he shed tears into the phone's transmitter. I listened as a good friend would; I even offered Jay my home as an escape. Trusting him implicitly and without reservation, I gave Jay a key to my home.

Eventually, he transferred to Atlanta. At the time, Christopher and I had been together for eighteen—going on nineteen months. I introduced him to a number of my friends, including Nicky—they instantly clicked, like soul mates.

Fenced within the very moment I saw Jay sitting next to Christopher, my love for him as a friend instantly turned to contemptuous stone. Jay looked over at me. Our eyes locked. He quickly looked away like I was a stranger. He didn't have the courtesy—the graciousness to come over to speak. But why would he? Jay had clearly chosen sides. It's disconcerting how love can morph into hate so instantly—within a breath. In this case, at the turn of the head. I guess that's why they say: there's a very thin line between love and hate. Jay had more than stepped across that line—he had hurdled it like an Olympic gold medalist.

I tapped Marty on the leg. He looked at me. I motioned my head at their table. Marty surreptitiously glanced at Jay and Christopher as their laughter wafted in our direction. He looked back at me. The expression on Marty's face soured. He shook his head, telegraphing the wry countenance of what I construed as my shared disgust. No doubt, Marty saw my discomfort all over my face like someone had thrown a bucket-of-it at me.

I continued to sit at the table in disbelief. My head forward. My legs tense as a racehorse's ready to run once the gate to the starting stall opened. I picked up the glass of water in front of me. Took a big gulp in an effort to swallow the bad taste in my mouth from yet another gigantic betrayal. It was as if Jay had committed treason. My take: Jay was most likely trying to get his black dick into Christopher's white-boy ass. Maybe he had. After all, the word on the street: Christopher was hanging his butt into the air for all takers—his very butt-sweat mixed with the ejaculate of his many sexual encounters. Assuredly, drawing them in like flies to shit. How apropos.

The server interrupted my stream-of-consciousness—mental

development of contempt for Jay as she took our orders. I randomly selected an entrée without any intention of eating. I'd suddenly developed zero appetite. There was always the possibility that if I'd eaten anything, I would have surely projectile-vomited it up—Linda Blair style like her character from The Exorcist. By the time the food arrived, I'd forgotten what I'd ordered. A seamless amalgam of brown and beige on a bright white plate sat on the table in front of me.

"Dig in boys, you're going to need your energy tonight on the town," Marty jested, with a toast of his beer.

His friends laughed. The small talk continued. Once again, I pretended to be interested and engaging but not as successful as before. I stared at the monochromatic plate of food. Pushed a few items around with my fork. Their ongoing conversations merged with the sound of clanging utensils in combination with that of the surrounding tables—displeased my ear drums.

I bided time until I could exit the restaurant. Preferably, with some measure of decorum. Hoping the guys would finish up their meals and get to Blake's—or to whatever gay destination they would hit first in the lineup for Friday night fun and adventure. Exit before my mind became too fraught with dangerous thoughts of how I wanted to pick up the knife beside my plate and with calculated force, deeply plunge it into Jay's heart to return the gratuitous favor of his phony friendship. Then, bathe in his blood. Before I really did stab him in the heart. And in the process, before I took a few stabs at Christopher. Two murders for one—payback, as they had so symbolically done to me.

I'd plead not guilty due to Homicidal Mania and no remembrance of the murders. That, I must have blacked out. The headlines: Deranged Stalker Stabs Ex-Lover and Ex-Friend in a Bloodbath at Uncle Julio's Restaurant: Patrons Aghast As They Run For Their Lives. In that event, instead of a bogus stalking charge—I'd be facing the felony of capital double murder without possible reasonable doubt. Certainly, not with a roomful of eyewitnesses.

It was still fairly early in the evening when Marty and the guys dropped me off. Everyone was cautiously quiet as the car rolled into the driveway.

"You sure you don't wanna go out with us to Blake's?" Marty sincerely asked.

"I'm quite sure… but thanks. I've had enough fun for one night,"

I sarcastically offered. "But have some fun for me."

He leaned over for an affectionate hug. Once out of the passenger seat, a guy in the back hopped in to replace me. The car door shut. I offered a quick wave at the guys. Told them goodnight and happy hunting.

I barely functioned enough to insert the key into the lock of the front door—the galvanizing events of the night had left me mentally spent. The only thing to smile about was the sight of Dugan looking up at me through the glass.

The house was intensively absorbed within an eerie quiet—except for the sound of Dugan's paws on the wooden floors as he escorted me through the subdued stiffness to the lounge in the den; he immediately jumped on it.

I laid down—more like collapsed. Dugan scooted on his stomach to cuddle up beside me. My mind reeled in total disbelief and bewilderment of how incredibly hostile the evening had become, until I plummeted into a tormented sleep.

An hour must have traveled before I woke to Dugan licking my face—a cue that he needed to go outside. I sat up on the edge of the lounge holding my head with both hands as if it would fall off my shoulders if I didn't. Following slipping minutes, I got up. Dugan eagerly headed to the back door. It squeaked open. The milk-warm night air met me under a silvery moon as I watched Dugan run off. I waited.

Once he returned, we re-entered the cool air of the house. I plopped back down on the lounge—Dugan jumped on top of my torso before he lay down making himself comfortable as he affectionately stared with innocent black eyes.

"Who's my good boy?" I asked as I scratched his snout.

The moonlight intrepidly seeped through the windows, intermittently obscured by swiftly journeying clouds. Beams of silver came and went and then came again—pushing fitful glow-after-glow into the house. A broken pathway washed its way across my feet, continuing into the kitchen and meeting itself piercing the skylight with untold millions of converging rays of soft luminescence. Soon enough, it disappeared again in lingering moments. The moon's light continued to go and come as the drifting clouds dappled the sky.

As those clouds, my mind drifted as well until it dwindled back into indisposed sleep—offering shelter from the harshest of truths. That night had reminded me: hate can be a very valuable ally—perhaps, even a friend.

sugar and poison

Hush, little baby, drink your spoiled milk.
I'm fucking crazy, need my prescription filled.
Do you like my cookies?
They're made just for you.
A little bit of sugar, but lots of poison, too…

Milk and Cookies
Melanie Martinez
Jeremy Dussolliet
Rick Markow

The persistent ringtone of my cell saved me from the ending of a phantom-like dream. Caught within a muddled-minded state, I fumbled to retrieve the cell wedged in one of my jeans' pockets.

"Yeah… hello?"

"Hey, Randy. It's Kelly."

His call caught me between two adverse worlds.

What… what time is it?" I stammered.

"Almost nine. Am I disturbing you?"

"No… it's all good"

"Sounds like I woke you."

"It's okay."

"What you doing?"

"Not much. I'm not doing anything."

It took a few moments to realize it was still Friday night. Uncle Julio's—Friday night.

"I was thinking about coming in town… wondering if I could see you?"

My mind mentally lapsed for another moment as I sat up. Dugan remained undisturbed.

"Sure. Sure… I guess. Why not?" I rejoined, somewhat tentatively resuscitating myself.

"Okay! Great!" Kelly stated, with added zest. "What's the address again?"

"381 on Seventh Street. Just off Charles Allen Drive. Remember?"
"Got it. Be there in a few."

Once awakened, my head careened from the earlier events. As was common, blame inundated my illogical reasoning: it was my fault I'd run into Christopher by agreeing to go out for what I thought would be an enjoyable dinner. But instead, a dinner quickly gone bad—like unexpectedly ending the same at Zocalo.

Before Kelly's arrival I popped a lamotrigine and two more clonazepam—my intermittent magic pills, including the antidepressants to battle the internal brawling. Intermittent in the way a car's engine with a damaged starter relay doesn't always crank. Of course, a Viagra was necessary for Showtime at the Apollo—always a tough crowd to please. Again, I was quite aware I'd been taking considerably more than the prescribed quantities of drugs—way-more, much like candy from a children's Pez Dispenser. But in Kelly's case, he wasn't coming over to play cards—unless it was strip poker.

At our first meeting, his boyishly sweet face had pulled me in: Kelly's lean six-foot and well-toned swimmer's build, caramel eyes, long full brown hair, and an adorable heart-shaped birthmark the size of a Washington quarter just under the areola of his left, generously-sized nipple had solidified the deal.

He was a junior at Kennesaw State University, a half-hour's drive up I-75 North. An art major, so we'd at least had something in common. Quite talented, possessing accuracy in the execution of the human form—surmised from the captured images of drawings he'd shared from his iPhone.

After a period of making-out the night of our first hook up, Kelly became extremely shy when I began unsnapping his jeans. I soon discover the reason for his reticence. Kelly was born with a condition clinically referred to as microphallus or micropenis—an abnormally small penis.

While the size of Kelly's dick was unimportant to me, I sensed how it would be a difficult situation for him—especially in a gay world where size-matters tends to be the paradigm. Where the supremacy of size meters the quotient of desirability to a huge number of proverbial size-queens for a nice big and juicy projectile. For that, I was inherently dismissive of such hedonistic nonsense—vastly preferring quality over quantity in any value assessment. Rather preferring his pretty boy-next-door face and pleasing ass, and the distraction they offered.

Having stated that, however in full disclosure: among the manifold gay mixed bag of proclivities exists the little dick subculture where inordinately small penises are coveted and objectified. Something for everyone's taste and desires.

That first time—the more his jeans and underwear were removed paralleled the increasing gradation of coloring in Kelly's face to fire engine red. He began to stutter. Stammering apologetically for not being well-endowed. I recall telling Kelly it wasn't an issue for me. That, with a face like his no one should care one way or the other. Even though I knew many would. For that reason alone, in the rough and tumble gay world he would be subjected to disappointment and few second dates—even hurt by jokes not directly addressed to him concerning the size or lack thereof. That is, until Kelly crossed paths with the right man. The one who would appreciate all he had to offer—certainly, desire more than a body part. Know, what a prize Kelly was.

As the first time, I'd attempted to relish our night together. To find comfort in being with such a sweet and beautiful young man—just on the other side of twenty. To enjoy those exquisitely delectable looks. His soft voice. The feel of his desirable, tender body. And to my advantage, Kelly took equal pleasure in the feel of an older, muscled man on top of his smooth and yielding skin as his tight ass was pertinaciously pounded.

With all that had happened since, for the most part, everything for me was felt on the surface—depthless including sex. Kelly had quickly become a temporary fix as the others were who followed the breakup. The ones who knocked on my door over the last six months—all as momentary as the umbrageous, navigating clouds obscuring the mooned-sky. If it had been a different time—it may have been a contrasting story—certainly, concerning Kelly.

Now, I'd considered sex as a cardio workout session—nothing more. Nonetheless, the Viagra was a trooper and kept me going like the Energizer Bunny overriding any emotional conflicts to hinder my performance. The company usually only offered limited distraction.

If I were nothing else—as I'd always been, I was a serial-pleaser.

All that was needed was chasing-lights signage in large letters over my front door pulsating the night: CHUMBLEY'S PLACE—EVERYONE MUST LEAVE SATISFIED OR YOUR MONEY REFUNDED IF UNFULFILLED AFTER SERVICE IS RENDERED. GUARANTEED.

Kelly presented himself at the front door smelling of strawberries—as if he'd taken a bath with them floating in the water. Within minutes, our clothes were scattered on the floor and Kelly on his knees sucking my dick. He was sugary sweet as he was poison. I'd allowed Christopher to get all up in my head again, due to what had gone down at Uncle Julio's after seeing him and Jay so buddy-buddy. I wanted to fuck both out of my mind—hoping, I could accomplish that feat by using Kelly. And I needed the distraction offered by his pretty warm ass from those earlier night events that could have easily turned bloody.

I won't lie. I felt like a predator with such a young boy in my bed, even though of the legal age of consent; Kelly was scarcely on the other side of twenty—pushed-up and aligned with my skin, hardened-muscled from countless workouts, steroids, and the passing of time itself.

I was thirty-four at his entrance into the world. The fact Christopher was thirty-three, although only a year's difference, there had been nothing sweet about him. I never saw Christopher that way—never saw him as innocent, at least not in the way I did Kelly. With him in my arms I was reminded of a verse from a Mick Jagger and Dave Stewart song, "Old Habits Die Hard." The verse: "hard enough to feel the pain." It had been a night of both—pain and old habits.

"Jesus Christ. I'd learned nothing," I cursed myself, even though Kelly had searched me out as had Christopher.

He'd found me on a popular gay sex site—as many of the others had. I trolled them out of loneliness and feeling disconnected—unattached. That night was Kelly's third visit to my bed.

I released him from an encapsulating embrace. Threw Kelly backward on the bed. Hovered over him like a dog on all fours. He gaped his legs wide. Still shy about his condition, Kelly covered his genitals with both hands. I leaned back in a kneeling position as my eyes glazed over him. Kelly's body had never seen the inside of a gym.

Still, it was perfection in its natural state. Physical beauty is a gift, and Kelly was indeed blessed in that respect. I recall him sharing, the only exercise he liked was running three to four times a week covering five miles on each jog.

"You're beautiful… move your hands away. You don't need to be shy around me," I assured.

Kelly did as I'd insisted; a slight smile flattered his face. Leaning back forward, I kissed around his small erect penis leaking of precum before I began to lick it; but first, I slid my hands under him to take hold of his amazing ass cheeks—before I rubbed my face on his crotch. Before I moved my hands and slid them over his body—stopping long enough to play with and then suck his ample-sized nipples. That alone—sucking his nipples was enough to make me cum. But I didn't; I wanted to save it. I wanted him to feel unreservedly desired—wanted him to know he was the prize in the fullest of measure.

I climbed back on top of Kelly—took the missionary position as he wrapped his legs around my waist. We kissed—my eyes remained open so I could admire the beauty of his face. Watched how it altered as I slowly entered him.

After pounding Kelly's round ass—firmly and hard, I rolled off of him. Physically depleted of energy, I was ready to call it a night. That is, until he inched his alluring body until it was on top of me. Making mine, his bed.

Kelly lifted his head from my chest; his long hair brushed over my flesh as Kelly's brimmed lips sultrily kissed mine. They lingered generously—tasting nectarous. In the subdued belated hour, I found it difficult to take my sight off of Kelly's faultless face so close to him; his eyes glowing like shimmering gemstones as they captured what little light was in the room—wittingly ensnaring mine as did the youthful splendor of their gravity—near impossible to look away or break the kiss. "Better they be savored," I thought.

Then, without warning, his sweetened lips pulled away as his head returned to my chest.

"Thank you," Kelly whispered.

I didn't respond. Caught speechless. Wishing everything were different; and knowing I should be the one thanking him.

Breath-to-breath, Kelly again lifted his face to grant another saccharine kiss. Our eyes locked afresh. This time, for barely a few seconds before mine were able to look away—perhaps pusillanimously. Suddenly, I found it difficult to face the reality of the moment I'd found myself entangled—the very tick of time that had been staring back at me in the mirror image of Kelly's gaze burning my eyes—burning them through the years passed.

I leaned back against the headboard. Little time had passed before I heard the boy sinking into sleep. If I'd been a smoker, I imagined myself lighting up a cigarette and taking a drag while my gaze intensely returned to every inch of Kelly. Although my eyes watered from the irritation of the mounting hours—still, I couldn't pull them off him. So, innocent. So young. So unbelievably desirable.

A deep, hard twinge inflamed my chest. Abruptly, I felt swallowed-up in shame and guilt. My head exploded with voices all too familiar. I couldn't help but wonder how many more young men I would take to my bed—as older men had taken me in a different lifetime.

I had to wake Kelly. I couldn't let him spend the night. To do so would have made it all too personal—but it had already become so; and as much as I wanted to keep Kelly for myself—I knew I would be of no use to him—not in my state of mind. Still, to let him go felt as if I were casting Kelly out into the black of night and into a harsh world at that.

"Kelly… Kelly," I breathed.

I shook him gently. Kelly jerked.

"Hum?" he sleepily mumbled as he repositioned himself up against me like a drowsy cat and moved his head on my lap.

I kept watching Kelly—kept searching his innocence. He blinked his eyes open before closing them. Kelly moved his hand to my penis. Cupped it and my balls.

"Kelly," I spoke again.

He looked up at me. I quietly smiled. Again, a part of me couldn't help but to desire to have Kelly all to myself. To keep his innocence safe from the world. To take Kelly to California. To be happy with him. But I knew it was a fool's dream.

"Time to head home, Kiddo."

"Can't I stay? You don't want me to?"

"Of course, I do… but it's been a long day."

"We can just cuddle," he compromised.

I told Kelly that if he stayed, we would end up doing more than cuddling. That, I would be climbing on top of him throughout what remained of the yawning night. And as much as I would like that, I needed my sleep. That, there would be other times. At that, I piloted my hand over his face. Leaned down. Kissed him on his forehead.

Gradually, I slid from the bed. Within a breath's time—I looked over my shoulder at Kelly before grabbing the underwear from the floor. Still mesmerized, I watched him rub his eyes awake as he looked in my direction. In the undefinable way Kelly looked at me, I almost changed my mind to let him stay.

He stood. I walked toward Kelly and captured his nude body in my hands. Kissed him as I ran them up and down the smoothness of his skin.

"You fool," I damned myself. "He can be yours. Don't let him leave."

We walked within the nebulous stillness of the hallway toward the front door. The silvery night had remained as it seeped through the glass and washed over Kelly.

"You have no idea how beautiful you are in this light," I softly spoke.

"Me?

"Yes. Yes, you."

"Will I see you soon?" Kelly asked.

"What do you think?"

He smiled. Took that as a, "yes."

"Well, goodnight, Randy.

"Goodnight, Beautiful."

I stalled at the door—wanting to hug him again and taste Kelly's sweet lips before letting him leave. Sadly, I observed his youth walk over the porch and down the steps. His image was soon engulfed in halos of the moonlight.

Back in the bedroom, I took more pills. Always more pills. Dugan had already jumped up and taken a spot at the foot of the bed. He eyed my movements. The feeling of loneliness obfuscated the room—all too unpalatable from the onset of the confusion that lay siege to my mind.

I reached for the iPod on the bedside chest before lying down—before pulling the white comforter over my body much like a shield. After adjusting the earphones, I searched for Adam Lambert's version of Roland Orzabal's, "Mad World" written for Tears for Fears. Tears and fear were too-well-known by me having felt fear too much—having cried the same. I set the song on repeat.

And I find it kind of funny
I find it kind of sad
The dreams in which I'm dying
are the best I've ever had
I find it hard to tell you,
cause I find it hard to take
When people run in circles,
it's a very, very
Mad world

Yes, I personally did, "find it kind of funny" as I found "it kind of sad," that "the dreams in which I'm dying are the best I've ever had."

I patted my hand on the bed for Dugan to lie next to me. Motionless, I stared into the void of nothingness until the song entangled me into sleep. A few more threads unraveled. More, more—and more.

thunder before the storm

A low rumbling slowly advances from somewhere in the distance—it vacillates indiscriminately while scattering the pristine redolence of rain far and wide. Slight. Cool. Refreshing. You breathe. The scent is drawn through your nostrils and fills your lungs.

A sudden flash of lightning startles—you jump as it crackles and slices the low-lying thickset formation of clouds that begins canvassing a once clear-blue sky. It's a definite warning a storm is moving in. But you're fooled; you think there's more time—more time until you need to run.

A clap of thunder quakes. The sky swells. The air thickens. It becomes unstable. Its disposition—petulant. More thunder mounts. It roars. Another flash of lightning follows as wind whips and streams—persistent and forceful as the approaching storm builds in intervals.

Thrusts of electrified bolts flash—they're angry. The intervals become closer as the storm strenuously grows in vigor. Boisterous, ashen-colored amassing clouds roll in; they become grayer until blackened. They consume what little blue remains—take total possession until what few of the sun's rays that are left are gone as if they never were. It's an invasion.

The closer the time between flashes of lightning and the sound of thunder, the more expeditious its encroachment into your world. Now, you sense the need to run for cover—but it's too late. Within seconds, the storm has ripped through your being—throwing all the elements of your psyche far from all reality. Before totally aware: you're drenched within the torrent.

I would have thought spending time with Kelly would have closed the night on a good note; and the shock of seeing Jay with Christopher together at Uncle Julio's would become nothing more than a warning I could no longer be certain who my friends were—decipher between friend or foe. Certainly, the latter pertained to Jay. I wonder who would be next to turn on me; to take the wrong side. But that night, I had no idea the marked degree of tenebrosity that arrested my mind; the storm just over the horizon. No, that night wasn't over—not by a long shot.

The 15-watt bulb in the lamp on the dresser—spilled a silky-thin glow sheathing the room. Within minutes after lying down, my eyes opened unbidden. I lay there seemingly without purpose. Pillory thoughts teleported in and out of my head—hijacking my mind; my brain refused to consent to sleep regardless of the number of pills I'd ingested.

I picture abandoning the bed. Walking into the kitchen. Opening the fridge and retrieving a bottle of a Sauvignon Blanc. Downing the first glass before taking the bottle back to the bedroom. Still, my mind drifted. Thoughts continued to shift until they returned to the past—to some three years to that late November morning of 2006, of my beloved mother's funeral.

I stood in the long aisle leading from the stage to the open double doors exiting the chapel, inviting in a brilliant translucent empyrean-like light. Bright, magical rays of airy yellow-gold—speared through. Those big double doors—the final ones to walk through to gain my freedom. Two cages had been unlocked that day: my mother's and mine.

I pressed warm hands bidding farewell to the people leaving Mother's service as I felt many of their love for her. Minutes before, I'd internally shook behind the podium giving a CliffsNotes version of her so-called life. I remembered how fictitious it felt speaking to a full crowd of her dearest friends, neighbors, church members, some unfamiliar faces, and what was left of our small maladjusted family.

Behind me, an oversized flat screen flashed fifty photos of her—all animating her life. An anthology of my mother's story and the truth of it hidden behind the eyes in each image: of the innocence of a sweet little girl; of her youth beaming with dreams; of a blossoming beautiful young woman; a mother; a battered wife; a widow; years before and after, where mental afflictions dominated her existence; of maturing, unraveling years; a woman's life so unfulfilled and tortured; of the slow ignominious alcohol-and-drug-besotted downward end of her journey. Each picture leading to that day I had to say goodbye. The tears wept were not those grieving her death, but rather the life she rightfully deserved but never lived.

As I turned to walk away from my mother's grave—a promise was made: my feet would never again walk on Middle Georgia soil underlaid with red clay—much less, return to Warner Robins and certainly never stand in front of that house on Shirley Drive. And with that promise, I found added release in the knowledge I would no longer have to drive those some-109.1 miles back and forth between it and Atlanta as I had for years. And over them, even at the short distance of an hour and a half, I'd always drive my car faster north to Atlanta than going south to Warner Robins—to ensure breaking through the invisible barrier of the portal that divorces the two before it closed. Afraid if I delayed, I would be physically trapped as I was mentally. And toward the end of the drive, at a curve to the left on the Interstate, once passed, five miles or so ahead, I was able to breathe again at the sight of Atlanta's skyline.

And on that day, as the sun seemingly pushed years of darkness away, I never would have imagined: I would imprudently put off moving to California; foolishly become involved with someone half my age and as a result, live a lie; that the day would come I would spiral downward—as I'd watched my mother; attempt suicide more than once; become a prescription drug addict while using alcohol as a binder; wrongly accused of being a stalker; loose myself in the flood of a tempest. No, never would I have imagined steering miles off course—and away from the resolutions of that November day.

blackout

Two weeks before Uncle Julio's Friday night collision—William called in the mid-morning catching me still in bed. At quick assumption: another one of his check-ins. Verifying I was doing okay since the court case. William's calls had become more frequent—annoyingly-so, even though the best intentions of a good friend.

"Yes, yes… I'm good," I stated before he could ask.

"You must be in a mood," William pried.

I smirked.

"No. Just getting the day started."

"It's almost 10:00, Randy."

"Yes, I know. Needed to sleep-in today."

"You sure you're, okay?"

"Yes, Doctor. Just like I said the day before yesterday," I lied.

"Good. I'm glad to hear."

"You keep calling so much… Russ is going to think we're fucking."

"Well, you can ask him. He's standing next to me."

"Oh… did he hear?"

"Yes," Russ laughed. "William has the phone on speaker."

The interchange continued as William humorously expressed his partner would know better—know, we weren't doing the nasty because he was too old for me. I passed over the comment even though I knew it was meant as a joke. In the background, voices clamored as announcements of plane arrivals and departures. The distinct sound of a jet in take-off flight.

I asked William if they were flying off to Bali or some other exotic destination. Within a few more words, he informed they were at Hartsfield–Jackson. That, they were flying to his house in the Laguna Hills but decided to surprise me for the day and take a much later connecting flight.

"Get your butt out of bed and pick us up," William insisted.

"Oh… okay. I'll leave after I take a quick shower."

"Just put on a T-shirt and jeans, Randy."

"Okay… okay, I'll be there in thirty. Delta?"

"Yes… can't wait to see you. We'll be waiting at the curb."

As soon as we arrived back at my place, Russ grinned. They had both acted a bit odd during the drive back—despite the usual small-talk.

"Where're your bags?" he asked.

"What bags?"

"Your travel bags. You're coming with us."

Some surprised silence followed on my part as they both looked at me.

"I can't. What about Dugan? I can't leave him," I insisted, as he wagged his tail looking for some attention.

"Can't a friend watch him… what about calling, Mitch?"

"It's too last minute."

"Then… can't you kennel Dugan?" Russ asked.

"No. I never do. Dugan doesn't like other dogs. He's a people person."

I could tell William was thinking of another option.

"Hey… I'll call Delta. Surely, we can get him on the plane. He's a certified emotional support dog."

As kind-hearted as William's plan was, I just couldn't drop everything. Pack a bag and leave town with or without Dugan.

"Well, that would all be great, but I also have to finish an artwork for a designer this week," I lied.

But the real reason for rejecting the trip was because I just wasn't up to it. And I knew if I told William, he'd continue to worry about me.

With more discussion, I'd managed to convince them that I did want to go, but if the fictitious art was finished I would. They bought it. Instead of packing my bags—the day was spent shopping at Phipps Plaza and lunch at the Ritz Carlton next door. Later in the early evening, after dinner at Einstein's, I returned my surprise guests to the airport.

The tempest increasingly gained volatile potency as that night advanced—until I was sucked into a black hole. A blackout. Undeniably, due to the combination of the assortment and number of the pills I'd taken throughout that day and into the night, along with the consumption of alcohol—in a frantic search for some numbing delivery system to alleviate the emotional agony—as my mother had done for years.

As I was later voiced: that same night, I'd called Oliver to drive me to Jason's Deli. I understand from what I was told, I ordered a good portion of the menu and ate most of it. Thereafter—I reportedly made a dramatic spectacle; and if it wasn't for the fact that the manager on duty was a friend, was the only reason the police weren't involved. As the shameful epic saga continued, I'd slapped Oliver. The act pressed him to call Marty, who brought Hal and Mitch for reinforcements.

By their accounts, I'd increasingly became more unruly. Eventually, they forced me into Marty's car to return me back to the house. After some deliberation, it was decided to call for an ambulance.

Accordingly, by the EMT lottery, I was ignominiously offloaded in the ER of South-Central Atlanta Hospital. Its location on the far side of Ponce de Leon Avenue—a thoroughfare serving as the dividing line between the well-to-do and the dirt poor.

At the time, one of the derelict neighborhoods of Atlanta where you don't want to be after dark. An area squeezed-in with crime-ridden housing projects overrun with gangs, drugs, and prostitution. Many of its residents born within that section of Atlanta—never left the boundary lines the entirety of their lives unless in a casket.

While at the hospital—this ordeal having taken place on the night of July third, one week after William and Russ came to take me with them; Marty contacted William to spill the upshot of the debacle.

After the plot and characters of the novella was read to William, he called the ER doctor on staff at South-Central. William informed his counterpart of our friendship as he did of his concern I was in crisis; and that the staff should keep a close watch on me. William and Russ were returning to Miami the following day with another layover at Hartsfield-Jackson.

Layers of nebulous images drift in my mind—even still: a man lying on a gurney with an IV in his arm; enclosed in a tiny area surrounded by white cubicle curtains; the man pulls the IV from his arm; it and the small white strip of tape falls to the floor; he manages to exit the hospital without being ostensibly detected or physically detained; confused, he wonders into the nocturnal. Indeterminate time passes. A second layer is pulled: the man finds himself looking up at the storied, golden-domed Georgia State Capitol building.

It remains a quandary of how I managed to maneuver on foot for the better part of five or so miles in such a condition of disorientation. Directionless. Muddled. Spaced out. Concurrently wandering streets and pathways. Stumbling like a common drunk in the dankness of godless hours of a summer's night. Somehow managing—unsystematic as it were, by normal methodical movement of the human body from the hospital to Downtown Atlanta and backtracking to the Capital. Concurrently, lost between the contrasting shadows.

I vaguely remember attempting to appear sober—with only random streetlamps to cast the way; whichever way that was at the time. All the while—surely slurring to Marty on my cell phone. Bidding to direct him while Hal was at the wheel to my ever-moving location. Marty subbing as an animated GPS as the co-pilot and Hal the pilot of the expedition to find the runaway patient; and only clues to work with as if I the prize at the end of a scavenger hunt. Their single goal was to liberate me from that night of hell—and my state of discombobulation before being mugged or arrested for public intoxication. But what public, at that hour?

As told: I was rescued some hours later—around 3:30 a.m., rescued at the Folk-Art Park on the southwest corner of Ralph McGill Boulevard and Courtland Street. I'd presented myself with two badly sprained ankles and a broken flip-flop. Apparently, I insisted Marty and Hal to transport me home as if they were Uber drivers. And, by no means—call another ambulance.

I hailed to a massive, blinding headache dressed in the khaki shorts and T-shirt worn the night before; Dugan lied next to me—chewing on the surviving flip-flop. The hazardous misadventures had scrambled my brain into runny eggs such that I didn't first realized it was July 4, 2009.

From the bed—I spied an empty bottle of wine and one of SKYY vodka on the bedroom dresser. I'd obviously had downed both, even though I'd never been much of a drinker until 2009—certainly, understanding because of having alcoholic parents, I'd feared I might become one—plus, there was the fact that I was an extreme health-conscious individual. But for the sake of full disclosure, there was this one time when I was twenty-years old throwing up in the bushes after attending a party. Despite all, I'm sure I can partially thank Christopher's gift of his restraining order for my sudden leap into the bottle.

The tempest that begun mounting weeks before in my mind—the angry echoing sounds of thunder and the blinding bolts of lightning, that had both reached their merged apex as I wandered the streets of Downtown Atlanta, had ceased that next morning. All that remained was again, the hammering hangover; but the turmoil had quelled—unexpectedly, my surroundings eased to calm as the once dominating and overshadowing rolling darken clouds dissipated. And so, I knew that morning, the time had presented itself—to keep the calm and prevent the thundering and lightning from returning.

accounts payable

There are no new beginnings in life—only new directions to be taken on one's journey between birth and death…

I laid in what seemed the ruins of a life lived thousands of years before my birth, surrounded in the rubble of crumbled stone and debris. The demolition not caused by age and weathering of those years, but that of my own doing as I watched the flaking of that life's depiction as if illustrated on the ceiling above my head.

It's exacting to transmit in words how acute—how arduous the weight of disappointment or even the degree of self-loathing felt every morning for some time to follow once released from the hospital. I'd stopped looking directly in the glass, back-coated with silver and mounted in a contemporary frame above the bathroom vanity—afraid of what I might see standing in the backscatter of the reflection. If anyone were to judge me, none could any harsher than I did myself.

The shame I fed on was poison. I'd backpacked enough of it—much of which was never mine to carry. But this was a different mutation of a beast awakened from centuries of hibernation. Uglier. More treacherous. Mentally damaging if I wasn't already enough—an incompatible and aversive variety of self-abashment.

Chills and fever indicated the hemorrhoid hadn't improved despite ointments and hot salted baths. Concerned of septicemia—William had me examined by Dr. Thomas. I'd sensed my primary physician's attitude had altered toward me. Any attempts to hide it elucidated the obvious—evident in fixed eyes and a perfunctory voice. Not merely discontent with the events of July fourth, but perhaps frustration he was unable to help me from the beginning. I felt a stiffening line between physician and friend being drawn at the disbursement of the latter.

William's and Russ', some fourteen-year relationship remained strained for some time as a result of William's overly-attentive preoccupation with my well-being and willingness to do anything to ensure I'd be okay. Understandably, Russ had felt pushed into the background. Again, deduced by Sandra from some of her observations of their interactions while I was hospitalized. To her, it was clear that Russ was jealous and conceivably always had been of me and my tight friendship with William. As well, he'd remained pissed that William had canceled their month-long trip out of the country.

Hal and Mitch split not long after my parole. Not surprising, considering their relationship had already been bearing in that direction for some time—slowly morphing from lovers into housemates.

Hal wasted little time acquiring a replacement—finding himself in the throes of a new love. Two months later, a wedding date was highlighted on the calendar—as they had already registered at several exclusive boutiques, Bed Bath & Beyond, and department stores for preferred wedding gifts.

After several romantic overtures by Marty—he eventually grew tired of my subtle rejections and stopped trying. But he remained loyal. I was grateful to Marty for not running as I was for his continued support when many long-established friends turned their backs. Especially since our friendship was new—having begun a few months before the July event. I do have to give him credit for seeing something in me other than—crazy. If I were ever ready for another try at a relationship, it would be difficult with suicide survivor on my dating résumé.

I obviously didn't jump off the nearest tall building once released from Davy; but the ideations were always floating around somewhere in my mind—even playing hide and seek. I often believed, a deemed accident would be better. The idea, taking me back to the thoughts I had at times while in college of crashing my car into a telephone pole or even a tree. And as much as I wanted to after Davy—especially, at times wedged in periods when it felt impossible to keep breathing, I kept thinking of Sandra and what the second failed attempt had dragged her through: heartbreak, fear, worry, and the past. And as a result, I told myself it was too soon and even that I should give life a chance to win out over death. To try as hard as I could. To dig my fingers deeply into life while trying to keep out of Death's shadow.

In some inexplicable way and to a point, I was learning to exist with the sadness, loss, and emptiness—the crippling depression but that's not to say I didn't walk to the edge many times in the process; but you haven't gotten to the end of this story that you're reading—at least not yet.

There have been a number of stories addressing a percentage of people who have jumped off the Golden Gate Bridge—and no doubt it applies to many other bridges around the world, and even buildings as it does to other avenues and survived. The moment that they took the leap; they regretted they had and were grateful to be alive.

Phil Donahue, the creator and host of the long running (1967-1996), "The Phil Donahue Show," who was also a writer and film producer wrote: "Suicide is a permanent solution to a temporary problem." After some research, I couldn't find anything about him ever trying to commit suicide. And regardless of how much respect I had for Mr. Donahue, I wouldn't call him an expert on the subject nor would I anyone in the field of psychology and psychiatry unless they have tried to take their life. From where I'm standing—so to speak, there are so many things wrong with his blanket statement as there is only one that is right—depending on an individual's set of circumstances. The problem with blanket statements is that they can never apply to every human.

I'm grateful for those who have survived a suicide attempt and happy that they did and feel that way, but as I've shared, I wasn't. Personally, I wish we lived in a world where no one wants to or finds themselves in that position and doesn't try or succeed at meeting such an end. But I won't be shamed by anyone concerning my situation. And although it may be viewed as a contradiction in some respects—any shame I carry in regard to myself is a different matter altogether.

A number of acquaintances and some friendships nurtured over the years seemed to dwindle more as the weeks moved forward while I stood in place. Understandably, Russ kept some distance between us and my situation. However, William, Marty, Hal, and Mitch stayed close even though I knew they would eventually have to resign from their full-time babysitter positions. Sandra kept hers despite my insistence she stop worrying about me so much and get to living her life. But if it wasn't related to my art in the various galleries, with interior designers or a request for an art donation from a nonprofit, the phone rang less often until it was mostly telemarketers.

In dissection: a stalking order added to a graphic suicide attempt led people to credit—I'd gone crackers. One gave believable legitimacy to the other. Together, they made for one hell of a sensational story—stacked the cards up and against me like a new skyscraper being erected in Midtown. It confirmed that Christopher's lies were spreading. I wondered how much longer those would spin like filthy clothes in a washing machine.

The first few times I trained at Ansley Mall's LA Fitness were unnerving due to noticeable stares of jetting eyes along with rumbling whispers. In avoidance, Mitch worked out with me at the Buckhead's location—five miles north of Midtown. I didn't wish to be the freak in the freak show that had returned from the dead for the entertainment of others. As well, to evade the possible questions I wasn't ready to answer—that is, if anyone were to ask. And if they were, I was certain they wouldn't want to hear the truth. The compression bandage hiding the horrific and telling fresh scar on my left arm—wasn't really concealing anything. Possibly, bringing more attention.

It was as if I'd been physically released from one prison only to be locked up within the walls of another—while mentally remaining in both. The latter's walls were made of those stares and whispers. Existence became robotic—isolated as it was insulated. A shadowy wide line separated what was from what is until there was no delineation between the two. The periods of panic, fear, and depression came and went—each return staying longer than the one before as the days and nights elongated like pulling taffy.

I eventually returned to the Ansley's location. The rumors and accusations were going to continue regardless whichever gym I utilized.

I'd convinced myself that by hiding only added to the sensationalism and it was better to be seen. Although bothered by it all, that too wasn't going to change anything so I may as well stand in the center and let it all circle around me. There was no escaping it or even me. Besides, the gym had always been a lifeline—and if I ever needed one, I needed it after being released.

Working out was one of the few things I knew how to do well; and it did offer a temporary psychological outlet. I returned to cycling various combinations of anabolic steroids and force-feeding. They were going to see me coming anyway—better to give them something bigger to watch entering the doors. Still, it didn't make it any easier.

Hotel del Hell sent a whopper-of-a-bill for the accommodations and services rendered from Davy's accounts payable department. The total—almost enough to purchase an upper-floor condo in one of the expensive Midtown high rises with city views. Davy's great efforts to retain my presence as long as possible to milk my health insurance company had backfired. Blue Cross Blue Shield refused to pay a major portion due to Davy's breach of the terms of their agreed contract: failing their legal obligation to request permission "To Keep and Treat" since I survived the surgery but required further care.

The oversight and since I was the insured, gave me total indemnity from compensating the hospital. Releasing me from any possible financial burden. I equated it to refusing to pay a resort hotel bill while on vacation because of bedbugs, and roaches in the room service food while rats scampered about the hallways.

Still, Davy was relentlessly determined to get payment over the year that followed. Bills continued to overflow my mailbox—even receipt of one the day before the one-year anniversary. Several, necessitating stern legal letters from Allen threatening to set into motion the original lawsuit against the hospital that had obtained my release. Besides reiterating every infraction, including attempting to commit fraud and unlawful detention—some new charges were added for good measure. In other words: to back the fuck off! In conclusion: The Patient Advocate's office sent a pseudo apology letter—but worded such to show no responsibility on their part. Basically stating: we're sorry you had an unpleasant stay.

Shortly following the first bill—the kicker arrived in my mailbox:

Blue Cross Blue Shield dropped me like an over-baked hot potato. Surely, to save their shareholders' and CEO's billions of dollar profits. I was left out in the cold with a pre-existing medical condition: crazy. Plainly, my many years of paying premiums made no difference. For the next several, no company would touch me. Self-employed, I was on my own paying out of pocket for healthcare: doctor visits, psychiatrist, therapist, and medications. All adding up to a sizable dent in my wallet.

of what remains

A velvety breeze chaperoned the cooling air of October as it journeyed westward. Once green-filled trees of summer amassing Piedmont Park—a block down and across the street from Outwrite Books and Coffeehouse at the corner of Tenth and Piedmont, continued their transition into deeper shades of oranges, yellows, and reds while others stood almost barren. Aromas of the sleepy season had been heightened by a constant and steady rain that washed the morning hours into the afternoon—giving way to a shy sun peeking through the low-slung cloud cover. I saw that as a good sign—the sun even as shy as it was.

In the emergence of evening, I stood unsure outside the well-known bookstore tightly holding a worn copy of "Alabama Snow" in my right hand—tight enough that my fingers were almost numb. Within a fenced mind, I watched people walk in and out of Outwrite. Some offered hellos while others nodded in polite gesture. A few stopped to offer a greeting and a hug—both of similar warmth. Others looked before quickly redirecting their eyes.

Square blue Post-it Notes stuck out of some of the pages of the book—identifying which short excerpts I'd planned on sharing. Each one was highlighted in yellow after spending part of the day reading them aloud as if preparing for a role in a movie.

I felt emotionally torn as I idled at the busy corner—second guessing myself as I wondered if I'd made the right decision to agree to do the reading rescheduled from early August. But after days of probing thoughts, I'd decided I may as well show myself instead of continuing to hide while hoping for a positive outcome. I was nervous—more like, scared shitless. It had been almost three months and one week that had passed since being admitted to Davy.

The reading was designed as a fundraiser for the local LGBT+ youth organization, YouthPride and their suicide prevention program—Evolve! Regardless of what I may have thought about life at the time—perhaps guilt-driven among other emotions, I felt I owed something for having survived.

Thirty or so long and wide minutes later, with a pounding heart, I faced an audience of curious minds. I'm rarely nervous speaking to groups of people; but this was an exceedingly different situation. My nerves were deep-fried. My eyes broadly scanned the room—but not stopping long enough to make direct eye contact with anyone.

I glimpsed a few of Christopher's soccer teammates sitting in the back with some of his buddies from the gym—each one a link in the long chain that helped disperse the rumors that continued hopping around Midtown in one salacious version or another like fleas on scratching dogs in the Atlanta Humane Society on Howell Mill Road. I doubted that any of them had read the book but instead were there hoping to see a mess of a person. They weren't in attendance to support YouthPride—and certainly, not me.

Even though the events of Christoper's stalking accusation, the following court case—both taking place some five months later, including the Fourth of July suicide attempt that resulted in my forced confinement in Davy's mental ward—collectively took wide-screen focus over the context to "Alabama Snow."

The book had nothing to do with those events. It had already been released before they had taken place. I'd only written about the break up and the January frantic attempt. It goes without saying, I wish I hadn't included it or woven Christopher into the book. But it seemed like a good idea at the time—to add another layer since I was in a relationship. And because I wrote about it, I felt it was necessary to share how the relationship ended—Christopher having walked out at the time I was close to completion. But the reality is that I'd completely steered away from the intent of the book. From the first word I'd typed, it was meant to be a story about the relationship between a mother and son—not about a mother and son and some guy named Christopher.

I did attempt to extract him—but I found myself overwhelmed as I spent hours staring at the computer screen and unable to focus much of the time. It seemed impossible; I'd woven Christopher too tightly into the story. My mind became disjointed—everything around me seemed disjointed and impossible. I lost focus. At the time, I didn't realize just how disjointed I'd become.

Eventually, I had to come to a decision: either leave Christopher in or walk away from the book and let it die—at that point, it seemed toxic. But as overwhelmed as I felt, to do so—to walk away regardless of it being toxic, it seemed as if I was letting my mother die a second time.

Of course, since I left Christopher in, I should have only written how the relationship ended and left out my mental meltdown of a soap opera—certainly, not the drama of the suicide attempt. But by then, I don't believe I knew who I was, much less what day of the week I was standing in. Still, I'd opened that door due to including that first attempt in January, which is why I wanted the reading to be a fundraiser for YouthPride—hoping the organization would move to the forefront.

Unquestionably, after the court case was dismissed due to the evidence, only those in the courtroom on that day were aware of the verdict—whereas no one outside did. And because of that, Christopher kept it to himself and told his friends otherwise—presenting himself as the victor and me classified as a convicted stalker. It's not like I had a press conference on the steps of the Superior Courthouse to declare mine. His buddies were riding on those rumors that had become fact due to covering up the true outcome of the case.

If anyone in attendance was bold enough to ask a question relating to those rumors—which was a concern and as awkward as it would be, I'd somehow have to redirect the focus onto YouthPride and dismiss the elephant in the room. I wasn't doing the reading to defend myself or set the record straight concerning Christopher's embroidered stories—as if out of the tabloid, National Enquirer; the book wasn't titled: "Cock-And-Bull." And even if I wanted, most people are going to believe what they want to believe. If any of his friends or anyone else were hoping I would bring Christopher up, they'd be disappointed; I had no intentions of reading anything from the book about him.

Marty, Hal, Mitch, and Sandra sat together in the front row with William and Russ, who'd flown-in for the event. I was relieved to see Russ and glad they'd ironed things out. My eyes momentarily hovered on their supportive faces as I reservedly smiled. Hal shot a thumbs-up as Sandra winked and mouthed, "Love you." At the sight of them, I breathed a bit easier.

As the event was about to start, I felt like a hypocrite standing in front of everyone; although I was good at it—acting, the role: presenting myself as though I was okay when I clearly knew I wasn't. Another face—another story, similar to others who'd survived suicide and pressing prevention; while addressing that hundreds of millions around the world don't. Still, hypocrite or not, I knew it was important to reiterate the message that there are people who care. People reaching their hands into the darkness to pull others out.

The only part I wasn't acting was the one that I cared about others—even as I continued teetering on the tightrope while the mayhem taking place inside my head persisted. Hopefully, the professionals at YouthPride—their message, would reach anyone in the audience who might be in emotional crisis; then I would focus on the story of a mother and son.

The owner of Outwrite presented himself. He spoke about the night's event before introducing the director of YouthPride. After ensuing some well-delivered words, addressing the importance of the organization's presence in the community as a safe place for LGBT+ youth to gather—a haven of commonality and its educational significance on health and other aspects, he transitioned to the head of the Evolve! program.

Impassioned, she eloquently spoke of saving young lives—many discarded throwaways into a harsh world where they find themselves on the streets: from being kicked out of their homes by parents unaccepting of their sexual orientations, runaways from abuse and violence at home, bullying among other factors. And on the streets: easy targets for drug addiction, victims of more abuse and violence, sex trafficking, and even death. She ended with the staggering statistics of resulting suicides. By her profound dedication to saving young lives, the head of Evolve! had moved the audience, evident by the swell of applause.

At my introduction, I handed over a check as she generously offered an appreciated, plentiful hug before taking her seat. The room quieted. An occasional cough and the scoot of a chair over the floor was heard. I momentarily stiffened in impaired consciousness at the microphone. Adjusted it to my height, more so to afford some time. Time to gather thoughts. My eyes blear over the faces looking at me. Surely, they were wondering what was next. My mind drifted. I felt exposed. A short wave of panic rolled. I cleared the poignant trepidation caught in my throat.

Surrounded by those in attendance, again, I questioned if I should have waited longer. Still, I knew I couldn't just run back out the front door into the fall air. I had to do this, panicked or not. Do it with as much self-control garnered from within. Hopefully, with some grace.

As standard, I reintroduced myself as unnecessary as it may have seemed. I wholeheartedly thanked the representatives of YouthPride for the valuable services they offered to our young community as I did for their presence at the reading. Next, my appreciation was delivered to the bookstore owner and his staff.

I spoke briefly about the first suicide shared in "Alabama Snow." Because of the public knowledge, versions of it whether correct or not, at my resistance, I felt I should speak about being confined at Davy due to a second attempt and left it at that without going into any further details.

Otherwise, I stuck to the plan—transitioned my focus to the excerpts identified by the Posted-it Notes: a life-long relationship between a mother and her son—the child who stayed behind until she parted this earth and only then was the umbilical cord severed; the secrets we shared and those we kept from each other; the encapsulating ugliness and unfortunate events—as what little good that remained in spite of them; how collectively they affected us both mentally—at times, straining our bond and others that reconnected; how we were so much alike; of how I'd always tried to save her from my father—even after his death, her drinking, and mental afflictions but failed; how eventually I came to understand, I couldn't even save myself.

I'd purposefully selected more palatable selections to read as the assemblage came in and out of focus due to my eyes tearing up at times. At some point during the telling—surely psychological, the scar on my left arm began to burn. It felt like it was ripping open the more I read—but only I could see the gushing blood as it spilled onto the floor.

In spite of the humiliation, I felt because of leaving Christopher in and writing about the January suicide attempt, among other things, there was a silver lining found in my inbox some weeks following the reading: an email from a guy in Washington State. It was short—the email thanking me for writing "Alabama Snow;" and because I did and was so open, it saved his life. I responded to ask for the back story. He allotted his partner of some 14 years left him for a younger guy when he thought they were happy and shared a deep love. He'd no idea that his ex-partner was seeing someone else; and that the day before he left, he'd imparted his love from him.

The next day, the soon to be ex pulled the sun out of the sky when he boldly announced the relationship was over. The emailer felt abandoned, drowning in loss, and had lost sight of his life. But it was the cruelty of how his ex-partner left—the horrible words he spoke before he made his exit. Soon after, thoughts of suicide took over his mind.

As well, I inquired how he ran across "Alabama Snow." He conveyed he was looking around on amazon.com and found it. Something told him to order it. And once he finished reading, he didn't want to act on his suicidal ideations. His email made me pause—made me not completely regret dispensing the full scope of the story—at least, momentarily.

blood money

I kept a considerable amount of cash in key safes. Each one hidden under three of the four deep false bottoms of the built-in, wall-to-wall and floor-to-ceiling bookshelves in my home office of the Seventh Street house. Before its purchase, the money was secured in a large safety deposit box at SunTrust Bank. The fourth, hid my watch collection.

By comparison, a small amount of the money was mine whereas the majority—a considerable sum, had been couriered to me by associates of Mills Gunn. A multi-millionaire in New York City, who I met while on a trip to Acapulco, Mexico.

In my first book, I'd shared parts as other elements surrounding my association with Mills—but in exceedingly limited detail. And I didn't portray him in the blinding light as I came to know Mills for a number of reasons. Even though I used a fictitious name as I did the other people in the book—if he'd found out I'd written one and read it, it would have been obvious to Mills I was writing about him.

Either way, the fact remains if I'd exposed more, could have led to possible legal consequences—and more so, repercussions outside of the law—even face possible death. After many years, I'd hoped any acknowledgement of me in relationship to Mills had dissipated. That is, until out of the blue, a writer whose work had been published in various well-known publications found out about me.

At the time of my chance meeting with Mills, while sunbathing on the deep-sloped beach outside my hotel; I knew nothing about the stranger other than he was considerably older, short, and wasn't attractive—and sure, his thick blonde curly hair was a wig. In the days following, it seemed uncanny I kept running into Mills and his small entourage for the duration of the trip—to the point I felt creeped on. Even one of his buddies cornered me, "You should be nice to Mills." The interaction—of what there was of it, caught me off guard as it seemed rather threatening.

Within a few days from leaving Mexico, Mills lobbied for my phone number. Although I had zero interest, I hesitantly gave it; but certain nothing would come of it due to my disinterest, and because he lived in New York City. But I was wrong.

Upon returning to Atlanta, Mills began calling—essentially hounding me to visit. His persistence eventually wore me down; a number of weeks after our meeting, I was flying first class on a Delta jet to New York at his expense. I viewed it as a free jaunt and nothing more. But as it's often stated: nothing is free. However, my position about Mills quickly shifted once we walked outside of LaGuardia, where a Rolls-Royce was Doris Day parked; a tall, thin, and older Black gentleman stood next to it dressed in a chauffeur uniform awaiting.

That first trip slipped into several more a month for two or three day visits—sometimes, flying me in for an overnighter, where I returned to Atlanta the next morning. Ultimately, I begin staying for longer periods. Then, one evening, over dinner in some swanky restaurant, Mills surprisingly made it clear that he didn't want me to see anyone else without asking how I felt about him.

My disinterest in Mills hadn't changed even as attentive as I found him to be; but certain he would eventually grow bored. Until then, due to the lure of the magnitude of Mills' wealth and lavish New York lifestyle, I planned on sticking around: the two-story condo on Park Avenue, chauffeured around in not one but three Rolls-Royces, and the monthly allowance he ended up allotting among other perks. At that first meeting in Acapulco, I would have never thought Mills possessed such wealth.

He was one of those older men who had an appetite for pretty and younger. Beauty is much like currency—a commodity to be bought and sold. Mills' wealth drew many who possessed both, equal to his hunger. Other than looks, I believe one of the attributes that set me apart from the competition, was my perceived innocence and the assumption I wasn't impressed by money when I unquestionably was but acted otherwise.

In order to maintain the facade, it was important to be independent and not ask for anything related to Mills' wealth—not even a pack of gum. To do that—asked for something would give me away. Give away my interest in how much I could profit in the way of gifts before Mills grew bored and replaced me with a new pastime.

Until then, I would show affection—even fake love if it got that far. Nonetheless, I doubted it would—Mills didn't seem the type. However, while playing the game, I never thought I would find myself plunged into the deep dark side of him with limited ways out.

That first day I spent with Mills, we'd ventured to Soho to check out galleries and later do some shopping. The snow had picked up from the night before when I arrived—quilting the city.

"Randy… get whatever you like."

There was a lot that I wanted like a kid in a candy store but reframed—at least for a while.

"You need something heavier," Mills insisted, as he pointed at a selection of wool jackets. He chose one and sized it against my body. I noticed the hefty price tag.

"Yes… this will work."

Mills placed it on a display table of perfectly laid-out winter scarves. He pulled another jacket from a different section—leather, body-fitting, and short-waisted.

"What size are you… medium?"

"That's very generous, but really… not necessary."

Mills looked disappointed—perhaps slightly bothered by the rejection.

"How about these leather gloves?"

"Seriously, I'm good… aren't you hungry? Let's go to lunch," I suggested.

Mills took both jackets, a few scarves, and a pair of gloves to the counter—clearly, no thank you wasn't an option.

We were both bidding to show our best side; but I was winning at the challenge—I'd gotten a head start. Even within the first minutes of our meeting, I sensed a prevalent emptiness accompanied by darkness—like an aura bordering Mills.

Once we started—whatever it was after my first visit, as much as Mills attempted to keep aspects about his life hidden and me within a fairy tale, that darkness surrounding him widened. The only way I can best describe it, is to use the phrase, "a leopard never changes its spots." To be more scrupulous, it's better phrased: "only for so long before they begin to show themselves again." For Mills to change his character—his nature, was only possible in short intervals.

Although I hadn't noticed during what brief interactions we had in Acapulco, I soon became aware that Mills had a heavy cocaine habit. I'd been around drug use before—certainly, in the modeling industry and knew the signs; I kept any knowledge of it, as other discoveries when they came into light, to myself. But a lot or little light, it was clear, Mills was a man filled with secrets and hidden agendas—certainly, a questionable one.

Inklings of salted breezes prevailing from the southwest, altered Mills' mood from the tenseness of the city to a low key atmosphere. Mills appeared relaxed and not so tightly wound like a 10-day watch as he habitually was in the city. He had little interest in doing much of anything—preferring sticking close to the house. But I knew that had much to do with me. And other than that, Mills wanted sex which I found barely tolerable. Cold. Stiff. Awkward—but thankfully, quick. The only concern I had was his wig coming off amidst the act as I continued playing the game. My only concern about sex with him was Mills' wig falling off. In fact, the only real thing I found pleasure in was being at the beach.

Often, a few trusted friends lounged around the pool while his houseman served drinks. Donald, who I came to find out was a close friend of Mill's, was also the man who'd approached me while in Acapulco; and instructed that I should be nice to Mills. Donald also had a young lover. With time, I began to see Donald as a friend, and it became obvious that he quickly took a liking to me.

One Saturday afternoon, while sunbathing next to me, Donald mentioned the opposite of what he'd told me in Mexico as he looked around to make sure Mills wasn't in earshot. He was actually in the house at the time.

"Randy… you need to be careful," he spoke in almost a tapered whisper.

Donald wasn't able to express why due to Mills' untimely exit from the house. He sat down on the edge of my lounge and rubbed my leg.

"You two enjoying yourselves? Mills asked.

Donald discreetly raised an eyebrow in such a way that told me the same—to be careful.

"Oh… yes. Such a gorgeous day," Donald responded as we both smiled at Mills.

Other than intimate dinners at the house, either alone or with some of those friends, and that of a few others' homes on the island—we seldom went to the dock. Certainly, never to the popular nightclub, The Pavillion. Showing his possessiveness, Mills forbid me from walking the narrow boardwalks alone—thickly flanked by pitch pines, sassafras shrubs and trees, and other native vegetation where guys had sex under what light was offered by the moon—or moonless nights in the dark where moans and other repetitive heated expressions of pleasure escaped through the foliage, without him or one or more of his friends—a few of which I found rather handsy. In fact, Mills would have been happy if I never left his side.

In shelter aggravation, one of the very few times I challenged Mills, I insisted that he'd nothing to worry about concerning me talking the boardwalks alone if he was going to spend the majority of his time at the house—expecting me to do as well.

"Look… Mills. I'll wear a chastity belt if that's what it's going to take to ease your mind," I joked, even though I knew he'd prefer to keep my dick and ass under lock and key.

"Funny, Randy."

In all actuality, I wasn't joking—more like annoyed but trying not to let it show in the tone of my voice or on my face.

"It's obvious… you think, I'm going to go wild in the bushes with some guys. You know that's not me."

But admittedly, I probably would if I'd crossed paths with the right flavor; but it would be too dangerous—certainly, with so many eyes on me. And if I did, it would be my bad luck if he knew Mills or some of his friends. With someone like Mills, most people knew I was with him—even those outside his circle.

Mills looked past me. But his annoyance with me was clear.

"It hurts you'd even think that."

An edgy pause followed.

"You don't even like to walk the beach… how many times have you with me? Perhaps, twice? You know I love it… the beach… especially here."

Another pause charted.

"Okay… okay. I guess it's okay."

I felt restrained as usual. The fact I had to assure Mills otherwise, was like asking for permission. His controlling weighed heavier and heavier with time. But I wasn't going to exchange one cage for another—the other obviously, Warner Robins.

The awareness he needed to govern every aspect around him, including people—and even me, were all flashings caution lights. Still, they weren't enough to make me walk away—the money retaining its strong hold.

Unanticipated, Mills asserted he didn't want me to see anyone else without asking how I felt about us. I found it somewhat troublesome on two counts: again—not first asking, but his decisiveness on the matter wasn't surprising, and I'd yet to have spoken the "L" word or had he. But in regard to Mills' insistence of my fidelity, it had more to do with ownership and the only dick he wanted up my ass was his.

Mills certainly couldn't monitor me when I was in Atlanta—or didn't believe so. Conversely, regardless of Mills' continued affection and generosity, I wasn't foolish to think he was being faithful—sure, he likely was fucking other younger men when I wasn't around. In all actuality, I didn't care who he fucked. Again—I wasn't in the relationship for love but only money.

With overseer eyes, Mills began to widen the crack of his world: more dinners out in the city; Broadway shows; attending various events, and parties hosted by more of his friends, where before, I'd yet to meet.

A few black tie events were at his close friend, Roy Cohn's—or should I say, his partner in crime. But I'd met Roy sometime before. There had been a number of intimate dinners at his brownstone with Mills and me and his younger lover, who was around my age—while two Afghans lazed around on a Persian rug or one similar.

Roy's demeanor was rather standoffish, but never rude; he actually gave me the creeps and had crime written all over his face. The first word that entered my mind when I'd initially met him was, Mafia. After dinners, Roy and Mills often stepped into his office and closed the door while leaving me with his lover and the dogs.

At populated events, Mills often unapologetically pulled me away if he saw me interacting with men he seemed to be threatened by—certainly, handsome ones. Clearly, Mills was marking his territory like a wolf in the wild.

Mills cut off a famous clothing designer at one of Roy's black tie events. As the designer was approaching me, after seeing us smiling at each other from some yards away. After a brief exchange, the designer walked away while slightly shrugging his shoulders and winked.

Pissed. I would have appreciated an introduction since I'd started modeling again. It wasn't as if Mills had walked in on us fucking in the broom closet. Afterwards, he made it known that he told the designer to stay away from me.

"Seriously, why did you do that?" delivered with a dense inflection of anger even though I knew Mills didn't like to be questioned.

He stared; Mills' eyes roughened like sandpaper. I'd noticed earlier they were somewhat bloodshot and glassy. He sniffed and then sniffed again—Mills had been sniffling on and off during the evening, starting in the car. It was clear he'd been snorting. I turned and walked away without speaking another word.

In weakened retaliation, I avoided him until Mills brought me a glass of champagne. My inclination was to throw it in his face. Instead, I felt obligated to engage in conversation with my owner like a good dog with a leash attached to the collar around its neck.

Roy and another man walked up to Mills and me. Mills glanced over; Roy rigidly studied me as always seemed to be the case.

"Randy… give us a few minutes alone."

I stepped away. A muffled but feverish conversation immediately pulsated as I headed in the direction of the banister overlooking the staircase leading to the first floor. I leaned in against it. Men and women dressed in formal attire casually walked up and down—some caught in conversations. Others drank. The brownstone had been abuzz throughout the evening.

The designer and two female models stood at the landing. I glanced back at Mills; he was still absorbed in the conversation with Roy and the other man. My interest returned to the staircase and of course, to the handsome designer and the women as they engaged an older couple; I'd hoped I could catch his eye again.

After a few passing minutes, one of the women la bise the older before the small group broke apart. The designer and models took a few steps downward before stopping to speak to another one of Roy's guests. Then, as I'd hoped, he looked up at me—smiled, as he'd done earlier and nodded before directing his eyes forward as they took a few more steps. Then, the designer looked back. Smiled again. Our eyes continued to watch each other. Soon, they were soaked-up into another group of guests.

"Fuck Mills," I thought.

On our return to the Park Avenue condo, Mills offered an empty apology.

"Sure… it doesn't matter."

Marcus pulled the Rolls in front of the condo building; I didn't wait for him to walk around to open the car door as I stepped out and hastily cut through the fevered night, passing the doorman without offering the usual hello; and as with the chauffeur, pushed through the glass doors of the entrance—disallowing him to do the same.

I was quite aware it best not to push the intensity of how upset Kew's brazenness of blocking one of the most prominent fashion designers from introducing himself had humiliated me. He wouldn't even have cared anyway of how I felt about being censored—more like instructed, who I could and couldn't interact with. Mills would view it as an act of defiance on my part; and that would be dangerous.

I'd already crossed the line by walking away at the party and then later, rushing out of the Rolls. I knew I had to step back from the boiling anger. And as much as I would have preferred to sleep in the guest room, I had no choice except to lie with Mills.

His leg crossed mine as I'd awakened from a grappled sleep. My skin crawled in disgust. Mills' cum had solidified on my stomach—what little there was of it. I felt cheap—cheap like a bargain-basement hooker. But the knowledge wasn't lost on me that I too was in the same profession; the only difference, I was paid in $1000 bills disguised as an allowance for doing chores in the bedroom.

I asked Mills for permission to have some time to myself.

"Why is that?"

"I thought it would be nice to take a long walk in the park… that's all."

He briefly stood silent in the sleek minimal kitchen as my body leaned against the countertop. I waited for an answer as if a kid wanting to play on the Jungle Jim with the other children.

"Sure… I have some things to take care of anyway… you go and enjoy yourself."

I couldn't help but think, "He must have a dead body to get rid of."

Whispers of spring caressed the air as I walked unhurriedly along the Lake—barely looking up from the ground to notice the breathtaking views of portions of the city partly hiding behind lush overlapping canopies of trees of various heights and widths, and shades of green. Perhaps, it had gotten to the point I was beginning to take New York for granted.

Caught within mixed emotions having stopped to sit on a bench, small tracks of time were lost as blurred images of people walked by and others jogged; I took an inventory of my life—past to present.

As much as I would have preferred to stay away from the condo all day, concern swam Mills might be wondering what had taken me so long to return—that is, he had first. If not, I knew Mills would ask the doorman. But concerned or not, a detour was made to Fifth long enough to purchase my mother a bracelet at Bergdorf Goodman.

The doorman greeted and informed Mills was out—so it was the latter.

"Mr. Gunn wanted you to know he wouldn't be back until around 6:00."

Apparently, by Mills' eager attention that evening, he'd patently understood why I walked away from him at the party and later rushed out of the Rolls and into the building once Marcus delivered us to the condo. But in spite of the lapse of some 24 hours, I remained bothered by his actions; and glad my flight back to Atlanta was the next day.

"Why don't I take you to a nice dinner… do you have a preference?"

"No…you pick. Anywhere is good."

"Well, I want to take you somewhere really nice," Mills asserted.

"You always do… and I hope you know I appreciate you for that and many other things," I threw Mills a bone.

On the way, Mills handed over a small, gift-wrapped present. I imagined it was his way to offer a more noteworthy apology. The gift was an AMEX card. That told me, Mills had never looked in my wallet; it was the second I been given by another man.

"I was going to give it to you a few weeks ago."

"Thank you... you shouldn't have."

"It's time you had one."

I leaned over. Placatingly kissed Mills.

"Is there a limit?" I shamelessly asked.

"Hum… " Mills sniffed followed by another. "Just don't break the bank."

I kissed Mills again in the same manner as before.

Mills instructed Marcus to take us to Lutèce on 50th Street. The French restaurant was always packed and near-impossible to dine there without a reservation made well in advance; but as always, Mills got what he wanted.

The stylish hostess greeted Mills as soon as we walked in the door.

"Mr. Kramer… we weren't expecting you but it's always a pleasure."

"Good to see you as well, Manon.

Within five minutes or so, we were seated. Although I'd taken four years of French, I wasn't a fan—finding the shi shi restaurant to be over the top and certainly too fussy for my taste. Plus, it made me feel out of place as all the five star restaurants I'd been taken to by Mills as well as other well-too-do older me—nor, did I like French cuisine but pretended otherwise. After all, one of my jobs was to make Mills happy.

I excused myself to the restroom where I bent the other AMEX into four pieces before wrapping them in toilet paper and flushed them—flushing three times, just in case. It was a precaution—I didn't want to be caught with two AMEX cards. If I had, Mills would have grilled me about it, and I didn't want to tell him that it was given to me by another man.

As the distance of the relationship managed to move forward, Mills' cold and ruthless side became more apparent. It was as if he had another persona with a darkness in his eyes—that I should have seen all along. Having once believed a number of the questionable things I'd heard about Mills were just rumors, including his and Cohn's possible ties to the mafia—I came to believe otherwise, that they were more fact than fiction.

Mills' control and jealousy remained never-ending; it was pushing me away. I was growing weary of faking being committed and fulfilled sexually but I had to keep up the act of a devoted pet in every way—the façade while in New York. I began discreetly seeking out sexual pleasure while in Atlanta even though I was certain of what Mills might do—what he was capable of if he found out. Yes, I felt guilty. Still, I hungered for some good hot sex that I couldn't get from Mills.

Although the changes in Mills were caution flashing lights, they weren't enough to make me try to escape—not just yet. The money and lifestyle still retained its strong hold. Plus, to walk away from him would be a mistake—like a prize horse breaking out of the barn, and I was already playing with fire. I was walking a treacherous path; but perhaps, I had since the day I met Mills in Acapulco.

Astonished and totally catching me off guard, Mills insisted—not asked, I move to New York and live with him. He offered an E Class Jaguar as he did to set me up in an art studio, and there were more perks. However, Mills expected me to stop modeling which I'd started again sometime after Bradley's death.

Most young men would be satisfied—jump at the chance to get the car, an AMEX in their wallet; the presents; the allowance and of course, keep the lavish New York lifestyle. But that wasn't enough for me; although I'd already been purchased, I wasn't moving only for him to eventually ask for a refund when the next young man came along and caught his eye.

What really surprised me was that Mills didn't seem the partnering kind; and like many men around his age, Mills couldn't watch himself grow older through another person. But like most of us, I knew he had a strong need to be loved—regardless. And Mills was afraid of having one of those young men walk away before he decided to cut them loose.

If Mills expected me to pick up my life in Atlanta and relocate—to alter my future plan of getting back to California, which he already knew about after having told him on the day he found me on the beach in Acapulco, I decided to roll the dice. I wanted to negotiate to see how far I could push Mills for more—for big dollar items I didn't mention in my first book. And depending on what he agreed to, would tell how much Mills wanted and cared about me. The only concern, regardless of his wealth, Mills could be very frugal at times. I'd already figured out he wrote off my allowance as a business expense—as he would an employee.

Mills had already agreed to provide for my mother, but I added a specific request—much like a codicil to a will: purchase a nice home for her and deed it in her and my names. One other item remained on the list. I knew I was pushing it: a house, of my choosing, in the Hollywood Hills—and both the Jag and house would solely be in my name. I knew due to Mills' wealth—the expenses of the requests were chump change.

He'd agreed to the purchase of a home for my mother, but concerning the one in the hills of Hollywood, Mills retorted.

"I'm a New Yorker through-and-through," He stressed unyieldingly.

"I know that… Mills. It's not like I'm asking you to move there."

He looked at me with a staggered gaze. I held it; the living room went silent while thoughts stumbled through my mind as I considered the best way to keep Mills from dismissing my request.

"Think about it as a vacation home."

I moved from the club chair and sat down beside him on the sofa. I was certain Mills felt I was asking for too much; but I knew he would see it that way even before I asked. And I knew, to get him to agree would be like twisting thick metal with my bare hands.

"We'll talk about it later," Mills stiffly said.

That was his way of saying no. But I wasn't giving up. Mills could easily afford it. The money would be chump change.

"You know I told you in Acapulco… that LA was in my future plans… I'm willing to meet some kind of compromise."

Now he looked pissed that I was pushing as I'd thought Mills would—but I didn't care. I'd nothing to lose as long as Mills cut me loose if he felt I was using him as others had.

I lied and told Mills that I wanted us to be together; and I'd be crushed otherwise. But it had all been a lie since the moment I stepped into the Rolls that first time at LaGuardia.

I again reminded Mills that moving to New York would sidetrack my plans. So, if I was going to let that happen, I needed to have both worlds: New York and Los Angeles.

"Mills… you likely think I'm being greedy… but that's not the case. And if you think about it and try to see it from my viewpoint, you might just understand."

Mills looked away then back at me.

"It's your money and obviously your choice."

I held a pause to see what he might say.

"Give me a few days…"

That wasn't the answer I wanted to hear.

"Mills… if I move to New York, then I'm going to be living your life and not fully mine."

Increasingly, I grew more frustrated and even angry. But I knew I had to hold them in and not let Mills see just how upset I was. I was pushing my innocent act over the line, and I knew it.

"Randy, I said I would think about it. But first, I need you to run an errand with me."

Mills looked at his watch like he was going to be late to catch a flight.

Three days later, Mills called me in Atlanta and caved; but with stipulations of his own. They weren't unexpected: I could only go for short periods—a week, maybe two at a time; he likely join me on occasions, but due to various business obligations, only stay a few days, and on those when he wasn't, one of his people would have to remain until my returned to the city.

All along, Mills was basically having the chauffeur do the same thing when I was in New York. At the times he had business to attend to, Mills would leave Marcus with me while Mills cabbed-it. But Marcus had to stand guard, so to speak—whether I was shopping or having lunch. He was never allowed to not keep an eye off me; and without a doubt, reported back to Mills on a continuous basis about my activities.

Besides the collar around my neck with an attached leash, I may as well have a tracking device around my ankle. The stipulations weren't unexpected. I could live with them; all I cared about was the house and my name on the dee—and because Mills had agreed to all my requests, I felt important to him as it gave me some control of my own over Mills as well.

knee deep in shit

My unsettled mind staggered on the upcoming move as I walked the early-morning beach—the new-day sunrise momentarily sat on the horizon, offering a pinkish haze met by graying clouds. Mills was sleeping in, which meant the morning belonged to me.

The dog managed—if only briefly, to snap the leash hooked to his collar. Even so, I was on an island surrounded by water. There was only so far, I could run—or rather swim. The irony hadn't gone unnoticed that I'd basically agreed to continue my confinement within the tight margins of Mills' control, but also to two islands. But that wasn't the worst of it: the Devil had acquired another soul—even if it was for considerable money.

Each imprint of footsteps taken, were washed away by the rolling surf before another could be made in the sand—clean salted air mixed with the smell of rain-to-come filled my lungs, as I listened absorbedly to the ocean, and the surrounding reflection it extended.

Growing angrily, darker clouds surged inward—pushing the grayness until it surrendered—attested by a bolt of lightning as it flashed and speared the ocean; a startling clap of thunder chased. Birthing raindrops fell, but I didn't run—determined to stay until the sky opened up and completely soaked me. Maybe even wash me out to sea, assisted by the increasingly churning wind.

Echoed voices of laughter found its way to me as I looked further down the beach. Two guys ran in circles—one trying to catch the other until both jointly pulled themselves down into the surf.

My mind suddenly flashed like the lightning had minutes before. Thoughts of Bradley charged. Three years ago, we were those two guys; although, it seemed like more—like more days had come and gone. Days that slipped away. Still, it hurt—the loss. I wondered what Bradley would think of me now. But I knew whatever he did, Bradley would still love me. I too began growing angrier as the sky; it wasn't supposed to be this way. I'd unquestionably trade all that Mills offered and more—and more and more and more, to have Bradley back, and me returned into his arms.

Mills looked—rather scoped me from across the table as the houseman served breakfast. Occasionally, I broke eye contact to look at the pool through the rain splashing against the large windows. The drops that had fallen on me earlier and increased to a steady rain, had grown into a downpour—accompanied by more lightning and thunder. I was certain the pool would be overflowing soon enough.

"It's really coming down," I told Mills, as if he couldn't see the rain for himself.

"I'd say so… you certainly were soaked when you returned."

"I've always loved the rain… I like to jog in it."

Mills looked up while buttering a slice of toast.

The morning walk had given wider clarity of the situation I'd found myself surrounded by. Over the last many months, I not only had become Mills' prisoner, but the same to his money and the glamorous life it provided—but by then, I'd realize more than ever, it was a dangerous one. Nevertheless, it's not like I woke up one morning and suddenly realized it—realized, the fire I'd been playing with. Perhaps, a part of me had begun to thrive on it—the danger. At the time, I remembered a boy sticking one of his mother's Bobby pins into the wall socket of my bedroom. In a split second, the electric shock jolted as the socket popped; in chorus, its current ran from my fingers up my arm. The room instantly filled with a burned smell; the socket and cover plate turned black. It's reasonable to conclude, I was lucky.

"Are you set for the move? Two weeks, Randy… two weeks, I expect you here as agreed."

"Yes… I will."

Even though I was living it—caught up in a world of money, it was more akin to a fantasy than reality. Two extremely different worlds—my left foot in one while the right in the other. The line between—sharp as a razor's edge. That fantasy, similar to a Cinderella-like fairy tale. I was just waiting for the stroke of midnight in order to see what the outcome would be—not all fairytales have happy endings. Hence, the razor's edge; and certainly, Mills wasn't Prince Charming even before his fortune had taken hold of a poor boy from Middle, Georgia. And overtime, I came to see Mills as more like the evil step-mother who held the purse strings. I wondered, would I be lucky as I had been after sticking the Bobby pin in the socket—once both feet were in his world?

The assigned date of the move—the closer it came, the more it seemed to be barreling forward. And each day that passed, the more I second-guessed myself while taking inventory of what I knew about Mills. What I'd learned from seeing and hearing—most concerning, if only heard partly from around the corner. And then, there was the involvement Mills had engaged me in—as if I were his apprentice. At that point, I was certain Mills was capable of anything. And I had no doubts, that if we were on a sailboat with one lifejacket and it was sinking, Mills would take it for himself and leave me to drown.

Having once suspected Mills was laundering money—why else would he go most mornings to check the receipts of his businesses. My suspicions were verified the afternoon two big men in black suits stood on either side of the gates of a long driveway leading up to a mansion. Mills parked the Corniche. He grabbed the black briefcase from the backseat.

"Stay in the car. I'll be back shortly."

I watched as a third man, positioned at the front doors, opened one for Mills. Before entering, he quickly looked back at me. From where I was sitting, it appeared so cloak and dagger. The only thing missing was that Mills wasn't wearing a black trench coat to match the briefcase.

He didn't return for a good 30 minutes without it. I remained quiet as Mills had when he returned. I didn't need to be a Bloodhound to smell—Mafia.

On one occasion, I overheard Mills tell Roy, "No one's going to find him." That wasn't the first time I got the impression someone else went missing. Much earlier in the relationship, we were at a restaurant having dinner with ten or so of his friends. I sat across the table from Mills. Among the various conversations, I overheard something similar from Mills telling the person next to him.

Within a span of a month, he had me deliver a briefcase twice to a tall thin and ball-headed man waiting in a deli while Marcus remained in Mills' limo.

"I've got to catch a cab across town. You'll be doing me a big favor."

"Sure… "

"Don't say anything. He'll know what you look like."

I didn't ask any questions—either time.

Guilt began setting in—joining the standing fear I had for some time of what might come. Even though, early on, I was satisfied with what Mills was giving me as I stated in my first book; it wasn't always the case as the relationship moved forward. I eventually started using Mills by the means of deception—as so many young men had before me. And aside from that, I didn't want to be pulled into his questionable dealings more than I had. I didn't want to be his errand-boy. What was next other than delivering briefcases?

The fact remained; I could never love a man like Mills—never even come to have strong feelings. I didn't really like him—even disgusted at times. It had become more exhausting to pretend otherwise, especially while engaged in sex. I needed to be consumed. Held. Kissed. Made love to as Bradley once had. I wondered how much longer I could keep up the charade. How much longer, could I keep living with a collar around my neck—every move watched? As questions built, Mills' money didn't seem to be enough. No amount would be—contrary to what I'd believed earlier when the Rolls Royce first turned onto Park Avenue.

the 17th

Early Tuesday morning after having returned from Fire Island the evening before, I passionately kissed Mills at the elevator—managing not to gag from his tongue down my throat. Marcus was waiting downstairs. I'd switched my reservation to a morning flight the night before.

"We'll pick you up on the 17th."

"Can't wait," I told him, still uncertain.

"Call me with the details once you decide which house you picked for your mother."

"Okay."

"We'll get started on the one in California… " Mills paused. "Once you get settled here."

I hugged and kissed Mills again for show.

A sense of relief lathered as the Rolls pulled away from the curb heading to LaGuardia. I looked back at the condo building through the back window; again, knowing what I might be giving up if I made a firm decision not to return to New York—unless I had a modeling gig.

"How was your weekend… Randy?

I'd broken Marcus from the habit of calling me Mr. Chumbley, except when Mills was around. I didn't like the formal aspect, and I'd come to like him. Being very astute, I'd a sense he knew I wasn't that excited about relocating to New York; but never said anything.

"It was enjoyable. Had an early morning walk yesterday on the beach while it rained… before the downpour that followed. But sill, I like walking in the rain. What about you, Marcus… what did you do"

"Spent some time with my grandchildren. It was nice."

During the flight, the list of questions rattled. Although I'd planned to return to the apartment upon arrival—instead of I-75 North, I merged South. I'd decided to surprise Mother; and look at the three houses I was considering. Lori, the realtor, had informed me that they were still on the market.

Rather than utilizing the key, I knocked on the door. Mother's face instantly lit up when she opened it. Her arms reached out to hug me. In an embrace, I kissed her on the cheek.

"I didn't know you were coming… "

"Well, I can head back to Atlanta."

"Oh no you won't. You spending the night?"

"I can't. Wish I could… next week. Okay."

Mother frowned, more so jokingly—but I knew it carried some weight. Some disappointment.

"You just missed Siggy."

"I'll give her a call later to say, hello."

As I crossed the threshold—a chill coursed. I followed Mother into the breakfast room where we sat down at the table. She put her hand on top of mine.

"You look good, Mom."

"You're just saying that."

"No… I'm not."

We had an early dinner at the Waffle House. A comfortable walking distance from the house, my mother often sat in a booth having morning coffee. She'd spent so much time there; Mother had become somewhat of a fixture. She once told me, "I like to watch the people who come and go... all kinds. I've gotten to know most of the regulars… and the staff."

I was sure, Mother went there to get out of the house. At times, I wondered if it bothered her as much as it did me—the house. An image of Mother switched-on. An image, sitting all alone saddened my heart. But I knew sometimes, Siggy and-or Joann would go with her as they took Mother to other places.

A towering, middle-aged woman with a pleasing face scurried in our direction. Ketchup—along with something else soiled her apron—a hazard of the job.

"Mary!" she called out with a level of excitement. "I haven't seen you since they changed my schedule… but I'll be back on mornings… soon enough."

She scaffold down to hug Mother.

I placed the menu back on the table, already knowing I couldn't eat anything except a salad; everything else was greasy. I looked up and smiled at the friendly waitress.

"Now… who's this handsome young man?" she asked while eyeing me.

"Randy, my younger son."

The waitress introduced herself as Kim before Mother had the chance.

"He has your eyes."

"It's a pleasure, Kim."

"He's polite, too. You raised him right."

Kim took our orders; patted Mother's shoulder before turning to deliver them to the counter. I glanced at the time on my watch. Lori was expecting me, in roughly an hour and a half.

I walked Mother back into the house. By then, it was 5:12.

"You going to be okay? I should get back on the road," I told her, not wanting to hold Lori up. Or did I want Mother to know about the house hunting until everything was set in stone.

"You sure you can't stay over," she expressed again.

"How about we go to Beals this Saturday."

I gave her a big hug; kissed Mother on the cheek as I did when I'd arrived.

"Call me when you get back… watch out for those big trucks."

"You know I will."

Mother always told me that—referring to semis.

I offered another hug before taking a step back. Mother looked up with her sad almond-brown eyes.

Torn. I was torn between the house I'd decided on for my mother and living in New York to acquire it for her. After seeing her—looking into her eyes that day—although, I had since I was a little boy; nothing seemed so important anymore. Nothing for me, that is: Mills' money, the Jag, and even the California house. There was something about that day—that moment in time sitting across from her at the Waffle House in that shit town, that had resonated with me—that followed me. Pellucid, but not. Definable, but not. In line-sight, but not. And I had less than two weeks to figure it out.

Less than two weeds to decide—decide, whether to bolt or stay with Mills and take my chances. But even to bolt, might be a challenge.

With a degree of acquaintance with Mills' daily routines, I played a game of probabilities. I'd call the Park Avenue condo when I was fairly certain he'd left for the day and leave a message on the answering machine—even with the maid. I did the same at his businesses. As well, I didn't answer my phone and let the calls go to my machine.

When I returned to Atlanta around eight that evening, two messages from Mills were waiting.

"You didn't call. Where are you?"

"Randy… call me back."

Mills called a number of times up to around 10:00, leaving similar messages—each one, seemingly more demanding. Just when I thought he'd given up for the night—two more broke the small hours. I'd considered telling Mills; I was at my mother's after having fallen ill. But I knew he'd asked for her phone number, and I didn't want him to have it.

I'd planned to take my chances for two, 24 hours periods; but due to Mills' aggressiveness, I thought it best to answer the phone the next night.

"You're not coming… are you," he spoke with heated irritation.

I hesitated.

"Mills… Mills, I am. I just need a little bit more time."

"I don't believe you… you'll be sorry if you don't take that fight on the 17th."

I hesitated, again.

"Randy, I'm serious!"

"Please give me some more time to spend with my mother."

The 17th, Mills yelled.

"Look… I'm not going to be threatened."

"Randy!" he pushed harder.

"I'm hanging up. We can talk when you calm-down… when you understand my situation."

A number of days had passed; but Mills' calls continued. Thankfully, his anger had lessened to some degree—or so I thought.

"I'm going to fly to Atlanta tomorrow."

"Fuck," brain waved… knowing, I had to think quickly.

"Not just yet… my mother's coming for a few days," I lied.

"Bullshit."

"Mills… have I ever been dishonest to you?"

"I'm beginning to question," the anger in his voice returned.

And he was right; I'd been bullshitting.

hog-tied

Although afraid of Mills, the hostility riding on his threats had significantly fueled that fear. Within the days that tracked, I'd noticed a stranger hanging around the grounds of the apartment building. I elbowed it to paranoia and nothing more. I was living in Midtown—after all, and cruising for one's next sexual meal was much like a past-time for many to satisfy their hunger. But concern shifted the night I noticed a shadow of a man sitting in a car—with a bird's eye-view into the large windows of my bedroom.

Those suspicions shifted into the oozing hours; I was startled by unforgiving banging at the front door—such, I believed within seconds, it would be kicked in. Then, it stopped; but only long enough to begin again at the kitchen door leading to the back hallway. Soon thereafter, both doors were equally assaulted. At that point, I realized, it wasn't one man—but two.

Beyond frightened, I managed to dial 911.

"Some… someone's trying… trying to kick in the doors of my apartment," my voice shook as panic welded each word to the next—shortening breaths.

My address stammered from my mouth to the dispatcher. She asked me to repeat it. As I did, I conveyed that I wasn't sure how much longer the doors could withstand the aggressive attempts to break through. Although it seemed much longer, within minutes, I heard police sirens in the distance; but in Midtown Atlanta, they could be headed anywhere. And those were as they weakened. I held my breath. Thought about climbing out the window but I was two stories up and no fire escape. Then more sirens were heard. They grew louder. Even louder. I knew those were just blocks away. The banging stopped.

The following day, Mills called.

"So, I see that you're still alive."

"What do you mean?"

"I'm only concerned about you," Randy. "Nothing more, but you need me to keep you safe," he added.

I knew he'd sent the two men—I just reframed from making reference to what had transpired the night before. To do so would be unwise. Mills would have denied it anyway. But he knew I knew he had. As I've stated before: Mills wasn't the kind of man to say no to.

The question: What was his plan? To have me hog-tied and forced back to New York, or my throat slit and left in the apartment? As much as I didn't want to return to Mills and his control and ownership, I obviously would have preferred the first.

knots in a ball of tattered string

The two goons who'd forcibly attempted to kick in my apartment doors were never seen again; but that's not to say, I stopped looking over my shoulders. And even though Mills' calls continued, they weren't as blatantly threatening—but hung low like fruit rotting on vines. Even still, threats or not, I felt the collar around my neck loosening; and thankful, I'd remained alive.

My plan was to stay as far away from Manhattan as humanly possible. But that changed, when I was hired through the agency to do in-store ads for Barney's men's wear. Fortunately, it only required being in New York for just over a week. Still, it felt too close to home—or rather, what almost became my prison. I obviously didn't tell Mills—I was in the city.

As more time passed, Mills' anger appeared to pass as well. But I could sense there was some lingering resentment. With more time, his calls became more sporadic. But when we did speak, it seemed as though Mills viewed us as friends at a distance; but that was totally one-sided—his. Having remained suspicious, I played along while wondering what might be down the road. After all, I still knew what I knew. And if any shit was going to fall—I didn't want it to fall on me.

"Come out to spend a few days in Fire Island."

"That's very nice of you to offer… I'll come another time… if it's an open invitation."

"Of… course," Mills responded somewhat adversely.

Not long after I'd turned down the invitation, the calls weaned off but didn't stop entirely until about a month later. I was certain, he'd met another slice of young flesh—waiting in line. It was better that way; and I finally thought it was all behind me—that Mills was behind me or so I wished. But that wish didn't last very long. Fast forward some-seven months later, like a bolt out of the blue, I received a call from him again. Even after all the time that had passed, Mills' voice still incited a level of anxiety.

Mills had practically begged me to come. It was a side of him I'd never seen before—or expected. Desperation plagued his voice like a fatal disease.

"Why is that? Why do you need me to come after all this time?"

"I'll explain everything once you're here. I really need you… Randy."

"I don't know. I don't think it would be good for either of us."

"I did a lot for you… and was willing to do much more."

"It was a trade-off, Mills. One sided… and I didn't want to remain under lock and key."

Mills started sniffing. Then he cleared his throat.

"I didn't want to lose you."

Against better judgment, I booked a flight out of Atlanta that late Friday afternoon. Mills was waiting in the Rolls. I'd expected to see Marcus standing outside; but instead, a tall and wide virile Brazilian, without the chauffeur's uniform greeted—whose name I don't remember.

"Mr. Gunn is waiting for you inside," he spoke with an infused accent—before opening the back door of the Roll's.

Flagrant tension immediately filled the car—as if waiting for a guillotine to drop severing my head from my body. Déjà vu electrically charged as if I'd never left. As if—I hadn't escaped.

"Appreciate you coming," Mills' voice quivered, as he leaned in to hug me.

A chill, as if from a New York's winter's snow storm, briefly caught me—I'm sure Mills saw apprehension in my eyes as he did in my stiffened body language. The last time I saw him was the morning he'd dropped me off at LaGuardia—two weeks before I was supposed to return to New York to live with him.

"What happened to Marcus?" I was surprised not to see him waiting by the Rolls."

"He… he retired. Marcus was getting too old."

I suspected there was more to the story. Certain—Marcus was replaced rather than having hung up his uniform of his own volition.

"That's too bad. I really liked him."

Mills didn't comment either way; he just looked at me with sadness confined within his eyes.

The Brazilian maneuvered the Rolls away from the curb and around and through what appeared to be much like a parking lot of cars. After our brief verbal interaction, Mills fell within himself as he turned his head away to look out the window.

Although not knowing why Mills seemed to urgently need me to come, I sensed it was something serious. Surprisingly, I felt a sense of empathy; as our brief exchange slipped into silence—occupying the majority of the drive to the condo—only disrupted by sounds of traffic. The driver kept his eyes forward except the few times he looked at me in the rear view mirror. If he was a chauffeur, then I was Queen Elizabeth.

As we exited the Rolls into the night air lit up by the mass escape of lights through the windows of the surrounding lofty buildings, I was surprised the doorman on duty remembered me. Perhaps, I really had returned back into an element of time—I felt the same, stepping into the Rolls at the airport as I had that first time. My mind flooded with a variety of feelings and images—especially, that of the first night of my arrival when Marcus opened the door for me outside the Park Avenue address; and stepped out into a delicate flurry of snowflakes falling on my face and melting seconds later. The only thing that seemed to be wrong—out of place: the absence of Marcus' friendly face.

Abandonment of any readable emotions, Mills' eyes scanned the room through the low light before they landed on me sitting on one of the living room's white sofas. He, on the matching one directly across from it. Mills periodically sniffed the small drops of mucus from his nose as he kept repositioning his body out of agitation.

"Tell me what's going on that has alarmingly distressed you… such that you wanted me to fly to New York."

Mills delayed before responding.

"It's this young guy I was seeing."

"Was? You must have pretty strong feelings for him… "

"Does that make you jealous?" Mills asked, as if to hurt me.

Knowing him, an element of that statement may have been meant to, but it was clear that any jealousy belonged to Mills concerning this new guy; and it was eating him alive inside as if there were a frenzy of piranha in his gut.

"I'll always be… in some way. If knowing that will give you any pleasure in me walking away from you and everything else."

"No… Randy, it doesn't."

Mills had been dumped for another man just more than a decade younger—but apparently, Mills money hadn't. He thought the young ex and his new older lover were playing him. Still, Mills wanted the boy back—at any cost. That was evident.

Regardless of how I felt about Mills, I was oddly anguished to see him in such a condition—he didn't seem like the man I left. But rather, to some degree more human. Or it could have been that I hadn't given Mills enough credit in that area when we were together.

Clearly, this boy had brought Mills to his knees. But that didn't mean, I'd ruled out Mills' state of mind had more to do with his possessive and jealous side. That was the man I knew—the man I ran from.

"Randy, I gave him a gold watch just days before he told me it was over… he said, get it for me so I did."

Mills looked as though he was going to break down. That too, was surprising. Mills had always been in control on many levels, including watching every step I made.

"You were unlike him… never asking for anything, until you negotiated what you wanted to relocate. They were valid requests under the circumstances."

I avoided any interjection so hopefully Mills could get things off his chest.

"Why didn't you stay… why didn't you come back instead of letting things go?" Mills unexpectedly asked.

"I think you know the answer, Mills… it's not as simple as you put it."

I explained that I became afraid. That, he knew I knew too much. Going further with my explanation, that despite his generosity, I felt expendable; and as much as I wanted the lifestyle, it didn't feel like I belonged. Maybe not even good enough.

"I would never have let anything happen to you as long as you were with me. And you did belong. You're so beautiful, and I was proud to have you."

I didn't know how to respond. I offered a tapered smile before glancing away then back. And there was that troubling statement again: nothing would ever happen to me as long as I was a good boy.

As I hadn't mentioned the attempted invasion of my apartment shortly after the time it took place, I wanted to at that moment. I wanted to know why. Clearly, it was a message with a number of possible outcomes. Certainly, to scare me. Was it to force me back to New York? What if I refused? Did he really want me that badly or had I bruised his ego such that he wanted me dead?

"Mills… I need to ask you something."

"Sure… what is it?"

I hesitated.

I want… ," I delayed again.

"What, Randy?

"It's really nothing. You have enough to work through."

"Do you need money?"

"No… no, it's nothing like that," I stated, then changed the subject.

The more I thought about it while sitting across from Mills, I realized that unlike the boy, I didn't leave Mills for someone else. Perhaps, that ended up being my saving grace.

Mills soon returned his focus to the boy.

"He'd kept asking… and I kept giving. Even after he left, he came back for more."

Where I hadn't felt guilty before, oddly I suddenly did at some level at the time knowing I'd played Mills all the same—but I was in a whole different league. I'd set the price much, much higher for me than some cash, gifts like a gold watch and others. Mills never apprehended that—as far as playing him, not even when I began negotiating for more—when he already was basically giving me the code to the safe, I asked for the whole bank. But the homes were reasonable requests under the circumstances—as Mills agreed.

The fact I eventually gave them up, along with the rest, and as the dust settled, certainly made Mills believe I was a good person. And the fact Mills was so generous, told me that he was in love with me—in his own way or his own definitions of love. For men like Mills, love is control, ownership, and jealousy.

When I look back, I'm amazed I was able to walk away still breathing. Remember, I was just some young guy who was playing mind games with himself—more like, my past and the present at the time and flying by the seat of my pants or more like, my ass. Without question, what I was doing was rawly instinctive and fear-based. But back to the guilt I began feeling, actually had nothing to do with playing Mills for his wealth, but his love—and regardless of his definition, and that he was a volatile dangerous man, I had no intentions of returning it nor would I have been capable of doing so.

"He treated me like a YO-YO," Mills expressed with amplified confusion trailed by anger as he got up to pace the room. His words rambled faster; I expected Mills to hyperventilate.

"You need to take a few slow breaths… sit back down."

Mills didn't take my advice as he kept going on and on—still pacing.

"Mills… please. You're out of control. This isn't like you."

Still, he continued.

"I… I was giving and my ex's new boyfriend was too... he was giving the boy his dick up his ass," Mills boiled.

"Listen to me. Take a seat. Please."

"I can't. And that's all this guy can give him because he doesn't have any money."

Knowing Mills had lost ownership of the boy to someone else, his jealousy took on a vengeance of a wounded animal who still had some will to live left. Mills' face was covered in despondency and bitterness. Unless he settled down, I knew Mills' jealousy would likely get its retribution; and I knew about getting retribution from a very young age, although the surrounding circumstances were very different.

"I could fucking kill that... ," Mills blurted, not finishing his intention.

"Kill who, Mills? I asked, feeling I should walk away from the whole situation. I was way over my head.

He didn't answer. Just looked at me, then walked across the living room toward the bathroom and closed the door. I knew Mills went in there to snort. After all this time, he was still trying to hide his habit from me.

"I'll just tell Mills, I need to take a walk around the block when he comes out," I thought. But actually, instead, hail a cab once outside back to LaGuardia and leave my bag upstairs. But as much as I wanted to, he'd view my act of ducking out as deserting him and a form of betrayal, as I knew he'd felt in spades when I didn't move to New York.

Mills wanted to drive out early Sunday morning to catch the ferry to Fire Island for the day. Needless to say—it was a somber and resentful filled drive. Mills had talked himself into exhaustion starting when I arrived. I knew he hadn't slept in days. I heard Mills up and down both Friday and Saturday nights walking around the upper floor of the condo. I actually didn't sleep much at all. I mostly laid awake looking at the ceiling and listening. At the time, in those disconcerting few hours of night, I oddly remembered how I would do the same as a kid when my father was on the warpath. I was concerned; concerned and afraid to leave him alone; afraid of what Mills might do, again, knowing him as I did. And especially after his unfinished comment, "I could just fucking kill." That wasn't just an idle threat.

I drove the Corniche. The weather met us with a slight chill and low fog—both eventually dissipating. I hoped by doing so—by going to the Island, I could get Mills out of his head; but as much as I attempted to keep him off track, Mills kept U-turning back to the boy and the new boyfriend.

Once we got off the ferry and to the house, Mills seemed somewhat calmer much like the island being that it was the off-season we were encased within. He'd stopped talking about the boy and his new boyfriend. I don't know if Mills had finally talked himself out for the time being or if it was the serenity of the chill in the air—its crispness. The tapered breezes that rustle the bushes and lazy Pines while what colored leaves were left on Aspens and Maples and Oaks, slowly swirled in the air until they found rest on the ground. Even they had lost some of their vibrance and left more subdued in color. The slower than slower pace. The near-empty boardwalks. By all accounts, nature had taken back Fire Island from the humans.

"Let's take a walk. We'll even go to the beach… I know you love it there. Remember, I met you on one."

His suggestion took me by surprise. As I'd earlier shared, I could hardly get Mills to walk with me when I was with him.

I took it as a positive sign as it was welcomed. Plus, to get out of the house and walk around The Pines might give Mills a new perspective. Or so I'd hoped.

"Oh, yes… I do. I recollect it well," I let out a controlled laugh.

"God… Randy. I wanted you from the moment one of my friends pointed you out while we were sitting under our palapa."

Found off guard, I questioned how to address Mills' confession—if at all.

A wrestled pause charted.

"So annoying… you were so annoying, Mills but in a good way," I verbally reacted. The latter of the comeback was for Mills' benefit. I wrapped my arm round his shoulders like we were childhood friends.

We walked through the chilled, repetitive breezes carrying the sea air as I warmed my hands in the pockets of my jacket. Mills lagged a few steps behind at times until I circled back around to get us realigned side-by-side on the beach. The surf spoke loudly as it aggressively rolled up under an unpredictable onion-colored sky. My thoughts began to slip backward. Even though it had only been under two years since I met Mills on a beach in Acapulco, it seemed as if much more time had passed. As Mills remained thankfully quiet for most of the walk, I reread some of the pages out of that storybook life in a city called New York. But in reality, it would always remain make-believe even if I'd moved there for a day or a month or however long I could survive the restrictions, and my heart void of true love as I'd known it so well with another man only a few years before. Hours, days, months, and years—love, regardless of one's definition, heartbreak and loss, all were knots knotted in a ball of tattered string.

The Corniche broke down while returning to the city. We sat on a bench outside the train station, eating Häagen-Dazs ice cream bars.

"Remembered how I'd have Marcus stop to get a pint of Rum Raisin when we were returning to the condo after being out."

"Yes… yes, I do," I warm-heartedly smirked.

Admittedly, it was one of the sweet things Mills would do. He'd always had several in the freezer when I came to New York. And aways a gift-wrapped present on the bed upon my arrivals. Yes, pleasant memories—but when you strip the layers, those sweet things and gifts are like bait on the end of a line; and you're the fish being reeled in to be fried and eaten for dinner. But, again, I could say the same concerning what my objective was and how to get it. Mills was my fish at the end of my line. It was an alluring pretty face and a tight smooth body that were the bait.

"I'd wished you'd moved to New York as we'd planned," Mills resurrected the topic again. Each time he did, I felt like a cad.

"You mean… as you'd planned," I thought.

Despite everything I knew about Mills—I couldn't help but feel sorry for him as we sat there.

While waiting for the train, I did tell Mills that he should get away, even visit me in Atlanta although I really didn't want him to. I knew I didn't have to tell Mills that the boy was using him, that was a given. It comes with the territory—again, rich older men and pretty boys. Mills had had a lot of them, and I did remind him that there were plenty more where the boy had come from. But it was clear to me, in this particular situation, that both the ex and the new boyfriend were using Mills and he knew that as well.

When I left New York, despite any dangerous anger disguised as despondency I interpreted in Mills, I was sure that he'd have a new pretty young man in his bed within weeks if not sooner. I did call a few times to check in, only to find Mills anger was still burning through him. I just kept hoping any fears I had for the boy would not play out. Most of all, I was relieved to be out of New York.

Nearly a week later, after returning from New York, I'd received a call from a friend who was absorbed in the gay lifestyle—globally. If there was some be-all and end-all massive event, from "Timbuktu and Back," Cary was there. Including, religiously, spending summers on Fire Island.

"Have you heard from Mills?"

"I was just in New York."

"So… so, you know."

"Know what?"

on the lam

Mills returned my call within two days after I left the message with his son. The conversation was relatively brief with little information.

"I appreciate you checking in on me… Randy."

"Of course. Are you okay?"

"For now. Will… will you come back to New York?"

At the Park Avenue condo, Mills vowed innocence. Self-defense. Solicited my belief.

"Randy… you do believe me? Tell me you do."

He got up and walked over to sit next to me. Mills put his hand on my thigh; he squeezed it.

"How should I answer?" I questioned myself while Mills frenziedly stared at me like a dog waiting for a bone.

"Tell me what happened?"

"Have you heard anything?" Mills questioned.

I paused.

"Well? Have you?" he edgily pressed; his stare remaining frozen.

"All I know is you were shot. That's why I called, Ross… it's… well, I have no words."

I knew it would be a mistake to tell Mills anymore, including whether I believed him or not. Obviously, I didn't; and surely Mills was aware of that. I'd rather he just be honest. But knowing Mills, I knew he never would. I sat there waiting for what elucidation was to come that hung on his tongue.

In some way, knowing it happened two days after I flew back to Atlanta, I felt partly guilty. I should have stayed a few more days knowing the gravity of Mills' emotional pain. Consequently, if I had, the older boyfriend would still be alive. Furthermore, I should have known Mills was planning something—I would think, handsomely paying the new boyfriend to stop seeing the boy; but that's not what had taken place.

"I was at one of the volleyball games… gave his new lover a ride home. He invited me in for a drink."

"Where was the boy?

"Out of town… he was out of town," Mills repeated.

"I'm flabbergasted you would even do that… give the guy a ride."

"Yeah… but I'm trying to make peace with all of that."

Mills never made peace with anything unless doing so benefited him. He had to be faking his willingness—I was certain.

By Mills' account, while in the apartment, he was attacked by his ex's new lover.

"He… he went crazy on me."

Mills voiced the altercation involved knives, resulting in him mortally stabbing him in self-defense. Again, I didn't believe a word of it as far as being started by the boyfriend. And even as notorious and vengeful as Mills was, I knew the possibility of him getting the upper hand was extremely thin. I would have thought that Mills would have had someone else do the actual deed—like his chauffeur or anyone who was also connected with the Mafia; and that assassination could have been carried out at any time.

As I may have stated earlier, I came to believe Mills was indeed capable of having someone killed, but again, I can't imagine him achieving it himself or wanting to. After all, Mills wasn't one of the men attempting to kick in my apartment doors.

The aggressiveness and intensity of the blows were something Mills was incapable of executing—a result of his slight build. But that's not to say, regardless of physical attributes, people aren't capable of doing passionate acts whether good or bad. Certainly, when jealousy is the motivation. As also shared, Mills was an extremely jealous man that I'd experienced first-hand. No one takes anything he has branded, unless they want to pay a hefty price.

Perhaps, my saving grace, after he'd settled down concerning changing my mind about moving, was that I didn't leave him for someone else. I'm sure the boy was being watched, just as I had once been.

The following day after the attempted break-in, Mills called.

"Are you ready to move?"

Sitting there, a chill seized as I remembered what Mills once told me, "As long as you're with me, I'll never let anything happen to you."

If murder had been on Mill's mind—being the cunning man I knew and setting aside the intensity of his jealousy, he'd know it would be too soon regardless of who carried it out. Everyone, including the police would know he was guilty and likely view the murder was for hire.

Mills got up. Walked over. Sat beside me. Put his hand on my thigh. Squeezed it.

"Randy, I'm just not sure what to do," he said, as if a kid who'd wrecked his father's car and was afraid to come clean.

"Afraid," I thought. "Hardly," not with his money and resources—certainly with his arrogance riding shotgun.

I wasn't that naïve; but I kept acting as if I were.

I looked at Mills. Slightly shook my head—once again, sure he'd something planned after the boy had left him if he wasn't going to return permanently to Mills' bed.

I adamantly believed it played out differently. Apparently, knowing the boy would be away, the madness of Mills' inflamed jealousy took over and he'd lost all sense of reality; and he saw it as an opportunity. I don't know the status of the chauffeur that night; Mills didn't mention him in his depiction, and I didn't ask. But I'm sure he'd considered involving him to kill the boyfriend and dispose of the body as well. Then, Mills could have told everyone that he did pay the boyfriend off to disappear. That would be the best plan, and more believable; and it wouldn't matter how soon the murder took place.

That best plan lost in madness, murder-by-knife would have to be quick so the neighbors wouldn't be alarmed by the scuffle and possible yelling—an element of most fights. And for the odds of success, surely, Mills knew to bring a knife to the volleyball game—like a switchblade that could easily be hidden on his person. Then, once in the apartment, he would have to surprise the boyfriend. But knowing Mills, he likely had planned to murder him at the game when no one was around. Perhaps, in a bathroom—anywhere in or around the game, but more likely outside.

Evidently, Mills didn't find an opportune place at the game, so that's why he offered him a ride home. And if that were the case, and if I'm correct, the fight apparently started in the kitchen. When the boyfriend had his back to Mills, that's when he would have struck. But Mills didn't anticipate the boyfriend becoming aware of the switchblade—giving him enough time to grab a knife and fight back.

A car would have been necessary for a quick getaway. I'd heard that Mills owned a Mercedes, which I was never aware of, or had I ever seen one parked in the garage alongside the three Rolls and the stretched limo. However, Mills could have purchased one at some point after I left him. And what I earlier shared: during a dinner out with a number of his friends, I overheard Mills talking to the man seated next to him about someone who'd stolen one from Mills.

"Whatever happened to that guy who stole your Benz?"

"No one's ever going to hear from him," Mills replied, as he seemed to purposely look in my direction. That conversation solidified in my mind that indeed Mills was capable of being involved in murder.

In recounting the story, Mills left out the fact that they weren't alone in the apartment which is understandable in his efforts to make me believe he killed the boyfriend in self-defense. Mills apparently was unaware of a roommate upstairs, who'd heard the brawl and called 911before barefooting it to the main floor.

While the older boyfriend was dead or dying, in Mills' efforts to eliminate any witnesses, he proceeded to chase the roommate around the dining room table; and throwing glass containers on the floor in an attempt to corner him. Fortunately for the roommate, the police arrived. Mills was ordered to drop the knife; and when he didn't, he was shot resulting in significant damage to one of his eyes. I've forgotten if it was the left or the right; but I vaguely remember Mills wore an eyepatch that still revealed part of a scar.

Tried for murder; the trial was deadlocked. Having eventually told Mills to spare the bullshit, he confessed that two of the jurors were paid off and also threatened.

For the third time, my presence was requested. The singular reason I kept chronically returning, as I've mentioned a number of times, was I'd remained afraid of Mills and the murder intensified that fear. As I've also consistently shared: I knew what I knew while in the relationship with Mills and telling him no was never a wise choice.

Following Mills and his Brazilian chauffeur collecting me, we immediately went to a bank; I waited in the lobby. Mills retrieved an impressive jewelry collection from a safe deposit box—one of many, to be auctioned at Christie's. Subsequently at lunch, Mills brazenly made it known he was preparing to leave the country; in preparation, everything was up for sale.

"Why are you telling me?" I don't want to know anything… anything more than I do, Mills… you're pulling me deeper into all this and into more danger. And… and, if found out, I could be seen as being complicit."

"Randy… you're the only friend I have left. They're all keeping a wide distance—if that.

I remained seated when I would have preferred to run. Mills mistakenly thought I was his friend, or he was just returning the favor of me having taken advantage of him. Seeing me as a friend or not, I have no doubt he knew I was cautious of what his next move would be as if we were playing a treacherous game of chest greased-up for me to give up my queen; but I was sure, he was greasing me up for more.

As my first summons, where Mills had several near-breakdowns concerning all the drama caused by the boy breaking things off, we went to Fire Island. At breakfast on Monday morning, before my return to Atlanta, Mills informed me that I needed to give him a window of time to leave the country.

"Fuck! You want me to do what?"

"I need your help… to give me a window of time to escape… I'm going to be tried again. I have to… I have to leave."

"What about your buddies in black… you know, your associations with the Mafia."

"I know I'm being watched. I need someone they would never suspect… "

"So… I'm the lucky fool."

"Look," Mills sniffed. "I'll make it worth your while."

"The only… worth my while, is to leave and not end up in jail or worse."

"You don't have a choice."

"How are you even out of jail?"

All I could do was bury my face in my hands.

"I'm out on a sizable bond."

"Really… any judge would know you're a flight risk. Wait. I forgot for a second. You've got some friends in pretty high places… how much. Wait, don't tell me."

And I didn't want to know. Besides, I already knew that Mills had more money than God stuffed away—untraceable, in many places around the world.

In my first book, I only wrote about the telegram Mills told me to send to his attorney; maybe that was just one request—or should I state, ordered. Maybe Mills had actually asked me to do more—like he'd given me a grocery list. And would have to. I was trapped, and I'd already put my life on the line when I was with him. But I wasn't only afraid of Mills, but his associates-in-crime.

I also wrote about the card I received in the mail after Mills had left the country. He'd written what a wonderful friend I'd been and that he wanted me to know that he appreciated and loved me. It's true about receiving the card and the brief note that he wrote. I also shared that there was money in the envelope; but that's not true. You have to remember that Mills was alive at the time and on the lam; even still, I thought the card would be the last time that I would hear from Mills; that I was finally free of him. But once again—I was wrong.

The next day after the receipt of the card, a courier knocked on my apartment door. I signed for a box full of money. I can assure you that it wasn't a thank you gift; it was another way to keep me tied to him and what I'd done. It was actually, blood money; and Mills had made me a criminal.

Maybe a few years later, Mills contacted me through a third party. Maybe, I knew all along where he was.

I've read some mistruths concerning what really happened, and others about Mills, separate from the murder—that just don't have wings to fly.

Much earlier, I shared that many years later, I was contacted via email by a reporter-writer. He'd found out about me after I'd thought I was well hidden from those past events surrounding Mills. But apparently, I wasn't.

Terrified that I'd finally been caught, I didn't wish to expose myself any more than I may have been to the authorities. Expose, the things I'd done to help Mills. Certainly, not fill in any blanks; and there were many concerning him. Nevertheless, I did want the reporter-writer to know, in spite of the man who Mills was, is that he desperately wanted to be loved. But a man like him never found it or even could—only his money did. And for many of us who were drawn to it thinking it was free except for giving our bodies—that was rarely the case. The cost is usually exponentially much higher.

partners in crime

I wrote Sandra two letters days before July 4th. My hand shook; I could hardly read my own writing as tears fell onto the stationary. The first was to say goodbye—to tell her, I was sorry and heartbroken to leave her and Dugan behind. I asked Sandra to forgive me; and try to find solace in the knowledge I was at rest; and begged her not to follow.

"Dear Sister, please do your best to go on with life… keep searching for the happiness that has eluded us and our mother. Do it for all of us. I know I leave you with a massive burden to carry in your heart… "

I asked Sandra to take care of Dugan—that I needed her to look after my boy. A check for $25,000.00 was included for her and Dugan to take a long vacation somewhere by the sea. And that a trust had been set up for her that Allen would oversee.

"You will feel my spirit watching over you… I know you will."

In the second, I revealed to Sandra about the money in the three key safes as I did the watch collection—as I did about the safety deposit box. I conveyed; she was the only other person that could access the deposit box at the bank. I'd included the key in the envelope as I shared the location of the keys to the key safes in the office. I wrote that it was a sizable amount of unreported money, and it must remain such. That, I was giving it to her but to keep it a secret from everyone and never deposit any of it into a bank account. Instead, move it into a safety deposit box. Both letters were sealed and taped along with a few other letters with a copy of my will—Allen, obviously in possession of the original. I placed all the letters in an oversized envelope—sealed as well, with Allen's address and phone number. Left it in plain sight on top of my laptop on my desk.

After my release from the hospital, Allen returned the envelope. Considering that I'd survived the ordeal after coming out of surgery, he didn't distribute the letters. I'd put the envelope away in the filing cabinet in the closet of the office and forgot about it. That is until one morning, I was sitting at the round desk in my home office drinking coffee while checking emails.

While in lapse of thought, I looked around the room. Being anal-retentive, I noticed the art books on the bottom shelves weren't stacked as I'd kept them: precisely, perfectly stacked in a pyramid.

I got up to stack them back in the proper order. Concern probed. I'd not removed any of the books or accessed the safes in months—before or after returning home. I proceeded to remove the books from the shelves and the shelves themselves to reveal the safes. After retrieving the keys to unlock each one, I discovered one was already unlocked. Four banked-wrapped bundles of hundred-dollar bills and some loose cash were missing. Totaling just over $3000.00. Four watches were gone: two Nixons, a Montblanc, and a 1969, Breitling Chronomat. The Montblanc, valued at over $5,000.00. The Breitling, at least $9000.00 if not more. The Nixons combined, roughly 1,200.00.

Although the Breitling and the Montblanc were insured, the Breitling had been a gift to Bradley. Obviously, holding extreme sentimental value as it was rare. The other three watches and the money aside, the theft of a watch represented the stealing of an extraordinary part of the past—pilfering, the most precious thing I owned: the memory of the happiness I found with Bradley, and even a part of Bradley himself. It, and those memories were all I had left of him.

In the event my home caught fire, the Breitling would be the only object I would take—even at the risk of burning in the flames myself.

A handful of people had been in and out of the house while I was hospitalized. Except for William's failed FBI sweep for my illicit steroids—I couldn't imagine any of my friends would go snooping around. And again, the compartments under the bottom shelves were well hidden unless someone were to have x-ray vision. Even though Allen hadn't, again, given out the letters, I felt the need to be confident the one to Sandra concerning the key safes and watches hadn't been opened. I retrieved the large envelope from the file cabinet. Closely examined it—going as far as sleuthing it, using a magnifying glass to for any signs it had been opened and resealed. Afterward, I was convinced it hadn't. That only left two probable culprits. Probable but not conclusive.

Distressed by the stolen Breitling, a state of panic followed suit. I didn't care about the other watches or the money. I called Allen only to get his voicemail. I left a message before calling his secretary. She informed that he was in court. In the meantime, while waiting for Allen's return call, my mind spun searching who could have taken the money and the watches. And I mentally questioned who had keys to my house.

There were five people: Sandra; Christopher, who never gave the house key back or did I think to ask for it; Nicky, but she was from a wealthy family; William, also wealthy; Allen and Oliver too, were very well off financially; Jay, who wasn't and hadn't paid back the three thousand I'd loaned him the year before.

Although they had keys, several other people had access to my home while I was in the hospital. But my mind eventually pointed to one person. One person, who had enough access and for a period. And due to that access and amount of time, I could have slipped up at some point and that person could have discovered there were false bottoms to the bookshelves.

It was just a matter of when the money and watches were stolen. And why weren't all the key safes taken as the entire watch collection? Then, there was the matter of the keys to the safes. But they wouldn't have been that hard to find since I kept them, with the keys to the cars in a contemporary box on one of the shelves.

Shortly following the discovery, I had a locksmith change the locks. Then, took Allen's advice and immediately started checking pawn shops within the vicinity of Midtown. He thought it would be the best avenue if they hadn't already been sold.

By the fourth, I found the Breitling and the Montblanc. I explained to the proprietor they were stolen along with two Nixons. He'd tensely asked if I'd made a police report. I hadn't but stated otherwise—hoping that would allow me to get them back at a fraction of their value since I'd brought it to his attention that he had taken in stolen merchandise. But I would have pretty much paid anything to get the Breitling back.

The owner insisted it was just the two. But I believed otherwise, that the Nixons had already been sold. I also made it known to the pawn shop owner that the watches were a part of my watch collection and had been documented by photographs and were listed with my homeowner's insurance. Which they were.

Even if I'd called the police, I had no solid proof to substantiate who I suspected before I searched the pawn shops. My accusation would be weightless. And it would be my word against someone else's. Besides, my word could possibly be viewed as that of a crazy person due to the July 4, 2009, event. Or even a lie on my part as revenge.

After haggling, I offered twenty-five hundred for both and another two-hundred-fifty for the identity of who had pawned them. The owner responded, "I don't want to get involved." Another one-fifty changed his mind. His description of two people was enough to be certain of the collaborators.

six

the cowboy and the horse he rode in on

On that sunny arctic mid-morning, the air had a cutting rawness. My third lap around the Arrivals level of Hartsfield-Jackson Atlanta International, I spotted him standing on the curb looking all like Canadian—Bruce. I figured, if I were going to meet someone that wasn't a one-night stand, perhaps he should be an out-of-towner. That kind of logic may not have made any real sense—but nothing had in quite some time. For that, Canada seemed sufficiently out-of-town.

Bruce looked like a Tom of Finland outtake: a muscular frame, competition-perfect body, filled out his attire. A nicely-fitting, snowy-white crewneck sweater showed off to-die-for pecs; an open, waist-length, brown leather jacket, I was certain was Banana Republic; distressed Levi's, showcased a porn-star-perfect shelf-of-a-bubble-butt and a noticeable protuberance in the front. All enough to rush a tingling sensation throughout my anatomy.

Express-dispatched from Toronto—Bruce looked exactly like the many pictures he'd emailed over the few past months. He had advertised his features and benefits well, like a seasoned telemarketer. It was an effective sales pitch. I had made an impulse-purchase the first time Bruce dropped the suggestion he should come for a visit. Before I knew it, it was all arranged: to spend a long weekend getting to know each other.

I wondered if he would be a fulfillment-purchase? His sales pitch—like a late-night infomercial on the higher-up cable channels that came with a guarantee. But a guarantee of what? Nonetheless, the merchandise standing on the curb—melted the chill surrounding all that hotness. Bruce was clearly, one piece of exquisitely delectable eye-candy in the flesh. I remember trying not to think too much about his arrival. "Just let it happen," I told myself. Too much preplanning and forethought in such situations seem to militate against the odds of a favorable outcome.

Bruce was two years older. We'd met, where else—online. He stood out among the rest that stressed the Internet cables with men and boys looking for sex, anonymously or otherwise, and perhaps some for a partner. Bruce seemed unique—breaking the de rigueur mold. Not one time in his emails or during lengthy phone conversations, did Bruce steer in the direction of sex. A surprising tactfulness that caught me off guard from the usual hunt. Although Bruce did inform, he was a top and only a top. More surprisingly, Bruce never asked how I was hung which is often the first or second question asked.

Phone conversations eventually outnumbered the emails. Bruce made me smile—even laugh. Things I hadn't done or felt in a very long time. At least, not since Bradley. But the longer our exchanges continued—the more I wondered when it would all end. Come to a screeching halt; as I questioned, if it was just the building of male lust masquerading as possible true feelings?

Bruce had no idea the tall order of my admittedly spectacularly inflated expectations. If he had, Bruce most likely wouldn't have booked a flight from Toronto to Atlanta. For years, up to Bruce, I was consciously unaware I'd been sizing every man up to Bradley. At my Canadian's arrival, I would be doing the same.

I eyed Bruce, looking for the approach of his ride. His image grew larger as the car inched along. So did my labored anticipation, aware I was getting closer to something. Those first moments, once Bruce got into the car, would be telling of what might come to be. Would we hit it off face-to-face as we did via exchanged emails and on the phone?

A car pulled away from the curb—my cue to take its place right in front of Bruce. I told myself, "Breathe. Just breathe. Please fucking breathe!" Yes, I was nervous. He'd flown-in to spend four days. I questioned: if it was wise, and were four days too much time for a first meeting? I was taking a rather bulky risk with Bruce. He wasn't coming for a coffee date. Certainly, not from Toronto to Atlanta for a Frappuccino.

superman

During the drive to the airport—I wondered if Bruce would be pleased once he saw me in the living, breathing, flesh? Certainly, after we'd spent some one-on-one time together. I knew those first few minutes—perhaps even seconds would determine how the rest of his weekend visit would fare. And if it were a bust—having found me undesirable, we would awkwardly part ways with a handshake or an uncomfortable hug—disingenuously promising to get together again before he made a quick getaway.

I didn't want to disappoint him. Bruce wasn't flying a thousand miles for a slam-bam hook-up when he could cross the street in Toronto for that. Bruce had made it clear: he was looking for more. As much as I wanted someone in my life in that long-term, warm, and fuzzy way, with my track record and a résumé with the line items of mental meltdown and suicide attempts—that was a lot of pressure and apprehension for both of us.

Even with those concerns, I had a good feeling about Bruce. Call it positive thinking. A first in a long time—positive thinking. Still, I didn't want to jinx it. Certainly, avoid stepping on any cracks while walking down a sidewalk. He'd said the same about his gut feeling concerning me shortly before his travels to Atlanta. I knew we both were betting against some big odds. We'd been playing poker, the last few months; Bruce felt he was holding a winning hand. But it was the other way around—I felt I had a royal flush. All the same, it was a gamble for both of us. Bruce was coming to see if that feeling was as real. No more hiding behind pictures, texts, and small talk over the phone—although we did engage in a few serious discussions.

Bruce would do more than just hear the inflections in my voice as he had over the phone. Face-to-face sharing the same space with only inches and not miles between us, Bruce would see my lips move accompanied by facial expressions and body language—as I would his. More importantly, Bruce would be able to see my eyes react. I'd just hoped he wouldn't read desperation in them.

I remained brittle and raw on the inside. The walls I'd built hopefully to isolate myself from any more pain, resulting in more bitterness and disappointments—a barricade to deflect life's bullets of injury to the heart and even those of the soul had become a maze. Not that they were succeeding and their intended purpose, the day came—all those walls started crumbling at a time I was running out of emotional bricks and mortar—and time. Valuable time. I needed that someone to hold me tight again without breaking me—as Bradley had. Bruce certainly had the arms to do just that: hold me tenderly or break me in half.

The endearing conversations with Bruce had sparked an ounce of hope there was another proverbial Superman—somewhere within the spectrum of Bradley; a White Knight who had treated me as his prince until the day came, he was no longer around. Perhaps, I'd been allotted the one—my quota and that's why anything disguised as a relationship was volatile resulting in short lifespans with problematic endings. Still, I wanted at least something close to what I had. Only close because I knew Bradley was irreplaceable. And I was willing to accept someone in the vicinity of him. I needed salvation from the plagued emotions—occupants of a barren wasteland. The things that couldn't be box-up and taped-shut with industrial packing tape. Much of the same things I wrongly believed my mother could. The feelings of emptiness, loss, and loneliness had returned. Sleep afforded little amnesty.

Those relentless nightmares continued to come at me as I grew restless of sleeping alone without human substance. God, how I missed Bradley since his memory had returned to the surface. At least I had Dugan. I hoped Bruce would be more than a well-wrapped outer shell. He wasn't riding in on a white horse but in a white Air Canada plane with a huge red maple leaf on the fin of its tail wing. Perhaps, that would suffice for the white, well-groomed, galloping steed.

Not until our later phone conversations, did Bruce get to know some of my story concerning the July 4, 2009, suicide attempt that hospitalized me for several weeks. Even a few of the gory details—although, admittedly, a CliffsNotes' version with a few pages torn out—of what had gone down before and after the breakup, and some of the surrounding instability. It would have been unrealistic to try to keep it a secret from Bruce—unfairly so. But I didn't want to empty the whole bucket of bloody water over his head. The last drops would have to wait. Wait until if there was evidence that we had a chance of any staying power and Bruce, not just a shiny new toy.

He would obviously find out eventually. It was too colossal of a sink-hole—too enormous to contain, especially if it were to get any bigger. I didn't want to pull Bruce in with me. Still, I felt obligated to be somewhat candid. He had a right to know in case Bruce didn't want to deal with the excess weight of my truckload of baggage—be afforded the courtesy to step away before the investment in a plane ticket. And, he had to know I was going to leave Atlanta at some point. That, I had to make it out West. If I was being completely honest with myself: I wasn't emotionally strong enough—yet. And wasn't even sure if I ever would be due to the fluctuating plummets into depression, and the mornings I woke feeling an overwhelming sensation of death encircling me.

Astonishingly, Bruce had shown a lot of compassion. The concerns he expressed were only for my well-being. Bruce didn't flinch. He didn't run in the opposite direction. The emails continued as the phone still rang. Knowing the crux of the matter—hadn't deterred him.

Bruce squatted beside the low-profiled XJS. I pressed a finger on the button to retract the window; the car heater gave way to the cold chill of the outside air rushing the interior. Still, I felt overheated as strong manly hand with long and thick fingers rested on the top of the passenger door. I'd noticed his nails were perfectly trimmed, manicured, and lacquered in the most discrete, masculine, clear-coat matte polish. His honey-brown eyes met mine. They locked. I swallowed hard. Really hard.

"Hello. I'm Bruce," he introduced, with a mischievous smile.

A line of recalcitrant honking motorists seen in the rearview mirror angled for an inch of curb space, piled up like bumper cars in an amusement park. A seemingly bad-tempered traffic police officer whose mission in life was surely to monetize with incentive fines—at a nanosecond's indiscretion in premeditated vehicular dawdling, his annoyingly ear-piercing whistle.

"Hum. You look kind of familiar… "

"From where?" Bruce jokingly asked, followed with a wink.

"I think I picked you up the last time I was cruising the airport arrivals for hot men in need of a ride. Do you happen to need a ride?"

Bruce chuckled.

"But seriously… nice to meet you in the flesh."

I hadn't spent much effort getting ready to retrieve a guest: a quick shower; a pair of old jeans; a black T-shirt; a North Face gray hoodie; well-worn Nikes, long retired from the gym; a few spritzes of Egoiste Platinum by Chanel. If all else failed, at least I wanted to smell good.

As I eyed Bruce, I remember thinking that I hoped I looked better than my pictures. But I wasn't going to get all worked-up over something that might be a waste of both our times. I thought it best for the first impression to come-off as relaxed and casual. Although I'd hoped when he saw me, Bruce would feel I was worth the price of his plane ticket to Atlanta. So, what was the point of getting all dressed up like a beauty queen?

My reticence generated a latent prompt to break eye contact. I managed to resist. At that moment, I wished I'd put a little more effort into my appearance. I clasped my breath. Bruce was no longer a collection of pictures stored in a file on my laptop or a voice over the phone. His buzzed hair revealed a distinct widow's peak. Bruce sported an exquisitely timed, two-day facial scruff. His presentation was the personification of sexy.

A grating beeping horn interrupted the moment, followed by a stream of sudden short-and-shrill tweets of the traffic cop's whistle as. He flailed his arms. Translation: move-the-fuck-on. The officer's patience clearly was wearing thin—on hair-trigger, prepared to criminalize my very stationary presence.

"Hop in before Whistle-Happy gives me a ticket."

"I thought you were never going to ask."

Bruce stood up. His face disappeared replaced by a crotch in my frame of vision. The car door opened with a click. A hand pulled the back of the passenger seat forward. A bag bounced into the back. His body took possession of the seat.

"The electric prompt is on the right side of the seat," I instructed, seeing that his body was cramped.

Bruce and the seat slid back.

"Thanks. I need the leg room."

"I can tell… by the way, the seat warmer switch is next to it."

"Seat warmer?" Bruce chuckled. "This is a warm day compared to

Toronto."

I turned the steering wheel. Pressed the gas pedal with a heavy foot. Screeched away from the curb before the police officer could blow his obnoxious whistle. Superman turned his head back in my direction. His gaze returned like that of a combat sniper's, in the scope on a rifle. There was that smile again. A visceral tingling filled my abdomen. I felt like a schoolboy anticipating his first kiss—wondering if he could get it right and pleasingly enough.

a new bod in town

Bruce had suggested that we get-in a good workout directly after his arrival. I thought it to be a good idea. It offered the time to interact in a familiar, mutually comfortable environment—doing what we both liked. Plus, a gym workout would help sustain the mystery a while longer. That is, if we both felt a spark; and if so, prevent us from jumping each other's bones in the first few minutes after arriving at the house. Although admittedly, in the forefront of my mind, I was eager to get Bruce naked as soon as I could since the sight of him at the airport. I managed to resist the devil made me do it impulse. Plus, I wanted him to make the first move. That is, if my Canadian liked what he saw. Bruce had his left hand on my right thigh the entirety of the drive back—I saw that as a good sign of his interest.

After a quick introduction to Dugan—his approval important and dropping off Bruce's bags; we collected our gym attire. Within the fifteen minutes of a somewhat irregularly pulsating drive, several flirtatious grins were exchanged—we arrived at LA Fitness. A small miracle we'd made it alive and not killed in a car accident due to my eyes directed on Bruce instead of the road most of the drive.

The moment we walked through the doors, we entered a wormhole into another dimension—light years away from the rest of humankind. An independent world within itself. We maneuvered our way through the somewhat crowded gym—the nucleus of male gay existence immersed in loud music intermixing with random spotty voices, clanging weights, and that of grunts and moans from physical exertion in a desperate quest to obtain the body-beautiful. Later to be displayed on the dance floors of the clubs around town—shirtless, of course.

As if in slow, deliberate, and prudent motion—like two characters in a Martin Scorsese film, hungry eyes and thirsty mouths followed as heads turned to the imposing introduction of Bruce. The captivated onlookers' primitive instincts instantly triggered with overwhelming, flooding, racing imagery: the sexual ecstasy of lust; wet hardness; man sweat; smells of arousing, potent body odors; dark corners; heavy, measured breathing; thrusting movements; pain and pleasure—dismissing all lucid thinking and caution.

A new hot bod was in town with a handsome, manly face. Most of us are slaves to beauty. Certainly, many gay men. We worship muscle under exquisite flesh of the male form. We want to be cocooned in and smothered by it. We want to own it. Devour it and be devoured by it. That was Bruce. Exquisite. Sublime. Celestial. Magnificent, as if he were genuinely a creation of Michelangelo, come to life from the ceiling of the Sistine Chapel some four-hundred and ninety-eight years ago; come to life from fresco transformed into flesh and blood.

In the locker room, the stares enhanced. Penetrating—to the degree of intrusive. Like a pack of wolves circling while closing in to ambush their prey. Guys lingered as Bruce came out of his tight jeans and sweater. Until stripped down to a black pair of Armani underwear. Jaws dropped. Involuntary gasps heard. Bruce's body was ripped, the perfect combination of lean and bulk. But I already knew that from his pictures. His skin: smooth, toned, blemish-free, and tanned. Although Bruce was the focus of objectified celebrity attention, he never let on. No doubt, used to being the center of attention in most settings—clothed or otherwise.

On the gym floor, Bruce's snug-fitting black tank revealed spectacular pecs, delts, and guns to cause an ogling frenzy by those who'd missed the locker room show. Gray athletic shorts gave way to meaty quads and calves—that is, if eyes moved below his unambiguous bulge outlining a sizable, flaccid penis. Bruce wasn't trying to flaunt his junk. It would take the duct tape and paraphernalia of a drag queen's wardrobe to keep it under wraps.

I found considerable satisfaction in flaunting Bruce at the gym every afternoon of his visit. Many acquaintances—who seldom said hello, continued to grill me as to the identity of the new piece-of-meat. My response, in a polite manner: he's a friend from out of town. But that wasn't enough to satisfy their hungered curiosities as if chickens pecking for kernels of corn. Some of the boys, likely in need of a diaper change. Others, wanting to have Bruce's baby.

easing into things

Following the gym or more-like—Gay Pride Day with Bruce as the Grand Parade Marshall and lunch at Panera Bread, we returned to the house for a well-deserved nap.

Bruce removed his red tank top and tossed it in my direction. My hand instinctively reached up to catch it as he plopped on the bed. Of course, Dugan jumped up—letting Bruce know whose bed he was on.

"It's mine now."

"Why do you think I threw it at you?"

I grinned.

"Want to shower?"

"Mind if we forgo it even though I'm a bit funky?"

"No… it's more than okay with me."

Dugan sniffed Bruce then began licking his face.

"I can see he's a lover and not a fighter."

"That's my Dugan… "

"Why don't you come lie down with us?" Bruce asked.

"You bet, Cowboy. I want to brush my teeth first."

I occasionally eyed Bruce and Dugan through the open bathroom doorway. My reflection in the mirror over the sink gaped back at me while I brushed—gaped back, as it questioned: why would such an accomplished man want to be with someone so broken like me; someone who had become the butt of jokes; someone who had been wrongly accused a stalker, regardless of being vindicated in court; someone who was labeled as crazy; someone who held his head down in unwarranted shame; why had he flown from Toronto to Atlanta, when men were surely lining up at his front door awaiting his return?

Absorbed within the stretched quiet of still air, I laid next to my Canadian who'd fallen asleep on his back. The unanswered questions stubbornly continued to reel my mind on a continuous loop. Dugan had already moved to the end of the bed. I remained fixed on my side as not to disturb Bruce—my back to him as my eyes scanned the bedroom.

I felt the movement of the mattress as Bruce rolled on his side. His left arm slipped around my waist to pull my body closer to his. Bruce's chest against my back, not only offered warmth—but a sense of needed comfort.

A whisper eased into the silence of that afternoon.

"How long was I asleep?"

"Not long… maybe thirty minutes."

The smell of prominent body odor, potently-sweetened, transuded from Bruce's pores—distinctive and arousing. All the same, I was glad we hadn't rushed into sex. Actually, more relieved. Without forethought and unexpectedly, an image of Bradley flashed under my closed eyelids. One of many occurrences that came and went over the years—but they had flashed more frequently since early 2009. As well, I'd begun dreaming of him again; dreams of us together visited as I slept—as if Bradley had a key to my mind. And in many ways, he did. All welcomed. All seemingly real as life itself. And while I slept, I knew those dreams gave me solace only to awaken with tears.

With time—a few years after I lost him, those images and comforting dreams I had of Bradley eventually began to slip away. In some ways, their retread was embraced. My heart just couldn't take the pain they had left me with—leaving me to mourn him over and over.

The image of Bradley that afternoon—undoubtedly, was triggered by Bruce's arm around me. Out of all the men I'd been with after Bradley, Bruce was the closest to mirror him. Lying with him was as if a part of Bradley had returned. I felt it. I felt Bradley, as if he was once again beside me. My heart wafted toward his memory as a tear left one of my eyes; rolled over my cheek down to my lips. Bruce's voice carried me back to the present.

"Is this good for you?"

"You… you won't get any complaints from me," I responded, as I cleared my throat.

Bruce's lips tenderly kissed behind my neck as he squeezed me tighter. Then, even tighter. And with each squeeze, I left his bicep flex. Then, again and again until the kisses as the squeezes became more sporadic. With one last kiss, Bruce's face soon nuzzled into the curve of my neck. His breaths became deeper. My eyes closed. The silence returned as we both were pulled within a cloud of sleep.

Soundless time had given way to the narrowing of the day—and the light of the bedroom as well. Undiscovered until Dugan nudged his snout at my face, awakening me. He needed to go outside. Skillfully, lifted Bruce's arm from around my waist—careful not to disturb his sleep as Dugan had mine. Successful, our movement left him undisturbed.

The unforgiving air impaled with sharpened cold—rushed the den the instant the door opened. Dugan dashed out into the elements that held everything living at its mercy. Not faltering, he was back within minutes as Dugan shook himself warm. I closed the door before freezing into an ice statue. We returned to the bed—to another source of agreeable heat.

In the sedated hour, I was soothed to just be—just be next to Bruce once again. Sheathed in the satisfaction of his presence. Listen to his hypnotic-like unbroken respirations even though we'd made plans for later. But I'd rather allow Bruce to remain in his slumber—perfectly fine in continuing to share the bed. The earlier overwhelming questions, by then, had slipped from my mind. Or maybe it was Bruce's presence that finally had pushed them away.

As my eyes were about to close, Bruce's arm returned to take hold of my waist. Once again, my body was against and aligned with his. But that was temporary. His hand moved up until it reached my chest. Bruce began to rub it from pec to pec before rolling me onto my back. He climbed on top of me. I felt the strength of his weight. His lips locked mine. The dominance of the increasing size and hardness of Bruce's penis: obvious. The only barriers—our gym shorts.

"Jesus," I thought.

a drive into the night

Our silhouettes showered in the low light of the bathroom; temptation called as we washed each other's bodies…

Dressed and after kissing Dugan on the head and giving him a treat, Bruce and I headed out. In intrepid defiance, the temperature had fallen once again—pushing Atlanta into a cold snap. Apparently, tepid by Canadian standards. Bruce requested the car's top down. I obliged although my ass was freezing—the seat-warmers of the XJS seemed inadequate for the intensity of the Siberian-like weather.

The car traveled through the clear and brisk impulsive wet-cold infusing air, under a nearly-full polished moon—incandescent and beaming, surrounded by a smoky luminosity as I showed Bruce parts Midtown.

I took a sharp right turn off Peachtree Street into the posh, stately Ansley Park neighborhood. The more Bruce leaned into me from the passenger seat—his left arm securely around my shoulders before moving his hand to rub the back of my neck under the scarf that wrapped it, served to defrost my body.

Once back on the main drag, abundant light poles glowed down and outward. Resplendent—they haloed through the frosted, deep gray and darkened air. They merged the faster the long, sleek, black Jag raced like a jet up an almost empty Peachtree Street—running yellow traffic lights seconds before changing to red. Within minutes, we'd made it the six or so miles to the heart of Buckhead. From there, the car continued left onto West Paces Ferry Road to view the mansions of old-moneyed Atlanta, and those of the nouveau riche.

The hour approaching midnight, I headed back southward. Stopping off at R. Thomas Deluxe Grill: the popular twenty-four-seven eatery. A long-standing destination for an eclectic crowd: the night owls—perhaps vampires, too; straight and gay; preppy-to-hipsters; professional to chill; aging hippies; bead-bedecked earth-mothers; tatted-and-pierced punkers. The famed gathering of diversity, situated on the west side of the main drag—the virtual border between Buckhead and Midtown, filling customers' bellies since the 1970s. The décor—couture kitsch to down-low tacky. Its saving graces were the cultural interlace, is the food.

The well-known and colorful proprietor has a fancy for the husbandry of exotic tropical birds—dozens maintained in cages outside the premises. Some trained to greet and converse with patrons in quite intelligible English phrases. Every time I've gone there, I instinctively long to open the cages and set them free from their captivity and involuntary labor. Birds are meant to fly free.

We sat, warmed near one of the patio heaters, at a small round table covered with a 1960s-patterned tablecloth—maybe older. Customer chatter and discontinuous traffic noises bordered. Bruce had been attentive since the moment he slid into the passenger seat of the car. Never once did I notice him look at another guy in the gym or while having dinner. Although like the gym, in R. Thomas—the roving eyes fancied Bruce as they slowed then stopped on his countenance. As in the car, he insisted on sitting close to me.

Although circled in a packed room, it felt as though we were in our own orbit—as we talked about everything yet nothing. I was more open to conversation than I'd been at lunch as we shared our entrees. The wine could be thanked for that.

Netted in our dialogue of those assortment of topics, was my dithering concerning California. About how I felt I'd wasted too much precious time—while seemingly on some quest to find a way to pull myself back into one person. To be whole again. Bruce suggested that sometime soon we should meet in Los Angeles for a getaway. It sounded better than nice. Our late-night dinner of sharing food and conversation lasted minutes past 3:00 a.m.

The raw gelid-night air met us exiting the restaurant. As in the car, Bruce put his arm around my shoulders. Again, pulled me closer as we navigated our steps down the steep-sloped parking lot to the car. The further away from the restaurant, night breathed silence. Only a few spattering stars' brilliance managed to strain their light through the dark sky—leaving the multitude cloaked by the expansiveness of the city lights.

Each exhale of crystalline-like breath was carried on a visible, misty cloud from the condensation. Effortlessly suspended in front of our faces until the little cloud drifted a short distance and then dissipated. Swiftly followed by another and then another before the one before was completely gone. Bruce unexpectedly stopped me in front of the car. He physically turned me to face him—eyes to eyes while wrapping both his arms around my waist. A warmth rushed through my body—from fingertips to toes. My heart jumped. Then, jumped again in my chest. He pulled me in until there was nothing between us but clothing—not even air separated us.

I managed to hold his deliberate and inquisitive—almost invasive gaze, as if Bruce had me in a mesmerizing trance. As if I'd been spellbound. Bruce's penetrating silver eyes seemed to have accessed into my inner being—as if having found a fracture allowing admittance to search through it attentively and laboriously. Peering under every scar—causing a small quake of fear to rumble. There had only been one other person in my life that made me feel so exposed—so vulnerable, even more so than Bruce was at that moment. I didn't want him to look too sweepingly and fathomless. There were things no one should ever know. Certainly, not Bruce. Know of the pile of grotesque secrets I'd kept hidden. Those that would have to die with me. The space around us and everything in it: the cars, the buildings, the moon above, the sky, and the air itself began to spin.

I fully expected Bruce to say something. I waited for his mouth to open—for words to be liberated by his lips but he continued to silently stare. Sudden shyness compelled me to look away; I fought it. Yet, I was too fainthearted to blink. Too afraid if I did that in a glimmer of time—a nanosecond, less time needed to take a breath, Bruce would abruptly disappear. And I'd be left standing alone in the deepest, most interior part of night.

A smile eased on his face. It leaned toward mine. Our noses touched. He tilted his head slightly. A kiss followed. Our lips touched sparingly but luscious before our mouths opened. The kind of kiss that only happens in old-time movies on the big screen. That kind of kiss that leaves you wanting more.

Bruce took the car keys. Mindful I'd consumed one too many glasses of wine. Besides being irresponsible if I did get behind the wheel, I certainly didn't want to damage my Canadian package. The XJS shot out of the parking lot and back onto Peachtree Street. Bruce maneuvered it as if a race car driver. I leaned my head back on the headrest. The feeling of pure exhilaration progressively pumped the faster he drove—the faster the black Jaguar sped south cutting through the night back in the direction of Midtown. As earlier, the streetlights and those from the surrounding buildings increasingly blurred together as did the thoughts in my mind. I didn't even feel the cold. I deliberated what the rest of the night offered? Even if—I was ready for it?

a nina simone kind of night

A good-natured Dugan was waiting at the door when Bruce and I returned in the edging hours before sunrise. My house guest squatted to show him affection, scratching his head that progressed to innocent play-fighting.

Dugan's tail increasingly wagged until at the speed of a ceiling fan on high. As the new-found friends played, I inserted a Nina Simone CD, set on repeat, in the stereo located inside the Art Deco chest under the main double windows of the living room. One final pat, offered by Bruce, left Dugan wanting more attention—enough never being enough for him. I'd a sense that I might feel the same.

Bruce stood up. Took my hand and led me up the diffused, feeble light of the hallway in the direction of the master bedroom. At the doorway, he packaged me in his arms and kissed me—enkindling hunger for more while weakening every bendable joint in my body.

Entangled within the passionate kiss, Bruce walked me backward. Stopped at the foot from the bed, then released me from his arms and the prolonged kiss. He began to disrobe my upper body—garment by garment until the scarf, coat, and shirt piled on the floor. Unbuckled my belt. Unsnapped and unzipped my jeans. Pushed them down enough to expose black boxer-briefs, and a leaking hard penis sticking up passed the waistband.

Bruce moved his strong hands to capture my face. They cradled it with a gentleness. But there was no denying the crushing strength they were capable of. I didn't care. I wanted Bruce to crush me. He returned his opened lips to mine as our eyes united for ineffable minutes—until Bruce's lips broke the breath-robbing kiss at the push of his hands on my chest. My body fell backward without warning onto the bed. From that position, I was looking up at a giant.

I watched as Bruce removed his clothes. As each garment fell on top of mine, anticipation once again raided. That of touching his bare skin. Running my hands over it. Licking it. And the feel of it against my body.

Bruce wrestled the shirt off bulging muscles. The last garment to fall. It dropped from his fingers as the rest had, exposing a massive torso.

Thoughts abandoned expect for those of him—too captivated by his six-foot-two unimpeachable frame: broad, muscled shoulders; massive biceps and triceps; explosive pecs; washboard abs; the more than impressive size of his uncircumcised penis and large-egged testicles.

Bruce's dark chest hair appeared naturally short—thinly covering his chest. It trailed narrowly down his abdomen between ripped muscular abs to the navel. My body ached with lust as my lungs drew hungering breaths at the sight of this mountainous man in all his naked, and mightily glory.

Bruce leaned forward. Smiled. His body fell downward, landing on either side of mine as his hands and arms balanced him inches from my face. The mattress bounced at impact—the bedframe surprisingly left intact despite the abruptness and weighty poundage. I was happily trapped. Bruce could confine me if he wished and as long, without any struggle—without any protest.

"I think I'll need… need more than a long weekend," Bruce confessed as he hovered.

I didn't utter a word in response. My head may have spun from the wine earlier at dinner on the drive back to the house, but at that point, it was all Bruce. An agog quivering seized.

The inches between us quickly vanished as Bruce lowered himself on top of my body. The stone hardness of his erection commanded dominance as it pressed. I spread my legs. Raised my knees. His balls dropped between them. Bruce's tongue licked my lips as his eyes lanced mine—holding an unflinching gaze. I reached for them—his balls to feel their weight in my hand as Bruce's lips took mine. My mouth welcomed his tongue. It tangled with mine mixing our saliva until it ran over my chin.

Unwanted by me, our lips separated as Bruce lifted his body off mine. But only inches as before. My hand released his balls. Then, Bruce took it as he did the other and slid them over the bed sheets. Up, until they were restrained over my head.

Bruce returned his lips to mine. His tongue probed deeper into my mouth. Deeper. And then deeper before he moved it downward over my chic; soon continuing to my neck and further to between my pics.

From there, Bruce's tongue moved to my nipples. Teasing them first as it circled each areola before he began sucking. Then, biting. Then, milking. Each bite. Each suck became harder and more intense as he alternated from nipple to nipple. The growing intensity reflexively arched my body. His eyes looked up at me as his tongue traveled to my penis. Bruce licked the leaking precum before his mouth took its head. Slowly took the full length of my penis between his lips to my balls. Sucked it up and down. Then, sucked back up one more time—even slower. I was about to cum like a sixteen-year-old boy fucking his first girl.

Bruce released my hands. Leaned back on his haunches. His beckoning eyes traveled my body. I waited for Bruce to move. To return. I reached out to grab his dick and balls. I tightly pulled at them. Still, Bruce didn't move.

I caught his roaming eyes. Locked mine on them as I enticingly began to spread my legs again. Inched them wider apart as I moved my feet back to raise my knees. And the wider I spread my legs and the higher my knees, they were telling him to climb on top of me. Telling Bruce, I wanted him there. Wanted him—on top of me and between my legs.

Without a word of explanation spoken, the invitation was undeniably clear. Bruce knew that. He replied with an immediate RSVP of, yes. Within seconds, Bruce was exactly where I wanted him—where he'd been invited. Wittingly, once again, our four lips met with evocative passion. Our mouths became wetter. Tongues again entangled as Bruce's massive body trapped mine between him and the bed.

Bruce calculatingly moved on top of my body. His dick rubbed against mine. Both oozed precum. Fluid. Slippery. Wet. The more Bruce picked up his pace, the more profuse their discharge became. And the more his muscled thighs pushed mine further apart. Tart and vinegary sweat covered our bodies as it soaked the sheets of the bed. A collision of intense intimacy and primitive instincts, that had been building and integrating since the moment Bruce got into the Jag at the airport.

He moved his arms until his biceps were under the bend of my knees—lifting my ass. His movements increased. I tightly wrapped my legs around his waist. Our tongues continued to probe deeper as they tangled, secreting more saliva. I was deliriously lost in the moment of the caliginous night. My mind removed from reality. Then, it happened. The large mushroom head of Bruce's dick broke through the sphincter of my anus. The pain close to making me pass out. My scream only muffled by Bruce's tongue and held within his lips. Immediately, all movement stopped. Still, the head of Bruce's dick remained in place. We were both frozen until our lips eventually parted. Bruce raised his head from my chest. His eyes directed at mine.

"Randy… I'm sorry. I didn't mean for that to happen. Really. Are you upset?"

Unspoken moments hung as my eyes closed then opened again. As I held my breath.

"It… it's okay. I'm okay. Just don't move. Give me a few seconds."

"I didn't hurt you… did I?"

"No. No, I'm fine. I just need for the pain to subside."

Bruce mellifluously kissed me. Again. Then, again. He rested his forehead on mine. Bruce suddenly seemed vulnerable. Our bodies, still connected by the head of his penis in me. We were both well-aware his precum, perhaps even his semen was leaking into my ass. But rather, I really didn't care. I wanted it. I just didn't know how Bruce felt about it.

Either way, the pain was too intense. Enough that my eyes began to water. I needed him to pull out—regretfully so. And Bruce knew that. Knew he had to pull out. He worked his tongue back into my mouth. Dug it deeply until I had no air. Then, in one quick movement, Bruce pulled out. The pain, equal as to when the head of his penis entered. His lips left mine once again.

"I'm fine. Don't worry… I'm happy you're here."

Bruce smiled. Kissed me again before he moved his head to my chest. It had been a long and intoxicating day that had pushed deeply into the blue of night. Admittedly, I'd been too confident that I would be able to take Bruce. But we had more time. I rubbed my fingers over his close-cropped hair—damp with sweat as were our bodies. I leaned over and reached outward to pull the top sheet and comforter from the floor. Pulled them over our bodies. Looked over in the corner at Dugan still on his doggy bed—pouting. I smiled at him. Tapped my hand on the bed. Pointed a finger at the foot of it. He jumped up. Wagged his tail before making himself comfortable.

Bruce and I—Dugan of course, remained undisturbed in the solitude of winter; unaware of the occasional gusts of wind rustling the limbs of the leaf-barren trees around the house. The Nina Simone CD continued to play. Her songbird voice lilted from the front of the house; down the long hall and into the bedroom—there, barely more than a whisper.

breakfast: the most important meal of the day

I sat up. Pushed back against the headboard as I rubbed my fatigued eyes until they squinted open. I knew they must be bloodshot. The bedroom was blurry. The air, washed with the smells of sweat and sex. My body was drained of energy. My nipples—sore and raw. I knew without touching them.

A ray of light from the large picture window over the tub wedged into the room through the partially opened bathroom doors—I was thankful the drapes were still drawn closed containing the morning outside. I turned to find Dugan on the bed looking at me—but that's nothing new. I wondered where my Canadian was. He's not in the bed next to me.

Then, I heard noises in the kitchen. Bruce must be there—there in the kitchen. The hint of the smell of coffee wafted.

"So... you're finally up."

I looked over at the clock on the dresser. It's minutes past ten o'clock. Bruce stood naked in the doorway. Two large mugs of coffee were in his hand. "Damn," I thought. "He could sell a shitload of Maxwell House coffee like that." Its aroma—teeming. My dick instantly became erect like helium being forced into a blimp-shaped balloon.

"I guess I needed the sleep... I see you made coffee."

"Yes... I think I remembered how you take it. Chocolate milk with vanilla protein powder, right?" Bruce second-guessed himself as he spoke in a raspy voice.

He walked to the bed and handed over one of the mugs.

I took a much-needed sip. Then, another.

"It's perfect. You did remember... thank you."

But the coffee being perfect had more to do with Bruce having made it, than the correct ratio of chocolate milk and protein powder.

"Come sit beside me."

Bruce propped himself against the headboard. Leaned over to deliver a good morning kiss that may as well been gift-wrapped on my chapped lips. As expected, Dugan walked right over me to get to Bruce. I rolled my eyes.

"Well, you really have made a good impression on my dog."

"That's because… I'm so lovable."

I smiled as I took another sip.

"Oh," he exclaimed. "I let Dugan out… and found his dog food in the fridge. So, he's all taken care of. Now, I can have you all to myself."

He kissed me again.

"Want to get cleaned up and go out for breakfast? My treat."

"I'm up for that," I replied.

"By what I see sticking up under the sheet… you're most definitely up for something."

Bruce took the mug from my hand before I could finish. Turned away long enough to place both on the bedside chest. Seconds later, I was on my back after he'd pulled me from the headboard. Then, rolled on top of me. Placed a hand behind my neck. Drew my face to his. Kissed my lips unrestrainedly—once again, I was entrapped under his exceptional mass of muscle.

I knew I liked him, and it wasn't because Bruce was hot and had a big dick—to boot. Or more so, the fact he seemed to desire me—why, was unimportant. Regardless and even in light of the affection and moments of tenderness Bruce showed, I was quite aware I needed to contain my emotions. Had to draw them back. Not allow them to get the best of me. See the weekend for what it was—and nothing more.

I caught a breath as he broke the kiss. Bruce lifted his face. Mischievously, looked at me before his tongue licked its way down my torso until it reached my fully erect wet cock—on the verge of exploding. His mouth lingered at its slippery head flowing precum. An unchaste fever swelled. Bruce tongued up and down its shaft before sucking my cock as if it were a lollipop. Then, he stopped. Bruce's eyes trailed back to mine with a studied gaze as he stood up. Walked around to the side of the bed. Pressed his massive thighs into the edge of the mattress until his dick was inches from my face.

Bruce proceeded to slap his meaty cock against it. Then, rubbed it over my lips several times before leaving it there—its heaviness noted. Once back in his hand, Bruce slowly stroked it—calculated but firm. He determinedly let its engorged glans brush over my lips again, before pressing it between them. I obviously knew what this Goliath wanted. My mouth opened—wide, to take its mushroom head. Its urethral delivered much wanted milky nectar: a hint of saltiness and the strong, sweet sourness of Bruce's manhood.

With each stroke, the more it oozed into my mouth—the more I swallowed. The more it mixed with my saliva and Bruce's streaming precum—both abundantly running down my chin onto my chest. I inched backward on the bed. Rose up enough to lap the precum like a thirsty dog left out in the heat of summer. I stopped long enough to take several more life-giving breaths.

In its fullness—Bruce inched the mushroom head into my mouth. Moved both his hands to the back of my head to moderately aided its movement; I carried on with the challenge before me. The further, the more its size stressed the corners of my lips. Regardless, it didn't deter me from trying. I wanted it.

I began to gag. Still, I persisted. Bruce's precum continued to copiously discharge. I repeatedly gulped his juice. It trailed down my esophagus on its way to my stomach as some continued to escape and cover my face and chin—until it eventually ran down the gap between my pecs.

Aware of how much I was struggling, Bruce snaked his cock out. Although my strained lips were disappointed, I knew my mouth and throat needed a break. Bruce got down on his knees and licked up the flow; he sucked what had made it to my navel. Bruce held it in his mouth—rushed his lips to mine. I opened mine as I drank it—the mixture of saliva and precum.

"Get on top of me. I want to try again."

transient

The retreating moonlight shadowed Bruce as he stood inches from me—as I looked up at him from the bed. In marked contemplation of outlying thought traveling further than the bedroom and into the future, prematurely—like an infatuated pigtailed schoolgirl, I wondered if he would love me one day and abundantly as Bradley had several decades before the encapsulating last two days?

The impression Bruce had made over the previous months from a distance, and since his arrival in Atlanta was permeating. Would I have another tangible chance at something real and solid? Would it be as never-ending as the universe—a universe, I once gazed upon with Bradley on many idyllic and romantic occasions, when everything around us went silent except for the sound of our breaths—as if we were the only two people left alive on Earth?

In some ways, I felt like we were. I wondered: if I was just being a fool to even entertain a life shared with another man again was nothing but a fantasy? But I already knew the answer in my heart—still, my mind pressed-on.

Bruce pulled at me. Pulled at every emotion—from fear to lust, and even that of loss. Every emotion I'd experienced in my life up until him. He lit a light on both the darkness and even light itself, as if I'd switched out a fifteen-watt bulb with one radiating the intensity of a hundred in a lamp. And certainly, there was nothing pedestrian in the way Bruce reminded me of how I once was in love. That white-hot captivating love. Inexhaustible. Simple. Complex in conjunction. That in itself—the possibility of such love again was frightening. In all actuality, a love with no descriptive words. Not any. Meaningless. Pointless and weak adjectives—some, nonexistent but felt. Weightless words in comparison to that of authentic undying devotion and loyalty where only piercing eyes, longing lips, gentle hands, and uninhibited thrusts can only speak the language. The kind I'd carried for Bradley that had gone into hibernation at my insistence. How else could I have survived the loss of him?

Now that many thoughts—memories of Bradley had awakened and rushed back like a lover returning after a long absence of years, following the July 4, 2009, event, could I even love Bruce if he indeed wanted me in such nonverbal definition? Either way, by then, I'd become fully aware my heart had been dying for years—starting at some point in my childhood and accelerated when I lost Bradley. That dying, and the pending death only prolonged momentarily in the arms of other men who in truth meant nothing to me up to and after Bradley.

He had been the only man capable of stopping that pending death. That is, until it returned like a cancer coming out of remission the day Bradley died and the knowledge—I would never be held in his arms again. Would the recurrence of that dying prevent me from loving anyone in that true nonverbal definition once lived—once breathed in every second spent with Bradley? Or, instead, would I have to continue to lie to myself and settle for much less as I had been for years? Was I lying to myself concerning Bruce as well? Would it only be a mosaic of members of the United Nations coming and going in sexual trysts of the flesh void of any degree of love—they, no more than band-aids covering a bleeding, wounded heart? Was Bruce also one of those band-aids? Was it even fair to allow him to love me, understanding I didn't even know if I would be alive in the next weeks or months to follow if I fell into despair again. Bruce's love, no matter how great—not enough to stop the bleeding.

My eyes continued to scrutinized him, as they move in slow motion up and down and side to side over his form: his face, from his hairline to his square chin; its deep dimple more defined by his facial stubble, that had become darker since I'd picked him up at the airport; the hairs on his chest that grew in the deep valley between his hard, large pectoral muscles; how they and his biceps flexed; how long and thick his dick was; how each of his balls hung hefty on either side of it, his dick and balls so big that they didn't seem real; how his hands reached down toward the mattress as his arms brought them, until they were on either side of me; how his body grew bigger and wider the more Bruce bent over me to get back in bed; how all of him grew bigger and wider the closer he got until Bruce was on top me again.

He kissed me, then rolled over my body to the other side of the bed. This time, on his side. Bruce's left elbow speared the mattress. Its hand balanced his head. The other arm rested across the umbilical region of his abdomen. I moved my body to mirror his. Bruce opened his mouth to speak but then closed it as if he'd misplaced his thought. I waited for whatever it was to pass through his enticing lips. Instead, his eyes roamed my face as mine had his body, until they focused on mine. I attempted to read Bruce—what was circling in his head behind them, but us sunk into them. Goosebumps coated my entire body like a garment.

"What?" I asked. "What were you going to say?"

"Nothing. I'm just looking."

Modesty and self-doubt momentarily washed over me as if from a large bucket of dirty water.

"Is this some staring game we're playing?"

"Can't I just look at you, Randy?"

"Of course, but you're so quiet."

"Don't you think the silence is nice?"

"Well... yes. It is."

At that, Bruce extended his hand to touch my face. Ran the back of it over my cheek—slowly and lithesome like that of a single, falling leaf as if its descent from the tree limb to the ground had been delayed by a slender, passing breeze. Such assiduous tenderness by Bruce suddenly pained me as it drew more memories of Bradley back to the surface.

If I believed in reincarnation, I would have thought it was Bradley coming back to me. That, it was Bradley rather than Bruce less than an arm's reach across the bed. My eyes quickly closed to prevent Bruce from seeing them begin to water—to keep my tears under their lids.

The intimacy surged vulnerability and exposure—making me want to run. But I didn't. I didn't run. At that extracting moment, all I wanted from Bruce was sex. Sex to deaden the unfeigned pain that symbolic cut had swiftly brought. Sex to push the memories of Bradley back. Sex had been my own form of therapy—short-lived, as it were. But therapy all the same. At least it kept the bottles of sleeping pills in the drawer and not in my stomach.

What simmering warmth of closeness that had accumulated around the bed since Bruce first laid with me two nights ago, somehow had chilled starting the moment after he touched my face in that way. But that hadn't been the first time Bruce had—had so tenderly touched me. Perhaps, the accumulation of such affection after too many days and nights of loneliness that had frozen my flesh was just too much. Too much-too soon. Even, too much-too late.

I knew then, I would have to pretend—to perform. Act. But it wouldn't be the first time. I'd pretended and performed enough over the years; it had become second nature. Instinctive. And I knew I had to stop thinking about Bruce attached to romance. Stop thinking as if I'd shot all thought out of my brain with the pull of a trigger.

Bruce leaned in to sweep his lips over mine. I slightly turned my face such, that he would miss; trusting Bruce didn't think it was intentional but only coyness. I smiled instead, hoping that it would be enough. Enough to make him believe nothing had changed concerning how the sight of him and his touch had stirred me just moments before that leaf slowly fell to the ground. Bruce reached out his arm. It wrapped around my waist. Without effort, Bruce pulled my body over the sheets to him.

throwing caution to the wind

You love the best way: with a touch of madness and reckless abandon…

Ariana

I knew what was about to happen—what was coming. What had started the night before. Even if I had wanted to resist, it seemed useless at that point. I needed to prepare myself. My body starved for his dick to enter my ass. Then, reason took over my desire for Bruce to push his cock in at that edging moment.

"Did you bring condoms? I mean… do they even come that big?"

"Yes, but they're special order," Bruce winked.

I wouldn't be surprised, but I knew he was kidding.

"I've some in my toiletry bag."

Bruce lifted himself off my wet, sweaty body. The mattress recoiled from the lightened weight. I turned my head in his direction. As if a voyeur peering in a window in the middle of the night, I watched Bruce as he walked toward the master bathroom—his erect cock probing ahead of him. I was still amazed by his physical omnipotence with a confident stride. Bruce's muscled, powerhouse, basketball-sized butt cheeks shifted in movement with each step.

Bruce looked back wearing a mischievous smile as he entered the bathroom. Once again, the voyeur—my gaze remained unbroken. Bruce leaned over. Unzipped the kit sitting on one of the black Mies van der Rohe Barcelona ottomans in front of the dressing closet. Rummaged through it. Pulled out a string of perforated condom packets—indeed prepared. He turned and paced back to the bed. The closer Bruce's approach, the sharper the XL Magnum in gold print came into view. I wonder if they would even be large enough.

"Dear God," I allowed.

Bruce raised my legs into the air; he opened them wider as Bruce rubbed his face between my butt cheeks. His tongue tantalized my hole with featherlike licks. My urge was to moan loudly in response to the intense pleasure offered as if we were in some cheesy porn movie made in a cheap motel room on the southside of the city, but I held back in muffled exhalations.

The licks grew aggressive and longer. Up under my balls. Over them. Up my dick. Then, down again. Up and down. Bruce only stopped to spit large mouthfuls of saliva in my hole before continuing. He ate on it—and the more he did, the wetter it became until my hole was dripping. I burned for more. More. More. More, of everything he was doing. Bruce's tongue pushed in. Pushed deeper. Fucked my hole harder.

I reached back on the bedside chest for the packets of condoms. Grabbed them as if each were filled with cocaine for a desperately needed fix. Bruce brought my legs back down to the bed—my feet to either side of him as he leaned back on his buttocks. I quickly tore one off in a sweat and handed it to Bruce.

"Are you sure?"

"Yes. Yes, I'm damn sure."

He ripped off the perforated top with his teeth. Spit it out to the side. Bruce's fingers purposefully rolled the condom over the head of his dick—continued down its remarkable shaft while stretching its elasticity close to the point of ripping. With questioning eyes, Bruce looked at me as if asking a second time for permission. Undoubtedly, the look in my eyes surely once again answered the question.

I watched as he reached for the tube of lube from the chest. Popped the cap. Squeezed out a double handful. Proceeded to spread it over and in my hole. I raised my legs. Placed a foot on each of his frontal deltoids. Waiting. Longing. Anticipating. But first, he would make me wait for it as Bruce gently inched his long and thick middle finger in. Deliberately, he moved it in and out in slow repetitions. Then, two fingers. Then, Three.

Reflexively, my neck arched my head back toward the headboard as all three fingers jointly moved in unison. My eyes closed. My teeth gritted. My back arched as well as my sphincter painfully expanded to accommodate them. My entire body surrendered. Bruce placed his free hand on my chest to hold me down as he continued to finger-fuck my hole—I wondered if the prelude would be enough.

Bruce's hand dug it fingers into my left pec. Then, the right before his thumb and index finger pinched and twisted the nipple of each—giving them equal time. Gently at first until he had them in a vise-grip as if using pliers. Until they burned. Pinching and twisting, as he continued to finger-fuck me in heated acceleration.

Buffered moans amplified as they streamed from my lips—ones expressing pleasure regardless of the concentrated pain, pushing to the edge of hedonism. My body was possessed by sporadic movements—fingers of both hands dug into the wet sheets and mattress in a death-grip.

The more Bruce finger-fucked me along with the extreme vicing of my nipples, the more I wanted to feel that pain—more pain. My breaths plunged; my hands released the bedding and moved to aid Bruce's fingers—pushing them even deeper. me.

"Randy… you look like you're going to scream."

"It's okay. I'm more than okay."

The contortions stopped. I look at Bruce with carnal eyes.

"I'm a big boy… keep going," I insisted, in drawing gasps of air as I wiped the sweat from my forehead.

"It's just going to take more lube. Lots of it," I added.

Bruce placed a pillow under by butt for support. The thoughts of sexual gratification amassed throughout my body. Bruce momentarily looked down at his enormous member as he stroked it. His head tilted back. Seconds later, his eyes returned to mind. He looked at me as if asking for permission. But Bruce knew permission was a given.

He rubbed his dick up and down the crack of my ass—knowing, exactly what he was doing as I felt the weight of its thickness. Its rigidness. Up and down. Repeatedly, up and down—oozing more wet, thick precum. Up and down until Bruce was ready to align it with my anus—or it seemed as such. Seemed, as if he was about to. But first, Bruce circled it with his dick's mushroom head. Teasingly, around-and-around numerous times, before he finally pushed it in.

The immediate pain seized as it broke through. I managed to restrain most of the begging screen it triggered behind my gritted teeth. What of it that escaped, trailed whimpering moans. Bruce stopped. I took in a deep breath as he kept the mushroom head in. My anus throbbed. Throbbed. It throbbed. Seconds later, Bruce pulled it out and then pushed it in again. I gasped each time. Out and in. Out and in. Out and in, guided by his hand. And with each of my gasps, Bruce slowly inched in the shaft as well. Slipping both in deeper. Further. Assertively.

As the seizing pain increased, the more I wanted it regardless. Heated sweat covered our bodies. It dripped. Soaked. More rolled from my forehead into my eyes.

I pressed the other hand to his abs.

"Stay still… don't move."

I needed a minute or two for the wave of pain to wane.

"Do you want me to pull out?"

I shook my head in a definite, no.

Moments later I nodded, yes—yes to keep going. I moved my feet from Bruce's delts downward, wrapping my legs around his waist. He leaned down to surround my lips with his kiss, while still holding his penis to guide it in. I held on to his biceps. That alone—holding onto Bruce's biceps as the sight of his body was a rush within itself. He inched his dick in. Another inch—then another. And another.

"More lube," I blurted out as I gritted my teeth.

Bruce accommodated. Squeezed more on without pulling out the part in me. Lucky for me, it was an extra-large tube fitting of an extra-large cock. He inched it in more as I breathed in and out. I let go of one of Bruce's biceps. Brought my arm to my mouth. Bit down on it. He picked up a steady rhythm of short ins-and-outs. Pushing his cock in more, then back out. Then, more, then back out. Still, trying to loosen me up. My anus throbbed. It seared. But I had no intention of asking Bruce to stop a second time.

As much as I attempted to continue to hide the increasing pain, he saw the discomfort on my face. Still, I didn't want to give up. I refused to. I was going to do what it took to take all of it. I knew I could eventually take it as I had with Bradley's—whose cock was equally ample. But I was younger and I'm sure real love and trust had made it so much easier. For moments, I closed my eyes and pretended it was Bradley's dick inside me. His lips on mine. My legs around his waist. His strong body holding me down.

"Randy… you're still in pain. I don't want to rip you open."

"No… no. I keep telling you, no. Just keep it in. I promise it'll get easier for me. I don't want to disappoint you."

"Disappoint me… that's not going to happen?"

I knew it was the drag of the condom adding to my inability to take Bruce's cock—regardless of the amount of lube. Surprised, it hadn't broken as the other one had.

"Take it off… the condom. You're just too big."

The moment riveted—caught in the clutches of desire: both mind and body. If Bruce was willing, there was no turning back until I had what I wanted. Any consequences—be damned.

"What?"

Bruce stared at me.

"It's okay. It's okay, if it is with you."

Not another word was shared. Bruce pulled out. Indecision was apparent on his face—or so it appeared. I hoped Bruce wasn't thinking, I was being reckless by asking him. But I knew I was.

Moments seemed like minutes as I continued to wait for Bruce to say something. Anything. But I fully expect him to get out of bed. But he didn't. Bruce just kept looking at me.

My legs took back possession of his waist. Each of my hands reached behind to secure them on Bruce's butt cheeks. I waited. Then, I got my answer as he pushed his dick in—picking up a steady flow again. I held my breath as before. Bruce inched in. I refused to coward despite the sharp, jagging, motherfucking pain.

With each short thrust, his cock made it deeper. Widened my sphincter. A third of the way in. Then, a fourth. Then, half. There he stayed as Bruce made slow, measured thrusts. I pushed at this butt cheeks. My head tilted back again. My legs took a tighter hold as my ankles locked around Bruce. Sweat oozed from our pores. Bruce's rained on me. Bathe me in primal, diaphoresis perspiration—filling the bedroom. His precum filled my ass as it dripped to the sheets. My precum rolled off my stomach.

The more Bruce moved, the heavier his weight became—the tighter our bodies pressed together. Bruce rocked and pushed harder. His thrusts, more calculated and precise—in and out. They escalated into fraught movements, plunging drives until his massive manhood had taken all my ass. The headboard hit against the wall surrounded by the windows. Another followed. Then, another and another. Each one louder than the one before.

He moaned. I moaned. My hands held the back of his head while pressing our wet mouths together. Our tongues searched as they sucked. Soon, they proceeded to fuck each other's mouth—robbing breaths. Our lips fed off the hunger as Bruce's facial stubble scraped across my face. His movements slowed then built-up momentum as Bruce crashed over and in me. An orchestration of rhythmic alternating thrusts of caged desires. Longer. Shorter. Slower. Impelling. Lunging. Unintentionally edging on violence.

The impelling and measured thrusts intensified from Bruce's powerful body driving his dick—pushed me moments within reaching climax. No longer capable of constraining the unidentifiable while encased in the rush, semen and prostatic fluid shot between our stomachs—without having touched my cock.

Bruce's voice staggered low and husky.

"I'm about… fuck… "

Several earth-shattering thrusts followed. Then, more. Always more. My ass throbbed in measured successions. With one final deep thrust, there was no mistaking the charge of loaded cum that shot from his large balls through his phallus in rapid, sporadic, repeated jerks. Hot, ecstatic loads of seed jettisoned into my ass. Again. Again. Still more. Even more. The involuntary peristaltic orgasms—astonishingly overwhelming. Reflexively, my thighs constricted his waist more; my ankles locked tighter to keep Bruce's dick inside—until the last drops of his semen. I wanted all of it.

Bruce's body went limp on mine—as his lungs labored for air. Bruce raised his head enough to lock his lips on mine before pulling out. Then, rested it on my chest before rolling off me. Bruce soon lazed into sleep. I listened to the tempo of his breathing. Relaxed. Velvety. Mellifluous. Time and space seem to have lagged until it wholly stood still—the world had stopped. I tried to refuse to let my mind wander outside the bedroom—certainly, not any further than the brick walls of the house on Seventh Street.

My eyes circled within the gray-flannel color of the dim bedroom. I turned on my side—my back to Bruce. The throbbing eventually lessened to a soothing, rhythmic pulse and an occasional sharp stinging. Soon, my eyes closed. I sensed the force of the body next to mine. In the isolation of the quietness, my mind was unable to resist the compelling beckoning call of a one true love that Bruce had resurrected. I couldn't help but wish—if I turned around, Bradley would be next to me.

a new day

Sedately and by design, the genesis of another unspoiled morning hesitantly peeked over an imperfect horizon line. However, any invasion of its light was denied into the room by the bedroom's draperies—drawn closed. Impetuous, it soon found entry through the adjoining bathroom's window as it reached inquisitively between the slight opening of its double doors. With caution, giving birth to random shadowy interior images. Eventually and with conviction, it would fully extirpate what little lingered of the night as its intensity pierced and lengthened.

I'd awakened minutes before with the sensation of Bruce having been inside me that had lingered throughout the night. The wetness inside and between my butt cheeks had, as well. As had the pleasure received from the pain. I reached to pull the sheet up; it was stained with lube, semen, and spots of blood. All the makings from the perilous night's hunger.

The expansion of Bruce's hairy chest stuck to the smoothness of my back. His arm hadn't moved from around me. For moments, I was grateful to be wrapped by it—emotionally calm and soothed by the rise and fall of Bruce's chest as his lungs breathed in and out the morning. But, again, my mind dwelled on Bradley while sweet Dugan slept peacefully sprawled on his side—remaining at the foot of the bed.

"How I wished Bradley and Dugan could have known each other," my mind drifted. But the last seconds I'd spent with Bradley and these with Bruce, had spread as wide and long as the universe. As I had many times, I tried to push mental reflections of Bradley further back into the mind. But that had never completely worked. And at those penetrable moments, it was as if the very heart of Bradley had found a slice between Bruce's chest and my back—regardless of how closely our flesh meshed.

I remained motionless, refusing to turn my eyes in the direction of the clock. I closed my eyes. The world could stop on its axis, for all I cared. Even better—if its hands could travel back to some-forty years before.

In the hours before, while the black of night still retained ownership of the sky, I'd fallen in and out of a provocative but much needed sleep—the nearer it came to relinquish itself to morning. My restlessness, out of concern that what was left of it would slip away too soon.

Each time I'd awakened dazed, required reminding myself that this wasn't a dream that would melt like a dusting of snowfall over the ground—once the sun was high in the sky. That Bruce wouldn't melt like the white into nothing. And that everything I'd experienced for the past two days and nights with him, was as real as the flesh that covered my body. The very flesh that shared his. But, as the night before, when thoughts of Bradley had fallen into sleep with me—they awakened alongside me as well.

By the time more of the outside light feathered within the bedroom, Bruce stirred awake.

"Good morning," he greeted.

"Hey. How did you sleep?"

"Like I was in heaven," he answered.

My heart quickened.

"And you?" Bruce asked, as he nuzzled his face into my neck.

"Off and on."

"What… did I snore and keep you awake?"

"No… no. You barely made a sound or moved."

Bruce kissed my neck and the back of my head.

"How did I manage to luck out with someone like you?" he questioned.

I didn't answer. I wasn't sure if Bruce had lucked out. Instead, I moved my hand back to caress his head.

If I could have died at that moment, I would without pills or a razor blade—and possibly happy to some degree. Irrevocably so, as if every single onerous emotion between January of 2009—actually, since my mother's death in late November of 2006, and that very moment at hand, they would be no more than sudden gusts of tempestuous wind—seconds gone. Seconds forgotten. Seconds never lived. Finally at peace safely clasped in the arms of a good and caring man. And with my back to Bruce's chest, again, I could pretend it was Bradley's arms that held me. That's why I didn't want to move an inch in either direction—certainly, not behind me. He, too, was one of the ghosts I walked within their shadows, but perhaps Bradley's, to attempted to shield me from and hinder the others.

Well into mid-morning—the collecting sporadic sounds of an awakening inner-city drifted ethereally from outside the house; glided in the chilled air like soft music heralding a new, clear, and bright Saturday. The Atlanta mid-winter briskness had rebounded into comfortable sweater-weather. Sunshine drenched the blue skies without a breath of wind as if Mother Nature couldn't make up her mind.

We landed at Joe's on Juniper for lunch. Beforehand, I'd popped a few much-needed Advils to lessen the pain from the activities of the night before—as if I'd undergone some serious anal surgical procedure. A car ride would have been easier on my ass, but we took the leisurely thirty or so minute walk from the house with Dugan pulling on his leash, cutting through the pristine Piedmont Park and up Eighth Street.

Upon arrival, as expected, Joe's outdoor patio was full of people seated at tables, while many others stood in small to medium groups drinking and chit-chatting waiting to be called from the list. One look at Bruce, the host with pink hair and a nose ring pushed us to the top. As a thank you, although I'm sure the punker would have preferred to give Bruce a blowjob in a bathroom stall—he discreetly slipped him a folded Benjamin Franklin.

We were both famished—for obvious reasons while Dugan was always up for some people-food, especially his favorite: sweet potato fries. Pink led us to a table on the expansive brick-laid patio by the white picket fence, paralleling the eponymous street—Juniper for which the famed restaurant and bar was named.

I noticed several guys from Bruce's gym fan club refilling their imaginations, while other vicarious gawkers' GPS aimed directly at him as if Bruce were a sex club destination. Clear, by the OMG looks on their faces and pointing fingers.

Bruce devoured two entrees and a plate of chicken wings. Dugan patiently sat under the table, blissfully dog-happy when I slipped him a sweet potato fry. After brunch, Bruce wanted to walk around to see more of the neighborhood. Once back at the house, the plan was to head to the gym. But first, I required more Advil.

blurred

The night before I was to take Bruce back to the airport after his first visit, he was stretched out shirtless on the bed. A happy Dugan snuggled up next to him enjoying Bruce's affectionate attention. I was leaning in the doorframe of the bathroom brushing my teeth—zoned out, staring at Bruce's biceps and the sexy hair of his armpits.

"What do you think about me flying back in mid-February?"

The suggestion was much contrary to when Bruce earlier first mentioned returning within a few more months as in March or perhaps April.

"Hey, that would make it around Valentine's Day. We can do the whole dinner out thing."

I kept brushing.

"I'll even bring you chocolates and flowers."

The mention of an earlier visit slowed my brushing as toothpaste—so-not-attractively, ran out the corners of my mouth and over my chin dripping down onto my chest as if I were having a convulsion.

The new plan had totally taken me by surprise; I hurriedly thought of how to respond to such a romantic plan—necessitating, more time to assimilate. And in order to do that on the spot, required more brushing. At least, my dentist would be proud.

I held up a finger to indicate I would answer once finished with my oral hygiene. I walked back to the bathroom sink. Spit out what toothpaste had remained in my mouth. Rinsed. Toweled the excess from my mouth and chest before returning to the support of the doorframe.

"Are you going to cover the bed in red rose petals, too?"

"If those are your favorite flowers."

"Actually, white tu… " I stopped myself. About to tell him they were white tulips.

I closed my eyes. My heart sank as thoughts pinwheeled back to Bradley. A mental image of him walking toward me holding a bouquet of white tulips seized my mine. I took a hard swallow.

"Randy… you with me?"

I pulled my thoughts back to the existing moment.

"What… oh, of course."

"You zoned out for a second." Is something wrong?"

"No... no, of course not. I guess... I was just thinking about what kind of flowers I like the best. There're so many," I deflected.

"So... then I should get an assortment."

"Ah... aha, is this going to be one of those lesbian second dates? You know... that involves a U-Haul?" I quipped.

"What, you don't want me to come back?" Bruce asked, making a fake clown frown. "I know your pup does."

"Rest assured we both do," I stated. "But not that soon," I thought.

How else could I answer? I didn't want Bruce to feel rejected.

My Canadian returned to Atlanta six more times. In-between visits, phone conversations continued as before we'd met in person. On the calls I wasn't up to talking, I'd cut them short. Lied about an early-morning doctor's appointment or an art installation. Anything that sounded believable—convincing.

On other occasions, I didn't want to talk; my brain was either shredded by confusion or bee-hived in depression. Again, I wasn't going to allow Bruce anywhere near the darkness I felt. I wasn't going to pull him in, much less let him know, even though Bruce had told me not to worry—that he would not leave me to fight it alone. But the truth is: the on-again-off-again battle with depression is a battle that can't be fought by an army regardless of how many psychiatrists, therapists, and rattling bottles of prescription pills lead the charge—at least, that was the case for me as it was true for my mother. Thankfully, since meeting him, many bouts had come less frequently.

More than anything, Bruce had become a lifeline to hope. And as much as I'd vacillated between slowly distancing myself from him emotionally and then pulling him back—I needed that lifeline; and I needed him.

During Bruce's fifth visit, he openly—without pause, confessed deep feelings for me. I, too, had developed a stronger connection to him much more than primal lust. Even in the realm of love. At the same time, I felt I wasn't worthy of Bruce or his love.

A mid-evening dinner at Gilberts on Tenth Street, we sat at an intimate two-top by the open, clear-paneled windows of the double garage door that looked out over a radiate midtown—alive with lights projecting from short buildings and august skyscrapers. Vague images of people walked past outside in the newness of a fall-filled night. The interlace of music and voices of other patrons seemed faded, as if we were contained in our own little bubble.

Bruce held my hand on top of the table. I remember staring into his eyes trying to find myself in their reflection but didn't. That concerned me. Troubled me. Made me wonder why.

That night, detailed plans were ironed out: I would holiday with Bruce in March. The excitement outlined his face at the thought of showing off his native land to his not-so-new American friend.

"I can't wait for us to lie in bed while looking out over Toronto from my penthouse," Bruce spoke with eagerness.

As we continued to converse over our dinner in the honeyed-sepia atmosphere, Bruce also suggested we meet in Los Angeles for two weeks. During one of them, he wanted to drive a large stretch of the PCH.

"Each day… let's drive as many miles as we want. We'll stop along the way to beach-it and spend each night in a different hotel. What do you say?"

"Sounds wonderful," I replied, even though I knew I wouldn't do any of it with Bruce.

Even as much as I attempted to smother my fears, they kept drawing breath—quickened from the depths of their lurking place. Their grip, reaching up and firmly holding me down. As a result, I was immobilized by the sheer terror of truly allowing myself to fall in love again, and the slicing panic of losing it. I couldn't risk having that love yanked as if ripped from my flesh and the bloodletting that would follow—as it had with Bradley. Besides, no matter how strong my feelings had grown for Bruce, he deserved someone capable of loving him fully—not use him as a crutch or a substitute for a ghost.

After Bruce's first departure, I'd spent weeks in a state of vacillation, weighing the odds to the point of becoming an off-and-on psychological cripple. As much as my heart wanted what we'd shared on each visit to follow, therapy had taught me I couldn't depend on someone else to ensure my happiness or carry it on their shoulders. I fully knew that would always be the case—I would always need someone to carry it for me.

Again, uneasy concerns about the bouts of depression added to the equation. Even with medication, they would come and go at their own calling. I didn't want that for Bruce. Feasibly, that is proof enough concerning how much I cared for him. I didn't want Bruce to go through what I did for years—watch my mother ride that roller coaster of mental calamities. All connected, as they took over her life right before my eyes—almost to the end.

As close as we were, I never really knew if she ever found any measure of peace and resolve from what had been done to and taken from her, or if I ever would. I'd no idea what was in store for me. If my disease would progress as hers, stockpiled with the enumeration years—even with a kitchen cabinet crowded with medications. And even the periods she was doing well, it was only a matter of time before it all circled back to a blinding dark place.

I couldn't put Bruce through that: slowly watch someone he loved, become a shell of a person. Empty. Dry. Brittle. A person to crumble at any moment, the pieces too sifted and impossible to stack back into a human being. Bruce wanted three things for and from me: love, companionship, and happiness. But I knew I needed more of them from him then he did from me. Knowing that and moving forward would be selfish. I would wonder every day: would this be the day that I would break his heart and mine? And I was certain those wavering bouts would eventually end us.

We'd discussed my fears at some length. In keeping, Bruce had been patient. I asked for more time. As expected, he said everything possible to mitigate the gravity of my concerns, including offering anything I needed to help bring me to him.

I backed the car out of the driveway to return my Canadian package to Jackson-Hartfield one last time. At least, I was certain it would be. Almost a year had passed since the first time I'd picked Bruce up from the airport. A cold rain—as cold as I felt inside washed the night. The windshield wipers were set on a ten-second delay. Almost exactly the time needed to clear my view apace with the raindrops collecting on the glass—equaling the tears I was trying to hold back. I intentionally drove under the speed limit to slow the bleeding in my heart.

As always, Bruce held my free hand every mile. I questioned, as I had again and again if I was doing the right thing—letting Bruce go.

I was tempted to pull the car over to the side of the Interstate. But I didn't. I didn't, even as much as a part of me wanted to. As much as my heart warily hung between us as did the air.

Narrowly, twenty words or so were spoken. Perhaps, too painful—too entangling with uncertainties. Instead, our occasionally connecting eyes exchanged thoughts and words that didn't need to be verbally expressed but rather seen in reflections.

Upon arrival, I inched the XJS toward the International Departure sign. As the car came to a stop at the curb, I switched off the engine. Bruce and I faced each other; our eyes searched as we sat quietly while time circled around us.

Bruce waited until the very last minute to open the car door. But before, he took my face in his hands. Pressed our lips together in a fervent kiss, embodying all I'd felt with him over the past many months—from lust to love to joy to sadness and to heartbreak. Afterward, we exited the car. Bruce captured me in a long embrace.

"I… I already miss you," my voice faltered.

"Me, too."

What else could he say, or me for that matter?

Bruce winked. Then slowly turned to walk away. Fixed, I watched. Again, as before, that feeling he was my last chance revisited. The realization—terrifying. After a few paces Bruce stopped. Turned. Looked intently for minutes while the rain fell upon us. Then, the inevitable, Bruce turned away and continued onward—immersed within the multitude.

seven

nip and tuck

I met a new morning deciding to have a facelift. Just like that. Like I'd chosen to have granola and mixed fruit topped with vanilla yogurt, instead of an egg-white and turkey omelet for breakfast. It all seemed so sensible as I weighed the positives and negatives of going under the knife. The idea had been seeded by a sudden obsession at the discovery of a bit of a neck-wattle that appeared a few days before. It caught my eye while shaving in the bathroom. Over the days that followed, I scrutinized it like a scientist searching a cure for some deadly disease—turning my head left and right and up and down, while attempting to push it back where it belonged, back where the jawline meets the neck. My analysis: bothersome and a clear sign I wasn't getting any younger—instead, older.

A billboard-sized neon sign of aging gape fixedly back from the mirror-of-time that no amount of Neutrogena Men's Age Fighter Moisturizer or some skin-tightening, anti-aging, serum purchased at the cosmetic counter of Saks Fifth Avenue from the lady with fake eyelashes and bright red lipstick or ordered from QVC would stop, much less, turn back the clock. None of it would slow the marching forward of age. But some nip and tuck would.

I set out on a quest to find a renowned surgeon—seeking recommendations. My first call was to a friend in her sixties who'd just recuperated from a facelift and looked amazing. Addison invited me over to take a closer look at her results.

"Sugar, it's one of the best things I've done since I divorced my second husband," she proclaimed, as Addison sipped on her second dirty martini with three olives while we lounged in the sitting room of her lavish, Tuxedo Drive estate.

After interviewing her plastic surgeon and two others who were recommended as well—the second, by my primary physician. Well-meaning as Dr. Thomas was, he broke HIPPA laws by calling the surgeon before the interview to share sensitive medical information about my attempted suicide some two years before without my consent. The plastic surgeon insisted I have my psychiatrist evaluate me beforehand. "Screw that!" I thought. I highly doubted having a facelift would send me into a psychotic nosedive. I went with Addison's. I wasted little time in scheduling surgery for the day after Thanksgiving.

After some three hours under the knife-of-youth, my face and neck were bandaged under layers of gauze. Two drain tubes hung low on either side to divert fluid from the incisions into egg-shaped plastic collection bulbs. The look, certainly a first prize winner at a scary Halloween costume contest. Quite alarming for small minds—enough to make little children tremble in extreme terror.

After surgery, I was delivered home by Sandra; and a friend who'd flown in from Colorado to nurse me. Little did they know what an annoyingly difficult patient I would become. Upon walking through the front door of the house, Dugan took one look, growled before quickening away. He eventually came around and realized it was me. But to be sure, he spent a lot of time sniffing, not only the bandaging wrapping my face but my body as well.

The flesh of my face felt like it had been pulled to the four corners of the Earth—well, I think it actually had. The three weeks to follow were considerably uncomfortable; especially, the first several days and nights to follow. The prescribed pain killers offered little assistance. As a result, I walked the rooms of the house into the early hours of the mornings as if I were a mummy. A lot of explicit cursing seemed necessary—enough to make a vicious conniving she-devil, if not a sailor proud.

Once the bandaging was removed, I looked as if I'd careered through the windshield of a car—twice, after hitting a Georgia Power Company electrical pole head-on at top velocity. De-mummified, a chin bra was required to be worn twelve-hours a day for two weeks, and ice packs every twenty minutes or so for swelling.

Naively, I was certain I would be back at the gym in no time—two weeks, tops. Certainly, at the very least, able to do light lifting and cardio, dismissing the doctor's no weight training for two months and even then, to take it extremely slowly. I more than underestimated my body's abilities.

As the healing had gone slowly—time eased by at an equal transport. The varying, rambling thoughts in my mind calmed as if they'd made a temporary truce. That winter, Atlanta had a couple of wet gloppy snowfalls—teetering on the meteorological distinction between rain and snow, contrasting the conventional storybook wind-driven drifts. Still, somewhat magical—all the same. Dugan and I took long walks of welcome seclusion, slogging through a picturesque Piedmont Park dressed in slushy white icing covering the sleeping grass and dripping from naked tree branches.

I often went to movies at the Midtown Art Cinema in the middle of the day when the theater was near-empty, choosing to sit in the center under a ball cap. Other times, catch a later show while in the back row, hidden from the rest of the movie-goers. My face still somewhat bruised and puffy like a freshly baked biscuit. Those movies as the park, gave me the opportunity to escape the world for hours-on-end—and even from myself.

As I look back, I don't regret having the surgery. Not a single nip and tuck or stitch—they each were worth every cent. And certainly, I don't miss my arch-enemy—Mr. Neck-Wattle.

a stranger and the leonardo

With one phone call to American Express—rejuvenation escorted me off the plane at Josep Tarradellas Barcelona–El Prat Airport. Some fifteen miles later, in bumper-to-bumper traffic, I found myself among 1.6 million plus Spaniards and who knows how many tourists in the expansive, cosmopolitan city of Barcelona. A city I've loved since my first shoot there a lifetime ago—the capital of Spain's Catalonia region with 2000 years of rich history, culture, and art. Birthplace of celebrated Spanish artists to the likes of Joan Miró and Antoni Tàpies, and a favorite, Salvador Dalí—actually born in Figueres, a small town near Barcelona.

I knew a little Spanish. Enough to get directions to the nearest restroom. Having taken four years of French in school, I relied on a Spanish-English dictionary, patient and accommodating Catalans and Spaniards alike (Spain having two languages) stopped on the streets, and the tall, extremely attractive concierge with cajoling, coffee-colored eyes—a Spanish version of Clark Kent at the Leonardo Boutique Hotel. I would have welcomed his knock on my suite's door for further personal assistance, especially inquiring if I needed help breaking in the large, comfortable, bed. But alas, the only knocks were those of the room maids.

Antoni Gaudí's, Basílica i Temple Expiatori de la Sagrada Família seemed somewhat unchanged as I stood before it once again. One man's vision of eternity—its first stone laid in 1882, when Gaudi was thirty-one-years of age. Some forty-four years later, the innovative Catalan architect died at seven-three—hit by a tram as he was crossing the street on his way to his beloved Sagrada Familia, which he'd dedicated his life to. I can thank my English-born, handsy, art history professor in college who loved his red wine for that tidbit of information. Still, awed, and mystified—my neck bent back as far as humanly possible. The afternoon sunlight glissaded behind the edifice—illuminating facet-after-facet. In the spectacular besieging afterglow, I could easily conjure-up choirs of angels—cherubim and seraphim, floating on the necromantic air while lifting their voices into the firmament.

Some days were spent visiting places like Parc Güell, admiring its whimsical sculptural structures. Absorbing hours lingered by in the Museu d'Història de Barcelona district—walking narrow medieval streets of the Gothic Quarter in a refreshing drizzle. Returning one sunny day to meander the bustling market—vendors selling their wares of exquisitely-crafted leather goods, jewelry, and other vernacular items. Another day, on the steps of the Catedral de la Santa Creu i Santa Eulàlia—eating lunch while people-watching. An overcast afternoon was employed at the Cementiri de Montjuïc—a massive and majestic reliquary with towering views over the Mediterranean. A drifting sense of peace carried me as I touched statues of grieving angels crying for those laid to rest—guardians kept the Devil from pilfering the souls of the dead. Others were captured sitting in ladened reassessment on the beach—looking out over the Balearic Sea contemplating life, and how I'd arrived at that very strand of existence.

I'd little interest in visiting every touristy spot likely on a long list of the average American traveler from dawn to dusk. Rather, preferring to become adrift and then absorbed into obscurity within anonymous crowds as if the city itself had swallowed me up. A city where no one knew me or anything about me as I walked among the multitude. Hinging twilights were welcomed to sauntered city streets as if I were someone else who didn't have a care in the world. Someone else even unknown to me as if a stranger passing by on the sidewalk or the other side of the street. Someone not broken into millions of pieces, but whole and happy. Perhaps, like a slithering snake shedding its skin—I too, attempting to do the same with each step. Attempting to free myself of mine and discard Randy, while discovering a new version of myself coming alive in the City of Barcelona.

Streetlights increasingly flickered as a waning day was summoned by the night—much like a mother calling her child for dinner before the escape of its last spoon-full of light. My shadow casted long and thin the more the lamps fully spotted the sidewalk. I was left to wonder, what or who might be waiting in a doorway or around the next corner. But I carried no fear of such in this foreign place—realizing, every part of my life had been foreign as well.

Eventually, I'd stopped at one of many quaint restaurants—the mixed-aromas of food grumbling my stomach to dine. Afterward, as the evening expanded into the somniferous hours, I purposely continued my walks aimed to do so as far as my legs and feet could shuffle me along until they tired—at times, until the kiss of daylight. If I'd gotten too far astray from the hotel or too lost, there was always a taxi to return me back to the Leonardo.

Once back in my polished top-floor suite, I'd video-chatted with Sandra to check on her and Dugan—the nine-hour difference usually caught her having morning coffee while Dugan finished his breakfast. After sharing the events of my day and evening, and being informed of their plans, I'd crawl into bed dressed in fine linen sheets. Often, my last thoughts and feelings as my head rested on the pillow were those of liberation in knowing I was some 4,566 miles from Atlanta, and the chaos I'd been living within on and off there. The geographic knowledge of knowing I was separated by the North Atlantic Ocean gave comfort as well. A certain contentment found in the surrounding facelessness—the moment I'd disembarked the plane at Aeroport de Barcelona-EL Prat. Each day of the two weeks, I counted them like gold—like a pirate would before burying it for safekeeping. Mapping out his hiding place with X marks the spot.

As that gold piled, and three days left in Barcelona—I'd stumbled onto a lovely corner café. Strings of softly-lit outdoor lights glint the night as they crisscrossed above round white-shirted tables, and chairs on a cobblestone patio. Along with the combinations of delightfully delicious smelling food and that of the night air itself, the ambiance offered, made for a perfect romantic atmosphere. Agreeably proven, by the young man and women dreamingly gazing into each other's eyes—the lights illuminating their exchange of flirtatious smiles as they sipped wine while holding hands under the table.

A distinguished elderly gentleman sat surrounded in solitude—his tan, wiry short-hair dog was curled up by his chair. Two middle-aged women talked while making exaggerated gestures with their arms and hands. Sometimes giggling. Others, shrugging their shoulders while leaning inward as if telling scandalous secrets—surely, the neighborhood's busybodies.

My bowl of gazpacho had been thick and filling. The ensalada mixta with cherry tomatoes, white asparagus, and artichoke hearts topped with a light olive oil and vinegar dressing—served with Spanish flatbread was refreshing. The dish of gambas al ajillo delicious. All consumed with the aid of a bottle of Albariño—a light white floral wine that effortlessly slid down my throat.

The after-dinner evening stroll was leisurely paced amid the warm and tamed breezy air back to the Leonardo. I took in the vitreous night with an unexpected hint of citrus as I walked the tight cobblestones admiring the varying architecture—conceptualizing the lives of the people in their back-lit apartments—stories high, some atop storefronts of retail spaces; their windows casting a fractured sallow-yellow radiance out into the streets. Many having expansive balconies, displayed ornate ironwork. Block after block of connected buildings and a few surreptitiously separated by darkened alleys.

Unexpectedly, I happened to pass within inches of a dashing Spaniard. Steps slowed as our eyes curiously but cautiously made contact. His were dark as the sultry night sky over us. Tall and lean. Firmly built. Sported a well-kept, closely-cropped beard that framed his face. Wavy hair. Long, that curled down over his left eye. I watched as he pushed it back over his forehead during our chance passing—taking place within a gasp of air.

My purposeful, guarded footsteps slowed even more. I looked over my shoulder while proceeding at a snail's pace—hoping. Hoping, he might stop under the next streetlight. And he did. He stopped. Unambiguously, our innocent glance widened into a prolonged stare, of perhaps a more investigative nature.

I paused, before turning around—the Albariño, a source of courage. I nodded, hello. He offered a quick wave. We both took a circumspect step toward each other. At that moment of anticipation, my heart began instantaneously beating quickly in my chest. My face flushed—too, partly attributed to the wine but more so him. I wasn't or rather didn't, feel the least bit intoxicated—just light-headed and hopeful of what might come of the night. Hopefully, a novella of romance and hot passion.

My Spaniard's name was Alejandro. We lingered in the thinning hours under the streetlight examining one another with courting eyes—the obscurity of a capsuling night enveloped la ciudad de Barcelona. His English was no better than my Spanish. But I wasn't about to invite him to my hotel room to engage in detailed dialogue—certainly, not for a Spanish language lesson; but rather, one of entangling flesh.

The morning was still innocent like a new born baby when I awakened from a brief sleep—tired but feeling reborn. Alejandro slumbered—his body partly pinned me to the bed; but I had no desire to move. Its sheets were twisted and pulled to the floor and sodden with a night captured by the greedy yen of aphrodisia, untamable restlessness, and unanticipated tenderness.

I explored every part of his face—every inch of his body until the emanated light filled the room and clothed our naked bodies. After he opened his eyes, Alejandro adjusted his position fully back on me.

Without any protest, I eagerly allowed Alejandro to take my body again—visiting the night before. Some two hours later, the depth of our eyes said our goodbyes as we stood outside the Leonardo Boutique Hotel. I watched as Alejandro walked away, trusting he would look back as he'd done the night before—but didn't. He didn't look back. Nevertheless, it was a fairy tale that briefly fluttered from the pages of that novella.

I spent the day before my departure at the beach reading and starting a new journal. The first line: fue un día hermoso, como lo había sido la noche anterior.

That last night while packing my luggage, the hotel phone rang. The cajoling, coffee-colored eyed concierge was at the other end.

"Mr. Chumbley… you have a guest who wishes to come up to your suite. His name is Alejandro."

I glanced over at the stylish woman—perhaps mid-sixties in the first class seat next to mine. She'd practically talked my head off for the first two hours of the 10 back to Atlanta. She excitedly spoke about her American-born grandchildren while showing off pictures. I politely nodded and smiled, while offering forced compliments—to the point of inciting a migraine. After being served one-to-many glasses of champagne by the flight attendant, and to my relief, she finally reservedly snored herself to sleep.

A part of me—the part that had never truly felt free except with Bradley, wished to keep traveling from country-to-country like a vagabond. I'd rather be lost in the world than in my mind.

Surrounded by the dimness of the cabin and too wound up to join my traveling companion in slumber, I pulled a notepad from my black leather satchel. The overhead spotlight illuminated the pad on the tray table as I jotted down the title of a list: "The Insane Travels of James Randall Chumbley."

Egypt and the Greek Islands were the top two destinations with ten more to follow. The last, The Maldives in South Asia. But those places would remain in my mind—at least for a while and for two reasons: I would miss Dugan too much, and for the first time in some years, I was concerned I'd been spending too much money like it really did grow on a tree in my backyard.

Although I was excited to see Dugan and Sandra, my stomach sickened once I was through customs—mostly, because now I had returned to Atlanta. I wanted to turn around and board the next flight to anywhere on that list.

spoiled mapo tofu

I stopped training at LA Fitness' Ansley Mall location. The initial reason: I didn't want to continue playing dodgeball with Christopher or that's at least what it seemed I was doing at times. Of course, he'd no obligation to stick to certain times to train for my convenience so I wouldn't run into him. Nor was it an ongoing world dilemma of a consistent several times a week; just once was enough to make me uncomfortable. I switched to the Georgia Tech, Spring

Street gym just under a two mile walk from the Seventh Street house. I found the walks enjoyable. The one going, made for a good warmup and returning home provided a good cool down. Plus, both offered head-clearing space. However, changing did prove to be problematic on two counts.

An incident arose due to a new member at Spring Street. A relatively handsome guy caught my eye. Handsome enough for a second glance.

Occasionally, we'd pass each other within a foot or two—enough to give the police an accurate description if he'd been a bank robber while I was making a deposit: mid-forties, buff, tall, brown hair and eyes. Each time, he said hello accompanied with a pleasing smile. I returned the simple greeting as we went on to resume our individual regimens. As had been my usual modus operandi, I continued to keep my head down—especially while training at the gym. Then, one random afternoon, in mid-hellos, he stopped me as I was walking away.

"Hey. Hold up," he called out.

I turned, taking the few steps back toward him.

"Hello again," I replied.

"It seems we're on similar training schedules."

"Yes… it would appear so. I find it nice to get in before the afternoon onslaught."

"We always say hello in passing, but I've never stopped to introduce myself. I'm Brent Morehouse."

"Nice to officially meet you, Brent. I'm Randy Chumbley."

An awkward silence followed.

"I think I've heard of you."

The smile erased from his face.

"Are you an artist and writer… or something like that?"

"Yes, actually, I'm something like that," I answered, with a slight laugh.

Another moment of silence followed—maybe more. Brent cocked his head.

"Are you Christopher Wallis' ex?"

The question caught me off guard. My first instinctive impulse was to say no. I preferred to divorce any association with Christopher. Certainly, that we'd been partners or our paths had ever crossed, for that matter. Plus, the less I heard his name the better—for both of us. Although disinclined, I responded.

"Yes."

My answer was followed by even more silence. Brent's stare took a sharper focus. His jaw marginally dropped.

"Ah… so you're the crazy stalker who tried to kill himself," he cockily pronounced.

I broke eye contact and walked away without acknowledging his impertinent comment. Brent obviously ran in the same circles as Christopher—still propagating his lies, which Brent had confirmed. The encounter was upsetting. Not only had it caught me off guard, but I found it mentally inhibiting. While walking away, I thought of the Hydra in Greek Mythology—the serpent with many heads, was much like those lies. Cut one off and two more grow in its place.

Brent's comment was bad enough; a few weeks later, another surprise caught me off guard. But this one had teeth. To add more insult to injury, I looked across the gym to spot Christopher talking to a few of his buddies. At the sighting, I was quite perplexed. With three LA Fitness locations within a five-or-so mile radius, the third at Atlantic Station—there was no justification for him to show his face at Spring Street. And I don't believe it was just a coincidence. I have no doubts that one of his friends who also train at the Spring Street location had mentioned I was training there. Other sightings followed. I viewed Christopher's appearances as a deliberate show of imperious disrespect—rather childish.

Some might think I was giving Christopher more power over me due to the unraveling caused by seeing him, but that wasn't the case. He was no more than a bad reminder—more like getting the runs after eating spoiled Mapo Tofu. Admittedly, after the second sighting, I took a few days off.

The Saturday morning to follow, I'd awakened in a warm sweat induced by a nightmare. Christopher was the leading character. A baleful feeling of death surrounded me. I felt unsure. Unsure like everything else. Unsure of the days and weeks to come—much less the seconds, minutes, and hours. Unsure of the past and present and the future. Unsure of the rest of my breathing days. Unsure of my purpose as I lie in bed encased in the milky haze caught within the four walls. Unsure if I even wanted to move an inch. Fucking unsure!

The only thing I wasn't unsure of: I needed to take a clonazepam and a lamotrigine. I took two of each.

The compressor of the air conditioning unit outside the window kicked-on—whirling the motor's fan mimicking the sound of disturbed circling bees. Its abrupt launch, an indication the inside temperature had risen above seventy-six degrees. A welcomed, fresh cool stream of oxygenation exited the vents in the ceiling—expanding throughout the room while stirring the existing, still air.

The hour remained questionable until I glanced at the clock announcing late morning. Regardless of my mental state, I had to make myself get out of bed—for nothing else, expect to take Dugan out and feed him. Afterward, and some play time with Dugan, a cold shower helped as did the meds. I mulled over heading to the gym or waiting to go later. I decided to go and hoped Christopher wouldn't be there at the same time. Hence, the game of dodgeball commenced. I would have to, once again, take my chances. But first, I had to stick a two-inch syringe loaded with stacked anabolic steroids in my ass to stay on schedule with my current cycling period.

a bottle of belvedere and 150 bucks

Finding comfort in the flesh is temporary—in one's soul, it's everlasting…

Despite understanding sex wasn't the answer or mentally healthy, I'd slipped back into random sexual encounters that still left me more isolated. Nonetheless, as much as I tried to resist the urge, the more I wanted it—the more I wanted sex. Like alcoholism, I was becoming an addict—an addict of the flesh.

Hours were spent in the chat rooms. My front door began to revolve again. On many weekend nights, I walked the eight blocks from the house to the Atlanta Eagle—masked in the anonymity offered by the perishing hours. Depopulated. Abandoned. Uncertain. The hours, when sound is more imperative than sight; and what can't be seen in the emptiness of light.

In the masquerade of shopping up and down the aisles of cereal, canned goods, frozen foods, and produce—a hook-up was the top item on the grocery list for a different kind of nourishment—offered at the Midtown, twenty-four-hour Kroger next to Ansley Mall on Piedmont Avenue. So-dubbed, for its legendary all hours gay cruising and hook-ups. Whether in the light of day or cloaked by night, they came to feed their appetites.

Sunday morning had arrived late; or rather I had. I'd awakened horny with wood. While stroking with one hand, the other reached for my laptop on the bedside chest. Once on, I began cruising the gay sex sites. Clearly, contradicting myself—not wanting casual sex but at the same time, repentantly dipping into the very places to procure the act for mental distraction.

An array of profiles presented themselves on the screen. Each person looking for something: some wanted an NSA hook-up; others, nasty pig sex; a cute bottom advertised via pictures, to be pounded by a muscular top with at least an eight-incher; another horny soul, to be gangbanged; a heavyset guy, desired to suck and swallow—no reciprocation necessary, before work; a middle-aged couple requested a third to spice up their lackluster sex life as if ordering a Domino's pizza with extra cheese.

They all may have wanted different variations on the same theme but for the most part, I knew some—as I, were trying to fill up the holes inside them. Then, there were the others who just wanted sex as if a sport like basketball and didn't need a void to be filled—just a touch down. I was fully aware; those brief encounters would only serve to augment my own void. It wasn't the first time I was drawn to the screen like a moth to a flame—and likely, it wouldn't be the last. The realization it was a dead end, still didn't always stop me from pushing the power button on my Mac.

I viewed the modern age of the multitude of sex sites as a winding avenue on the Internet. A pick and choose online one-stop shopping from the comfort of one's home while sitting in front of the computer. An avenue lined with pictures of men: blurred faces, some clear while others faceless or eyes blocked out or even headless torsos; in jeans to jock straps to nothing; dicks and asses for the taking; a short or long list of desired appetites, top-bottom-versatile and more, to from fine dining restaurants to quick eat-and-run delis—mostly the latter; among others.

It's a hunt to find the right man or men to wear or for him or them to wear you. Maybe both. And then were the pic collectors. Certainly, nothing like when I was a teenager flipping through the men's underwear section of an old, thick, Sears Roebuck & Co. Catalog—where imagination ran as thoughts did, "I hope I have a body like that one day." And unlike the catalog, the search on the Internet usually leads to a knock at the door. Or a door-slam, if the person standing there had posted someone else's pics or those from ten years ago. While on those travels, I often felt like a middle-aged mongrel dog trying to find its next bone. Eventually, all the profiles ran together like thinning watercolors.

The ubiquitous ping sounded as a text box popped up on the screen—announcing an invitation to message-chat.

"Hey man. Like your pics. Nice pecs."

His profile's inventory included, he was twenty-five. An array of images showed a blonde, smooth, pretty-boy.

"What's going on?" I typed, perfunctorily.

"Not much. Just hanging in my hotel room."

"An out-of-towner?"

"Yeah... Nashville."

"What's your name?"

"Johnny."

"Yours?"

"Randy."

"What brings you to Atlanta?" I typed.

"Trying to make some money."

Awe, lucky me... a prostitute looking for his next paycheck, I thought, as our online chat continued.

Suddenly, I felt like a hypocrite for thinking that.

Johnny shared he was staying at the Wyndham in Midtown not far from my house. I asked him how's business? Johnny expressed it was slow for a sunny, summer day. But he'd figured most gay men were in Piedmont Park taking advantage of the sun. He'd gone bar-hopping the night before with friends and ended up with a killer hangover.

Out of curiosity, I asked how much does he charge his clients? Astonished, I made the inquiry. Astonished—I would even entertain paying for sex.

"It depends."

"On what?"

Johnny charged one-hundred-fifty for a quick hook-up, and five hundred for the night. From his pictures and my younger experience, I knew Johnny was selling himself short. Clearly, he wasn't a pro.

Johnny went on flattering my ego—surely, to secure the purchase. I thought for a moment. Then, another few.

"Sure. Why not?"

"You have anything hard to drink? I need some of the hair of the dog…"

"Hungover?"

"In the worst way."

Thirty minutes later, with an unopened bottle of Belvedere in my backpack and one-hundred-fifty-dollars in my jean's pocket—having popped a Viagra before exiting the house, the automatic double-sliding doors smoothly functioned, giving allowance to the lobby of the hotel. I made a beeline to the bank of elevators further back and to the right. An elderly couple greeted with head-nods as they exited. Uneasy and edgy, I pressed three.

I stepped out into a deserted hallway, lined in beige and off-white striped wallpaper. The carpet felt thick under my feet; the whimsical pattern made my eyes blur. I stood for a moment, determining which direction to proceed to room 315 as told by Johnny. The signage directed to the right. I dutifully turned and walked to my port of call. The only sound was my flip-flops, each flop, rhythmically echoing off the walls, breaking the muffled silence. The room was at the end of the hallway. I lingered momentarily in front of the door—staring at the numbers before I knocked.

The door opened wafting conjoined smells of sweat, sex, and booze. But my mind was more focused on who was standing there—standing just on the other side.

"Shit," my mind flashed at the sight of him—strikingly-beautiful in the flesh like his pictures.

Johnny stood dressed in a pair of jeans unbuttoned at the waist and shirtless. His wide smile gleamed as he ran his fingers through thick, blonde-white hair back from his forehead revealing walnut-colored eyes. His body: tan; smooth; well defined, but not overly muscular. Johnny motioned me in. At that very moment, I knew he was unquestionably the pro, and I was the rookie.

"Hey… come on in," Johnny invited, in a disarming Southern drawl.

I smiled. Walked into the dim room—the draperies drawn closed.

"You're as handsome as your pics, Big Boy," he gratuitously complimented.

"It's been quite a while since I was a boy."

"You know what I mean," Johnny responded.

"Sure, thanks."

I wasn't quite sure if he candidly thought I was as handsome as my pics, or if that was only part of his practiced professional come-on. After all, his job was to make his clients feel good. I pulled the vodka from the backpack and sat it on the dresser.

"Nice shit… thanks."

"No problem."

I dug the wad of cash from my pocket. Laid it next to the bottle as Johnny approached. He slid his hands up my T-shirt. Pressed his body into me, then coyly lifted his head until his lips reached mine. His, were full. Pink and soft. Cogently, I surrounded them with mine before slipping my tongue deep into his mouth. Johnny welcomed it as he began sucking, like it was a baby's pacifier. Slow. Measured. Consistent. He tasted of sweet, innocent youth—but no doubt, this kid had lost his, some time ago. I pulled Johnny in closer; my penis engorged with blood.

His lungs took in a pant of air as my lips parted from his. Then, a second pant, before he managed to speak.

"Your chest is fucking massive… just the right amount of hair," Johnny observed, as he ran his hands over it.

I sat down on the edge of the unmade bed—the generic, white hotel sheets were well-tanged. Both they and the under pad, were pulled from the corners exposing sections of the mattress. The top blanket—mostly on the floor, was covered in monochromatic geometric shapes. Johnny stood over me as he pulled off my T-shirt.

"You got some bitchin' abs. Nice big arms, too."

The adulation made me uncomfortable, finding them somewhat overdone like a baked chicken.

"I'll say… you're quite nice to look at yourself."

Instantaneously, I felt stupid telling him as if I were some desperate old man. He already knew that—that he was beautiful.

"Glad you like," Johnny smilingly responded.

He slipped out of his jeans and underwear. Kicked them across the room. Proudly, Johnny stood in front of me. His penis was average but still nice. I wanted to lick his stomach but didn't. Johnny got down on his knees. Began sucking on my nipples while fondling my junk. I wrapped my arms around him again. Moved my hands lower until I had his round, ample ass in their grip.

"Man, you're nice and hard. Yummy," he added.

Johnny looked up at me quite convincingly, as if he were being authentically affectionate. But I wasn't buying it, reminding myself he was a call boy, and I was nothing more to him except cash.

I found myself wondering, "How many times had he'd been fucked in this hotel room over the last few days?"

Johnny was doing and saying all the right things—skillfully. Surely rote. Surely spoken to many a john. Every complimentary word given like a waiter for a bigger gratuity. Speedily, I wasn't feeling it emotionally or physically. Thanks to the little blue pill—like rubbing a dog's belly, only my dick showed any interest in screwing the boy. However, my heart was indifferent. My brain faltered—playing twisted mind games: you're getting old, better get as much ass as you can while the getting is good; so, what that he's a prostitute; a hot piece of ass is still a hot piece of ass; doesn't matter that this isn't real affection; so, what, fuck him and leave; it's no big deal.

Then, that annoyingly pesky unraveling started, accompanied by a queasiness working up from my gut—pushing to the surface. I tackled to focus on the hot boy in the room. Not the argumentation in my head. I told myself, to imagine how good Johnny's hot ass would taste before I slid my dick deep inside it. The voices in my head were screaming so loudly, I was sure Johnny could hear the heated debate.

"Hey, Rand… Randy… you with me? You zoned out there for a bit. You, okay?"

The voices slipped away. My eyes focused back on the prostitute. I pulled Johnny up from the floor. Pulled him on the bed until his stomach was on mine. Johnny rested his chin in the valley of my pecs. Brushed his impeccably beautiful hair out of his eyes again as he lifted his head to look at me.

"Am I not doing something right?" he implored. "Are you uncomfortable being with a prostitute? You did say this was your first time."

"No… no. It's not you. Most of us are prostitutes in one form or another."

"Well, I was wondering. You're nice and hard. I'd like to have some of that."

"I'd like to give it to you," I volleyed.

At that, I rolled Johnny off me. Stood up from the bed. Pushed my jeans and underwear to the floor. Stepped out of them.

"Now… I really want you to fuck me," Johnny smiled. "You're making me horny… and it's not because of the money."

"How about we lie here for a while?" I suggested.

"Sure, man. If that's what you want."

That disjointed afternoon, I laid on top of an amazingly beautiful guy. To fuck Johnny would be like using him—like other older men had and would, to momentarily reach back in time to recapture their own youth—eclipsed and stolen by time, as they licked the sweat from smooth and tender flesh. Reached, to rediscover the desired intensity of sodden lust. Reached, for the rejuvenation offered from the consumption of sweet-salty cum as if drinking from the fountain of youth. And the wet-warmth of the raw exhilaration found as they slipped their dicks in unaged ass.

I'd become no different than those men who had been knocking on Johnny's hotel room door before me and those who would after—as I'd used others like Johnny but without having to pay in green currency. And like Johnny, in my own youth, I allowed those older men to rent me to relive their youth as well. But maybe there was more to it than money. Like me, then younger and now older, maybe Johnny needed the attention—starved for it, and the money was only an offshoot. But I never would have settled for pennies on the dollar as he was. Not even despite my low self-esteem. And because of that, pennies on the dollar, in Johnny's case, the older men were getting much more out of the arrangement. But Johnny was worth more than any monetary number, or so I thought. Maybe I had been as well—no matter how much I'd walked away with in dollars, but empty-handed in other ways.

All the same, I couldn't stand the thought of becoming one of Johnny's anonymous johns—my face, eventually to blur and mix with the others within hours, if not days. To blur until the outlines of our faces are erased. To blur, as many of those from my past had, and erased as well as if they never existed. As if—my flesh had never been touched by them. Even still, I wanted to find some transient comfort. A few ounces of serenity. Again, I just didn't want to be alone that Sunday afternoon—even if it was with someone who had been selling his body. Again, who was I to judge him? Being that it didn't make Johnny any less of a person. He was surviving. I would have to be satisfied with Johnny in my arms and be in the moment—digging for every ounce of willpower not to think about yesterday or into tomorrow.

I repositioned our bodies. Put my arms back around him. Then, pressed my dick into the sweet, deep crack of his ass as. My eyes soon closed—venturing to disembarrass my mind before dozing off; only to be jolted out by another bad dream sometime later. By then, Johnny had also fallen into the layers of sleep. I'd found some succor I'd sought upon awakening—human flesh against mine. But we were just two strangers with no shared past and no future. Nothing less and nothing more than the time that passed, as we lay together on the bed in the confines of the walls of that dim hotel room of the Wyndham. I soon fell back into a light, peaceful-laced sleep somewhere between reality and fantasy until I awoke. I checked the time on my wristwatch. Almost an hour had passed.

"You awake?" I uttered.

No response. I asked again.

"Yea… yes," Johnny answered, in a languid volume.

"I've got to go."

"You sure?"

Johnny turned his head; he looked at me.

"I feel I didn't earn my money," he sleepily added.

"Sure… you did."

"If it means anything, I think you're fucking hot."

I blankly stared at him a bit longer. I didn't feel I was. Rather, again, like I was paying for the compliments.

I eased out of bed. Johnny continued to lie there until he rolled completely onto his back. He watched while I redressed. As I slipped my feet back into the flip-flops, I looked away and then back over at Johnny. Still lying there so invitingly. His beauty summoning. A moment later, I turned to grab my backpack.

"Sure… I can't at least give you a blow job?"

He stood up; got off the bed. Walked up to me.

"Yea. I'm sure. No worries. It's not you."

"What about the vodka?"

"Keep it."

I took another long gaze.

"Take care of yourself… okay."

After those last few words, I turned away. Negotiated for the door. Johnny followed. I turned for a last look—still coveting him but knowing it was pointless. Knew it best to go before I changed my mind. And again, I spurned that proclivity to use him as a piece of ass—as I'd sporadically done others since 2009.

I opened the door. A maid pushed a cart around the corner.

A few feet down the hallway, I looked back. Johnny remained outside the hotel room door—watching. I offered a brief smile before turning my head back forward.

"Hopefully, he'll eventually land on his feet and won't remain on his back," I thought.

eight

nutter butter cookies

It's quite amazing what three months can do. Over summer break between my junior and senior year, I went through a metamorphosis after becoming a major health nut. I stretched—growing from 5 feet 10 inches to 6.1

Generally, five out of six or seven mornings, before sunrise, I'd hit the dismal streets jogging—eventually, progressing up to five or so miles. The younger years—cowered by abuse and violence, filled with arbitrary days walking to the Dairy Queen to get a soft-serve vanilla ice cream cone dipped in chocolate for under a dollar, finishing it halfway back to the house only to return to get another for comfort were long gone. So were—Nabisco Nutter Butter cookies.

One late morning, after walking into my bedroom, Mother caught me on the floor lying on my back at the foot of the bed—using the lower end round metal bar as a barbell and the bed as the weights to do chest presses. That afternoon, she purchased me a proper weight set. As Jack LaLanne, the television personality—fitness and nutrition guru as my motivation and with constant use, along with a good amount of sweat equity, my body quickly transformed into toned lean muscle. What acne I had cleared up and I grew out my hair—Jim Morrison style.

On that first day of my senior year at Warner Robins High School, a lot of students first thought I was the new kid. That is, until they realized I was Randy Chumbley—but improved. Although still shy and unsure of myself, I engaged with some of the girls who flirted, as they and others watched me in class and in the hallways. Many, of which, had never talked to me since starting high school. Eventually, one of the prettiest girls and I started going steady.

Surprisingly—almost to the point of shock, even Bobby Maze, a muscular and nice looking athlete took notice. He played football with my brother and buddied around. First, I'd occasionally caught him staring at me while in the school cafeteria having lunch from the table where he and the other jocks and their girlfriends sat together. Not the killer stare I' d been used to, but one of a more inquisitive nature. The same Bobby Maze who dated one of the cheerleaders, Amy Gray. The same Bobby who bullied me between classes and in PE, as well as in the locker room the year before.

Within a short span of time, Bobby's glances morphed into subtle brushes up against me—whereas the year before, one of his popular bullying tactics was to push me in the direction of the lockers. Initially, I thought the first brush was accidental—that is, until one of the brushes included his hand touching my ass as he passed from behind. Bobby briefly turned around to face me while walking backward.

"What's up, Randy?" shooting his usual cocky smile.

He quickly looked around the hall—surely to assess if anyone noticed him talking to me.

Those were the first unthreading words he'd ever spoken to me up until that incident.

"Uh... just heading to chemistry."

"See you around... then," Bobby responded as he quickly turned and disappeared around the corner.

If Bobby wasn't brushing up against me, then he was walking the halls while holding Amy's hand. Even then, Bobby would throw me a side stare.

Bobby's attention got as far as the late-evening I was walking to my car leaving the Houston Mall. I ran into him as he was about to get into his blue 1971, Plymouth Satellite. Bobby blocked me from passing. Pushed me up against his car. Grabbed my crotch and proceeded to sloppily kiss me. I managed to push him aside before he could jab his tongue down my throat. Bobby stood back, glared at me, seemingly upset that he'd been rejected.

The old Bobby quickly returned, when he got back in my face—not to try again, but to express, "If you tell anyone... I'll beat your ass."

Not long after, I started going steady with a pretty, long-haired blonde girl. As I understand it, Bobby still lives in Warner Robins and married to Amy. They have four grandchildren and two great-grandchildren.

The surprising attention continued into college. It was a new semester; the array of colored leaves fallen from the trees were carried on the wind as I watched them through the large studio windows swirl and dance, thieving my attention from the art professor.

"James… James, are you with us? It's your turn."

As I got up and walked to the front of the class, I noticed a new student I'd not seen before sitting at the back. An older woman who reminded me of the famous model, Lauren Hutton caught my eye.

As the class dispersed for the door, she stopped me.

"I liked your presentation," she complimented.

"Thank you… I hope you weren't the only one."

"I'm sure everyone did. I'm headed to lunch. Can you join me… or do you have another class?"

I came to find out she was a well-off divorcee—not quite old enough to be my mother but close, taking art classes more for a distraction than anything else. I imagined she had become bored and took them to fill some of her time away from charity events and lunches with some ladies' social club.

Not before long, I found myself at her beck and call. Once or twice a week, long nights were spent in her bathtub submerged in bubbles while drinking champagne. No doubt, I wasn't the first college boy who ended up in her tub and bed.

An equal opportunity college student for all ages, I later met a tall and fit architect old enough to be my grandfather. At the time, I was painting backdrops for the Macon Little Theater. Such the romantic, he'd prepared candlelit dinners at his beautiful, Asian inspired, contemporary home in Macon. Being well-known in the community, he was Skittish about being seen in public with someone my age. I must say, he was damn good in the sack.

Betsy and Monica were rivals for my attention—resulting in a lot of friction between them. But their commonality was the all-girls, Wesleyan College. Betsy had already graduated a few years earlier when we'd met while Monica was still attending.

The round-bellied British Art History instructor regularly invited his students over in the evenings for wine. I never went—no matter how many times he personally cornered me. My favorite art professor shared the instructor and head of the Art Department often talked about me, and it wasn't related to my work. However, that might be why I got A's in my classes when I likely should have gotten B's, and my senior art show was in the top five.

Randy was a grade-school teacher who lived in the Massey apartments in Macon when I moved into one of their efficiencies—within walking distance to the Mercer campus where I was taking post-graduate classes. Macon and graduate classes because, again, my mother wouldn't remarry or move to LA even if I tried to pry her out of the house and that town with a crowbar.

I'd told Mother that I had to get out of Warner Robins, and I was moving to Macon some 20 miles away. That first week, I spent the night at the house. I felt as if I was abandoning her.

I used Randy to feel safe. Plus, he was good at fixing my car when it broke down as he also did maintenance on it like changing the oil. He eventually wanted a relationship. Although at first, I only pretended; but over time I became attached to him and came to believe I loved him.

At the time, Randy was engaged to another teacher. When he expressed, he was going to break it off with her, I told Randy not to. It was around then that I was moving to Atlanta. I was invited to the wedding in Florida. We had sex the night before the nuptials.

Driving back with two friends, I felt sick to my stomach and thought about opening the car door and jumping out. I guess I felt abandoned even though I didn't want Randy. Today, I clearly see the pattern.

It seemed the moment my car crossed over the city limit line of Atlanta—it wasn't long before my life surprisingly shifted for the better in unexpected ways. And what attention I started noticing beforehand my senior year of high school and while in college, expanded exponentially. Even considering my self-esteem issues, situations arose where I was aware—much like my mother had been the center of attention when she walked into a room, people took notice of me.

Many of them, men old enough to be my father if not more, boldly made their approach. Being a new face surely helped—evident by lingering gazes. I like it, as if I were a mannequin on display. And the more I was noticed, the more I wanted to be. But that had started as a child in need of love. Later, crossing over to sex and the high I received as a young man to be desired and even the payment received. And for segments of time, the attention was good for my ego to the point, I thrived and fed off it. With time, that need to be wanted made me an addict.

Nevertheless, it didn't matter how many staring eyes watched or the mouthed, OMGs I caught; eventually as had often been the case, I would start feeling ugly and not worth a second glance. Intellectually knowing is one thing while what one feels emotionally is totally different. The emotions usually trumps the intellect—at least, that has always been the case with me.

My insecurities would regain control. Once again, I would feel out of place. When able, I pressed myself to appear as if I had been born with a silver spoon in my mouth. Not to put on airs but give the impression I was something—worthy and far more than a small-town boy dripping wet behind the ears. All, to keep those insecurities on the other side of that city limit line.

Not long after my arrival, a photographer approached me in the store while I was working on a display in the men's department.

"Pardon me, I'm Tate. I couldn't help but notice you. Have you ever modeled?"

"Randy. Nice to meet you. But no, I haven't."

"You have a great look. I think you'd do well."

"Are you serious? Do you mean porn?" I laughed.

"No... fashion and product representation."

"Um, I don't think that's for me."

"Look, here's my card. Give it some thought call me... okay?"

I was surprised as I had been the first time I was scouted while taking graduate classes at Mercer. Two people approached me while I was studying in one of the patio areas. They were looking for college students to represent a line of clothing. And even more so, some twenty years later while in the lobby at the Four Seasons; when an older, well-dressed gentleman, who owned an agency in New York, stopped me and similarly asked the same—if I'd ever modeled. I lied and told him no. As I look back, I wish I'd been honest and told him, yes; and I would be interested. He, too, communicated I'd do well—especially for commercials. He gave me his card; but as the second time, I never called.

Not bothering to call Tate, he determinedly came looking for me about a week later. I was easily to found, much like bait walking around the store. Tate told me he'd talked to another photographer and on his recommendation, alone Nick wanted to see me. Again, I hesitated.

After more convincing, I gave it. A few days later, I found myself in Nick's amazing studio in a refurbished old warehouse just east of Downtown. He seemed like a nice guy. Even one of his kids was running about.

"So, Randy… I understand you don't think modeling is for you."

"Yeah. Never even given it any thought."

Nick looked me over.

"Surely, you've noticed people look at you. I would imagine, a lot… even hit on."

I laughed, too shy to answer right away.

"Well… well, the saleswomen in the couture department always tell me I should be on a soap."

"I can see that… but it's obvious to me, you don't see yourself the way other people do."

Nick then asked me to give him a few hours to take some test shots.

"My assistant is in the back. We have everything here."

It wasn't long before Nick called to show the images he'd taken. I was certain they sucked. But when he presented a stack of them, I didn't even recognize myself. Still, I wasn't convinced I stood a chance in Hell at getting paid for my looks in such a cutthroat industry.

"Randy… I knew it the first time you walked into the studio. Your self-esteem may be in the toilet, but your looks aren't. And regardless of how you see yourself, you carry yourself well."

"I appreciate all you're saying, Nick… but."

"No buts, Randy," he cut me off. "Of course, it's a long shot, but most things are. I just have a feeling about you."

"Nick… I don't feel it."

"I wonder why?" Nick spoke under his breath but enough for me to hear.

"What?"

"Nothing… will you let me see what I can do? Trust me. Okay."

Within a week, I received a call from Apex Model Management in Atlanta. Later, to find out their main office was in New York with two others besides Atlanta, in Los Angeles and Miami. Two former female models, Ronnie and Barbara were the agents at the Atlanta office. Nick had taken it upon himself to courier my pictures over.

After the agents looked me over as if I was a prize cow at an auction, including stripping me down to my jeans and taking Polaroids, they sat me down for some discussion.

"It's clear, the camera loves you… and Nick agrees. Just leave it up to us. Okay?"

"Like I told Nick… I just didn't know."

Subsequent of some arm twisting, I signed on the dotted line before I left the agency.

As a new face, there was a lot to learn. And it was a long-shot—modeling. Each of the agency's offices kept copies of a book filled with their models from each city. Comp cards—a small collection of recent pictures and measurements of height, weight, eyes, and hair color, along with clothing and shoe sizes had to be kept updated. Each model had their portfolio of pictures and those from gigs they'd done.

Go-sees were necessary where models would be scrutinized to see if you had the look casting agents wanted—sometimes referred to as cattle calls. I was just another face and a body among many. Those cattle calls were the worst for my self-esteem—usually feeling out of place with no business being there. Many times, I wanted to run back out of the door as I waited to be seen with other models. But Gary and the Atlanta agents took me on like a high school group project as they continued to believe. I certainly didn't myself. Apparently, I got lucky. Due to Apex Model Management having four offices, Ronnie and Barbara pushed my pictures. Doing that, and the fact Gray was well known and respected as a photographer, his recommendation and those pictures seemed to be a huge help in getting me noticed.

It wasn't long before I began getting optioned for jobs in Atlanta. I basically kept the modeling to myself, not wanting to tell friends. Getting booked for some while passed over for others. In the beginning, the money was enough to buy bird seed. Around 250 bucks a day of mostly sitting and waiting, painted with makeup, clothes being ripped off my body and then redressed. But as my portfolio slowly grew, the more jobs came my way—resulting, in more money.

Within the same timeframe, Britton's New York's corporate office relocated the East Coast VP of Merchandising, Oscar Barfield, to Atlanta—along with a few buyers, and a new visual merchandising supervisor named Jud for the downtown store to oversee the staff of twelve—including me. Short and muscled, who swished his hips when he walked. Along with Jud, I'd met the buyers but had yet to personally meet the VP. That is, until the day I was on the second floor waiting for one of the elevators.

When the doors opened, the VP and Head of Finance, Thomas King stood inside talking before they walked out. Thomas was in his 60s. A warm man with an even and friendly temperament. I liked him. Thomas had been welcoming from the very first day I started, telling me his office door was always open if I had any issues or needed anything having to do with work or otherwise. We occasionally had lunch in his office or walked over to a little café across the street at Peachtree Center. In some ways, Thomas took me under his wind knowing I was new to the big city life. I came to feel like we were friends.

And so much so that one morning I embarrassingly tapped on the frame of his door. Thomas motioned me in while on the phone. I took a seat and waited. My crotch area had been itching for a couple of days. I didn't know why. I confided in him. Thomas leaned back in his desk chair and chuckled.

"You really are a newbie, Randy."

"What do you mean?"

"Well, I don't think you're going to die. I'm pretty sure you have crabs."

"Crabs?"

"Yes, pubic crabs. But… it's not a big deal. I got them twice when I was your age."

Thomas told me to take a few hours off. Go to Woolworth across the street to buy a box of pubic lice treatment; and instructed on what else I needed to do.

Once they walked out of the elevator, Thomas said hello and asked if everything was going okay as he placed a hand on my shoulder.

"Yes, I'm jumping from one project to another."

"Have you met Vice President Oscar Barfield?"

"No. I've not had the pleasure."

I reached out my hand to shake his. The doors of the elevator they exited had closed. Another pinged opened. Several customers stepped out.

"It's nice to meet you, Mr. Barfield."

"You as well… call me Oscar. No need to be so formal."

The VP held my hand longer than your average handshake as he keenly looked me in the eyes and smiled. Barfield was handsome. Tall with a medium build. Perhaps, early 50s with graying temples.

Thomas went on to inform the VP: I was one of the youngest on staff to oversee the large storefront windows when it came to women's fashion.

Another elevator came and went. More customers exited. The VP expressed he was very impressed with what work of mine he'd seen. He winked. An awkward pause followed as the VP kept looking at me.

"Well… I should get on with it. I'm sure you both have a busy day, but again… very nice to officially meet you," I expressed.

I turned to face the elevators. Heard the ping of one's approach from a higher floor as I watched the flashing red indicator numbers above descend. As I continued to wait, a commotion from behind caught my attention.

I turned my head to see the VP in the middle of a trip but caught just in time by Thomas.

"I should watch where I'm going," I overheard the VP.

At that, I walked into the elevator.

At the end of the day, as I was in the parking garage walking to my car, I heard Thomas call from behind.

"Wait up, Randy… "

My pace slowed. Thomas caught up. He looked around the garage, then back at me.

"Hey… what's up?"

"Goodness, I… I need to start that diet I've been putting off," Thomas said, between deep inhales of air.

He was a bit on the heavy side.

"Did you notice Oscar trip as we were walking away from you at the elevators?"

"Yes, yes I did… but pretended not to."

Thomas laughed.

"I think you have a new admirer."

"Who?"

"Do I really have to tell you?" Thomas grinned. "You didn't notice how Oscar ogled at you like a girl with a high school crush?"

"Well… I think that's somewhat of an exaggeration."

Thomas took another labored breath.

"The VP trip because he was looking back at you. He wasn't watching where we were going and tripped on my foot. And… he's been asking about you on and off today."

"I think he was more interested in my work."

"That, too. But… trust me. He's really into you. Just wanted you to know… got to run."

Thomas headed to his car, still panting for air.

the unwelcome house guest

Some six months had passed before I got my first modeling job in Atlanta. Despite the support and encouragement by the agency, and more shoots at Nick's studio, I continue to feel like a fish out of water—finless. Nervous and unsure, I almost ran off the set; but somehow, I managed to do a decent job. And fortunately, the photographer was a friend of Nick's and already knew I was green.

Shortly thereafter, a few more followed. Besides nerves, I had another issue. My new supervisor didn't like the fact I was dividing up vacation days in order to juggle them with Britton's—especially when my first job in Los Angeles required four days. The fact that we had 12 people on staff, taking a few days here and there shouldn't have been an issue. I think it had more to do with the fact that my supervisor didn't like me after I rejected a few of his advances.

On a Thursday evening, my apartment mate, Tom, had a casual dinner party of twelve friends. In advance, he'd suggested I invite Jake if I wanted who I occasionally dated—the epitome of tall, dark, and a young John Wayne handsome. We would be eleven and twelve at the table.

Jake had a best friend, Chip. At our first meeting, I didn't realize they came as a package deal. A two-for-one priced item like a Wednesday special of the week at Kroger. The three of us sometimes caught a meal together, and a few times out to bars. Within weeks of that meeting of the two-for-one special, there were instances of Chip's flirtations. At first, I didn't take his advances seriously—seemingly rather harmless. I was still learning about this new gay world, its boundaries and rules. Although I would come to learn there were none—boundaries or rules where Chip was concerned.

It's not that Chip wasn't good-looking with his towering linebacker build, but there was something about his personality that was questionable. The unwanted advances escalated. I became emotionally troubled by them: the ass and crotch grabbing; purposefully brushing against me; pinching my nipples through my shirt; gyrating me from behind, his hands firmly on my hips; leaning in to whisper bellicose sexual innuendos. I struggled to remain cool. Attempted to keep my distance. When situations arose where distance was shortened, I continued enduring Chip's unreciprocated solicitations—remaining optimistic they would stop at some point. Preferably, sooner than later.

They progressively got creepier. Even frightening. Chip seemed to take great delight—as if thinking I would be flattered by sharing, he jerked-off to a clothing ad of me in a magazine he'd kept under his bed with his cum towel. That knowledge prompted a more direct approach to the situation—hopefully, to nip things in the bud by bluntly addressing the actions of my unwanted suitor. I lied and told Chip I liked him as a friend, but that was as far as my interest went. I was sure telling Chip he disgusted me by not respecting boundaries wouldn't be helpful in deterring him. And despite my contempt, I still didn't want to hurt his feelings—as if he had any.

Pulling Chip aside didn't stop the advances, rather serving to fertilize them. Making him more aggressive as if Chip received some morbid gratification in knowing—in seeing how they rattled me. I began opting out of hanging with them both. Made-up excuses to leave when Chip showed before his chance for a good grab.

I'd made it clear to Jake there were to be twelve guests, and I was only inviting him and not the twin. Though no earth-shattering surprise, but not expected, Chip was in tow sporting a big, Cheshire cat grin as he stood over and behind Jake when I opened the front door.

Twinges of dread bounded around within the mucosa of my stomach. That evening, there were fifteen guests for dinner—one uninvited. At that moment of opening the door, I'd no idea of how calamitous the night would end.

The entirety of the dinner was shrouded by Chip's presence. Unremittingly, I continued to keep an uninterested distance—one measurable as if a yardstick were duct-taped around my waist for accuracy within an eighth of an inch. I refrained from looking directly in his direction, sitting at the other side of the table. But it was necessary to keep a covert knowledge of Chip's location as if I had a radar sensor implanted in one eye.

As usual, he brashly threw looks attempting to catch my attention that were deliberately ignored. I was learning there wasn't anything subtle about him, and Chip wouldn't know a boundary line if it were made of barbed wire and strangling him around the neck. At one point, I dropped my guard; Chip followed me into the kitchen—attempted to pin me against the refrigerator door. Force his lips on mine. Thankfully, Tom came in prompting Chip to back off. I jetted for the bathroom. Locked myself in for a good ten minutes. Sat on the toilet hiding my face in my hands out of frustration—while gathering some wits.

With the conclusion of dinner—stomachs satisfied by Tom's excellent cooking skills and sections of wine, I was relieved. I wasted little time cleaning up with the help of one of the dinner guests—while my watchdog eyes continued to keep a lookout for Chip whereabouts.

The guests began to dwindle out the door as Tom was busy talking to Chester, his older boyfriend of some five years. Jake asked if I wanted to go out for an after-dinner drink with a few others, as Chip stood in the doorway of the kitchen—his linebacker build filling it. I declined for the obvious; but couldn't if I wanted to.

I'd been hired for a shoot scheduled early the next morning at the Peachtree Western Hotel in Downtown Atlanta. My role was a young executive enjoying the accommodations of the newly renovated hotel. I knew it best to stay in and get to bed—fresh for the assignment.

Jake gave me a hug as I discreetly kept an eye on Chip.

"Okay… I understand. Good luck tomorrow. I know you'll do great," Jake encouraged.

I watched as he walked toward his twin until they disappeared into the dining area.

Tom popped his head into the kitchen.

"Randy… you need any more help?"

"I'm good. Just a few more things and I'm off to bed. Oh… thanks for an exceptional dinner."

"My pleasure. David and I are heading over to the Armory."

My focus returned to finish cleaning up as the few remaining guests dwindled from the apartment—their conversions with them. The front door closed.

Ten o'clock was approaching while I'd finished straightening up from the dinner party and completed a strict bedtime regimen of beautification practices. Following, I checked the front and back doors for reassurance they were securely locked. There was considerable crime in Midtown, including several occurrences of burglaries in my apartment building, as had been in others on the street. Exhausted, with brushed bright shiny white teeth and a freshly washed and moisturized face, I shut off most of the lights before falling into bed.

Although still new at being in front of the camera, modeling jobs hurtled apprehension the night before—as if having a final exam in a class I'd skipped the entire quarter and never cracked open the textbook. Then, there was the continued fluctuating badgering of my self-esteem—that voice in my head, much like a bully, asserting I wasn't good enough as it always had since childhood. Not good enough, despite the new jobs and the amount of encouragement from Kip Lang, his associate who stumbled across me at Britton's, and the two women who managed the agency. At times, it was enough to make me want to stop. With bending effort, I had to seriously attempt to psych myself up to show up—in such a way, transforming into another person. Still, there remained times, I thought the clients were out of their minds to want me.

I positioned a pillow to rest my head as I laid on my stomach. The dinner had been spoiled by Chip—his game of cat and mouse. As troubling as he'd been by invading my boundaries, I reminded myself that I'd brought other goliaths in the past to their knees, and it wasn't for the purpose to suck my dick. With concentrated and slow breathing, I attempted to shake out any negative thoughts from my head. I relied on an old technique from childhood. I'd close my eyes imagining I was weightless, floating out of my body and drifting up into the sky until I was flying among the stars in a universe that had no beginning or end. Oftentimes it worked.

Near the onset of sleep—believing that night was over while pushing it away, I had no idea that I was mistaken. It wasn't. It wasn't over. Certainly, unaware how it would land on top of the accumulation of past events that had piled—or how the many months to follow would add to my definition of self.

a mouse caught in a trap

A shade of raven subtlety sponged the room. The lamp I'd left on in living area casted a low haze thinning down the hallway that leaked into my bedroom. The sixty-something-year-old apartment was without sound except for random creeks of the aged, brick building and the night-active mice's occasional scratching and scurrying around in the confines of lath and plaster. There was an ongoing rodent problem; the apartment manager had been slow at addressing. The infestation to the degree that earlier in the evening before the arrival of the dinner guest, a lone critter speedily ran out of the oven when I opened it to insert a tray of dinner rolls. Of course, startled, my hands flew into the air as did the tray of rolls.

Then, it happened. In a flash. No forewarning. Descent into sleep gruesomely disrupted. An abrupt forceful grab at the waistband of my boxers jerked me back through a foggy channel to devastating lucidity. A lightning-quick, hard, tug, immediately followed. Lifting my midsection. The boxers ripped from my body. The sound—shredding.

Before there was time to mentally process—to turn my head around, a heavy poundage of heated flesh left me immobile. Trapped. Hot, heavy breaths circled my head as did dank body order. Within seconds, a hard, large penis stabbed through my anus—inciting eldritch, spine-chilling terror. The thrust at penetration, the intensity of it almost enough to make me lose consciousness. I managed to force a bawled scream of bloody murder as it repeatedly jabbed into me.

Incalculable shock and confusion took over—disorienting. A

recognizable panic fueled my struggles to get from under the heft of the hindrance disabling movement—as if I'd been pinned down under a car. The attack, brutal. Harrowing. The rapist at least twice my body weight. I screamed out again, "Get the fuck off! Goddammit!" Within seconds, it all came into ugly focus.

My assailant's implacable and rancorous thrusts became progressively more erratic and deeper. His large hand hastily covered my mouth, suppressing the screams to near extinguishment while making it strenuous to breathe. The other arm and hand tightly wrapped my abdomen, making it—combined with the weight, impossible to wiggle free. Tears flooded my eyes from the incendiary, fear, and the pain.

The disorientation and panic clogged my brain until I realized it had to be Chip. I was certain—obvious by the unblemished sound of his voice.

"You want this. I know you... you do. You fucking tease," Chip lambasted, in a low aggressive tone.

His piggish sweat slithered my back. I bit down on the hand covering my mouth—hard enough to draw blood. Its taste pervaded my mouth. Chip tore it out, but not before I had some skin clinched in my teeth. I gasped to replenish air into my deprived lungs. Then, took advantage of the moment to scream out, but it was quickly curtailed.

"You little, bitch!" he gruff. "So, you want it rough. I can give you, rough," Chip repeated, as if he'd been gentle up to that point.

Chip shoved my face into the pillow. I strained for freedom while gasping for more air—fully convinced I was fighting for my life, and sure that was his objective to suffocate me in the process. The impalement continued like a knife; I felt meager seconds from death the more oxygen was restricted, and from the paroxysm of rage delivered in sadistically inflicted torture. But still I grappled—regardless how futile. My survival mode conjured intrinsically by childhood, instilling fighting back to the very last second even as impossible as the circumstances were.

I found myself almost grateful for the onset of his profuse precum which had at least eased the abrading of my ass—convinced, he wasn't using a condom. Automatically came the overwhelming and incapacitating terror of being infected with HIV and an STD. The headboard of the queen-sized bed knocked against the wall until it began leaping and scraping over the hardwood floor. Moments later, he was done. His body jerked with continued, intensified thrusts as he ejaculated in my ass. I wondered what was next.

The room felt bereft of life. Sucked out. Colorless. Silent, except for Chip's lumbering breathing: his body, feeling even heavier like dead weight; the knocking of the headboard and the bed due to his last ferocious thrusts; the squeaking of the mattress askew on top of the box springs. Breath was regained as Chip lightened his force on my head pushed into the pillow. The mental observance I hadn't suffocated made me wonder if Chip would soon have his hands around my neck. My survival instinct kicked in stronger than before. I struggled again to get from under Chip. But he was still too heavy and kept his arm around my waist—his hand, locked my flesh. I knew if I scream again, I'd only be silenced as before.

"So… this is what you've been giving Jake… a nice fuckable ass," he whispered, as his teeth pulled at my ear.

The low growl of his voice rumbled evil. The stench of his perspiration dripped with the sweat like a steamy rain as he raised his body inches from mine. Chip hovered, as if deciding what to do next. It seemed an eternity. Finally, he got off the bed. I turned my head enough to watch Chip as he menacingly towered-up as though a malevolent monstrous ogre—his pants and underwear down. His boots still on. His shirtless torso exposed. I remained fearful he would jump back on top of me and start again, if not choke me to death as I'd believed earlier. Again, too afraid to scream thinking to do so would irritate him, and that would be my end. I just wanted Chip to leave.

He wickedly laughed, surely proud of what he'd just done. Still eyeballing me, Chip pompously and in an enthusiastic depraved gesture of exhibition, shook his bloodied dick at me before putting his underwear and jeans back on. He grabbed his tank top from the floor. Stood stiffly back up. Threw the tank around his neck—not bothering to put it on.

Moments later, Chip began to nonchalantly walk backward to the doorframe. A grin of superiority flashed from his face like a neon sign. I watched Chip in searing hatred, but not straight in the eyes. I remained frozen. I kept praying he would hurry up and fucking leave, but Chip remained standing in the doorway.

"I'll be back for more, Cum Dump Boy," he threatened.

I kept quiet.

"You'll need a refill soon... bet mine's the biggest rod you've ever had."

Still, I remained silent. My teeth clenched. He kept staring.

"Tell me you want more, Randy!" Chip demanded.

He took a few steps toward me—then, stopped.

"What... you so smitten that you can't speak? Don't you want to thank me?"

As before, I remained quiet. I didn't expel a word.

"Randy... boy? How does my hot cum-load feel inside you... you can feel it, can't you? Damn! That was a hell of a deposit."

Clearly, Chip was taking pleasure in his persistent merciless taunting. Undoubtedly, needing his ego stroked—wanting praise for his criminal action.

"Yea... yes. I... want you to come back," I forced from my mouth, hating every quivering word. Hoping against hope his self-admiration would be placated enough to finally leave the apartment.

"Now... that's my boy," Chip's words slipped off his tongue like a twisting rattlesnake's.

Chip winked with great exaggeration. He backed out of the room and disappeared into the hallway. I held my breath until I heard the front door open.

"See you soon, Lover," he yelled out.

A few long breaths later—the door slammed shut.

inch by inch

Perturbation erupted. Caustic fear clawed. Breath hindered. The sheets twisted and ripped—stained in Chip's sweat and my crimson blood. His piggish odor gagged in the air of the room. I had to get up—I had to. If nothing else, I had to get up to clean myself. Tremendous apprehension guardedly inched me off the bed—trembling, unsure if Chip had indeed left when the door slammed. The protracted throbbing in my anus was acute, like being scorched by fire. Irregular, short, and piercingly sharp sensations stabbed with undiluted, blistering pain. A thin stream of blood ran down each of my legs as cum dripped out my ass.

Biting and nagging fear persisted. Paranoia swamped my head. I still wondered if Chip had remained in the apartment; and the slamming of the door was just a tactic to make me believe he'd left but was hiding to toy with me for his perverse gratification. "If only Tom would come back from bar-hopping," I thought—more hoped. But sure, he wouldn't return to the apartment until much later, if at all. Tom often spent the night at his boyfriend's place.

I faltered in discomfort toward the bedroom door. The more I moved, the quicker the blood ran down my legs. At the doorway, I stopped—seconds from passing out. My head spun, as did the apartment. My eyes blurred in and out of focus. The doorframe supported my unsteady body. Otherwise, I would have met the floor.

I waited before attempting a few more steps. Still shaking as I peered around the doorframe toward the living room—eyes scanned the area like a video camera. A few distrustful breaths, my hands pulled me around the frame into the hallway. Enfeebled, they pressed against the cold plaster wall—guiding my body. I stopped again. Listened for any sound that would indicate I wasn't alone. My heart pounded like a drum, fully expecting Chip to suddenly jump in front of me like a psychotic clown in a Jack in the Box.

Dead air filled the apartment. I waited longer while listening—although unsure if I could even trust my ears for any possible movement and noise. Every creak of the old building made me wonder if they were Chip's footsteps. Another mouse raced in the wall. A car drove past the building. The heavy-footed neighbor upstairs walked across the floor. Knowing he was there, offered a slight degree of confidence—he would surely hear me yell if I saw Chip lurking in a corner.

After more auditory deduction, it appeared he'd indeed left. I corralled more nerve to limp over to lock the front door—marking a path of drops of blood on the floor. The same to the back door of the kitchen.

I managed to make it to the bathroom. Quickly, I locked the door behind me. The fevered thought of AIDS returned. My mind raced with theatrical images of me thin and lifeless in a hospital bed—my mother crying over me. The same at my graveside. I told myself, "Snap out of it.

"Think, Randy. Think," I told myself.

At that, I realized there were boxes of enemas in the cabinet below the sink. Grabbed one containing two. Reached for the bottle of hydrogen peroxide and another containing iodine. I quickly unscrewed both caps on the enemas before discharging half the liquid in each bottle down the sink. Replaced it with a combination of the peroxide and iodine. Some liquid spilled on the sink, rolling over the edge down to the small octagon patterned black-and-white tile floor. The solution fizzed; it turned pinkish as I screwed the caps back on.

I eased my way down to the bathroom floor and onto my back. Raised my legs high and spread my feet wide on top of the rim of the tub for support. Inserted one of the enemas into my anus while eating the pain.

The homemade concoction stung as I squeezed every possible drop out of the plastic bottle. I discarded it to the side. Closed my legs. Raised my knees to my chest and held them there. I proceeded to rock my body. I remained in the position until I felt the urge to get on the toilet. Still, I remained, holding everything in as long as I could retain the solution.

At the last possible moment, I reached up a hand for the top of the sink. Pulled myself up toward the toilet. But I'd waited too long. The solution broke out like a dam had burst. "Fuck," I yelled, more from the torrid stinging, rather than the mess. Regardless, I lay back down on the floor—in the mess. I took a few minutes before inserting the second enema. Repeated the process.

The second time, I made it onto the seat within a slice of a second. The dam broke again, as painful as the first. As what exploded on the floor, the toilet water turned red with blood, the iodine and peroxide mixture, and what of Chip's semen I could discharge—I knew he'd fucked me too deeply to get it all out. Besides, if Chip did infect me with anything, it was already in my bloodstream. If that were the case, the enemas were pointless. Nevertheless, I had to try.

Exhausted, I slid from the toilet onto the floor. Crawled to the tub. Reached through the plastic curtain to turn on the water to hot. Switched the lever upward to divert it to the shower head. Water gushed as steam soon fogged the room. I sat with my arms wrapping my knees to my chest as I watched the trail of red make its way down the drain. The hot water rained over me until it became freezing. In veracity, I didn't feel the cold for some time after the hot water had been depleted. I didn't feel anything except for the throbbing and nauseating, gut-wrenching fear of what that night had brought.

I considered calling the police. But refrained. It would be pointless to report the rape—only serve to humiliate me more if that were possible to be any further self-abased. To do so, would give way to them making a joke out of it and a good laugh: a gay man being raped about another. As with my father years before, not even the police could protect me now—as they hadn't then.

On some occasions when my father was drunk—on overdrive, the yelling from our house lurched to the neighbors. At such times, it gave them concern to call the police. Once an officer arrived, my father would go outside and shoot the shit with him as if they were talking about football. The officer soon drove away without having checked on us. We were left defenseless. As then—I remained on my own.

I cleaned the bathroom floor. Changed the sheets and pillowcases of the bed. There was little sleep to be had by the time I finished up and returned to bed. My ass continued to seep—spasmed with needling pain throughout what was left of the night. Listening.

During a break from the shoot, I called Jake to tell him what happened. My ass still throbbed, and my pride shattered like Venetian Glass. I'd already started blaming myself—for not assimilating the gravity of Chip's unwanted advances seriously enough. Rather thinking, they harmless but overt horny guy—disrespectful at that even though, again, they began fighting. Still, I would have never thought Chip's would end so violently. Obviously, my father had done enough damage for several lifetimes; I'd also blamed myself for his violations, when the impeachment was never mine to take proprietorship.

Of course, I questioned what I could have done to prevent it—prevented Chip from taking that license. That, self-imposed entitlement of authority. That is, other than taking a knife to my face and disfiguring it so I would become undesirable to others. I'd mistakenly associate them with the actions of every other guy in Atlanta and elsewhere on the hunt—which I'd hot-footed found out shortly after moving to the big city. It's not like Chip was the first guy to grab my ass or be sexually obtrusive. But just because I was gay and frequented gay bars, still didn't give anyone the right to take free license once I walked through the door, grabbing along with unfiltered, blunt, and crass sexual come-ons.

take ten

Smothering night came again. Suddenly. Lunging. Aggressive. Fragmented. Searing its footprints on my soul along with many others. The befallen rape by Chip had been harrowing as my life was finally beginning to flourish—as I found an allotment of happiness in the Emerald City. Now, the city of newfound hope had been greatly tarnished—the Emerald City wasn't so polished anymore.

The excitement of doors flying open—being noticed in a crowded room where not a single person had any knowledge of the dangerous and turbulent early years of my past had dulled. The rich hope that enchanted me, almost tangible enough to hold in my hands along with the sparking desires to live every second to the fullest of a new unfolding life—had wilted like the white flower of a magnolia tree does within minutes of being picked.

It left me feeling powerless once again. Helpless. Less than human. Disposable. Certainly, mortified. All the detracting things I've been given much currency in as a child. It seemed the violence was shadowing me from Middle Georgia. Waiting for an opportunity to strike again—and it had.

As that childhood, I wanted to forget the abhorrent events of the rape. But how could I? They—those events, along with everything else seemed to be my normal. All of it—the ugliness and unbounded darkness, thread-by-thread were woven into the fabric of my being. And now with it: that of which Chip had casted.

On every journey backward—mile-by-mile, was much like passing through a corridor. Both sides of the Interstate were lined by deeply-rooted and massively dense tall trees, making an impenetrable fortress wall built by a multiplicity of species: oak, varieties of maple, sugarberry, American yellowwoods, and lanky slash and shortleaf pine. All at the mercy of invasive unbridled kudzu climbing, coiling, and trailing the trees—turning acres into massive alien-like creatures.

As the car returned me back in time to that town and that house, I knew I risked being sucked into that past limited existence as Chip had me. Hesitation possessed each time I inserted the key into the door and heard it unlock; and walked into murky shadows of distrust. What light surrounding the house outside refused to follow me—consternated to shine through its windows. Surely in fear it would be trapped there—as I had, and that light would be swallowed up in all that pernicious, unending night.

Like the events of my childhood, the act of rape also left me angry, vengeful, and unforgiving. It had reached deep within my core pulling up the caustic, penetrating, sharpness of rage. The same I'd felt twice before. The latter at seventeen—once again, that rage thirsted for more blood. But this time, for Chip's.

A few aspirins fell on the bed as I shook the plastic container minutes after awakening at four-thirty. I couldn't get the ones in my hand down my throat fast enough to hopefully ease the inexorable throbbing. Excruciating pain to even move an inch, made me think twice about getting out of bed. The warm bath helped after I managed to make it to the bathroom without passing out—only to return as I lay hold of both sides of the tub to come to my feet so I could shower the soap from my body. I questioned if I would be able to stand, much less walk, most of the day at the shoot. But I didn't have a choice. I had to show up regardless.

Olfactory memory retained Chip's smell as it had the unforgiving weight of his body. My brain—relived the nightmare while gouging an old wound. Chip's act of extraction served to suck me back into a time warp—back to those impounding years in Warner Robins. And like that kid, that morning, I could never seem to scrub the filth or its poison entirely off my skin.

The portal opens. Light flashes. Then, flash again. Darkness falls. I walk through. The memories rustle awake. Trails to the forefront. They whisper. Images enlarge and the whispers increase in volume the closer it all comes to the surface. The shed smells of liquor as if a gas main had broken. My father orders me to stand in front of him—orders me to take off my clothes. The sound of a zipper follows. He exposes himself in the shed.

I start crying. He places his hand on my shoulder. Forces me down to my knees—to the dirt. Moves his hand to the back of my head. Gruffly pushes it into his crotch. With the other, takes another swig of liquor from the bottle. I stopped crying knowing it's pointless—it won't change what is about to happen. Later, he sits down in the lounge chair outside the shed. Watches me as I rake leaves and pick up fallen debris from the trees as if nothing else happened.

I walk back through to the present. I dressed. Gathered, like picking up seashells on a beach, the mental fortitude to prepare for the shoot at the Peachtree Western Hotel. I put one of many masks worn before—assigned that ability of habitual repetition of learned behavior. Rote. Acting like everything was hunky-dory to the outside world.

I present myself as expected. Act as though the events of the night before had never taken place as I stand in front of a large, seamless, white, Cyclorama wall. The photographer motions to the makeup artist to wipe the nervous sweat from my forehead. His camera clicks repeatedly as he moves forward then back. Steps to the left. The photographer tells me to look up then down then left then right. To look straight into the lens of the camera. To sit in the chair to the left of where I'm standing. Lean back. Lean forward. Stand up. Run my right hand through my hair. Now both. Hold it. Don't move. I feared it—the camera. Fear it will somehow capture the horror of the night before on my face. Fear it will see through the mask.

The makeup artist as the wardrobe girl makes me feel asphyxiated as they fuss over me between takes. Even the lighting tech irritates my hyper-neurotic state—always inches or a few feet from me. He feeds my paranoia. It felt like he was Chip lurking, waiting for the opportunity to grab at me. They all do—everyone associated with the gig, including the other two models. The studio space seems to keep shrinking. I feel the walls closing in. The loud music makes me want to scream. I existed on the edge. My eyes and ears bled desperation. I fight the overwhelming urge, the air-sucking suffocation to run off the set and out the building.

"Now tilt your head down and to the left while your eyes are on the camera. Smile."

I force another. Then, another and another.

"Good, Randy… let's take ten."

I'm relieved. I need to sit down. But first, head for the restroom. My asshole feels wet. Feels like it's leaking blood.

Later, I called Jake. He answered. I can hardly tell him about last night. Not sure where to begin. I stumbled on my words.

"Randy, just tell me. What's up? Why do you sound so frazzled?"

Following a few hesitations, I managed to pull the words out of my mouth. He didn't speak a word at first. I waited. I cleared my throat. Then, cleared it again.

"Didn't you hear what I just said? Chris raped me last night after everyone left the apartment. I thought he'd left with you."

"Ah… ah. Really? He wouldn't do that," Jake insisted.

The wardrobe girl called my name. I looked back at her while raising an index finger to let her know I'd be there in a minute. She returned a thumbs up.

"Come on, Randy. You're exaggerating."

The response stunned me.

"He did. Chris did, Jake!"

"You're being dramatic."

"The fuck I am!"

"Look, you must have led him on."

My voice freezes. I hung up the phone.

I'd later found out that Jake had fundamentally given his blessings to Chip—like I was property to be haphazardly passed around or put on loan. It all made sense remembering Jake's impervious reaction when I'd called him—my ass still on fire.

the arrangement

Squirrelled with keeping my distance from Chip, my supervisor at Britton's became more of a problem concerning time off to model even though it was mine to take. Much to my surprise, it appeared being in front of the camera wouldn't be as short-lived as I'd believed.

The agency was gradually receiving more calls about my availability—not only locally but for some gigs in Los Angeles. Pushy Jud—attempting to throw his physical weight around, insisted I make a choice and soon: to keep my position at Britton's and stop modeling or keep modeling and quit the department store. I was unsure of why it was a big deal with him. Britton's had 12 visual merchandising personnel, and all my reviews have been better than good.

I had money saved, mostly generated from those rich older men. But I knew there was an expiration date stamped on my ass. Plus, I'd never planned on getting paid to be some older man's play toy. Or did I feel good about myself for doing it. But not feeling good didn't stop me. Plus, having the money helped to do more things for my mother.

Even though things seemed to be going my way in front of the camera; I couldn't bank on the modeling to really take me to the big time. And as I wrote in, "In the Arms of Adam: a diary of men," due to my low self-esteem issues while attending Mercer University—most days I anticipated someone from the admission's office to interrupt class and announce I wasn't good enough to be a student at such a respected educational institution. That fear reached modeling. I fully expected a similar scenario of some bigwig walking in on a shoot and stating, "Get him the fuck out of here… he's not good enough to be a model!" Due to the insecurities, riding on paranoia—not knowing it was a persecution complex at the time, I figured I might need a job to fall back on once I was exposed as a fraud.

I talked it over with Thomas, including my self-esteem issues and I might need a job to fall back on if my face broke the lens of the camera. He suggested I make an appointment with the VP. I was hesitant.

"I don't understand how that would help my predicament."

"Randy, you know the man has a thing for you. At the very least, he can get Jud off your ass."

" … I don't know. Even though it seems to be working out… the modeling, I feel silly letting people know."

"Well… what does your agency have to say about your future in it?" Thomas asked.

"They, as Nick, believed I could make a real career out of it. Even move into doing more commercials… I've already done one locally. Barbara and Ronnie feel acting's in my future. But tell me to relocate to Los Angeles after I get a few more gigs."

"Randy… I see that. After all, you're a beautiful young man… so innocent looking."

"If only he knew," I thought.

I blushed. Lowered my head. Seconds later, looked back up at him—bashfully.

Thomas scrutinized me as if he's dissecting.

"You've got to stop being so hard on yourself. You still can't see what we all see when we look at you."

Even with Thomas' support, I felt odd. Even stupid.

"I can get you transferred to one of our stores out there. They'd take you in a heartbeat."

I took a long sigh.

"I still can't get my mother to budge out of that small shit town."

"Then, go anyway. You can't keep putting your life on hold for her."

My eyes watered. The sensation of a small tear rolled down my check. I brushed it aside with my hand. The thought of leaving Mother behind pained me in the worst way.

Thomas noticed.

"Are… are you okay?"

"She put hers on hold for me… for all her kids. And suffered through a brutal marriage as a result."

"I'm sorry, Randy. I didn't know."

"See, that's why I can't walk away from her… leave her all alone. I'm stuck in the middle of two worlds, Thomas. The one I'm trying to run from… and the one I'm trying to run toward. But… but it's more like running in place," I aired.

I brushed away another tear before it could get caught in the corner of my mouth.

Thomas went quiet for a moment. Looked as if in deep thought. Then, he spoke.

"Leave it up to me. I'll speak to Oscar about your situation… even prime him."

"What do you mean?"

"Just call his secretary. Make an appointment before you leave today."

I figured I didn't have anything to lose. The secretary got me in to see the VP just before lunch the following day. I was nervous as a cat surrounded by a pack of Doberman Pinschers while I sat in the small waiting area of the offices on the sixth floor of Britton's. Beads of sweat rolled down from my armpits under my shirt.

"Randy, can I get you something? Water… a soda," Sheila asked.

"That's very kind of you… but I'm fine."

"It shouldn't be much longer. He's on a call," she winked.

Minutes later, his door opened. Oscar stood in a dark blue suit with a red silk necktie. I was certain, a Karl Lagerfeld's. I wasn't sure which was better looking, the suit or the smile on his face.

"Randy… good to see you. The windows look great with the new

Norma Kamali line. Stunning. I'm hearing good things about you from the buyers and women's clothing managers."

"I appreciate you saying so… Mr. Barfield."

"Come in and have a seat."

The VP closed the door. I sat down in one of two, black Wassily chairs facing a sleek lacquered white desk. He walked around me. Sat on its edge with his hands on either side gripping it, and his legs stretched out. Crossed at the ankles. I noticed his polished, laced brown leather dress shoes.

"I guess you forgot we're on a first name basis," he smiled.

"Just… just thought I shouldn't in front of Sheila."

"She calls me Oscar as well."

"Oh… okay."

"So, I understand you're in a bit of a quandary with Jud… as Thomas tells me."

I explained the situation in some detail as the VP listened: Jud's bitching about asking to take more of my vacation's days separately; his ultimatum to stay or leave, that I had to make a choice between continuing to work at Britton's or modeling; my self-esteem issues; concerns about health insurance if I were to take a chance and quit my job.

Oscar moved away from the desk. Walked behind me. Put both hands on my shoulders. Began to massage them. I remained nervous as I had in the waiting area. Hoped the VP wouldn't notice it from my voice or body language, and how I resist looking him in the eye.

"How does that feel?" the VP asked, leaning his head close to my right ear.

His lips brushed it as he spoke with control.

"Good… it feels good."

"Your shoulders are so tense, Randy,"

He moved his hands from my shoulders down over my chest. My body tingled. Still the nervousness waited for what was next. But it wasn't the first time an older man had been so attentive. I actually came to thrive on it.

Shortly thereafter, Oscar moved to the other Wassily chair. Adjusted it to face me. Sat down. Boldly and confident, he confessed a strong interest in knowing me better. Agreed, the modeling was a good opportunity not to be passed up. Understood why I felt the need to keep a reliable job. That, we could make an arrangement, assuring to secure a position at Britton's but still come and go as needed for modeling—whether for a day, days, or a week—if not more. One that would be hush-hush. Kept from Human Resources. That would get Jud off my back, and he would no longer be my supervisor.

On the spot, the VP changed my title to Visual Merchandising Advisor. A bump in salary as well. The new position would get me out of the mother store to review the visual work of others. Or rather, the disguise of doing so. I still had to occasionally work in the mother store when I wasn't on a gig. There was just one catch: sexual favors when Oscar wanted to see me at his apartment, which I would soon find out was rather lavish. Overnighters, too. And call him VP while engaged in sexual acts. I surmised he got off on that.

The unexpected proposal more than caught me off guard. If anything, I was hoping VP Barfield would tell Jud to be supportive and work with me for a while; and not push me into a corner of having to pick right away.

After a long period of silence on my part and maybe some shock while the VP waited, I said yes. It seemed I was just handed a free ticket to ride—freedom to come and go. But as it's often said: nothing is really free, certainly, concerning that steady paycheck and the health insurance I wanted to have to fall back on. I had to earn it in another way by being fucking good in the bed—engaging in sexual encounters with the VP.

Technically, as with those other older men, that made me a prostitute—sex for pay even if I wasn't walking the streets and having sex behind a dumpster or in a sleazy motel room—even in the backseat of some john's car. However, those kind of accommodations for such activity would seem more fitting for someone of my up bringing. But of course, many of us can rise a few or more notches above our born station in life—certainly, where we lie on our backs. But I saw it as trading favors for mutual benefits. The fact Oscar was handsome was an added bonus. Much like a Christmas bonus from Britton's. I just wondered if I'd made a wrong turn on the road; a road that didn't have another turn but only led to the edge of a cliff.

Not a soul. I decided not to tell anyone about the rape other than Jake. Foolishly, I thought he would man-up and end his brotherhood with Chip. But I was excruciatingly wrong. Eventually, I confided in Tom. Evidently, I'd failed to do a thorough job of cleaning the bathroom that night after laboriously focusing on cleaning myself out—get Chip out of my body. Tom had noticed some blood puddled where the cabinet of the sink met the floor. Just enough to concern him that I'd possibly injured myself in some way. So, I told him. He agreed calling the police would have been pointless, and it was best to keep my distance from Chip and Jake.

As I've partly shared, the rape triggered old feelings of inferiority, disgrace, shame, and the dirty way my father had made me feel, as did memories of Mr. Jones. How I used to take long showers to wash my father's smell off of me. Psychologists, often state children are resilient—many able to recoil back to some state of center after a traumatic experience while others never do. Being one of those others, I know today I've never completely recoiled or even rebooted from many of those childhood violations. They layered over like the skins of an onion After the rape, the mercury in my internal thermometer jetted up the hermetically sealed glass tube at a rate and speed, fast enough to burst the glass.

I made myself invisible for the better part of a month. Put my social life on lockdown. I kept a virulent lookout for Chip's old, sun-bleached, navy-blue, souped-up redneck truck with huge tires. It wasn't hard to miss, especially with the tailgate plastered with Georgia Bulldog bumper stickers.

A few nights that followed, that ghastly-inky one where he'd forced himself on me without any guilt or concern of how it would affect me while amassing more shit on top of shit, I'd noticed his truck parked on Eighth Street—a block down from the apartment. I'd no idea if Chip was visiting friends or fucking some trick—even forcing himself on another guy or even stalking me for his next opportunity to strike.

It wasn't necessary to see his truck to know Chip was driving by the apartment when I was home; I could hear the roar of its loud motor—even blocks away. The sound was unnerving enough; but also served as a chilling reminder of the night my father pulled his police cruiser around the back of the house. The night, I'd feared that would be the one—the one he'd murder my mother, siblings, and me.

Subsequent weeks that followed, uneasiness walked behind me like a bodyguard each time I was away from the apartment—especially after dark. I'd lied to the landlord that I'd been awakened by a burglar in the act of breaking into the apartment. I insisted he add an extra deadbolt to the front and back doors.

I bided time hoping Chip would grow bored and move on. But he remained persistent with episodes of brazen honking the truck's horn when he saw my black Alfa Romeo parked in front of the apartment. Even intrepidly bold as to stop in the middle of the street to gun the engine—no matter the time of day or night. I saw each occurrence as a threat to my safety—another warning from Chip, conveying he would be back as he told me that night of the rape.

I started parking around the corner, then several blocks from my apartment. I never left the car in the same spot twice, requiring parking it further and further away. The greater the distance, the more I wondered if I would make it home without Chip suddenly appearing out of nowhere. My heart fiercely thumped fear and heightened awareness: listening beyond any normal hastening of night; past the shrill repertoire of vociferous mating calls of the katydids, their increasing harshness circling and jarring my senses while splitting every nerve in my body like electric wires; crossing shadows on the street; vehicles coming and going; doors opening and closing; each rustle in the hedges that coaxed beads of sweat from every pore. All, elevating angst.

Despite operose efforts, Chip wasn't deterred. If anything, increasingly resolute—much like a wolf detecting the smell of trenchant fear in its nostrils. Within time, he usually managed to locate my car. Like some urban terrorist, he brazenly left notes on its windshield—disturbing and graphic. Each contained a veiled threat: Hey baby, we going somewhere tonight? What time should I stop by? Man, have I got another big load for you.

Chip increasingly became a phobia. Tom's boyfriend offered his guest room for as long as I felt the need to stay away from the apartment. The generous accommodations were swiftly accepted. After several weeks, I returned in anticipation the coast was clear. That perhaps, by not seeing my car over that timeframe, Chip might have believed I'd moved out of the neighborhood. Even out of Midtown. I'd actually debated moving to the suburbs.

Chip was a bully just like my father and as dangerous. The rape and resulting fear sent me back to hiding under that childhood bed. It awakened the nightmares. Caused me to lose my nerve. Shattered the belief I was no longer breakable after my father's death. His infringement returned me to where I was once more covered in the stench of ugliness. Revived a dead man from his grave—more like, tossed me in my father's coffin with what was left of his flesh and with his bones. The longer Chip persisted, the closer I came to a climactic point. This toilsome game of hide-and-seek had to come to an end as my father had.

As I once had put myself between my parents—I had to put myself between my fear and Chip. Since he had returned me to the past, I had to become that seventeen-year-old boy again that had strategized his father's death. Go back to the first night I stood over him with a shovel in my hand, while he was passed out on the shed's cot. The shed where he defiled and humiliated his youngest son. As well—return me to the morning he died.

While in hiding, the agency sent me to California for a week for a magazine shoot—temporarily putting my mind at ease. Because of the trauma the rape had caused and the wounds it opened, I'd considered shipping my car across country and never return. But, again, I'd remained tethered to my mother and her afflictions that were in many ways mine as her alcoholism—and still unwilling to remarry. A few weeks later I was in Chicago for three days to do a commercial for a high-end chain of clothing stores. It wrapped a day early. That night, I caught a flight back to Atlanta and drove directly from the airport to Warner Robins to spend a few days with Mother.

When in Atlanta, I was still required to occasionally show up at Britton's, and certainly—in the VP's bed. Otherwise, I'd sequestered myself in the apartment. At times, back at Tom's boyfriend's house. The self-imposed isolation within four walls eventually made me feel like I imagined the hamster I had as a kid, named Frank—years before my enlightenment that animals shouldn't be in cages.

It's possible, Frank felt trapped. Of course, I really wouldn't know how he felt—perhaps, happy going nowhere on the hamster wheel while locked-up, understanding that was all he knew since birth. That is, unless there was an innate longing Frank had to scurry around in fields. Unlike Sandra's yellow canary, Frank only existed a short time caged before escaping. So, I would deduce, Frank did want his freedom. I wanted mine, too—from my mother, the South and all it entailed; and of course, from Chip's cage and not end up dead like Sandra's yellow canary. Middle Georgia—was much like growing up in a cage and going nowhere in my own wheel.

trip the light fantastic

Cabin fever set in. Lying low in the apartment like I'd robbed a bank waiting for the heat to pass was making me restless—the weekends I was in town. My friend Todd, one of the first I made after moving to Atlanta called. It was a Friday night.

"Why haven't you rung me back?" he asked.

"Been meaning to… but you just beat me to it. What's up?"

"You want to go out to the Pharr… maybe Backstreet later?"

I thought for a moment. Wondered if enough time had passed to venture back out to dance?

"Come on, Randy. It's been weeks since I've seen you… you being out of town a lot and all," Todd pushed, in his Southern accent he always accentuated when he wanted to get his way.

Although I came close to confiding in Todd about what had taken place that vexed night of the rape—I didn't. I wanted him to know why I'd been in avoidance mode, but, again, kept it from Todd. One would think, as my best friend, I would. As much as I may have, I didn't wish to hear out loud what had transpired—the words spilling from my lips. As that little boy had, I kept quiet about the abuse—carried the shame that wasn't that boy's or mine, concerning what Chip had done to shoulder. Little did I know, after the rape, history would repeat itself with a similar outcome.

The Pharr Library on Pharr Road off Piedmont Avenue, located in the South Buckhead area—was a hot spot every Friday night. Usually, the first destination before hitting any one of the-some-thirty gay bars and clubs in the Atlanta area. On the first floor of an office building, its huge patio looked out over Pharr Road off Piedmont, blocks from the long and winding Peachtree Street.

Known primarily as, The Library because of its décor: wall-to-wall and floor-to-ceiling bookshelves of books. Not to be mistaken for any old library for studying, or researching your next biology paper, but for that of analyses and fact-checking of whom you might be taking home for a quick and further exploration of the human male body before hitting another club. Or would you find a middle-aged librarian with bifocals and her hair in a bun at the front door checking in and out books. If you were anyone or wanted to be anyone, or even if you didn't care to be anyone concerning the popular crowd—you elbowed your way through the hordes of early Friday night patrons—not a one pulling a book from the thousands on its shelves.

I would be remiss not to mention Benta, a Friday night fixture—more of an icon at the Pharr Library. A divorced, straight, middle-aged Scandinavian woman, attractive, short, and voluptuous. Her white-blonde hair styled in a gender-neutral cut. Benta, not only loved to twirl and shift her hips from side-to-side on the dance floor—always wearing white tops, and semi-full skirts to accentuate her dance moves, but the gay boys even more so.

If anything, I had to get out to dance—back into my newfound world of the beat-driven, urban night life of Disco. Dancing to the likes of Donna Summers, the Bee Gees, Chaka Khan, Chic, Gloria Gaynor, Thelma Huston, Sister Sledge, the Village People, KC and The Sunshine Band, and the like. I craved the sense of freedom dancing under a huge, reflective, mirrored disco ball—spinning from the ceiling over a crowd of strangers offered: a world within itself; dancing for hours-on-end blocking out the crap in my head; getting lost among hundreds of sweaty bodies grooving; engulfed in the sporadic, spellbinding, and hypnotic electric light show; guys randomly passing around little glass bottles of poppers (amyl nitrite) inhaled for a quick, warm euphoric head-to-toe rush. And yes, I needed those seductive glances of admiration if they weren't overly aggressive while avoiding the grabbing.

Once the Pharr Library hit its peak around 11 p.m., most ventured out to the Armory, then across the parking lot to Atlanta's version of New York's Studio 54: the large, multiple-level playground of Backstreet Atlanta 24 Hour Nightclub in the heart of Midtown on Peachtree Street. After other clubs and bars with closing times from 2:00 or 4:00 a.m., Backstreet was still pouring drinks for gays and many straight allies alike—having been grandfathered-in on its liquor license: acquired rights not subject to the last call for newer such establishments. The drinks kept pouring as the music kept playing twenty-four hours and seven days a week—every day of the year.

I began venturing back out—many times with Todd as I did that Friday night he called after the extended absence. It seemed my time away, including shoots, short trips back to Warner Robins, and Chester's guest room had done the trick. There hadn't been many of Chip's drive-bys or notes left on my car's windshield since I started spending more time at the apartment. I felt relatively safe. Occasionally, I'd spot the twins, but they kept their distance as I did mine. Still, I remained guarded—on high alert, as I had as a kid.

Admittedly, there were a few times I would be overtaken by a bout of PTSD at the chance sighting of Chip, even if he was keeping his distance. That severance of space didn't always prevent him from letting his gaze hang in my direction, usually accompanied by a discomposing grin. If that were the case, I would discreetly exit as swiftly as possible and move on to another venue—or usually return home to collect myself.

It wasn't that I was running away, but again, airing to caution. Even after a span of time, Chip clearly wanted me to run in fear so he could catch me. That's what he wanted: me to fear him. He needed control and dominance just like my father. It was repulsive enough as it felt cowardly, playing dodgeball with the clubs to avoid the twins. As well, it didn't help matters much when I would catch sight of them in the small confines of Midtown—in broad daylight.

After several weeks had passed since my last sighting of Chip, one of which I was back in Los Angeles for three days—I found myself at Backstreet with Todd on what should have been a typical Saturday night. As unusual, the club was packed like a can of sardines. I was in my happy place on the dance floor with Todd, "tripping the light fantastic" amongst the crowd—many snorting cocaine and while others stuck to poppers and always happy to share. I'd take a hit of poppers now and then as Todd, but not the coke.

Todd eventually ran off to have a drink with a newly made friend, who'd been grinding up against him. I continued in the absorption of anonymity in the middle of the huge dance floor. I wanted to be invisible—well, except to the shirtless, hot guy that had generously been passing his poppers back and forth. The night was looking quite promising. Still, I reveled in being transfigured into one with the masses—having no past or future, only desiring to own the present and the music. The music that seemed to make time stand still.

The DJ on the high stage played a remix of Donna Summers' pulsating, "I Feel Love." Prismatic, varicolored lights scanned over and through the crowd in such a fashion as I would imagine being on a mushroom high would take over one's mind—having no doubts, many of those blowing whistles and waving glow sticks around and above their heads to the rhythm had consumed among other party drugs as they screamed for more of Donna.

The night was calling 3:00 a.m. By then, it was squeezing room only—Backstreet had likely filled beyond the building's occupancy limit set by the Fire Marshal. After about an hour, and some unapologetic passionate making out with hot and shirtless, I excused myself to the restroom but told him I would be back over the ear-shattering music. At that, he landed a come-back-soon kiss on me.

Jake came into view as I wedged up the stairs leading to the main floor. He appeared to be sizing up a cute farm-boy-type at the mezzanine bar overlooking the dance floor. I was certain Chip had to be close by—but hoped not. That's when I saw him in the shadows, burning an unflinching laser stare. Chip jetted in my direction—knocking people aside like toothpicks. I struggled to the top of the stairs like maneuvering through thick pancake batter.

Once passed the bar on the main floor, I hurried toward the door leading out to the parking lot. Only slowing long enough to tell the doorman, Big Dog—his name self-explanatory, "Will you stall that… that big guy in the red T-shirt coming my way? He's been harassing me!" Big Dog gave me a nod as I bolted out into the lumpy and humid blackened air. A blurred, zigzagging line of people waited at the door as if to offer themselves like a sacrifice to the music stretching into the unpredictability of night.

Adrenaline moved my legs as I made it through the tightly parked cars in the block-long and wide, hilly lot. Continually, I scanned over my shoulder, just in case Chip was still in pursuit while looking for the parking attendant who was as old as Jesus—tall and lanky, Joe.

If you consistently tipped him well, Joe never forgot your face or name; and miraculously made room for your vehicle, even if all the spaces were taken. Maybe he was—Jesus. I scanned over the area and soon spotted the attendant and my car. The Alfa Romeo was wedged between two cars parked at precarious angles.

I handed Joe a twenty to perform a miracle in freeing the car and promised another five if he could make it quick without scratching it.

"I'll get it."

Joe briskly left. I looked back toward the club's entrance. No sight of Chris. Either he was only trying to rattle my nerves and had no intentions of catching up with me, or Big Dog was holding Chris up. Minutes late, but it seemed stressfully much longer, Joe pulled up inches from where I was impatiently waiting. I slapped the extra five bucks in his hand. Hastily jumped into the Romeo. Hit the gas—catching Chip's image growing smaller in the rearview mirror the closer I drove to the exit of the parking lot.

little rabbit

Ensuing that night, Chip wasted little time picking up where he'd left off months before. I'd been grossly mistaken it was over—that he was done. Like a rerun of the 1983, horror film Christine—the plot: an evil car with a humanoid-like possessive personality ruled by jealous tendencies, wheeled over people to their death who its owner was either friends with or another new one that came into his life. Chip was the car.

The phone calls started up again, some wordless heavy breathing while others of sexual whispers on the other end, if not hang-ups. Chip boldly knocking on my door or bedroom window in the middle of the night. Driving by my apartment, furiously gunning the engine.

Chip didn't seem to want to allow my release from his compulsive, sociopathic, persecution. Even threatening to contact the police the next time he stopped his truck in front of the apartment to gun the engine—its license plate fossilized in my brain, failed to deter his belligerence. But I knew it was an idle threat on my part, and irrefutably—Chip did as well.

As an alleged gay-on-gay rape, requesting a restraining order wouldn't have been taken seriously by the Atlanta Police Department. Their pledge to serve and to protect only applied to white people and not those of color or perceived deviant homos—certainly in the South. And, as I'd learned as a kid, they protected their own. Again, it would be another reason to give the police a good laugh at my expense. Besides, I didn't have any real evidence—out of disgust, having thrown away the notes threatening another sexual attack with those little drawn hearts he'd boldly left under the windshield wipers of my car.

Even though I had feared Chip as I had my father as a kid early-on, that changed as I got older. And as it had with him, my killer instinct was pushing its way up closer to the surface with each perceivable endangerment to my life Chip made. Much like my father, afraid or not, once again, I felt it might come down to kill or be killed. The fear I continue to carry, not only had to do with Chip—but what I knew I was capable of doing if pushed too far. I knew I had to come up with a more concrete plan to manage Chip. But I wasn't going to let him box me in again.

Chip viewed me as weak as my father once had. But I needed to change that impression. On a scorching and near-dead, dripping, weekend night, I spotted his truck parked blocks from Backstreet. At its sighting, I shifted into a different person—feeling the swift modification of my brain. Like an involuntary reflex—impulsively, I pulled the Alfa Romeo into an open space a few car-lengths past his truck. There, I waited. Waited for the wanderers to pass by: a few people turned corners, others intermittently ambled the sidewalks or crossed the street. I continued to watch and wait until they faded further into the distance.

At the all-clear, I took the opportunity—knowing I had a short window of time until more people headed in my direction, or a police car might drive by. But figured the surrounding darkness offered an advantage. At that, I exited the car. Opened the trunk. Retrieved a Phillips-head screwdriver and proceeded to puncture Chip's driver's side, front, oversized tire of the truck. Stabbing the screwdriver into his heart would have been a more preferred permanent solution.

Chip could consider himself lucky I'd only flattened one. My rash act of vandalism was to send a message, or perhaps that tire represented Chip. As he'd so brazenly done leaving those notes under my car's windshield wipers, I did something similar: with my apartment key—I scratched, "Fuck You!" into the driver's door and a heart as well. I knew the act would escalate my on-again off-again situation with Chip—possibly to a point of no return. But I couldn't help myself. I'd reached far-past my limit. Driving away, I realized it would likely make Chip even more predatorial.

And it did. But I doubt the message made Chip think twice about his terroristic-like aggression. The longer it irregularly continued, I wondered what was so special about me for Chip to target me. There's always someone better looking as there were plenty of eager hungry power-bottoms running about Atlanta, who would have openly welcomed Chip to plow them good and hard, and I'm sure he was—if not raping some of them, left me perplexed. Eventually, I figured out that Chip didn't want, "eager." He wanted power and to instill fear. That deduction, made during one of his late-night habits of tapping on my bedroom window while calling out, "Randy, let's play. Come on, let me in."

On a number of occasions, I called the police to inform there was a prowler around the apartment building. They seldom showed. Like all abusers, Chip thrived on fear and control. He wanted to instill that fear which made him feel powerful. Chip was much like a bully on steroids. Still, I remained determined to stop playing the tiresome game of catch me if you can. I wasn't going to run in circles—like a skittish, bleeding little rabbit in a den of wolves playing with it before they went in for the kill. Like those wolves, Chip could smell the blood and the fear. And like a wolf, he wanted more.

He'd every intention of making me bleed again as he'd jaggedly and without mercy had the night of the rape—I was certain of it. But I was going to live my life regardless. Go out when I wanted to even though the freedom dancing afforded, as that sense of safety of being lost in a crowd became tainted despite how vigilant I remained when I chanced-out for a night on the dance floor. Despite that vigilance, there were more disruptions—more infringements by Chip and more avoidance tactics on my part. I'm sure, so pleased with himself each time he got the jump on me as if a tracking device had been implanted in my ass. My disgust overwhelmingly built stories higher than the Empire State Building.

At the time, it wouldn't have entered my mind there was possibly some correlation between how I returned time and time again during my first two years of junior high school to cut Mr. Jones' grass after he'd molested me the first time in his new car. A handgun on the dashboard. A dirt road in the middle of nowhere. A hot summer day—the fireball of the sun beating down. His beady eyes. Sweaty. Plump. Red-faced. Intemperate, fanatic movements fiercely going at me—grunting and snorting as he frantically pushed his hand into my shorts to grab at my penis as the other pawed at my legs with clammy hands, while sloppily cramming his tongue in my mouth.

How that correlated with Chip—in how I sporadically kept venturing out to the clubs even though I knew he could step out of the shadows. The closest any realization of a connection was one of those nights Chip grabbed me from behind on the dance floor while sticking his hand inside my jeans. Cupped my penis and balls. An immediate sense of déjà vu found me in the kitchen of that house on Shirley Drive. Back to the afternoon I was face-to-face with my father, when I told him that I would kill him if he ever laid a hand on my mother again. I wanted to tell Chip the same—but if I did, that would give back the power I was trying to take back.

In fact—they all had to be connected: my father, Mr. Jones, Chip, and even Christopher thrown in there somewhere with them. With all four, putting myself in the way of physical and emotional danger—and me in some ways allowing it. As much as I try to analyze my relationship to them and their connection—my mind twisted into a knot.

After a few more close-calls following a period of a reprieve, the realization came that if I could conceal any fear—bandage the wound he'd inflicted, I had to act as though it all really wasn't a big deal to me anymore when we were in the same place at the same time. But I knew to succeed in my plan, I'd have to be convincing—tolerate Chip a while longer until he couldn't smell the fear or the blood. Laugh-off the liberties he'd taken over the past months when he sniffed me out like a dog in heat. Even flirt with Chip before walking away. Put up with the very things that made my skin crawl: grabbing my ass as if tattooed with his name, as he did the same to my crotch; the pinching; pushing his body into mine, forcibly attempting to open my mouth with his tongue. And to make it all convincing, I would have to also kiss Chip instead of fighting him off. Then, I thought, Chip would finally move on once he believed he'd lost his power over me, and I would be free of him.

So, I did. I did put up with Chip's shit a while longer despite significant disgust. My cunningness eventually did result in my goal. I'd been right to make him believe I wanted him. Chip stopped bothering me. He'd walk past me without stopping but rather throwing his glaring eyes in my direction. Still, if I'd thought it once, I did a million times, "Someone needs to end that motherfucker."

a leaden sky

After two short trips away from Atlanta, one to take my mother to Hilton Head Island for Mother's Day and the other—a shoot, it was a relief to return and not feel the need to look over my shoulder. A relief, not to worry about being harassed by Chip anymore. A relief, that the game of cat and mouse was over—certainly, putting up with his advances while acting like I couldn't wait for the next time he slipped his hand down the back of my jeans or to stick his tongue into my mouth when I was out and about.

A relief, not to be handled so gruffly like someone's property. As nerve-wracking as it was—the acting performance of tolerating Chip's presence and his advances had been worth every excruciating moment. He even stopped trying to get me to have sex. And I certainly didn't miss the terrorizing sound of the gunning engine of his truck. But there remained the worry of the possibility of being infected with AIDS—often inciting nightmares of my mother crying over my dead body covered in Kaposi's sarcoma dark lesions.

More trips to Warner Robins. And, all the while, as I had been, I continued to pray my mother would remarry. Pray, she would stop being mentally sick. Stop drinking. Stop having to lie awake in my old bed on my visits listening to her at the breakfast table sadly singing along to the records she played on the stereo. Stop hearing the clang of the bottle hitting the glass she drank from, or the pop of the beer cans. And when I wasn't praying, I kept asking my mother to move to Los Angeles with me. Still, amongst it all, I didn't realize my life was being sucked out of me. That, I was giving it all away.

Tom and his older boyfriend decided to play house. I moved in with an interior designer who resided in one of the top condos in the Plaza Towers Condominiums. Although intended to be a roommate arrangement, some weeks later, he began pressuring for more. Directly, I found a large one bedroom apartment on Twelfth Street—a few blocks from Peachtree Street.

Even though I'd run into Chip and Jake a few times—they kept their distance. Again, I thought I was in the clear. That is, until some weeks later at around 10:00 p.m., when I heard Chip's truck gun its engine as he'd done many times in the past. This time, in front of my new place. I was confounded, that after moving three times in a matter of a month, Chip found out where I was living.

The apartment's parking lot was in the rear, so my car was seldom parked on the street. It was likely he'd followed me home at some point from Backstreet and I didn't notice his truck trailing me. To be sure I wasn't imagining it, I turned off the lights before cautiously looking out the window. Chip's truck was idling on the street. His face shadowed by a near-by streetlight as he appeared to be scanning the building. My mind wasn't playing tricks on me. Chip was either curious, or up to his old tricks again. The fact he knew where I'd moved, raised a red flag.

Considering Chip's discovery of where I lived, I decided to err on the side of caution—even more so. I'd planned to stay as far away from him as possible. Concerns for my safety took on more air, although they had never fully deflated as Chip's tire had. I did think that perhaps it was just curiosity on his part and nothing else. But I soon found out Chip was back to his old habits. There were more drive-bys. At least he didn't have my new phone number—that gave me some comfort there wouldn't be any more heavy breathing.

I still occasionally went out, but back to being the skittish mouse looking out for the lurking cat. Standing my ground obviously was short-lived as it didn't have any staying power. After a few close calls with Chip at Backstreet—dealing with more of his sexual résumé, including an incident where I had to duck behind a car when he saw me leaving, and another where I had to jet around a corner, I decide it best I stay away from the club for a while.

A month later, the build-up of cabin fever ventured me out to the sordid Cove, on Dutch Valley Road off Monroe Drive. The classic single-level hole-in-the-wall bar and dance club aroused moral corruption that Baptist ministers raise their bibles to high heaven at their pulpits during Sunday morning church services. The Cove was another bar with acquired rights—often, the last stop before sunrise.

Outside the Cove's entrance, a shadowy variety of human forms waited in a long line in the tenebrous of the hour. Guys in their cars cruised the parking lot in the rear. A steady meandering went back and forth like a stream of ants from the Morningside Chase Apartments across the street, christened as Vaseline Valley—the reason for such should be obvious. During the summers, the hot hastening nights encouraged the necessity of skinny-dipping in the complex's pool. Others walked around peering into the open doors of the apartments to see what action could be had.

As a rule, I'd learned it's always good to make extra-nice, be super polite, smile big, know their names, and look pretty—usually worked every time with the doorman and bouncers of the bars and clubs to keep from waiting in the lines. Certainly, in inclement weather. An occasional slip of 20 bucks helped to be treated as if of celebrity notoriety.

A thick, varying fog of dirty white to gray pervaded with cigarette smoke, watered my eyes—met me the second I entered. In combination with the superabundant product from the fog machine for the employment of the dance floor, discharged throughout every inch of the establishment—was much like walking into a New York City blackout the deeper I made it into the bar.

Low ceilings and a bad ventilation system were contributing factors. All resulting in near opacity of visibility unless within a foot or two from another person. The perfect club to serve up a large helping of anonymity—just another sweaty shirtless shadow among a host of others shifting provocatively while stirring otherworldly desires on the dance floor—or elsewhere.

The soles of my shoes suctioned to the floor as if they hadn't been mopped since the Cove opened in the early 1970s. The bathrooms reeked of piss and who-knows-what other bodily fluids to be avoided at all costs. Mysterious and naughty—the Cove was alluringly sensual for this small-town boy. The strobing-colored lights over the dance floor—drastically swallowed by the fog over the throng of patrons, if not the case, would defuse the purpose.

The few times I'd hung at the Cove—I never saw the twins together or separate. That didn't mean, Jake and Chip weren't there at the same time, again, due to the limited vision. If you were at the Cove with a friend and lost them, a pair of night-vision goggles would be beneficial in finding their location. Even equally beneficial—for a half-decent look at the face of the guy whose throat you had your tongue down. Of course, there was the chance I got lucky and missed them coming or going, depending on the time of night. Although as usual, even with limited visibility, I'd kept a keen eye out for their sudden appearance.

I mostly went to dance and for observational reasons like a postgraduate psychology student gathering material for a master's thesis. Well, sort of. I, too, as the rest were on the hunt. On a hunt for either sex or just to feel part of something bigger than oneself. The sanctum was the place to end up if you were one to burn the candle at both ends—perhaps, in the middle as well. All the bars were much like churches, where many of us found our own kind of religion. And the music—our choir, never disappointed.

This was a slice of the seedier side of gay life, and for those who preferred to live in the silhouettes or tip their toes or deeper into the waters of the carnal flesh-eating passions. An exhibition of people: from the T-shirt and jeans comfortable; to the preppy; to the outrageous; fag-hags; boys-for-rent, some with their pimps; drag queens; transvestites; among others indefinable. At the long bar, they threw back vodka shots, or their poison of choice—some inebriated close to the point of hitting the floor. All the colors of the rainbow. True and loyal creatures of the night. Young and old, and in-between, were to be found at the Cove. That is, if you could see them.

The entrance to the dance floor was separated from the rest of the club with meat locker plastic strips—actually, quite appropriately so. I'd danced well into many mornings, greeted by an ardent and unforgiving eye-squinting sun as I stepped out of a fantasy world and crossed back into shackling reality. And as those nights passed, I'd removed my T-shirt. Struck it into the waist of the back of my jeans as the music beckoned. I too became a moving shadow in the mist. Like a warm, unfaltering, midnight shower, sweat covered my face and body the more I danced.

But, that night—before I could be purified by sunlight, an arm boarded through the opaque veil with gripping fingers. Immediately and strenuously, I was pulled from the dance floor into a corner—pinned. Chip had found me.

The smell of alcohol thickened his breath as he forced his mouth on mine. Chip's body—a boulder held me in place. His hands firmly groped. Oxygen scrambled in and out of my mouth. His, slid over my face to my ear. Baleful words spilled into it; my screams were absorbed within the resounding music while the thick fog left us invisible to the surrounding dancers. Chip jerked me around, bashing my face into the wall—contorting it into a mask of pain. Bit into the flesh of the back of my neck—like the wolf he was. Panic dominated my mind once again.

Chip unbuckled my belt and unzipped my jeans as I struggled. He pushed them and my underwear to the floor. I knew continuing to fight would serve to anger him more. I stopped thrashing. Stop resisting. It would be futile. Knowing it was better to prepare myself for what I knew was coming. At that moment, his dick sadistically impelled me—harrowing and perilous stabs of his incursions. Reliving a real-life nightmare agonized with each thrust. Tears flooded my eyes. The loud music faded away as I did into nothing.

The intermittent jetting of his load followed. Chip's irate thrusts slowed to a stop. I remember being relieved it was over as I waited for him to pull out. But moments later, he started again. Thrusting jaggedly—as if trying to stab his penis entirely through my body.

I waited for my chance to run. I felt his mass ease away as his breaths quickened. I took advantage of the moment. Hastily bent down, fumbled to pull-up my underwear and jeans. I squeeze out from Chip and the corner, but he grabbed me. Turned me like a rag doll to face him. Looked me square in the eyes, "How did you like my screwdriver?" Then, shoved me aside like I was nothing. Like I was disposable. Like I was just a cum dump.

Holding up the jeans, I made-way toward the exit through the swamped fog and the crammed dance floor—shoving people aside while zipping and snapping my jeans. Raced by the doorman. Around the back of the club—to my car.

Back at the apartment, I didn't bother to clean Chip out of me or shower. I shut myself up in my bedroom instead. Collapsed on the bed. Awoke later in the afternoon smelling like a bar. I didn't have to look—I felt the blood-soaked underwear sticking to my ass. I eventually showered. Checked the messages on the answering machine. One, from the VP of Britton's conveying he'd be back in Atlanta on Thursday. Two calls from Mother. By the slurred speech patterns of her liquored voice, I knew she'd started drinking again after an extended dry period.

I soon dressed and made the drive South—arrived as the sun's light squinted low. Mother sat at the kitchen table. A half-empty bottle of wine within reach. Patsy Cline's "Crazy" haunted—playing in a whisper on the stereo's turntable. A copy of Polo Male was open to a two-page spread I'd done months before—its pages, somewhat wrinkled. Mother lifted her head.

"Oh, my beautiful son. I didn't know you were coming. I would have fixed myself up."

"Mom, you look wonderful… really. Just as beautiful as ever."

But she didn't. She didn't look beautiful in her state of disheveled intoxication.

"You're always here… here for me," she added, as Mother lifted the glass of wine to her lips.

I spotted several empties on the kitchen counter as I sat down next to her. Mother took a smoldering cigarette from the ashtray—inhaled a slow drag. Seconds later, my eyes fixated on the stream of smoke she lethargically expelled from between her lips into the already smoke-hazed air. Mother coughed as she snuffed it out among the others in the tray. I reached for her hand. Looked into her blood-shot eyes. She looked so empty—depleted, like the bottles by the sink. I felt helpless, as I knew she was.

"It's okay, Mom… I'm here. Let's get you cleaned up."

The day had fallen under a leaden sky by the time I put her to bed. At its edge, I stood—looking down at her while offering a sympathetic smile. Her indolent eyes settled on me until they closed. I walked across the room. Turned on the television and the volume to low. The near-inaudible voices served as white noise. What little light the television emitted—a reluctant night light, barely kindled into the room as if keeping a safe distance from the sadness in our hearts. I laid down beside Mother while staring at the ceiling—not knowing what else I could do for her emotionally, or even for myself.

The headlights of a passing car driving west on Shirley Drive, ominously swept through the windows of the deep-gray room until disappearing down the street. I was losing hope for my mother. Still, I struggled to find some—some hope for her. If only an ounce.

Mother whispered out, but the faintness of her words were too quickly absorbed within encasing griminess of uncertainties.

"What did you say?"

I turned onto my side. Looked at her. Mother's eyes were partly open. I leaned over. Kissed her forehead. She slid a frail hand across the sheets. I took hers in mine.

"It's okay. It's all going to be okay," I told her, knowing it likely wouldn't.

Mother's eyes closed then opened—then closed again. Her feet fidgeted as she constantly rubbed them together. I watched until the alcohol and meds tunneled her closer into sleep. It seemed, the booze and pills were all she had left in life. I could only hope that in her dreams—the life she'd once planned could live on there.

Lying there, I wished I could have given them back to her. But all I could do was just lie next to her. Trust, at least—knowing I was beside her, Mother had some comfort. It seemed as if I would never completely escape this place. This town and house. They continued to pull me back in my efforts to rescue her from the misery and pain. I feared her life—what was left of it, would tragically end in Warner Robins.

nine

erased in time

I couldn't help but blame myself for the second rape as I had the first. As I'd blamed myself for most everything bad and ugly that had occurred in my life up until then. Blamed myself for not being strong enough. Smart enough. Acting fast enough. Blamed myself for not being anything. But another side of me knew better, despite questioning if I hadn't waited long enough to venture back out? Questioning, if I let my guard down—became too lax in my vigilance? Questioning, if I'd been too naïve—or even over-confident? Wondering, if I had misjudged my abilities once I'd believed I collected myself enough after being raddled and worse by Chip, that I could stand up to him? Fool him enough to think I was eager for Chip to have me in any fashion that suited him—when I was only playing along?

Once again, I'd became wedged. In order to wiggle out—once and for, I'd have to bide more time and wait. The very things, I did throughout my childhood. And to be on the safe side, even continue to plan—plan harder. Accumulate a successful one if it came to that again. All the while, be on the lookout once more—more guardedly than ever. And if need be, look for the right opportunity to strike.

I'd proven to myself that I was once good at making a plan even under extreme pressure; and at the last minute fueled by the raw emotions of fear and hate and the desire for revenge. All three had been the metals that had forged my sword and shield. Combined, they can also be much like gasoline spewing out of a person's pores—setting the world around them on fire. But, at least for me, regardless of all the waiting and planning in a live or die situation, I've always acted on the flames of those combined raw emotions.

I was sick of being the underdog when it came to Chip. It's not like I could just walk away. Just like I couldn't walk away from Mr. Jones or my father. In the end, I didn't lay down and die for them.

Within two weeks after the attack at the Cove, Chip was found murdered in his apartment—very-bloody-dead. The Atlanta gay rags reported the scene of the crime was brutal and bloody. That, it was analogous to a B horror movie. That, the murder was possibly a crime of hate or passion considering the excessive number of times a knife was plunged into his body. Excessive? As far as I was concerned—a few hundred more wouldn't have been enough. Wouldn't have been excessive.

I experienced a homogeneous relief Chip was dead as I had the day, I cleaned up what was left of my father. Maybe even the second he'd died. Maybe. And as that day, with Chip's demise, the distress and anxiety—the barking fear, left me. Now, they are all long-dead. All deserving of their bloody end. All well-rotting—their flesh returned to dirt in their graves, leaving nothing more than bones. My father. Mr. Jones. Chip.

The news washed through Midtown like a tidal wave, but there was no mention of Chip's murder on the six o'clock news—not even a short paragraph on the last page of the Atlanta Journal Constitution newspaper. Apparently, a gay murder wasn't considered newsworthy. Rather, gay bashings and the killing of homos were deemed more of a recreational sport. But, in Chip's case, was it murder or self-defense—regardless of the way the determination was extracted and how his punishment delivered? In my view, Chip got what was coming to him. Perhaps, someone—as others, understood the meaning of: preventive measures.

I'd been to Chip's small apartment shortly after meeting Jake. It resembled that of a gay frat house. A large collection of proverbial fag magazines: Blue Boy, Colt, and Honcho piled the coffee table along with VHS tapes of gay porn. Large posters of naked men plastered the walls like wallpaper. It was all the evidence the police on the scene needed to see; their homophobia, reducing felony murder to the misdemeanor of jaywalking.

Jake was the one who found Chip's body on the sofa, as the gay rags printed. Being such close friends and sharing everything, I imagine he may have known who accomplished the deed. Out of curiosity, some years later, I did ask a friend connected with the District Attorney's office to snoop around to see if there were any unsolved murders during the timeframe of Chip's demise.

The only details I offered—willing to give: Chip's real name; a physical description; that he lived in an apartment in North Midtown, and it was likely the police assumed it had been leased to a homosexual. As I expected, and even hoped for the murderer, there wasn't a record to be found in any computer file or any archived with Chip's name.

I guess it's possible to get away with murder—at least in this lifetime. It's highly probable, at the time of the murder, the police and the Atlanta District Attorney's office could have cared less about putting much effort into the murder of a gay man. As I'd thought, the paper on the clipboard the details of the investigation were written on, likely got as far as the trash can. The motto, "To Protect and to Serve" only applied to white people in good neighborhoods. Not people of color, and certainly not one more dead fag.

Thirty-eight years have been absorbed by time since Chip's murder. No one has yet to be charged for the crime. Good for that person. Good for him. Good for him for striking back. The lesson here to be learned: be careful whom you take advantage of—fuck with, because revenge can be very patient. At least, that's my understanding. I guess it is possible to get away with murder—at least in this lifetime.

On July 17, 2004, like so many who'd fallen to AIDS, the iconic Backstreet Atlanta 24 Hour Nightclub—a massive, three-level, 10,000-square-foot space died. Others, like the Armory, the Cove, and The Sweet Gum Head were dead as well. When Backstreet opened in 1975, at 845 Peachtree Street in the heart of Midtown, it was a glowing beacon beckoning gay men and their allies. The epicenter for untold numbers: many young from small-town America's Southland congregating in droves from all over Georgia and as far up the East Coast as North and South Carolina, down to mid-state Florida, west to Alabama and north covering Tennessee.

For young gay men like me, it was a rite of passage as we flashed our private membership cards upon entering its Golden Gates to Disco Heaven. Each time I walked through those doors was like passing through a portal into another world. I felt a little bit special and a little bit naughty at the same time.

All the bars and clubs formed the purlieus that played a role in many young men's lives. The gay establishments offered refuge. And in that refuge, came the freedom to be ourselves away from the repressive prejudices outside their walls. Allowed us to be authentic as we danced under strobing, multicolored lights and large mirrored reflective balls spinning from the ceilings as we found some temporary sanctuary—while our bodies and minds absorbed the music.

Sanctuary, from the families that wouldn't accept us—and society for that matter. Sanctuary, to live in the moment as the fear of AIDS lingered in our minds. From the fear of judgments. From our own personal struggles. At the time, many of us, searching for who we were and who we would become; deciding which road to take at the fork of youth into the future—at least the ones whose third stage of life was not stolen by AIDS, and even murdered because they were homosexuals. Still, in the moment, the music made us feel like we would live forever. That purlieus, was an island of magic and mystery—and even, of chance. Defining. Life-changing. Even haunting.

Many human transformations took place inside their walls and the shadows within: the self-discovery; again, that sanctuary offered, if only short, to escape the undesirable realities of the times; the passion and lust; falling in love for a moment, for a night, or for a lifetime; the driving beats of the music rhythmically pounding into our souls and taking hold of our hearts, pushing blood through our bodies as it did desires; and so much more—some indefinable by words.

Backstreet drew its last breath after the owners lost a long battle with the City of Atlanta, partnering with the Midtown Ponce Security Alliance, and one City Councilwoman leading the charge for its death—seeding fearmongering that the renowned club was ground zero for prostitution and drugs. At the time, the only remaining club in the city having a 24-hour liquor license. The last stab in its heart was the City's denial for its renewal. Eventually for all, last call for the last drink was announced. Their music went silent. All their flashing-colored lights flickered off. The shimmering, mirrored balls stopped spinning over their dance floors. Their doors were locked for the last time. Their walls that protected us, fell into rubble soon thereafter.

The attack on Backstreet was a subterfuge to push the gays out—and for the valuable real estate Midtown had become. Forgetting, that years before, it was the gay community that began the revitalization of Midtown like in other major cities. Restoring once beautiful in-town neighborhoods back to their original glory after being neglected between the 1950s and 1960s. These in-town neighborhoods were deserted due to the White Flight, also referred to as the White Exodus. Caucasians—racists-on-the-run, in a large-scale migration for suburbia and a color-free life from the in-town communities becoming more racially diverse.

Before the gays began resurrecting these in-town communities from their death, most straight people wouldn't have given a penny for them, much less a second thought. The same is true—of the city block where Backstreet proudly once stood. Yes, thank the fags for opening the doors of the return of the whites! Once mammoth cranes finished filling dump trucks and took the massive wreckage away, beginning with Backstreet, it was all expunged except in the hearts and minds of those still alive to remember its life-altering meaning to them.

For some twenty-nine years, Backstreet was an ardent part of in-town Atlanta—the Mecca of the Southeast. But it will never be as real today as it was then, and to know that you would have had to trip the light fantastic under that large, shimmering, mirrored disco ball, especially in the early-to-late 1980s, when that last call before that last dance in the other clubs may have very well been both for many men dying from complications of AIDS while they were literally dancing for their lives. But, again, in the moment, at Backstreet—they could live forever.

In 2008, the thirty-six-floor Viewpoint was built on Backstreet's unmarked grave. The only remains—the brick and concrete dust that settled under the foundation of the new structure. More high-priced condos in huge high-rises rapidly soared upward changing the skyline of Midtown.

Today, the vast majority who walk that part of the famed street at 845 Peachtree, at the corner of Sixth Street, have no idea that it—Backstreet, and the music ever existed. But I can still hear the music and feel the pulsating effervescent beats every time I passed by where it once solidly stood. Sometimes, I'll pause my steps and close my eyes—as people passed around, to be transported, like a river swiftly running backward, to find myself once again in the middle of the dance floor engulfed in the men, those colored-flashing lights washing over us, and the music pounding our heart.

Yes, the music. Long live disco. I guess like Backstreet and the others—our lives are eventually erased in time. To this day, no one has cared enough to rally to have a plaque secured in the concrete side-walk honoring Backstreet.

As far as the exsanguinating night of the rape at the Cove, it was the last time I danced within its smokey, white-gray fog. Hopefully—it would be Chip's as well, lurking within the obscurity it offered.

the in-betweens

In-betweens are shifting spans of time, coming and going—coming and going. Welcome. Aways, welcome. You want them to come and not go—those in-between times. They give a metered of time—a leave of absence from the madness of nothingness—more time not to die. Offering times of solitude that pull you out of the room of in-sanity; pull you back a few steps from the edge of the sidewalk, seconds before stepping onto the street in front of a speeding bus. Still, you are vulnerable. The door to the room of insanity is still a few steps ahead. Still waiting to open. Still waiting for your entrance. The bus is still speeding toward you.

Those spans of time—the in-betweens, are much like calling heads or tails with a coin. A span begins the moment the coin—positioned on the nail of the thumb and held down at the bend of the forefinger is flicked into the air and ends the second it lands. Each span can last seconds to minutes, one day to the next, a day to weeks, and if fortunate, even months. It's a span of time when time itself can stand still—as if the coin were suspended in the air. But once the coin lands, you walk back out of that period of solitude the in-between offered, and once again you find yourself standing in front of the door to the room of insanity. Find yourself standing on the side-walk watching the speeding bus headed in your direction. Hopefully, that door doesn't open. Hopefully, you don't step into the street. Hopefully, you find yourself among the living and not surrounded by that nothingness—wrapped like a blanket within madness. I know them as they know me—those in-between times. I know them as I know what waits outside—we are well acquainted.

Time outside of the in-betweens is lost. Hours arbitrarily amassing into days, weeks, and months over sixteen seasons of those four years. Lost time—collected in a box on a shelf but not forgotten. My sanity, always in flux. Me, waiting for the in-between to return, when I dove into deep periods of depression: periods I felt my sanity slip away, only to be replaced by fears of madness catching up with me—sensing it on my heels; fear that I would completely become my mother, as I witnessed the same happen to her. Those periods came and went—like people passing on a busy sidewalk: some moving slowly, others in a hurry—all going somewhere, but seemingly with some purpose.

Still on edge, most days, I managed to workout, robotically spending hours at the gym, attempting to feel normal—the normal I'd once known. Training was the only thing I did well. Nights outside of the in-between: high doses of clonazepam, along with lamotrigine were necessary. The combination allowed me to become semi-able to briefly get lost in movies with Dugan in the bed with me. The movies helped to push the realities of my life at arms-length. But I was always apprehensive—even terrified, of what mornings would bring.

Clonazepam is a highly controlled medication. My psychiatrist only allowed thirty a month. One a day, was nowhere near enough of what I needed. Accordingly, I bought considerable contraband quantities—as I did Xanax and Valium, from the dealer who sold me various steroids. I became hopelessly addicted to clonazepam and lamotrigine—often popping them throughout the day like breath mints—sometimes, downing them with a few shots of vodka. I knew the risks but left outside of the in-betweens—were far more terrifying.

I suffered through those excruciating periods of lost time I couldn't fight anymore, no matter how many times I picked up the sword, only to drop it; four years to feel completely whole; four years coming unglued and then glued again; four years for my life to flow without getting tangled in those desperate periods between the in-betweens; four years of being in and out of flux; one thousand, four hundred sixty days to be exact. That's how long I waited in and out of the in-between. At times, I'm still waiting.

Spending slow-footed time in Piedmont Park with Dugan, aided the ability to remain longer in the in-betweens. Although we rarely braved the bustling weekends—the air brimful with the patchy, wavering tones of people's voices mixing with laughter and that of nature: walking and jogging; riding bikes; parents pushing baby strollers; children skipping with young delight, apart from the few throwing temper tantrums; couples holding hands; shirtless guys playing football and other activities. All the things I didn't—couldn't be a part of outside solitude's door. Even if I faked it—and I was once an expert at faking it, however exhausting at times.

During the weekdays, Piedmont Park was virtually empty except for a random person here and there. I remained stationary while the rest of the world seemed to move forward. But stationary was better than being trapped in the nothingness—eyeing madness while it eyed me. It was better to remain in the in-between as long as possible—as long as it would allow me. Unlike those people, I would walk without purpose. I didn't even know what purpose was anymore, despite many successes and all the beauty life afforded in blocks of time over the past years—that had suddenly been swallowed up in that void of insanity: in the void of nothingness. If there were any purpose in the in-betweens, it was to exist and stop thinking about death.

Introspective and unhurried walks around Piedmont Park with Dugan became a ritual. Following, I sat for unnoted epochal spans on the same bench—day into day under a massive, majestic oak that graced Dugan and me with its company. Its lush protective canopy of abundant leaves offered shade through springs and summers while capturing the sun's rays before allowing passage to meet the ground. As time marshalled, the oak's shadow on the grass stretched longer and longer as it was pulled by the hours.

The oak's brown-black barked trunk had become thickened and abraded by its many years of existence. Its branches reached far and wide and up, like a giant's arms, hands, and fingers—heavily knotted as those of an elderly man with arthritic joints.

The bench faced a wide, well-traveled path of little interest to Dugan as he lay under the bench. His long, bull terrier head rested on his stretched-out front legs and paws. Dugan's paws, usually on my feet as if I would float away like a helium filled balloon without them holding me down. Patiently, he waited to be offered one of many dog treats from a Ziploc bag I'd filled before we'd left the house—three blocks away. And on those days sitting on the park bench, Dugan watched the squirrels romp, from tree-to-tree, and from branch-to-branch, but he didn't try to catch the squirrels. He never moved from his position, except to lift his head to retrieve the treats from my hand.

On the other side of the path, the bench looked out over an expensive, low, meadow—once part of an eighteen-hole golf course back in the 1930s. Late spring and summer months, people sunbathed on towels on the other side of the meadow that sloped upward, referred to as Oak Hill—a quick walking distance to a granite structure, as old as the park, that was, at the time, a restaurant named Park Tavern. The stone building had gone through many iterations as the park itself since it opened in October of 1887.

I speculated about those people who found recreation and camaraderie in the park, and the various events that took place there—all those many years ago. Imagined women dressed in their long proper dresses as they held lacey umbrellas to keep the sun off their delicate faces. Men walking beside them, in suits and wearing top hats.

While sitting, I watched the seasons migrate from one to the next—mild days, to warm, to hot, to decidedly chilly. Some days the sky brought gentle rain and others, downpours. Still, I remained on that bench—although, Dugan surely would have preferred we head back to the house. He'd move from under the bench. Shook the rain from his coat while giving me the eye as if saying: "Are you kidding me? Are we just going to stay put?" Perhaps, I stayed, trusting the rain would wash my soul clean.

During the light to moderate days, I tilted my head back, watched the raindrops jump from leaf-to-leaf and branch-to-branch, until they sprinkled my face. The oak's lush and compact canopy gave protection from most of it in the spring and summer months like an umbrella. But in winter, it stood barren of its leaves. Even still, I sat on that bench with Dugan in my lap, as I held the handle of a large black umbrella. But still, I sat on that park bench like one of George Lundeen's life-size human bronzes sitting on other benches in public places.

At times, the winter months hurried sleet. On occasion, even a smattering of snow—but it rarely actually snows in the South. However, when it does—when the snowflakes whispery ride the cold, wind-pushed air drifting or rushing downward to languidly mantle the sleeping ground, it abounds with a sense of calmness in the disguise of purity. And the more abundantly it falls, it covers all the surrounding ugliness.

I'd watch the flakes gather onto Dugan's white coat before the warmth of his body melted them into his fur. And like during the gentle rains, as if a little boy in relished glee, I leaned my head back with opened mouth to catch the snowflakes on my tongue.

The thicker it layered the ground, voices carrying laughter tunneled from behind us as people collected. Kids and adults alike reveling while they slid down, challenging the large hill some yards to the west. Making use of anything, from cardboard boxes to trash can lids and actual sleds. Even on their stomachs and backs. Some picked up enough speed to make it across the road below, that ran along the lake. Dugan and I stayed until the world around us was as white as he was. On the walk back to the house, there were six footprints—Dugan's and mine.

When I began to feel madness pull at me, pull me closer to solitaire's exit and that of the park; my hands gripped that bench as my breaths did—attempting to remain in place. Hoping not to be kicked back out into the nothingness and the insanity where it lived—where it called my name.

While sitting there on that park bench, my mind would ping-pong. Wondering many things, including much in the past—as if I hadn't visited it enough. Mostly my thoughts were caught by the echoes of love. My desperate need for it. The loss of it. Why some people were able to hold on to it and others, not. Why I was never allowed either but only carry it in my heart and not in my arms.

As I heard the songs of the wind rustling its abundant leaves, I would talk to Dugan and the tree as if he and it were able to understand every word of the human language that came out of my mouth. But it didn't matter—it didn't matter, if Dugan or the tree ever spoke back. Regardless, it was just important to tell the oak every possible thing about me. I had a strong sense that it did listen and did so without judgment. Other times I sat in silence of heart and mind and let nature do the talking.

I wondered if the oak could feel joy. Pain. Wondered, if it was ever sad. Wondered, if it were anything more than a tree or knew the difference between itself and a shrub. If it had a heart beating somewhere under its bark and within its rings. A soul. A mind. And if the latter, what it thought about the world around it? About the people who passed by it every day and night. About me. I wanted the majestic oak to tell me stories of all it had witnessed since it first germinated from its cup-shaped acorn—determinedly began digging its roots into the rich dirt a good hundred-and-fifty or more years before. Still, after all that time, it stood strong and proud to be a tree in a park.

In the in-between, as the oak and even the bench, and of course, Dugan offered a transient departure from thoughts of my own self-execution—protection from myself. It gave me the opportunity to reflect, to analyze and to learn more about myself and why I'd become the way I was—why everything seemed to have changed overnight in early January of 2009: from light to darkness; from joy to sadness; from beauty to ugliness; from hope to nothingness; from life to death.

As I sat on that bench, I counted how much time had passed since I was released from Davy—how much time I managed to stay alive. I made it this many seconds. This many minutes. This many hours. This many days. This many months. I made it one more day. Two more. Three more and so on. That's how many more twenty-four-hour periods I managed to breathe in air. All the while, I waited for those pieces—all my pieces to find each other again. Waited for them to come back together to make me whole. And unlike those serene days in the park when I heard the wind rustling the leaves and branches of the tree, on the days I was caught in emotional torment at the very edge of the in-between—I felt it blowing through me. Blow through all the holes left by those missing pieces that scattered far and wide—so very far from center.

There were times I never thought I would find myself again. Never come back to center. I feared there were too many; too many fragments of myself to reassemble. But I knew they were somewhere. Alone. Petrified. Wandering. Lost. Drifting. Looking for home—looking for me. Looking for what few pieces that had returned. But I needed all of them—if not, most to return. To collect. To find each other. To return to center with the rest of the pieces waiting for them as I was—even if they were damaged—as I was.

Like Dugan, that great oak was my friend. I hoped it thought the same of me and Dugan. So, in the in-between, I sat on that same sun-bleached park bench under that mighty oak—patiently waiting for it to tell me why I should keep living.

Encapsulated within the solitude of those itinerant days looking over the meadow, my trance-like thoughts chased the wind—even outside the margins of my immediate existence waiting for the in-between. The closer to the edge, to those margins, the park circled counterclockwise as if the bench was a ride on a miss-directed carnival carousel with scary painted horses carved out of basswood. The mirrors perhaps manifesting a life as creepy music played. The faster it wheeled in reverse, the further it took me back to revisit a past that had been visited too many times before—to where I found myself standing in front of symbolic, unopened doors as the park blurred until it wafted from color to black-and-white. As the wheel slowed, and my thoughts chased back within the wind—back to that immediate existence, to my relief, the color returned—but not without hesitation.

Some days, I just sat there with little thought. Others, I opened some doors as I re-examined certain aspects of my life. I questioned: my belief system; moral code, if I had any; if God really existed or some afterlife, and if either, would I be transported into light or returned to darkness as I had in my bathtub. Would I be judged for my sins—my grisly actions only, or would the extenuating circumstances be considered as would my undying devotion to my mother and sister, my kindness and generosity as other defining factors and characteristics that made me, in-part, a good person? Would the bad be weighted with that good—and would the latter outweigh the other?

snap of the rubber band

Other than how it may have appeared, I forged attempts—although successes and failures or somewhere between to hold it all in. Hold it together so my guts wouldn't spill-out of the old emotional stab wounds and gush onto the floor—even when the periods of calm were habitually interrupted by the unwelcome rushing of searing depression and latitudes of violent episodes of metaphorically swinging steel baseball bats of anger toward me and life itself. My emotions continued expanding and contracting like rubber bands. And much like rubber bands, the more they expand and contract—they always snap.

Unless you've live it—it's beyond description of what it's like to lose direction after a large block of time when I'd managed to regain progress—believing I wanted to go on living. Feeling as though I'd found my way through the thick of the woods that were too heavily amassed and therefore hindering sunlight from filtering through the canopy of life.

Then, the topography changes. The canopy thickens even more until all sunlight is blocked, and confusion and self-doubt returns. There's a sudden shift. My core compass spins like it's caught between two polar fields—life and death. The darkness races toward me. I run in the opposite direction. It catches up. Pulls at me as I attempt to pull away. Back and forth. Back and forth. Back and forth. The darkness pulls. I pull. The air thins. I wonder if the next breath will be the last. The pulling snaps the rubber band. I take a pill or two, or three.

I told myself: this is just another set-back; eventually, I'll get there; I'll get back; I've come too far to stop; I'll get to okay as long as I keep fighting the sudden urges of self-destruction.

More push and pull followed. More stress on the rubber band as it expanded and contracted again—closer to snapping.

When I felt it about to snap, the majority of my thoughts wavered more to destructive; but a few held steadfast: don't fight; just give in; you know you want to die; no—stop listening; keep going; keep fighting; stop fighting; give in; don't make yourself suffer anymore; you're just fooling yourself; you're a fucking mess; broken beyond repair; you're weak like your father told you; no, you're not weak, you proved it to him; you can do this, damnit; no, no, you can't.

The thoughts I once had in college about driving my car into a telephone pole or tree returned. The emotional pain was insistent—ruthless. Make sure to unsnap your seat belt. No! Don't. Yes! Do! Do it! Do it—dammit! crash the Jag! The Rover is too big—you might survive. Yes, better to crash the Jag! Fucking do it! Everyone will think it's just a tragic car accident and not a suicide.

I'm aware that I'm at the point of out-of-control. Falling backward. The abyss of emptiness is steps behind. The rubber band is now taunt. Then, it snaps. I know I have to stop the evil voice in my head. The one that wants me to die. At the risk of dreams and nightmares, I'd take sleeping pills to put myself under. Not enough to die, but enough to save me from that voice's torment in the waking hours. Yes, it was better to sleep than crash the Jag. Still, medicated or not—there are no guarantees when the voice beckons.

john doe

His name is John Doe. Why? Because that's the name the police will give him when they find his body: John Doe, an unidentified disfigured corpse. Hopefully, too decomposed to find any evidence to connect him to me during the autopsy.

While the rest of the world seemed to sleep—swaddled in the arms of a merciful night, I lay awake restless on edgy blades. Mostly in fear of unwanted dreams I wish not to be entangled within if I were to close my eyes. And as I fear dubious dreams, I do the same of the day that will follow the night. My mind beseeching time to protract and thus delay tomorrow's arrival—to keep its distance. For with a new day, it's another one of uneasy uncertainties to combat to live through. Until then, the night cocoons me from the day before and the one to come. Not only do I fear its light, but I am untrusting of myself—and that what both will perchance brew.

I fitfully turned my head from the flat screen to the clock on the dresser across the room, ticking its way toward Sunday morning—eyeing it as if time itself were a mortal enemy. My mind spun as the clock ticked—its hands crossing twelve moving west away from midnight. The more it did, the more I felt I was moving away from center.

At least Dugan appeared to be in a peaceful doze like a baby after a bottle feeding and diaper change, while I watched a Sci-Fi marathon of the television series, Supernatural—and I don't particularly like Sci-Fi movies. But I take no shame in admitting that Jensen Ackles and Jared Padalecki are eye-candy and quite candidly, I have a huge crush on Misha Collins—preferably naked and covered in whip cream from head to toe. The red cherry is optional—well, depending on its precise location.

I'd hoped to get my mind straight or, at best, find an escape from reality in the misdeeds of demons, ghosts, vampires, and the like. At the moment Jensen Ackles' character, Dean, was about to decapitate a gnarly biker vampire, my cell rang on the chest to the right of the bed. After recognizing the name, I took another look at the clock. It was twelve-thirty-five.

John Doe was just another random guy from the gym. On occasion, he'd asked for a spot on the bench press. Eventually, he asked for my number while suggesting we should hang out sometime. So, I did—give him my number, that is. John Doe was short, with the body of a well-trained gymnast. Perhaps, mid-to-late thirties. I found him somewhat attractive and no doubt sex with him had crossed my mind. But he ran with a tight group of gossipy queens I didn't care much for. Plus, I was in one of my sobriety periods from sex. Misha Collins on the screen was enough—and no, I didn't have my hand inside the shorts I was wearing at the time jerking.

Over the phone, John Doe conveyed he was out-and-about and wanted to stop by. Obviously, a booty call. Not up for one that night, I told him I could use the company, and it would be cool if he wanted to hang out for a while, but made it clear I wasn't feeling up to having sex if that was his intention. John Doe asked me to text him my address. I did. Within the course of some twenty minutes, he knocked at the front door. My decamp from the bed disturbed Dugan's sleep as he perked up his head. I motioned him to the dog bed in the corner of the room. The disappointment of his dismissal was obvious as his eyes turned meek-like. A few minutes later, John Doe and I were lying side-by-side a foot or so apart. At his arrival, I explained the flat screen in the den wasn't working and I'd yet to replace it, so we'd have to watch the show in my bedroom.

He was dressed in jeans that were deliberately frayed above the knees for that worn look, a light-blue Ralph Lauren Large Pony Polo, and a pair of wolf-gray Nike Roshe One athletic shoes with the large white swoosh. Yes, he looked rather sexy.

At that thought, I suddenly realized I should have at least put on some gym shorts and a T-shirt. I remember thinking: I might be giving John Doe mixed signals by my lack of dress and us on my bed, as we commenced in small talk about the gym and what he'd done earlier in the evening. Pretty much—the usual Saturday-night-bar-troll before his appearance at my door. It was obvious, John Doe had a bit of a buzz on and not from one-too-many gin and tonics. I thought I smelled the hint of weed.

"You mind if I take off my shoes?" he asked.

"Sure, make yourself at home."

John Doe sat up to untie them before kicking his Nikes off onto the floor. Thump, thump.

"Got anything to drink?"

"How about a Rolling Rock? I have a few in the fridge."

"Sounds good."

"I need to take Dugan out... give me a few minutes, then I'll grab them."

"That sure is a pretty dog. What's his name again?"

"Dugan," I answered, aware John Doe's buzzed state affected his short-term memory.

"Cool. Cool."

While getting off the bed, my guest requested to use the bathroom. I took the opportunity and scrambled to grab a black T-shirt and pair of gray gym shorts from the bottom drawer of the dresser. Dugan was already at my side and quickly followed me out of the bedroom as I dressed in the process. Upon returning with two Rolling Rock, John Doe was still in the bathroom. I sat his beer down on a coaster on the chest by the side of the bed where he'd plopped down earlier. By then, a good fifteen minutes had passed. In another five, he pranced out—butt-naked like a show horse. "Damn," I thought, but regardless of his pretty body, I still didn't want to mess around.

"Well, I did tell you to make yourself at home," I joked, to make light of an uncomfortable situation.

Ostensibly, an uncomfortable situation—but clearly not for my house guest.

"I like to walk around naked," he proudly responded, as he sat down on the bed with his back against the padded headboard.

"Uh-huh... good to know. So, you're a bit of a nudist, I take it?"

"Something like that. I enjoy giving my neighbors a bit of a show now and then."

"I see. Too bad mine are likely in bed asleep by now to miss your performance... but you can always go over and knock on their door," I hoped.

My humor was obviously lost on John Doe. His little show-and-tell increasingly ushered me toward annoyance. I wasn't amused and realized the mistake of welcoming him over or trusted that he would behave. Of course, I should be flattered but I wasn't. Then, I noticed a little bit of white confection-like powder under his left nostril, and I was certain he hadn't recently baked any funnel cakes in the last few hours. Rather, he'd obviously snorted coke in my bathroom, which rapidly escalated the situation. I knew I needed to get him out of my house.

The unraveling worsened. My mind searched for stratagems—of ways to gracefully ask John Doe to leave when I should have just walked him to the door—naked or not and opened the front door to usher his exit. But before I had a moment to come up with an out, naked gymnast guy with about a five-inch boner decided to crawl on top of me. At first, it seemed like innocent horseplay. A bit of rough and tumble in the bed. Still, I wanted no part in it. John Doe hadn't taken me seriously about not being interested in sex, but just company. I'll concur, in gay lingo, company and sex can be construed as one in the same: synonyms. Then, he attempted to pin me down. That was a huge mistake on his part. Still, I attempted to keep my cool.

"Hey… I told you we were just going to hang a bit."

"Yea. I know. As in getting off."

"No, that's not what I meant. I thought I'd made that clear when you called," I disputed.

"Come on. You answered the door in boxers. What… you some kind of tease?"

"I didn't mean to give you that impression."

"Well, I'm here to play."

John Doe was strong for someone his size, and solid—even though, I had a good twenty-five pounds or more on him, and several inches taller. My anger rose like a thermometer in Death Valley as his hand grabbed my flaccid, uninterested penis. I aggressively push him off to the side.

"Just relax and have your beer," I said, irked at the unraveling of the night and the mess I'd gotten myself in.

I soon found John Doe to be a persistent little fucker. As I was about to get off the bed, he grabbed my shoulders from behind and pulled me back—not understanding the definition of no. John Doe took advantage of my position on the bed—flipped around on top of me trying to wrestle. Big mistake. I hated wrestling: a throwback from childhood, my older brother always bullying and pinning me down added to the things my father forcefully made me do. As John Doe continued to restrict my movement, my mind flooded with images and smells and sensations of past events, all racing my mind. Like magnets—they reunited. The past and the present explosively collided, and my panic along with that anger went into pipe bomb mode.

He pinned my hands—his hard-on pressing. Backflashes of entrapment laid siege of my mind. I struggled to get the upper hand.

"What the fuck!" I instantly blurted out. "Get the fuck off… you… you little shit!"

"Awe. Don't be such a crybaby. I'll show you what a little shit I am," John Doe, boasted.

He became increasingly aggressive—his hands firmly around my wrists like restraints. An instant flashback of being tied down in the bed at Davy added to my distress. My wrists burned from the friction of the constant twisting and pulling to free them. Eventually, I flipped on my side. Still, John Doe wasn't letting go—the situation continued getting gravely worse by the second. Lighten-quick, he moved behind me. In an instant, John Doe had me in a chokehold.

"For a big guy… you… you're such a pussy," he belittled.

"Look, dammit, I told you to get off!"

"What, you can't take it?" Joe Doe taunted.

"Goddammit!"

"You're right, I'm going to get off… I'm horny," he played on the words.

"Hey, this isn't okay!" I harshly abashed.

"I bet what you need is a good fucking," he exclaimed.

"Man, stop. You're crazy. STOP! NOW!"

John Doe was getting off on his sick shit just as Chip had many years ago. At that, my unraveling continued. My fibers—wearing thinner and thinner as we both sweated profusely.

Suddenly I snapped. In a split second. I felt it in my brain. I heard it, like a bone breaking in half. Loud and clear. I'd split into another version of myself. I felt the rapid transition: from good to bad, to pure evil—inside of my being. I wanted to hurt him or worse—leaning toward the latter.

I broke his hold. Forcefully, jabbed John Doe in his side with an elbow. Rolled on top of him. Took control. My anger was in overdrive. My hands mechanically reached for his neck. At contact, they tightly clutched it. The look of supremacy on his face retreated to one of surprise. John Doe resorted to repeatedly spitting in my face; a few chunks hit my eyes. I felt the blood pulsing through the carotid arteries on either side of his neck. John Doe reached up to grab my wrist, trying to pry them away. It was fruitless. His body struggled under me, kicking his legs and feet while trying to speak. Pure adrenaline had taken over my body as the look on his face turned to desperation.

"Who's the pussy?" bulleted from my mouth as my hands squeezed tighter around his neck and he grappled for breath.

rage

Sometimes—rage gets the best of a person. At others, it's all a person has. At least, this is what I know. What I've learned. What I've lived. And, yes, on occasion, it's gotten the best of me and the worst outcome for others.

Rage pulsates through my blood like a virus. It has, as long as I can remember. Perhaps, it is—a virus. And as it's much like a virus, it's a force not to be fucked with. Never. Its stems, like thorns of a honey locust tree. Punctures like the sharpest of steel. Draws blood—in my case, the blood of the unimpeachable. Anger and hate are one in the same. Both—are mine. At times, I feel they are all I have.

My hands retained their firm hold around John Doe's neck. It wasn't horseplay or S&M. He'd started this bullshit. He managed to spit in my face again. I saw red. as his legs and feet violently thrash. I had no plans of letting go anytime soon. A hint of cyanosis set-in on his face. A bluish pale-blue color replaced his pinkish flesh—his lips darkened.

Like bullet points for a business presentation, a precise plan presented itself in my head—twelve. One: to drag him into my art studio to prepare him. Another: to make sure none of my DNA was on his body. A third: to put his dead body into the boot of my Rover. There are many roads between exit 242 and the airport, where I could dump a body in an out-of-the-way wooded area.

John Doe continued to strain to speak, but it didn't matter. He had already said enough—shoveled his own grave. He continued to thrash about; in the process, he peed himself. The smell of urine strongly permeated the room and wet my inner thighs. His stare was rigid. Perhaps a last nonverbal plea for his pathetic. egocentric life. For another breath.

John Doe's eyes bulged fear as he sucked for oxygen. Gasping. I still straddled him. My hands still choked him. Again, his voice grappled.

His hands weakly floundered for my neck. More haggard sounds weakly exited his mouth—between efforts to clear his throat. John Doe's consciousness dwindled. His body suddenly went still. I loosened my grip around his neck, then pulled one of my hands away to wipe the sweat from my forehead. John Doe opened his eyes again. Attempted a flimsy swing at me. All so pointless.

I leapt out of bed. Grabbed one of his ankles. Pulled him off the bed onto the floor. Thump.

"You… fuck. I'm calling the police," he hoarsely threatened.

I laughed. Then, laughed again—wickedly so while dragging John Doe over the tightly woven wool onion-colored sisal rug of the bedroom. John Doe reached to grab the doorframe. With one hard tug, his grip was severed. I wasn't even sure why I was dragging him—the rage still controlling my actions. Then, a moment of clarity came then went. I continued to pull John Doe by the ankle, his arms and hands thrashing for anything to secure him down the hallway. Its runner bunched. I kept pulling.

John Doe reached for the black pedestal positioned against the wall displaying a life mask a gift from an artist. Both topple over, shattering the mask. That alone, made me want to finish what I'd started on the bed. Instead, I kept dragging John Doe toward the den and back door. His eyes remained wide. Fear still covered his face.

Once in the den, he grabbed the curved stainless-steel leg of one of the Mies van der Rohe Barcelona chairs. Dragged it with him. I stopped.

"Let go… touch another thing and you're dead on the spot."

More raspy words exited his mouth.

Then, I tugged hard. Then, harder. Then, again. Enjoying each one. Enjoying how scared John Doe looked. Once at the back door, I released his ankle. I opened it. Helped him up and pushed him out. John Doe stumbled. Fell down. Nonplussed, grappled to his feet while struggling to maintain balance. He then looked at me.

"You… you going to give me my clothes?"

I returned into the house. Quickly gathered his shit before rushing back outside. Tossed them in his direction. Like a mad hatter, John Doe fumbled for his belongings. But who was the mad one? He hastily headed toward the open gates as I watched him disappear into the disjoined ink of night.

ten

anna

Anna came highly recommended. Mid-forties, medium-height, and thin with short graying brown hair. My first impression was of a nice woman with a pleasant disposition. During the interview, it was obvious she wasn't a dog person apparent by Anna's body language while she sat on the Ralph Lauren sofa. A curious Dugan sat on the floor by her feet—interested to know who this new human was in his territory. When Dugan tried to lick her leg, Anna moved her feet while shifting her body.

Another tell-tale sign: she never once patted him. I reassured Anna that Dugan would lick a robber to death before he would bite one. To put Anna to ease, I motioned Dugan over while we continued to talk. To further alleviate her evident anxiety, I let Anna know he was usually with me when I worked in the art studio or was out of the house; but there would be times, Dugan would remain in the house when she came to clean—particularly, when I was at the gym. Contrary to my perception, Anna responded that she would be fine. I hired her that day.

Once she started working, I did make sure Dugan was indeed with me most of the time as I'd informed her. Even still, there were times, to her annoyance, Dugan would follow Anna around. Especially when she vacuumed, and he would play-fight with the machine.

Within a month, they were pals. I was certain from the beginning; Dugan would win her over. I'd catch Anna petting or scratching him behind the ears, and giving Dugan treats out of the big glass canister on the kitchen counter. She grew on me as well; I found myself at ease on cleaning days with Anna in the house—actually, looked forward to seeing her each week. I'd given Anna a key so I wouldn't have to be home every time she came. Anna was very thorough and meticulous.

She would usually come on Wednesdays and stay a good part of the day. Although there were times I needed her for an extra half-day. In the beginning, I'd refrained from sharing much about my bouts of depression when I hired her, rather mentioning it was something I occasionally struggled with—expecting there would be times my mood would decline.

When those darker periods presented themselves, I kept some distance—again, mostly by staying in bed. I'm certain Anna had noticed my medications while putting away underwear, T-shirts, and such in the drawers of the dresser—and when I unintentionally left them out. Even more so, I was sure Sandra had discussed with Anna some of what happened in July of 2009—likely her way to make sure someone else was looking out for her brother when she was away.

Anna never said a word about it, but after a month—she unexpectedly began bringing me a weekly bounty in a Tupperware container filled with fresh-baked oatmeal raisin or peanut butter cookies with whey protein powder in the mix. The protein, I was sure, because she had seen me make shakes in the blender with the whey before heading to the gym. It became clear—Anna was taking more of a personal interest in my life.

saying goodbye to seventh street

It had been a worrisome time consumed with two weeks of packing up a household of many years: furniture, cherished belongings and boxes of memories. And, of course, art from the house and the art studio.

Those belongings—collected over some three decades wrapped in brown packing paper. Others in well-read Atlanta Journal-Constitution newspapers, and the local gay publication, Southern Voice from stacks abscond from ubiquitous kiosks around Midtown. All taped-up with other boxes of varying sizes and stacked in every room of the house.

After some-fifteen years, three days following the third anniversary of July 4, 2009, I sold the Seventh Street house. It had stopped having any semblance of a home for some time. Perhaps, in reality, it never did.

With Dugan at my side, we stood in the middle of each room saying goodbye to the house and those years. It was a mixed bag of angst, regrets, and gratitude addressing revisited memories of events—

good and bad. Some unwanted—certainly, the two suicide attempts.

In contrast, there were many others cherished times of happier days and nights of the amazing things that had taken place inside those walls and under the roof that contained my life there were welcomed; the years before 2009; my home nestled on the densely aged, tree-lined street three blocks from Piedmont Park in a coveted intown area of Atlanta.

Patricia and Willam: made sure the lawn was well manicured: the shrubs were trimmed; the flower beds were refreshed with perennials and annuals; the English ivy that climbed the taupe-painted brick trimmed as well; white orchids on the living room coffee table and the den; the house spotlessly cleaned. A house that was once photographed for a magazine featuring a Southern artist of some prominence. A house I loved with beautiful, well-appointed furnishings arranged on tightly woven wool-onion rugs; and fine art hanging on the walls.

A house where intimate groups of guests gathered for many dinners—and larger ones to celebrate friends' birthdays. Others for fundraisers—or just because I felt like having a party. Christmas tree decorating events. Holidays spent with Mother that sometimes included Sandra when she was able to take leave. Spring cookouts to welcome the remarkable season before the entry of the stifling heat of August—were spent with neighbors and friends in the backyard while drinking wine; the air suffused with the clang of glasses as we toasted various people and things to be recognized laced with conversations and laughter. And of course, the equally lovely fall weather after the crazy winter, where one day it was freezing and the next warm.

Primed or not, it had gotten to the point I could no longer bear to live in that house waiting for the walls to close-in any more than they had; and the roof to collapse

It's stunningly tragic how a pound of despair can asphyxiate a ton of joy. Looking back, I don't know how I could have allowed that to happen. All the same, it had weakened me allowing the ugliness from yesteryears to rise and break through my flesh. Nevertheless, the house I once loved became one of shadows and a house I came to hate. I'd overstayed my welcome and it was time to go. In the years I lived on Seventh Street, there had been three deaths: my mother's, and the other two were mine.

After the furniture and boxes were carried out and loaded in the moving truck, I watched it drive away. A once full house was now vacant—all that was left were echoes.

Dugan's and my reflections in the glass looked back at us as I inserted the key into the lock. It clicked. In those defining moments, I felt as though I didn't know him—that man. But hoped—whoever he was, he'd be the keeper of all the bad I'd experienced on the other side. Therefore, it would remain there—remain with him. If not, hide in the cracks. I'd once believed something similar when I'd locked the door of the house on Shirley Drive, after my mother's death. But I was wrong. "Maybe this time, I'll be right," I hoped.

I've always believed houses catalogue a living history—most everything that took place. They retain bits and pieces—including, echoes of heartbeats of those who once resided within their walls. In relation to Seventh Street, everything since it was built in the early 1920s—all steeped into the plaster walls behind countless layers of paint and wallpaper; and under many layers of wax covering their wooden or linoleum floors. The same is true concerning Shirley Drive—keeping record of a broken family.

I wasn't unaware, in those last moments that I stood in the vacancy, its sale would be the first of five over the next four years. A continuation of the long search since childhood. A prolongation, to find a safe place indeed called home. That is, except for the short reprieve found with Bradley who you will come to know. To this day, I've yet to find those elusive four walls; and that safe place—not only from the past, but from myself.

It all felt bittersweet as I turned around to face the street. Dugan followed as I took a few steps to the edge of the porch. There, I stopped. Looked back to face the door before turning back around and continued down the steps as we proceeded to walk to the car. Moments later, I opened the passenger door of the XJS. Dugan climbed in—the Rover had already been moved. I told myself to resist the overwhelming urge to look at the house again: "Don't look back whatever you do."

Once in the driver's seat, I glanced at Dugan. He was looking out the car window at the house. I think he knew—surely, he did. Then, I reached over to scratch his head.

"I guess we need to be going, my sweet boy. It's time for us to move on."

Dugan looked at me. We sat there for a few minutes—but I did. I did look before starting the car. I told myself, "That has to be the last time." Knowing it would be in my best interest, even when coming back to visit friends in the neighborhood.

Inching out of the driveway for the last time, it felt much like leaving a funeral of a dear friend who had been sick for years—mourning their loss wearing sackcloth and ashes. But I knew I was mourning the loss of so much more.

I slowly headed west, still wanting to look back as the urge tugged at my neck. I asked myself, "What's the point? The point of looking back?" I knew there wasn't one and kept my head facing forward.

On a Thursday morning, I sat at a nicely polished large conference table at O'Kelley & Sorohan Attorneys at Law, LLC. I felt nothing—as if every nerve in my body had been cauterized. My brain, too.

Friend and agent, Cole sat closely beside me as the closing attorney went through the settlement statement. He had equally been a therapist-of-sorts—helping me with my fluctuating emotional state as other aspects throughout the process of selling the house and the search for a new residence.

The copy in front of me remained untouched as the buyer and others flipped through the document. I could barely hear the attorney's voice and interjection of others finding the flipping of the pages to be vexatious.

"How you holding up?" Cole looked over to whisper.

"I want to get out of here," I mouthed.

"Soon enough, my friend. Just a few more signatures and then, I'll take you to lunch."

When I told Anna I was selling, with hands on her hips, she adamantly made it clear: she didn't pack or unpack. Eventually, Anna changed her mind and brought her younger son, Timothy, to help.

the loft

I wondered if I'd just made another mistake—taken another wrong turn. Regardless, I had to leave Seventh Street.

William had asked why I wasn't moving to California? He'd relocated back West with Russ into a home in West Hollywood a few years after 2009, while keeping the Laguna property.

"I thought you'd be moving to Los Angeles by now, Randy. I'm surprised. California was always the plan… right?" William spoke with perplexity at my decision to stay.

"Right… bu… but I think it's best I wait a while longer… a year or two," I told William, just to throw some dust into the air As a smokescreen. "Besides, the new loft is beautiful."

The act of waiting hadn't a thing to do with it—moving. I just didn't have a good excuse as to why I wasn't—at least one that I clearly understood, much less one William would. I'd obviously used Christopher's pleads and the disguise of love to stay three more years. It seemed my desire to move to Los Angeles had grown small, if not microscopic—I wasn't sure.

I'd purchased a recently built two-story loft in the Castleberry Hill district, a few miles from Downtown—roughly the same distance from Seventh Street.

It felt Alien. The newness of the loft was alien. Cold. Empty as my heart—leaving me unsure how I felt about it now that my life had relocated within its perimeter. The day before, I had stood in another empty house I knew like a longtime friend—only to find questioning if the loft and I would remain strangers if not anything more than casual acquaintances regardless of how beautiful it was. If we would keep our distance? But what I did know, free of uncertainty—it would never be home.

Beforehand, and having already grown apprehensive and weary by the third viewing, the hunt for a new house took several months from a formidable and strenuous long list—twenty-one properties to be precise as thoughts of California lightly drummed in the back of my mind: too small; too big; shitty neighborhood; nice neighborhood, but not nice enough; too close to Seventh Street; too far away; too traditional; hell no; maybe. Several months, like searching for the mythical white unicorn with a golden horn projecting from its forehead.

Cole may as well have pinned a picture of each house on a wall. Blindfolded me. Spun me around until I was dizzy. Then, pointed my finger at one. Eventually, and I'm sure to the relief of Cole, I arrived at a decision without any success of finding the unicorn. Still, I wasn't sure. The loft was an abstraction of some conceptualization of an unresolved mind. Nevertheless, it was the one I'd chosen. Perhaps, time would tell. And that was one of the elements I required: an intermediary period of more time.

I was its first owner; no other mortal had resided—existed within its walls before me. Accordingly, there were no sins committed there for which to repent, or ghosts from other people's lives to endure that remained within those walls. A place that didn't know happiness or sadness or anything in-between. But, if the loft was going to know misery, and even the possibility of degrees of joy—it would only know mine. The loft was without history. Without a pulse. Without breath. Without eyes and ears. Without teeth to bite. Certainly, it didn't know death—including that of a human soul. It was a blank canvas.

Its sleek, open contemporary architecture was a desirable aspect. Most of the furnishings from the Midtown house fit within the space illuminated by the forty-foot, floor-to-ceiling windows. A wide balcony looked out toward the Atlanta Falcons Stadium and CNN Center. Off to the far right, the tall columns of Centennial Olympic Park that were lit at night; and part of Midtown and Downtown Atlanta seemed within arm's reach. The lit columns of the park reminded me of Los Angeles International Airport. As if apropos, the Art Deco themed Bank of America Financial Center topped with an open-lattice steel pyramid adorning a beacon of light, was in view—as it was from the backyard of the Seventh Street house.

Once all the boxes, art, and furniture were in but not appointed, I'd spent the equivalent of a week sleeping a good part of the time when I wasn't at the gym. Some mornings, I awakened believing I was still at the house. But instead of a quiet neighborhood, I was living in a denser urban area of old and new construction—concrete and steel.

It would take some time to adjust—transitioning from one environment to another. Dugan would as well.

That first night at the loft, from the living area downstairs, I watched Dugan manage to walk midway up the stairs as if he was warily on a lake of thin ice, then turn around and maneuver down. Likely he was thinking, "I'm having none of this." I resorted to carrying Dugan up and down the open-air concept stairs.

Surprisingly, days later, while lying on the bed reading in the master bedroom suite, I heard his low growl. I looked over. Dugan stood on the top step. He looked at me—seemingly bewildered. I was as well that he'd come all the way up to the second level. If Dugan could speak, I imagine he would ask, "What the fuck am I supposed to do now?" His dilemma reminded me—to my amusement, of how Dugan used to climb on top of the outdoor patio table countless times at Seventh Street by using a chair seat as a step; but he always waited for me to lift him off.

After that, it was clear Dugan had enough of blazing new trails. When he wanted to lie on the bed, or on the lounge in the mezzanine that looked down over the first floor, Dugan would lie at the bottom of the stairs with his head resting on the first one—waiting on me.

I assessed that Dugan was spooked by seeing light through the contemporary open-risers of each stair that made them appear to be floating. That surely, sending his dog-altimeter into panic mode. But Dugan's misadventures didn't stop with the stairs. Although he liked the coolness of the concrete floor on his belly, at times, he had issues walking on the slick surface—difficult for him to always maintain good traction due to his claws.

Even though trimmed regularly at the groomers, the wicks of Dugan's claws were long which limited how closely they could be clipped. If cut too short, the wicks bled and made for one pissed-off dog. So, like the stairs, I usually carried him. Other times, I pushed Dugan from behind while he was lying on his belly or pulled him with his leash that connected to his harness at the chest—Dugan, wagging his tail like it was playtime. I was certain he loved it, because Dugan would often have his leash in his snout while looking at me—at times, that he didn't need to go out to do his business.

Anna continued to work after the move. From watching me carrying Dugan around, she took it upon herself to find a solution to his dilemma with negotiating the slick concrete floors. She researched online and discovered some doggy shoes with traction that greatly helped. But it took three pairs before he stopped chewing them off his paws. Even still, Dugan and I continued to play our sliding games.

Happily, he did seem to like the balcony. I left the tall sliding glass doors open enough for him to freely go out and back in at his leisure. Dugan often spent time sunbathing as he napped, requiring the application of sunblock on his nose and snout. Occasionally, I would catch him curiously peering through the vertical railings at people and cars passing below. I believe the balcony was his favorite part of the loft.

I took my time unpacking. For the good part of a month—both levels of the loft remained full of stacked boxes as if it were a warehouse. But I knew it was important to position everything sooner than later—it's just I didn't feel like it. That hesitation, surely a derivative of the West Coast—possible subconscious to keep most of my belongings boxed. Several times, Anna asked when I was going to seriously unpack.

"It's like a maze in here," she would say.

"I'm working toward it, Anna… I am."

One Wednesday, Anna didn't look very happy. I still hadn't made much progress. I found her walking around the first level with Dugan trailing behind. Anna's hands were firmly on her hips as if she was trying to keep her skirt from slipping down.

"How can I clean the floors with all these boxes everywhere? Am I supposed to dust them as well?" she barked, in a tone fitting of a drill sergeant.

I couldn't resist snickering.

"Oh, so you think I'm being funny."

I playfully shrugged my shoulders and threw Anna some puppy dog eyes, even though I knew it had to be annoying with the boxes everywhere. It was clear she wanted me to get the lead out of my ass but, again, I didn't have my heart into it. And I didn't want to share why; even though I was pretty sure she did. I just didn't want to concern her.

"Oh goodness me," she huffed.

"Okay… okay. I'll unpack one of them."

"Just one? Make it two," Anna commanded.

I smiled.

She looked back at me cross-eyed. That told me, she was half adamant and half messing with me.

"If you don't behave and get this done by next week… then no cookies for you!" she insisted, as if I were a kid.

By the following Wednesday, I'd only unpacked maybe three more boxes. Perhaps, four. Anna kept her promise.

"Well, I'm taking the cookies home," she huffed, while putting the container back into her big cloth carry-all.

I flashed a funny frown, but Anna ignored it and went about her work.

That day, I had to leave for an appointment with my therapist. After the session, I went straight to the gym. By the time I'd returned home, Anna had finished for the day. She left the cookies, and a note that she had taken Dugan out. Even before I left Midtown, Anna had gotten into the habit of looking after Dugan's needs at the times I stayed in bed a good part of the day. Including, coming up to get him and carry Dugan down. But, during those periods, I usually managed to take him out and feed him in the mornings. Then, I would leave him downstairs to wait on Anna's arrival.

By the following week, I still hadn't made much progress with unpacking—sure Anna would scold me like a teacher would an unruly child for not doing my homework. Upon arrival, she let out an exaggerated sigh while shaking her head in more disapproval. Anna rolled her eyes while raising her arms in the air.

"What am I going to do with you?" Anna grumbled, as she handed over the weekly container of cookies.

I smiled and gave her a hug. Then, Anna picked up the list from the counter of extra things I needed her to do.

About to leave for the day, Anna informed: as she had waived her no packing policy, she was doing the same concerning unpacking; and like before, she would bring Timothy over in a few days to take care of it herself. In the process, telling me, "But you're going to pay big."

At that, Anna let out a few huffs as she headed for the door.

"Thanks! You're the best," I called out, as the door closed behind her.

As promised, Anna arrived two days later with Timothy to help unpack the remaining boxes. They were already at the loft when I returned from an early workout. I left it up to Anna to place the contents where she knew I would likely want them—using the old house as a template. It ended up being a two-day job, including finishing the arrangement of the furniture. I did pay big and gave Anna a raise. The loft may have not felt like a home, but it looked like one.

a new year's resolution

Some six months after moving into the loft and floods of kaleidoscopic emotions, another New Year's Eve had rolled around. I'd managed to survive another one-hundred and eighty-something days. The days and nights within reach of a new year, trundled back and forth like a ball caught in a ravine in perpetual motion—much like my life had been over the past three years of back and forth at varying degrees of movement and speed.

Dugan and I were curled up in bed around nine o'clock. As usual, he'd tunneled his way to a warm and comfy spot under the comforter—likely dreaming about the doggy treats in the big glass canister on the kitchen counter, like kids dream about candy in the candy aisle of the grocery store.

That fleeting last night of the year was no more than another random one as far as I was concerned. In fact, I couldn't wait for the hands of the clock to cross over to 12:01 a.m. The gaiety served as only a reminder that it should have meant more to me—certainly, another year still on this earth: the urban carousing of ongoing celebrations in the neighborhood; the shifting clamorous sounds of the popping and bang-bang-banging of firecrackers; the hissing and whistling of skyrockets shooting at a waxing, crescent moon. All stimulating expressions of astonishment on the faces of onlookers as the resulting light show reflected in their eyes and colored their faces, as they exploded miles into the night sky. I just wasn't one of them—one of those countless people.

The hoopla—seemed distant and surreal outside the confines of the loft. Still, there was no escape as the ensuing eruptions of millions of spattering lights passed through the large windows, coloring the walls as well as those faces—a constant shifting of flashing the night. I'd politely declined a few, well-meaning invitations—not willing to fake merriment, but a few bottles of champagne would have been nice. All the same, I was content to just be with Dugan.

While countless numbers of the world's populace filled the streets—by time-zones, cheering on the magical midnight hour wearing glossy, funny colored cardboard hats and blowing paper roll-up party whistles representing untold hopes, dreams, and resolutions for a better, more promising year to come—I waited for my trusty sleeping pills to hush the intermittent noises associated with the bombing of the sky. To abandon and anesthetize all of it. Those sleeping pills—my only lover to bring in the New Year. And of course, Dugan—his body tightly aligned against mine so closely, one would believe he was an appendage.

In the late Sunday morning's brightness of New Year's Day, Dugan literally rooted me somewhat awake as his snout nuzzled my face in the sublime innocence of his sweetness. I, on the other hand, was still caught within the languid retreat of grogginess of a drug-induced hangover. But he wasn't going to leave it at that. As if telling me to get the fuck up, Dugan began licking my face. At that moment, befuddled or not, I told myself, "Nothing mattered but that moment of incorruptible purity with him next to me."

But no matter how much Dugan bathed my face, it would take a while before I was clear-headed. The inevitable result of the continued, open-ended mode of taking more than the prescribed number of sleeping pills as I often did—at times, dangerously enough to possibly induce a coma. I needed to pass through REM sleep into the deeper stage of NREM where dreams and nightmares are uncommon although rarely successful in that quest. As well, I was still very much relying heavily on the medications prescribed by my psychiatrist—searching for an analogous hope that slipped in and out of my mother's fingers during her life. Once caught, holding it tightly until it slipped away again like a bird longing for its own freedom in flight. Still, she awaited its return like an old lost friend—until her last breath. Now, I'd been doing the same.

By that New Year's Day afternoon, the haziness diffused within my head. Dugan and I dressed befitting the nipping weather for a walk in Centennial Olympic Park. He, in a black-and-white plaid fleece sweater with a little hoodie he always shook off his head. I wore a black sweater and plaid scarf to match with Dugan's. We walked the boundary of the twenty-some odd acres, crisscrossing the green space a few times. In the process, an array of people passed us while others wandered different areas of the park—all hopefully enjoying the semi-clear day as I, and surely, Dugan.

We eventually took a rest on the steps overlooking the center-piece of the park, referred to as the Fountain of Rings: five Olympic rings inlaid in the concrete surface shooting streams of water fifteen to thirty feet in the air as if dancers. In summer, kids and adults alike would cool themselves in merrymaking from the heat in the world's largest interactive water fountain.

While seated, I contemplated the twelve months to come—the things I wanted to accomplish despite the flurries of light to darkness, and times of grayness. I wanted to make it a better year than the three before. I also thought about the aged oak in Piedmont Park I would sit under with Dugan at my feet for hours at a time in the stillness of heedful solace—while still in the Seventh Street house. I made a mental note that Dugan and I should visit our old friend again—that oak tree.

I'd retreated into the arms of seclusion—once again, closed my bedroom door to interludes of strayed sex. Predominantly an aftershock of my past reckless behavior. I wouldn't define myself as happy then—cutting in line of okay, but I did feel peaceful a good part of the time. Peaceful enough to travel—take a breather from Atlanta. Six or so weeks apart, Dugan and I spent four days in Charleston at the Belmond Charleston Place—just because. The second trip, a chill week with Darcey in Malibu, two of those days and a night spent in West Hollywood. Although the return to California delighted me, there were mixed emotions of should-have, would-have.

The getaways had been exactly what the doctor ordered—literally, to jump-start a new perspective for the new year. Upon my return, I felt somewhat revived and more clear-headed. I could see a vague aura of contentment in front of me, or so I'd hoped. But, unexpectedly, but not surprisingly, the newness wore thin within a few weeks as the aura—about as long as it takes for the latest model of a car's new smell to wear off once it's driven off the sales lot.

The nightmares picked up speed. No doubt, partly triggered by my encounter with Brent at the gym. They pulled me far back into the past once again. Still, I did what I could to tug forward. I reminded myself at that juncture—in that New Year: I'd survived two attempts on my life; despite failures, I managed to continue to fight the depression and suicidal ideations since Davy—no matter how teetering; that I had outlasted my time locked up there.

Enduring those things and so much before them, I wanted a happy ending—of some sort when in reality, not everyone gets their happy ending. But that didn't mean I wouldn't stop trying even when others had failed no matter how extensively they tried. I don't think anyone wishes to died—rather, it's the emotional pain they want to be beheaded. To be executed.

To obtain it, I knew the road ahead might continue to be long and wide. A maze of more twists and turns to be traveled. More internal battles to fight and truths to make peace with. That is, if I could stay alive long enough to lead me to that happy ending. Perhaps,—a New Year's resolution.

murmurs of old ghosts

I hear their voices calling—louder and louder until they howl my name like running wolves…

Psychiatrists are known to be proponents of concession. Sigmund Freud, Austrian neurologist and founder of psychoanalysis believed the average person spends six years of his or her life dreaming. Those dreams cover a wide spectrum: pleasant experiences offering feelings of calmness and safety; the erotica of sexual encounters; intense blood-curdling nightmares; others, not remembered.

Freud theorized dreams are keys to unlock repressed conflicts, including deeper truths of a person's life that lay hidden—beyond reach in the subconscious. Much like those deeper truths I'd suppressed for years; the very ghosts I'd been running from had finally caught up when I found myself in a massive labyrinth that seemingly had no exit—at most, one I couldn't find.

The dreams and nightmares continued at random over those four years—some even to this day, though I'm far from where it all began. Many awakened me as if on the edge of death looking down into that abyss of nothingness. Wakening me in a heated lather of perspiration, frenzied, and quivering for my life. First, some elusive. Others, fuzzy pictures of places, people, and situations of impaired definition. Rather, arbitrary shards of glass that mirrored a vast landscape of frail truths wrung from bygone events.

Two-plus decades before, those shards had settled into the innermost, darkest alcoves of my mind where they remained dormant—concealed from light that would expose their jaggedly, sharp, and soul-piercing teeth. Once their captive, I was exposed to obscured reflections in their eyes of inflictions and the possible acts I may have performed as a result, as others I was capable of staging—all part of my normal existence. The very occurrences from which I ran—expecting never to face again. Thus, my subconscious permitting only diluted versions that were tolerable—while protecting me from those that hideously weren't. But I somehow have always known—the past is seldom escaped. No disinfected breaks. A portion of its poisoning, sobering grotesqueness remains in the blood such—one day, a staggering price will have to be paid.

At times, the dreams—like dust settling on stacked boxes containing the forgotten belongings of past residents in the attic of an old house—thinned and tapered. Only occasionally, they swirled and broke the surface of consciousness as if from a rapid gust of wind rushing through an infinitesimal space of a window seal. The stay of execution proved to be too good to be true as they grew and matured back into full-fledged nightmares—returning with vengeance. Unrelenting. Barren of mercy. Their intensity paralleled the gaping periods of depression.

The more formidable exasperated that depression and anxiety—reopening suicidal ideations. As much as it was needed, at times, sleep was dreaded. I'd no idea of what might be hungeringly gnawing-down on the other side of my eyelids. I feared the waiting disturbing thoughts and malevolent nightmares would return once I closed my eyes. Both, void of pity. Averse to return to the depths from which they once lay in repose in the chasm of a vacuum.

As before, the dreams pilfered the nights—kept repeating variations of twisted scenarios. Some convoluted and distorted, and inaccurate in miscalculated measure—layering real past events, while mixing confusing faces and places like old home movies reels taken on a vintage 8mm Bell and Howell Zoomatic camera, one superimposed on top of another. Some films had no recognizable meaning to my life while others lay bare underlying truths between the layers of those reels—

undeniable or challenged.

They grew like invasive kudzu taking over an aged cemetery and the surrounding landscape—proliferated into vivid imaginations with splinters and specks of reality. As they collected; the larger those dreams became. Within the expansion, stood what looked like the worst possible of human beings. I awakened depleted. Surrounded by the stench of death. Disoriented. Consumed. Gasping. My mind reached for the present while attempting to run from the pending danger—questioning: if this time, was it too late. If there had been a knife by the bed, I would have plunged it into my heart. It was already bleeding, anyway.

The falling dream I had while at Davy—returned. New ones followed. I'm in a crowded courtroom. Mannequins—hard and plastic. Their faces, painted like carnival performers. Their heads, with lifeless eyes, turned in my direction. Arms raised. Fingers pointed—condemning. Others, wrenched back to childhood featuring my father. A little boy running in the dark—endlessly running deeper into blind nihility.

That same boy, a teenager, covered in blood standing over his father's dead body. Then, with blood still on his hand as he stands in front of the house on Shirley Drive. All of them—thieves of magnanimous sleep. Some mornings, although appearing as, I was unsure if I'd awaken. Unsure if my mind had completely crossed back into the present realm and concrete physical world—severed from the illusory simulations of some virtual reality. My eyes mentally struggled to open. The sense of a powerful, weighty, and hostile presence hovered inches above my body. The energy pinning, inhibiting movement—perhaps, attempting to pull me back into the dreams and nightmares of the other world.

"Get up! Get up and run!" my inner voice screamed, but still the invisible weight held me down.

The voice was imperative that I open my eyes and get out of the bed—to run or be suffocated by the force.

In efforts to elude them: I meditated in bed, repeating over and over that the thieves of sleep would pass, and I would be okay; traveled my mind to places I'd yet to visit; beckoned remembrances of exhilarating times lived to the fullest, and those possibly to come; welcomed loving dreams of my time with Bradley and how he made me feel protected from anything bad. All aided by anxiety and mood stabilizing medications, in ambition to invite life-affirming influences to punctuate sleep—as Dugan lie by my side. But still, those thieves returned night after night. And because I had little success, as my mother had, I turned to increased doses of medications—exceeding what was on the labels of their containers, and the consumption of alcohol. They too failed me as the dreams and nightmares expanded and reproduced.

With the uninvited homecoming of murmuring ghosts, so did Chip's from the early 1980's, as it crept into REM sleep—and me, into its clutches. With the extension of time, after some twenty-nine years, he'd returned from the grave—clawed his way back as if his memory had always been inches beneath the surface of the deception of serene waters.

Like it all happened yesterday, I found myself standing in Chip's apartment—blood everywhere. The questions to be asked are many. Was it just a dream void of realities, or was I being put on trial by his ghost at my most vulnerable for committing what would be viewed as a serious crime? Had my subconscious critically weakened—ruptured by the years of stab wounds that covered every inch of flesh? Had they eventually deteriorated the barrier of defense that once protected me from reality—from another secret? Was I facing my own reckoning—my own damnation?

Once again, I was a young man walking through a deadened, deep cobalt night. I turned the corner of the Armory. My footsteps proceeded toward Sixth Street, paralleling the bar. Strong vibrations of the mesmerizing music reaching far past its walls compelling lost souls to come to dance their troubles away until the sun returned. Others, to delight in merriment and abandon. Both, seeking a sense of freedom. I stopped in my tracks at the sight of Chip leaning against the driver's door of my Alfa Romeo parked on the poorly lit street. He appeared over-served as he attempted to steady his linebacker's body against the car.

Within moments, I was against the car and sealed in the embrace of Chip's brute strength. Passionately enthralled in a protracted, bewitching kiss without struggle or protest on my part as if we were lovers—as if I possessed immeasurable avidity for Chip rather than the indefatigable revulsion, preferring to believe he was dead and not alive. As other times, I awaken in frightened perturbation; the sheets soaked in a lake of sweat as chills splintered my bones.

I sat up in fright. Sweat collared my neck as it rivered down my breastbone and further. My eyes dubiously searched through the naïve, weak light. Hurriedly, I reached to switch on the lamps atop the bedside chests. The resulting introduction of more luminosity extracted the night from the bedroom as it disavowed Chip's ghost back into the darkness of the waylays of my mind.

A fragile reassurance was found once I realized I was in the loft and not the apartment I'd shared with Tom a lifetime ago—further pacified as Dugan rested his snout on my lap; his studying eyes focused up on me. Surely, a restless sleep of body jerks and tossing and turning, stirred from the invasion by Chip's intransigent unforgiving ghost had alarmed my faithful protector. But not even Dugan had the superhero capabilities to safeguard me from the intrusions that possessed sleep or what befell years before. Or could he challenge every ounce of what I'd felt then—that had been resuscitated with Chip's ghost: the oppressive fear, the paranoid worry, hysterical panic, and the ongoing turbulent sickness in my stomach. All of it lay in bed that morning—Dugan and I were far from alone.

Chip's ghost kept assaulting sleep as he once had my body; time hadn't been a buffer. The revisiting imagery of those events, too real. Too threatening. Too exacting.

the haunting

The nightmarish-dreams' invasions persisted in waves—stewards of bashing assaults inflicted on my psyche. If I wasn't already completely entangled within the bowels of madness before—I may as well have been. And if not, they were trawling me through the black muck of yesterday. Each one—raising the heavy red curtains of a stage where I was surrounded by adversaries as they recreated past occurrences while their rotting flesh peeled from their bones. A Shakespearean-like horror-stricken play based on real life where I played the protagonist.

Like home movies recorded on the reels of 8mm celluloid rolls in a vintage Bell and Howell Zoomatic camera and played on an old, pull-up projector screen, one film was superimposed on top of another. Amateur films that captured everything. Every truth. Every horror. Every violation. A documentary made but never intended to be viewed again. My mind took the place of that old movie camera.

Chip would be standing by the bed, looking down at me as he did that night of the first rape. Then, suddenly, he transformed into the image of my father. But instead of abuse, we consensually made love on the cot in the shed. He was the same age when he died—my father, but I was thirteen and not a young man as I was when Chip terrorized my life.

In one reel, my eyes startlingly opened wide. I'm on my back in my parent's bed. A waning sun flagged a beam of light through the double windows. Tiny dust motes floated within the sunbeam as it crossed the room appointed with the French-style furniture that Mother loved. The dancing particles circled and drifted—suspended in the beam that gradually withdrew as the sun made its exit pulling it and the remaining light with it.

Deadness surrounded. The stench decay encapsulated. I looked toward the window. My father lay on his side as if he had also been watching the light drawn back to the outer side of the windows. The back of his head, blown out—gummy like macaroni and cheese that had grayed from being left out on the kitchen counter for days. Blood soaked the sheets—covering my naked body. My father then rolled over to face me. At that, I awakened.

Each night rolled quickly over into the next. Then, the next. The next and the next slipping past daylight. The home movie rolls making that whirring and clicking sound. Blurrily, the film rolls. I'm a boy running down a dirt road in the middle of nowhere. Whir and click. Without any separation of time, I morph forward as if a time traveler to a young man still running. Whir and click. Once more, I'm a boy again. Whir and click. Mr. Jones has a firm hold on my wrists. The weight of his fat, round belly pins me face down—heavily on the grass in his backyard. I'm struggling to break free. Crying. The air is profuse with the nauseating smell of freshly cut grass. Blades of it chokingly clump in my mouth. I can't spit it out. I can't scream. It tastes like broccoli and dirt. It's waxy, like I would imagine that of a green crayon.

Mr. Jones' khaki pants are down around his brown oxford shoes. They dig—his shoes, through the blades of grass down into the dirt as he fucks me in the ass with his small dick. My eyes focus on a large pile of red bricks by his patio. I see my lawn mower. I keep looking—looking at the pile of bricks. Looking and thinking. Wanting Mr.

Jones to stop. Waiting for him to get off of me. The film keeps rolling. Whir and click. Whir and click. Whir and click. Scratches and black spots distort some areas of the film. Whir and click. Whir and click. Whir and click. An image of Mr. Jones falling face-first into the pile. A dead Mr. Jones.

Whir and click. I'm a young man standing over his body holding one of those red bricks. I'm smiling. Whir and click. Whir and click. I'm a boy. It's spring. I'm walking in front of dead Mr. Jones' house. His car is parked under the carport. It's no longer shiny but covered in dust. The yard is unkempt. Grass is at least a foot high. Full of weeds. One of the mower's front wheels squeaked and wobbled over the cracked sidewalk. Whir and click. A hand slightly pulls open the draperies of a front window of the house as if to peek out. Whir and click. I pick up the pace. The toe of my shabby sneakers with worn soles catches a broken section of the concrete. I stumble a bit. I tell myself, "Pay attention. You don't want to fall and bust your head open as Mr. Jones had." I smile again. Whir and click. I directed my eyes forward. Head to the next block. Whir and click.

The nightmarish-dreams serve to push me closer back to suicide—closer to that threshold between life and death where I had stood more than once. As those dreams came and went freely of their own accord, I reassured myself they would eventually pass like the ones I'd had before their return bombardment—that they were the sick part of my subconscious and the guilt of carrying secrets that betrayed me by resurrecting the dead. Whir and click.

At my yearly physical examination with Dr. Thomas, I asked him for a recommendation of a psychiatrist; one who I'd feel comfortable with and not ashamed or judged. I'd stopped therapy at some point before—having been talked-out, being evasive, and just fed up in general; and I'd grown tired of stumbling from bar to bar.

He was quick to recommend a psychiatrist at Northview Mental Health Clinic associated with the Northview hospital just outside I-285 perimeter that circled Atlanta. A Dr. Hortman, who also offered therapy. A two for one doctor.

"Randy, you'll really like her. I'll call Dr. Hortman this afternoon to let her know you'll be making an appointment… and would appreciate if she could see you as soon as possible."

I thanked him as he wrote down her information. But even with the recommendation, it didn't guarantee I would mesh with Dr. Hortman. And in the event, we didn't, I hoped the search would be a quick find and not a long-drawn-out scavenger hunt I'd experienced; and I needed to keep the drugs in a steady flow.

I was able to obtain an appointment with Dr. Hortman without much delay. I brought my five-inch thick, three-snap-ring notebook binder with all my medical records. I found Dr. Hortman, sincere and welcoming

Right off the bat, I felt it was a good fit by the way she greeted me, and the kind tone carried on her voice. Her compassion, apparent in her eyes. After that initial session, Dr. Hortman said it was clear I was in distress—especially after I shared some information concerning the nightmarish-dreams that had relevance to my life. Limited relevance, of course as I fed her. She wanted to get started right away. One session each week to begin with.

After first reviewing my mother's mental history I'd shared, analyzing my depictions of my father, the resulting childhood environment, reading previous psychiatrists' and therapists' notes—most of which she found inconclusive, and many questions from Dr. Hortman during the first three sessions, she surmised my depression had been triggered while I was a kid. But that I didn't know it was depression because happiness was foreign, and because of that I didn't know what it was—what happiness was even though I saw the smiling faces and heard the laughter of other children.

"Your focus as a child was on the welfare of your mother and not yourself. That little boy knew, not only did he have to protect her from his father but from herself... that's a lot for a kid to handle, James. I see that a lot in my profession," Dr. Hortman, explained.

I watched her closely as she continued.

"And I'm certain, you're gravely suffering from other afflictions that were never fully addressed in the past that will have to be analyzed."

Dr. Hortman added, we had started a new journey that we needed to take together to insure a better understanding of my psych.

Over the weeks to follow, Dr. Hortman started out slow as if I was in kindergarten all over again. I started out slow as well, as I fed bits and pieces of a savage start in life and what those years possessed. But most of it was already in that binder on her desk. There were more questions concerning my father's brutality and more addressing my mother's mental illness. And concerning their alcoholism. About his suicide and more—before and after. The more questions about my father's death, the more I sweated. I was growing extremely uncomfortable with each probing question, while still guarding what information I gave and what I held back. Dr. Hortman' questions began to feel like perfectly good teeth were being extracted from my mouth with pliers.

I hung in there as I continued to guard my answers—but felt what I'd imagined a pig would at a barbecue. That is, if the pig knew it was up next for the skewer.

To make it easier on me, I gave her a copy of " Alabama Snow." As I expected, Hortman had many questions about Christopher and the first two suicides—especially the second. Those too in the binder, but she wanted to hear the answers from me. Particularly concerning Christopher, because she believed as I eventually did, he was the trigger that sent that freight train in my direction.

Dr. Hortman earlier addressed childhood traumas that caused me to develop PTSD. A condition I wasn't even aware of having—at least, not by clinical definition. As I shared other events with her that took place years before I met Christopher, she furthered reiterated what was trigger, again, was my PTSD amplified actions—how he coldly and abruptly ended the relationship without closure, added to the cheating; the events surrounding the restraining order; the slanderous lies; the court case; how, as a result, I felt ostracized by my community; among other related factors Christopher brought it to my door.

"It's all about connecting dots, James. As far back as you can remember until ending up in Davy," she conveyed. "It's much like a puzzle, and we need to piece it together," Hortman added.

In the process, as a result of her initial analyses the more she learned about me, Dr. Hortman made changes in my medications—more adjustments.

Hortman wanted to know details about my father's abuse and violence, especially after she'd read "Alabama Snow." She wanted to know about his deemed suicide—but I left deemed out of the description to avoid definition. Eventually, I shared about Mr. Jones and the molestations. About the rapes by Chip as well. But not the outcomes of either, even though she'd asked.

I portioned many things as Hortman patiently listened. Certainly, my love for Bradley and all that surrounded it as well as what beat inside. Dr. Hortman was the only psychiatrist or therapist I had ever talked to about him.

Also sharing, Sandra had told me that while I was coming back to consciousness, I'd called out his name a number of times. And that I began having dreams about us starting in January of 2009, after a long period of only rarely experiencing them. As well, I shared the dream I had about Bradley while locked up at Davy. Dr. Hortman conveyed my concerns were valued about his drinking—certainly, understandable since I lived in a world flooded with alcohol.

I told her I still blamed myself for his death. Hortman felt otherwise, but I insisted I didn't want to debate it. She respected my request. I came clean about the favors I traded with the rich older men when I was younger—basically prostituting himself. And that much of the time, I felt all I had to offer anyone was my outward flesh.

It all made sense to her—the rich men and giving my body because of the sexual abuse I experienced as a boy and that perpetrated by Chip also while a young man. Hortman associated it to a loose form of transference. More, self-objectification, where I viewed myself as an object and not a whole human being of any inner worth.

I revealed my hatred for Christopher to the point of being dangerous. Of how, in some ways, he represented them. But I assured her I had no intentions of acting on any thoughts of harming Christopher—although, a part of me instinctively wanted to. Dr. Hortman seemed to understand why I'd made that correlation with Jones, my father, and with Chip and why I hated all of them.

Of course, she encouraged me to find a way to release my hatred—that she would do what she could to help in our sessions and advised anger management classes. I explained it was an impossibility. That, I'd attended some in the past, but the outcome was unsuccessful. Her knowing that, I sensed she knew forgiveness also was unattainable for me to give. So, Dr. Hortman spared me the lecture of how it was harming me. In truth, it wasn't. As that forgiveness was lost in a void, I felt no need to even forgive myself or carry any guilt—apart from what my mother had to see that September morning.

I came close to breaking down during that particular session. Why, I wasn't completely sure. It could have been for any number of reasons and some I did know—why I wanted to cry. Perhaps, it was because I knew—as with all the other medical professionals, I was lying to Dr. Hortman by omission. It was obvious that she was doing all she could for me—much more than the other had; and I felt bad about spinning her wheels. I did want to tell her everything—tell Dr. Hortman the truth. All of it. She deserved to know.

At the tick of a clock, if ever I felt the need to unburden myself at whatever cost, I did then. Unburden myself of all that I'd kept hidden and for so long; and if not hidden, then withheld to the point of lying—otherwise omission. Only telling part of the story and by doing so, leaving myself out in the cold—so to speak. Therefore, all I could continue to divulge was what had been done to me and not what I'd done to others. Those very things—those acts, that were at the root of my mental destruction—the valuable pieces of the life and death conflicts that encased me.

I grappled within myself—internally, those lies vs those truths came to blows as did the game of smoke and mirrors vs transparency. All the while, well aware that no matter how desperate I was to be free from the monster under my flesh—yet again, out of the need for self-preservation, those truths would have to remain in the dark; patient-doctor confidentiality law wouldn't protect me regardless of how many years ago certain acts had taken place. For that, I would have to go to confession; but I wasn't Catholic and Dr. Hortman wasn't a priest.

My eyes went wet.

"If you need to let it out, James. It's okay," she comforted.

Hortman picked up a box of Kleenex from off her desk.

"No… no, thank you. I'm fine."

I held back as much as I could. I didn't want to cry.

"Okay then."

Dr. Hortman set it back down.

As I walked out of Northview Mental Health Clinic after that late morning session, the rain slowed to a drizzle. The sun broke through the cloud cover as it freed rays of light shimming the sidewalk.

what's in a name

The pleasant blonde receptionist behind the sign-in counter at Northview informed Dr. Hortman was running late. I smiled and took a seat in the discerningly tasteful waiting area with a few other patients. By then, I'd been seeing Dr Hortman for a number of months.

Dugan also had a doctor's appointment—rather, veterinarian for his bi-yearly check-up. I'd planned on rescheduling, but Anna insisted she would take him. Sandra was coming to the loft in the late afternoon to spend a few days. I wasn't up for a visit—more like, a check-in as if she was a home visiting nurse.

While waiting, I contemplated what mental afflictions sat with me as I discreetly eyed those few waiting to see their psychiatrist. Much like those I was locked up at Davy with—each one had their own story regarding what brought them to Northview. But unlike Davy, these patients were upper middle class to affluent with health insurance. However, concerning the latter, I was still paying out of pocket.

We may have had nice addresses, drove nice cars, and money in the bank, but mental illness obviously doesn't discriminate like addictions don't.

My eyes landed on a well-dressed older woman sitting across from me. She nervously fidgeted with her pearl necklace. The 3 carat round diamond platinum ring on her finger was hard to miss.

She looked over at me and offered a lonely smile. I nodded and gingerly smiled back. I could feel her loneliness that dwelled within her being—the isolation she'd wrapped herself within. See into her soulful eyes. It was obvious neither one of us wanted to be in that waiting room; but we were there all the same. Perhaps, she and I were looking for some salvation—some freedom, from our mental afflictions that boxed us within ourselves; and by society. In the accumulating minutes to follow, an astute looking middle-aged man came out to escort the woman back to the offices. I continued to watch until the door closed behind them.

Twenty or so minutes later, Dr. Hortman popped her head into the waiting area looking for me. At eye contact, she waved me back.

"How are you?"

"Fine... thanks. Yourself?"

"It's been a hectic morning. Sorry I kept you waiting."

"No, it's okay."

"I appreciate you understanding."

"Of course."

I followed Dr. Hortman down the long hallway. Large, well-executed equal-sized black and white prints hung on the wall that led to her office—sleek in design. I took my usual spot on the contemporary couch. Hortman shuffled through a stack of folders on her desk and pulled one out. She grabbed a pen. With both, walked toward me and sat down in the modern square club chair to the left of me.

"So, anything new since last week?"

"Pretty much the same. You know, gym, Dugan, Anna being bossy... like my sister. In fact, she's coming later today for the weekend... oh, and thanks for updating Dugan's emotional-support animal papers."

"I was happy to."

"Sometimes I swear Sandra and Anna are in cahoots. They mother over me as if I'm an infant... watching my every move. It's like I have three watch dogs... Dugan, the third," I declared.

"Well, they're just looking out for you. It's good you have them. You need their support."

"You're right."

"You must bring Dugan with you at your next appointment," Hortman said as she smiled.

"Sure, I'll do that. I'd love for you to meet him. Dugan's at the vet right now, getting his six-month checkup. Anna took him for me."

"Great. Are you and Sandra... Dugan of course, going anywhere soon? I think you told me last week you might... that you were thinking about it."

"Maybe... my sister wants to fly somewhere for a long weekend."

"That's definitely a good plan. Getting away will be good for you both."

"Last week, when we were about done, you mentioned that you heard from... Hal, I believe. One of your friends that supported you before and after you were released from Davy."

"Yes, it was a nice surprise. I hadn't talked to him or the others in some time."

"I see."

"Yeah… he just wanted to say hello and tell me about his new boyfriend. Hal told me they are seriously in love. I'm just waiting to hear about the one guy that finally sticks."

"Sticks?"

"The one… so to speak. The one that isn't a stand-in for a serious relationship."

"Explain."

"He'll have a new one in a matter of weeks. Hal always says that they are seriously in love. Each one of them. I'm just waiting to see if he stays with one for more than a few weeks."

Dr. Hortman let out a slim laugh.

"What about the rest of the guys?"

"Well… I don't see them much at all."

"Do you know why?"

"I imagine, they've just moved on from all the drama… mine, of course. Can't really blame them. I know the whole mess affected them negatively."

"How do you feel about that… I mean, the ones you don't hear from much?"

"It's sad. Actually heartbreaking… especially concerning William. And I'm still trying to deal with the whole betrayal of Jay."

I was sure they needed space from the ugly mess and again, drama as I'd conveyed to the doctor. Plus, they had their own lives and problems… and I couldn't expect them to protect me from myself forever. Not anymore. But I remained grateful to them… and even more so, for the love and support they gave Sandra. But Jay was a whole different situation.

Dr. Hortman quickly switched gears as if driving a five-speed race car around a sharp corner. Then, hit the brakes.

"James, as we've discussed a number of times, you've always been the protector… a fighter, beginning from when you were a kid."

"Yes… I know, but like you said, we've already discussed all that."

Repeating the subject, I wanted Dr. Hortman to stop. To stop mulling over what we already had while putting more of her psychoanalytical spin on some of what had taken place.

My ears began ringing. Random thoughts whispered as fear

pumped through my veins. I didn't feel safe—antsy. Once again, I was mentally propelled—suddenly, back to that house; Dr. Hortman's voice switched off. The sunlight in her office retreated out the window until I was left surrounded by darkness. I wanted to run—but where?

"James... James. What's wrong? Are you okay?"

The doctor's voice returned.

"What?"

"Are you okay? she repeated. "You're white as a ghost."

"I do?"

"James?"

"I...sorry. I just had a flashback. Back to Warner Robins."

I felt embarrassed.

"Do you want to stop for today?" she asked.

I thought.

"No. It's okay. I just had another one. You know... we've talked about how they come out of nowhere... I'm find... really."

I lied. I wasn't okay but said I was to try to play down what had just happened. "Please go on to what you were talking about."

"Well, tell me. Are they coming more often?"

"No... no, not really," I lied again.

Dr. Hortman looked concerned. Again, I repeated that I was okay.

Dr. Hortman proceeded to communicate that she only wanted to revisit a few things. I yielded as she pressed the gas pedal but in reverse. And by doing so, it felt as though the tires of that race car were running over me while I laid on the asphalt of a highway.

Although again, I didn't feel it was necessary, Hortman repeated past events as if I were watching a movie many times over about a boy and a villain. A movie casting a scared boy named Randy and his father. A boy who went to great lengths, again, to protect his mother, knowing by doing so—he would be offering himself as a sacrifice to his father's abusive retaliations in hopes of sparing her from much of it. A movie including, about the boy's rising suspicions that his father might abuse his sister; and how he tried to watch over her. I just couldn't tell Dr. Hortman how the movie really ended.

"I know things didn't work out for your mother as you had hoped after all you did... after all you did to try to protect her, even after your father had been dead for many years, and up until the day she died."

"Shit," I thought, as I internally questioned some of those past actions and how they didn't procreate the end result as intended like Dr. Hortman had stated. But her statement served as only a reminder—a trigger, of how I had failed. Triggering the flashback. Then, Dr. Hortman accelerated as if preparing me for test questions for a college final exam.

She detailed: because of all of it, I paid a hefty price. Not only as a result of those childhood violations, but interjected they accrued from lies, broken promises, betrayals, and even disappointments. Including, the promises I'd made to myself—idealistic as they were, that I could fix everything and by doing so, it all would be okay. Even though, again, I didn't want to hear it, I knew she was right.

Dr. Hortman looked down at the open folder.

"Have you seen Jay since that evening at the restaurant?"

"No… and I hope I never see him again."

"You know, James… concerning friendships… they can be a promise, too."

I quickly looked at my watch.

We both were suddenly distracted by a loud voice passing outside her door.

"Hey, hey George… hold up!"

Hortman momentarily waited.

"Speaking of the flashback you just experienced out of so many, I think that razor blade and prescription bottles of pills… as your first attempt, had been waiting for you for a very long time. Before you ever knew who Christopher was… actually, years before he was born."

My mouth gaped open. As other statements, I knew Dr. Hortman was right: ever since I was a young man, I'd been dancing with Death. The room turned cold.

She paused again. Taking a few moments to flip through some pages in the folder.

"I'm actually getting ahead of myself. We'll talk about that in our next session."

The doctor flipped back a page. Jotted down a notation.

"Okay… getting back on track, the stalking order was another betrayal after you were doing it again… protecting someone you cared about. Jay was a betrayal as were other friends who walked away after having known you for years."

Once again, repeating what I'd already given much thought to—certainly, concerning that back-stabbing, Jay.

At that point, my anxiety was drilling through the ceiling. I just couldn't think about what a fool I'd been for being too trusting for my own good. I noticed she looked at the clock on the wall. Then, back at me.

"I'm about to make a correlation that will hopefully shed new light on some things."

Once again, Dr. Hortman paused. Looked around the room as if to give herself more time to accumulate thoughts. I waited. Moved to the edge of the couch and waited. Then, waited some more while trying not to look at my watch again.

"Let me ask you a question. In fact, I have two."

"Okay... sure," I replied, while wondering what was coming next. What was about to exit her lips.

"Do you know why I don't call you, Randy... knowing you prefer people do?"

Now, I'm the one who paused before answering.

"I... I figured it was for professional reasons... most professionals call me by my first name."

Yes, that's true. But if you remember, I stopped calling you Randy after a few sessions with you."

"Yes, I do... that you stopped."

"And I did, because of something that I came to realize."

I waited for the doctor's explanation.

"I call you James, because that's who you need to fully become now and should have been for some time."

My eyes remained on Hortman as she further spoke; her words were caring as she expounded: that in my childhood, at some point I got stuck.

"What do you mean?"

"It's like a part of you stayed that boy. However, you matured in many ways but in others, you didn't."

As confused as I was listening to Dr. Hortman, I tried to get to a point where I understood what she was trying to explain. Eventually, I told her I wasn't getting her point.

"Okay... let me put it this way."

Dr. Hortman started again. She stated: Randy is the one with self-esteem issues. He is the one that doesn't feel worthy. He is the one who is still fighting his father in his head long after he died. And when I'm faced with traumas, Randy sometimes surfaces. But despite all that, James is the one who made lots of things happen for himself with Randy in tow. Despite all my successes and the positive things, I've done in my life, Randy is under my skin telling me otherwise. It's time for Randy to grow up—to mesh with James, as Dr. Hortman put it.

"I don't know, doctor. I think my self-esteem issues and not feeling worthy aren't going to go anywhere… even though I do know better."

"Well, we'll keep working on them in future sessions. They're why it's important that we revisit uncomfortable things… like I just did."

"Okay," I didn't demur.

"Aren't there lots of times that you still feel like that little boy?"

At that question, I understood.

"Yes… there at times. Times that I feel afraid when I have no reason to be. And I still fight those poor self-esteem issues to this day… when I know better."

"We're going to stop for now. But I'll ask you the other question sometime later. I think I've put you through enough for today."

"As I stated early… I didn't want to rehash certain things. But now I understand why it was important."

A light flashed in my head. After that session—I started asking friends to call me James-Randall and introducing myself as such. That version of my name seemed to fit better at that point. I included Randall out of love for my mother, who gave me the middle name so she could call me, Randy. Dr. Hortman had been right as she had been astute. I knew she got me—at least, to certain degrees. The flashing lights persisted.

charcoal-to-black

"Who knows, James… but if you believe Bradley was alive today… you and he would still be together and living in Los Angeles, then that could very well be the case."

I slid my hands under my thighs—sat on them while listening. With just the mention of his name, my mind traveled in reverse. The past became the present. Instead of years, only seconds had passed—like walking back into a room after just having walked out. My heart felt as if it was blistering.

"James… "

The doctor's voice returned me to the present. I wiped a tear from my cheek. Then, another one fell.

"Are you okay?"

"Yes… fine. I'm fine."

But I wasn't—I wasn't, okay.

"We never know where the twists and turns in life will take us," Dr. Hortman caringly said.

"Yes. I… I of all people know it can flip in a mere second if that—even stop dead-cold. But if Bradley and I remained healthy and from harm's way… yes, I know we would."

My eyes closed. Quiet tears seeped under their lids. Seeped, for what should have been.

I was tempted to reach for a tissue from the box on the side table next to the couch. The box, that every psychiatrist and therapist have in their offices. The, cry me a river box of tissues; but I didn't. I swept the tears away as I removed my hands to look at Dr. Hortman.

"But it's my fault. It's my fault we're not together. It's my fault he's dead. It's my fault that I'm so pathetic!"

Dr. Hortman remained quiet as she jotted down another note in my folder before speaking.

"It's not your fault, James. It's not. And you're not pathetic. You're human."

I didn't respond right away. Instead, turned my head to look out the window watching random people walking in undetermined directions—at least to me. Then turned to look at Hortman. I kept placing the blame on myself. My fault, I couldn't protect my mother and sister from my father. I'd earlier told Dr. Hortman that he did eventually get to her. That, Sandra had called from Germany to tell me. I also eventually told Dr. Hortman what my father had made me do in the shed. I went on—placing more blame on my shoulders .

"You can't keep beating yourself up for things that were out of your control."

Silence flooded the office. I glanced back out the window. My heart was beating as if it was about to explode.

"No… it's my fault… certainly, concerning my sister. I could have stopped my father sooner."

"Stopped how?" she asked.

I could feel myself spiraling as I could that rage.

"It's… it's my fault that I waited too long. Waited until the last minute before I… I."

"I what, James?"

At that, I realized I couldn't finish that sentence.

"Nothing. It's nothing… "

Once again, my mind drifted—transporting me to that late afternoon of July 4, 2009. Instead of being in the bathtub, I was a spectator standing in the doorway of the master bathroom: a hand holding a razor blade; it, slashing through flesh; the water turning red.

"James… did I lose you, again? You seem to be a million miles away… and struggling."

Once again, Dr. Hortman's voice retrieved me from the past.

"I… I was thinking about July 4, 2009. The memory came out of nowhere… seeing myself in the bathtub."

"Why do you think you revisited it?"

I rubbed my forehead with my right hand.

"I guess from talking about all that I feel was my fault."

I communicated: I guess it was because, earlier in the session I'd brought up Bradley—if only momentarily. Then an image of Christopher's face unexpectedly wedged between us. It made me think about how so many people believed I tried to kill myself because he left me; and I even may have thought that myself at the time. Even publicly said: Christopher was the love of my life; as I'd written in, "Alabama Snow" but admittedly, I was so messed up in the head. All sorts of memories of life events seemed to be rushing at me both night and day. In dreams and nightmares, too.

Furthermore expressing: Christopher wasn't the reason or was he the love of my life. That I regretted the statement and was humiliated because of it. That, I wanted to vomit every time I thought about stating such and even him. That maybe I should run to the restroom and up-chuck in a toilet, so I don't mess up the beautiful carpet in her office.

It'll always be out there. I could have another addition printed and revise my thought process at the time. Still, there's so many books out there; and even if it were to have a second edition, I don't think it would make any difference.

The quiet transitorily returned.

"Remember last week when I told you I was getting ahead of myself?"

"Yes… I believe so."

"About how I thought you might have been on a path toward committing suicide years before?"

I listened.

"Yes, you did let Christopher into your life. But it's not like he is a child."

Dr. Hortman continued, conveying that as she understood it: I had no initial thoughts concerning him other than being there for another person after he reached out to me about something I'd shared in my first book. Once again, I was doing what came second nature; helping others. And after a number of emails, we met but it was Christopher who fueled anything more.

"But… "

"No buts, James. Yes, it was you who decided to stay. The rest is on him."

"I still have to take responsibility for believing I had strong feelings for Christopher that grew over a short period of time. Then, I foolishly bought his story of how he was in love with me… resulting in allowing him into my life."

"Yes, we basically have agreed on that."

Hortman dove deeper by stating: obviously, none of us have a crystal ball and we don't always make the right decisions. Many as a result of outside factors and-or beliefs. Moreover, articulating: although, having not analyzed him as a patient, she thought from what all I'd shared concerning Christopher, there was a thin line between narcissistic personality disorder and sociopathy. That, he likely wanted everyone to think I was a stalker to save the embarrassment of being publicly under the influence of alcohol and possibly drugs, by putting a negative focus on me when I tried to step in to help him. And Christopher used what I had said: about him being the love of my life against me. Then, not much later, the public knowledge of my suicide attempt also played a huge role in giving more credence to that I was mental—of which I already knew it had.

"Christopher doesn't have the ability to feel empathy and remorse. He is manipulative. He's aware of those flaws but hides them. He's only out to get what he wants… and no doubt, you were a target. He saw an attractive older man with a good life. A nice home and two nice cars and equated them to money. You proved that by being so generous."

"By far, Christoper was the biggest mistake of my life. I almost have to laugh," I smiled.

"Why is that?"

"Just the correlation between… the love of my life and the biggest mistake… at this point, it just seems funny. Do you see what I mean?"

"I do. Also, he was out to get revenge for you mentioning the warts."

"I know… and I do understand the need for revenge."

"Have you ever put two and two together… I mean, seen the connection between you staying for Christopher and how you've always had a strong need to be loved?"

"I do now."

Since I brought up the suicide and Christopher, Dr. Hortman wanted to talk more about the subject minus him.

"As you know, we'd spent some time talking about the first and the second suicide attempts. What I want to know, is if you've had other thoughts of hurting yourself at any period before 2009."

My thoughts momentarily hovered before deciding not to. Not to answer the question directly or otherwise. I didn't want to go there. But then, I changed my mind and told her I had. Told Dr. Hortman, about the wavering thoughts of crashing my car that had started in college and continued for a few years later. And then those, after Bradley was gone.

"Did you ever get close?" she asked, while looking at me with probing and gaping eyes.

"Once… maybe twice."

Hortman made another note in my folder. I was glad that she didn't ask for details.

"Let's talk some more about your father's then."

"Must we?"

"I think it's important… certainly, due to the circumstances of how he died."

Dr. Hortman brought up the research on the probability of the increased risk for someone to have suicidal thoughts and actually act on them, if a family member ends their life in such a way. But that didn't mean it happens in every family.

"It's a complex interaction of genetics and environmental factors, James."

I confessed I'd fantasized about killing him. I'd used the word fantasized, because I didn't want her to think I was really serious or that I was capable. I felt telling her would raise some concerns.

"I'm sure I told you I was happy that day. I found great relief in knowing my father was dead… but my heart was torn up for my mother."

"I understand… with all I know about your childhood, I do believe your attempts really had very little to do with what your father did. Although I believed they were connected to what you experienced as a child and as a young man."

I did convey that I wasn't sure, due to my childhood, who the real Randy was. As I've stated a number of times, I was always playing a part. One role or another. Not only to attempt to protect myself and hide truths, but also who I thought people wanted me to be.

"Does that also have to do with the prostitution?" Hortman boldly inquired.

Although I'd shared certain aspects of that life, the question caught me off guard.

"It sounds so cheap and sorted. I mean… that's how I felt at times. And, yes, I was playing a role."

"You know, James… a number of children who are sexually molested end up in the sex trades… similarly, children who are battered may get involved in an adult relationship where the woman and even some men are abused by their partner."

"I didn't go looking for it… I mean, these sexual arrangements with older men. They always approached me… but admittedly, it got to a point that I put out signals. Like being overly flirtatious or occasionally glancing and smiling at them. I sometimes could tell by the way they carried themselves and the clothes they wore… certainly, the car they drove. But mostly, how they looked at me as if I had a sixth sense about it."

"So, you got to the point you were quite perceptive."

"In the beginning, it was awkward for me. But I quickly learned not to have sex with them right away. I took it slow. Made them really want me in their beds. They had to ask me to have dinner… more than one time… and depending on what restaurants they took me to, I knew. But still, I wasn't going to let them bed me in exchange for a meal."

I'd shared an early experience when I started going to gay dance clubs in Atlanta. One Friday night at the Pharr Library—a rather small club was always packed on Friday nights. It got the name, because most of the walls in the club were cover—floor-to-ceils with shelves filled with books.

I was standing among the crowd. Despite the loud music, I was close enough to overhear a guy I'd only met once tell his friend who was looking at me and showing interest, that he couldn't afford me.

"At that time and before I met Bradley, I had an arrangement with an older man, but we never went out in public… and… there was no way he could have known."

"Quickly getting back to your father… again, from what you're told me, it's obvious that he was deeply troubled."

Dr. Hortman extended: she would imagine that since I knew very little about my father's childhood other than his mother was unwed when he was born, there's no way of knowing what his childhood was like. But there was always the possibility it could have been abusive as well. And if that were the case, as some children who are abused, they grow up to be abusers. Touching on the fact that he was in two wars, my father likely had PTSD. She further verbally illustrated: back then, in the military culture with an expectation of masculinity, it was called: man up and get over it. Unless it results in suicide, if gone untreated, it can last a lifetime. One of many symptoms, is intense explosive anger.

"Clearly, you have it as I'm sure your sister does. Undoubtedly, so did your mother. Surely, so does your older brother but his way of dealing with that childhood is by walking away."

"I've always thought that… but still, it wasn't right concerning

Stephen."

Over the sessions to follow and as the nightmares and twisted dreams continued, I remained reluctant to share much more. Doing all I could to keep the buoy above the waterline in order to navigate me away from those dangerous truths. Again, preferring Dr. Hortman to use that binder as a reference book of study. Plus, again, I'd grown wacked from telling so much like the constant rerun of a movie. Once again revealing viciousness and vulgar details with them—most in the binder as well.

And of course, I had to keep on my toes concerning all that I'd kept hidden from the résumé of the other psychiatrist and therapist. Plus, I was too apprehensive to give the impression I was undeniably sicker than they believed. Feasibly, not acknowledging—even to myself, the slope had become steeper with each dream until it was too steep to climb back up. Inch-by-inch, leading me closer—closer to Hell. With each revisit of the old ghosts, the more I slid downward until I could see the gates open to welcome me as if a vacationing lodger.

Dr. Hortman labeled them as by-products of my PTSD and prescribed prazosin. Among others, she wanted to do Image Rehearsal Therapy (IRT). I was threatened by her suggested course of therapies. Convincingly, I managed to put her off—expressing hesitance to face the nightmares in the daylight any more than I had and preferred to give the prazosin a chance. Disappointingly, the medication had no effect. It may as well have been a placebo. Growing more concerned, Hortman continued to pressure me. I remained unwilling to engage in any form of therapy I couldn't control, or that would dig deeper into my psyche. At all costs, I had to protect myself from reliving too much, and therefore, risking full disclosure—thus exposing myself. As a safeguard, I proclaimed the nightmares had become less frequent—when in fact, they were increasingly mounting and equally disturbing.

At their pinnacle, Christopher re-entered. The dreams and nightmares of 2011 grew more massive like a huge ball of smoke and flames. A young man running out of a firestorm, with my father, Mr. Jones, Chip, and Christopher in ruthless pursuit.

Resisting sleep, my nights were spent watching movies with Dugan into the uncertain hours of night. Besides the great comfort he offered, staying awake was a precautionary measure for self-preservation from the onslaught of the ghosts that hovered—waiting to release the dreams and nightmares profuse with muddled realities and phantasms.

Once sleep became too overpowering, they laid beside me with their chilling demonist dreams and nightmares: Christopher and I lay on the cot in the shed; we danced at Backstreet, years before he was born; he and Chip had sex, as they did with my father and Mr. Jones while I watched standing naked and covered in blood. Again, reels of film playing on top of each other. Again, all seemingly taking on a life of their own. In most of them, at some point, I was holding a razor blade to my hand. Whir and click.

masters of the night

The most sinister of the merging dreams and nightmares raged on—repeating various iterations and returning like boomerangs. Each version—more fearsome than its predecessor. Whirl and click. Once again, the light had been ripped from the sky. Late in the decaying hours, the specters—masters of the night, came out to play their evil games. Although not close enough to reveal their ghoulish faces, I knew them as their silhouettes walked and leaped around looking for prey. The air: hot and muggy. Thick. Inhibiting. Ominous. The increasing dreams layered as others had. Many—like watching old, silent black-and-white movies where the images shimmied because the perforations in the rolls of film slackly fit into the sprocket holes of the projector.

I lagged in measured paces as I hesitantly followed Chip up the two flights of stairs of the six-unit apartment building in North Midtown—my hands tucked deeply in the jeans' pockets. With each one—each step upward, was a step closer to discovering now the dynamics of this segment would twist and distort into a horrifying finale.

At the front door, he fumbled with the key to unlock it. The glass globe light overhead was noticeably cracked as if someone had thrown a rock at it from below. In the dream, we had been out heedlessly dancing at the Cove—the crime scene of the second rape.

I stood in the center of Chip's living room. The light—grainy.

Shades of charcoal-to-black. Fuggy. The apartment smelled like ass and dirty socks. No doubt, ground zero for fucking—lots of it.

Sweat poured from my forehead as if fostered by a toxic fever. Within labored breaths, abruptly, the space detonated sporadic glaring light: dark to white to white to dark. A pizza box lay open on the floor; a single slice was left partly eaten. It appeared to be pepperoni with extra cheese. Empty beer cans and bottles littered the coffee table. Others scattered the room as if left where the last bit of alcohol was swallowed.

My mind spun. Thoughts circled. My eyes blurred—like riding a playground merry-go-round. My hands remained in my pockets as before. Chip took a firm grab of my ass as he walked past me toward the television. He inserted a porn tape. Straightaway, the room filled with thumping music and the moans and long, panting breaths from men pleasuring one another. From there, Chip made his way in the direction of the sofa—likely sourced from the Salvation Army. He turned around. Chip's smoky bar, bloodshot eyes scoped me. Whirl and click.

He stripped off a red, tattered, Georgia Bulldog T-shirt—a white cartoon bulldog mascot wearing a sweatshirt with the letter G printed in the center. Chip tossed it at me. But missed. Seconds later, he picked up a half-empty bottle of beer from the coffee table and gulped the remainder—surely, hours warm. Some dribbled onto his massive chest and down his stomach. As Chip set it back down, the bottle wobbled before it rolled off the table onto the floor. My eyes followed it until a wall stopped it.

"Let's play. Don't you want to play, Randy? Just like we've been doing?" his words sloshed, as he plopped down on the sofa.

Trepidation chased. The need to run to the door pried at my legs. Shaking, they remained.

"Come here!" Chip demanded. "Come here and sit on my lap."

The frame froze; Moments later, it jiggled. The dream continued. Whirl and click.

"Don't make me come get you," he threatened.

Chip stood. Unsnapped his Levi's. Pushed them down over ample legs to the floor. He'd gone commando. No doubt, to be sure everyone could see the protuberance of his cock while at the bar—an advertisement. Chip sat back down. Spread his thighs. A rock-hard cock for a drunk profusely seeped precum.

"Ran… Randy. Come on, pretty boy. I… I've something you want, and it wants you."

I still can't move.

"Goddammit! Come the fuck here!" he yelled, stroking his rod while grinning with pride.

I manage to take a few steps toward him as if pulled by an invisible rope. I stopped. The frame jiggled to my father sitting on the sofa. Whirl and click.

"Come… come on," he slurred. "You don't want to make me mad. You know what happens when I get mad."

I stepped closer. Whirl and click. Chip jiggled back into the frame. He pulled me down until my knees met the floor.

"That's a good boy. Now… raise your arms."

I did. Chip yanked my shirt upward until I was bare-chested.

"Stand up. Ta… take off your jeans and under… underwear."

I bent over to untie my Adidas. Kicked them toward the front door. I don't know why, I just did. Perhaps, it was instinctive—mechanical. Then, reluctantly, unbuttoned and unzipped my jeans.

"Hurry up, dammit!" he yelled.

I pushed my jeans along with the underwear to the floor. Stepped out of them. I quickly grabbed my shirt from the sofa and threw the jeans and underwear with it in the direction of the door. At the time, I didn't know why—I just did, again, instinctively. Without forethought. Mechanically.

Chip pulled me down to my knees again. Locked me in place with his massive, tree-logged size thighs like a vise at my waist. He reached for my nipples. Twisted both with his fingers. My teeth clenched. My eyes teared.

"Stop. STOP! It hurts."

"Awe… you can take it," he slurred.

Like with my father, I couldn't. I couldn't take it anymore. None of it. My eyes continued to water from the savagery of the pain, and more so—what I quaked was to follow. I attempted to pull away, but Chip's thighs still impeded any resistance. The tears rolled down my cheeks. The tears—as before, pleasured Chip as they had my father. I'm certain years later, my mislaid heartbreak had done the same for Christopher. Any pain given was their gratification. The more tears that fell, the harder Chip pinched and twisted my nipples until they bled from the friction. Constantly, he pinched and twisted... pinched and twisted.

"Su... suck it. You know you want my cock down your throat. Go on. Suck it."

They were similar words my father had barked with such ugliness and hatred as he stood in front of me. Chip shape-shifted back to my father. Those two words—sissy boy, triggered a terror-within-a-terror flashback. I followed his orders as I'd done the same for my father. The film jerked back to Chip. Whirl and click. He pushed my head down with one hand—directing his penis with the other while forcing it into my mouth. Deeper he pushed. The corners of my lips felt as if they would tear. I gagged for air—chokingly. To fight, I steadied my hands on top of Chip's thighs to push away. The effort, pointless. He was too strong. I grew weaker from the lack of oxygen.

My gag reflex set in; I wanted to vomit. The retching noises came rapidly. I pounded my fists on Chip's thighs trying to get him to stop while, again, attempting to push myself up off my knees. The mass accumulation of his body sweat made it impossible as the slippery flesh prevented any purchase. My struggles only goaded him to apply more pressure—exhausted more of my strength. Chip's cock corked my esophagus, blocking a fiery vomit of fermented stomach contents and caustic gastric acid. Any ability to breathe was fully compromised. Dizziness set in. Chip's laughter faded; the light in the room became dimmer. I knew I'd pass out within a minute, perhaps seconds. I had to do something or die.

In a last-ditch effort, I took what energy was left and bit down on his cock. Chip yelled out, "What the fuck!" as he pulled my head back by the hair.

"Let go... you little cunt!"

Chip wedged his fingers into my mouth, tearing at the flesh of the corners more. I stopped biting down—my strength diminished. Chip scraped his dick out between my teeth and lips. I tasted my blood from the splits on my lips. Finally, I could breathe. I rolled over on the floor as I gasped for more air. Chip grabbed my hair again; he pulled me up to my feet as he stood.

"You motherfucking bitch boy," he degraded.

Chip forcefully backhanded me across the face. I fell back down to the floor. Whirl and click.

"I… I need some water."

Chip pushed me in the direction of the open kitchen area behind the sofa. I stumbled. Looked back. He had sat back down. Whirl and click.

I stood unclothed at the dirty sink. Food-grimed dishes with utensils were stacked around and in it. My mouth and throat hurt like fire. One hand steadied me as the other reached for a glass on a shelf. My body quivered. My hand shook as it filled with tap water—more spilled back out over the rim than stayed in the glass. I was unhinged—a door ripped totally from its frame. I sat the glass of water on the counter without taking a sip. Looked back at Chip still sitting on the sofa that partitioned the kitchen from the living area. Looked at the back of his head. His huge neck and broad shoulders. Whirl and click.

"Get back over here, sweetie!" he mocked.

My movements slowed. The images clicked frame-by-frame-by-frame. I turn around. Chip still faced forward. My mind started spilling again. I pulled at a drawer knob. The drawer creaked as it lagged open. I looked back to see if the sound had alarmed Chip. It hadn't. Another image: a kitchen knife in my hand—anger had tightened my fingers around it. Next image: cat-like, I walked toward the back of the sofa. Next image: I stood behind him with the knife at my side. Chip's right hand gripped the base of his dick. Repeatedly, he slapped it against his abs. Slap. Slap. Slap. Whirl and click. I'm seventeen again. I'm seventeen standing behind the same sofa. Standing behind Chip sitting on it. Still facing forward while he's calling me.

"Randy. Randy. Randy. Randy… come here."

The images to follow were like a Shakespearean tragedy. Like it was all too real. It felt as such in the dream. As if it happened that night. Perhaps, it did. The fire quickly raged through my body—flaming with intensity. Scorching. Blistering. Demanding. My fingers clutched the knife as if programmed to kill. I raised my arm. With one quick unemotional thrust, I plunged it into Chip's bare chest—delivered from behind.

The frames moved faster until one froze again. Whirl and click. Chip let out a breathless, muted yelp. He attempted to get up but couldn't.

A strenuous inhalation of air followed. A gurgle. The reel began rolling in hyper-motion. I plunged the knife a second time. Then, a third. A fourth. A fifth. With each, the squishy wet sound of blood. The smell flooded my lungs as it did that day of my father's demise—pungent in the air with that of sweet charcoal smoke and that of sulfur. It covers my hand and arm—Chip's blood.

Another reel started. I'm on my knees in the living room of the house on Shirley Drive; I'm cleaning the deep-green carpet soaked in blood—the color of darkened red wine, with a large sponge and scrub bush. I repeatedly wring the sponge into a bucket. The bloody water is filled with pieces of flesh and hair. The armrest of the sofa is red as well—the blood caught in the weave of the upholstery. The wall behind me, streaked in red. Everything is red.

The frame skipped. Whirl and click. I'm back in Chip's apartment. The knife is gripped even tighter in my hand. I've lost count—the number of stabs. The blood slowed spurting in pulses out of Chip onto the sofa and floor. I walked around for a better look. I stared at him. Waited for Chip to move. Expecting him to open his eyes. To move at any second. But he didn't. Chip didn't move. His chin rested on his bloodied chest. Arms to his sides. Motionless. Lifeless. Quiet. The bloody knife still clutched in my hand. Whirl and click.

I guardedly walked toward the front door. Pick up Chip's T-shirt he'd tossed at me earlier. It appears clean, untouched by the blood. Whirl and click. I'm back at the kitchen sink. The knife, still in one hand. The T-shirt in the other. The knife dropped in the sink. The metal clanked. I reach for the glass of water with my bloody hand. I drank what water was in it as if trying to put out a fire in my belly. Finished, I washed the glass and the knife. I wiped down the counter using the shirt before I wrapped the knife in it.

The frames shift. Whirl and click. They stop. I feel locked in time. Waiting. The projector started up again. I'm back standing near the front door of the apartment. Gathered my clothes while looking at Chip's big, lifeless body. It all felt so normal—familiar. Chip didn't look so scary anymore. I lay the shirt-wrapped weapon on the floor. I dressed. Take back possession of the wrapped knife—aware it's evidence of a crime. My feet arrested a few more steps. At the front door, both my hands held the wrapped knife; I reached for the knob with the tail of the T-shirt. I turn it. Opened the door slightly. Looked back just to assure he is dead—that Chip is dead as I'd possibly done the same, in another place and time.

Whirl and click. A quick flash of light blinded me. Seconds passed. At that, I'm not in Chip's apartment. I'm standing inside the front door of the living room of the house on Shirley Drive, but I'm not seventeen. I'm in my early twenties. My father's body is on the sofa. I felt nothing. Just empty, like I'm dead too. Dead like Chip and my father. The light flashed again. I raised my hand to defuse it. Whirl and click.

I'm standing outside under the broken light. Disembodied voices scurried down the street. Elongated, eerie, and malformed shadows passed under streetlights until they disappeared further down and around a corner. It's the demons—soulless creatures—in search of shelter before the sun comes back around. Within the hour, its faint glow will start to hallow the city. All that remained was the silence as I continued to stand under the broken light. Whirl and click.

I'm at the bottom of the stairs. I followed the sidewalk—each footstep precise as the one before. My white Adidas filled the frame. They picked up their pace. Several blocks away, the images slowed. I stopped. The T-shirt wrapping the knife fell like a feather into a storm drain. The air around me is thick and heavy. I'm thick and heavy. I notice a single drop of blood on the top of my right shoe. Whirl and click. My tongue licked my thumb to wet it. I leaned down to wipe the blood off. The approaching new daylight started to shatter the night. Whirl and click. I'm driving my Alfa Romeo. In the frame to follow, I parked the car in an open space close to my apartment. Whirl and click. I woke in my bed. I'm still dressed in the same clothes as the night before. My right hand and arm, still covered in blood. The sheets—stained red. Whirl and click.

a ticket to ride

I arrived at a merciful stretch. The malformed dreams and nightmares decreased. And with the dulling of their canine teeth, the depressive periods did as well. The patchier, the more I experienced a resurgence. An intramural strength, I once possessed within, pushed upward. I was hopeful the roller coaster's bearings were wearing out—soon bringing the long ride to an end and its last run over the amusement park after some three years. Hopefully, I could finally step off. Stop entertaining the ideation of crossing death's threshold one day, while stepping back into life the next.

I felt my state of mind was much healthier after additional adjustments of medications and Dr. Hortman' continued guidance and sustaining care in my well-being; helping me feel like a person and not a number with emotional issues. And for the umpteenth time: not sit there and "realize what a very bad thing" I'd done.

Months later—soberingly I was jolted out of sleep soaking in the sweat of dejection. Shaking like a tree branch in a windstorm just moments from snapping at the next pummeling gust. The sensation of wretched torments of death, accompanied with the alpine anxiety of desperation, surrounded me. The dreams and nightmares returned as if only having given me an ephemeral pardoning—long enough for them to reload. Unyielding. Problematic. Feral. Assassins. Quick invasions, rapaciously taking custody while leaving few nights unsoiled by their animus as if fired from rocket launchers. At their core, more recurring, unwanted thoughts, and remembrances. The more they reinterred the hours, the longer the periods of depression left me impuissant. Mornings were erratic as I raced for my medications. Once again, days stood bedeviled—uninhabited without purpose. The suicidal ideations ascended to plague at my resolve to stay alive.

During periodic visits to the loft, Sandra concernedly apprised how she often heard me frightfully talking and mumbling loudly in my sleep—ample in deposit to wake her in the first floor's guest room. Sandra shared how she would race up the stairs, to find me thrashing in bed as if fighting a formidable adversary. By her account, Dugan would be standing on the bed watching as well. When he saw her, he would jump off and scurry to her.

Reluctant to wake me but wanting to at the same time—Sandra conveyed how she would sit on the top stair with Dugan beside her. Watch, until I seem to settle down. Then, motion for Dugan to return to bed as she would to the guest room. My emotional immune system had already been greatly challenged enough—I knew I was facing another internal battle like the one leading up to early July of 2009. I knew this period was fucking serious. The truth be told, my birth certificate was more of a-ticket-to-ride than anything else—the last station closing in.

This new series of dreams and nightmares vividly continued—still baselining actual events. More layering. As real as life itself as the ones before. Mind-warping. Fucked-up. As if I was constantly being pulled back in time. As if my skull had split open and spilled them out—the events. Whirl and click. I walked into the living room. The disagreeably dank smell, repulsive. Forbidding. The light, monotone. Dim. Ashy. Just like it was. Instead of my father, it was Christopher who lay on the sofa with the barrel of the rifle on his chest. The muzzle, in his mouth. His finger on the trigger. I looked at my left hand. Turn it over. See the burn marks. Christopher's face looked in my direction. His eyes wide open. They grotesquely jetted at me.

Inside a captured breath, the sound of the rifle reverberated like an atomic bomb. It shook the house like an earthquake. Clumps of Christopher's hair, pieces of skin, and brain matter covered the sofa and carpet. Blood splattered the wall like a Jackson Pollock abstract. The odor of blood fumigated the living room like Raid roach killer. Yes, that fucked-up. But he was still alive as Christopher stood and walked toward me—as if right out of a script from an episode of American Horror Story. Face-to-face, he opened his mouth. His snake-like tongue licked my face. The enormity of it awakened me. Clearly, the nightmares were not going to retreat as before. Rather, reside in my head like a messy house guest that had overstayed their welcome—moved-in without asking my permission.

Mental terrorists planted landmines in my brain. Whirl and click. I stood at the podium—white-knuckled the edges. My back to the crowded courtroom of the Superior Court of Fulton County. The surroundings, fuzzy as if looking through Vaseline smeared glass. My vocal cords strained for speech to defend myself against Christopher's accusations. Without success, nothing exited my mouth—as if a mute.

A larger-than-life judge loomed high over the bench pointing her finger and laughing hysterically. With blood-red eyes, Christopher, his sister, and brother-in-law joined in. The bailiff did the same. Behind me, the body of onlookers in the courtroom stood pointing fingers and laughed as well. Terrie, too. All of them, exaggeratedly leaned forward and pointed while they laughed—an eerie convulsion of howling. Like oversized, freakish, characters from the Alice in Wonderland storybook on crack cocaine. I—Alice, looking for the exit from the rabbit hole. The combined laughter, deafening.

In the nightmare, I fell onto my knees. Covered my ears. Shouted for everyone to stop. Upon awakening, my heart soared to escape my chest as if about to go into cardiac arrest. Vanquished by their unhindered persistence, over a short span of time, I ingested sleeping pill after sleeping pill—dangerously so, not to end it but in hopes of quickly passing through REM sleep into the deep stage of NREM, where dreams and nightmares are uncommon. I wasn't successful.

For a short time, I kept them to myself. The same, concerning the return of the bout of depression that continued its incline on the backs of those night-time specters. I remained certain they were still coming for me. I feared the loss of myself all over again. I could feel them—their dominance taking territory of my mind.

I'd questioned why I was having thoughts of Christopher again—even in the maze of those malformed dreams? Months would pass without a single brainwave dedicated to him. That was, until I spotted him at LA Fitness on Spring Street, some days before I had the nightmare about him taking the place of my father. Two more followed closely—nights apart.

Realizing seeing him again had triggered them, I adjusted my workouts to mid-morning or early afternoons. The weekends remained a crapshoot. I just wanted to be free of him—never lay eyes on Christopher again. I found it bitingly contradictory; he told the judge that day in court he was afraid of me. So, the sight of me at the Spring Street gym location should have sent him running out the doors as if running from a fire. Instead, Christopher kept coming back.

As I'd spent months planning my father's end, I lay awake in the seeping darkness of mind thinking about Christopher's. About how he would die one day. Whirl and click. Caught in the clutches of another nightmarish-dream, I was raddled awake back from the depths of the unknown as blood gushed from Christopher's throat in a crowded LA Fitness.

The more often the sleeping hours were ravished relentlessly by their force, the realism and intensity widened and lengthened as if dreaming through a magnifying glass. After weeks of waking in cold, dank, sweats—in limited degrees of acuteness, I confided in Hortman the dreams and nightmares had returned. I had to find the off button. I needed her to stop them from returning and by doing so, keep the monster in me dormant.

I'd already shared meeting Brent at the gym when he referred to me as a crazy stalker—as I did of Christopher's repeated appearances. But I didn't, concerning the performance in the congested gym. Only that he was standing in the living room of the house on Shirley Drive when having a nightmare about my father's death.

Dr. Hortman' professional assessment: the nightmares were night terrors. She believed Brent's statement was another resulting humiliation aiding in egging them on, triggering my PTSD from childhood traumas. Dr. Hortman was also certain, the blatant exhibition of Christopher's narcissism—showing up at the Spring Street gym location had rooted his appearance in the night terrors. I was diagnosed with another disorder to add to my résumé: Parasomnia, the abnormal behavior of the nervous system while sleeping. Dr. Hortman also assessed—as I was already aware being in the middle of it, my past and present and the in-betweens were colliding. She believed my childhood and those two years with Christopher were mangled in my subconscious; adding, the night terrors might be my subconscious working at resolving the conflict in my mind. Unquestionably, a war raging in my brain. But I knew her assessments were incomplete because I left out the most important and damning part.

In addition, Hortman believed the night terrors were also taking place because I'd never made Christopher pay for what he did—never held him accountable for his illegal corrupt, false accusations that I was a stalker and violent toward him. Plus, spreading his lies around that set fire to my character and reputation. I'd let him get away with it all—again, basically murdering my standing in the community. Fundamentally, I'd rolled over and played dead. Stalking is a serious crime. Again, one I never committed. But one with serious repercussions for the accused as I found out the hard way. But Christopher walked away without any repercussions. Regardless of my innocence, the accusation alone is damning. If I'm going to be damned, then let it be for what crimes—if they can indeed be called crimes than ones, manufactured by a blatant snot-nosed liar.

Dr. Hortman agreed, as I'd earlier shared with her, Allen's adamant legal advice that I sue Christopher. If I'd followed through, she felt there was a good possibility I wouldn't be sitting in her office but rather would have walked away from most of it and be living in

California. However, she cautioned me to be aware, if the night terrors continued, I could very well lose touch with reality and possibly do great harm to him. But, again, those thoughts had already infiltrated my mind. Dr. Hortman was concerned sleepwalking might arise. She adjusted my medication again while adding prazosin to help reduce the intensity and frequency of the night terrors. She also wanted to start Image Rehearsal Therapy.

Within the professional analysis and assessments, Dr. Hortman agreed Dr. Albridge at Davy should have never—as it was highly unprofessional and emotionally barbaric, have told me, "You need to sit here and realize what a very bad thing you did."

That, I never belonged at Davy and should have been transferred to a private hospital as I had requested. That, Albridge didn't even deserve the title of doctor in her opinion. I got the sense that Hortman knew of Albridge's grave lacking's as a psychiatrist.

I did share with Dr. Hortman: I was possibly aware of a few incidents of what I believed were sleepwalking. That, one early morning, I woke to the sound of Dugan's licking peanut butter and grape jelly from his snout. The same, along with part of a banana and breadcrumbs on the sheets and remnants of what appeared to be a sandwich on the floor by the bed.

Unless Dugan had more skills than I was aware, he certainly didn't get out of the bed after I'd fallen asleep, head downstairs, open the fridge, retrieve the peanut butter, jelly, and loaf of multigrain bread, retrieved a banana from the fruit bowl and slice it to make a sandwich on the kitchen counter. Once prepared, carried his midnight snack in his mouth back upstairs and jumped on the bed—although Dugan did love bananas and peanut butter. I'd always shared mine with him. A half-consumed glass of chocolate milk was on the bedside chest. None which I recalled: the sandwich or pouring a glass of chocolate milk during the night.

Whatever was transpiring, I'd sensed this, yet another new battle would be demanding. I staved off as much of the moon as possible from crossing the sun to avert The Third Coming and my own apocalyptic end.

the diversion

Roles change in life. Certainly, when it comes to family dynamics and unforeseen events reversing those roles. Oftentimes, as parents age or become incapacitated—and for other reasons, they eventually convert back to children as their adult children switch places and become the parent. For others, early-on in their young lives, many children take on the role of parent—as I did for my mother. Little sisters become big sisters, due to the same, for one or more of their siblings—as Sandra did for me. After I was released from Davy's psych ward, she became my big sister protecting me from myself—as I had once tried to protect her when we were children.

Sandra may as well have moved in. A lot of her clothes did—as other personal effects. She often stayed for long periods. I feared if my ongoing roller coaster emotional hell-ride didn't eventually come to a halt, it would continue to negatively impact her life—as I know our mother's had both of us. Our father's impact, more like near annihilation, is a given. At times, I managed to muster-up the good face—hoping Sandra would be convinced I was okay. Even the periods I was hanging on the edge, no matter how long or short they lasted. Despite all my efforts—the July fourth event stuck with her like a second skin.

As I'd written about: I cleaned up the macabre scene of our father's death to spare Mother from seeing it again and prevent Sandra from seeing it at all. But I wasn't able to save her from the gruesome scene in my master bathroom the day after I'd ingested the pills and slit open my arm.

Sandra's metered visits afforded opportunities to smooth animosities collected over conflicts between siblings in our adult lives. Perhaps, even reconcile a few differences and issues surrounding our mother's life and death. Sandra had become a different person—surely, a constant transformation by the time of her retirement from a 20-year military career. We were able to get reacquainted, or rather versions of the layers the years had added—to each of us. The people we'd become leavened by the separation of an ocean due to much of her deployments in Germany, and the rest at army bases in distant states from Georgia.

Other than the times she returned to the States for visits, our communications were limited to issues concerning our mother over infrequent long-distance phone calls. Although we hadn't completely severed each other—like our brother had us and our mother from his life and that of his family.

Sandra, Stephen, and I would always be reminders of a childhood we wanted to forget—but never would. Still, there were remnants of who we'd been as close sister and brother, defined by that shared childhood. And as I may have mentioned, Stephen wasn't around much of the time—more of a stranger than a brother. Regardless of how reacquainted we'd become, and as long as we live, the big elephant will always be in the room—those crippling family dynamics.

After William, Russ, Marty, Mitch, and Hal had broken away—my once gallant protectors, Sandra continued to be. As my strong ally and a friend as much as she was a sister. I have my assumptions as to why they turned away, but those are of little—if any, importance today. Although I'll always remain grateful to them—not for intervening, but for all they did after—including embracing Sandra. I wish them well.

By November of 2012, once again, I felt mentally pushed within inches of the darkness—the moon had picked up momentum toward the sun. I held what little ground was left, staying just inside the separation line dividing the light and that darkness—hope and hopelessness. Attempting, yet again, from allowing the black that had totally eclipsed in 2009 from doing it again. I began to wonder if it was the light, and not me, that was giving up as the murky shadows reached closer to that line of division.

Sandra had arrived on the first Friday of that November. The weekend to follow had been quiet for the three of us—Sis, Dugan, and me. We watched movies in bed and ate popcorn late into the hours of Saturday morning, Dugan more interested in the popcorn then the flicks on the flat screen. I hit the gym in the mid-afternoon while they napped. I put on another good face for her benefit—while stuck in a holding pattern like a lone pilot out of contact with air traffic control, left to blindly navigate in circles to find a safe place to land.

That evening, we dined at No Mas! Cantina. A popular Mexican restaurant—a mainstay of the neighborhood and a lovely walk from the loft even in the chilled air. Sandra filled up on salsa and chips with a side of guacamole while rolling out her Southern charm like red carpet at a formal gala, flirting with the gay waiter. I couldn't help but smile when she told him, upon ordering our entrees: "I'd like a lot of extra dressing on the side with my salad. I like a little salad with my dressing… if you get my drift?" Once the entrees arrived, she was stuffed after ordering a second helping of salsa, chips, and guac. The girl could eat and still maintain a respectable figure. By the conclusion of our meal in the crowded restaurant abuzz, to-go boxes were required.

Sunday mid-morning, we took Dugan for a walk in Centennial Olympic Park to people-watch. Dugan—always the center of attention anywhere we went. Kids came up to ask if they could pet him. Some frequently, animated with childhood excitement, would ask the same question: "Is that the Target dog?" I'd always say, "Well… of course he is."

Monday morning, I was startled out of sleep by Sandra's calling my name while shaking me as if the loft were on fire. I looked up at her and then over at Dugan standing on the bed beside me.

"What… what is it?"

"You were intermittently babbling incoherently and crying… loud enough it echoed throughout the loft," she explained in a panic. "I didn't want to wake you… kept waiting for you to stop, but then you began screaming."

"I was? Really? I don't have any recollection," I told Sandra, even though I was fully knowledgeable.

"You were calling out for Bradley like you did while in recovery. I clearly remember."

"I did?"

"Yes, you kept saying… don't go. Please don't get in your truck."

Sandra asked me who Bradley was. I told her he was someone I once loved from a long time ago and left it at that.

I'd been drifting in and out of nightmares throughout the night. Jolted awake only to be thrown back asleep and once again captured in some monstrous place in the province of the dream world. Again, I didn't want Sandra to know I had any remembrance of such. I didn't wish for her to worry.

"You, okay? You're wet as if you've been standing in the rain."

"Um, yes… yes. I'm fine. Sorry I… I alarmed you."

"You need to get in the shower," she insisted. "I'll get it started," she added.

"Thanks, Mom," I half-assed clowned. "But let me lie here a bit longer first."

"Okay. Do you want some coffee? I just ran the Cuisinart."

"That would be good."

Dugan settled back down on the mattress. I looked over at him as he eyed me.

"I'm fine. I'm fine, my truest of friends," I told him, as I reached to scratch his head—more for my comfort than his.

What Sandra didn't know was that before she came for another visit, I'd been over-medicating again and drinking due to another penetrating dive into a depressive state; the approach of the holiday season added fuel to it and the returning thoughts of death as well. But I was somewhat confident I'd managed to keep it all from her.

Soon showered, I dressed in a fresh pair of pajamas before returning to bed. I heard Sandra's steps make their way back up to the second level. I looked over from the bed. She stood on the landing with one hand holding the railing and a large mug of coffee in the other.

"Smells good, Sis," I commented, as I sat up against the headboard.

"Well, you look all refreshed," she stated. "But why did you put on another pair of PJs?" Sandra added, while raising the mug before walking over.

"I was up too late watching movies with Dugan… the usual. I'm still tired and guess I should have skipped that horror flick," I stated, to give reasonable plausibility for the commotion I'd made in my sleep.

Sandra walked closer to the bed.

"Just as you like it," Sandra stated, as she handed over the mug.

"Thanks."

Seconds later, Dugan perked his head before standing up at full attention.

"Is that turkey bacon I smell?"

At that, drawn by the scent of food, Dugan slid off the bed and headed to the stairs to wait to be carried down.

"Yes, and Dugan knows it," Sandra laughed.

I mechanically got out of bed long enough to carry Dugan downstairs. Told Sandra to only give him a few small pieces. That, the vet had been on me about Dugan losing a few pounds. Sandra offered a pretentious smile as she shrugged her shoulders.

"I'm Dugan's aunt. It's an unwritten rule that I'm required to spoil him, you know."

"Well, try to hold back… don't let his cute face sway you."

"I'll do my best, Randy."

"Right," I quipped. "Like you ever listen to me."

"Well, I'll feed my dog-nephew and take him out."

"Thanks," I said, as I headed down the stairs.

Halfway up, Sandra's voice stopped me as she asked again if I was sure I was okay. I reiterated, she shouldn't keep worrying and fussing over me.

Once back in bed, I knew I could stop the act—at least, for a short time. An hour or so later, I made it back downstairs to find Dugan sunning in his usual spot on the terrace. Sandra sat in the downstairs living area, flipping through a fashion magazine.

"Finally," she stated, as Sandra looked up from the mag. Do you want some scramble egg whites?"

I told her I was okay for now. That I might make a protein shake later.

"Okay then," Sandra muttered, as she returned her attention to the magazine flipping through its pages.

My movements were mechanical: I filled the mug with more coffee, and the last of the chocolate milk from the carton; added two tablespoons of the whey; got one of Anna's oatmeal raisin protein cookies from the container in the fridge; walked over and sat down in the matching black Grand Le Corbusier chair across from Sandra.

She adjusted her posture as I sat there. As I continued to fight the edginess—fight, the anxiety having a field day. Both, brought-on by the ruthless night's sleep due to the nightmare. Fight, slipping with Sandra about what was banging in my head. She had her own issues to deal with, and I knew mine added more shit onto hers. I didn't want that.

"You sure nothing's wrong?" Sandra persisted in her probing. "You know I have telepathic powers."

We both smiled.

"You're driving me a bit nuts with the mothering, Sis. And, by-the-way, your so-called telepathic powers aren't working very well to-day."

Sandra shifted the topic of conversation about what we were going to do for Thanksgiving, knowing I'd stopped giving the lame holiday-of-a-lie any credence or acceptance since the last one with Mother at the Seventh Street house.

"Why don't we go somewhere… fly to St. Thomas for a non-Thanksgiving vacation. I could use a tan."

"Sounds like a good idea. Let's talk more about it later," I told her, but not knowing if I could emotionally go anywhere.

I didn't even want to venture far from the loft; except I'd been forcing myself to do a few things with Sandra. I'd even lost interest in training at the gym but still made myself. And of course, my scheduled psychiatrist appointments.

"Hey… listen. I know we were planning on heading into Midtown to grab lunch… but I just want to lay low today. Is that okay with you?" I asked, not wanting to keep pretending I was perfectly fine the rest of the day.

"Whatever you want to do."

I heard the disappointment in her voice as Sandra looked back at the magazine. Still, I had to get her out of the loft for the day. I didn't want my sister to suffer along with me. Knowing, in many ways, our pain was very similar.

"Hey… better yet, why don't you go shopping in Buckhead. Take my AMEX and treat yourself on me," I offered.

Sandra looked back up. Her eyes lit up as a smile grew on her face.

"You sure? You know I'm dangerous with a credit card… es-pecially if it's yours," she laughed.

"Yes, I'm aware of that fact. But… you deserve it. I want you to splurge. Get whatever you want."

"Okay. It's your money."

"Yeah. Get a mani-pedi… hair… the works. Buy a new outfit," I insisted.

"Hmm," she uttered, pinching her chin between her thumb and

forefinger. "Does that include shoes?" Sandra, clarified.

"Sure."

"Oh… don't tempt me."

"Like I said… the works."

I got up. Walked over and offered a big hug. Sandra reached up to put her arms around my neck.

"I love you, big brother. You know that… right?"

"Yea. I know. But I think you love my AMEX more… so, get out of here and go shop to your heart's desire."

Sandra kissed me on the forehead and headed toward the guest room she'd essentially commandeered. I returned upstairs to get the card from my wallet. Once ready, Sandra reappeared in the kitchen where I was sharing a banana with Dugan.

"I'm about to leave."

I pulled the card from the top pocket of my PJs. While handing it to her, I teased by quickly pulling it away before Sandra got a firm grasp.

"Having second thoughts?"

The second time, at lightning speed, she yanked it from my hand.

"It's mine now," she claimed.

"Oh… I'm just playing with you."

Dugan and I followed her to the front door.

"You need me to bring you back anything?"

"Yeah… if you don't mind. I'm out of chocolate milk."

"Sure thing," Sandra answered, as she hurried to her car.

Back upstairs, I took a few minutes to stand at the railing of the mezzanine's lounge area overlooking the loft. The sliding glass doors of the terrace were wide open, letting in the gentleness of the remarkably beautiful clear and bright November day. I tried to cherish the moment and breathe it in—to remember it.

Dugan crawled beside me in the bed. Looked up at me with his sweet eyes as he rested his snout on my chest. His weight against me felt protective. Made me feel peaceful. I was glad Sandra was finally out of the loft. More importantly, knowing she was happy to have a carte blanche shopping day. I just hoped my card didn't disintegrate from too many swipes. My diversion tactic worked, even at the expense of the possible hefty AMEX bill to come the following month. I closed my eyes. With effort, I attempted to force out the pessimistic babble in my head—stop the onset of a merciless spiraling free fall.

Shortly, the front doorbell echoed. Like a Pavlovian response, the source of the sound reminded me: a designer was sending her assistants to pick up three large, commissioned artworks that afternoon; they were for a Marietta medical building. It completely slipped my mind but favorably, the art was wrapped and ready to go.

Once her assistants were gone, I wasted little time returning upstairs and directly to the dresser across from the bed. I pulled opened the top drawer. Grabbed the prescription of clonazepam and hurriedly jiggled out two.

Sandra returned to the loft in the late afternoon. She called out like an alert system as she ascended the stairs with designer bags rustling—extracting me stupefied out of sleep. The smell of a well-spritzed, fruity-sweet perfume aroused Dugan. I imagined one of her many purchases of the day.

"You awake, Randy? I'm back."

solar eclipse

The brightness that had filled the loft before, was replaced by the soft hues of a pale yellow-orange glow of the setting sun. It washed the listless air as the day poised for its closing. The room would hold what light was left until it eventually grayed with the approaching inevitably of nightfall. My breath, shallow. My heart—numb. My mind, uncertain. The night to come potentially lethal. Little did I know those hours to follow would be ones of returning desperation, and of such magnitude. Or was I aware, there were still things—abominable chattels, hidden so profoundly in the catacombs of my soul that would return like ghosts riding on squalls of revenge.

"You awake, sleepyhead?" Sandra asked as she shook my shoulder.

"I… I'm, now," the words fumbled as my eyes opened and traveled in the direction of her voice.

Fiercely in need of a clonazepam—perhaps two, I wanted to hasten from the bed to the dresser's top drawer. But I resisted the automatic impulse of a docile brain that the drug had created. If I did, again,

Sandra would know there was something wrong in my head. Admittedly, I was fully aware of the addiction—whether the drug itself, or some emotional attachment out of wont.

Both her hands were full. Holding a considerable load of bags—various sizes, as if Sandra had been Christmas shopping for a family of nine residing in the 30327 zip code of Buckhead: Gucci, Kate Spade, Nordstrom, Saks Fifth Avenue, among a few others—their store logos blocked under the overzealousness of quantity.

"Did you have a good sleep?"

"Yeah. I feel rested," I lied, as I wiped my clammy forehead and held my hand there for a few moments as if testing for a fever.

"Well… I can't wait to show you all I got," she giggled. "I even have a surprise for you."

Despite my volatile emotional state, I was happy to see my sister excited. As with Mother, I never wanted Sandra to ever feel unloved. Unwanted. Abandoned.

"Oh, goody," I replied, as I slowly sat up.

Dugan scooted off the bed in his funny way: lying on his belly as he inched his front legs to the foot before sliding off the extra-thick mattress—surely wondering if there was something in one of the bags for him.

Sandra walked plopped the cargo containing her treasures on the floor.

"I walked a good twenty miles shopping," she exclaimed, while letting out a sigh.

Dugan raddled the bags as he probed his snout into several.

"Looks like you cleaned out the stores… but more importantly, did you max out the card in the process?"

"Perhaps."

Sandra laughed; her excitement as bright as a 150-watt bulb.

The part of me that remembered happiness was indeed that for her—happy. I didn't care even if she'd spent a small fortune.

"There were several huge sales… I saved a ton!" Sandra exclaimed, possibly thinking she'd done me a huge favor by not breaking the bank.

I smiled as I slid back against the headboard.

"I've all the receipts in my purse… you want them?"

"Just leave them on my desk."

"Don't you want to see how much I saved?"

"I'm sure I will when the statement comes... and thank you for racking up some Delta SkyMiles for me," I jested.

"Splendid... so we can take that trip."

"It would appear so."

"Great! Oh... I stopped by MetroFresh... picked us up some dinner and... I remembered the chocolate milk. Did you ever eat today?" Sandra, mothered.

"I had that protein shake," I lied. "I'm good for now. Just put mine in the fridge."

"You sure?" She asked, again.

"Yes, very."

"I'm going to put on some of my new finds to show you."

"Sounds good."

Sandra gathered the shopping bags. Dugan seemed perplexed; he looked back at me. As she started her descent downstairs with the truckload of bags, I asked Sandra to take Dugan out and feed him first—as I had, and she'd done that morning.

"Of course."

Taking advantage of her exit, I walked to the dresser. Apprehend two more clonazepam—I'd been craving like a pregnant woman does pickles and ice cream since the moment Sandra had awakened me upon her return. I then met Dugan at the top of the stairs. Picked him up in my arms as if he was a big baby. By the time we landed on the first level, Sandra walked out of the guest room. Within seconds, they were heading for the front door—Dugan wagging his tail. After locating the carton of chocolate milk in one of the bags Sandra had left on the kitchen island, I took a few big swigs without bothering to use a glass. Chocolate milk always had a calming effect on me.

Much earlier that afternoon, while Sandra racked up SkyMiles, I'd been dragged awake as if by meat hooks. One of the night terrors returned. Widening the crack of the subconscious—taking further possession of sleep. In the terror, again, as before, Christopher had taken the place of my father. The phantasm, much like watching an old rerun. The only difference: after the pull of the trigger and the explosion, instead of the surrounding area, I was the target of the bloody, human debris from head to toe—including my eyes. Blinded, I reflexively and frantically wiped the wet and smelly remains for the return of sight.

Once my vision cleared, I found myself in the shed behind the house with my shirt off and the apparition of my father standing in front of me; this time, taking a swig of Jack from the bottle after having finished off a number of beers. The shed lifted from the ground and spun up into the air, leaving my father and me encased in a dusty whirlwind.

As was the circumstance of others before, I felt trapped within my body upon my mind's return to the present and reality—at least what I thought was real, back in the bed of my bedroom. Any attempt to move was impeded by a massive, pinning weight on my body. Still, I struggled but remained as if a quadriplegic. Once able to move, I sat up in bed in a sweaty fright—my head gyrated. Feeling as if I'd been beaten to a pulp, my breaths were quick and shallow as an acute sense of extreme dread shook my body to the core. That shadow of darkness—stiffened.

A wave of nausea overtook my constitution. I floundered from bed to the master bathroom. Fell to my knees in front of the toilet. Lifted the lid in time to vomit up liquid. As had been the habit; after returning to the bedroom, I downed the several clonazepam clenched in my grasp. Upon returning to bed, I pulled Dugan into my arms as I attempted to fight my way through the surrounding obfuscated shadows—until the mental exhaustion shoved me back into sleep.

the descent

As much as I'd wanted Sandra out of the loft, I was relieved she'd returned from her day of shopping. Perhaps, I thought her presence would push the shadows back into its walls. I retreated back to my bedroom where I sat quietly in one of the Barcelona chairs—but my mind was anything except silent. Once I heard Sandra re-enter the loft with Dugan, I got up to splash water on my face and brush my teeth before putting on a robe to join them downstairs. I desired another fix of chocolate milk as I did their company.

Dugan and I sat in the heartening, graceful light of the living area as Sandra changed into one of her new designer outfits. She made the first floor her runway until each one had been presented. I could see the dollar signs rack up in my head like that of a banknote counter. But, again, no matter. She was happy.

"So. What do you think?"

"I love them all! Sensational, Sandra," I exclaimed, in forced enthusiasm.

"You don't have a favorite?"

"Well... the fact you're wearing each one makes them so."

"Awe... you think?"

"Just telling it like it is."

A buoyant smile lifted her cheeks. Sandra shyly shrugged her shoulders in delight like a little girl who'd just finished her first dance recital to the roaring applause of parents.

In appreciation of my approval, she walked over and gave me a big hug and peck on the cheek.

"What do you have planned for the rest of the night?" I asked.

"More dress up... I guess. Maybe watch some television while I eat."

"You? You going to eat yours? We can sit down and eat together."

"No. Going to call it a night. We'll do something fun tomorrow... maybe hit the Botanical Garden and then take Dugan to Piedmont Park. What do you say?"

"Sure."

"Okay, then. I'm going to head back upstairs."

Sandra smiled.

I picked Dugan up securely in my arms. A few steps up, I turned to look back at Sandra where she remained standing in the soft surrounding glow of the loft; the smile hadn't left her face.

frailty of night

Dugan scurried from my arms onto the bed. I watched as he circled on the white comforter until he plopped. My knees met the flood at the bed's edge as if I was about to pray. But for what? Still, perhaps I did or rather my heart did. Did, for Sandra and Dugan but I felt no need to pray for anything else; certainly, nothing else for myself. What good would it do? I'd been praying for years: for my mother, for Sandra, and for myself. For our emotional pain to heal and for happiness to find us since our individual searches had seemed to leave us further from it. And because of that, left us more lost. More alone. More afraid. All for the same and other individual reasons.

What made it worst—if worst were possible, was the rhetoric I had enough of from the mouths of some therapists and even psychiatrists asserting that I could do better—try harder. Then there were the life coaches—the books they wrote, and the Dalai Lama wannabes on social media preaching the same as if they knew our individual hearts and souls—as if they could look inside them. And as I've mentioned: I told the same to my mother before I really knew—experienced, what unforgivable emotional pain and torment felt like. Before I had lived it as she had—and was still living it while trying to mask it.

I laid my head on Dugan's soft white fir as if his body was a pillow—my arms wrapped around him. By then, the frailty of night had completely taken over: surrounding my world or what there was of it.

Restlessness followed. I stood. Walked through the bedroom pass the top of the stairs toward the short hallway that led to the mezzanine. There, its railing supported my weight as I looked down to the first floor that I'd just left. It, as the entire loft, was washed in the echoing hazes of thinning city lights; welcomed in through the floor-to-ceiling windows. My mind drifted as if it had left my body—time seemed to spin backward until it lapsed.

I walked back toward the bedroom and to the dresser. Rifled the top drawer. Took two more sleeping pills, another clonazepam, and a mood stabilizer—well-aware, I'd taken too many in a day's time but unaware those additional pills would serve as transporters to travel deeper into those treacherous catacombs like going into a battle stripped of armor and weapons.

I returned to Dugan and to bed. I pulled him closer. Dugan made me feel safe from the dripping night. Soon thereafter, my eyelids grew heavied until they closed; and my body as my mind were blanketed by sleep.

By Sandra's account, in the shrinking hours, the somber quiet of the loft was disturbed as she was startled awake by a sudden lurid thump, followed by several more in succession—all loud, all random, all thick, combined with moans and garbles before there was silence again.

She hastened from the guest bedroom into the expansive area of the hall to find me laid-out on the concrete floor at the bottom of the stairs. Fearful I was unconscious or worse from the apparent pratfall, she called out my name while gently shaking me until I began to moan again. Sandra wondered if I'd broken something until moments later, I slowly came back to half-life after more moans and added gibberish. She told me my eyes then opened as I managed to sit up with the help of the stairway wall.

I can only surmise: I'd gotten out of bed to make it down to the kitchen for a swig of chocolate milk from the fridge. A habit in the middle of many a night, and as I've shared—finding it of some comfort like mother's milk. Being out of it from the consumption of pills, I must have had a misstep, resulting in a dangerous and certainly, less than conventional descent. Sandra delineated that she'd asked if I needed any help, but I'd brusquely responded in a drunk-like state that I was fine and to leave me alone.

Disregarding any harshness and attempts to swat her hands away, Sandra managed to examine me: a few lumps on my head and some blood muddied my face—but no alarming broken bones as far as she could determine. But Sandra said she held concern for possible internal harm due to the twenty-plus stair free fall—astonishingly, without breaking my neck.

Although appearing to be physically intact, Sandra later shared that she'd told me to remain still while she called for an ambulance. In response, again, as shared, I grabbed her arm and hostilely yelled: "Don't you fucking dare!"

She floundered in precarious moments. If my angry words went unheeded, Sandra would hate herself in the event the fall had caused serious trauma unseen by the eye. On the condition it was just a tumble resulting in nothing more than bruises that a man of my size and thickness could possibly withstand, and an ambulance were called, Sandra knew I would be on a rampage for days-on-end.

My abrasiveness placed her in a difficult quandary; left her hanging in the perplexity of uncertainty. Plus, she wasn't stupid. Sandra knew I'd been heavily medicating, despite my stage-acting to cover my prescription drug consumption. She knew me all too well. And regardless of if there was no physical harm, either way, I was on a collision course.

As Sandra made the decision to side with caution and make the 911 call, I began to inchmeal my body to the bottom stair. Sandra paused. In the unsettling state that engulfed that night, she watched. Her words were: I'd drowsily looked up at her and spoke, "Sorry. I… I'm fine. I'm fine. I'm so… so sorry." Then, sat there as if gathering wits of what to do next.

Apparently, minutes later, I reached up for the railing to lift my butt onto the bottom stair. Sandra continued to observe while her mind jumped from one synopsis to another of how the night would culminate. Then, I went up backward, stair-by-stair at the pace of a sloth on my butt while continuing to grab the railing for support. She followed in case I might have another fall. Once at the top, Sandra described how Dugan leaped from the bed. And as if a guide dog, how he walked next to me; using his snout seemingly to steer me as I crawled across the bedroom in the direction of the bed. From there, I managed to climb up. More varying pitches of moaning commenced as I curled up in a ball. Shortly, Dugan jumped next to me.

Sandra further expounded: she'd moved one of the Barcelona ottomans to the side of the bed. She sat in the shredded shadowy light while holding my hand. Dugan's head was on my chest while he looked at her as if he knew—as if they both knew something but unsure of what. Sandra listened as I continued to mumble sporadically while she counted each of my breaths until I drifted back off into a quiet sleep.

Sandra returned to the lower level. Put on the coffee and waited for sunrise. And with her, Sandra shared she was accompanied by an uneasy feeling that lingered in her gut of what was left of that absorbed night filled with taxing precariousness. That, it was a harsh reminder—harking back her long wait in Davy's ER with my friends some three years before.

loss

Death is not the greatest loss in life. The greatest loss is what dies inside us while we live…
Norman Cousins

I don't know how many stab wounds a soul can endure. How many times—if at all, it can fully heal. How many times it has to face death. Perhaps, too many. But what I do know from personal experience—is that parts of it can die, leaving a cavity through which our very essence is left vulnerable.

In many guises, my mother and I were two humans living parallel lives of destruction—not of our architecture. We existed in a small world of pandemonium—all circling around her and the past. My past, as well. Our pasts were one as our presents. Although neither one of us ever doubted the weight of the love in our hearts for each other—as mother and son, there were occasions we'd argued and even screamed in frustration. Hated each other. Even, scorned. The source of the conflicts was centered around three things: crazy, alcohol, and her husband—my father. I always believed I was trying to pull her from a volatile existence swimming in the combination of psychiatric drugs and consumption of alcohol and his evil. But, maybe as well, I was trying to save myself.

Every time I heard her cry behind the bedroom door prior to and after my father's expiration, I experienced a death. Every time she mistook me for him—another death. Each time I passed her sitting at the breakfast table with a bottle of alcohol, downheartedly singing along to those old songs playing on the turntable, bedimmed in amassing shadows reaching inward from the outside through the jalousie windows while mourning what could have been her life—another.

Every drunken stupor I witnessed, knowing her heart ached for comfort. When I put her to bed and lay beside her until the booze and medications pulled her into a restless sleep, all-the-while wondering if the kindest act I could do for my beloved mother was to gently put her out of her misery—another death was experienced. Each time I put her in the hospital against her will, both our souls faced a death where there are no defining words—inexplicable representations. Many deaths were experienced over the three years Mother was committed to Central State Mental Hospital in Milledgeville, Georgia.

Surrounded in the crystal-clear sunlight of an August morning, I stood on the sidelines outside the chapel on the day of my college graduation. I felt awkward in my black gown as I held the cap in one hand and the scrolled diploma in the other—the diploma I achieved for my mother. I watched other graduates with their families and friends as their combined abundant joyous celebration filled my ears. But there was none in my heart and my mother was nowhere in sight. I wanted to run. I did run.

As I hurried away from the crowd and across the stately-manicured grounds of Mercer University toward the stairs that lead down to my car parked on Montpelier Avenue—with each stride, the more the sounds of the merriment in the air dissolved like sugar in water. Once I reached them, I saw my mother precipitously trying to maneuver the steep incline upward. It was obvious that she was intoxicated. Instinctively, I rushed down in fear she would fall backward.

I took hold of her arm to steady Mother. Once back at the top and on solid ground, I consoled her for not witnessing her son's college graduation—telling Mother through her tears, that it was okay as I placed the fancy diploma in her hand. She held it tightly as if afraid it would disappear at any moment. And at that tenuous moment, another hardened death occurred simultaneously between our heartbeats. At that, I knew I wasn't moving to California anytime soon. That knowledge, another death for me.

As I'd shared in my first book, the door to the living and dining rooms were seldom opened after my father's death. But it was more for me than my mother. Each time I came within a few feet of it, chills ran up and down my spine as I felt the reach of the hands of my father's ghost—reaching to capture and pull me through that door and back to that day.

There were many nights I saw his image standing on the other side while it stared at me as if the door was made of glass. The truth be told, I'm captured by a macabre penchant to relive that event—more times than I can count. Surely, that is punishment enough. My mother did seem better after the internal shock had run its course. I believe she eventually unearthed the truth of his death, but we never spoke of it—how could she not know what her middle son may have done, and to what extent, to protect her from the man who mentally fragmented her, bruised her body, and made her bleed.

On many occasions, after I hugged and kissed my mother goodbye before driving back to Atlanta, I habitually got out of the car before pulling out of the driveway or having driven around the block, I would return to the house to hug and kiss her again; knowing my leaving her, Mother would feel a strong sense of isolated loneliness, and perhaps that of abandonment upon every departure.

Like others, I've lived through the dying of many internal—intimate personal commodities as much as the birth of others. For four years, I stood by emotionally impotent watching as death took parts of me from within—piece by piece. And, as hard as I endeavored to gather up those dead pieces and revive them, death kept lurking to take them back, but only some of me and not the whole. As much as I wanted to live, in varying measures—I wanted to die as well as those things had inside me. That desire was always there: the desire to stop breathing. But it wasn't just over those four years that many valuable life-sustaining emotional assets died and been resuscitated and died again: love, trust, belief, and hope had died many a death.

red velvet cup cakes

A few years after my release from Davy, I began stockpiling sleeping pills again as I had before July 4, 2009. I'd managed to sway Dr. Hortman, due to bouts of insomnia and the resulting exhaustion, it exacerbated my mental afflictions. Further conveying, I wasn't having suicidal ideations when I was. Dr. Hortman bought my story as well; but it took more convincing even though she was aware, the haunting dreams and nightmares did interfere with getting ample sleep. I was basically given a loaded gun in a prescription bottle.

At the inward creeping of light from the outside world, Sandra returned upstairs. As earlier, she sat by the bed watching me sleep. As more light pushed into the room, Sandra noticed random red stains on the sheets near Dugan. Her first reactive thought was that of blood. Panic pushed her due to the distressing events of the night, my history, and the returning periods of severe depression I'd failed at hiding.

Immediately, Sandra returned to her feet. Rushed around the bed to take a closer look and another examination as she'd done after the fall. To her relief, there was nothing alarming as if I'd cut myself, and again, I appeared be physically intact with no signs of self-harm. She discovered additional red stains near the bed on the large onion-colored sisal rug. Then, I noticed the wine bottle wedged between the bedside chest and the bed. Near the bottle, were two empty pill containers. Once in hand, the labels identified them as sleeping pills. The uneasiness in her gut quickly shifted to that of a five-alarm fire—escalated at the sight of a third container at the foot of the dresser.

As I was later told, Sandra shook my shoulders and slapped me. Then, harder a second time. At that, I partly opened my eyes. Broken moans followed.

At her description, I finally spoke, "What… what the fuck are you doing?" Her mind somewhat put at ease; Sandra decided to call my friend, Phil. Over the phone conversation she filled in the details of the harrowing night, including that I'd told her not to call for help; and the morning discovery of wine stains and the bottle, and that of the empty pill containers. Shortly thereafter, Phil arrived at the loft—beforehand, stopping long enough at his favorite bakery to purchase a box of red velvet cupcakes with cream cheese frosting. I remember him telling me, from years ago, "Red velvet cupcakes fix everything."

Within the week following, Sandra and Phil verbally painted the events of that night and daylight to follow. I listened as if they were talking about someone else: upon his arrival, I seemed okay other than appearing as though I'd been on a serious drinking binge. They removed my pajamas before forcing me under an ice-cold shower. I was obstinate. My vocabulary suited for a whorehouse as I'd apparently threatened to cut off Phil's balls and feed them to Dugan.

As they filled in the canvas like paint-by-numbers: after the shower, Phil and Sandra dried and dressed me in a fresh pair of pajamas. Together, propped me up in bed. By their account, I seemed more alert and no longer angry, but rather talkative. Making jokes as I devoured one less of a dozen red velvet cupcakes they fed me—Dugan having managed to snatch one in his snout out of Phil's hand.

By the time I'd wolfed the last one, my face was smeared with red cake and cream cheese frosting making me look much like a clown in the middle of applying makeup. Dugan made quick work of the small to larger pieces of cake on my pajamas and the bed—while he licked my face clean as well. As Sandra and Phil later told me, I remained locked within a buzzed-out daze for several days.

Fully back to reality, Phil sat me down to get as much out of me as he could about what happened that night.

"You weren't very happy with us," Phil revealed. "I'm not exaggerating. You were a fucking mess… in fact, quite scary," he added.

I told Phil that I was beyond sorry; and I didn't know what to say except that I hated knowing I put them through hell.

He expounded that I cursed and bitched them out—fought them the entire time Sandra and Phil kept me in the shower.

"You're a big guy… I think the only reason Sandra and I managed, was because you were out of it. Otherwise, who knows how it would have turned out."

Phil asked if I'd intentionally taken the pills. I told him I didn't remember anything after having gone to bed; but admitted that I was fighting some dark depression for days while trying to hide it from Sandra. And that the suicidal ideations were banging around in my head. Phil kept pressing me if I was being honest. And I kept telling him that I was. I worried that they would gang up on me and as a result, I would be forced into the hospital.

I did what I could to reassure Phil. Sharing that Sandra wanted me to take her on a non-Thanksgiving vacation; that we'd briefly talked about the day before. Going further to tell him I had fully planned on making the arrangements for us and Dugan to travel to Puerto Rico. But Phil's expression was telling. He didn't seem convinced I didn't remember taking the pills and I'd done so intentionally.

"Seriously, Phil."

"Okay, I'm going to take your word on it… but first, do you have any more sleeping pills stashed away?"

"No. I guess I took them that night. Please, let's just drop it. I'm fine now. You don't need to worry."

"You're planning on telling your shrink… right?"

"I don't think I can. I don't want to."

"Both Sandra and I think you should."

"Okay… I'll consider it," I lied.

"Well, you need to do more than that. But just know if you do anything like this again… "

"No, I won't."

As I began to tear up, I was relieved Sandra had taken Dugan out for a walk. I knew if she saw me crying, it would just upset her more. I knew I'd done enough damage to her emotionally. I guess we both had experienced another death the night of the fall and then that morning. I sorely hated myself at that very moment.

"Hey. Listen," Phil changed the topic. "I remember when I first met you, James-Randall. Goodness, I don't think I'll ever get used to not calling you Randy."

"It's okay. You don't have to call me James-Randall."

"I know I cut you out of my life when you told me you didn't want to date me… that you just wanted to be friends."

"Yes, I remember."

"It was too hard to be around you and want you at the same time. I couldn't handle it. It hurt too much," he confessed.

"You don't have to explain. I understood."

We were both so young. It hurt me too when Phil walked away from our friendship, over some thirty years' ago. But he wasn't the first. Back then, it seemed as though friendship and sex were one in the same. If I'd heard it once, I'd heard it a hundred times.

I liked Phil but my feelings didn't go any deeper than a friendship. The day came when he stopped returning my calls. So, I knew. I knew our friendship was over, and I knew why. Then, out of the blue, shortly after I'd purchased the loft, he found me on Facebook and sent a friend request along with a message. We met for coffee within a week and picked up where we'd left off. Phil admitted he'd heard why I was at Davy as he did about the crazy stalking rumors. That's what eventually prompted him to reach out.

"But you came back into my life when I needed a friend. And you're a good one regardless of how much time has passed," I said, about to choke up again. "All those years didn't change anything as far as I'm concerned."

Phil hugged me.

"God, I feel like shit about that. All of it… walking away from our friendship and taking so long to make up for it."

I told him that he had made up for it that morning by being there for Sandra and me.

"I just want you to promise me… promise… "

I cut Phil off again. I knew I couldn't promise anything as much as I may have wanted. The night of the fall had proven that.

"I'll be fine. Don't worry anymore."

I wasn't going to admit anything to Sandra or Phil. And certainly not speak of it to Dr. Hortman. And although I survived the ninety pills downed with a bottle of wine, specifically a Petit Cheval Blanc that was a loft warming gift I'd been saving for a special occasion and didn't break my neck on the fall down the stairs—it was another death, all the same.

ramifications

Fringed somnolent palms swayed in the warm tranquil breeze high above a secluded beach house; I rented the second week of December on the island of Eleuthera in the Bahamas. More so, out of guilt for what that November night had emotionally propelled at Sandra—and the dark tunnel, as my gruesome second suicide on July 4, 2009, had forced her to travel through over the stemming days that followed both. Again, we were somewhat estranged when I attempted my first in early January, some seven months before the second—the attempt, unknown until I exposed it in the writing of "Alabama Snow."

Dugan and I kept to ourselves as Sandra had much of the trip. We both sought some degree of solace and the need for recovery—unknowing of the delineation of possible ramifications that might make chase, not allowing me to see another year roll around or much of one. I feared more for Sandra than I did for myself of what may come. That fear ate at me and would continue to live within if I remained unable to find the emotional strength to combat my demons and silence those old ghosts while hindering their long reach. But mostly—finally purchase forgiveness for myself, for not only actions taken in the past but my inability to forgive the dead.

The emptiness still loitered as I looked to the water, seeking a sense of self and measured sanctuary, having once been endowed with profuse peace by the ocean. Small allotments of both were gradually found then taken away—then given again, as I felt baptized in the outreaching glow of the sun rises as Dugan lay in the lounge chair next to mine, never having been a fan of the repetitive foaming waves as he had the same at other beaches over the years since he became a gift in my unsteady life. Sandra preferred to sleep-in late most mornings.

As the days progressed, I remained stationary by the water's edge—sometimes unburdening on the pages of a journal. The salted breezes circulated levels of comfort as I walked the long, pink-colored, sandy beach—often feeling like the only human left on the earth; the green-blue water did offer repose and a sense of consistency as the waves washed over my feet and then returned to the sea—but ephemerally. As my life had always been give and take, the same was true with the ocean. With each wave that washed the shore, I felt that limited measured comfort but once the ocean took it back—the isolation returned. Any real and lasting stability, seeming extremely temporary as my existence had since 2009.

The house came with a mozo, who resided in a casita at the back of the property. Felix, a friendly elderly gentleman native to the Commonwealth saw to our needs: preparing meals and chauffeuring as he did dog sitting. Due to the increasing intensity of the sun in the afternoons, Dugan spent curious time following him around. My boy returned to me in the late afternoon hours. Sandra sometimes would join us.

A sense of reassurance hovered over me, knowing that another day was ending—meant another day lived as a fading horizon began to swallow up the sun. But not before transitioning the blue sky floating on the water in its variations of striking, phenomenal, colors of red, orange, red, and sometimes a mystical purple—until the blanketing of night, and with it, the showcasing of uncountable stars appearing as if at the passing of a magic wand. As other times, the unending scope of the universe offered a truth that my mental afflictions, which had been the bane of my existence, were of no importance as I was—insignificant and nothing more than a microscopic speck, if that, compared to its glorious magnitude that went on forever without a beginning or an end. But I had an expiration date—whether of life's plan or that of those afflictions.

Upon our return, against my wishes and despite discouragement, Sandra insisted on staying for an undetermined timeframe. She wouldn't take no for an answer—and it's obviously why.

a last resort

A part of me felt torn knowing that upon moving to California, I would be leaving her behind; but this time, in the cold hard ground. And chances were, I'd never return to the South—and thus, unable to lay flowers upon her grave…

The providential cognizance wasn't lost on me that I survived the events of that disintegrated night. But I didn't correlate surviving as luck—rather as a curse as I had the other attempts.

On the outer fringe of the many weeks following the holiday vacation, my mind was progressively ravaged by what I was told. Sandra and I agreed never to mention that night again. However, it would stay with us as the July fourth attempt—for the remainder of our lives. Nevertheless, in my solitude, embittered tears of self-reproach leached from my eyes like boiling oil of how deeply I knew my attempts, again, must have traumatized Sandra although she never outwardly let on.

I worked to roll back into some daily routines—looping in twenty-four-hour segments. The replication of a human on autopilot; a robotic machine with emotional malfunctions. As futile as it had been at times, once again, I assayed to program myself not to feel any emotion aided by prescription drugs and alcohol, as my mother had. To become mentally numb in the seam of confusion and distress—the residuals from much of the past thirty-six-plus-months amplified by circling back periods of depression that had repeatedly disarmed my defenses.

That November night had pushed me back into a maze of disorder. Those residuals, more concentrated within the unsure hours where the delineation between sanity and insanity—life and death is at its most attenuated. A dogfight ensued while I lay awake looking vacantly into the woolly air. It was staunchly perspicuous—Atlanta had become a pending deathtrap. More so than ever.

I did keep the third attempt from Dr. Hortman. If I hadn't, there was the concern she'd hospitalized me. And if not confined to another ward, Hortman would suspend prescribing sleeping pills—even though sleep was a high-stakes gamble of how often the hammering of the vexed dreams and nightmares would return. But, again, I needed those pills for those impossible days when I had to knock myself out to live to see another sunrise.

Aside, I would no longer be able to replenish my supply. But again, not telling Hortman wasn't the first truth about my life I had deflected to prevent it from boomeranging back in my direction—or I'd attempted to outrun. That night had been too disjointed to comprehensively maneuver through or manipulate enough. Impossible to make it appear any less alarming than it would be to Dr. Hortman—even if I stuck to the story: the overdose was unintended.

For that, the next few sessions grew exceedingly uncomfortable. Difficult to train my eyes directly toward hers. Watching the truth alter Hortman' facial expression. Letting her down and disappointing her with the beastly knowledge I'd fallen from grace once more. Uncomfortable, knowing I was betraying her trust once again after her having diligently dedicated herself—working to help me move forward. A task meant as a collaboration in which I was supposed to be a willing participant. Despite my avoidance, Dr. Hortman had noticed I'd fallen backward, even though I kept denying it. It was much like she could read the swelling thoughts in my head. See the deceit on my face and by my body language.

After further sessions, during one while I sat in Dr. Hortman's office as I had for the past some eight months, she politely smiled and asked me to hold tight until she finished writing a few notes. I'd assumed, concerning the patient before me. Sitting there, I felt as if something was brewing and about to boil. She briefly looked up at me a few times from her focus on a folder, then returned to her attention and continued to write.

"Sorry about that." Dr. Hortman apologized, as she closed the file.

"It's okay."

She went quiet—perhaps in some analytical contemplation. Picked up the pen. Gripped it in her hand. Thumbed the plunger in a rhythmic motion. Click. Click. Click. "Something's up," I thought.

I felt like a kid who'd been called to the principal's office for cheating on a test. All along, I knew I'd been cheating Dr. Hortman from the truth.

"James-Randall… it's good to see you. How have you been feeling."

"You, too. I'm okay."

"What about sleep? You're still looking tired. Still having issues with parasomnia?"

My mind pulled away. Wafted back to the beach. To the sensation of bubbling white foam of the temperate waves wash my feet.

"James… "

My attention reluctantly returned.

"A few a week. Sometimes… more."

"It seemed for a time… you were doing better."

I conveyed to Dr. Hortman, I felt I had in some respects. Sharing: while in the Bahamas I did a lot of reflection. That on a few late nights, while lying on my back on the sandy beach, my eyes searched the star-filled universe. And on those nights, I thought about how insignificant I was in comparison to its vastness. That my time there had afforded some rest and even sleep a few hours without the disturbing dreams and pursuing nightmares—or I didn't think I'd experienced them. But that, I distinctly remember the night before our return when I'd awakened in a heated sweet from one of them while feeling the pull of death.

"Have you told me everything?" Dr. Hortman unexpectedly asked as we bounced glances. "I'd hoped the prazosin would have been more effective," she magnified.

A paused shadowed; I looked away. Yes, the probing question at that moment was unexpected. But one, I'd been concerned might come up sooner or later. Another one to deflect.

I repeated to her what I had before. What I had lied about, that I didn't know. But, again shared with Dr. Hortman they have always been correlations to past events—like jumbled pieces not always fitting together in the right sequences as those life events while others did more concisely. As a follow-up to my statement, Dr. Hortman expressed she never understood why I didn't make it clear as to what many of those events were. I felt by her quandary, Hortman was getting too close to the core of my deceptions.

"As I've already tried to explain… "

I stopped myself. Paused. Searched.

"Maybe it's all just too much for me to… to explain, that is."

I expounded the best I could—thinking I'd done so enough without damning myself to her. But I reiterated to one degree or another it was everything surrounding and inside that messed-up childhood and beyond. Perhaps, certain events my mind wouldn't let me remember but their imprint remained.

Certainly, up to the loss of Bradley and how I still deeply feel it—had always even if at times it wasn't so raw and at others, it was as if I'd been skinned alive. And later, Chip's violations. I even went as far as admitting to Hortman that I often raged with anger and hated—at others and myself. And then there was the undeniable fact, I was much like my mother emotionally. What I may have inherited from her in my DNA and that which was from living it.

Much earlier when our sessions started, I'd told Dr. Hortman about Chip having raped me twice and even about Mr. Jones—certainly, my father's contributions. As I did, they never had to face any formal repercussions. Surprisingly, she never asked what had happened to Chip. And if she had; I'd tell her I didn't know. Not even a simple clarification he was dead or by what means

The air in the office became boney; I wrung my clammy hands in my lap. I began counting to myself to push the thoughts of what I'd done, and those leaching days at Davy out of my head. But it was too late as my mind flashed back. Flashback to images of Mr. Jones face down on the pile of bricks. My father's body on the sofa and the resulting blood at the shot of a rifle. The repeated thrusting of the knife into Chip's chest. To that of Davy's begrimed thirteenth floor. All spinning around me, as I sat feeling anger and an emptiness as reality pulled away. Then, the sound of Dr. Hortman' voice brought me back to the present.

"James-Randall… James… "

I took in a few deep breaths.

"Let me get right to the point," Dr. Hortman quantified.

I remained glued in the chair, my eyes wide. Surely, with a look like a deer caught in the headlights.

"Although you've made progress… I feel not to the degree I would like. In fact, you've been withdrawing. And I'm concerned the repeated horror flicks… as you put them, may eventually push you to another attempt."

I suddenly felt challenged. Concerned. The office blurred. I was sure Hortman was processing. She stood up from behind her desk. Walked around it over to one of the club chairs by the sofa and sat down next to me. Dr. Hortman comfortingly looked me in the eyes again. I looked away as before, then back again. Hortman paused a moment—almost in hesitation. She then gazed out the large window of her office that looked over a green grassy area with large trees before returning it back to me. I felt it coming—the point.

"James-Randall… I think if you earnestly want to try to live life to the fullest that you can and find some happiness… then you need to make that long-overdue move to California. As long as you stay here, you'll just keep going in circles with the fluctuations of depression and the night terrors as the nightmares… the messed-up dreams that are haunting you."

A blank look must have covered my face. Nervous tension grew.

"I want you to seriously consider leaving Atlanta."

"I… I'm not sure what to say," I responded.

"Say that you will. Say you'll test the waters… so to speak."

"I've already given up on that dream."

"James… have you really? Entirely?"

She didn't give me a chance to answer. Instead quizzed me again, if I'd given any thought, even a moment's to moving to the West Coast since I first told her I'd given up on it? I admitted on occasions.

"You've talked about how much California means to you in a few sessions. At times, even with a slight smile on your face… a somewhat bittersweet one in my view."

Bradley came to mind as I momentarily closed my eyes; my heart seemed to empty of blood.

"But…you've kept putting it off for the needs of other people… and questionable reasons. And fear. But I think it's a fear you must face. There's no one in your way except yourself… "

I conveyed it was too late. That, as she knew, a part of me has always lived in the past and for too long. So why risk anymore pain? That, I now have a beautiful new loft I purchased last summer; and though it doesn't feel like a home, at least it was more than comfortable. And at times, it seemed to be a safe place from the world.

"Well, there's a big difference between comfortable and happy."

She referred to the idea as food for thought—to give it serious consideration at this stage of therapy. But Hortman clarified: she wasn't telling me to leave but rather believed it would be good for me. That, I might surprise myself. That, after some time had passed, California just might be the best therapy for me. And that, I could hopefully make real peace with Bradley's death as other issues. Then, she recapped her concerns of me succeeding at ending my life at some point if I remain in the South and certainly, Atlanta. Again, unaware of the third attempt in November. I knew she was right. I'd known it myself—felt it was inevitable.

"What do you have to lose? Spend a few months there. Rent a house on the beach… and stay a while even if it hurts."

I started to speak but paused. I couldn't seem to finish the rest of it. Couldn't gather the remaining words. And the few I did, seem to have rolled over a cliff. I knew too, that Dr. Hortman saw something deeper in my eyes as she kept her complete focus on my face.

"I have a question for you, James."

"Okay."

"When Christopher asked you to stay for three more years… did you think of Bradley? Was he even on your mind as you were preparing to move after your mother's passing and before you knew him?"

Dr. Hortman reminded me of the answer of no that I gave her at an earlier session, after she'd asked if I really wanted Christopher to move with me to California once I'd agreed to stay longer in Atlanta.

"I did. Bradley was on my mind a lot. Even at my mother's service.

I told Hortman, I'd put two pictures of Bradley and me in my mother's casket along with many other things. How I stood by it with my hand on top of hers and talked about him and everything. Including, that we planned on them meeting. About how Bradley insisted, he would convince her to leave Warner Robins and move to LA. And, how I believed she would have. Like, I believed she'd instantly like him. And then she would know Bradley was good for me as she would see the love we cradled. I told her about how I lied when I'd suddenly returned to LA after he died but told her I was going for another modeling job instead; because I didn't want her to know my heart was breaking—how it bled for him.

I choked up. Covered my face with my hands.

"Are you okay, James?"

I let out a long breath. A breath that perhaps I'd been holding for years on end since the phone rang that devastating night.

"No. No, I'm not okay… I wished I'd died with him that day."

Dr. Hortman moved her hand to my shoulder.

"Do… do you think you possibly used Christopher as an excuse not to move to LA when he asked you to say without fully being conscious of it?"

Hortman believed: perhaps, at some point while in the middle of my preparations, I started feeling some reluctance—some emotional angst of returning to live in California. That it all circled back to Bradley, even after all the time that had passed.

She was right. I remember feeling some sense of relief after I agreed to stay. Dr. Hortman helped me realize I stayed because of Bradley and not for Christopher.

"I also think your mother was a contributor to you delaying. Again, consciously unaware, you somehow felt by moving you would be deserting her even though she had passed."

At that moment, I wanted to run out of her office in grief. Run out the building. Run to the street and into the middle of traffic.

"Another question about him… okay?"

"Sure."

"Why haven't you written about Bradley in your books?"

A humming sound like that from a neon sign filled my head.

"I… I've never shared anything about him because he belongs to me… and my memories of us are mine. They're sacred. I never wanted to share him with anyone. I guess that's why."

An image of Bradley lifting me in a bear hug flooded my mind.

Again, Dr. Hortman went on to ask, after everything that had taken place since 2009, to the present, if I'd be okay giving California a chance.

"I know this can be perceived as a trite question…. but I'll ask it anyway."

"Okay… sure."

"What do you think Bradley would want you to do?"

I repositioned my body. Cleared my throat.

"He'd… want me to. We both knew that was where I belonged, with or without him."

"So, don't you think you should… more so for you?"

eleven

exiting atlanta

I stood on the roof of the loft scrutinizing downtown Atlanta. The hour—placidly late. The moment clung to the humid air, saturated in a vapid haze of disquiet that lingered from the suffocating heat of an interminable day of indecision. It wafted over the city like a once pure-white bedsheet—now stained with the scum of an impure heart and the spilled blood of a broken soul.

Millions of lights illuminated outward from the windows of the myriad facets sculpting an impressive Atlanta skyline, comprising a vast architectural variety of buildings as they pushed through the baked haze of that mid-summer night. The mix of the old and the new—configured a modern-age city as it towered upward in the quietude. A near-full moon was juxtaposed between two skyscrapers like a large silver Christmas tree ornament in the concrete and steel jungle.

The silence fenced me. The air—remarkably still. Either the human race had ended, leaving me the last person alive or I'd fully been overtaken by the consuming isolation of loneliness to the degree of being incapable of seeing another living creature if it were standing right in front of me—nose to nose. If I hadn't known better, my eyes were fixated on an oversized photograph of the city—arms fully extended and clutched in my hands. The solitude, that defining of a life lived on a seesaw in a children's playground, but the only games played were rated for adults on the edge.

I'd only resided in the loft about a year since its purchase—almost to-the-day, in the middle of another sultry Atlanta summer. As if apprehended by time, I'd been fast-forwarded to July of 2013. Another year had come and gone totaling thirty-two, but the last one had felt like years rather than some twelve months. That night, on the roof looking out over the city, any attachment once felt had morphed into contempt. I'd become a stranger to Atlanta as it had to me. They say, all things must come to an end. Atlanta had come to that—as if it met its death. Better the city—than me.

Although I'd taken the advice of Dr. Hortman to finally leave Atlanta and the South, I felt much like a child being ripped from his mother's arms. And once again, I was concerned it would be a volatile transition as it would be emotionally stressful—until I found the right patient-doctor fit from the list of referrals she provided. I hoped whomever I found was as great as Dr Horman.

To hopefully minimize my concerns, she afforded four months of medication refills. And told me to check-in, and she would do the same. Dr. Hortman had been right about making the move—likely having been priming me for most of the past year to go after my sharing what all California meant to me. I knew I had to as she did. And if not, then jump. No more waiting to see. I'd used them all up—the waiting to sees. My life had come down to one of two choices: move and possibly live or stay in Atlanta locked up in my loft with Dugan and die.

Furthermore, as long as I kept my feet on Georgia soil—I'd continue walking over the dead bodies of the ghosts that chronically haunted me after they surfaced along with little Randy in January of 2009. I anticipated how much of the pain would follow me—preferring it to remain behind. But I wasn't fooling myself; I knew some of the pain, as those ghosts would always be my shadows. As I'd learned very early in life: I could never outrun all of the past or the injury of it. But maybe—just maybe I could get a good running start.

Besides Dr. Hortman, and the friends that hadn't walked away in 2009, I found myself contemplating what I'd feel ripped from—the more Atlanta's skyline dwindled in the rearview mirror as I drove south on I-75, merging onto I-85, and then I-20 West? Almost the same route I'd planned on taking once finishing high school in 1974, in my 1968, yellow Mustang Fastback.

Not surprisingly, little came to mind. Then, I thought of how I'd miss the summer rains. Yes, the rain—those plenteous Southern washes. That thought of missing rain, prompted the memory of the 1972, chart-topping hit, "It Never Rains in Southern California."

I'd miss Anna, too. Miss, seeing her on Wednesdays as other extra days. Miss, her funny disposition and occasional harmless sarcasm. Miss, helping Anna at times folding my laundry as other things. Miss, finding those baked cookies she left on the kitchen counter every week. As she'd waved her policy of no packing and unpacking boxes, Anna did the same concerning helping with my exit.

Earlier in the day, we worked at wrapping what household items were left while Dugan supervised. That, too, took me back to the summer before. Anna joked of how she'd miss him more than me. I knew Dugan would miss the balcony, but not the stairs between the first and second levels. As far as lying in the sun—there was plenty in California for him to enjoy.

As Anna was about to leave, I gave her a parting gift: an envelope securing a check and a note. I made Anna promise not to open it until she'd returned home. My eyes teared. I saw her as a friend—a dear one, at that.

"Now, now. No tears," she said. "We'll keep in touch," Anna promised, as she hugged me and kissed my cheek.

"I'll call you before I leave, and once I get to California. You can always visit. Say you will… I'll cover your plane ticket."

"Oh. You just want me to come to unpack," Anna joked.

"No… I just want those cookies, and I want you to come because I love you, my friend."

Anna smiled and kissed my cheek again. She began walking to the door. Dugan followed. Anna squatted to kiss him on the snout.

"You be a good boy and look after your daddy."

Anna looked over at me as she stood up. She winked. Opened the door and stepped outside. She didn't look back. Once the door closed behind her, I bawled like a baby.

My gaze adhered constantly over the city as many layers upon layers of thoughts—from joy to bereavements, zipped back to the very day my car crossed the city limit sign. Despite years of baggage still carried, then I was that young, wide-eyed, man looking to build his own life and find his dreams while biding time to go West. Then, believing it would be a short stop; I never calculated, almost thirty-two years.

Nevertheless, over that unanticipated extended timeline: I'd witnessed the city evolve into a beautiful world-class metropolis—the fifth largest in the country. Together, we both had gone through many reconstructions—many growing pains. Now, I was saying goodbye. But more than a goodbye, and as much as I needed to finally exit, it felt like another death. And like a death, like it's said when a person's life flashes before them, I was experiencing the same.

Within the first chapter of my existence in Atlanta, as well, I carried the ingredients of hope, promise, perseverance, compromise, and a nice helping of the good luck of being in the right place at the right time. But in the mix of it all, the great loss of an amazing man and, again, the life that was stolen from us by his death.

To this day, Bradley's death was as it remains the greatest loss of my life. Somehow, I eventually managed to step forward. And where others would have eventually left that childhood and Bradley's death in a box, I never really did—never closed that box. I realize that more than ever today. And it will remain open until I die. It's just how I was made over time. Plus, among it all, as his death was my greatest loss, Bradley was also the greatest gift I was ever given by being in the right place at the right time—and the circumstances that brought me there that night of our meeting.

And with each step forward, there were many steps backward. I honestly think the only thing that kept me going up until 2009, were those many masks I wore and the three people I had become. And because of them—those masks and those three different people behind them: I took hold of the sundry opportunities that presented themselves—many by just walking into a room as I've also stated before; included, are the parts of the world I was able to see; the accomplishments; passions lived with laughter and love of friendships built through community and volunteerism. Much of all had become foreign those last watery four years—all overshadowed by the blanket of depression that had nearly suffocated me to death as it had those many positive experiences.

The sun would be returning to the sky soon. In those outermost prickly hours as I looked up into an almost starless black sky, I recalled how I'd barely survived that move a year ago from the house to the loft—some six or so miles apart due to nearly thirty-six hours' lack of sleep, hoarded in emotional instability. Now within a few days, I was about to drive over two-thousand miles. I wondered what this upcoming move would be like. There was concern—more than, but I knew, again, I had to do this. I had to make the move and not think too much about it in fear of seconding-guessing the decision. Unlike the lyrics from the Albert Hammond's and Mike HazleMillsood's song—will you tell the folks back home I nearly made it; I had to do more than nearly make it. I had to make it.

I'd already purchased a home in the desert some ninety miles from Los Angeles: a mid-century with amazing views in the foot-hills of the small city of Desert Hot Springs. Located, ten miles east and with a higher elevation than the flat plain of Palm Springs. Both guarded on three sides by the San Bernardino and San Jacinto Mountains ranges.

The dwarfing vastness of the desert offered a sense of peace that at times made my emotional issues feel smaller. Plus, it was only some 90 miles to Los Angeles and about the same to Laguna Beach. The ocean offered peace as well. Both a calmness somewhat similar as I found at times sitting under that old oak tree in Piedmont Park with Dugan. At the time, the plan was to wait a few years before moving into the City of Angels. Baby steps. And I needed those baby steps; but this time, I was mindful of their necessity.

Perhaps, too, I chose the desert more so because I needed time and that's why I didn't move directly into LA. More time to come to grips with the return of the flooding memories of Bradley's death—of our death.

As Dr. Hortman had surmised: I was afraid of returning to live in LA after the stretching years—and certainly, without Bradley. I needed to take it slow and not have too many expectations—if any.

The Jag and the Rover were already a third of the way West on a car transport. The movers would arrive first thing that morning; a cleaning crew would come later in the day to give the loft a final once-over, alt-hough Anna had left it spotless for the new owner.

My thoughts stayed fixated on the details of the move and to the road trip across the country with Dugan and my sister. Like I could never leave our mother, I didn't want to leave Sandra behind. Besides, I knew she needed to get as far away from Georgia as I did. We would be driving her car, having decided to take our time and make it an adventure.

Finally, a home in California was waiting. Again, it just wouldn't be in Bradley's arms as it had been. I preferred to leave Atlanta un-noticed. None of it began to feel real until we crossed over the Georgia-Alabama line. That realness grew with each of the 2,173 miles traveled. Still, I knew the South would try to call me back, but I didn't have any intentions of answering. It was time to stop trying to die—finally time to go home and live the best I could.

land of sunshine

I became passionately acquainted with the Land of Sunshine and in particular, the Hollywood Hills shortly after my arrival in Atlanta when hired for a one-liner in a commercial. Even though having done several local fashion shoots and one other commercial for tennis wear, I white-knuckled with apprehension each time I received a call from the agency informing me that they had another job lined up. Leaving me each time to think, "Surely, they must be out of their fucking minds."

That same trepidation and thought—but amplified, once I found myself in Los Angeles; the city of the beautiful, full of both seasoned models and those bussing it in from all corners of the United States—many, in hopes of one day memorialized with their own five-pointed terrazzo and brass star along Hollywood Boulevard. So, again, what was this kid from Middle Georgia doing hanging among them?

Within days of the call for my first gig in the City of Angels, I learned it was dropped in my lap courtesy of the photographer, Kip. His influence and connections were a driving force after he'd sent one of my reels and some photographs.

At the production, I pretty much felt as if I'd just gotten off the bus. That is, until Garrett. One of the makeup artists; a good-looking, brown-eyed and hair, tall and lean, corn-fed transplant from Wisconsin. I well-remember his white skin. Thinking, at the time, it must be unusual for someone living in the state that seldom knew rain, but rather sunshine and endless beaches, would have such skin untouched by the sun.

During breaks, Garrett hadn't made it difficult to catch-on he'd taken a shine to me: a purposeful stance closer than necessary while he performed touch-ups; his leg casually brushing against mine; how he leaned in; the way his hand re-positioned from my upper arm to the shoulder; occasionally, a touch that lingered on my back; a beguiling stare transfixing my eyes as he patted beads of sweat from my forehead—an ardent look that translated: "I really want to fuck your brains out." The latter, certainly not in his job description and a look with which I'd already become very familiar. The attraction was shared, as the attention helped keep my mind off my insecurities.

That late Friday afternoon, after the commercial wrapped, Garrett timidly and in an endearing fashion—seemingly out of character for what I perceived as a confident guy, offered an invitation to join him and some friends for dinner. I jumped at the chance. Later that evening, as arranged, Garrett collected me in a white Mustang convertible with red leather interior at my hotel in North Hollywood near Universal Studios. It was fall and the air, relatively chilly with the top down.

A brisk drive later; we arrived at Casita de Campo Mexican restaurant on Hyperion. With the expected décor, I followed my escort thought clamorous conversations—unmistakably, full of an assortment of gay men with wandering eyes and telling seducing smiles. I stood behind Garrett as he lingered in the middle of the dining room. His head moved side-to-side, reading the crowd for his friends. My low self-esteem meter suddenly—rose into the red.

Garrett soon reached around and took my hand. "Follow me," he said, with a smile. I did. He made a beeline to a table in the far corner with an unobstructed view of the room. Two nice-looking men sat drinking beers while waving us over. Garrett made the introductions as we took our seats. The years since have erased their names. One was a young actor-in-the-making, Malcolm and the other, Steve, perhaps twenty years older, a public relations director for a popular soap opera. My shyness subsided the more I felt welcomed by the small group of friends, and the more Garrett placed his hand just above my left knee and gave a reassuring squeeze. The conversation was pleasant and engaging as eyes ricocheted from table-to-table.

Upon finishing dinner, Steve extended an invitation to a party up in the Hills. I was thrilled to be invited to continue the evening with these three handsome and well-mannered gentlemen. Garrett and I followed them in his Mustang. Steve, with Malcolm riding shotgun, drove a two-door, black, convertible Cadillac Coupe De Ville like a race car. The two vehicles traveled along Fountain Avenue to Santa Monica, then onto Sunset until they took a sharp right turn onto Hollywood Boulevard, winding upward into the Hills. The increasing height and magical city lights below, were dizzying as the cars drove up higher—in continuous, snaking, circles.

Once having arrived at our destination without a speeding ticket, the drivers parked behind a line of cars on the side of the narrow road. Our small entourage walked along a walkway flanked by a glass wall of falling water that led to a stylishly lit contemporary house set back in the hillside. Steve opened the front door without knocking. Straight away, we were greeted by Blondie's song, "Rapture" accompanied by scattered sporadic laughter and conversational chatter. That night—the very moment I walked into that house; another world opened-up. One even better than that boy sitting inches from the television, mesmerized by Cher in all her glory.

A toney gathering socialized. As expected, several pretty people stood out. Two, recognized from a soap my mother watched and recorded VHS tapes to send Sandra while she was stationed in Germany. I was never a fan of daytime television—invoking images of bored and lonely housewives living unfulfilled lives. Instead, existing vicariously through concocted storylines of lust, infidelity, mayhem, and even murder. All the while, many of their husbands spent their lunchtimes screwing their secretaries while their wives sat in front of the television between household chores. Perhaps, that's why the soaps were so popular: for a few hours a day, those discontented housewives could forget just how sad and ordinary their lives truly were. Possibly, my mother found a small period of escape as well, within the storylines and actors of those soaps.

Garrett shared that Steve worked with a main producer on one of the shows—also, owner of the house. I pretended to be interested but not impressed; even though I definitely was. As usual, out of my element, I felt out-of-place. But there was nothing new about that annoying feeling. Still, I was determined to belong. I was becoming a quick study and did my best to keep self-doubts and insecurities corralled. All of it was new and even raw: the modeling, the attention, and physically in California—and I was loving it all.

Garrett's attentiveness from the day and dinner continued. He left my side briefly to acquire two glasses of wine from the bartender behind a long kitchen counter with every imaginable liquor set out like a mini skyline of a sprawling city. Since dinner, I'd wondered the dimensions of his interest. Wondered if Garrett's curiosity went any further than my ass, or was there a sincere intent to get to know me? Could there be something more in his mind to develop? I was eager to obtain a direct human connection to the West Coast: a boyfriend.

Without fail, he remained the considerate gentleman as we talked. Garrett's body language, along with his eyes and smile were encouraging.

Encouraging, I wouldn't be waking up alone in the morning. Once the: "So, tell me more about yourself," expected question was posed, I gave my usual answer: small town Southern kid, college graduate working my way west with a brief stop in Atlanta. Any more details requiring truthful answers would have been a second date deal breaker. As Garrett poked for more, nervous perspiration dampened my armpits. Luckily, one of the guests pulled him away after a brief introduction—leaving me standing alone in the room of strangers. Mingling was yet a social art I'd come to fully master.

the view

The wall of sliding glass doors were wide opened as if to welcome in the magnetic allure of that clear and crisp California evening, filled with the magic of a fairy-tale. As the open doors welcomed in the night—the night beckoned me outside. The nervousness of feeling awkward was inching away; I walked out onto the long, expansive balcony bigger than my apartment back in Atlanta. Instantly, I fell in love for a second time with the expansively mesmerizing views. The openness, dwarfing me as I leaned out wanting to become captured within the enchanting night air—only braced by the railing from falling forward, and tumbling down the hillside.

My eyes remained locked in a trance-like state, absorbing it all like a dry sponge. In the fullness of time, I was standing at the pinnacle of the city where I'd belonged—where that teenager knew it had constantly beckoned. Irrevocably, as with the first inhalation of air when I walked outside of Los Angeles International Airport for the first time. Every fiber in my body told me so. Yes, I was the closest I'd ever been to happiness other than the day of my father's death. But that was a different kind of happiness—more of relief, tethered to the sweetness of long-awaited revenge.

My gaze lingered over the night. Or was it the night taking stock of me. Whichever, it was exquisite. This boy had made it all the way from Warner Robins, Georgia, on the opposite side of the country to Los Angeles, California—finding himself in a house in the hills of Hollywood. One of those life-changing moments that one never forgets—at least, not me. I just had to find a way to make it permanent. What Warner Robins? What Georgia? What South? What father? What childhood? At least that one night—except the concerns for my mother—they had all been sucked into outer space until the sun burned them all to ash. Burned them to ash in a fiery blaze that California night.

Regardless of how incongruous I'd felt earlier walking into that world, this was where, again, I belonged. Ripe with desires and lust. Over-the-moon happy—as if California was a lover in my bed. My imagination—impetuous, ran with wonder. Wonder of what it would be like to live the life, I speculated most of the people in attendance lived every day. The thought of returning to Atlanta in two days kicked at my heart. And, if indeed I were one of those people, it would be a rags-to-riches story—and much more.

Then, the thought of my mother pawed its way into my head. My happiness turned to sadness. My mind's eye saw her in that house. I debated her state at the time, even though we'd talked on the phone after I'd returned to the hotel from the wrap up and before Garrett had picked me up. She seemed fine at the time but all-the-same—I knew she felt alone. I questioned if she was sleeping with any comfort at that moment or sitting at the table in the low light of the breakfast room smoking cigarette-after-cigarette and drinking while listening to all those sad songs. At that, guilt collared my neck.

A couple stood at the far end of the balcony: a lean, pretty, long-blonde-haired woman nuzzled in the arms of a Rock Hudson-type. She and I happened to catch each other's eye. The woman smiled and cordially raised her glass of wine to me. I returned the gesture in equal measure and in appreciation of being noticed. Other than them, I was alone with the room behind me abuzz. By the increase in the decibel level of voices, the party had grown in number.

Moments later, a voice interrupted my admiration of the view.

"It's a beautiful night… don't you agree?"

I looked to my left. A tall classically handsome man, perhaps pushing fifty-five with movie-star black hair, graying at the temples, stood a few steps from me as if he'd materialized from the night air.

"Yes, quite amazing," I replied, turning my head in his direction.

"I get to enjoy it most nights… I'm Aaron," he introduced, as he moved closer and leaned on the railing as well.

"Randy… my name is Randy."

"It's a pleasure. You know… if the air is clear in the morning, you can see as far out as the ocean," he spoke as his eyes scanned me.

"That must be something to see… so, this is your lovely home?"

"Yes. Yes, it is."

I slightly looked over my shoulder. Again, wondering what had happened to Garrett then returned my focus to Aaron. His smile widened. I looked back at the view then returned my sight to my unexpected host. He brushed his arm against mine. My first thought was if his comment about seeing the ocean in the morning from that vantage point might be a subtle invitation to spend the night—coming across as somewhat of a pick-up line. Or just wishful thinking as his mysterious dark eyes pulled me in.

"It would appear you could use more wine. How about a refill?"

"I… I'm fine, thanks. This last bit is enough for me."

"Well, if you change your mind."

"Sure, you'll be the first to know," I unintentionally flirted.

It was just the way the words came out of my mouth that might perceived it that way. But Aaron was clearly a player. Call it a feeling and some experience. The giveaways were his smooth approach and devil-may-care manner.

If Aaron's earlier comment about the ocean in the morning was indeed an invitation, I'd find myself caught in a quandary if both Garrett and Aaron were sending the same message. But I came with Garrett and felt I should leave with him. Either way, the night would have the last word.

A light and genial conversation continued as I shared with Aaron I'd come to the party with Garrett and his friends Steve and Malcolm. Garrett had yet to return. Briefly I took my eyes off Aaron to look over my shoulder to see if Garrett was in eyesight; but by then the living area was packed. Aaron had moved over until we were almost shoulder to shoulder. His hand occasionally touched my back as we continued to get acquainted.

Eventually, Garrett and his buddies came out on the balcony and joined us. Somewhat unsteady on his feet, Garrett tightly put his arm around my waist and kissed me on the cheek as if laying claim to me. The heavy alcohol on his breath told me Garrett had one-to-many cocktails while enjoying the party. After more conversation—all being well-acquainted, Steve let me know they would soon be leaving as he nodded his head toward Garrett to acknowledge that. That, he was overserved.

"You about ready to head out, Randy?"

I hesitated. I really didn't want to leave and go back to the hotel. I could have stayed on the balcony all night just enjoying the views. At that, Aaron jumped in to offer he would see I got back.

"If you want to stay a while longer, Randy… I can have a car take you to your hotel when you're ready. The party is just getting started."

I looked at Garrett, and then his friends. Garrett made an exaggerated frown.

"Come with us, Randy… we're going to stop off and… and get a night… nightcap at a club on Sun… Sunset."

Both his friends shook their heads, no.

"We need to get you to bed," Steve insisted.

I gave Garrett a hug and told him I wanted to enjoy the party a bit longer and that he really should get to bed.

"Awe, Ran… Randy. Are you mad?"

"No. not at all. No reason to be," I offered. "Call me at the hotel in the morning. We can meet for breakfast," I added, convinced Garrett would be greeted with one hell of a hangover and would not be venturing out too early.

Aaron's comment about the ocean had been an invitation after all. Except to check out of the hotel and a dinner at Brenner's, I didn't leave his home until Monday morning after an unexpected three nights and two days lost in the head-spinning exhilaration of the weekend. I did call Garrett in the late morning the next day. I was right, he was too hungover to get out of bed. I didn't want to blow him off for the rest of the weekend, so I kept my plans vague.

Aaron called a town car to return me to the airport. I looked back as he stood on the street until the car snaked to the right down the hill. I resented every mile back to LAX—as I did upon boarding the flight back to Atlanta. But Aaron was right. You could see the ocean in the distance from his balcony in the mornings. At the time, I wasn't quite sure if I stayed the weekend to be with Aaron—or if I did more so for the view.

sex, love, or a savior

Aaron and I stayed in touch to a limited degree. If Garrett knew anything about my interlude weekend with the producer, it was never mentioned over numerous phone conversations. Upon my return to Atlanta, he'd left several messages. The first, again, apologizing for his inebriated condition at the party. Garrett expressed he wanted to make it up the next time I was in Los Angeles. The interest was mutual, but the notion was left up in the air—left to future circumstances to determine as we occasionally continued to talk. Garrett eventually started dating a guy; they moved in together. But, by then, we'd developed a long-distance friendship and would hang out when I was out West.

Several months had passed before I was sent back out to the city I loved. Unexpectedly, I revisited that magical night in Aaron's home in the Hills. After drinks and dinner, we shared a sexually charged night from sunset to sunrise that made the first encounter seem like a dress rehearsal.

As amazing as it was, the second go-around told me nothing would come from seeing him a third time. As I'd suspected, Aaron was a player—not of the settling-down human species. Although still naïve, I wasn't that disappointed although I would miss the view from the balcony—actually more so than I would miss not seeing Aaron again.

By then, I was growing confident by degrees. More comfortable in my skin for longer periods. During those times, I did see the beauty on either side of my flesh in the mirror. Concerning the outside, many visions of the ugliness of childhood had been temporarily flushed as if using extra strength Visine. More and more the exhilaration—the excitement molded a whole new person each time I walked out of LAX. I discovered attributes extraordinary about myself—smothered by many layers of abuse. I was learning my looks had great power over men, rich and poor alike. But that power had to be controlled as it came with a price. One similar to which my mother had paid—and one of many exacted by my father's obsession to own her beauty; to take ownership and control.

It was also becoming exceedingly apparent: men, as a whole, were either fun and games or disappointments—certainly confusing at times especially if I wasn't sure I was truly capable of maintaining a relationship as much as I wanted one. That is, if I could even find a test subject with some promising results, like a study for a cure for a disease. And if I did, I wasn't sure if I could delineate between lust and love, and a savior. A savior like Dennis, who I wrote about in my first book, had been in some ways. The older teacher, who lived in the Massee apartments in Macon while I was attending postgraduate courses.

Dennis was a rescuer; he was safe. And I certainly was so far from knowing what being in love was all about then. All I knew was, need. We were both seeing women the whole time he was fucking me. I know he eventually came to love me, but I never felt the same deep down inside. In all frankness, I was just using Dennis for that need to be saved. Still, I was too tightly tied to him in a sick way. And I felt severed when he got married because I told him: I was moving to Atlanta. That, he should marry the woman he was seeing. Then, I had sex with Dennis the night before the wedding. My need stronger than any resolve to abstain. It was all fucked-up from that day we met. Especially, on the drive back to Atlanta as I manically contemplated jumping out of a moving car on I-75, feeling as if I was being abandoned—as was my need.

Maybe all I was—was a sexual conquest. Another notch among many on their bed posts. At least that was what I was learning. It's discouraging—more so, that one of those notches wasn't the one. It's laughable: a whore selling his body for money and-or love. Either way, I would come to learn to use my looks to my advantage. At the time, even in the event I found the one, he would have to understand my mother would remain a priority—at least until she remarried, that is, if she ever did. The reality was growing like an unsightly furuncle on the chin: finding love wasn't going to be a slam dunk. It wouldn't be that easy to bump into, Mr. Let's Settle-down and Be Happy. My odds would likely be better of rear-ending a stranger on the 105 in Los Angeles, and the driver being the one.

Sporadically, I returned to the West Coast—mostly for work. A few trips, to test the waters if there was any depth to two encounters after Aaron and Garrett, and at the request of another older man that was paying me. But they proved to have lackluster outcomes. The older man became abusive, hitting me like he could because I was his property. I guess I was—his property sense again, he'd basically purchased me. None of them, not even worth the cost of the round-trip airfares. Regardless, my love affair remained with Los Angeles. I wasn't going to give up on that one.

Yet to find the one human connection that would securely attach me to the City of Angels, I felt as if in a competition. A race to find the one—the blue ribbon. After all, Los Angeles had plenty of guys from whom to pick. Too many temptations—much like Miquel Brown's 1983, disco song, "So Many Men So Little Time." Unlike its lyrics, I wanted to settle down with one and never have to give my body to another. In the interim, sex was, again, a distraction from reality. More so, being desired even for the exchange of money grew more addictive and the act of willingly being taken was transforming. But the only positive outcome—proved to be for my bank account.

then entered bradley

"Do you love me in this hour of light, in a city, in a room, in a morning?"
Walter Holland

I thought other men would eventually begin to wane the memory of him. Fade how he looked at me with those ice-blue eyes; the feel of his touch; the smells of him; of his lips capturing mine and their taste—dear God, their taste so intoxicating; the way his body felt against mine—its weight each time we made love and once finished, how he would hold me, his body wrapping mine as if it was a blanket; the passion and ecstasy; the sound of his voice and the words he spoke—especially, " I love you, Randy… and will forever."

Yes, I hoped as each man who fucked me more and more and more, the imagines of him would become only an outline—until my mind could no longer sketch him. Until everything. Everything. Everything and each moment had escaped.

I've sporadically mentioned Bradley throughout this telling—but not in any expansive commission. In some instances, expressing the powerful pull he had on me. Now, I'll share part of our story from the beginning until our demise—but never, the end of love. In fact,

I came to understand true love—almost from the very moment my eyes met his.

I know all too well the advancing years can be forgiving as they can be ruthless. They can push memories—cherished, or our worse-lived nightmares to the background. But within those gathering years or at any time in the course of one's life, they—those memories can unexpectedly be resurrected; and with that resurrection, the more painful they are—submerge us in merciless and crippling despondency.

It was so many years ago. So many years swallowed by time. So many years since the unforeseen day came, I tried to forget one man—forget him as much as I immensely loved him to the point of unyielding heartbreak. At a time when some would say I was too young to know real love. But they would be wrong. I was fortunate to be consumed by it and freely so. It was real—free of any doubts.

Although I've never shared what is written on the fragile pages made so by time, the words penned from the depths of my heart remain as strong as they were when written—inspired from first sight and first touch. Those words painfully read so many years later from the journal dedicated to him and dismissing what I've stated concerning Christopher in "Alabama Snow," I've only known one true love encompassing a soulmate and friend.

Somehow, I knew there would be no other like him—despite the few men before and the many after Bradley, regardless of how exceptional some of the others may have been; they could never compare. But I didn't love any of them. I just tried to believe I did. And yes, I didn't even know what love felt like until Bradley in each captured breath from his lungs.

Those other men's faces were nebulous by the years, if not sooner. Most of their names forgotten overnight or eventually lost within life's vicissitudes. But the memories of Bradley—of us, came and went notwithstanding how hard I tried to keep them of us at bay.

Out of all the years of my life, I've only known one home. Not a house with windows and doors and floors and ceilings and steps and a roof, but in the embrace of one man. He was all those things and more—immeasurably. Bradley was life itself. He was the oxygen that filled my lungs. The blood that ran through my body. The heart that beat in my chest. He was the waves washing the sand on beaches as he made love to me. He was the sun that warmed me. The moon and the stars that lit up the darkest night. He was the man I'd been looking for since I was a boy to save me from my father. Bradley was constant.

Mother had called the Friday night before I was to take a red-eye to Los Angeles on Sunday. We'd planned to spent the weekend together beforehand.

"Son… I just don't feel up to it. Let's put it off until you return. Okay?"

Knowing something was up, I dismissed what Mother had told me; I drove to Warner Robins early Saturday morning. As always, I heard the lie between her words. The one of several—too many times. Even: "It will never happen again. I'll quit… you can count on it." Not to mention the ones my father fabricated to his children as those he'd promised Mother early on. It got to the point I knew instantly that if I heard either one of them say: never again, quit, or count on it—all were lies in the making. In the making over and over, until at a very early age I finally learned that any word that equated to a promise was nothing more than a lie. Promises were antonyms. Too many to distinguish between what was true and what wasn't. And I knew all about lying.

Deceptively, I'd gotten very good at it. Learning by my own actions that I didn't need to speak a single word in order to tell a lie. I just had to get away with it. Get away with whatever it was that I did, no matter how horrible it might have been. Between my mother's spoken lies and my nonverbal ones, I would state that it made me feel as if our whole lives had been a lie. I wish that were the case because tragically, the reality was too ugly. Too monstrous. Too damning. Too heartbreaking. The lies were our lives. Lies lived and lies to die by. The only truth in the lies was that we were telling them, or again in my case—not speaking of them in order to protect each other. They, those lies however presented, only served to change us in the worst of ways.

That Friday night over the phone, I not only heard the lie but also that certain sadness in her voice that meant she was about to dive into a bottle of liquor for temporary comfort that she would never find at the bottom once it was empty.

"But… Mom, I want us to hang out before my flight leaves on Sunday night."

"No. No don't come. I need to rest. Call me Monday when you get to LA. I love you, Son."

The phone line went dead.

I knew if everything was okay, Mother would want me to come. She would never pass up the opportunity to spend time with me. We'd planned on driving to Macon for lunch at Beall's 1860 restaurant—on College Street. Located in the historic section of Macon, within walking distance of the Mercer University campus. The Beall's mansion stood out with its strikingly beautiful, white, neoclassical massive Corinthian columns lining its front and sides. On Sunday, we were going to church and attend the after-service luncheon where she liked to show off her son as she had dozens of times.

I arrive at the house to find Mother disheveled and intoxicated. She was difficult and dismissive from the moment I walked in the door. Angry that I'd come, but it was clear as to why: she didn't want me to see her in a disheveled state which I was already well-familiar with. Mother was agitated with garbled speech as she repeated the same thing: "I told you not to come!" Not only a sign she'd spent the night drinking but hadn't been taking her medications properly. The whole scenario was like watching reruns of a bad movie I'd seen untold times with the same unhappy ending. As her son, I desperately wanted to rewrite the ending. And as much as I tried—deep down inside, I knew the movie would always end the same no matter how many attempted rewrites.

An empty bottle of vodka sat on the kitchen counter next to the sink filled with dirty dishes. Another, half-empty, on the breakfast table. I picked them up as Mother yelled not to pour them out. But I did, fully knowing it would add to her disgruntled state of mind; it had to be done. Afterward, I did my usual sweep of the house before cleaning up the kitchen as she continued to sulk.

At times, she viewed my actions as controlling; still, I had to keep doing whatever I could to protect her, whether she was doing well or otherwise—for both our sakes. I was always grateful for the long stretches of sobriety. But when Mother fell off the wagon, she fell hard. And as impossible as it may have seemed at those times, again, I couldn't blame her. I understood why and how wounded—how broken she was. And when I clearly saw her emotional, life-sucking pain in my mother's eyes—it felt like being crushed by the world for both of us.

Mother had been doing remarkably well until our phone conversation the night before. But as I'd done before, when Mother was in such a state, I nervously gave her half a sedative or sleeping pill. Nervous, because I didn't know what medications were possibly in her system, along with the alcohol. Still, I took the chance to settle Mother down in order to get her in bed. Thereafter, I would keep checking on her to make sure she was still breathing. Disturbingly, as I'd thought on many such occasions when she was at her extreme worse—where I saw no hope for her but only continued misery, that once she fell asleep, I should smother her with a bed pillow to end my mother's tormented life. At times, it seemed the kindest act I could do for her.

By evening, I called her trusted friend Siggy. She agreed to come to the house first thing in the morning. It wasn't the first time Siggy had been willing to help—when my older brother should have done so. I told Siggy over the phone, I was supposed to fly to Los Angeles Sunday night for a shoot but was going to cancel.

"Honey, she'll be fine. I'll make sure of it. You go. You have to or your mother will hate herself if you don't."

Knots snarled in my stomach, still unsure if I should make the shoot in Los Angeles. Siggy continued to reassure she'd watch over Mother and not to worry. A few hours before the flight's departure, Siggy practically pushed me out the door.

Under a moonless night, the car raced north on I-75—my stomach nauseated as a foreboding mind wondered if I should turn back around. I barely made it to the plane, as I ran to the departure gate as if being chased by hungry lions. Stopping long enough to present my boarding ticket before continuing my hast, through the jetway to catch the red-eye. The last passenger to board as the cabin door was about to close.

Although still teaming with worry, it felt good to be back in Los Angeles. The shoot had been long and made taxing by the photographer, but I managed through the day only to have to do it all over the next.

Somewhat still jet-lagged and emotionally frazzled after a day on the set and still worried about my mother, it was difficult to relax in my hotel room much less fall asleep—even after I'd called twice to check on her. Mother seemed to be back on stable ground. Shaky but better. She told me she was sorry and not to worry. Siggy confirmed it. But how could I not—not worry? I always did about my mother. Always. Worried that one day I'll find her dead from a combination of alcohol poisoning or over medicating herself… likely both, when I drive back to Warner Robins. How heavily it weighs on my heart. The fear I feel each time I walk back into that house. How the thought keeps me awake some nights as I see her—see Mother's breathless body lying on the floor or in bed in my mind's eye.

I tossed and turned on the bed. Got up and down. I soon gave up trying. I needed a distraction. Perhaps, even sex. A temporary fix like a drug addict that promises it will be their last one and then they will go clean. My mother's stopgap was alcohol—mine was in the arms of strangers.

I took a cab to the Gold Coast bar on Santa Monica Boulevard in West Hollywood. The crowd was thin which meant fewer men to choose from. I felt a few eyes on me, but not anyone I wanted. I was beginning to think I shouldn't have even bothered. Then, with the slight turn of my head, I saw him leaning against the bar at the far end and looking at me. Tall and thickly built. Rather handsome. Dirty-blonde hair. Tough looking. Blue-collar type. He looked safe. Safe like he could offer comfort. I took a stool in the middle of the bar. Ordered a club soda with a lime. Gave him a look with a casual smile before taking a sip of my drink. He returned it—the smile. At a closer look, he appeared to have a kind face with deep dimples and a square jaw. I took another look. This time, holding his gaze as if I'd cast a net. He offered a second, wider smile. Damn, I wanted him just by his smile alone.

"You have a chance," I thought. But I needed him to be interested enough to walk over. As a rule, I never made the first move. So, I waited. But I waited too long—or so I thought.

Within minutes, I was cock-blocked by a lean shaggy-headed guy who took the stool next to mine, blocking the delightful view. "Fuck," was my next thought as I could see "Shaggy" looking at me from the corner of my eye.

"Name's Clint," he said, wasting no time in making a move.

"Randy," I politely responded.

"You want to get out of here?" he asked, without even offering to buy me a drink first.

I felt his right hand move to my left thigh.

"Annoying guy," I thought.

I moved it off—sure, he'd get the hint. But he didn't.

"Awe… man, you're hot. I'll show you a good time."

"I bet you would, but I just came out for a drink… nothing else."

Clint moved his hand back to my thigh and slid it upward. He grabbed my crotch as if I was his bitch. I jumped back off the stool. It toppled over to the floor.

"Fuck man! I don't come with the drinks!" I reflexively said and loudly.

"What. You think you're better than me?"

There was no point in responding. I quickly glanced over at "Dimples." I felt embarrassed. He was staring, likely enjoying the short comedy at play.

I decided to leave and return to the hotel. I offered a last glance at "Dimples" before turning for the exit. A few steps from the door, I heard, "Hey, hold up." I stopped and turned around. There he was wearing the same smile. Taller than I thought. At least six-four.

"That's a lot of man," I thought.

His gripping ice-blue eyes were like deep churning ocean water. A few days' scruff covered his square, cleft chin.

"Hey," was all I could manage out of my mouth. His eyes had basically left me speechless.

"I bet you get that a lot."

"Get what?"

"Hit on and grabbed."

I shrugged my shoulders. It was one of my phobias and I did get grabbed a lot and hated it but didn't say as such—not wanting to come off as conceited.

"Clearly that guy had too much to drink," I answered, instead.

"Or something… maybe you should have a bodyguard."

"You looking for a job?" I joked, then coyly smiled.

"I just might… where're you heading in such a hurry? You just got here… I saw you the minute you walked in. You're hard to miss."

I blushed.

"I guess back to my hotel."

"So, you're not from here?"

"Atlanta."

"Oh… I'm Bradley."

"Randy. Glad you caught me," I said, still overpowered by his eyes.

He asked what I was doing in town. I didn't want to tell Bradley for a modeling job. It would sound so lame. I told him it was just some uninteresting production work for a few days. Thankfully, he didn't press for details.

"It's still early. Have you had dinner?"

"No. Actually I haven't."

"There's a great place around the corner. Kind of a hole in the wall, but the food is good. Want to go?"

"I like those type of places," I responded, but what I was really thinking was that I'd like anywhere as long as this guy was with me.

Of course, I accepted the invitation. I had no plans of letting this man out of my sight, at least not for the rest of the night.

Bradley led me to a booth in the back. We waited for the server. I was at a loss for words.

"Say something… anything," I thought.

But I didn't. I just kept looking at Bradley and around the joint.

"I bet you're the shy type."

"Pretty much. I don't mean to be boring."

"You're not… you'll warm up to me," Bradley smiled, as his dimples showed themselves.

"You're like a big teddy bear… so I guess I will."

Bradley let out a chortle laugh.

After dinner, I didn't want the night to end. Fortuitously, Bradley asked if I'd be interested in a drive. I found myself back up in the Hills as Bradley drove around. Eventually, he pulled in front of a smoked-glass gate, the flat roofline of a white house was noticeable on the other side.

"I thought you might like to hang out at my house for a while… that is, if you want," Bradley suggested. "There're great views from the rooftop," he added.

"Sure. I'd like that."

My heart jumped; a warm feeling washed. The gate slid open revealing a low profile L-shaped contemporary home. The landscaping, purposeful. Large white round pots, filled with high and low native plants lit from above flanked either side of the wide alcove.

Upon entering the double glass doors, we walked into an open white space. Monochromatic furniture, accented with pale grays and black fitted the architecture. Pedestals for impact, showcased sizable pottery low-lit by recessed lighting as were a few impressive canvases on the walls. At the far end, large sliding doors led to the backyard highlighting a glistening pool filled with inviting serene blue water.

that first night

Tranquility wrapped as we lay on our backs; a thick blanket stretched corner-to-corner under us on the roof. A brusque chill captured the inert air. Still, I felt warm within the measure of a foot from Bradley—our bodies parallel. The ether, a satin-black and a moon as big as life itself. To this day, I remember how its light bathed Bradley's face. Remember the occasional shooting stars, their trails glowing like long arrows as they cannonballed through the thermosphere—although light years away, seemingly within arm's reach. Together, we listened around the silence. An owl hooted, either to locate others or to exert its dominance over the hillside. Coyotes yelped in the far distance. When we talked, I found the tone of Bradley's voice calming—offering a feeling of safety. His stocky build, a sense of protection much like a fortress. I remember everything—everything, from our first night together. Everything, as if that first night was last night.

As I hoped with each inhale of the night, eventually Bradley slid his large right hand over the blanket to mine. First, touching it with his index finger before completely grasping mine gingerly in his. At the same time, we turned our heads away from the sky to look at each other. Then, Bradley rolled onto his side. I did the same as he inched his thick left arm across my waist until he cupped my side. Bradley pulled me over to him. Slowly, he brought his face closer. Our eyes searched. Searched, until they became transfixed—penetratingly so.

"Can I kiss you?" he whispered.

"I was hoping you would."

Bradley smiled. His face inched closer—closer until our lips pressed. I soon found myself under his weight. Bradley's hands moved to my hair. His fingers combed it as we continued to kiss. I've never been kissed with such genuine tenderness and coaxing passion. I was left breathless. Breathless, as if the oxygen was being stolen from my lungs—and freely so.

I ran my hands up and down his broad, muscled back. Bradley's taste was manly. Satisfying. Intoxicatingly arresting. I knew then, he was the one. Assuredly. Within a matter of hours, between the moment he stopped me in the bar to when he took my hand on the roof and then kissed me—I knew. Bradley too, had captured me as the chill had the air.

"You're pretty amazing, Randy."

I was cautious to respond as I mulled words over in my brain. Luckily, Bradley kissed me again before I could respond. My mind chased. Moved way too fast. Ridiculously so. I already had thoughts of us living together for the rest of our lives—growing old, while still encased in love. Even though same-sex marriage wasn't legal at the time, I knew what China pattern I wanted. The wedding ceremony would be on the beach at sunrise—elegant but simple. Both of us dressed in matching white shirts and slacks, and barefoot on the sand. Our small gathering of friends would hate having to get up so early. But they would get over it.

Our vows would be exchanged as the sun began to rise above the horizon—bringing forth a new day, and our new life together. Our gaze would remain unbroken until the last word of enduring devotion was spoken. I would likely tear-up in infinite joy. Actually, I knew that I would. Bradley would smile as he winked at me. He'd place a ring on my finger and I, one on his. Then, we would seal our promises with a long, demonstrative kiss. A kiss that would remain on our lips for the remainder of our years. And once our mortal lives had ended, the love that bound us would go on living throughout all space and time. All of it—a life together and beyond. Yes, it was all settled in my mind.

I lifted my left arm to check my watch for the time. We'd been on the roof for a good five hours since arriving at Bradley's home around nine.

"I don't want to… but I need to be back on set in four hours. I guess you should take me back to the hotel," I regretfully informed Bradley.

I'm sure he heard the avert disappointment between my words. We both sat up. Bradley ran his hand up and down my back.

"Or… we can sleep on the roof. I promise to get you back in time," Bradley suggested, as he leaned into me.

I told Bradley I was more than tempted. But I knew I might not be able to sleep, leaving out the part of the cause being attributed to how Bradley made me feel. How he made my mind race, and my body crave him. But surely, he already had an idea—an indication of the pull he had on me.

"Well, let me tempt you some more," he coaxed.

Another coyote called out into the night. Then, another.

"I should warn you, I'm a squirmy sleeper and will likely roll right off the roof… that is, if I'm even able to fall asleep."

Bradley put his arms around me. Reclined our bodies back down on the roof. Once again, taking my lips passionately. Engulfing my body within his arms as he had before. I felt safe. Secured. Protected. That was enough; I ended up staying. Bradley went downstairs. Minutes later, he returned with a comforter and pillows. An alarm clock, too. Bradley reassured that he would hold me so tightly, that I wouldn't roll off the roof.

The pages of that journal recounts some of what I wrote about Bradley during a break from the shoot; the day after our chance meeting and the night that followed under an enraptured sky:

2

I'm so tired today but it's worth it... meeting Bradley, that is. Still, I have to stay on my toes. The photographer is so demanding. But I'm happy. Crazy happy. How did I get so lucky to meet this man??? But I feel it was meant to be... meeting ~~Bradly~~ Bradley.

If it wasn't for Siggy helping me with Mother I would have never come to LA... never made that flight. And I'd be toast with the agency. Still I feel guilty leaving Mother while she's in ~~another~~ another broken-hearted drunken state. But I know Siggy will take good care of Mother.

I want to kiss Bardley again. God, those blue eyes and smile!

Last night was magic. I've ~~ne~~ never felt such a strong pull... well, I've ~~so~~ never felt much of anything until him.

I'm glad we didn't have sex although I wanted to. It's just I didn't want him to be another

3

random casual fuck. I want it to be more. It might if I could just get the hell out of fucking ~~to~~ Georgia! I belong in California!!!

But I'm so stupit! Stupit! ~~Stup~~ Stupid! I'm sure he has tons of guys after him. Bradley was just feeling sorry for me because of that ass who was hitting on me at the ~~bar~~ bar, that's ~~proba~~ ~~pr~~ ~~probably~~ probably why he talked to me when I was leaving and took me to eat, ~~Ma~~ Maybe?

I'm confused... he took me to his house. I loved lying next to Bradley on ~~the~~ the roof of his house and looking up at the stars. That has to mean something.

Bradley knows I'm going back to Atlanta ~~tomorrow~~ ~~Tomor~~ tomorrow. I wonder if he'll call me at the hotel tonight??? I want to see him again!!!

Well, they're calling me back on set...

leap of faith

A landscaping architect, Bradley co-owned a successful company with his sister, Joy. Obviously, his passion by how he talked about it—his work. Bradley was a hands-on kind of boss. Liked to get his hands in the dirt with his crew as he oversaw the work of celebrities' homes and upscale commercial properties. His sister handled the business end. The occupation was in their blood, having grown up on an expansive strawberry farm in Santa Maria—still operated by their father and uncle. Bradley was country music, boots, cowboy hats, and pickup trucks.

While affluent business-wise, he was far from the perceived atypical white-collar type. For all outward accounts, Bradley was blue-collar as they come, and he looked the pa

rt in his tight-ass jeans and boots. T-shirts wet with sweat and dirt soiled. No doubt, turning heads in his Ford Flareside pickup with the company's logo emblazoned on the doors. When you saw Bradley—you saw a fucking man's man and not some imitation. Yet, he looked mouthwatering dashing in a tuxedo—attending charity functions and events for his family's, Beal's Foundation benefiting underprivileged kids coupled with scholarship grants in agricultural studies. If Landscape Architecture Magazine had a yearly "The Sexist Landscaper Alive," Bradley would be on the cover in those size 14 boots and a stretched out, sweaty, dirt soiled tank top showing off all his manly might. He was all the icing on the cake, and the topper was his killer smile.

When I would visit Bradley after his workday, I never wanted him to take a shower. His body perfumed of earth and sweat; I wanted to feel his big hands and unwashed body all over me like skin lotion. He'd throw me on the bed, the sofa, kitchen counter, even the floor, and take me as if he were a caveman. Other times he was as reposeful as falling snow. I wanted to be branded by his flesh, his dick, his lips, and his smell—his everything.

He'd often sing along to whatever was playing on KZLA radio while driving his truck—seeming to know every country music song ever written. His all-time favorite, A Tender Lie by Restless Heart. I'd heard him sing it so many times that I knew the words, backward and forward. Although his voice was about as out of tune as an old piano left out in the rain, I never grew tired of listening to him.

That first charmed night with Bradley, expanded wide and long into months. Countless others were spent gazing at the heavens while making love—not sex. His kisses were tender before they would crescendo into passionate and ravenous raptures embraced in his strong arms as I welcomed Bradley inside me. And like that first magical night, we often fell asleep on the roof. His arms wrapped my body as if he never wanted to let me go and I felt the same—just as he'd promised our first night together. So closely—as if my flesh were his and his mine. As if we were of one skin.

Then, that night came. That moment. That instant, when I heard the words, I'd been longing for. Maybe even desperate to hear from Bradley's lips. Free of questions. Free of any doubts. Free of hesitations and vacillations. Each one, so perfect in all their magic. But they weren't magic. They were as real as the large moon that dominated that night sky. As Bradley did the same to me.

Like unbounded times before—the heavens as witness, Bradley thrust inside me as the intimate and unbridled passionate hours went unnoticed but only felt. My naked body eagerly held captive by his as if our souls integrated. Mine warmed by Bradley's and his, were by mine. I never wanted him to stop, but when the climax could no longer be held back, Bradley's heated cum flooded inside me like a river.

Still, Bradley's dick remained in place as our sweat-soaked bodies did. As our lungs labored for more air. As our bodies and minds fed on more heated cravings. As his penis and my stretched sphincter and anus pulsated. As my legs around his waist—unwilling to release him. As our lips and tongues refused to relinquish the moments caught in the abyss of unmeasured time. But that night, it was more; that is, if even more were possible. Thinkable. Imaginable.

He rose on his elbows. Bradley's hands caught my face. They held it as his eyes penetrated mine. As they searched.

"I love you, Randy. I truly do."

Bradley's words raced joy through me.

At that moment, I felt complete, but I had for some time. More safety surrounded me—held by his arms.

"I feel the same… I have for some time. Actually, from that first night on the roof."

Bradley kissed me. I kissed him. We kissed each other. The world went still; but our hearts kept beating—one for the other. Our penetrating eyes lingered. Continued to search, but they had found what they were looking for. We both knew it. Not another word was spoken. That is, until I did. Until I spoke.

"Take me again… until the sun comes up."

Whether Bradley and I were in his bed, on the roof of his home, or my bed in Atlanta—even in the bed of his truck, all I cared about was being with him. Just the two of us was more than enough for me—I didn't need or want anything but us—to be with not only my love, but my finally-found human connection. At those times, the world's population went out of focus as did my worries and insecurities. As did Warner Robins, and sometimes even my mother's mental afflictions and alcoholism.

When we were together, all my attention was dedicated to Bradley and him alone. I'd fallen hard, and like a superhero, Bradley caught me. My heart was his. Bradley felt like home—I was home with him. Bradley was the right one for me. Everything I could ask for in a friend, a partner, and a lover.

I stepped back from modeling, finding it a huge relief—only taking jobs on occasion in Atlanta or Los Angeles, and very few out of the country. Although the agency wasn't delighted by my decision, they respected it not wanting to totally cut me loose. Thus, and to my relief, no need for the sporadic, mutually advantageous affair with the East Coast VP of Britton's which I didn't tell Bradley about or wouldn't. One of several secrets to keep to myself. But I was used to keeping secrets. Or would Bradley ever come to know of the few rich older men who had filled my wallet. My days as a prostitute were over—or so I thought.

I told the VP I was in love and of my future plans about moving to LA to be with Bradley. There was no animosity at the dissolution of or our arrangement—it was just sex after all. But he did continue to support me when I needed time off. Britton's and my job title remained a near-perfect cover. I went back to work. By then, the manager who disapproved of my special treatment had tragically succumbed to AIDS. And I could finally focus more on my art, which Bradley encouraged.

We had met before the eruption of the AIDS epidemic—when very little was known, and it would be a number of years before a test was developed. But soon after Bradley and I became serious, we stopped using condoms. We knew it was reckless, but the need to be free of any barriers is what we wished.

I had to feel him—skin-to-skin, as I did for his cum to ejaculate deep inside of me. I did feel a lot of guilt as I saw so many die. And there was always the chance one or both of us could have been infected. Bradley died before that test was developed; and since I've managed to remain negative, chances are he was as well. But that doesn't mean having unsafe sex was less careless. We were putting our lives in danger all the same. Still, I would have done it all the same.

Again, one limitation remained that kept me fettered to the South: my devotion to my mother and her needs. Bradley understood—from what I shared why I was so bound to her. And, he knew, I couldn't totally free myself from the South until she, in my fever-swamp fantasies, remarried or moved to Los Angeles. But admittedly, I was close to giving her a final ultimatum. Although I would always remain devoted to her, it was time to break away. But I knew at the same time, I'd remain shackled to certain events—certain actions taken.

I'd yet to officially come out to my mother, even though I'd often wondered if she knew. But I had dated a girl in high school for a short period. And there were a few others while in college. As far as Bradley, all I shared was I had a good friend in LA that I occasionally talked to over the phone and hung out with when I was there doing a shoot. That's all she knew. In an attempt to keep her guessing—if that were the case, my friend Nancy would sometimes drive with me from Atlanta to see my mother if I were going for the day. My continued attempt, or so I thought, to keep Mother in the dark that her son was gay. Besides, Mother loved Nancy as she did her. And I'm sure, my mother thought would make a great daughter-in-law.

At Bradley's encouragement, a plan was put into place: when Mother was in a good place emotionally, on one of his visits to Atlanta, we'd drive to Warner Robins so she could meet him. I instinctively knew, she would take an instant liking to Bradley. We'd tell her about us. It would be obvious to her how much Bradley meant to me and me to him.

Perhaps, indeed he could convince my mother where I failed, regardless of the increased pressure I'd applied in gauged amounts to the wound I unintentionally inflected by telling her I had to live in Los Angeles. And by her not agreeing to relocate, she was putting me in an impossible predicament of choosing her over the city I loved, and now Bradley.

I was aware, Mother knew my restrained threats were weightless and therefore, she'd never packed the first piece of luggage. But hopefully, if she understood there was a chance of my having to give Bradley up if she refused him as well, I hoped that would be the incentive she needed to sell the house and leave Warner Robins. And by doing so, she would not only have one son—but two who cared deeply about her. Two that would support her in every way possible as I had been trying to do alone. Bradley and that alone should make her pull out the luggage from the bottom of her bedroom closet and start packing.

Possessing a generous heart, Bradley insisted Mother would live in his pool house until we found her an apartment nearby. His abounding generosity was another marker of his unambiguous love for me. Bradley was certain he could change her mind. It would be an adventure for her. I hoped desire for it—an adventure, still lived somewhere in her. Like how she had insisted that while my father was stationed in France, that they live on the economy instead of base housing. Like the time she switched buses to visit New Orleans instead of taking the scheduled one back to Warner Robins after a high school reunion—Mother didn't share, until before she died and as I wrote about in "Alabama Snow."

I knew Mother wanted me to be happy as I wanted the same for her. Well, I was bringing "my happy" to meet her at some point—much sooner than later, or so was the plan. Bradley was just as anxious as I for a life together. For us both to be in Los Angeles living under the same roof. I knew it would be scary for my mother, but I'll tell her to take that leap of faith—with Bradley and me holding her hands. We do it together—the three of us. It all seemed the perfect scenario.

until it hurts

I've already stated: any measure of love I've known was a mother's love for her child, but it rode on pain. Growing to understand by experience from a young age, which continued into adulthood, I wasn't sure what love was in its purest form void of pain—or even, if such a love existed. But in my senior year of high school through college and beyond, I did know infatuation and desire but those were of the flesh and not the heart. Still, I wanted that thing called true love: a desperate boy wanting to be loved without any conditions or restrictions.

Having limited parameters, I questioned if love was possible for me—certainly, feeling unworthy of it. As I wrote in my first book: as a very young child I did believe my parents loved each other at one time. I still have faded memories of picnics where my parents laid in each other's arms while I played with my siblings. And I do remember my mother sitting in my father's lap in the living room after they had a vicious argument some hours before or days after. But eventually, that love or what I perceived as love between them all went to hell where it died.

I also wrote in my first book: the night of the day my father met his end; Mother woke me from a guilt-galloping sleep to drive her to the mortuary so she could sit with his body. Perhaps, she needed to remember their early years when they first met and within weeks, ran off to get married in Mississippi because in Alabama, there was a waiting period and Mississippi had none. That was a storybook kind of love, where the pining desire to be joined as one was overwhelming. But in retrospect, I believe they were just two beautiful people who fell in love with each other's beauty.

I still have the beautiful picture of my mother she sent to my father while he was stationed out of the country where she wrote on the back: "My darling, I love you. This dress makes me look bigger than I am." At the time that picture was taken, Mother was pregnant with my older brother.

That night, she sat with her husband's body—her need to do so, maybe meant Mother must have forgiven him. Although I could never imagine her doing so. As I drove her surrounded by the blackness of death, I felt like shit—even worse. But as I'd witnessed for many years before that night, by all outward appearances due to horrible events, signs of love that once lived between them had died—stabbed right through their hearts. It was in a grave rotting just like human flesh long before that bullet raced through her husband's brain.

Today, I understand more about my mother than I ever believed I did. That, she was not only searching for relief from the isolation and crippling pain caused by the mental afflictions she lived with, but perhaps more so of what she lost concerning love on many levels and in degrees—importantly, searching solace for a vanished love. As I've always been like her, the same is true in that respect: needing an unyielding love. We were as we will be—kindred souls.

But things were going to be completely different between Bradley and me and nothing like my parent's heart-crushing and deadly end. Again, ours was well on its way to become that unyielding and undying love. The one I questioned but still imagined, had come to life. Then, after some mouths together, the universe bitched-slapped me in the heart when I came to recognize the second limitation well-hidden behind my towering love for Bradley. And if it weren't for that love, I might have seen it sooner although I wish I'd never made note of it. Never.

Again, the first—my mother's repeated resistance to relocate to Los Angeles and thus impeding me from being with him without the distance of miles between us. For that, my initial love of California had moved to second place. But after meeting Bradley, it raced back. And the same is true concerning when I'd first thought my home was within the boundaries of Los Angeles—but, again, after meeting Bradley, home became within the boundaries of his arms. California aside, I would have lived anywhere with Bradley. Even in a hovel—and an overdrawn bank account.

The realization of Bradley's connection to my parents had grown slowly as if a plant I'd purposely rationed only drops of water. I didn't realize it until a few months into our relationship. As much as I attempted to deny it. Attempted not to face it. Attempted to tell myself I was being ridiculous to even give my suspicions poundage—that commonality, although to lesser degrees, had been right in front of me. Within months of my denials and dismissiveness and suppressing suspicions, I gradually suspected he was a highly-functioning alcoholic—and being that, too close to my childhood. I'd rather been repeatedly dragged naked over jagged glass in a field of broken liquor bottles.

I continued to sway myself into believing my concerns were baseless. That, I was troubled for no reason. After all, I'd been tipsy if not drunk at times. But the latter was few and far between. And I wasn't a prude. For a while, I actually believed I was wrong in my assumptions. That, Bradley was just a big man who liked his beer and usually handled it well. Still seemed to remain in control. Still loving. Still kind. Still attentive. Sometimes even silly. Made me feel like I was forged from pure gold. Made me feel I was alive. Certainly, infinitely loved. That, I was worthy. I never felt flawed when we were together.

Unlike my parents, he was a happy drinker—upbeat. And unlike my father, Bradley was never mean. Never hurt me. Never violated or degraded me. He wasn't a monster like my father had been, and not a mess like my mother could be at times. And I knew he would do anything to keep me safe from harm. Also, unlike my parents, I reasoned that Bradley only drank beer. I'd never known him to drink hard liquor—but liquor is liquor, beer or otherwise.

During the periods he drank more—usually on weekends when we were just hanging around his house or my apartment, the smell on his breath was strong enough that it sometimes flashed me back in time. Heaved me to the unwelcomed reminders of my father's smell as liquor exuded from his pours—his alcoholism, instigating those eruptions of abuse, violence, and the acts of violations. Acts concealed from the rest of a compressed world that began and ended at the property lines—and only known to my journals hidden in the back of my bedroom closet. A squashed world that may as well have been a junkyard—a maze of crushed cars, like that life and seemingly without an exit.

As Mother had done in the middle of the nights, but not anywhere close to those blocks of times with calls of boozed distress and at times, mania that often required me to drive through those middle hours that were more than just darkness of night back to Warner Robins or catch the next plane—Bradley began occasionally calling in diminutive hours as well. Alcohol aside, Bradley called me every night when we were on either side of the continent. Those were planned so we could tell each other goodnight.

"I miss you, Randy. Miss you so much. You need to be with me now!" Bradley would tell me.

So many times, I told him it was killing me that we weren't together full-time. Killing me not to be able to wake up with him every morning and fall asleep every night in his arms. When it came to saying goodnight and ending the call, Bradley would tell me I had to hang up first. Then, I would tell him that he had to. We'd go back and forth until we agreed to count to three together and then hand up the phones at the same time. But that didn't always work. Neither one of us would hang up first.

And because of that, our conversations continued another hour or more. I'd close my eyes as I listened to his deep voice, imagining Bradley holding me while I repeatedly ran my hands like feathers over his back. There were times I'd eventually fall asleep—Bradley's voice, again, so soothing with the phone's handset still in my hand. Eventually, I stopped giving any more thought to those periods he sounded like he'd had too much to drink. Those periods he seemed to be hanging on intoxication, either over the phone or in person where I saw and heard distinct markers of alcoholism—impeding some of his words.

So, I held my breath. Still kept my concerns hidden—and certainly, how they pulled at me. How they opened the pages of bookmarked gruesome details from childhood. I gave it more time. Told myself anything but the truth. Told myself that any concerns regarding Bradley's drinking were only residues of my parents and my mother's ongoing struggles with the bottle. That, I was projecting.

The Bradley I'd known for over half a year and some-months, continued to be loving, attentive, devoted, and, again, silly at times like an overgrown kid, but always reserved around the edges. Again, always in control. Always a man's man. And he was my man. Characteristics that pulled me into his arms, as his eyes and smile had, and above all—the respect he showed me the first night of our meeting. For long periods, I continued to overlook that commonality. In his defense, Bradley didn't always drink too much and at times, not at all. But when he did, my lips still accepted his passionate kisses as I did welcome him deeply within my body, with my legs wrapped around him. Again, my concerns remained silent—I didn't want the glass bubble I'd created around us to shatter.

Then, the night came that I could no longer ignore the truth—stop trying not to accept it. We were leaving the party of one of Bradley's friends, Roger. As we approached his truck, I reached for the keys in his hand. Bradley pulled it back.

"I'm fine, Randy… I'm good to drive," Bradley claimed.

"Sure, you are but let me drive us home. The cars are parked bumper-to-bumper."

"Naw. You worry too much," Bradley wielded his alpha male dominance.

I stopped. Looked at him—my face grimaced in annoyance. He continued to ignore me. Instead, Bradley jumped in the driver's seat. I relented, to avoid any further argument. Bradley started the truck. Put it in reverse, and while backing out, Bradley almost side-swiped a car within inches.

"Watch out… you almost hit that car."

"But… I didn't."

If the near miss wasn't enough, he backed into a mailbox—rolled over it and flattened it like a pancake. We turned our heads to look at each other. Bradley shrugged his shoulders; his embarrassment was evident. Excruciatingly long moments later, I opened the passenger door. Slammed it. Hard. Then, Bradley exited the truck.

"I'll take the keys now," I demanded.

Still Bradley was resistant to relinquishing them.

"Give me the fucking keys, Bradley! I'd like for us to make it back to the house in one piece."

At that, he tossed them over.

We went back into the house so Bradley could tell his buddy that he no longer had a mailbox and why. They boisterously laughed about it, which pissed me off even more.

"I… I'll replace it for you," Bradley told him.

"I know you will. I'm not worried… but let Randy drive," Roger insisted.

Already having the truck keys in my hand, I dangled them in the air before saying goodnight—for the second time.

Once back at the house, I headed to the bedroom. Bradley plopped down on the bed and stretched out.

"Don't be mad."

I didn't say a word. He watched as I stripped down to my underwear.

"I'm liking what I see," Bradley allowed.

Still, I said nothing. I walked into the kitchen. Poured him a glass of water before returning. Once back, Bradley was naked with a massive erection.

"Come over and get in bed with me."

Although tempted, I shook my head no at him. Bradley frowned. From the top right-side drawer of the contemporary vanity, I retrieved a bottle of aspirin. Shook two in the palm of my hand. Took the glass of water and aspirin to Bradley. He reached out to rub my stomach.

"Take these and drink the water. All of it."

"I'm fine, Randy."

"Yeah… fine like the mailbox you flattened?"

"Yeah… I guess you're right."

Bradley frowned again but did down the aspirin and finished off the glass of water. I took the empty glass from him and set it on the bedside table, then crawled into bed. Kissed Bradley several times. He then pulled me on top of his massive body.

"Not tonight. You scared me, Bradley."

"I'm sorry. I… I really am."

"I hope so."

I looked at him for a moment before rolling off Bradley and turning over on my side. My back to him.

"Goodnight, I love you."

Bradley sighed and let out a long breath.

"Love you, too. You know that… right?"

"Yes. I know. So, don't do that again. We can talk in the morning. Just hold me."

Before my eyes closed—within those rare and matchless small moments of that night while sheltered in his arms, I told Bradley what my mother always told me when she'd squeezed my hand so tightly that it hurt: "That's how much I love you. I love you until it hurts."

"Bradley."

"What, Babe?"

"I love you like that… I love you until it hurts. So, squeeze me until it hurts like my mother used to squeeze my hand."

He pulled me to him. Kissed the back of my neck. Indeed, Bradley did squeeze me. I felt the oxygen in my lungs pushed out into the air of the bedroom. As every time before, I never wanted Bradley to release me.

scrambled eggs

Disquiet dwelled to the degree I was unable to fall asleep. The evenly-paced light snores of Bradley's slumber that often offered comfort as I laid beside him—hadn't. Hadn't, due to each exhale of breath still hinted of the beer he'd consumed. The uneasiness built. And I was still mad. A lot mad. Not necessarily at Bradley, but at the curse of alcoholism following me the entirety of the miles between Warner Robins and Los Angeles.

I carefully lifted Bradley's heavy arm from around my body—momentarily pausing to look back at him before getting out of bed. I quietly crossed the room to the dresser. Opened a bottom drawer for his favorite, XXL well-worn, faded blue UCLA T-shirt to put on. Backtracking, I took the bed throw tossed on a club chair as I slid open the sliding glass door to wrap myself as I walked across the well-manicured lawn to the lounges by the pool. The chill in the air was most evident as the moon in its third quarter.

Lying there, I scanned the peacefulness of the night sky as I did that of the backyard. The luminating pool light broadly washed me within my surroundings in a transparent floating sapphire glow that reached through the glass of the floor-to-ceiling and wall-to-wall sliding doors of the master bedroom. From the lounge, I watched Bradley continue to sleep.

"I belong somewhere… to someone. I belong here and to him," I thought, regardless of how troubled I was at the time.

Surely, many others' first instinct would have been to run. But how could I? How could I run from the man who had electrified me—awakened me? The man I immeasurably adored. The man who made me happy. Who melted me by just the sound of his voice. Soothed and excited me at the same time by the feel of his flesh against mine.

How could I run from being the beneficiary of the insane desire stirred by the slightest brush of his lips? How it swelled inward each time. The man who offered safety in many ways—certainly, while wrapped in his strong arms. Whose ice-blue eyes I drowned in every time he looked at me. How could I return the gift granted to be able to share the same space with, and to look at Bradley in amazement accompanied by that sick feeling in my stomach that being willingly imprisoned by love conjures up, knowing that if it ends—I would surely die a painful death of poisonous heartbreak?

Bradley found me in the kitchen making breakfast in the mid-morning hour. His image suddenly came into view, reflected by the windows facing the side yard. Bradley stood in the open doorway leading into the room—his frame filled it, wearing his reliable print boxers watching as he occasionally rubbed his eyes and yawned.

His approach played like a short film through the reflections of the windows' glass. I pretended to be oblivious—disinterested as Bradley pressed his body into mine. He slid his large hands around my waist. Then downward to the unraveled hem of the shirt that was several-sizes too big for me. His hands teasingly lingered there for a few moments before little by little moving them upward underneath the T-shirt toward my chest as I felt their calluses. My body tingled—goosebumps surged over my flesh.

Bradley knew exactly what he was doing and why. Even so, I attempted to remain unfazed as I continued to scrambled some eggs. However, my stemming sexual arousal was evident by an erect penis tenting the T-shirt.

"Just don't tickle me," I thought, that would make me laugh out of control and lose my stance as weak as it was.

Bradley's lips brushed the nape of my neck; his hands leisurely moved back down until he wiggled a finger into my belly button. At that, I almost laughed but managed to keep my lips somewhat pressed together but my body jerked in response.

"Smells great."

I didn't respond as I plated the eggs with mixed fresh fruit. The toast popped up from the Sunbeam stainless toaster. Bradley slid his hands back up to my chest. Moved one long enough to wet a finger using his mouth—circled each of my areolas with it. Kissed my neck more. I creamed the T-shirt.

"Are you still mad?"

"More importantly… how's your head?"

"It's okay… I'll survive. The aspirin helped."

"You might want to pour yourself a cup of strong black coffee," I suggested.

Bradley did.

"Let's just sit and eat," I insisted, as I resisted the compulsion to turn around and kiss him.

I told Bradley we needed to have a serious talk. I knew if I didn't—if we didn't talk about last night, the worry would keep eating at me. I needed to get it off my chest. That way, I would gladly give in and let Bradley sweet talk me back into bed for the rest of the morning. He took a seat on the long white sofa. I sat in one of the Woodrow Box chairs. Bradley looked at me while waiting for me to speak.

I pulled the metaphoric curtains wider—shining it out. Telling Bradley how my parents' alcoholism—my father's abuse and violence still profoundly manacled my life. How my mother's paralysis to alcohol continued to hold onto her pitiable existence and how it kept breaking my heart for hers. How my father would drive his car with my siblings and me as he drank. The floorboard of the vehicle scattered with empties as they rolled around with each turn of the wheel. I hoped by doing so, Bradley would have a clearer picture as to why I was so angry and spoke harshly to him the night before.

I encouraged him to consider Alcoholics Anonymous.

"Just try a few meetings. I'll even go with you."

Bradley didn't give an answer either way, even though I shared that I sometimes accompany Mother to hers in Warner Robins. I also imparted how my older brother was often cold to her. That, I felt he'd basically detached himself from our mother emotionally even though he bore witness as to why she drank—why she attempted to drown herself in liquor. And by my brother's indifference, how it added more pain and heartbreak on top of what she'd been sludging through for years.

After pouring my heart out to Bradley, he surprisingly hit the defensive default—insisted he didn't have a problem despite the events of the night before. He even seemed pissed I'd even brought it up.

"Randy, I don't have a problem. I now get why you were upset with me. And I'll admit… I should have given you the keys to the truck to begin with."

"Well… at least you're willing to acknowledge that."

"I'm never going to put you through that again… and I'm sorry your childhood was like that. Really, I am."

"I appreciate that… but tragically, it's millions of children's childhoods and I hope you're serious about never letting what took place last night ever happen again."

"I promise… why haven't you ever told me what you went through?"

I thought for a moment.

"Because… because it's not your burden to carry. And what I do from it, will always be a part of me and I don't want it to affect our relationship. Let's not talk about it again. Not about that."

Bradley stood and walked over. Got on his knees. Laid his head in my lap. I ran my fingers through his hair. Then, he looked up at me. Again, those eyes. Those eyes that I knew saw my soul.

"Just remember, I'm here for you. And as I've promised, I'll help you with your mother. Again, get her to move. You know I'd do anything for you."

I didn't respond. Just smiled. Then, I thought if I should ask Bradley: do you love me enough to stop? But I didn't. I didn't because I knew that love itself wasn't enough—at least from years of personal experience. And that love wasn't a cure for many of life's disconcerting circumstances. It would be a mistake for me to have asked him that question. Our love for each other—or whatever it was, had nothing to do with his drinking just like a mother's and son's love for each other hadn't a thing to do with my mother's—or her inability to completely stop.

I'd heard quite enough promises in my life. Too many broken ones. Even though I knew Bradley thought he sincerely meant it, all I could do was hope. His insistence that he didn't have a problem, didn't make me happy. Made me sad. But I was glad, at least he, again, did admitted he was wrong not to let me drive us back to the house. I already knew Bradley was as stubborn as he was big. And even with his hard attitude on the subject, I also knew Bradley well enough to know that he was embarrassed. I didn't want to rub it in too deeply.

Once again, I backed off. Refrained from pushing the matter as I'd done a convincing job on myself: I was, again, being hyper-sensitive to the subject and maybe the problem was me. I went silent again, although my worries continued to breed within. Still, they were unspoken—swallowed in order not to mess up what I had with Bradley. Yes, I would keep loving Bradley. I had no choice in the matter. Hope that regardless of his laissez faire attitude, Bradley would slow down on the drinking. Keep hoping that he would see that if he continued, how it would negatively affect not only me but our relationship. And because I knew he was embarrassed; I felt the need to comfort his bruised machismo. I got up from the chair and joined Bradley on the sofa. Cuddled up to him as if I were a puppy. Rested my head on his chest. Then, all seemed fine in the world—our world. Rather, I pretended as such.

After a period of floating in the tranquility Bradley's arms offered, he got up. Stood like the giant he was. Reached out his hand to mine. Pulled me up. Pulled me to his warm body. Bradley looked down at me. With his hand, he lifted my face up at his. I knew Bradley saw the wetness that glazed my eyes.

"Babe," he spoke. "Let's crawl back into bed. I want to hold you as close as humanly possible."

"Okay… but don't think you're going to get any," I smiled. Then, jokingly added—with a straight face, "I'm not some boy toy."

"Oh, but yes you are. You're my boy toy… and only mine."

Bradley swept me up into his arms such that my head spun. My body tingled. Seconds later, I was on the light gray sheets dressing the mattress looking up at him before Bradley lowered his body on top of mine. He kissed me with such uninhibited wanting. My whole world was in his eyes looking back at me.

Blindly, he reached for the remote on the bedside chest to partially lower the electric window shades. They mechanically hummed—slowly squeezing out the bright mid-morning sun until only a smooth pastel-yellow hung. Bradley mantled me in his protective arms. Warm. Strong. Sheltering. Lovingly. Time wafted as did my mind.

"Dear God… don't ever let me leave this man's embrace. Never not let me know his kiss or be freed from his love. And if not… then kindly let me die at this very moment. Let the last beat of my heart be his as that of my breath," I thought.

Hours later, we showered then dressed in shorts and T-shirts—Bradley's didn't stay on very long. The balance of the day was spent working on the grounds of the house; tending to the landscaping. But mostly, my tending was watching him. Afterward, Bradley made dinner. Later, accompanied with the night, we took a naked midnight swim under a full titanium silvery moon.

hope springs eternal, or does it

The less Bradley drank the more optimistic I became. Spilling greater detail of a childhood drowned in booze seemed to make him attempt to keep his drinking at a minimum. I continued to hold onto the coattails of hope despite knowing how ragged they were from Mother's struggles and my father's madness it helped trigger. But Bradley and my parents were three different people. Lived different lives. Still, alcoholism doesn't pick and choose. Doesn't discriminate against who walks into a liquor store or sits down at a bar to drink until in a state of intoxication.

I've already stated that my mother's pain was too deeply seeded. Sown in violence. Fertilized in abuse. Watered by fear. I didn't know the source of what I perceived as Bradley's addiction. However, I did wonder if something had happened in his life before me that made Bradley drink more at times. But from what I knew, for the most part, his childhood had been idyllic. Still, that doesn't mean it was always the case: idyllic. And there was the chance he had the propensity in his DNA that had surfaced at some point. But I was more inclined to believe his drinking began from partying in high school and throughout college. Then, socially until it became a habit. Even still, as I was trying to save my mother—I was doing the same where Bradley was concerned, while hoping alcohol wouldn't infect the life we'd committed to share.

Once again, I was trying to save someone instead of myself. And as I have done countless times, putting my heart in harm's way. And quite aware, one of the very things I'd been running from—was what I was running straight toward. Actually, I'd already arrived at the risk of facing the possibility of more disappointment—but disappointment and I were long-time friends. So, I did what I'd always done as what I was presently at the time doing concerning Mother: holding onto hope that she would eventually stop drinking altogether. That, she would once again stay sober as she had long enough to receive a one-year sobriety chip at an earlier point in her fight. A proud day in both our lives. Mother had specifically asked me to attend that meeting to present her the chip. Some doctors as laypersons might gage: being a child of alcoholism, I subconsciously sought out what I knew; subconsciously drawn as some women and even men abused as children end up with abusers as adults. But I fell in love with Bradley long before I suspected he had a problem.

In respect to Bradley's drinking, I never asked or expected him to completely stop as contradictory as that may come across. Again, I wanted him to slow down for his sake—make him aware, not knowing what was in store within the next few years concerning his degree of consumption. That if it would get to the point, it would become a daily thing. And I didn't want to worry about Bradley—especially when he was in Los Angeles and I was in Atlanta or some other place for a shoot.

Admittedly, I knew I was too programmed to alcohol—it being a normal as a child, and it continued with my mother at the time I was with Bradley. Again, distrustful of my feelings resulting from extreme exposure, I was pushing the residuals on Bradley of the past and the present. Much like the opposite of living with the genie in the bottle, but the mistress of addiction and the bottle that harbored her. By contrast, bottle or not, I couldn't fathom a life without Bradley. The man that was the dream: undying love, California, and that house in the Hills. But regardless of the house, I would have lived in a shack with Bradley—with an overdrawn bank account and even put up with his periods of drinking. What was one flaw—as monumental as it was, compared to all the good and the beautiful he had to offer?

When we weren't in the same city, I could usually tell during some of those late-night phone calls if Bradley was drinking and if so, to what degree give-or-take a few bottles—and definitely, when we were together. Although Bradley had been tapering off since I'd share more with him—I wasn't naïve enough to believe that was always the case when we weren't together. Certainly, when he was out drinking with his landscaping crew and buddies. But I would give hope as much leash as it needed. Or did I want to be a nag even if there were times he drank more when we were together unless he became obstinate.

Wanting to do my homework, having grown close to Bradley's sister, I turned to Joy. Feeling comfortable enough to approach her with my apprehensions. Joy shared that, on rare occasions, she'd been concerned as well. But, as I was aware, since his over-drinking came in waves, she never confronted him. First as I had, she viewed her brother as a big tough man who just liked his beer.

"Randy, I've never seen Bradley as happy. That hard-headed and stubborn brother of mine loves you. You've broken through his gritty manly outer shell. I have no doubts about it," Joy shared.

Of course, hearing that from Joy sent me flying over the moon. I told her that her brother had changed my outlook on life in many ways. Including, some aspects of my past. And I too, was deeply in love with her brother. I also ask Joy if Bradley had mentioned the uncomfortable confrontation we had some months before, concerning him backing up his truck over his friend's mailbox after a party.

"Bradley did. Who do you think he told to have one of the crew replace it? Yours truly. That was a special-order mailbox. And... it wasn't cheap."

Joy shook her head.

"I'm sure it wasn't. I could tell even in its demolished state."

I went on to tell Joy that I'd asked for his keys as we were leaving the party, but that Bradley had told me he was fine to drive. Then, after he destroyed the mailbox, I didn't take no for an answer. That, it was the first time there had been any friction between us.

Joy further shared that since it only occasionally caused her concern. she eventually let it go. Especially because it never interfered with the company's success. But she agreed that the incident with the mailbox should have been a wakeup call for Bradley. Joy promised she would keep a closer eye on him.

"Randy... you know being the stubborn alpha that Bradley is, he would never acknowledge it if he indeed had a problem."

"I know, Joy. And that's what scares me. It scares me for the both of us."

"You know... my brother and I share everything. He told me about the alcoholism in your family. Bradley feels really bad... he told me so, and that he never wants to hurt you like that."

I was encouraged when Joy shared that she had also noticed Bradley's tapering off when she was around. Still, as I've shared: on the occasions I felt Bradley had too much to drink, I continued to remain silent. But like I did with my mother, I began pouring some of the beers in the fridge down the sink when Bradley was asleep. He never seemed to notice. I put up with the beer breath as we made love—as I allowed him to take me in full. Alcohol or not, I wasn't going to deny him or myself of our most intimate of moments. He wasn't my father. I took them in full—those moments.

In time, I returned to the stance that Bradley just liked his beer. Again, I was the problem. And as I've stated early on: even if it's not true, the more you believe it is then the more it seems so. But in Bradley's case, that belief system was a whole different context in every way. It was no longer one, two, or three-too-many beers, but my primordial fear of alcohol itself. But, like Tammy Wynette's song: "Stand by Your Man," I was going to do the same. Bradley was my man, and I would keep loving him. And I did. I believed I loved him as much as anyone could possibly love another human being. Each day that passed, I loved him more than the one before. As long as he never yelled at me. Hit me. Disrespected me. I would keep loving—my man.

So, I lived for those enamored cherished lost hours of circling mad affection on the rooftop of the Hollywood Hills home: talking; laughing; listening; gazing into the heavens as intensely and deeply as we did swimming within the vastness of each other's eyes, while making love witnessed by the moon and the stars; even under drizzling rain drops.

Plans continued to tell my mother together: I was gay and in love. To tell her once again after so many other times, to sell the house and move to California. But this time would be different. This time she would say, yes. Bradley would be by my side, and together we wouldn't accept no for an answer. Bradley insisted he'd pack Mother up himself—carry her onto the plane if he had to. Dear God, how I loved him for that.

Then, it happened again after I'd put Bradley's drinking aside—focusing on our love and not alcohol. That old friend, disappointment revisited—punched me in the stomach once again. A second incident one night after dinner, Bradley's seasoned pride got the best of him when I asked for the truck keys. At the request, annoyance soured his face. But I stood firm—stood my ground. Told him, I would have the restaurant call a cab to pick me up. I waited and then waited some more until he relinquished them. Once home and in bed, that was the first night—out of all those we'd spent together that Bradley didn't hold me in his arms as we slept.

The next morning, Bradley was back to his old self. Back to the man I knew—the big, strong, loving man. So, again, I went silent. Just kept loving him even though I was mad, beyond disappointed, and afraid. And because of my disappointment and fear, I decided to lie to Bradley for the first time. I even felt guilty about doing so. I told him that, after speaking to my mother on the phone that morning, I felt I should fly back to Atlanta that afternoon and drive to Warner Robins. That, she wasn't in any shape to be alone.

I missed Bradley the second he released me. His hands slowly slid down either side of my torso until they tightly held my waist. Our lips had yet to part. Then, they did but thankfully, Bradley leaned his head down to kiss me again. Then, they parted once more. And I missed him a second time.

"Call the minute you land in Atlanta," Bradley told me, as he always did. "Promise me."

His hands moved up to hold my face. Bradley eyes, dead center, looked into mine and mine, his.

"Yes. Yes, I promise," I answered, still looking up at him, my eyes unable to keep a single tear from rolling down my cheek.

Bradley wiped it with his thumb and then rubbed its secreted liquid over his lips. Again, he brought them back to mine. At that, I wrapped my arms around him. Stood on the tips of my toes to kiss Bradley on his neck.

He held my hand as we walked across the front yard and out the gate. The cab was waiting at the bottom of the driveway. Again, Bradley wrapped me in his arms. Squeezed me. Kissed me again.

"God… I wish you didn't have to leave early."

As Bradley finished that sentence, I felt like shit. A large pile of it.

"Me too," was all I could say as my eyes flooded again.

"You know, I can go with you. Just run down and tell the cab driver it will be a few more minutes… and I'll throw a few clothes in a bag."

I paused to think of what to tell Bradley.

"I wish you could but it's better I go by myself. I don't know how bad Mother will be."

My lies kept cutting me in half.

"I understand."

Our arms stretched out until the fingers of our hands slipped apart. Bradley winked. I kept looking back as I walked toward the cab. I waved before getting into the back seat. Bradley did as well. I began feeling home sick for him. With that, I missed Bradley a third time. The cab began to pull away. I almost told the driver to stop. I wanted to scream it out but didn't.

Once the driver dropped me off at LAX, I still hadn't stopped silently crying. My heart still hadn't stopped aching so much, that I called Bradley before the plane was about to board. I needed to hear his voice. Hear Bradley tell me that he loved me.

sooner than later

I dodged the erratic flow of traffic while crossing to the parking garage of the airport. The cars' headlights squinted my red, tired eyes as if it were a bright, sunny day. But it wasn't. The night had fallen hours before. While the plane was still in flight, I hid a few times in the lavatory. Did the same during my layover in Houston—locking myself in a stall. I sat on the toilet and buried the flow of tears in my hands covering my face. Despite how upset I was with Bradley, I missed him. I'd wished I stayed. Wondered if I'd made a mistake rushing out on the tail end of a lie. But I was scared.

I pulled the driver's seat forward. Tossed the carry-on bag in the back. Stood there. Another car waited to take my space. The driver honked his horn. I turned my head. My eyes scowled at him before I pushed the seat back. Got into the car. Dug into my jeans' pocket for the keys. Held them in my right hand as it shook. I began to cry again. I felt the distance between Bradley's and my heart. The driver waiting honked again. This time, I ignored the asshole. Rolled down the driver's window. Stretched out my arm. Shot him a bird. My message was clearly delivered as he proceeded further down to look for an open space.

Feeling lost and reluctant to return to the apartment—regardless of the late hour, I decided to drive straight to Warner Robins from the airport to check on Mother. Doing so, would make the lie I told Bradley a half-lie. I knew seeing me would make her happy even though pulling into the driveway would do the opposite for me—as it always had. I kept longing for the day; I would never have to return.

Once I arrived. I called out as I entered the back door so as not to startle Mother. She was indeed happy. Her face lit up like a hundred candles.

"Son… this is a surprise. I thought you weren't coming back from LA for another few days. But I'm so happy to see my beautiful boy."

I hugged and kissed Mother on the cheek.

"The shoot wrapped early. I decided to catch an earlier flight back," I lied.

"But… why so late? "You know I always worry about those big trucks on the road."

"I just wanted to see you."

"Have you been crying… your eyes are so red. You look upset?"

"No… really. I think it's just allergies," I lied, again.

"How about some coffee?"

"No thanks. It'll keep me up. But I'll take a glass of juice then I should head to bed… I'll take you to breakfast in the morning."

I called Bradley once I'd finished brushing my teeth and washed my face. He answered on the second ring.

"Hey… you, okay?" I spoke quietly, so Mother wouldn't hear.

"I've been tossing and turning all night."

"Something wrong?"

"No. No. Just miss you, Randy. It's good to hear your voice."

"Yours, too."

"How's your mother?"

"She's sleeping now."

"I wish you didn't have to deal with all that. That's why we need to convince her to move."

"I know… I know. Believe me, I know."

"I want you to be able to stop worrying about her. She'll be happy here, with us."

And I did. I did want to be able to stop worrying. But now, I was about both of them. I'd hoped Bradley would clearly see the correlation between his and Mother's drinking. My love for this amazing man and my mother made me feel like I was standing in the centroid triangle. At times, I felt the three points closing in on me: Bradley, Mother and alcohol.

"I need to get to bed… but I'll call tomorrow. Okay?"

"Sure. You get some rest, Randy. I love you."

"You, too. I hope you can fall back asleep. It'll be daylight for you in a few hours."

After breakfast at Waffle House, Mother and I stopped over at Siggy's. I enjoyed watching them interact as if they were close sisters. I guess in some ways they were. At times, it felt as if Siggy was a second mother to me. Harper Lee's, author of "To Kill a Mockingbird," adage, concerning 'you can't pick your family, but you can your friends,' certainly resonated with me when I would watch Mother and Siggy in the best of times. And as I've shared, I could always count on her during Mother's worst of times. I guess I should mention Charles Dickens since I'm somewhat quoting him from, "The Tell of Two Cities."

Back in Atlanta, I tried to stand firm—resisting the desire to call Bradley; but I couldn't. I faked a raspy voice and coughed when he answered the phone. I told Bradley that I'd apparently caught a bad cold, and I was going to sleep as much as I could.

"I'm sorry to hear that. Wish I was there to take care of you."

"You're sweet," I coughed. "I know you do… me, too. I should be well in a few days," I added as I intentionally cleared my throat.

"Are you sure? I can catch a flight."

"No. Don't. I don't want to take a chance on getting you sick."

"Tough guys like me don't get sick."

After that conversation, I didn't answer the phone even when I heard Bradley leave a message. As painful as it was not to reach for the handset—I'd wait an hour or so to call him back. Every part of me ached for him. I wanted to hear Bradley's voice—not in a message but in real time.

It was hard to stay mad at him for long. But, again, it was the situation coming at me from several directions. As weak as I was when it came to him, I knew it best not to be so readily eager to call Bradley. I needed a few days to think things out. Perhaps, Bradley needed them as well. Needed them to hopefully realize just how seriously his drinking negatively affected me. And I needed to formulate a plan so I would be in his arms—sooner than later.

the lucky ones

True love is rare. It's as innocent as a puppy and immensely passionate and wet as a heated summer storm in mid-August…

As it seemed Mother was improving for longer periods, I saw a glimpse of light return to her eyes as hope was heard in her voice. I was left cautiously happy for us both; and above all—immensely grateful. But still, there were setbacks. Each one, an expansive disappointment. Each one, another death for us both. Each one, as if a single leaf didn't have the will or strength or any more life left to hold onto a tree branch any longer in mid-fall and died as it fell to the ground. Each one, an endless circle of uncertainty—as well. Again, for us both.

I guess I was looking for a miracle among miracles and then some. A similar miracle I'd waited for as a child that never came. But even with each good stretch, I should have known I was only setting myself up for another anticlimax to come within days or weeks, or months. And when each one ended, I felt as if I'd failed her and me—at the same time. I should have known better from past experience; but I'd hoped my mother would triumph. That, my miracle would finally present itself after such a long delay.

While I was a sophomore in college, Mother did indeed triumph for almost a year after meeting a man named Eddie. He eventually asked for her hand in marriage. But to my cutting heartbreak, as I'm sure his, Mother rejected Eddie's proposal. But I knew why—why she said no when Mother seemed so happy with him. Why, she looked for excuses not to marry the man who wanted to give her a big slice of the world that she deserved.

The why of it: too often, when Mother looked in the mirror, she only saw a faint shadow of herself void of the remarkable woman she once was. She could no longer see her true worth or her amazing beauty that everyone else did. At those times, all my mother saw, were the layers of ugliness—the ugliness my father had strained her with that she was unable to scrub off. And as far as the happiness I saw, I knew some of it was a disguise. We were the same in that way. As I may have shared: I'd seen the reflection of ugliness looking back at me as well. But for me, that stopped when I met Bradley.

I began to bear the onset of guilt from spending as much time as I could with him, stealing time I should have been spending with my mother. But his light was too strong—a light at the end of a long and treacherous tunnel—especially, when I was once again safely encased within his arms.

Instead of juggling two lives, I was juggling three—but I felt lucky Bradley was the third—despite his own desire for alcohol. Mother's periods of depression, even when she wasn't drinking, were thieving more and more of her life—a horrible waste to witness of a brilliant woman. Then, when she slipped back into the bottle, it too pilfered even more. And the combination of both with the medications her psychiatrist prescribed was a volatile mix. Both Mother and I were trapped but for different reasons.

On occasion, instead of being on an even keel during periods of sobriety, I began noticing Mother experiencing intense mood swings from her depressive lows to manic highs. First, over the phone and then later in person. At the time, I didn't realize that bipolar disorder was surfacing until we met with her psychiatrist. She had fought enough battles and didn't need another mental affliction with which to go head-to-head.

Knowing Mother as I did myself, I knew a part deep down inside of her being was trying to continue to fight. And I had to continue to fight with her. From her psychiatrist's revised assessments and what I'd researched and was already aware of, the drinking was throwing a set of wrenches into the formula of therapy, medications—I knew she wasn't, again, always taking as prescribed—and her will, along with the PTSD because of years of my father's unrelenting dominance were altering her brain structure even more. Her genetics were a given, but I still believed if it weren't for my father, Mother would have lived a reasonably good life. And, again, I also knew, every day she continued to stay in Warner Robins—what that town represented, was a factor as well. It was a cage. And as long as she refused to move, she would never escape and fly away.

I also placed substantial blame on my older brother—and later, his wife as they built their own family, for walking away from the woman who gave him life. As children, we all lived in that house of hell, and he witnessed much of what Father had done to Mother as we all were casualties of his ruthlessness. I'm convinced if Stephen hadn't turned his back on our mother, she would have been so much better off to have two sons instead of one, and later an extended family of a daughter-in-law and three grandchildren as they each were brought into this world. Stephen or his wife ever shared with Mother that her first, second, or third grandchild was on their way. Or was Mother in the delivery room as she should have with each birth. But Stephen's wife's mother was.

Although Mother would often avoid discussion—talk to me frankly concerning her alcoholism despite the many times I'd intervened by either being with her at the worst of times or finding her hiding places; I knew the same was true with Bradley. As Mother had, he continued to hide his periods of over-consumption from me when I was away. But I knew. I knew and had seen enough in my young life to have earned a bachelor's degree in alcoholism.

As always, Siggy kept me apprised when I was away. I religiously kept her up to date with my schedule, as far as being out of Atlanta. Siggy told me when Mother was going to Alcoholics Anonymous meetings and when she wasn't. She would even check Mother's medications to see if she was taking them.

With the news of our mother's newly diagnosed condition, I told Stephen he had to step up and be the son his mother needed, but my words were ignored as they had in the past—but at least I needed to keep trying and hope he might grow a conscience and a sense of morality. See the responsibility owed. As before, my attempts once again resulted in heated arguments in person and over the phone.

"Stephen… I just wish you would embrace Mother. The woman who gave us life and stayed in a horrendous marriage for her children when she had a chance to leave."

Stephen didn't respond.

"Mother is continuing to maneuver a slippery road… and by your indifference, you're adding more grease. She needs the support of both of us. And I need some freedom."

"You're such a dramatic fag, Randy."

"You don't know shit about me. Besides, this is about Mother. Not how you assume how I live my life."

Stephen could be a hothead. I didn't want to antagonize him anymore than I had and possibly make things worse. Certainly, not push him any further away than he already was. Again, Stephen didn't respond. But he didn't have to—for me to understand what I'd always known: he was devoid of any compunction of familial connection as far as we were concerned and by distancing himself, seemingly void of any moral responsibility—at least that was my take. But I could hope that one day he would change.

"You shouldn't be embarrassed by Mother's drinking and mental conditions… as I've tried to hammer into your brain since the day you walked away. You know what the bastard put her through. And by turning your back on Mother, you basically picked up where he left off… at least emotionally.

"I've got to go."

The phone clicked off, quickly followed by the repetitive dial tone. In this case, much like a slap in the face.

With everything I'd experienced and my education by trial by fire with both my parents, I should have never expected Bradley to attend Alcoholics Anonymous meetings. And I failed to think about what a proud man he was. How Bradley's pride would never allow him. Even if he gave one meeting a try, I figured he would walk in and then turn around and walk out. I couldn't mentally picture Bradley—a big, strong, and confident man sitting in a circle talking about a problem he'd been denying. He'd never speak the first word even if he managed to sit still at a group meeting—likely mad at me for my insistence. Or would he want to hear the other stories; possibly concerned he might see a piece of him in them.

But I couldn't blame Bradley. I knew because I couldn't keep going back to Al-Anon, although I'd tried several times—attending some meetings then stopping and starting while in college and for years afterward. It was just too difficult to sit in those circles. Too difficult: looking at the faces; watching their expressions; seeing the same tears in their eyes, I'd cried as well; hearing their pain—feeling theirs, my mother's, and mine. All mixing. All coated with helplessness as I heard some of their stories that were too close to home. The weight of it was too crushing. But I did go to Alcoholics Anonymous meetings with Mother when I could, to show support—to rally her on.

Then, there was the worrying. The praying. The bargaining with God. Begging my mother to completely stop. For me those meetings were reminders, and I didn't need to be reminded of what I had lived with my father, as I was continuing to do with my mother and her relationship with the bottle. Although I did give the meetings my best shot—even if I wanted to run out of the room every time. I came to realize it was hypocritical of me to ask Bradley to go.

I called Bradley after my abortive conversation with Stephen. I told him I was wrong to insist he go to Alcoholics Anonymous and why. More urgently, I shared, my mother's mental state was deteriorating rapidly with the onset of her bipolar condition.

"Babe… do you want me to knock some sense into your brother?"

"Well, even as big as you are… I doubt it would do any good. Although I'd love to see you knock him on his ass."

"Just say the word."

I had to laugh. I needed to laugh.

"I'm concerned you don't fully know what you're getting yourself into, Bradley."

"Why don't you let me worry about that."

But I was worried. Worried about the cesspool he likely would be stepping into.

"You know I'll convince your mother… like I've been telling you. I made you fall in love with me… didn't I."

"You know you didn't convince me to fall in love with you. All it took was for me to turn around in that bar and look into your eyes. I was so lucky that night."

"I think we both… are the lucky ones," Bradley proclaimed.

empire chandeliers

Over three and a half weeks had passed since I'd looked into Bradley's ice-blue eyes. But, as always, we continued to talk over the phone several times a day—including, into the hidden hours of the night. It's not because I didn't want to see him—I did. I did, more than I wanted anything else. The more time that passed, the harder it was for me to breathe. If I didn't see Bradley soon, I feared the moon would crumble out of the night sky. That—I would crumble, too.

Knowing that, I kept promising myself I would never leave him despite what looming concerns I had pertaining to Bradley's drinking. Regardless of how the sound of the split-second click of the aluminum pull tab meant to me from the past. How disturbing it was. A reminder of the many times my father would drink from morning until night, and fear of what was to come. And then much later, my mother did the same. Click. Click. Click.

Regardless of how many times Bradley grabbed a beer from the fridge—I wasn't going anywhere. I even decided I would start keeping beer in my refrigerator in Atlanta for him.

Every touch of his flesh on mine. Every whisper he spoke. Every time he glanced at me, I knew more and more I couldn't live without him. As long as I was with him, I was determined to be happy either way. I felt I deserved that—to be happy and not to think about anything but us.

God, if you had seen him standing in front of you—you likely would too even if you were as haunted by liquor as I was. Likely, only think of how manly he was. How handsome, while questioning if this man had gotten lost and ended up in your apartment by mistake because you'd left the door open after carrying bags of groceries in your arms. And you likely would do just about anything to keep Bradley from walking out the door. Sex would likely be the first thing on your mind as it was mine when I first saw him that night at the bar. But as I've shared, within a short matter of time, it became more than the desire for sex. All the same, you would probably settle for a quick—hit-and-run.

Once the sound of the pull tab clicked, all I wanted was to keep looking at Bradley as he walked toward me—my lips waited for his. Other times, the mischievous one that clearly told me what he wanted. Damn, I wanted it too. All of him.

I knew without fail; Bradley would be there for me. He'd swim out to sea to save me from drowning—even in a monsoon. Knowing that too, after I'd shared my conversation with my brother with Bradley, I also knew my family's drama wasn't going to make him run. But I also decided I was going to keep it to a minimum—sharing that drama, certainly between my brother and me.

My life was only going to be about us—Bradley and me. And as he had been, I felt Bradley wouldn't give up on my mother. That, he would keep supporting me and keep understanding I had to get her out of Warner Robins. And he would continue to understand I needed to spend more weekends with my mother until she'd adjusted to the new medication added to what she'd already been prescribed. And it was important that she took them.

Moreover, I had to do everything I could to keep her from falling back into the bottle, which meant I had to take her and sit with her at Alcoholics Anonymous meetings. Siggy took Mother two or three times a week. Plus, I wanted Mother to go to church every Sunday, and that meant I had to be there sitting right next to her in the pew as many Sundays as possible. Keep her out of bed as much as possible on those weekends. I didn't want to have to put her back in the hospital. With so many trips back and forth, I began to feel like I'd never left the fucking town I hated. That, it was eating at the life I had started to build on my own and more importantly, the relatively new one I'd started with Bradley six or so months before.

I began to resent my mother. Still, I managed to keep myself together. Mother was the one who needed the glue. And regardless of any resentment, the most important aspect concerning her was for Mother to feel loved. My hands were full, with her and Britton's. So much so, it was necessary to turn down a modeling shoot scheduled for the following month after promising the agency I would still do a few now and then. I'd rather spend that time with Bradley—stealing away if necessary. Luckily, Sandra called. About to go on leave, she was flying into Atlanta from Frankfurt to visit Mother. The news was a godsend. And I was going to spend as much of that time with Bradley.

During one of our late-night phone dates, Bradley said he had an offer for me.

"Look, Randy… with all you're dealing with, I want you to quit your position at Britton's."

"What? I can't do that. I mean… I wish I could but that's impossible right now. Plus, once I'm living with you in… I'm sure I can get another job at one of the big department stores there. Actually, the Head of Finance assured me that he could see to it that I get transferred to one of the Britton's in LA."

"Well, I think you should focus on your art… even keep modeling. Just give them a two-week notice. I have plenty for both of us."

"But… Bradley, I can't let you do that."

"Yes. Yes, you can. I want you to. I can cover all your expenses."

"If I were to quit, I have enough money in savings to cover me… but I should keep working, especially if Mother needs more than I've been giving her. Although I'm sure she's been drinking some of it."

"Randy… if you quit, you would have more time to spend with your mother and get away to LA where you belong with me."

I told Bradley, as tempting as his generous offer was, I would give my notice when I knew for sure Mother was coming with me to LA. That, I couldn't wait for that day. And that, if he could convince her where I'd failed, I would move regardless as cutting as it would be for me.

"I really need to see you. Why don't I fly to Atlanta this weekend… oh, I forgot for a second that you'll be with your mother."

"Not as much as I want to see you, Bradley. I'm missing you like crazy."

I told Bradley that my sister was flying in from Germany in a few weeks; that I would come then.

"That's great news. But I'm going to lose my mind if I can't see you sooner."

"I feel the same. Besides, I'm surprised you haven't given up on me and met someone new."

"That's not going to happen. Don't even think that."

"But still… "

"No, but… besides, I've already branded you."

I was about to say something, but Bradley spoke again before I could.

"Now… what are you wearing, or are you naked?"

The next afternoon, a Tuesday, my new assistant Carol found me in couture talking to the buyer and the department manager.

"I hate to interrupt, but can I talk to Randy for a second?"

I excused myself. Stepped aside to see what Carol needed.

"Randy, you need to come to the cosmetic department," she said, stiffly and seriously as if a car had crashed through one of the large display windows facing Peachtree Street.

"Is something wrong?"

"Just come. The store manager wants to discuss an upcoming event… and she said it can't wait," Carol's voice squawked, then she hurried off in front of me.

We took the elevator down to the mezzanine that overlooked the stunning first floor where eight, huge, pear-shaped, empire chandeliers sparkled as they hung from three stories above—and huge Roman columns. From here, we took the escalator down as I scoped out the cosmetic department to the far right from my moving, bird's eye view looking for Sofie. A stunning woman in her late fifties who was once a model from France, before making the transition into retail management some years later after marrying an American banker.

Having not seen Sofie by the time the escalator delivered me onto the marble floor, I accidentally bumped into someone. I looked over to apologize. But instead of a customer or employee, Bradley was standing there with his carry-on swung over his shoulder. For a few seconds, having been tired and feeling drained, I thought it was my imagination. But once I realized it was him, my breathing increased dramatically. My heart bounced in my chest like a rubber ball. My eyes became as bright as the empire chandeliers hanging from the ceiling.

"What… what… " was all that came out of my mouth before Bradley picked me up in his arms.

A huge smile on my face and the tears of joy, told the three women gawking behind the perfume counter how happy I was to see my big, beautiful man. One of them gave two thumbs up as another winked at me in approval. I buried my face in Bradley's neck.

"Someone better pinch me… so… so I know you're really here!" I whispered as I moved my face to Bradley's.

"Oh, you better believe I'm here. I couldn't stay away."

Still, in Bradley's arms, I turned my head around to find Carol rapidly but softly clapping her hands together as if she'd won first prize in a teenage beauty pageant.

"Carol… tell Sofie I'm taking the rest of the day off!"

"You can tell her yourself," she responded while motioning her head in the direction of the escalator.

Only as Sofie could, as if the lead model in a runway show, she glided down the escalator in an Issey Miyake, red and navy, striped, high-waisted, pleated, skirt with a cream silk blouse.

"Mon chéri. J'approuve," she said, with a wink. "I imagine… you're leaving for the remainder of the day."

"If that's okay."

"Compréhensible… now, run along," Sofie, amusingly insisted.

After an informal introduction, Bradley and I rushed out of the store. My man stayed until Friday evening. I popped into the store for a few hours Wednesday and Thursday, while he shopped and walked around downtown Atlanta. Carol covered for me on Friday. I'd noticed that Bradley didn't drink a single beer while he was with me. I tearfully dropped him off at Hartsfield-Jackson—waiting until the very last second to leave my apartment, not wanting him to leave and wishing I was boarding that plane with him. Afterward, I drove on to Warner Robins—hating every mile South.

hard love

There never seemed to be a right time to introduce Mother to Bradley, so he could help convince her to move to LA. To tell her, we were in love and wanted Mother to be with us. I'd given her everything I possibly could: love, degrees of protection, support, and encouragement—and time. Including, a college diploma. But, again, my conscience and love wouldn't allow me to move some two thousand miles away and leave her behind.

Although he said otherwise, I was concerned Bradley was growing frustrated. My insecurities were making me afraid he might meet someone else. Someone, who was better than me. I knew Bradley loved me, but my low self-esteem made me believe I wasn't even worth waiting for—certainly, with the baggage of a mentally ill and alcoholic mother.

I came close a number of times to packing my bags and getting on the next flight to protect what we had. To protect me from losing Bradley. But each time, I remembered the night I tried to escape Warner Robins and perhaps my mother while in college. I wasn't only disheartened but also still very angry, after she'd rejected Eddie's marriage proposal.

At the time, I'd been in bed; I felt the walls of the room closing in to the point I could see them in my mind's eye. My heart raced as my lungs seemed to struggle for air the smaller the room became—the advancing walls squeezing it out. I felt the sudden need to run—and run fast; although I had no idea where or how far. I just needed to get in my car and drive.

I wrote my mother a note expressing that I wasn't leaving her, although it may seem that way. That I loved her with all my heart and soul, but I needed some time—some time to figure out my life and I would call her later in the day.

I knew by my leaving; Mother would open a bottle as soon as she read the note. I knew worry and fear would be all consuming, but I was worried and afraid as well. But I also knew, she was going to drink sooner or later anyway whether I was there or not.

With the note in hand, I walked from my bedroom through the rigidness of the darkened hour. As torpid as that night, I stood in the doorway of her bedroom—my backpack filled with clothes and some toiletries hung off my shoulder as a sickness stirred my gut. My eyes were glazed by tears; my heart ached. Each beat pricked as I looked through the faintness at Mother's face and listened to her breaths as she slept. I kept telling myself: I had to leave.

Eventually, I turned away; but before I could finish a step, I was compelled to look back at her before slowly continuing to walk through the dim, and seemingly airless hallway toward the kitchen. I left the note on the breakfast table. My feet felt as if encased in concrete as I took the few feet to the back door of the house.

I made it to the Mustang but couldn't manage to insert the key into the ignition. I sat in the car with my hands tightly gripping the steering wheel, while fighting with my conscience. An hour must have passed before I returned into the house and tore up the note. I walked into my mother's bedroom. Sat on the corner of the bed, while once again, watching her sleep. Maybe the main reason I couldn't leave was because of what happened that October morning, two years before and the resulting guild I carried.

I was able to fly to Los Angeles as I'd promised Bradley—some two weeks after he surprised me that afternoon at Britton's. We spent several glorious days in Malibu and the rest of the time at his Hollywood Hills home. All I wanted to do was to cherish every second with him as I cherished Bradley. Make love all night. Sleep-in and make love again. Swim naked with Bradley in the pool. To lie on the roof with him holding me while we counted the shooting stars. I wanted time to stand still.

A few days before I had to fly back to Atlanta, we had an argument. Or at least it became one.

"Why don't you just stay this time, Randy. Don't go back. Just stay with me."

"But what about… "

Bradley kept talking.

"Look… if you call your mother and tell her about us over the phone… tell her that you're not coming back but you want her to move here, that we'll both move her… then she might. She just might."

I thought for a moment as I looked into Bradley's pulling eyes. My heart started to hurt—felt as if it was severing into two halves. One for Bradley and the other for my mother. I felt as if I needed to throw up.

My mind instantly conjured a vision of Mother dressed in a nightgown as she sat at the kitchen table. A spent bottle of whiskey inches from her and an almost empty glass in her hand. Her fingers gripping it tightly as if it might break at any moment—gripping it with such sadness and desperation. Stubbed-out cigarettes—a graveyard of butts in an ashtray on the table as well. One half-smoked among them, was slowly burning as its trail of smoke rose in the hazy density of the air.

Like a rerun of a movie, I'd seen it in person many times. Too many. Standing, just standing looking at her through the opening above the stove in the kitchen into the breakfast room. But this time—in my conjured vision, the handset of the phone was gripped in her other hand as my mother was trying to call me. I could hear the rings in my head. Ring. Ring. Ring.

As that night I was in college standing at the doorway of her bedroom, tears ran down her face as they had mine. And like that night, while I sat in my car, I knew she would feel like I was deserting her—leaving her alone in the world. Mother would feel the same listening to my voice on the other end of the phone tell her, I wasn't coming back from California.

Another vision followed of Mother dead on the kitchen floor. Scattered pills from empty pill containers next to her. At that moment and for the first time, I actually resented—maybe even hated her. But it was the situation that I resented and hated. Perhaps, I hated myself. Hated what I had or may have done out of love and concern. And if I had, how it must have traumatized her more than I thought. But, again, he was a monster. What was I supposed to do? But her destruction was his doing. And he deserved to die because of it.

Regardless, Mother was holding me back as my love for her was as well. Both chaining me to Warner Robins. Or was it also the nagging guilt more than anything else? My guilt for the end result. Then, too, maybe I'd pushed her too hard to be okay now that my father was dead. Expected too much from my mother. Foolishly thinking, it would be that easy to be okay after years of living with the bastard. Then, there was the resentment toward my older brother for walking away from our mother. Oddly, I held none of that resentment for Sandra for joining the Army, although I would have rather her not had—remembering the day I was at the recruiting station to pull her out. To tell her not to join and go back to college. It was just one huge ugly ball of wax—one constantly rolling and growing bigger.

"But Bradley… "

"Dammit, Randy!" Bradley yelled.

He threw the beer in his hand across the room. The act stunned me. Disheartened. Shook. I'd never seen him that angry, as I hadn't heard Bradley yell so harshly. From the chair, I rushed into the bedroom. Closed the door. Laid face down on the bed and began to cry. I was scared.

"Would I stupidly allow my mother to be the end of us?" I questioned.

Minutes later, I heard the bedroom door open. I lifted my head to see Bradley standing in the doorway. Just standing with his head downward. Then, he looked up and began slowly walking toward the bed.

"Can… can I lie down with you?"

I nodded.

Bradley pulled me close to him. Kissed my eyes before wiping the tears from my cheeks.

"I'm sorry Randy. I never should have yelled at you… never upset you like that. Will you forgive me? Please forgive me."

For the first time, I saw tears in his eyes—having never seen Bradley cry before. I knew none of it was Bradley's fault—but mine. I kissed him. I told Bradley it was okay. That, I was sick for making us both wait, too. Sick of waiting to be with him in Los Angeles.

"When I get back to Atlanta, I'll give my notice… I will."

I told Bradley that I would drive to Warner Robins and tell her. Tell Mother that I was leaving whether she comes or not. Tell her that I can't keep living both of our lives. That, I need my own and that she can have one in Los Angeles. A better one than in this shitty town—this shitty house full of pain. That, we'll both leave it all behind.

Still, the explosion had shifted things between Bradley and me. He began to drink more for the remainder of our time together. But that, too, was my fault. Thankfully, he still held my hand. Kissed me multiple times a day. Made love to me every night on the roof and then again in the mornings. Some mid-days, he would come home from work for more before heading back to his crew.

As before, while I was back in Atlanta, we talked several times a day and at our usual time at night without fail. I told Bradley that I'd given my notice at Britton's and told Mother what I promised Bradley I would do. But I lied. I couldn't bring myself to tell her but still planned on doing so. I didn't because she had slipped into another bad state of mind, and I didn't want him to know. But the news—lies or not, didn't stop Bradley from drinking. Again, as always, I could tell during some of our phone conversations when he would sometimes slur his words and by his speech pattern.

About a week later, I returned to LA. He kept asking me, when? How soon? Bradley was becoming more aggressive. I could even tell when we made love, he was angry. He'd start out gentle before Bradley would repeatedly and forcefully ram his penis in me. Several times, making me bleed as his thrusts became harder and harder—deeper and deeper. But he didn't seem to care each time I told him to slow down. Bradley ignored my yelps and whimpers of pain and kept going at me as he pinned me between him and the bed. But I didn't fight Bradley. Didn't try to push him off of me or attempt to free myself.

One day, Bradley had so many beers that he later vomited on the living room sofa. I ignored it all. Bradley seemed to get worse, although he did stop drinking the last two days, I was with him. But I knew he did that for my sake. Then, we had a big argument the night before I was scheduled to return to Atlanta—a silly, stupid, argument at that.

"Bradley, please settle down. I'll be living with you in a month."

"Are you sure this time?"

"Yes. Yes, I'm sure."

And I was. Then, I had to open my mouth—circle back around to his drinking because of how he'd gotten sick. Bradley started up again. It scared me as the last time had; I was being dragged back to my childhood even more so, when I'd thought being with Bradley would protect me from it.

He walked out of the room. Left me standing in the kitchen. I knew I would have to take action. I felt I had to take the hard love approach; although, it was weightless on my part. I just had to make Bradley believe it was otherwise.

So, I gave Bradley a choice: it was me or the periods of excess drinking; that, he had to get a handle on it once and for all; that, he had to choose one or the other. Not only was it difficult and gut wrenching, but I also knew I was taking a risk by using his love for me as a bartering chip.

But regardless of what I told him, if it didn't work, and even though I'd lived with alcoholism my whole life—I would deal with it with Bradley. I was programmed to accept it, and I knew I was an alcoholic by association—an enabler of self-destructive behavior. Even my own. I would go back to Al-Anon meetings if necessary. I wasn't going to lose Bradley. And I convinced myself that Mother would miss me enough to let us fly back to pack her clothes and return with Bradley and me to Los Angeles. I'd address selling the house later, although I'd rather burn it down to the ground.

After my ultimatum, the tension between us festered the rest of the day. In an attempt to smooth things over, I suggested we take a bath together as we had many times in the past. I filled the large tub with warm water. Bradley didn't want to engage in conversation, but I kept trying as I massaged and washed his massive back and chest. His softball-size biceps and muscular arms and legs.

Bradley remained quiet even as he wrapped his arms around me; I moved to lean my back up against his chest. Later that night, we had sex again. Not love, but more hard-driven sex.

fragmented

Sunday evening, I was rushed to catch a red-eye back to Atlanta but not because of any concern of not making it in time. I didn't want to leave—leave Bradley but I knew I had to. I had to go before my heart fragmented any more than it was. As it continued to do so—I felt more pieces of my heart separate. I had to keep a firm stand, again, to make Bradley believe I was sticking to my ultimatum.

Tears ran down my face as I looked up into his watering eyes that revealed marked disbelief. Bradley took me in his arms. He told me that this wasn't the end of us.

"I need you more than the breath in my lungs. Don't let it be."

Bradley held me tighter as my head nuzzled into his chest; and the tears from my eyes washed his partly unbuttoned shirt.

"I've asked and asked you to the point of begging. You'd slow down on the beer for a while… even stopped for periods but then started again. I worry about where we'll be in the next five years concerning it. You know my history, Bradley."

"I… I can try harder. I will. You know I'd do anything for you."

I told Bradley I knew he wanted to as he'd proven several times. And that, again, I was thankful. Then, when he started up again, there were periods I felt like I had to walk on eggshells as I did as a kid around my father when Bradley got hardheaded and mad. But we couldn't keep going around in circles.

Bradley's lips pressed into the middle of my forehead. They lingered. My heart began to melt. Every ounce of me hoped and hoped and then hoped some more—Bradley once and for all would get help. But hope had rarely been kind to me when it came to alcohol. It's a lethal infection. I had to stop it from spreading any deeper into our relationship.

Making Bradley believe I was leaving him was the only way I thought I could stop it—stop the unforgiving and ruthless spread. But, again, either way, I was coming back to him. I just had to try this one last attempt before giving in to have what I wanted. The man that I needed. The man whose love made me fly between the stars in the heavens.

Before I left to take the cab waiting outside, I painfully placed the key to his Hollywood Hills home on the kitchen counter—the home he'd told me was mine, too. The one he said was ours. Bradley attempted to force the key back into my pocket. That key, which was more than a key to a house, but one that opened a door to the rest of our lives together. Besides the home I had found engulfed within Bradley's arms, that key was to a house that was the only one I felt was home. I wanted us to live our lives on the inside of that door it opened. But once again, alcoholism began to sever my heart like it had one too many times behind a different door. To the door of the house on Shirley Drive—as it continued so with my mother's drunken episodes that came and went as Bradley's had.

"You can give me this key back when you're ready… when you take getting help seriously, Bradley. Don't shatter my heart. I love you more than I can possibly tell you. I'll be waiting."

As I turned away, Bradley reached out his arm to pull me back. He hugged me once more. Kissed me again. And then again.

"Remember what I said, Randy… this isn't the end of us. I won't let it be."

That Sunday evening, I practically ran out the door and down the driveway. But, as always, I wanted to run back faster to Bradley. Instead, I didn't look back. I knew if I did—I would. I would run back. Staying firm to pressing that "hard love" was the hardest and most heart-crushing thing I've done in my life.

I called Bradley once the plane landed to check on him. To see if he was okay. He told me again he was sorry. That, he missed me. That, he loved me. Then I call Joy. Told her what happened. That, I've given him the ultimatum.

"But regardless, Joy… I'm coming back whether your brother gets help or not. I'll just give him some time."

Joy told me that she'd drive over to his house. I asked her to call me back. That, it didn't matter how late it would be for me. That, I wouldn't be able to sleep anyway. A few hours later, she did. Joy did call me back as I'd been waiting—waiting on her while curled up on the sofa holding a pillow. The television was on, but I'd muted the sound. Before the phone rang, all I could hear were the aching heartbeats in my chest surrounded by the silence of the room.

"Hello… "

"Bradley seems to have calmed down. It's clear that he's mad at himself. Told me… he now knows just how acutely his drinking too much at times has hurt you."

I began to cry, but seconds later stopped myself. Closed the floodgates. But still, the tears rolled down my cheeks. At that moment I wanted to comfort Bradley. Hold him. Have him hold me but we were over two-thousand-some miles apart.

"Randy, try to stop worrying… my brother is tough as nails. And he usually doesn't show his emotions so openly except around you. He's just frustrated. Once you're living together, he'll be fine. That's all he wants."

"Should I call him back? I want to. I need to."

"Randy, I wouldn't tonight. You already did earlier when you got to Atlanta. Bradley told me."

I just felt numb—every inch of me.

"Look… I understand why you have to do this. I just hate to see Bradley sad… and you, too. But maybe this is what he needs. And… and maybe you both need some time."

"Whatever the outcome, I just don't know how long I can manage to stay away. And when I do come back, whether tomorrow or next week… or next month, I'm going to stay and never leave again. I don't care if he keeps drinking. I'll adjust."

"I'm going to spend the night with him."

I felt better. At least a bit knowing she would be there.

"You know I love your brother… right? That, I can't be without him."

I sat up on the sofa. Held the right side of my head with my hand before I brushed it over my hair. Then I started to brush through it with my fingers; but stopped halfway. Grabbed a handful. Pulled at it as I reassessed my decision. I began to hate myself. Just hated me. Hated the situation. Hated the world. Hated. Hated. Hated. Hated that alcoholism was coming between us. But then I realized, the fight was between me and alcohol—rather than Bradley's drinking.

"I know… I know without question, Randy. Despite the drinking… you and Bradley are good for each other. You two will work it out."

"Can you give me a second?" I asked

"Sure."

I put the handset of the phone down beside me on the sofa. Moved both my hands to my face. Covered my eyes. Seconds later, I spread the tears on my cheeks to the side. Took a deep breath. Picked up the headset again.

"I'm back."

"Are you going into work?" Joy asked.

"Going to call in late."

"Okay then."

"One more thing, Joy… keep Bradley safe for me."

Again, Bradley told me he was sorry; and I said the same. We continued to talk on the phone as if nothing had happened—as if I'd never ran out the door. As before, our phone conversations took place at least a few times during the day. If nothing more than to say, "I love you." And we always talked around 11:00 p.m., East Coast time—every night. Before that ring, I'd lie silently in bed thinking of us together while waiting to hear his voice and breaths again—never tiring of them. And as I lay there talking to Bradley, my eyes closed while longing to be beside him with every word he spoke.

Bradley did tell me he'd talked to his doctor about drinking too much at times. With that information, his doctor recommended a counselor.

"I'm going to make an appointment.

Still, again, there were a few times I knew he was trying to hide the drinking from me, again, as my mother had. But I never said anything about it. Bradley told me he wasn't going to let alcohol tear us apart. That, he would make it all right again. That was why he was going to finally see the counselor.

Each day that passed, it became harder and harder for me to stay away. So hard that I'd booked an open-ended ticket to fly back to LA and to Bradley. And each morning I got so close to using it. So very close. I was determined to have everything I wanted: Bradley and happiness. One and the same. And if Bradley didn't stop his periods of drinking too much or keep his appointment with the counselor, then I would have to change my mindset. That, I would be the one going to counseling to help me deal with it.

I drove to Warner Robins to spend another weekend with Mother. It was hard but I told her I was going to LA for a few months. I omitted the part about actually moving. But I did tell her I'd already given two weeks' notice to Britton's.

"Why did you do that?" she asked.

"I'm just tired of working in visual merchandising."

"Then, what are you going to do?"

I hesitated.

"I'm going back to modeling full-time," I lied, again.

I saw hints of the concern and heightened sadness on her face, similar to the day I graduated from college—when, as I've shared, Mother showed up intoxicated and missed the graduation. I was certain her state was because it had been in the back of her mind that once I'd finished college and she had that diploma in her hand, I would be leaving for California—having gone to college for her and not for me as Mother knew. All that diploma meant to me was much like a one-way ticket.

Looking at her face, I began feeling sick to my stomach for lying. Analogously, the same when I'd lied to Bradley several times due to his drinking. But now that was behind us since I would be with Bradley soon and for good.

I went on to tell Mother she should come, too. To think of it as an extended vacation. That, I was sure Siggy and Joann would be willing to check on the house as the neighbors would.

"We can ask Sal next door if he'd cut the grass. You know he will."

"What about the mail?"

"Mom… you worry too much. We'll have it temporarily forwarded. I want to take you all around LA."

"I just don't know, Randy."

I told Mother, I also wanted her to meet some friends that I'd made. Friends, really meaning Bradley. And if she didn't, then I would send her a check every two weeks until I came back. Again, Mother told me she'd think about it, but I knew that translated to, no.

I'd already told Bradley the night before.

"Oh, Babe! Really! This is really going to happen… I mean, you here with me in LA?"

But I could tell Bradley had been drinking some. Again, it didn't matter anymore that he had. I was certain, that once we were living together, even though I failed with my mother, I would save Bradley. I would save both of us.

"Yep, finally. I've already started packing… selling stuff and giving some things to friends. I don't have that much anyway. I'm ready… Bradley. I'm more than ready."

"You better not be pulling my leg, Randy."

I laughed.

"I'll pull it when you pick me up at the airport."

"I'll let you pull more than that!"

"Oh, yeah… ."

"Wait… what about your mother?"

I shared with Bradley what I'd told her and that I had a plan if she didn't come.

"I'll just have to see how it plays out. But… but I'm moving however it does."

"I know that's going to be hard for you."

"Yes, very. But I can't be without you anymore. I want to see you every day… every morning and every night. Am I being too needy?"

"No, because I want the same… so much. It'll all work out. I promise. It will Randy… for all three of us."

I went on to tell Bradley my plan if Mother didn't come. That after two months, we would fly back to tell her the truth that I'd moved. Tell her about us. He was happy about the plan.

"I told my mother I'd call her daily and fly back every few weeks, and… that she can visit anytime she wanted."

"I know you're going to worry about her."

"Yes… I feel guilty but it's time. I will, and I'll tell Mother that… that it's going to be heartbreaking for me, but she can change that by moving."

During that phone conversation, I told Bradley I'd called Sandra in Germany. That she understood knowing how miserable I was, feeling I had to stay in Georgia for Mother's sake. That, she would see about taking some leave and fly back to the States if Mother still didn't come with me. I also made Sandra promise not to tell our mother I was moving for good. Told her about my plan if Mother wouldn't.

Sandra agreed moving would be the best thing for her and would encourage Mother. I told Bradley that Sandra thought Mother likely would once the realization hit her. We were too close as mother and son for her not to. And I shared with Bradley, that I told Sandra all about him.

"He sounds yummy. I'm happy for you… for you both."

"I can't wait for you to meet him."

"Me, too."

By the end of the call, Sandra couldn't help but make a well-hearted jab.

"I knew you were gay before you did," she wisecracked.

I prayed Sandra was right. Regardless, I had to leave no matter how much it would tear me in half. I couldn't imagine living another day without seeing Bradley. Another night without being able to gaze into the heavens by his side or wrapped within his arms.

I'd planned on telling Stephen but doubted knowing I was moving to the West Coast would phase him one way or the other. He'd likely still remain indifferent—while continuing to keep Mother in the background of his life. But I hoped he would surprise me.

eleven p.m.

Tears are the silent language of grief...
Voltaire

I was wearing nothing except a pair of Bradley's boxers while lying in bed waiting for his call. The use of a safety pin was necessary to fold over a section of the waistband since he wore an XL, and I wore a medium. My emotions ran high with excitement knowing I would be with Bradley in a few days shy of two more weeks. But that excitement was accompanied by nervousness, too. I just wanted to make him happy—make us happy; and I wanted the same for my mother. Regardless of how ecstatic I was, I knew I wouldn't fully be at ease until I saw him in the flesh, and we were living in our house; and Mother had finally agreed to move as well.

Randomly, I turned my head away from the white ceiling to look at the clock on the dresser, then back at the ceiling. The ceiling: much like a canvas with Bradley's and my past and present already painted while awaiting years of more brush strokes depictive of our future together.

Five minutes after 11:00, passed. Bradley was rarely late. Then, ten. Then, fifteen. Then, thirty. The next time I looked, it was 11:45. "He's out again with his crew," I thought. "They must have finished a big job and are celebrating... and Bradley's lost track of the time. He's probably not wearing his watch I'd bought in Italy for him," my mind wandered more.

I excruciatingly waited ten more minutes before I dialed his number—only to get his answering machine.

"Hey, it's me. Guess you had a long day, and out with your crew... or maybe fell asleep. No worries, still call when you get home or wake up. Love you."

I placed the phone on the floor beside the bed. Restlessness increased. Longing chased. Desire hungered. My mind wandered through thoughts and images of Bradley until they continuously circled. I was enraptured. Happiness gathered knowing I would be with him soon. Soon, I would be falling into the magic of Bradley's ice-blue eyes. Soon, I would hear his deep voice tell me how much he loved me. Soon, I would feel his large, calloused hands pulled me close to him. Soon, I would be in the safety of his strong arms—Bradley's heated flesh against mine. Soon.

I rolled onto my stomach and adjusted a bed pillow under my head as I looked at two framed pictures on the bedside table. A candid one Joy had taken of Bradley and me sitting closely together on the beach at sunset: his arm around my waist as my head rested on Bradley's wide and strong shoulder, and another of our eyes locked in a gaze.

I burned for Bradley—for his body on mine as I awaited his call. The thought of him slowly sliding inside me—inside of what belonged to him stole my breath as it always did. It felt as if we were one—one entity. One heart. One soul. Magical and rare. My body twisted on the bed at the notion of Bradley's lips brushing over my neck as if they were soft and quiet gusts of winds—until they met mine at the moment he began to take me. Take me body and soul as his soft kiss became passionate, aggressive, and forceful.

I felt it all rushing through my mind and body. The sensation of the touch of his hands on me. How mine on his sparked electricity. His hand running through my hair as I laid my head on his robust hairy chest. I felt warm—Bradley's warmth. His breath on my neck on long exhales. His stubble. His scent—invoking stout earthiness. That of his sweet and pungent sweat—wet and heated procreated from hours of making love. Sex with Bradley was an extension of it—a testament. Two people speaking through raw emotions rather than words that could never define what we shared.

My body distorted more at the mental visualization of the tactile feel of Bradley's movements—easy, gentle, and affectionate at first for such a strong man.

"Randy, do you want me? Who do you belong to?" Bradley would whisper.

"Yes, I want you. I belong to you," I'd shyly respond in moans of pulsating pleasure, echoed from memory as if in real time.

Bradley's hands would entrapped mine above my head on the mattress as our fingers interlaced once he was fully inside—once he'd completely taken me.

Chills of excitement amplified—running unbridled as my mind continued revisiting our many hours of unmatched passion. Bradley was the drug—all-consuming and I was the addict. Every tough—flesh-to-flesh, every whisper, every moment of him engraved in my mind.

"Just a few days," I reflected. Those thoughts and those imagines—all of him, grew and hardened my dick as precum flowed. Flowed until I came soon thereafter without having to stroke myself. I smiled at the thought of Bradley tickling me before I caught my breath. Lightly at first, then more aggressively. And how I would resist twisting and laughing until I couldn't anymore. How he wouldn't stop until I begged him to.

I turned my head on the pillow to look at the opposite wall away from the clock. Told myself, "You're being silly to eye the clock repeatedly and obsessively." I closed my eyes. Still feeling all of Bradley as if he was in bed with me. I resisted looking again. I waited. Minutes that seemed like hours passed as I listened to the ticking of the clock—as it grew louder.

Sometime after 2:00—about three hours later, the phone finally rang. Instead of Bradley, it was Joy. My concern heightened as she could barely say my name. The quivering in her voice was enough to make my heart drop to my stomach.

"Joy… is something wrong?"

Her voice repeatedly splintered.

"Randy… Randy, I'm calling from Cedars-Sinai Hospital."

"What… what happened? Did something happen to Bradley?"

Joy struggled to explain that from the witness account, Bradley's truck swerved on one of the narrow winding roads less than a mile from his house to miss a car coming up in the opposite direction. At that, his truck careened down the hillside.

The accident had taken place at around 5:00 p.m. West Coast time. Each word of Joy's had been like the twist of a vise on my heart as I sat on the edge of the bed, leaning over with one of my hands on my forehead to hold it up.

"Is he okay? Is Bradley, okay?

"I… I don't know. He's still in surgery."

"Oh God," my voice shook as my body trembled.

"Look… I've… I've got to go but I'll call back as soon as I know something."

All I could do was pray as I paced every room in the apartment. My heart tightened. The vise twisted tighter. Tighter. And then tighter. "I should be there now," I berated. And because I wasn't, I felt useless. Helpless. I began to feel the pull of Bradley as I had thousands of times. I needed to be with Bradley. I kept walking into walls until I turned around to lean my back against one. I went weak at the knees. My body slid down to the floor. I raised my knees to my chest. Repeatedly hit my head on top of them as my arms tightly wrapped the calves of my legs as if holding on for dear life—for Bradley's life.

Consciousness of time collapsed as I waited in angst—unmeasured. Fear rushed. Uncertainty smothered. The news stole the air from the apartment.

Oblivious of the time—of how much had passed, the phone rang again. I grabbed the headset; the phone itself hit the floor. There was silence on the other end. Then, more until I heard Joy's distressed voice.

"Ran… Randy… Bradley didn't make it. He didn't make it… my brother's gone."

"No! That can't be… it just can't."

Hearing Joy speak those four words—Bradley didn't make it: I felt my own life leaving my body with each.

We both cried tears of unfathomable loss, knowing but not wanting to believe Bradley had left this earth.

"When can you come? Randy, when?"

I could hardly speak, much less answer.

Moments passed. Then, a lifetime it seemed. But it was life itself that had left—left with Bradley.

"I… I'll get on the next flight I can get. As soon as I hang up, I'll head for the airport."

"Okay. Okay. Just get here."

The headset fell out of my hand. Hit the floor, too, as my body did. The air was sucked from the room and with it, what was in my lungs.

I lay there curled up like a baby, but I knew I had to get up. Again and again, I tried but couldn't. The makings of vomit rose up the epiglottis from my stomach. Within seconds, it jetted over the floor until there was nothing but dry heaves of grief.

I felt the pull of Bradley again. I mumbled. Mumbled off a list of things trying to convince myself Bradley was fine, and he would call any second: I must have been in the middle of a horrible dream… that, that this wasn't happening; that Joy never called; that Bradley wasn't dead, and again his phone call would wake me; that, I would pick up the handset of the phone on the little bedside table; surely any minute, it will ring and I would hear his voice.

Again, I told myself—wanting to believe it, I was dreaming: yes, Bradley will call; he'll tell me what he did every night at 11:00, hey Babe, I love and miss you; then he would ask, how are you tonight; is there room in the bed for me, fully knowing there was even though his feet would extend out from the mattress; in a few days, Bradley will pick me up outside of the arrivals at LAX; pick me up in this Ford Flareside pickup truck; rush around to hug and kiss me; grab my carryon; open the passenger door for me; the Ford will pull away from the curb; Bradley will tell me, let's go home.

Eventually, with blood-red eyes full of tears washing down my face, I got up and made it to the bathroom. Splash water on my face. Went back to the bedroom. Opened the closet door. Ripped a shirt off its hanger. My hands shook as I buttoned it. Struggled on a pair of jeans. The same, as I slipped a belt through its loops. Managed to put on some socks and a pair of loafers. Called a cab knowing I was in too bad of a state to drive. Grabbed my wallet and keys before rushing for the door.

I threw the fare over the front seat to the driver. Stumbled out of the cab. I don't remember shutting the door behind me. Raced to the ticket counter. Slapped my Amex on the counter. Told the agent I needed to get to Los Angeles. She asked me if I was okay.

"No. No. Just get me to LAX. Whatever it costs. Please."

Two hours later, I was on the first flight I could get out of Atlanta to Los Angeles. Roger was waiting at the curb. My eyes were blood-red from crying throughout the flight. The entire time, I tried to convince myself none of it was real. It was just a nightmare. I'd wake up any minute. The phone would ring, and Bradley would be on the other end—like every night. But I wasn't sleeping. It was real. The nightmare was real

As soon as Roger pulled the car into the turnaround, Joy came into sight—standing in the doorway. Her arms wrapped her waist as if Joy was trying to hold herself together. Hold herself together from crumbling. The car stopped. The engine stopped. I too wanted to stop. Wanted my heart to stop beating. The driver's door opened. I didn't move—I couldn't. Too afraid to exit the car. Too afraid to walk into the house. I sat there. Numb. Shaking. Lost.

Roger walked around to the passenger door. Reached his hand through the open window; and placed it on my shoulder.

"You coming, Randy? I can only imagine how paralyzing this is for you."

Roger was right. It was. It was paralyzing. I was paralyzed. And so was my heart—but still it managed to beat. Now, it was no more than a machine plugged into an electrical socket.

Moments later, or it could have been hours for all I knew, he opened the door. Still, I remained seated. I looked over at Joy. She forced a smile. We were all forcing—pushing the reality away from each of our hearts. Eventually, somehow, I managed to place one leg out of the car; my shoe stepped onto the mix of white and beige pea gravel. It screamed—the gravel. Then, the other leg and the other foot. The gravel screamed again. Each step, each crunch, the graveled screamed and screamed and screamed as I slowly walked in the direction of Joy. Roger followed behind. More screams. Joy met me halfway. Embraced me as I did her. Cheek to cheek, our tears mixed on our faces.

"It's… it's going to be okay, Randy. My brother loved you so much," Joy's voice mewled in my ear.

When she began to release me, I pulled Joy back into my arms. I was fearful to let go. Fearful, for Joy to stop holding me.

As in the car, time passed unnoticed until Joy took a step back. Leaned in to kiss my cheek before taking my hand. She placed a key in it. I glowered down at it before closing my hand tightly around it. I instantly knew what it unlocked. I'd used it many times before. I hated myself within those moments. Hated myself, wishing I'd never given the key back to Bradley that Sunday night even though it was supposed to be temporary to prove some stupid point. The look on his face flashed in my mind as did Bradley trying to force the key back into my pocket.

"Bradley would want you to have this back. You keep it," Joy insisted.

I opened my hand to look at it again, then quickly closed it. I started to cry again. Joy took me back into her arms.

"I need to go to the hospital. Can I please… please go. I need to go."

Silence followed before Roger spoke.

"I… I'll take you, Randy."

white tulips

No matter where I am, I remain exactly where I lost him…
Joseph Olshan's
"Nightswimmer"

Bradley's body lay on a hospital bed that had been moved to a room for the family members of donors and those of notoriety. His body was covered in a white sheet except for his face, shoulders, and upper chest. The room was dimly lit. I froze at the sight of it. It seemed as if the muck of the world was working its way up my esophagus to be vomited out. I wanted to turn and run. Where, I didn't know. I just wanted to run.

Mr. and Mrs. Beal, like shadows, were sitting in chairs side-by-side while holding hands. They heard us walk in. Both turned their heads to look at us.

"Randy… Randy, you're here…" Mrs. Beal's voice broke, as she wiped her eyes with a white handkerchief.

"Yes," was all I could say as Roger nudged me forward.

I didn't want to cry for their sake. But the redness in my eyes and what tears that clung to my eyelashes told them my heart was breaking as theirs were. Breaking, as if a huge mountain had crumpled to the ground.

Mr. Beal stood. Nodded his head to motion me over. I approached while my mind attempted to gather words of what to say when there were none. Nothing I could, if I'd found any, would possibly ease their hearts. He reached out his hand to kindly place it on my upper arm.

"May I sit with you and Mrs. Beal?"

"Of course… you belong here, Randy."

Roger stood behind us as I took the seat next to Bradley's mother. Mrs. Beal reached out her hand to hold mine. It felt so frail as it shook. Her flesh was cold to the touch. I lightly squeezed it as Mrs. Beal's wet eyes—so full of pain, looked at me. She attempted to offer a slight smile as she dabbed each eye again with the handkerchief. The handkerchief that was soaked with her pain. I leaned in to hug her while I kissed her cheek. At that, the tears I was trying to hold back began rolling down my face. I remember thinking, "If only Bradley was here… he would make everything okay." Then, as it had been since I got the first phone call from Joy, reality punched me in the heart again. Again, and again. And again.

My mind futilely kept searching for words that might offer some comfort to Bradley's mother and father. But in all actuality, I knew that was an impossibility. All our hearts bled, and words were just words—all I could do was look at them as moments, then minutes passed while the silence around us wept.

"Why don't we give Randy some time alone with Bradley… so, so he can say goodbye," Mr. Beal said. "We'll come back in a little while."

"I can never say goodbye to Bradley… I can't. I won't," I thought.

"Yes, Randy. Go… go over and talk to Bradley," Mrs. Beal softly told me as well.

Her hand slipped out of mine. Mrs. Beal then patted my arm as if to tell me it was okay. I looked into her wet eyes again, then wiped mine. Mr. Beal placed his hand on my shoulder. I started to get up but couldn't seem to as I looked at Bradley's body some feet away. I tried again. Then, again, until I slowly managed to stand up on weak knees.

I nodded. They turned and headed toward the door. Roger followed. I watched them exit the room and the door close behind. I remained in place; closed my eyes. My knees felt as if they were going to give way. I sat down again.

"Dear God, this can't be happening… it just can't," I spoke aloud as my voice broke through the silence of loss.

I wanted to scream and scream but doubted they would be heard, smothered by the encasing sadness. I used the back of the chair to help me stand again. Without looking up, I took the first step to where Bradley's body lay.

I placed my hand on Bradley's forehead. Brought my lips to his. Kissed them gently—fragilely; fragile as the moment as every moment was. Brittle. Then, again and again. Then, again before featherly brushing them over his face.

"Hey, you… you look good," I told Bradley. "Handsome as always."

I waited, fully expecting a response. Fully expecting him to get out of that bed to embrace me while returning each kiss I'd given him. And then we'd go back to our home. But he just lay there. Didn't turn his head toward me as I desperately wanted him to. I needed him to. I needed him to. I needed him to. I needed Bradley to answer me.

"You can't be dead… Bradley, please look at me. Please. We have a life waiting for us. Tonight, we can go on the roof. Lie there and watch the sky until I fall asleep in your arms—until the sun rises."

Again, I told myself Bradley wasn't dead as tear after tear fell onto his face like the drops of a slow rain. I held his big hand. Squeezed it. Kept looking at Bradley's face. Talking to him. Again, kept waiting for Bradley to wake up. To see his ice-blue eyes looking at me. How I desperately wanted to—needed to fall into them.

I outline his face with my finger—every line and curve. Pressed it into the deep dimple of his strong chin. Circled it around and around. I brushed my cheek over his—cheek-to-cheek until my lips met his again. Again, I pressed mine into his as I'd done thousands of times. Maybe more. More tears washed his face. His lips. His eyelids. His strong chin. Over his shoulders and upper chest. I ran my fingers through his hair before wrapping my arms around Bradley. Laid my head on his chest. Kissed and kissed and kissed it.

I squeezed his hand again. Rubbed his upper arm. Watched the short hairs move as the open palm of my hand ran over them. Leaned over and kissed his lips softly again. And then again. And then more.

Emotionally exhausted, I pulled a chair over to the side of the bed. Sat down. Took Bradley's hand in mine again. I continued to talk to him. Told Bradley over and over how much I love him—not loved.

"No. You're not dead," I told him again. And again. And again. "You can't leave me. You can't. Don't. Don't leave."

There was no comfort to be found. But only solace in knowing

Bradley knew I was coming back to him. That, I would have been with him alive in just a few more days. Then, I became angry. Angry. Angry. So angry that I wanted to crawl into that bed with Bradley's body and die too. I looked around the room for something. Anything. Then, his parents and Roger walked back into the room.

"Randy, let me drive you back to Bradley's house," Roger said.

I just sat there, unable to move. I didn't want to let go of Bradley's hand. His father eventually walked up behind me. He put his on my shoulder as he'd done when I first arrived. Mr. Beal leaned over.

"Son. Go and get some rest. You need to rest, Randy."

Mr. Beal helped me stand. I kissed Bradley one more time that night. Roger walked over. Put an arm around my shoulders as Mr. Beal stepped back. I hugged Bradley's parents again. Roger walked me out of the room. Out of the hospital and out to his car. Again, I felt the pull of Bradley. Pulling me back to him. More tears for Bradley quietly seep under my eye lids. Seeped, for what should have been—for all we'd planned on the roof of a house in the Hills.

Joy was sitting on the sofa when I returned to the house, intently looking through a photo album—her eyes still red and swollen from countless tears of grief shed. It was one of many albums Bradley had shared with me that Joy had stacked on the coffee table. Albums filled with pictures of a loving family. Many of her and Bradley. That, of friends. Pictures of Bradley and me as well. Joy looked up.

"Sit down beside me. Can I get you something?"

I shook my head: no. Joy pointed to a picture of her and Bradley when they were in high school that I'd seen before. Joy began to tell me stories—some I'd heard before and others, I hadn't. Then, she flipped to a page with pictures of Bradley and me. I touched each one of them.

"Do you have copies?" she asked.

"Most."

"I'll make some of the ones you don't."

I leaned my head on her shoulder. Joy reached her arms around me. Tightly hugged me. She kissed my cheek.

"You know… I think I'm going to sell my home and move in here. I'll feel closer to my brother."

I nodded as we looked at each other.

"I think that's a good idea."

"Oh, Randy, this isn't fair to you or any of us."

My watery eyes blurred Joy's face.

"I want you to stay in the house as long as you want. Know you're welcome anytime. My brother would want that."

The following day, as Joy and I stood in the kitchen, I asked if she knew if Bradley had been drinking a lot that day.

"I don't think so. No one at the hospital mentioned it."

But I was convinced Joy was lying for my sake. She quickly changed the subject. Told me that she noticed I didn't pack a bag. Told me she would see to it. See to getting me some clothes and a black suit.

"I've got clothes here."

"Yes, yes… I didn't think about that. Of course, you do."

She turned to look out onto the pool through the large windows. Then, back at me.

"But… do you have a black suit?"

I thought for a moment.

"I have two suits here. Yes, two, and I know a tux in the master closet… but neither of the suits are black."

"Okay then… just give me your sizes later. I'll send my assistant to get you a suit. I'm sure you're not going to feel like shopping."

Joy was right. I didn't want to do anything. Certainly, not leave the house.

"What about black shoes?"

"No, just brown dress shoes and black patent leather for the tux… some athletic and loafers."

"I'll go get my wallet."

Joy told me that wasn't necessary. That, Bradley would want her to take care of me. I didn't volley about the money. I knew she was right. That, Bradley would want it that way.

A week later, he was put to rest. The church service, as the graveside burial, was amassed with family and Bradley's friends. The bereavement swamped. The tears fell as if from the sky.

I sat with Mr. and Mrs. Beal, feeling immeasurable grief and loss as my heart begged for Bradley. As I bartered with God. And along with those emotions, I felt cold steel anger as I had at the hospital. I felt cheated by life, feeling that Bradley had been stolen from me. Joy stood at the podium talking about her brother. Her eyes bleeding tears. Then, she read Helen Steiner Rice's poem, "When I Must Leave You." I felt as if Bradley was speaking to me as she read the first six stanzas of the poem, and in its entirely.

When I must leave you
For a little while;
Please do not grieve
And shed wild tears
And hug your sorrow to you
Through the years...

The surrounding air smelled of citrus and honey from the scent of white tulips. Everyone at the graveside held one. As Joy was planning Bradley's service, I asked if we could give one to those in attendance.

While the minister spoke, I stood off to the side. I remember feeling suffocated while I remained frozen in denial. I still couldn't accept the man I love had been ripped from me—Bradley and our life together. Then, Joy spotted me. She subtly motioned to come sit by her and her parents. I took the seat next to her in the front row reserved for family and a few close friends.

Bradley's coffin was topped with a huge arrangement of an array of white flowers and green palm fronds. Still, I refused to accept he was gone. Accept, he was in that coffin. But I felt covered in death as if I was the one who had died. Joy reached for my hand and held it. We remained seated; everyone walked by the coffin and placed their white tulip on top of the arrangement. I watched as many fell off into the deep, rectangular hole in the ground underneath. Then, Mr. and Mrs. Beal stood along with the rest of us. Bradley's parents stoically place their flowers. Then, Joy. Then, me. Followed by the remainder of family members and close friends.

The reception was held at Bradley's home. I told myself it was just a party, and he would walk up beside me at any moment. But that moment never came and never would again. There was no running away from that ruthless reality except in my head—but even there, it was only transitory. Even to hear his friends speak of Bradley in the past tense was cutting. I took seclusion in his bedroom. The sun washed the room, but it wasn't powerful enough to wash the darkness that had encased me as if I were buried in concrete.

I removed my suit jacket. It fell to the floor. The tie followed. I sat on the edge of the bed. Kicked the shoes off my feet with unyielding anger. Then, crawled under the sheets while placing all the bed pillows around me except the one under my head.

Numbingly, I stared through the glass at the pool. An image of Bradley chasing me around it—then catching me before throwing me in the water, filled my head as if I was watching us in real time on the other side of the glass as water splashed everywhere. Then, he jumps in to catch me again. Image after image, seemingly so real that I could hear our laughter.

At some point, Joy opened the bedroom door.

"I'm sorry, I just felt overwhelmed and panicked."

Joy sat on the edge of the bed. Tenderly rubbed my back.

"I do understand, Randy… I understand. We're all hurting in different ways. I know that… that, Mom and Dad… as you and I are deeply wounded. And I don't believe those wounds will ever completely heal. As young as you are… I worry about you. And I feel like Bradley is telling me to make sure you're going to work through this… through him not being here."

At first, I couldn't speak. I closed my wet eyes then opened them. Looked up at Joy.

"I… I don't know how to… how to exist without him."

The tears returned as my body began to shiver. Joy wiped them from my cheek, but they kept coming.

"I know people say this all the time when someone passes, but I know for real that my brother would want you to go on… "

Joy stopped before she could finish. She took a breath.

"Go on and have a beautiful life. You brought so much beauty and happiness into my brother's life, Randy. That big lug of a man loved you."

We both went quiet. The mixing of voices from the living room drifted past the bedroom door.

"Joy… my beautiful life ended the moment Bradley died. The… the beautiful life I'd been waiting for since I was a kid. The beautiful life… that started the night I met your brother."

I buried my face in one of the bed pillows.

"I'm sure Bradley thought of you before he went unconscious when his truck… well, you know. And… I'm sure a part of him fought to survive for you. So, so he could take care of you."

I didn't respond. What could I have?

"I'm here for you, Randy. I always will."

The moping silence between us revisited—staying minutes.

"Mom and Dad just left. They asked where you were… I told them you were likely in Bradley's bed."

"I should have seen them before they left."

"No, it's okay. They understand. My parents want us to drive out to the ranch tomorrow. That is… if you feel like it."

"Sure. Of course."

Joy had once told me that when Bradley came out to their parents, it took their dad a while to accept it; but their mom already had an idea even as masculine as Bradley was and played football in high school; and was a huge UCLA football fan.

As she also had shared: they liked me when I was first introduced but were surprised, I was younger and so shy; and that concerned them. That is, until they were eventually convinced what Bradley and I had was real. Joy told me she knew almost from the beginning. She said, I was much like an enamored puppy with puppy dog eyes. Joy knew I would be loyal and good for her brother.

Joy got in bed with me. Side-by-side, we said very little. But, again, what could we have said?

"You know, Randy," Joy whispered.

"What?"

"For some time, I've thought of you as a younger brother."

"Thank you… that means more than I can tell you, Joy. I was just beginning to feel like I was part of your family."

"You still are, Randy. You are."

Other than going to the ranch with Joy, for the next three days I laid in Bradley's bed. I couldn't think of anything else but him. My mind moved in a continuous circle of in-and-out denial. I cried until there were no more tears to cry. Sleep was impossible. I couldn't eat.

Both night and day, I walked around the front and backyards. Sat by the pool with my feet in the water—remembering our midnight swims. And each night, I laid on my back on the roof, fully expecting I would turn my head to see Bradley beside me. My mind was constantly replaying every aspect of our short life together. Playing and rewinding—playing and rewinding. Playing and rewinding so that I could see Bradley looking at me. So, I could hear his voice talking to me, especially telling me that he loved me. So, I could feel the fingers of his hand enlace mine. Feel his arms around my body holding it close to the warmth of his, on the roof and under the heavens. But I knew it was more than me caught in a loop. Undeniably, Bradley was there with me. He was with me every second. I know because I could feel his pull once again.

As I felt him next to me, I relived every sensation of him running the gamut: from tranquility to exhilaration to heartbreaking loss. And yes, I felt the pain of loving him and how that love began—how two people bonded under the wonders of the universe.

Then, the harsh reality took a permanent hold. It screamed at me louder than ever before to the volume my ears felt as if they were bleeding, reminding me those days would never come again—those days and nights of Bradley and Randy.

The afternoon before the next day I was scheduled to fly back to Atlanta, I'd planned on ending my life—having taken a utility knife from Bradley's toolbox. I drove his black Oldsmobile 442 to the cemetery. I placed more white tulips on Bradley's grave with all the others; the palm fronds had started graying. I laid on the ground next to it. A stanza in Amanda McBroom's song, "The Rose" sung by Bette Midler, couldn't be any more appropriate at that moment: "Some say love, it is like a razor that leaves your soul to bleed."

As if light were life, the setting sun told the end of the story. It's last words soon spoken as it slipped further behind the horizon before it was hidden from the sky. At the last few words, I pulled the utility knife from the pocket of my jeans. Slid the blade out. Put it to my wrist. Then, at the first sight of blood from the point just piercing the skin, I thought of my mother. Then of Joy; and Bradley and their parents. As if he was talking to me, I let the utility knife fall from my hand.

I spent one more night on the roof of the Hollywood Hills home looking up at the heavens, waiting for a shooting star to race by with its long, glowing tail. Again, feeling Bradley beside me. Again, remembering what he felt like—what we felt like together. Eventually, for the first time in days, I fell asleep until the sun's peering rays awakened me.

The evening before I was to return to Atlanta, Joy walked into Bradley's bedroom where I was once again lying on the bed, wearing his old UCLA T-shirt—that I kept, and surrounded by the pillows. Always lying on the side Bradley slept on.

She held a square black leather box with BREITLING imprinted on the top with a winged B logo above. The very sight of it slashed. It was the box containing the Breitling Chronomat I'd given Bradley some time ago. I set up against the headboard of the king-size bed. Pulled one of the pillows to cover my stomach. Joy sat on the edge.

"You know… " Joy choked up.

She took a few moments to collect herself.

"Bradley was never a watch person… I don't think I ever remember him wearing one… that is, not until you gave him this one. Bradley was so proud of it. So proud you gave it to him."

I listened. Kept looking at the box, then back at Joy as she continued to talk. Kept wiping the tears from my cheeks while holding the bed pillow tighter.

I remained speechless as my heart drained its last drop of blood while my mind took me back to the exact moment in time, I gave the watch to Bradley. Watched the expression on his face as Bradley opened the box. Saw his smile widen as he put it on his wrist. Remembered how silly he was that whole day, periodically asking, "Randy, do you want to know what time it is in Atlanta?" He'd set the watch to East Coast time instead of West Coast. Bradley told me he would change it once I was living with him.

I buried my face in my hands. My pain couldn't have been any more overwhelming—any more emotionally debilitating. The knife of loss couldn't have cut any deeper since the moment Joy told me over the phone, Bradley had left this world. That, he had left me. My mind grappled to speak.

"I… I can't. I just can't Joy. At least not now. If I take the watch back to Atlanta, it… it will make the reality of Bradley's death more real than it is. And… and I'm not ready to accept it. Not sure if I ever will. I know you feel the same."

Joy moved her hand over my heart. She nodded. My eyes zeroed in on a single tear rolling down her cheek. Then, another followed.

Reluctantly, my hand reached to take the box from Joy's. It shook as I opened it. I stared at the watch as my mind instantly rolled with more memories. Within seconds, my puffy eyes were drawn to the bedside chest. The chest where Bradley had always placed the watch when we went to bed.

"Joy… I," abruptly, I lost my breath.

My careworn eyes were drawn to the bedside chest. To the chest where Bradley had always placed the watch before we went to sleep. My mind wanders more. Rolled more. Rolled backward.

I looked back at Joy. Then, placed the box on top of the bedside chest where I knew it belonged.

"Joy… can we just keep it here. Keep the box with the watch on the chest? At least until I feel I can take it back."

Then, I explained why.

"Of course. Of course, we can. As… as long as you want it to stay there," she agreed. "Whatever you want, Randy."

Long silent moments staggered as we both looked at the box on top of the chest. Those moments absorbed within the vacuum of heightened dejection gripping the room—gripping our hearts, and beings to the core. Both of us searching to find some forced imitation of comfort when all we could do was lean into each other—to hug. The hug, stalling in our arms.

"I've got to make a few more phone calls… and check on my parents. Can I get you something to eat?"

"No. I'd just throw it up."

"Well, you rest. Just try to rest, Randy. Do you need anything to help you? I have some valium."

"I don't think anything will… "

My eyes followed Joy as she stood up. She ran her hand over my hair.

"You have such pretty hair. Such a pretty young man."

Joy lingered another few moments.

"I'll check in on you later."

I laid back down on the bed. Held the pillow in my arms. Looked at the box for what seemed like hours until the penetrable grief sunk me into sleep.

I returned to Atlanta nothing more than an empty shell. My new life as I knew it had died with Bradley. I blamed myself for his death; blamed myself for likely making him first believe I wasn't coming back. And because of that, it possibly had made Bradley drink more. If I'd just not pretended to walk away from him so convincingly. If I hadn't stayed in Atlanta longer than I did, I believe we would still be together today: two aging men lying on the roof of that Hollywood Hills home while locked in an embrace and looking at the heavens waiting for those shooting stars. A man like Bradley only comes along about as many times as Halley's Comet passes Earth—perhaps 75 some years or so. But it's more like many lifetimes. I'm sure of that. I once knew what love was. A love that has never been matched since the last time he kissed me.

Bradley was the only man who ever made me feel safe and deeply loved—made me feel he wanted me because of what he saw on the inside instead of the package that wrapped me. I often wished I had been in the truck with Bradley when it careened down the hillside. Wished we had died together. It's the way it should have been. I do believe some people carry a curse. Mine was the burden of alcoholism. As my childhood was destroyed by it, the real love of my life died because of that curse.

Joy did sell her house and moved into Bradley's. She didn't change a thing—left it exactly the way he had. Each time I returned to LA, I would visit his grave with white tulips. Sat and talk to him. At night, I'd lay in his bed looking at the box with the watch. Too afraid to open it. Too afraid to still accept Bradley was gone. But I knew his spirit was with me. And every night, I felt him holding me in his arms. Almost two years passed before I brought the watch back to Atlanta; but I've never worn it and only occasionally take it out to hold it to relive the day I gave it to Bradley.

After all the years that have evaporated—gone like shooting stars; I've felt Bradley's pull many times.

When I must leave you
For a little while;
Please do not grieve
And shed wild tears
And hug your sorrow to you
Through the years…

But start out bravely
with a gallant smile;
and for my sake
and in my name,
live on and do
all things the same

Feed not your loneliness
on empty days,
but fill each waking hour
in useful ways,

Reach out your hand
in comfort and in cheer,
and I in turn
will comfort you
and hold you near

Never, never
be afraid to die,
For I am waiting
for you in the sky

For You, My Love
Run unfettered in the ocean's
salted surf as if there is no
tomorrow.
Catch each of the sun's warming
rays reaching down for you.
In wonder, gaze up at the infinite
black sky as it calls your name.
Marvel at the stars so bright blazing
through.
So bright for you, for you my love.
Jump high to catch the midnight
moon.
And as you begin to fall asleep,
the waves washing the shore
will sing to you.

Bradley

twelve

broken flesh and bones

The overcast mid-July sky appeared the consistency and color of spoiled buttermilk. Even the surrounding air smelled sour; but all the same, it served as a barrier from a baking sun. As common and to be expected, the humidity was as heavy and dense as Duke's mayonnaise. I was mindlessly waxing my yellow Mustang Fastback under the shade it offered. Suddenly, my father's yelling voice blasted through the screens of the open jalousie windows.

"Mary Ellen, wash the fucking dishes!"

I heatedly threw the buffing rag to the ground. Stormed to the back door of the house. Opened it. Stepped into the breakfast room and slammed it behind me. Slammed it such, the force should have shattered every glass slat. I chased the yelling in the direction of the living and dining areas. The moment I stepped down into the living room, my father slapped my mother across the face. She stumbled back against the long and narrow mahogany library table that saved her from falling to the floor. Directly, Mother raised her hand to her red cheek. I reached for the closest object: a large lamp on the sofa side table. Hurled it at him. My father thrust his arm upward to deflect it from hitting him in the face.

"You're a pathetic… drunken bully," I abhorrently screamed.

My father's blazing eyes zeroed in on me as the lamp landed on the dark green carpet. He charged in my direction—his fists clenched like the heads of two sledgehammers.

Seeded by the sight of him once again abusing my mother, degrading her, and ordering her around—I instantly knew what had to be done at that moment, but not in the matter of attack I'd been planning for some time. Or was I going to allow my father to hit me as well. He had been warned.

The yards between us offered an advantage. I turned. Fleet-footed across the linoleum to the kitchen counter. Without pause, I yanked the knife drawer open with such speed and vigor, it came completely out. In an instant—within a breath, the knives clattered onto the floor followed by the drawer.

I leaned over. Picked up the largest one. Took possession of it—ready to strike knowing my father was seconds behind me. I turned around; we stood within inches of each other. His liquored breath, staggering. His face, beet red as sweat covered it and soaked the neck of his dirty-white T-shirt. My fist firmly clenched the knife as its tip slightly pierced his belly just enough that a spot of blood was visible through the worn and thin fabric.

From my peripheral vision, I noticed my mother loitering in the background. Panic shaped her face. Her mouth moved in fast animation, but I was too transfixed on my father to hear all that hastened from her mouth. The boiling heat of rage raced through my body. I was moments from crossing a line I couldn't step back over.

Pure, tainted, hate arrowed from my eyes. I have no doubt; my father saw it—the hatred of a monstrous evil ready to attack. The monster in me—the very reflection of himself, he surely saw in the irises of my eyes that day looking back at him. I ached to thrust the knife deep into him. Twist it until he bled out like a gutted pig. Slaughtered him open. Witness his intestines slither from his body onto the floor.

My father's bloodshot and scorched eyes widened. I teased the tip of the knife slightly inward. More blood seeped. The spot on his T-shirt expanded. I felt a rush of pleasure as I drove him back up against the refrigerator with the knife. I was confident, my piece of shit father knew if he tried to take it from me it would be too late. But I wanted him to. I wanted my father to try to take it. I was ready as our eyes remained locked. As sweat beaded his forehead. But first, I wanted him to be terrified as he had made us feel. I wanted him to know—he was about to die.

My mother's image moved closer into my peripheral vision. I glanced at her. Then, back at him. Then, back at her. Tears streamed down her face. Her lips still formed words; the volume of her voice increasingly heightened in my head.

"Ran… Randy. No! No!! Please don't!!!"

My focus returned to my father as my mother kept repeating the same words. He looked at me, then down at the tip of the knife and the blood it stole from his body. Then, I felt her hand on my arm. I looked back again—momentarily focused on the red blotch my father's slap had printed. Her tears still rolled from her eyes—eyes that had no signs of life left. It killed me to see my mother cry; it always did. Her panicked face wore distress—like caked-on make-up.

"Son, put the knife down. Please!" her voice quivered as she stepped closer.

Even still, I had to stab him. Not once, but for each tear dripping from her eyes. Each tear he'd ever caused them to shed. Besides, I was so close. I had my dear old daddy right where I wanted him; washed in fear.

"I could tell the police it was self-defense," I thought. "Just do it. Do it now! Be done with him!" my mind commanded as my eyes scanned back and forth from my mother's face to my father's.

My mother spoke again. Her voice pulled my eyes toward her where they lingered—lingered long enough to look into her soul. But still, I watched my father from the corner of my right eye. The knife—its steel, bridging us together.

I felt my mother's hand on my arm holding the knife. She tried to push it toward the floor, but my hand remained unmoved. Mother spoke again; but weaker this time. Fear and desperation carried on each word. And as her voice weakened more, so did my death grip on the knife. In due course, both her voice and her touch broke the invisible barrier that separated my innate and learned ice-cold hatred from rationality. But it was my mother's rationality—not mine.

Again, my eyes returned to my father—stared squarely into his. As I had looked into my mother's soul, all I saw in him was nothing—no soul, but only a dead heart.

Then, I spoke deliberately to him: "This is your last warning. If you ever touch my mother again… I'll kill you! I Will Fucking Kill You! I'll kill you… you miserable fucking bastard!"

I pulled the knife back, but only inches in case he tried to lunge. Silence ensued. It was as if the world had stopped turning. As if everything on the planet had stopped. The three of us stood like stone in a very average kitchen with dishes piled in the sink. In an average house on an average street in an average shithole town. But far from an average life—so much less than average.

"What the fuck are you waiting for?" my voice broke the stagnating, brooding silence. "Get the fuck out! Get out!" I forcefully screamed. And he did. My father stormed out. Slammed the back door behind him.

I walked to the jalousie windows of the breakfast room—the knife still white-knuckling my fist. I watched my father get into his blue Ford sedan. He erratically backed it out of the driveway—almost hitting a tree. Although he'd cowered away, I was certain only long enough to lick his bruised pride and to plan and scheme—again, as I had been doing. He likely was headed to some woman's bed where she would spread her legs, offering up her vagina so he could play like a man. But he was far from a man. From a husband. From a father.

I walk back into the kitchen. My mother still stood in the same spot—shaking. Just standing and shaking in her faded, green and yellow floral night coat. Standing—looking empty. Used up. Fragile. Standing as if unable to walk. My mother lifted both her hands to her face. I took a few steps until I was standing directly in front of her. She fell weakly into my arms. I wrapped them around her. She looked up at me. The tears still abandoned her brown eyes. I saw nothing in them. She was dead under her flesh. How her heart managed to beat—pump one more ounce of blood I didn't know. It seemed an impossibility. After that moment—I don't believe the world ever really started back up for her.

My father and I kept more of an awkward and cumbersome distance. At times, passing within inches without acknowledgment. He never looked me in the eyes again, at least not for some time. Then, the day came that he did—one last time. But before that, as I had been, I continued to closely watch my father's movements as if they were my own. Still, very much aware, an uncontrollable rage idled in his core but so did it in mine. That very rage I'd inherited from the sequence of the nucleotides in his DNA encoding the synthesis of his genes and whatever was left out. The balance due, sculpted by his nightmarish enterprises. That day in the kitchen had accelerated my plan—to kill him before he could kill us.

Over the next several months, I waited for my chance. Waited for him to get drunk. To pass out on the cot. I knew time was running out. I needed to strike sooner than later. Kill him until my father was nothing but broken flesh and bones covered in a river of his blood.

night of the katydids

While sleep was an ephemeral recess, it was paper-thin. One eye open. An ear to the ground. Waiting. Listening. Contemplating. Planning. An accurate working crystal ball would have been an essential asset—marking time for my father's next caustic emission. A heads-up, beneficial in giving a favorable advantage due to his volatile and heinous state of his mind.

What I feared most: My father's murderous crusade—the more increasingly I was certain the time paced closer. More than once, I'd envisioned that dreaded night as apprehension pilfered the air. Each night, I struggled to keep my eyelids open while listening for his car pulling around the rear of the house. Listening for the back door to creak open. Listening for his unfaltering footsteps walk through the breakfast room and kitchen toward the short hallway to the bedrooms. Listening for two muffled gunshots in the cloak of night—surely, he'd use a pillow to dull the shots. That's, what I would do. One bullet for my mother and the other for Stephen while they slept. Unquestionably, Sandra would be next unless he spared her for himself. I was sure—I would be last.

If the muted shots hadn't awakened me, no doubt my father would. Before pulling the trigger—he would want me to know, he was the end of me. Take great pleasure in my knowing. I knew that narcissistic, fist-punching bastard would find it gratifying. In his mind, pulling the trigger would be akin to my father stepping on a bug scampering across the kitchen floor.

My body paralyzed in the bed as I looked at his silhouette standing in the doorframe—the shadows of night in-transit on either side of him as he walked closer. Closer, until I could see my father's baleful grin and leering eyes aflame raking down on me. The hot steel of the gun in one hand—pointed at my head. The other, holding a bloody pillow. Me, dead instantly—as the bullet coursed through my brain.

My father would never look back. Soulless. Vacant of a conscience. Not a single gasp of remorse for the carnage left behind. The Ford's rear lights would flash red. Paused at the end of the driveway before turning onto Shirley Drive. Making his escape into what would be the most eldritch of nights. Pride, his reflection in the rearview mirror of the car as he green-lit the town with Sandra and whichever woman he was fucking at the time. Proud of himself for murdering his wife and sons.

Arrested within the shifting hours of a moonlit, late-season summer night smelling of oozing pine sap—my fear intensified. The air—impregnated with the rhythmic, repetitive sounds of katydids in the lean and tall pine trees as if the stylus of an old record player were stuck in a groove due to a scratch in the vinyl revolving on the turntable.

The rattling boxed-shaped fans in the open windows of the house were useless. Serving only to circulate the stifling, heavily burdened heat-fevered air of another summer simmering boil. Their circling blades—overworked. Overworked, to the point of breaking down as they attempted to draw it the copious humidity as if it was whipped butter and molasses—making it arduous to breathe. If the heat wasn't enough manufacturing buckets of sweat rolling off my body, the mosquitoes were as they navigated their way through rips in the screens to dive-bomb for blood.

From my bedroom, I heard a car pulling around to the back of the house. I knew it wasn't my father's Ford Galaxie 500—its engine made a cycling, ticking sound in need of servicing.

That inked, heat-infused night—concealed by the comparable darkness of the house wet with that mucked perspiration, I measurably made my way to the breakfast room off the kitchen. Crouching low, I peeked out the open jalousie windows to see my father in his tan, Robins Air Force Base police uniform as he sat in the military car—the engine still running.

I knew it was against policy for officers to drive any further than off-base housing, some seven miles out. Nor was it allowed to bring their firearm home; they had to be signed back in after each shift. Instantly, my brain clicked on high alert; adrenaline surged throughout my body. I questioned: "Would this be the night? Would this be the night he would kill us and drive away?" And the biggest question: "Had I waited too long to murder my father?" He turned the car's engine off.

Still crouched, I made my way through the breakfast room into that of the laundry for a closer look. As before, I kept my head low looking over the stool of the windows. The moon cast an eerie nebulous blue light—enough to see to the woods at the far end of the yard past the shed. My heart surely beat a million beats per minute as I spied and waited—like a guard dog.

From that vantage point, I observed my father pulling a pack of Lucky Strike cigarettes with a match book from the breast pocket of his shirt; the distinctive packaging with its red circle and black lettering was detectable. He tapped the pack several times against the palm of his hand before pulling one out. My father brought the cigarette to his lips before flipping open the matchbook. He ripped one off and struck it twice before it flamed, illuminating his face for brief seconds. The tip of the cigarette burned bright red as he took in a deep drag. Then, threw the spent match out the driver's window.

The thought of waking my siblings and mother rushed my mind. I had to warn them that he was in the backyard in his police car. That he was perhaps minutes from coming in the back door and from our pending executions. And if he did, we might not live to see the sunrise. I questioned if we had enough time to creep through the house and out the front door to escape the bullets waiting in his gun. Did we have enough time to hide somewhere in the neighborhood? My mind continued to race as I watched my father take one long drag after another on the Lucky Strike as he held it between his thumb and index finger—until it was down to the filter. He flicked it out into the yard.

The longer he sat in the patrol car, my brain expeditiously labored until I decided we should run the few blocks to the practice field of Warner Robins High School. There, we'd hide in the bushes at the far end of the field under the billboard that had the painted face of a large red demon with horns, and an El Bandito mustache—the school's mascot. Certainly, once he found the house empty, knowing his plan had gone awry and surely wondering why, my father would drive back toward the base by way of Valley Drive paralleling the field—the only direct route.

Once he reached the stop sign at Davis Drive, it was our cue to run back to the house. Quickly pack some clothes. Load my brother's 1969 Chevy Nova and drive to our grandparents' farm in Fayette, Alabama. It would be pointless to go to the Police Station with what would surely be viewed as the fanatical thoughts of a teenage boy.

My mother's known mental illness wouldn't help my case. Plus, again, most of the police were my father's buddies.

At roughly the moment I was about to wake my family, the police car's engine started. But my father didn't back it up. He remained in the car as it idled. Its exhaust fumes siphoned through the windows of the house—pulled by the fans at the other end of the house. I continued to watch and wait. Once again, he reached for the pack of Lucky's and lit another cigarette. Minutes later, he turned the engine off again. That served to validate the dense conviction that my father might still be pondering our fate. If I were to act, it would have to be at that moment. Waking my mother from a medicated sleep might prove to be difficult. Likely, Stephen and I would have to assist her in our escape. It would slow us down—but it had to be accomplished.

My father took a few drags before he pulled the cigarette from his lips. He looked at it as if mesmerized. Then it hit me: maybe he wasn't going to shoot us. Instead, perhaps retrieve the large gasoline can from the shed to burn the house down with us inside. If indeed that was what my father was planning, our deaths might be viewed as a tragic accident. There had been a few others set by an arsonist around town. He was on duty after all—a near-perfect alibi. He would get away with it scot-free; there would be no need to leave town. Then, there was the insurance money on the house, he would have for payment.

He opened the car door; moments later, stepped out. Stood as he adjusted the gun in its holster. Then walked to the back of the patrol car.

"You have to go… you have to wake everyone up now!" I told myself.

My eyes froze on him as I began to crawl out of the laundry room. Then, back through the breakfast area; to the back door. I reached up to lock the slide bolt.

"That will slow him down," I reasoned.

Suddenly, static came through on the patrol car's radio. I crawled back to the window. Looked out at the moment my father opened the car door. He sat back in the driver's seat with his right leg positioned outside. He picked up the communicator. The static combined with the loud sounds of the katydids made it difficult to understand the communication. But I audibly heard him say, "Ten-four."

My father then positioned his leg back in the car. Closed the door. The engine started up once more. He took a few more drags before the cigarette flicked out the window as the first. The red tip took to the air as if it could fly before it fell to the ground. The illumination of the red brake lights bled the night, followed by the white as he put the car into reverse. Without the headlights on, the car proceeded to slowly back out of the driveway—the tires crushing over yard debris.

I walked through the door to the dining room. Stepped down into the living area. Walked to the far window looking out to the driveway. The patrol car's brake lights flashed as it stopped before turning right onto Shirley Drive heading in the direction of the Base. My eyes followed as it went the short distance to the end of the street. The brake lights flashed again at the stop sign. The car took another right onto Peachtree Circle. Then, it was soon out of sight.

I'm certain, the call over the radio spared us—momentarily. I was certain of it, as I was that my father was still plotting our end as I was his. I knew the battle was upon me. A race to see who swung that sword first and got away with murder. I stayed awake for what remained of that night in case he came back—waited for the sun to remove the darkness from the sky; but no amount of light could take it from my heart. I knew I could not wait any longer. I couldn't live through another night in fear. The night the katydids serenaded the moonlight—I knew. I knew it was time.

perry mason fiction

Friday afternoon, the three fifteen p.m. bell rang. The praised welcomed sound—announcing another day of high school hell had ended. Certainly that, and the weekend free of it. I wouldn't have to return for two days. Still, I was trading a smaller hell for one of greater proportion—201 Shirley Drive. Normally, I'd find Sandra waiting by the Mustang for a ride home; but she'd made plans with her best friend, Karen. Our older brother remained a stranger—continued to seldom be seen at the house as he continued to leave me to stand guard for our mother and younger sister.

As my car turned the back corner of the house, prudent repose idled. My father's Ford was gone. I never knew his exact work schedule—

just that his patrol shifts changed every four weeks. That alone, wasn't always reliable. As I exited the Mustang, I purposefully didn't look at the shed located at the far end of the property. Knowing what I had been planning for a lengthy time.

I entered the house. Mother was sitting at the breakfast table spooning a cup of instant coffee. Within seconds, I noticed the handprint bruises on her upper arms. Although I didn't need to ask, I did after I leaned over to peck her cheek with a kiss.

"What happened… where did those bruises come from?" I asked.

"What?"

"Mother, the bruises on your upper arms?"

She didn't respond. But we both knew it was a lie. Not answering was pointless as it was a weak effort to protect me as much as I had her. I moved one of the breakfast room's chairs close to where Mother was sitting—still spooning the coffee as she stared into the void of the black liquid as if looking for answers.

I knew they were made by when my father's hands had forcefully grabbed Mother, at some point after Sandra and I had left for school. I hated many things about school, but mainly because I wasn't home to protect my mother from his violence, oftentimes leaving other bruises as it did black eyes. But if I had my way—it would be the last of them.

"Just tell me what happened," I insisted.

"No… it's not important. I don't want you and your father to get into another brutal fight."

"Brutal fight? I haven't even spoken to that pile of shit much less looked at him since that last incident."

"Randy… I wish you wouldn't use such language."

She didn't say another word. Mother knew I was right—that he was a pile of shit.

Ensuing additional entreating, Mother told me what had transpired while I was at school. My father had shown up at the house around noon, accompanied by two of his buddies. Not seeing Mother in the house, I surmised he must have believed she was with Siggy or Joann. Instead, Mother was in the laundry room off the breakfast area when they entered the house. Afraid, she stayed. Sat on a stool by the washer hoping they would soon leave. Shortly to follow, Mother heard the beer bottles flicking open as they took seats at the table trapping her in the laundry room. The only exit was through the door between it and the breakfast room. My father and his buddies began shooting the shit. Not her words—shooting the shit, but mine.

To my mother's torment, they were bragging over a prostitute all three had fucked a few nights before. She told me of her attempt to block out their voices by covering her ears with her hands—but to no avail. As usual, they were too loud and rowdy. The thin wall didn't help drown them out. By Mother's depiction, my father started talking about her. Of how he wanted to get rid of her. "Jesus," I said, though I wasn't surprised.

Mother told me she had silently sat in the laundry room for several hours. Once his buddies left, my father stayed behind. Weak and emotionally spent, as she stood up—the stool hit the side of the washer. The noise drew my father to investigate. Finding her, he grabbed Mother by the arm to pull her out. Once back in the breakfast room, she managed to break his hold. Ran to the hallway bathroom and locked herself in. By then, three o'clock was approaching. My father likely knew better than to stick around knowing my sister although unaware of her plans with Karen, and I would be at the house soon.

Mother delayed in the bathroom until she heard the backdoor close. Shortly to follow, the Ford started up. It backed out of the driveway. He was gone, but unfortunately not for good—yet.

On Monday morning, I had Mother call the school's secretary to inform her I was sick and likely wouldn't be back for a few days. I knew if my father saw my Mustang parked in the back of the house, he would stay away—certainly, after yet another incident within a month of the last, where I had the knife at his belly.

He showed back up. Tuesday. Late-morning. I headed to the shed to retrieve the shovel. Brought it back into the house and confronted him—breaking a period of silence as I conveyed what my mother had told me about what happened the Friday before when he told his buddies he wanted to get rid of her.

"I didn't say that."

"The fuck you did."

He attempted to take a swing at me. I stepped back. Lifted the shovel and pointed the metal point at his throat.

"You think you want to try that again?"

My father cowered.

"The only one in this house who's going to disappear is you."

He took a few steps back; the end of the shovel still directed at his throat.

"I've warned you enough times over the last few months. This is the last one… the last warning. If I ever see another bruise on my mother, I promise I'll beat you to death with this shovel and bury you in the woods behind the shed."

I told my father I'd bury him because I couldn't reveal the actual plan. And to bury him, was a feasible and believable option.

At that, my father went out of his way to walk around me. He quickly showered, put on his uniform and left.

After the recent incident and my father telling his buddies he wanted to get rid of my mother, my mind raced even faster to seal my plan for his end. I'd finally concocted what I calculated was a plausible scenario to offer up on a silver platter to the police once my father's lifeless body was found. Still, as I've already conveyed: I had to wait until he was immobilized by intoxication, disallowing him to make noise or defend himself. Patience would be a key factor. But I knew I was running out of time.

The bashing had to be screened by the midway of night. That way, my mother and siblings would be asleep as hopefully, the neighbors would. The slightest hesitation to administer the first blow was unacceptable. Instead, it had to be lightning quick. Hard. Precise. The main target was his nose. Bash-after-bash-after-bash until assured he was dead to the point of unrecognizable.

After making sure my father was dead—the gruesome deed done, I would slip back into the house void of any remorse. Cold. Heartless. No looking back and hopefully free.

I'd keep the story simple and concise. More importantly—sparing any long details that might trip me up in some drawn-out piece of Perry Mason fiction—if questioned more than once. After the gruesome deed, I determined it best to wait until the next day after school to call the police. My story: I found him that way. That's, all I would say. I would wait. I would wait for any other questions if asked with a look of shock on my face—hoping the questions asked were the ones I wanted the police to pose.

I would only offer: my father and several of his buddies were drinking and carrying-on in the shed late the previous night. That, I could hear them from the house. Later, I heard some loud quarreling and swearing. If asked for more details, I'd say the words were somewhat hostile and garbled. That, I was still half asleep and didn't know what the squabbling was concerning. Again, just loud voices and what sounded like scuffling. But it didn't seem to last long before it stopped. Then, there was silence. Several minutes later, I heard a car pull out of the driveway before its tires squealed onto Shirley Drive.

That was my story. Nothing more. Nothing less. I would tell them: that was all I remembered from a haze of sleep. If played out as planned—convincingly enough, the story would point the finger at one or more of my father's policemen carousing drinking buddies from the City's Police Department and-or the Base. Since many of them often hung out in the shed drinking while playing cards.

With trust, my limited sewn fabrication of events would give pause to the investigators. Silently make them wonder about each other as well as the rest; but possibly remain quiet, due to some code of honor of protecting their own—perhaps, severing to interrupt and possibly squashing much scrutiny. Those in charge wouldn't have any idea of those who were supposedly with my father that night of my manufacturing. They most likely wouldn't even want to know—especially, if it meant one or more police officers could fall under suspicion. Hopefully, the murder would be rendered unsolved.

Not long after I'd threatened my father the last time, the weather had rolled into fall. On the cooler nights, he'd sleep on the sofa in the living room—if he came home at all. The rest of the nights, if not on patrol, he stayed away and rarely around on days off. The more he made himself scarce, the more anxious I became with the mounting change of seasons; concerned the fickle, ever-changing Southern weather would encumber my plan. Thirty-something degrees one night and close to sixty or higher the next.

A high probability existed: my father had suspected something was amiss. By the sweeping change in my demeanor, he may have taken my threats seriously since he'd withdrawn after the incidents—highly unlike him. He would wrestle a thousand-pound alligator if it pissed him off—even if he was boozed. My father was an asshole, times a thousand, among many other damning characteristics; but he wasn't stupid. Without a doubt, he knew my loathing of him was unfaltering. He'd surely seen how it inked my face on that day; I'd threatened to kill him with the kitchen knife fisted in my hand, as he did on the day I held the shovel—my young eyes suffused with eagerness to attack.

How could he not know after all he knew he'd done? Not seen himself in my deadened eyes on those days in my inelastic silence; not seen the monster he'd constructed; not sensed my stewing tempestuousness to disembowel or decapitate him—perhaps. Not seen that seething hatred ready to bite for every violation. Perhaps, that scalding hatred—built over years exuding from every one of the some-five-million pores of my body, like the smell of the liquor he drank had perhaps given me away. It all redolent in the surrounding air like the bitter perfume of revenge.

what if, and maybe

There is usually always a choice. In some cases, hopefully—it's the lesser of two evils…
Aristotle
(paraphrased)

From Aristotle's, "Nicomachean Ethics," he wrote: "For the lesser evil can be seen in comparison with the greater evil as good, since this lesser evil is preferable to the greater one… "

As I shared in "In the Arms of Adam: a diary of men," it's true: my older brother called the night of Thursday, September 27, 1973, at my crappy part-time job to deliver the unwanted news that our father had returned after several days away on another one of his drunken escapades. That one of his police buddies drove him home after he'd rear-ended a woman's car. At the time, I remembered thinking: "Whose kid's mother, at Warner Robins High did he hit?" if indeed that were the case? And if so, would I have to deal with the embarrassment of the whispers in the hallways the following day?

After work, I hurriedly drove the seven or so miles back to the house; I had to make sure my mother and sister were out of Father's reach. A waxing crescent moon left the late-night sky dark as if it were hiding; and likely so for good reason—at least, in my compacted world. And as much as I may have wanted to hide, too, I couldn't nor would I. The headlights of the Mustang washed over the asphalt as if giving direction. But I didn't need that kind—rather, how to navigate the pending hours and perhaps days to come.

I crept through the backdoor into a house full of invasive shadows. The air was heavy with a familiar, encasing low pulsating gray-black eeriness. I guardedly walked through the breakfast room to the kitchen. Stopped. Listened as my father's ruptured loud snores migrated from the living room sofa. I was blood-thirsty angry—antagonistic, he had returned again as much as he was breathing. I'm surprised, the heat rushing through my body hadn't caught the house on fire and burned it to the ground. Calculating minutes must have passed before I surreptitiously walked to my bedroom. Closed the door behind me as if it were made of thin glass.

I didn't sleep that night. Couldn't. Furiousness—cling. Raged, that I'd waited too long to strike—been too overly cautious. That, I'd spent too much time concocting an infallible story I shared in the prologue. That story, once it became reality to tell the police I found my father's dead body in the shed the next day after the night before when I'd beaten his head in with the shovel. But I hadn't considered—never even crossed my mind about how capricious Southern weather can be in the fall and winter months: 70% one day and 30% the next. I was also angry: I didn't kill him at the time I had a knife pointed at his belly—I've yet to share.

As I lay awake in the solidified darkness, still in the clothes I'd worn that day, I knew I had to act—and fast. My mind raced in circles about what to do. What if it snapped that night—if not, twisted in a million ways? I knew it was all chance, but, again, I had to do something. Think of something—even, at the eleventh hour. Even at my own peril. Even if it meant risking my life. But, what?

I remember how my mind rocketed through several scenarios. All weak. All unbelievable. Fantastical. Every one of them—full of holes. I felt powerless. Even weak.

As I wrote in my first book: it's true, Sandra and I were in the kitchen the next morning after our father's return the night before. It's true, my father heard us as we were about to leave for school and drunkenly called for us to come into the living room.

If I'd heard that drunken, hung-over voice once—I'd heard it a million times. Indeed, my sister did go against my wishes while I remained in the kitchen. It's true, after a minute—if that, I gruffly yelled at Sandra, "Come on! We're going to be late!" But, what if, I was more concerned about what I needed to do—yet unsure, after a fatigued night had turned into clumsily planning of how to take advantage of the narrowed window offered by a forged note—still attempting to script a storyline even though daylight had arrived before the ending was written? Thus—leaving me surrounded within impetuousness.

This new shaky and premature plan in-the-making, had one key factor: the first part had to be orderly like my father was—anal. Anal—just like the Army had made him. The military was all he knew. Like we all knew him to be. Like, I knew from snooping and watching my father like a hawk for years. Tidy, like he was in his base police uniform and when he was going out on the town with his buddies—as always, the smell of Aqua Velva aftershave trailing. Stinking.

To pull it off or at least attempt to do so, hung in the balance of chance involving a list of things taking place in three acts—perhaps in the vein of a Shirly Jackson novel. Adding up to what I'd omitted and skewed from the first book concerning some factors addressing fully in the matter of how my father died. Again, all chance. A crap shoot. A shot in the dark. Regardless, again, I had to try. Remember, I was a desperate and fed up seventeen-year-old when it all took place—the product of madness, and perhaps mad as well.

This is where I have to be vague for two reasons. One: I'm physically sickened by reliving that day—and glaringly so. Two: as I've done before, I cannot outright confess to anything that I may have been involved in or to what degree that Friday morning in September. But instead, only offer questions and likelihoods.

What if, in ACT I, although unsure, in the middle of the night, while frantically under the gun, I left my bedroom and made it down the short hallway to my parent's bedroom? Entered. Closed the door behind me to set the stage for my incomplete plan—even as flawed as it was? Mother slept heavily medicated, some nights, in Sandra's—if my father was home, regardless of whether he was sleeping on the sofa or on the cot in the shed.

She'd practically moved into Sandra's bedroom and usually didn't awaken until the early afternoons. So, what if, I knew this new makeshift plan had to look convincing—convincing, like my first well-thought-out one that ended up like spoiled milk because it had been left out on the kitchen counter for too long? Spoiled, like my ordinal plan I believed was foolproof.

Maybe I went to my father's desk. Turned on the lamp. Rummaged through it and pulled out what I thought I needed—including his checkbook. Maybe I tore one out of the book. Folded it. Placed it in my back pocket. Then I left the checkbook and what I took from the desk, and in an orderly fashion placed it all on the top.

Next, maybe I opened the closet door—allowing the trapped musty odor to escape as my hands filed through the hanging clothes. Maybe I pulled one item out and laid it on the bed with a few other things I'd removed from the desk. Again, neatly like I knew my father would.

Maybe I took one last look around the room to reassure myself, I'd left everything in order. Satisfied, maybe I turned off the lamp and walked back out into the hallway shrouded by shadows. Closed the door behind me. Again, it was all a crapshoot. Maybe after I returned to my room, I scribbled a note on a page torn from a composition notebook; notifying the principal's secretary I was to be excused after homeroom due to a dentist appointment and would return when done getting a filling in a tooth. Forged my mother's signature. Folded it and put the note in the back pocket of my jeans with the check. Maybe I hoped that note would give me a window of time. Maybe I lied awake waiting as the remaining hours slowly stole what was left of the night.

What if I did leave school after homeroom? Maybe I drove back to the house; but first, maybe I stopped at the hardware store not far from it to purchase the rifle in order to implement Act II. And maybe I forgot to sign the check, and it went unnoticed by the young store clerk. Maybe, I hoped luck was on my side that morning—much like purchasing a lottery ticket and putting it in your wallet. But holding out on checking the numbers. Why? Each day you wait, is another day of hope that you might hit the jackpot.

What if, once I returned to the house after making the stop, I parked the Mustang in the driveway but only a few feet in, instead of behind the house? Then, maybe, opened the car door but didn't latch it close in order to make as little noise as possible. Maybe I was shaking a bit as I walked over to one of the living room's windows to look through the sheer lace curtains to see if my father had fallen back into his inebriated sleep—after Sandra and I had left. What if, that was the case?

Then, maybe I walked around to investigate through my sister's bedroom window where I'd hoped Mother was still asleep—and hadn't broken her routine. Maybe she hadn't. Then, maybe I took a look around the adjoining neighbors' houses to ensure no one was out and about. It was usually a ghost town at that time of the morning. Then, I stood frozen, caught off guard, as a white, four-door Dodge sedan with a dented rear quarter panel sped past the house before disappearing around the corner.

What if, I took another look around before I walked back to the car? Maybe I retrieved the rifle along with some washrags I used to wash the car from the trunk. But this time, I needed the rags so I wouldn't leave my fingerprints on the rifle. Then, maybe I walked along the edge of the driveway and angled my body more toward the house while holding the rifle vertically against my body so it wouldn't have been so obvious what I was holding. Maybe, my strides were quick—but not too quick as I followed it around to the back of the house.

Maybe, I stopped at the steps to the back door—my mind unsure and, again, growling desperately. Scared shitless at the same time. Consumed. My breathing lumbered. My mouth, dry. That congealed hatred for my father I'd shouldered for years—overpowering. All the while, wondering how it would all play out once I was on the other side of the jalousie-windowed door.

What if, on cautious breaths, I walked through the breakfast room? Then, into the kitchen? Maybe, I stopped at the doorway that led into the dining and living rooms. Maybe, I stopped long enough to listen to my father still snoring. Maybe, I felt reassured by the sound. Then, maybe, I turned my head to the left to look down the grainy hallway to the bedrooms. Grainy, in that the house was usually dark—even during the day. Maybe, I checked the time on my watch.

At that, maybe I wanted to scratch the impromptu, second-by-second provisional evolving plan. Turn around and ran out the back door? But didn't. What if, instead, I did walk into the dining room?

Guardedly closed the door behind me. Maybe my stomach soured due to my hit-or-miss plan mixed with frantic panic; and sickened by the putrid musky odor of the house that captured the thick smell of the spatial lengthiness of alcohol. Maybe my nerves were fucked—ricocheting off the walls. My heart, beating a million pumps a second. Maybe I needed to take in a few deep breaths of courage, but I didn't because I might miss my window of opportunity—and the quicker the better for me to implement Act III.

Perhaps, I stepped down onto the living room's dark-green carpet and walked the few feet around to the sofa where my father still slept. Quietly place the rifle on the floor near it. My body lingered—rigid. Nervous sweat soaked my armpits. Maybe as I stood over my father—the vulnerable part of me almost felt sorry for him, but it was an empty sense of sorrow. Momentary. Weightless.

Maybe I picked up the rifle, again using the rags. What if, I put its muzzle in his mouth? Put his finger on the trigger with mine on top of his.

Maybe that's really not how it had transpired. Maybe my plan was to return to the house and smother my father with a pillow if he was still asleep on the sofa. Simple. Easy. Clean. And if awake, I was still going to smother him, sure I could overpower my father—but hopefully, without too much of a struggle. Perhaps my thinking was: one way or the other, he had to be dead before I went back to school that morning.

Maybe when I did return to the house, he was on the sofa drinking out of a bottle of Jack with the rifle next to him. Maybe his plan was to kill himself after all, but he could have been planning on shooting Mother instead while we were at school. Either way, he would have to take a cab because his car had been impounded the night before in order to purchase the rifle. My father had obviously had the cab driver stop-off at Big A's Liquors on Watson on the way back from the hardware store. Maybe he felt he would need some extra courage to pull the trigger—but it's doubtful, and like alcoholics, he just wanted to keep the liquor flowing.

If you're thinking: why would the clerk at the hardware store sell some drunk a rifle, he would. My father often patronized it, and he and the owner were well acquainted. Plus, he rarely appeared as if he was a sloppy drunk; and his tolerance was fairly high.

If I haven't stated it, my father would drive drunk with us in the car when we were younger. And again, concerning not signing the check, I imagine my father—along with being intoxicated, was in a hurry. Being frazzled is a possibility, but I also doubt that.

There is also the possibility, he had purchased the rifle at an earlier date—even months or more before; surely another avenue for murdering his family that he couldn't have given a fuck about. And if that was the case, he only had the cab take him to the liquor store.

Maybe my father feebly looked up at me. Mumbled something before taking a sloppy swig of Jack. Maybe, I watched as some of it dribbled down his chin and onto his chest. Maybe, due to the lingering stench in the living room, I was about to vomit; not only due to the choking smell of booze but evidently, sometime that morning, he'd shit his pants.

Then, maybe, he tried to speak again.

"What the fu… fuck… Ran…dy."

Maybe he spilled some of the Jack when he took another swig. Maybe, I asked my father while looking down at him: "What's with the rifle?" Maybe he tried to respond: "The w… hat?"

Maybe, my father was finally able to half-ass tell me what he was planning. That he got the rifle to shoot himself. But he was afraid.

Maybe, I thought for a minute—no more.

Maybe, I told him: "You don't have to be afraid," as I squatted down in front of him.

Perhaps, I'd never seen him so pathetic—so lost and childlike as I did that morning, void of the rage and anger I was used to. Unlike the opposite that I all-too-well knew: the angry drunk, the out of control drunk, the scary drunk, and the monstrous drunk.

Maybe, I acted compassionately. Maybe, I put my hand on his shoulder. Told my father it was okay. Lied that it, everything that had transpired up to that morning was okay. That if he killed himself, he was doing the right thing and by doing so, that would make it all go away. Maybe, I told him it was okay to shoot himself and that I would help him.

Maybe, it was obvious he was so far gone; and at that point, he would do whatever I told him was the right thing to do. And I knew by being there that morning, only added to his confusion aided by the drunk the night before and the Jack he was consuming—working on the second bottle as I could see the first on the sofa beside him. The smell of it, taking me back to those times in the shed that I'd hadn't forgotten that seeded my own rage and hatred and disgust. Maybe, he took another big swig as I held the bottom of the bottle to force him to keep swallowing.

By then, maybe, I helped him lie down on the sofa. Maybe, I listened through the quiet of that morning to be sure Mother hadn't woken. Maybe, then, I stood to take my shirt off because I knew I had to use it to keep my fingerprints off the rifle. Maybe, I stood there looking over him in only my T-shirt as he watched me. Maybe, he was still holding the bottle of Jack—by then, empty.

At that point, maybe, I reached for the rifle—again using my shirt. Placed it on his chest as he kept watching me. Maybe, I saw his eyes begin to tear. Maybe, I told him again, he was doing the right thing and smiled. "You're doing the thing for all of us." But, maybe, that smile I smiled was for me and not him.

Maybe, I put his left hand on the rifle. Maybe, he started to speak and then didn't. At that, maybe, I raised my left leg to bend its knee on top of his hand to hold it and the rifle against his torso. Maybe, I reached for one of the decorative pillows at the end of the sofa and placed it on my father's body because maybe I knew I would need it.

Maybe, I smiled at him again; but again, as the first one, the smile was for me and not him. Remember what I wrote in the beginning pages of this telling?

"I owed my father nothing." I owed him nothing—not even a smile.

Maybe, he resisted a little. Maybe, I pushed the muzzle of the rifle between his lips. Maybe, I forcibly held it in place by covering his mouth with the pillow—my hand pushing down. Maybe, he struggled a little more again; but I had him trapped like he had trapped me for years.

Maybe, I saw not only real, dead, cold, fear and sudden panic in his eyes as they darted from side-to-side. Maybe, his whole body was shaking at that point. Maybe, with my right hand, I put his right index finger on the trigger as he tried to pull it back as I put mine on top of his.

Then, maybe, I pulled the trigger and felt the hard kick-back of the rifle; and felt the heat. The scorching burning fire of Hell. But felt no guilt or remorse for him. Again, I owed my father nothing. Maybe, my ears rang a shot rang out though the house. Maybe, I felt the kick-back of the rifle. But as I pulled that trigger, I felt the splatters of blood on my face. Saw the havoc caused by that bullet on and around me.

Maybe, I quickly grabbed my shirt—and not washrags as I would have in the first scenario, but rather the smoking pillow.

Whichever may have played out, maybe for a split second, I looked back toward the sofa—back at him, horrified by what the bullet did but not sad. How it shot out the back of his head. Horrified, by all the blood that painted the wall in large and random splatters, the armrest of the sofa, the green carpet, the brick planter between the living room and the dining room. Horrified, that my mother heard the shot but hoped she was still tangled in her heavily medicated sleep. Horrified, she would find his body. Then I looked away. Wondered, if I was caught up in a nightmare. Maybe, regardless, I was relieved what is it. Then, turned the doorknob. Opened the door. Reached my hand back around to lock it. Stepped outside onto the porch. Quietly closed the door. Maybe I hurried to my car. Started the engine. Backed out of the driveway. Nervously drove away.

Maybe, I looked in the rearview mirror. And while I was looking at my reflection, maybe I wondered if a person could be good and bad at the same time—so far on either end of the extreme sides of the spectrum. And maybe my heart cut into as if by contentious jagged glass—not for him, but for my mother. Maybe I prayed she wouldn't wake until after I returned home from school. That, she would remain under due to the meds, including the sleeping pills she regularly took. On the drive to school that morning, I'd already convinced Sandra to go home with one of her friends after school. Gave her a 20-dollar bill so they could go to an afternoon movie.

Maybe a block and a half away from the house, I had to pull the car over. Open the door and release the vomit, forcing its way up my epiglottis onto the street.

Maybe I thought my mother would receive an allowance of liberation once the shock of it all eased. That, all of us would be freed. Maybe I had to hope. Kept holding on to the lottery ticket a while longer. Maybe I justified what I'd done, as doing the wrong thing for the right reason—and certainly, again, our self-preservation. Chosen, the greater of those two evils. Either way, it had to happen; that night of the katydids, when their chirping waves consumed the thickened night had proven that.

Just maybe, I'd made it back to school but was late for second period. Maybe first, I went into the boys' restroom to wash my face. Maybe I'd brought my shirt or the washrags, again, depending on which scenario took place with me and pushed it or them down deep in the trash container of the restroom. Maybe, I acted like everything was normal even though it was so far from it. But believed—everything would now be okay. That, it was over.

Then, while sitting in class—my mind still back at the house, I was startled by the announcement that blasted out of the intercom: Randy Chumbley, meet your mother at the front of the school. Maybe I said fuck, fuck, fuck under my breath.

What if, that's how it all went down and the abhorrence my father and I carried for each other was over, but my hatred would remain? Or at that point, was that hatred directed toward me? But it actually didn't matter how that bullet was delivered. In the end, justice was served all the same as I was on my knees with my hands covered in my father's blood cleaning up the carnage. Perhaps, it was my blood to clean up. Maybe and What if?

I've often contemplated that morning. Often wondered, if life had just caught up with my father like it had me in 2009, and spilled over for the three years to follow; and he saw no other way out as I hadn't. That is, if my second version offered is the true version. But you'll never know. Regardless, as much as I hate to admit it: I am my father's son. I can be a monster as he was. Even long after his death, my father left his branding—seared onto my soul.

the dusk and the dawn

Are we not our own witness…

There's always more to everyone's story. Our stories in full are dictated memories on the pages of a book held within our minds. In actual fact, our minds are those books. But although written, many memories recalled cannot always be trusted when parts and pieces—remnants collide as one page is flipped to the next and the next. And then there are those written memoirs of horror we wish to erase but cannot; however, those pages are locked behind many doors with the others. But still, the shadows of their ghosts—grossly disfigured, are free to wander on the other side as they escape through the keyway. They hide deep behind the veil of darkness and with them, those shadows carry our nightmares.

There are times our stories, if not just parts, are screaming off those pages. The other parts remain untold, so as not to break through the ceiling of silence. Or at least, so we hope. On the other hand, the more we are willing to share—to read aloud and as more people do the same, we as humans come to realize that we are not so different and are part of a kinship of one kind or another that reaches around the world regardless of any borders drawn.

Although seen as strangers—some we may even pass within inches in public places, are only so on the outside. It is those closely similar life events and resulting emotions traveled which brings us together in those kinships without knowing it. Sometimes, too, we are running from many of the same ghostly shadows.

As far as that little boy is concerned, you would have had to live within his skin—incarcerated in the confines of his flesh that clings to that boy's bones to be privy to the key that opens the last door and walk over its threshold; to fully know every letter and punctuation of the rest of the story—even to comprehend it.

You would have had to live in his flesh every day and night. Actually, you would have to be that boy to know why he did some of the things he did. The boy who existed—struggled to survive, thinking each hour might be his last. Specifically, if you awoke to see another day before Friday, September 28, 1973, in that house on Shirley Drive in Warner Robins, Georgia. And with that stated, for me to fully know your story, I would have to do the same—live within your skin as well

Tragically, it remains standing today—that, house. One in from the corner that still holds many quaking truths and bloody secrets of that childhood—decades passed but not forgotten. A house still in possession of the voices of my mother, her cries of despair like those of her children. Certainly, impounding the actions as the raging of his father—and the echo of that bullet. The one I heard that day as I stated in my first book. But I did, in such a way not to tell all.

Mercifully, I'll never physically walk that street again or stand in front of that house as I'll not step over the threshold of the front door and walk back in—even though, I know abstractions of my essence will be forever trapped within as long as that house stands. How could they not be? And as I've stated much earlier, or will I ever set foot—living and breathing, on Middle Georgia red-clay soil again. Or will my dead body lie beneath it.

But I do not need to physically go back. Unfortunately, and to my hindrance, the acts that took place in that town, on that street, and especially in that house and the property it sits on—the shadows of those ghosts have all too often read aloud from the pages of my book. And then there are the images drawn on many of its pages. Images of our faces, that of every room, every corner in it, every crack in the walls including those of that shed and the stains on its cot, and those of the tall pines as that huge magnolia tree as well. That magnolia—its only saving grace.

It's the images that flash like those from a Kodak Carousel slide projector in my brain, repeating on an endless loop that is the most unbearable of all of it. All of it. All of it. All of it. I can hear the click the projector makes before each image flashes onto the walls of my skull. Those images are what haunt me the most as the acts that took place. Those actions—provoking those screams and the harsh voices interposed in the background. Stirring up immeasurable hatred from the past as those images flash, is a larger part of the collective reasons I wanted to die so desperately. It's those acts that took place under that roof that fashioned me—stitching the propensities of murderous thoughts and potential into a boy's brain as if he were a rag doll.

It took me many years to ask my sister what our father had said to her that morning—the morning of his demise when the dusk came to meet the dawn. That is, beforehand, when he'd called us into the living room as we were about to leave for school. I guess, I really didn't care to know for the longest time. Nor did I want to know what he might have said to me—if I'd gone in as well. That remains so to this day.

Sandra shared, she really didn't remember. Evidently, our father's words to her were lost to the years that followed. However, Sandra did tell me he was cut short when I yelled at her to come back so we could leave. But at my delivery of the question, Sandra could instantly see herself in her mind standing a few feet from him that day—as if it were yesterday.

Concerning those truths between the lines and in the margins—referencing my first book: "… I stood by my father's open grave and heard the rifle shots echo through the leaf barren trees up into a cloudless-blue sky. The Honor Guard—seven soldiers in dress uniform—stood in a row, stiff as boards. Each with three rounds in his rifle. Twenty-one bullets rang out in succession making three loud shots. And in truth, there was a fourth shot, silent to all but me. The first muffled shot—the one entering my father's mouth—rang in my ears that day, as I looked up to watch the bullets hit the sun."

I also did state: "somehow a part of me was there." And that part will always be there as it is today. As that morning—before and after, I've continued unraveling. The same part that, as long as I can remember, has always looked for a crack to escape through. Admittedly, I'm still looking for that crack. Maybe that's one of many the reasons why I tried so hard to die between 2009 and 2012, because I never found that crack. I could never escape.

No, there is no escaping any of it: the gaping echoing voices of cries and screams; words of hate that were spoken; the tears shed, even that of blood.

double-double cheeseburger

Yes, I've wondered what my life would have been like without Dugan gracing it. But I cannot imagine never having known this amazing creature—this steadfast friend and companion. This champion. Having the miraculous gift of his unconditional love. This gift of comfort, when many times—there seemed none to be found other than within reach of him.

In knowing all he has meant to me over the ten years of his life and still does, unequivocally our last four in Atlanta and the four in California we shared: was all the towering anguish, betrayals, and lies—the ugliness of three suicide attempts, counting on Death to end my emotional pain delivered in full by the many cutting losses in my life that were triggered—resurrected, following the morning of Christopher's cruel and heartless exit? That exit, leaving the door open and giving easy re-entry for the many ghosts from the past to enter and unleash their awakened inexorable wrath. Thus, resulting in those four destructive and incapacitated years. Again, was it worth it—worth knowing Dugan?

To even entertain answering that question, I need to reiterate that I had originally given Dugan to Christopher as a gift. But later, I took him back. The truth of the matter is that if I'd never become involved with Christopher, I would have never gotten Dugan for him—and if that were the case, Dugan would have never been in my life to begin with.

Nevertheless, the answer is that there is no answer. In effect, it's not about being worth it but the times Dugan's light amid me, offering thin layers of protection from the outstretch of blackness—the chase of its wide and long shadows. It's how Dugan helped to save me, at times when doctors and medications could not. It's about the legions of times I looked at his face, thus knowing it was possible to take another breath of life. About the days Dugan never left my side when I could not bargain for the emotional strength to leave the boundary of the bed.

It's about how he learned to read my varying emotions—many times, licking tears from my face. How he would nuzzle his snout in my neck and place his paw over my heart as Dugan peacefully lay next to me; my eyes lodged in a vacant stare at the television screen attempting to become lost in make-believe when reality was unforgiving and choking. It's about the many smiles he drew on my face and the welcomed laughter expelled from his quirky performances. The sound of his steady breathing during lifeless nights, donating grades of stability—the knowledge I was not alone. It's about the way he looked at me—how he watched over me all those years until his last moment on this earth.

At nine years old, Dugan was diagnosed with canine lymphoblastic lymphoma. At those three words, my knees gave out. I gripped the examining table to keep from crashing to the floor moments after the veterinarian delivered the crippling news. The world around me seemed to collapse. My heart fragmented. My entire body liquefied. As much as I attempted to dam them, tears flooded my eyes. If I'd ever needed to be locked up in a padded cell, it was then. At the time—I remember thinking, "I wish I could have it instead of my sweet Dugan." I'd taken him to the vet thinking he had allergies because his eyes had become red and droopy.

I was referred to a hematologist-oncologist, Dr. Simmons in Ontario, California who had made great strides with animal cancers.

Within days, Dugan began a protocol of chemotherapy treatments once every three weeks. After the first, he would not get out of the car to go into the facility. He panted unremittingly. I could see fear in his eyes even though Dugan was familiar with the smells and the environment of veterinarian offices, having gone to the vet every six months for checkups and booster shots since the was a puppy.

As a result, I carried him into the facility on each following visit. But every time someone entered or exited the double glass doors, Dugan lunged for them. In an attempt to lessen his anxiety, Dr. Simmons' assistant would feed him after each treatment while we were in a private waiting room. She also would put us in one when we arrived.

On our return home, I would go through the drive-in of In-N-Out Burger to get Dugan a double-double cheeseburger. Since they didn't offer sweet potato fries—Dugan's all-time favorite, I made them for him at home. Even though Dugan's regular vet had harped that he needed to lose a few pounds, it didn't matter. Under the circumstances, he could have all the cheeseburgers he wanted. Even I gained weight.

After six chemotherapy treatments, to all-embracing relief and incalculable gratefulness—Dugan went into remission. Sweeping exultation warmly ran throughout my body at the oncologist's celebratory news, as I sat on the floor with my sweet boy in the private waiting room. I knew I just had been given a gift; one not to be taken for granted. Dugan and I had a second chance. More time. More nights watching Netflix. More mornings, waking up on the very edge of the bed with Dugan up against my body—being such the bed-hog that he was. More time at the beach. More picnics in the park that overlooked the blue waters of the Pacific Ocean. More everything that was Dugan.

However, Dr. Simmons cautioned that there was a chance the cancer would rear its hideous head. But again, I knew then, I had to more than cherish everyday with Dugan—every single breath taken with him. Where I'd failed before, I genuinely began to learn how to live in the moment with Dugan. He was my longest relationship—my dearest friend and companion. Dugan knew me better than I knew myself. My partner in crime. I pinned hope that the lymphoma would not return and thus, allow Dugan to live out his natural life span.

My hope was crushed some eight months forward in mid-April—minutes past 2:00 p.m.

I was sitting at my desk typing. Matt Alber's, "Hide Nothing" played at a moderate volume on my iTunes. As usual, Dugan was stretched out underneath the desk on one of his dog beds—my feet sporadically tickling his belly.

Suddenly, something didn't seem right. I hit the pause key on the laptop. My concern accelerated as I noticed Dugan's breathing grew heavy. My gut told me what I feared most: the lymphoma had returned despite the chemotherapy treatments and every online remedy I'd searched, and those friends had shared as possible deterrents. Still, I hoped I was wrong. Hoped that Dugan was fine. That, I was worried for no reason.

Mere minutes later, I was rushing to the car with Dugan in my arms. Well within forty-five minutes—the XJS made a sharp turn into the parking lot of the cancer center. Over that timeframe—likely the fastest drive I'd ever made to Ontario.

Dr. Simmons' assistant took Dugan into an examination room as I waited in a private one. Some thirty minutes later, she returned with my boy to find me sitting on the floor. My back was against the wall. My legs spread out. My arms locked over my chest as if to keep my heart from falling out.

"Here's your sweet boy," she said.

Dugan hurried over. I raised my knees up. He took comfort between them as he licked my face. I repeatedly kissed Dugan on his snout.

"Is it back?" hesitantly I asked, without breaking eye contact with him.

Silence drew.

"Dr. Simmons… he'll be right in, Mr. Chumbley," she gently spoke.

But she didn't have to answer. I knew. She'd already answered the question by not telling me.

Minutes later, the doctor came in. Dugan began to pant. His eyes darted, the closer Dr. Simmons approached us. The doctor kneeled to pet Dugan as he looked me in the eyes.

"I'm sorry… he's out of remission."

The news sliced through me. Although anguished beyond translation, I refused to cry. I boxed my emotional state the best I could under the circumstances. I didn't want Dugan to see me upset as he looked at me with those beautiful and loving eyes. There was no more crying to be had—at least not for the moment. It was my turn to be Dugan's champion as he'd been mine the very moment I fell into despair in early January of 2009.

I moved my hands to hold Dugan's head. Pressed my face to his as I continued to scratch behind his ears. I doted on him as if everything was fine. That's how I wanted it. I wanted everything to be fine. Then, Dugan rested his head on my chest.

Following a lengthy discussion with the doctor concerning resuming the protocols that day, I eagerly said yes. Dr. Simmons diagnosed: Dugan was still young enough that he might go back into remission. Moments later, Dugan whimpered as he lifted his head from my chest and looked up at me. His telling anxiety and agitation increased as did his panting.

Without a doubt, I knew Dugan was telling me not to. Not to put him through the treatments again. I achingly changed my decision on the spot. I knew I had no other choice. I could not. I could not do that again to Dugan, due to all that angst I'd witnessed the treatments had caused my boy. I could not selfishly put Dugan through them a second time, no matter how desperately I needed him to live.

After further discourse, I questioned Dr. Simmons about how long I could keep Dugan with me without him suffering. He told me, feasibly for two months—if that. The oncologist educated me on what to look for so I would know when it was time to let Dugan pass through this life. Dr. Simmons gave him a shot to momentarily retard the spread and prescribed Dugan a steroid. Also, tranquilizers—at my request to calm him. I told Dr. Simmons I never wanted Dugan to enter a veterinarian facility again.

"I'll make sure Dugan has everything he needs. Just call to keep me posted. We've grown very fond of him. Our hearts are broken as well."

At that, Dr. Simmons benignly held Dugan's head in his hands. He resisted at first before he relented.

"You've been a brave boy. It's been an honor knowing you and your daddy, Dugan… even under these very difficult circumstances."

Then, he looked at me.

"I wish you both the best of luck. Again, call me if there is anything Dugan needs."

As I'd always done after Dugan's treatments, on the way home—I stopped at In-N-Out to get him a double-double cheeseburger.

sixty-two days

Dugan was rarely out of my sight. Even with the devastating news that he'd come out of remission, I did my best to see we carried on with life. But I remained in denial; I refused to accept the inevitable waiting down the road. Refused to accept what was to come. I could not accept that I was going to lose my best friend. Still, a part of me was quite aware time was not on our side.

Straightaway, I hired a photographer from Los Angeles to come to the house to take professional photographs of Dugan and me. The arrangements were made in advance for Dugan's veterinarian to come to the house when the time came. I also visited the crematorium to make the final preparations. The owner, Ruth, understood my wishes that Dugan's body could not be left alone in a dark room or a cooler—he had to be cremated without delay. In the event it was not possible, I had to know the procedure to preserve his body overnight at home. And that I would pay for a single cremation—not wanting him included in a communal cremation with multiple pets. Then, I would stay until I had Dugan's ashes in my hands. Every possible scenario was contemplated—to ensure Dugan made a loving and smooth transition.

Counting days since we'd returned home from the oncologist's office was avoided. Dugan continued to eagerly eat; he seemed happy. Out of paranoia, I checked his glands several times a day. By mid-May, I noticed an increase in swelling.

My sixty-second birthday was quickly approaching. I hoped he'd make it long enough to be with me. Reservations were made at the Art Hotel on Pacific Coast Highway across from Crescent Bay Point Park and Crescent Bay Beach below—for Dugan, Sandra, and me to spend June 19th through the 22nd. Since moving to California,

Dugan and I spent many enjoyable days picnicking in the park above the Pacific Ocean, while Sandra spent her time at the beach below. I read and wrote while Dugan lay beside me or rolled around in the lush green grass.

In the second week of June, the swelling became more rapid. Still, I kept hoping. Dugan continued to consistently eat; he never turned down a banana or doggie treats—certainly, not his own dog food and always eager for people-food. I gave him all he wanted.

Within days, I had to lift him on the bed. Dugan was no longer able to reach up enough to place his front paws on the edge, waiting for me to give him a boost up with my hands on his rear end. At times, Dugan's panting increased. To help settle him, I would give Dugan one of the tranquilizers Dr. Summons had prescribed. Lied on the floor next to him and softly rubbed his belly while feeding him pieces of a banana. That seemed to slow it down. Some days later, Dugan began to hide in a corner of the master bathroom. I knew that was not a good sign—but again, as long as he seemed calm much of the time and continued to eat, I told myself that it was not time.

That dreaded day came—June 16, around four o'clock in the afternoon. Sandra called me into the kitchen. The tone of her voice, pressing. Dugan lying on the floor panting incessantly. Heavy. Labored. His eyes wide and darting—panicked. His face, telling of urgent distress. Dugan had seemed okay that morning but clearly had taken a rapid turn for the worst.

Also panicked, but I acted as normal as possible for Dugan's sake since he'd always tuned into my emotions. My heart was racing as I grabbed the bottle of tranquilizers from the counter. Shook two out. Took a banana from the fruit bowl on the island. I lay down, face-to-face with Dugan—all the time talking to him. The banana instantly caught his attention as I peeled it. Stuck the tranquilizers in half before offering it. He gobbled it up without hesitancy. I ate the other so Dugan could see me—hoping he would think everything was normal. But that was really for me. I wanted everything to go back to normal.

"Can you hold on for four more days… maybe five?" I asked him in those desperate moments.

Dugan kept looking at me.

"Come on boy, my birthday is four days away… we're so close."

I was sure, Dugan's eyes told me that he might not as he weakly licked my face.

As much as I wanted the elusive impossible, I knew then I had to let Dugan go; I had no other choice if I wanted his pain, panic, and confusion to end. It was about what he needed—not about what I wanted.

Concerned about Dugan's attested degree of discomfort, and if the veterinarian could not break away soon to arrive at the house—I had Sandra call the office.

"Randy, he can't make it for a few hours. They have an emergency."

"Tell them we're on our way," I directed, not wanting Dugan to suffer another moment.

I asked Sandra to grab all the dog treats from the large glass container on the counter and bag them. She followed me as I carried Dugan out to the car. Sandra drove. I sat in the backseat with his head on my lap as he took treats from my hands. Upon arrival, an assistant waited in the lobby. Urgency absorbed time as she led us into an examining room. There, I sat on the floor holding Dugan while still feeding him the treats. Sandra sat uneasily in a chair, tears in her eyes.

Shortly, the veterinarian entered with the assistant who greeted us, accompanied by another. He wanted to move Dugan to a different room to administer the pentobarbital. I insisted it had to be done where we were. In advance, I'd requested Dugan first get an injectable tranquilizer to help calm him from fighting the pentobarbital. I lifted his face close to mine. Talking non-stop to him. Telling Dugan everything was going to be okay—that he would be okay. Dugan was still interested in the treats and wanted more. A few tears left my eyes as I continued to hold back the rest while I kept talking to my boy and smiling at him.

After the tranquilizer was administered, we waited for it to take effect; Dugan kept accepting the treats. The ones Sandra had brought were almost gone. I looked up at the other assistant. Without saying a word, she hurried from the room—within moments, she returned with packages of treats. At that, the veterinarian excused himself for a moment.

Dugan sniffed the bags as I collectively ripped them open with my teeth. I began feeding him from the palm of my hand as before.

Never stopping. One treat after the other as if coming off an assembly line to keep his focus on the treats and not what was going on in the room behind him. A second injection was required. Within a few minutes, the look of fear left his face; the glare in his eyes softened. Dugan's breathing settled some. He appeared more peaceful. His tail wagged a few times.

The veterinarian returned. He asked if I was ready. I said I was not—that I never would be, but I had to be for Dugan. He reached for the syringe of the pentobarbital from a tray. The veterinarian looked at me then Sandra, and back at me with a soft, compassionate expression.

"I know you'll never be ready for this… but do you want a few more minutes?"

I looked over at Sandra. Motioned my head for her to sit on the floor with us.

I reluctantly nodded without looking up, keeping a perfervid gaze into Dugan's eyes—sponging his living image in my mind. The same with his warmth in my lap. Dugan still took the treats from the palm of my hand. I laid my body over his. Moments later, I sat up returning eye contact as I blindly reached for more treats. Sandra placed more into my beseeching palm. Dugan eagerly kept eating them as if nothing was wrong.

I looked up for a few seconds at the veterinarian as he was about to inject the syringe of pentobarbital. My friend was about to move on without me—the dreaded reality, I feared since that day his veterinarian told me Dugan had cancer. Within moments, I knew Dugan would be gone. I smile at him. Kissed Dugan on his snout while our eyes were still connected. Then, his closed. I felt the life leave his body. The weight of his head was only supported by my hands. I rested it on my lap and leaned my body back over his. My arms embraced Dugan. He was gone. My sweet, sweet, boy had passed on. Sandra put her arm around me. Rested her head on my shoulder. The tears I'd been holding back poured from my eyes as I sobbed, drenching Dugan's coat. I sensed the engulfing draw of death.

The best part of me had transitioned from this life. I intensely wanted to follow him. The doctor and assistants left us with Dugan as I'd asked. I required time to pull myself together—if only temporarily or someone would have to call an ambulance to take me away. There seemed no movement of time even though minutes must have passed. Time had come to a halt. There was not yesterday or tomorrow or five minutes to come, much less one. Not even a second. More tears fell. Sandra and I wept.

Then, I asked her, "Will… will you please go ask them to call the crematorium?"

There was a pause. A few sniffles. Sandra wiped her eyes. She squeezed me before using my shoulder for support to gain her footing.

"Of course, you stay here with your boy."

I lifted my head. Watched Sandra walk toward the door.

one more night

I heard nothing caught within the grip of Dugan—everything about him: past, and the crushing present. Suspended in a trance-like state, the last some-ten-years with him flashed in my head. Every moment.

"Randy, did you hear me?"

I didn't. I didn't hear my sister speaking. I'd drifted backward in time. Seeing Dugan as a puppy pulling on a rope as we played tug of war. Him looking out the front door of the Seventh Street house waiting for me to come home. Remembered, when we stood in front of the Welcome to California state sign. I remembered it all. All the ten years of our life together.

I felt a gentle shake on my shoulder. It brought me back to the reality that Dugan was not sleeping in my lap, but dead. I looked up to see Sandra.

"What… did you say something?" I asked.

"They can't take Dugan… it's almost 5:00 p.m. It'll be first thing in the morning."

"Oh… " I remotely recall responding.

I actually was relieved—relieved the crematorium was about to close.

My thoughts were apprehended in an inscrutable dimension. If they were closed, then none of this was real and Dugan was still alive.

Still caught in a semi-impenetrable state, I stood with Dugan in my arms. An assistant rolled in a stainless-steel gurney.

"I'll help you get him to the car," she offered.

The gurney looked cold.

"No... no, I'll carry him."

Sandra led the way down a narrow hallway to the back door. The assistant followed. Then, Dugan and me. His head rested on my chest as I cradled his weight in my arms. Even though he was dead, the warmth of his body against mine comforted me. Still, I refused to accept that Dugan no longer had a heartbeat. Mine barely did.

The heat of the late afternoon sun and its light rushed the hallway in blinding unconcern as the door was pushed open. The four of us made the short walk to the car. I looked back at the assistant to thank her. She placed a hand on my shoulder. Her gentle smile spoke words that were unnecessary to speak—the translation, clear.

Sandra opened the back door of the Toyota for Dugan and me. Once seated, his head remained against my chest and his body in my lap. My head rested on his as the world around us kept going. Kept moving. Kept existing. But inside the car, it had stopped.

Sandra drove back in the direction of the house. This time, the drive void of the earlier urgency to the veterinarian's office. What was the point? There was none. Once we walked back through the house's double orange doors, Dugan would not be waiting. He would not perk up. Would not look at me. Would not wag his tail in delight. Or, run to me.

The car filled with silence—nothing but silence. It cocooned mourning and death. I remember not hearing the sound of the surrounding traffic. Sandra and I didn't speak a word for several miles. What could be said?

At some point later, I heard the trunk close. The driver's side car door opened. Then, shut. I looked up. Sandra sat in front driver's seat with her body turned to look at me.

"Randy, I got the two large bags of ice."

"What?"

"The ice... for Dugan."

I hadn't realized the car had stopped, much less turned into the parking lot of Von's grocery store.

"Okay. Good."

The owner of the crematorium had instructed, if Dugan could not be cremated until the day after he'd passed, the ice would help preserve his body until the next morning.

Sandra turned back around. I heard the engine start. I returned my attention to Dugan—not that it ever left. I kept patting his head. Kissing it. Talking to him. All I could think about was how lost I felt. How lost I became the second he'd stopped breathing. How lost I was at that very moment, and how I would remain so in the days and months to come.

The car backed out of the parking space. I leaned my head against the headrest as Sandra steered through the lot toward the main drag of Palm Drive. I shook my head left then right. Left then right. Left then right. I was angry. Angry. Angry. So angry, I want to hit something.

Sandra inched the Toyota into the rush hour traffic. Took the full right turn and drove up the hill toward the house. I stared at the palm trees lining the road as the car passed them. I just wanted to get Dugan back in the house—back to his home. Our home.

"It's going to be okay, Randy," Sandra comforted as she continued to drive.

I dropped my head and laid it back on top of Dugan. The tears flooding my eyes were pushed out by more. My throat closed up; I was suffocating. I felt the car stop and then proceed forward. I knew we had just crossed Mission Lakes Blvd. The house was only a few yards away.

I felt the car turn. I looked up as Sandra pulled the Toyota up the driveway. I could see the orange doors of the house. The car stopped. The engine shut off. We both remained seated. Minutes collected. Then, more.

"Let's get Dugan in the house."

"What?"

"I think we need to get in the house, Randy."

Sandra got out of the car. Opened the back door. Helped me out with Dugan still in my arms. Once standing, Sandra put her arm around my waist. Steadied and guided me as if I were a crippled elderly man up the three steps and then along the lengthy walkway to the front doors. She unlocked them, pushed the right door open. Then I stood to the side. The cold air in the house from the air conditioner collided with the heat outside. We were caught in the middle.

I carried Dugan across the threshold—knowing this would be the last time he'd ever enter the house again. Sandra closed the door behind us. My habitual instinct was to set him down on the floor but stopped as I was about to bend down.

"Dugan can't walk," I thought. "He can't walk because he's dead."

It hit me again that just a few hours ago, Dugan was alive when we left the house. Now that we are back—my boy is dead.

"Be right back… I'll get the ice from the trunk," Sandra spoke.

The front door opened. Then, closed behind her. I stood in place as I waited for Sandra to return. As if I needed her to push me down the long hallway to my bedroom. Soon, she was back. She'd wasted little time.

"Stay right there, Randy. I'll put these in the freezer for now?"

I nodded.

Moments later, still holding Dugan, I followed Sandra into my bedroom. I didn't know what to do. Didn't know if I should keep holding him or lay him down on the bed.

"He… he needs a large towel from the laundry room," Sandra said, before she hurried in its direction.

Sandra soon returned with one. I waited for her to spread the towel in the center of the bed. As if ceremoniously, I lay Dugan on it. There was a weak comfort knowing he was back on the bed. He did look peaceful—looked as if he was sleeping. I stared at Dugan expecting him to wake up at any moment. But he didn't—Dugan didn't wake up.

"I'm going to lie down with him… okay," I told Sandra.

"I think you should… and try to get some rest. Just know Dugan is home. He's with you where he belongs. I'll be back in a little bit. Call out if you need me."

"Okay… okay. Wait. Dugan's Frisbee. Will you bring it? And… and his Kong, too."

"Sure. I'll get them now. He really loved that toy."

"Thanks. Dugan really did. He'd carry it with him almost everywhere… remember?"

"Yes, I do," Sandra responded.

I saw a few tears on her cheeks.

"You know… he would never fetch it when I tried to teach

him."

"I remember that, too," Sandra smiled.

Sandra quickly returned. Placed it near Dugan's snout. The dimming light filtered through the white, wall-to-wall, and ceiling-to-floor semi-sheer drapes over the windows behind the bed. The descending sun—seduced the pale orange and nimbus yellow to follow behind the San Bernardino Mountains. Sandra returned to check on us—she stood in the doorway.

"I turned down the thermostat to 70… don't you think I should bring in the bags of ice?"

"I guess it's time."

Sandra left the doorway long enough to retrieve the bagged ice. I place one on either side of him. Then, asked her to lie on the other side of Dugan.

That evening, and throughout the night, I vigilantly stayed awake with Dugan's body up against mine—petted and kissed and talked to him while Netflix was on the flat screen. I had Dugan for one more night, and we were doing what we had done most nights: lie in bed together and watch television while letting go of the rest of the world. After a while, Sandra told me she would leave us alone but check in from time to time.

"Do you want anything to eat," she asked.

I shook my head, no.

"Are you going to be, okay?"

My red and puffy eyes told her the answer without me speaking.

"Well… call if you need me."

"I will… "

Sandra directed a loving smile at me. Then, she left the bedroom. I redirected my attention to Dugan.

She checked in on me several times that night. And each time, Sandra would sit on the edge of the bed. She kissed me on the forehead before reaching over to pet Dugan again and told him she loved him.

"You were the best dad to Dugan… he had a good life."

I wanted to respond but couldn't. Instead, I reached out my hand to hers. Sandra squeezed it.

I cursed the morning once the sun found easy entry into the house through the large windows. Damned it for coming too soon. I needed more time—more time with Dugan. I watched the clock on the bedside chest wanting time to freeze. At 8:15, I carried Dugan's still body back to the car—to take his body to the crematorium as Sandra led the way. As the late afternoon the day before, returning home from the veterinarian's office, silence stilled the air.

The owner was waiting.

"I'm so deeply sorry. I know how much you and your sister are hurting."

I replicated a smile.

"It's all ready," Ruth informed.

Sandra held her kiss on Dugan's snout for moments as she ran her hand over him. She stopped at Dugan's ears to scratch behind them. He used to love that—loved having the back of his ears scratched. She looked up at me. Smiled delicately. Kissed me on the cheek. Pulled away and took a seat in the waiting area. My tears dropped onto his white coat as they had on and off for the past some fifteen hours. I remember thinking as I stood there that morning, how snow-white he was.

A memory was triggered—echoed from my mind. A wonderful, vivid evocation like one of poetry: Dugan and I walking in a winter snow in Piedmont Park. I'd let him off his harness to run in an open area while people used anything from cardboard to trash can lids, to actual sleds to speed down a steep hill close by. I leaned my head down to kiss him yet again as he remained wrapped in my arms. At that moment, my knees felt weak as my heart. I had to sit down. I took the chair next to Sandra. Leaned over and cocooned Dugan's body with mine as I rocked him as if he were a baby. He was. Dugan was my baby. Yet again, my face rubbed over his coat.

"You take your time, Mr. Chumbley," Ruth offered.

I looked at my sister for some strength—to keep me from walking out of the crematorium with Dugan.

"It's okay, Randy. Go. Go on. Dugan will always be with you."

Sandra kissed me on the cheek again. She patted Dugan and scratched behind his ears one last time. Hesitantly, I stood. Made my feet move in Ruth's direction standing by the door to the crematorium room. She opened it. I followed her. The room baked like an oven. Once she slid open the chamber door, the heat instantly intensified like a ball of fire had rolled out, sucking the oxygen out of the room—out of my lungs. Automatically my eyes squinted due to the fiery flames. Acute as if the sun had fallen from the sky.

I kissed Dugan on his snout before rubbing my face over his snow-white coat. Again, as I'd done a million times and more, I told my boy, "I love you so, so much. We made it... made it to California together." And with each letter of each word, my tears still kept falling on my peacefully sleeping Dugan.

Ruth looked at me. I walked closer to the open chamber and the fire. At that moment, I felt the mobbing sorrow and the weight of my love for Dugan. The deep sorrow that had been weighing me down since I was first told he had canine lymphoma. I hesitated again, not wanting him to leave my arms. After long moments, I painstakingly placed his body inside. Ruth slid the opening shut. I wanted to open it back up to pull Dugan back out. Hold him back in my arms.

"Let's join your sister in the waiting area."

With sheltering kindness, Ruth placed her hand on my back to lead me out of the room. I didn't realize until I'd sat down next to Sandra that the intensity of heat had burned my left hand; I didn't ever feel the physical pain.

Quietude of an opaque morning dominated the waiting area—only interrupted by the occasional random spurts of brief conversation between Sandra and Ruth. I rarely interjected but rather offered nods and purposeless smiles.

Locked within a suspended state, I relived many flashes of Dugan's ten years of life: filled with his images and blessed appreciation of the many gifts he unconditionally gave me with unyielding kindness and protection—above all, the purity of love from one of Earth's creatures to another.

The sound of a buzzer brought us to attention. I looked over at Ruth.

"It's time," Ruth stated as she stood up from her chair.

Without prompting, I followed her back into the crematorium room. As before, the intensity of the dense heat trapped by the door immediately escaped the second it was opened—leaching out, instantaneously consuming the cool air of the waiting area while flash-drying the tears from my eyes and those rolling down my cheeks.

I stood stiffly as I watched Ruth put the heat-resistant gloves back on before sliding open the chamber door—its confined roaring heat once again was unleashed around and through me. My beautiful creature; my friend was now a pile of gray ashes.

Ruth carefully swept Dugan's ashes into a pan with a brush made of long and thin bristles.

"Let's step over to the table in the corner," she directed.

Ruth sat the pan down and stepped aside.

"Give them time to cool," she cautioned.

I hovered over Dugan's ashes. My tears went dry before they could completely bleed out from my eyes. But they kept coming—eventually, increasingly such, that the surrounding heat could not prevent all of them from dripping into his ashes. Whereas some hours before, when we arrived, they soaked Dugan's white coat. I waited as long as I could before I ran my fingers through them—through his warm ashes.

"Use this scooper," Ruth said as she handed it to me.

"No. I have to use my hands."

With as much care and love as Dugan had given me, I did the same with his ashes as I placed them into a small, but thick and clear plastic bag; then secured it close with the thin twist tie. I waited a few moments before placing the bag into the square lacquered burl oak box I'd already selected when making the preparations. Centered on the outside was a square brushed-metal silver plaque:

DUGAN

MY CHAMPION

LOVED DEEPLY AND FOREVER

July 7, 2008 - June 18, 2018

For almost two weeks, that lacquered square box sat on the right bedside chest—the side I slept on. Every day, several times a day, as I did each morning upon waking and each night before sleep, I placed my hand on it as I looked at one of the framed pictures on the dresser the photographer had taken of Dugan and me. My heart was still heavy. Nothing felt right.

Subsequently, one late morning, I knew I had to do something else for my boy. The thought occurred, I hadn't totally freed Dugan. I immediately called out to my sister—somewhere in the other side of the house.

"Sandra… Sandra, we're going to drive to Laguna."

Moments later, she walked into my bedroom to find me holding the box with Dugan's ashes.

"What did you say?"

I looked up at her.

"The three of us are going to Crescent Bay Point Park."

Sandra's eyes move to the box in my hand then back at me.

"You mean now?"

"Yes, now."

"Why?"

"I feel as if a part of Dugan is trapped in this box… I've got to set him free."

A lazy breeze guided Sandra and me as we walked over the green grass of the small park atop the bluff as if it were supple carpet. The very grass, Dugan used to love its soft coolness under his belly. Only a few shades of blue separated the tranquility of the sapphire Pacific Ocean, and the sky with sparsely scattered puffs of white cotton candy clouds. It appeared as though we were surrounded by the vastness of blue as we continued toward the left edge that overlooked the coved beach below; guarded by large rock formations on either side. In the backdrop, the houses of the Laguna Hills rose upward—tall and as wide as we could see. Except for the rhythmic sounds of the white-capped waves wild and determinedly washing over the rocks below, the world seemed at peace.

I constantly kept a tight hold onto the burl oak box containing Dugan's ashes as we continued to silently walk past the lush beds of evergreens native to Southern California; and a variety of beautiful flowers that languidly accommodated the breeze. Then, suddenly, I felt compelled to stop at one of them. As sad as I was, the heaviness that walked alongside seemed to lessen. I looked back out over the ocean. An image of Dugan rolling around on the grass captured my mind.

"Are you okay?" Sandra asked.

I looked at her with a slender smile.

"I think… I know this is the right spot. I know this is where Dugan wants to be.

Together we got down on our knees. Rays of the afternoon sun reflected off the plague on the box. With Sandra's encouragement, I opened it. Then I carefully untied the plastic bag confining Dugan's ashes.

"I guess this is it," I whispered, as if talking to Dugan. But I was, I was talking to him.

I removed the plastic bag. Gently shook out some of his ashes into the palm of Sandra's hand; then some in mind. We each placed several small handfuls deep into the bed floor until the bag was empty. I was comforted by knowing Dugan would have a breathtakingly beautiful place to rest—instead of the darkness of the box. I pried off the plaque from it with one of the keys on my keychain. Dug a hole in the dirt with my hand to bury it where we had placed his ashes. My boy was completely free. Sweet Dugan was now a part of the earth, and the ocean where it met the sky.

I often return to that very spot; each time, I take some of Dugan's favorite dog treats and place them inside the bed of those evergreens and flowers. I sit on the same blanket that Dugan and I did; but now, next to where his spirit rests while I read and write. Or just lie there on a blanket and talk to my boy. It's in my will that my ashes will be placed there when my time comes—when my time comes to rest with Dugan in that part that overlooks the blue Pacific Ocean and where, its soft breezes kiss the cool green grass that he so loved to lie upon.

My Dugan lived sixty-two more days after we left the oncologist's office for the last time—technically, passing through the door out of this life, four days before my sixty-second birthday. I am grateful, after all the stops and starts, the train wrecks, the sorrows to the happiness, the ugly to the beautiful and all the in-betweens, that I had Dugan by my side.

I'll always miss his physical presence, but I feel his strong spirit. Looking at the pictures of us makes me smile. Makes me happy-sad. I prefer to think of him as being somewhere in the house: lying under my desk, spread out in front of one of the large windows enjoying the warmth of the sun, moments from walking into whichever room I may be in, or jumping on the bed each night after I fall asleep to watch over me—to protect me.

author's note

So much more has been chronicled by a life lived regardless of its enterprises. Living artifacts intimately carried—bounded between the nethermost layers of flesh. They—portage, weighty and burdensome cargo to ferry year after year. Yes, so much more remains untold from those journals that were meant to remain sealed, including the bits and pieces I've shared in my writings. But, again, concerning "Unraveled," I've offered much for you to choose to give credence to or not. The choice given, to protect myself from possible consequences.

Time has not granted the luxury of wiping the amygdala section of my brain clean. Or blinding the visions of blood on my hands or how it first gushes then drips, drop-by-drop while draining life. The sensation of the feel of its warm, thick, wetness remains—as does the metallic inhalation of its smell.

Now, I find myself in the present finishing the last pages of this—my final book from those many journals. The last one, having anything to do with my life from birth until this moment. This one, the first and third, collectively making an awkward trilogy: a boy fighting abuse, humiliation, among other offenses and violations. A boy, full of shame, hatred, anger, and a taste for revenge. A boy, fighting to protect others and for his own self-preservation. A boy, searching for love. A boy, who lived a volatile life into young adulthood and beyond. A boy, who became and lived as three different people.

That boy, now an aged man, still feels unworthy at times despite having been once desired by many and despite many accomplishments and successes. Who still feels panicked. Still haunted by the ghosts lingering in the shadows and the caustic dreams and ravaging nightmares they carry depicting past events and deeds. As that boy, a man who still sleeps with a light on to bid the darkness. Who still awakens at times, feeling surrounded by Death. But as that little boy did: I still tell myself, "Everything is going to be okay. Nothing will hurt me."

My use of derogatory words such as crazy, loco, and lunatics are not meant to be disrespectful to, or stigmatize anyone who lives with mental illness—although it may be seen as such. I made use of them because that's how I felt locked up in the milieu of Davy's mental ward by most of the staff—certainly, the Head of Psychiatry. The same is true from people in my community over my last four years in Atlanta. As well, those stigmatizing and disrespectful words are used throughout society—by many who believe they will never be one of us standing on the razor's edge between life with death. But one day, some may very well find themselves there.

Depending on the source, some 700,000 people globally fall to suicide annually—referencing only those who succeed. Roughly, one billion people's lives are affected by one or more mental conditions of various degrees of severity. Mental Illness is a serious disease not to be dismissed or is the grave suffering of those who navigate its treacherous journey. It crosses all boundaries regardless of age, gender, race, or financial standing.

Its layered complexities do not have a statute of limitations, whether seeded in the DNA or by situational conditions or both—past or in the present, including traumas or combined with a range of other additional factors. Sometimes it can take years for the resulting adverse emotional damage of events to surface. Also, many people do not seek medical help due to societal stigmas.

I stopped therapy after some seven years. And although I withheld certain events and the truths surrounding them, I did experience revelations and answers. Since 2009, not only have I been diagnosed with ideations of ending my life, but clinical depression, anxiety disorder, and PTSD enacted in childhood. I remain under the care of a psychiatrist for medication management.

My story—as other's, is obviously not a fairytale where the ghosts are defeated, the dark clouds lift and all's right within my world. But thankfully, many people who navigate their individual journey greatly benefit by medications and treatments under the supervision of professionals and support of family, friends and in some cases, community so they can successfully manage their mental health.

However, in all frankness, I cannot make any promises that my story won't end by my own means. But I am grateful for many things: the extraordinary experiences I've had; an array of things I've been given and those I've been able to give others; the purpose

I found in community; the freedom to be an artist and writer, although, concerning the latter, I know I'm not some a literary genius but I don't have to be; what both have accomplished and offered to people; knowing that people see my artworks every day across the country and abroad and read my books, and addressing the latter, many sharing that by telling parts of my story I am telling theirs and it has been of benefit to them; and back to my are, it was given me the ability to help many nonprofits and the peoples they assist; some of the pain that has taught me; especially, the love I've been given.

On a last note: if you are one of the millions who struggle with mental illness, please know I wholeheartedly wish you healing, know you are loved, that you have my compassion and respect, and I wish you as much joy as you can gather in spite of what the illness steals from your life.

acknowledgments

I'm deficient in words to convey the weight of gratefulness to those who have supported me in many ways. To express how tall each of you stands—including, during the process of the written depiction of this book. I know each of you accepts me as I am. See all of me and not just the broken parts. To know better than to believe the lies while seeing through their mendaciousness.

My Mother, for bringing me into this word. The unwavering love you gave to me. The many nights you stayed up late to help me write my college papers and so much more. I wish you had the beautiful life you so deserved—were able to wear flowers in your hair.

My sister, I'm deeply sorry I put you through so much pain when you were already overburdened with your own—and our mother's, which we both will always carry. You were there for me. You stood by me. You did your best to protect me. You watched over me. Never forget, you are loved by me.

Anthony King, my friend and editor. Without your endless patience, encouragement, and dedication to me and this book, I would never have reopened any of those journals that began this journey. As you know, I've given up many times; but you kept reassuring me not to. I know it has been a frustrating endeavor for you, plowing through wordy and tangled sentences—many protruding outside the margins like an angry hernia. Certainly, frustrated by my dyslexia.

My friend and attorney, "Allen." We are brothers and you have more than a brother's love from me. Sometimes I feel, if it were not for you, I'd still be locked up on that life-sucking ward.

Karen C., my confidante. My dictionary and thesaurus. Thank you for picking up the phone time and time again.

Marty M., for all your support as well—for our lunches and conversations. How I miss them as I do you.

Randy H., thank you for your friendship and patiently listening without judgement.

I owe a deep debt of gratitude to "Marty," "Hal," "Mitch," "William," and "Russ" for rallying around me in 2009—especially, for embracing Sandra with much care and love. I love each of you.

Anna, for looking out for Dugan and me, and all those cookies you lovingly baked. Plus, rescinding your packing and no packing policy.

I must thank the wise old oak that stands in Piedmont Park for the time it gave me to reflect; and at times, a sense of peace under your canopy. The canopy, that often-offered shade and the soft light it filtered washing down over Dugan and me.

"Peggy," for your guidance and support while I was confined within the daunting walls of Davy's mental ward. And for showing me much respect.

My dearest love, Bradley. Regardless of the shifting of time, in no amount have I loved another person in the way I did you—still do. Certainly, once the memories I tried so hard to suppress of us surfaced undamaged by the years since I was last encased within your strong arms. Those memories—transporting me back to you where I've always belonged. You're the only true home I have ever known—my only shelter from chaos, fear, and loneliness. I'm forever grateful for the time we had, although short in comparison to the life we'd planned. How I wish it could have been so. Thank you for your exclusively exceptional, and fathomless love. Unbound. Irreplaceable. Authentic. So deeply. And thank you, for sharing the heavens with me.

And of course, my sweet, sweet boy Dugan. There are no words to express how much I miss you. But, one day, we will be reunited when my ashes are placed with yours as a small amount will be scattered on Bradley's grave. Until then, I think of you daily as I miss our many nights watching television. The light you brought into my life, did help me to battle the revisiting darkness. Thank you for trying to protect me—for always being my loving companion. It as one hell of a ride—wasn't it. When I leave this life, perhaps, I'll be home again with both you and Bradley. I pray to the universe—it will be so.

I must thank this book. As emotional and excruciatingly painful as it has been to write, in many ways it brought Bradley back to me in full. Perhaps, that's why, in some undefinable way, the reason it was meant to be written in the first place.

Also, thank you to the strangers who have read my books, many of whom have come to find our lives have much in common. I have always shared parts of my story for you.

www.ingramcontent.com/pod-product-compliance
Lightning Source LLC
LaVergne TN
LVHW010551100826
845148LV00014B/2690

* 9 7 9 8 2 1 8 4 3 5 8 1 3 *